Study and Teaching Guide

FOR

THE HISTORY OF THE MEDIEVAL WORLD

By Julia Kaziewicz

A curriculum guide to accompany

Susan Wise Bauer's

The History of the Medieval World:
From the Conversion of Constantine to the First Crusade

Peace Hill Press
Charles City, VA

This study and teaching guide is designed to be used in conjunction with Susan Wise Bauer's *The History of the Medieval World*, ISBN 978-0-393-05975-5.

www.peacehillpress.com
1.877.322.3445

How To Use This Study Guide

This Study Guide for *The History of the Medieval World: From the Conversion of Constantine to the First Crusade* is designed to be used by tutors, parents, or teachers working with both individual students and groups.

For each chapter of *The History of the Medieval World,* three sets of exercises are given. Some chapters also include a fourth set—map work.

I. Who, What, Where

This section is designed to check the student's grasp of basic information presented in the chapter: prominent characters, important places, and foundational ideas. The student should explain the significance of each person, place or idea in **one or two complete sentences**.

II. Comprehension

This section requires the student to express, in his own words, the central concepts in each chapter. The student may use two to three complete sentences to answer each question.

III. Critical Thinking

This section requires the student to produce a brief written reflection on the ideas presented in the chapter. Some preliminary exercises are also provided.

IV. Map Work [maps found on pages 781 & following]

This section uses a traditional method to improve the student's geography. In his *Complete Course in Geography* (1875), the geographer William Swinton observed:

"That form is easiest remembered which the hand is taught to trace. The exercise of the mind, needed to teach the hand to trace a form, impresses that form upon the mind. As the study of maps is a study of form, the manner of studying them should be by map-drawing."

Section IV asks the student to go through a carefully structured set of steps with maps (provided on perforated pages in the back of this book): tracing repeatedly, then copying while looking at the original, and finally, where appropriate, reproducing from memory. He will be asked to use a black pencil (one that does not erase easily) as well as a regular pencil with an eraser, as well as colored pencils of various kinds. Large amounts of tracing paper are needed!

Chapter One

One Empire, Under God

The student may use his text when answering the questions in sections I and II.

Section I: Who, What, Where

Write a one or two-sentence answer explaining the significance of each item listed below.

Arius—**Pg. 9, ¶ 1 & 2—Arius was a Christian priest who served in the Egyptian city of Alexandria, and believed that the Son of God was not divine himself; he was a created being. Arius was excommunicated from the Church by his bishop, and the door was shut on Arianism by the Nicene Creed.**

Byzantium—**Pg. 11, ¶ 3 & 7—Byzantium was rebuilt by Constantine as a Christian city, full of churches instead of Roman temples and filled with monuments from the great cities of the old empire. Byzantium became the new capital of Constantine's empire, populated with "men of rank" and decorated with Christian imagery.**

Constantia—**Pg. 4, ¶ 2—Constantia, half-sister of Constantine, was married to Licinius at eighteen in order to cement the alliance between her half-brother and the eastern imperator.**

Constantine—**Pg. 4, ¶ 1, Pg. 11, ¶ 2 and Pg. 12, ¶ 1—Constantine became the single ruler of Rome after defeating Maximinus Daia and Licinius. Constantine moved the capital of the Roman empire to Byzantium, and by 330, he succeeded in establishing one empire with one royal family and one church: Christianity.**

Diocletian—**Pg. 4, ¶ 1 & 2—Diocletian, a former ruler of Rome, had appointed a system of co-rulers to share the job of running the vast Roman territories so that no one man had too much power.**

Edict of Milan—**Pg. 6, ¶ 2 & 3—The Edict of Milan was a proclamation made by Constantine that legalized Christianity in all parts of the Roman empire. The Edict declared that anyone could practice Christianity open and freely; it promised the return of property that had**

been previously confiscated from Christians, and that all Christian churches be turned over to Christian control.

Incarnation—**Pg. 8, ¶ 1 & note, and Pg. 10, ¶ 3—The Incarnation is the central doctrine of Christianity: that God came to earth in the person of Jesus Christ. The official argument Christian leaders had over the exact nature of the Incarnation was ended when the Nicene Creed was sanctioned by the leading bishops of Rome.**

Licinius—**Pg. 4, ¶ 1 & 2, Pg. 7, ¶ 4 and Pg. 11, ¶ 6—Licinius, imperator over the central part of Rome, east of the province of Pannonia and west of the Black Sea, married Constantia in order to form an alliance with Constantine. Licinius was exiled in Thessalonica after Constantine accused him of persecuting Christians, and in 325 Constantine had Licinius hanged.**

Maxentius—**Pg. 3, ¶ 2—Maxentius, the 29-year-old emperor of Rome, was drowned in a fight against Constantine on October 29, 312 during the Battle of the Milvian Bridge.**

Maximinus Daia—**Pg. 4, ¶ 1 & 4—Maximinus Daia ruled the eastern territories of the Roman empire, territories that were constantly threatened by the aggressive Persian empire. Maximinus Daia was attacked by Licinius, and when defeat was imminent, swallowed poison and suffered a slow death.**

Nicene Creed—**Pg. 10, ¶ 3—The Nicene Creed asserts the Christian belief in "one God, the Father almighty, maker of all things visible and invisible," and is still used in Christian churches today. The Nicene Creed emphasizes the divinity of Christ.**

Section II: Comprehension

Write a two or three-sentence answer to each of the following questions.

1. Why did Constantine send Maxentius's head to North Africa?

A1.—Pg. 3, ¶ 3—When Constantine took Rome's throne, he had to send a message to the supporters of the usurped leader, Maxentius. Constantine packaged Maxentius's head and shipped it to North Africa so that Maxentius's southern supporters would understand that it was time to switch allegiances.

2. What made the battle between Maximinus Daia and Licinius in 313 a holy war?

A2.—Pg. 4, ¶ 3—When Licinius met Maximinus Daia in battle in 313, his army of thirty thousand men marched under the banner of the Christian God. Maximinus Daia and his army of seventy thousand men had vowed, in Jupiter's name, to stamp out Christianity in the eastern Roman domains. The presence of the Christian banner pointed out that the battle for territory had become a holy war, and the defeat of Maximinus Daia's large army by Licinius showed the grace of God was on Licinius's side.

3. How did Licinius guarantee Constantine's safety on the throne after defeating Maximinus Daia?

A3.—Pg. 6, ¶ 1—Wanting to make sure that Maximinus Daia's lineage posed no threat to himself nor to Constantine, Licinius murdered Maximinus Daia's two young children, drowned their mother, and put to death three other possible blood claimants to the eastern throne, all children of dead emperors.

4. How do we know Constantine was not a devout Christian?

A4.—Pg. 7, ¶ 2—We know Constantine was not a devout Christian because he continued to emboss Sol Invictus, the sun god, on his coins; he remained *pontifex maximus*, chief priest of the Roman state cult, until his death; and he resisted baptism until he realized, in 336, that he was dying.

5. What excuse did Constantine use to get rid of his co-emperor Licinius?

A5.—Pg. 7, ¶ 4 & 5—In 324, Licinius accused the Christians in his court of spying for Constantine and threw them out. This act allowed Constantine to claim that Licinius was persecuting Christians, which was illegal according to the Edict of Milan. Licinius surrendered to Constantine's army and was exiled to the city of Thessalonica.

6. What is the paradox of Christ's existence? How does Ignatius of Antioch describe this paradox?

Note to parent—Ignatius of Antioch is quoted on page 8 of the text. The excerpt in full reads:

There is one Physician who is possessed both of flesh and spirit;
both made and not made;
God existing in flesh;
true life in death;
both of Mary and of God. . . .
For "the Word was made flesh."
Being incorporeal, He was in the body;
being impassible, He was in a passible body;
being immortal, He was in a mortal body;
being life, He became subject to corruption.

The student may use any part of this excerpt in his answer.

A6.—Pg. 8, ¶ 7—The paradox of Christ's existence is that Jesus partook in both human and divine natures. Ignatius of Antioch described this paradox as a man "both made and not made; God existing in flesh; true life in death . . . being impassible, He was in a passible body; being immortal, He was in a mortal body."

7. Describe the difference in Christian beliefs between the Ebionites, the Docetists, the Gnostics and the Arians as described in the chapter.

A7.—Pg. 8, ¶ 3 to Pg. 9, ¶ 1—The Ebionites believed that Christ was essentially human, and divine only in the sense that he had been selected to reign as the Jewish Messiah. Docetists

insisted that Christ could not truly have taken part in the corruption of the body and so he was instead a spirit who appeared human. The Gnostics believed that the divine Christ and human Jesus had formed a brief partnership in order to rescue humankind from the corrupting grasp of the material world, and the Arians believed that God was One, and that the Son of God must have been a created being who did not share the essence of God.

8. How did Constantine come to be anti-Arian?

A8.—Pg. 10, ¶ 2 & 3—Constantine sided with the most influential leaders of the Christian church when Arius split from his bishop. Arianism created a hierarchy of divinities, with God the Father at the top and God the Son somewhere underneath. Because this was anathema to both the Jewish roots of Christianity and Greek Platonism, the leaders of the Church sided against Arianism and created the Nicene Creed, which Constantine supported.

9. In his support of the religion, what did Constantine offer Christians who lived in the Roman empire?

A9.—Pg. 11, ¶ 2—Constantine offered Christians the protection of his imperial power. He recognized Christian priests as equal to priests of the Roman religion, and exempted them from taxes and state responsibilities that might interfere with their religious duties. He also decreed that any man could leave his property to the church, and he created a new Christian city to be the capital of the Roman empire, Byzantium.

10. What happened to Arius after his condemnation at the Council of Nicaea? Why might Constantia have supported Arius?

A10.—Pg. 11, ¶ 5 & 6—After his condemnation at the Council of Nicaea, Arius hid in Palestine, but his theology did not disappear; it remained a strong and discontented underground current. Constantia might have championed Arian doctrines because Constantine had Constantia's husband Licinius and their ten-year-old son killed in order to ensure his throne.

Section III: Critical Thinking

The student may use his text to answer this question.

The first thing we learned in Chapter One of *The History of the Medieval World* is that when Constantine's men marched into Rome after defeating seated ruler Maxentius, they did so with the sign of Christ marked on each shield. Christianity was not only credited with helping Constantine defeat Maxentius, but also for bringing Rome together into one united empire. Write a paragraph explaining what gave Christianity the special quality that allowed Constantine to use it to keep his Roman empire together. In your answer, make sure to explain why Constantine made the Nicene Creed law.

Constantine saw Rome as an empire of different peoples, banded together under one rule but separated by their various cultures: "For centuries, it had been a political entity within which provinces and districts and cities still maintained their older, deeper identities. Tarsus was Roman, but it was also an Asian city where you were more likely to hear Greek than Latin in the streets. North Africa was Roman, but Carthage was an African city with an African population. Gaul was a Roman territory, but the Germanic tribes who populated it spoke their own languages and worshipped their own gods" (Pg. 6, ¶ 6 to Pg. 7, ¶ 1). Constantine saw that it was almost impossible for the people of the Roman empire to be loyal to two different cultural identities. How could one be both African and Roman, or Roman and Visigoth? However, one could have a cultural identity and a religious identity: anyone could be a practicing Christian no matter what their cultural identity, be it African, Visigoth, or Greek. Also, because Christianity had begun as a religion with no political homeland to claim as its own, it was more aligned with its practice and doctrine than with a place. This made it easily adaptable for use in Rome, an empire that was constantly taking in new lands and people within its boundaries.

While the belief in Christ could be held by any kind of person, it was no use to Constantine if people believed in different versions of Christ, or had different ways of practicing. If he was going to use Christianity to unify Rome, it had to be the same religion everywhere. Constantine made the Nicene Creed law in an effort to homogenize Christianity in Rome. If one believed in Christ, then he also believed in the government that deemed that belief right and lawful. Thus, in Constantine's view, believing in Christ meant believing in Rome.

EXAMPLE ANSWER:

Constantine saw Rome as an empire of different peoples, banded together under one rule but separated by their various cultures. He saw the difficulty in converting someone loyal to the Visigoths, or Greeks for example, into someone loyal to Rome. However, anyone could believe in Christ without giving up all the parts of their own cultural identity. As a religion with no original homeland, Christianity was suitable for use in Rome, an empire that was constantly taking in new lands and people. While the belief in Christ could be held by any kind of person, it was no use to Constantine if people believed in different versions of Christ, or had different ways of practicing. If he was going to use Christianity to unify Rome, it had to be the same religion everywhere. Constantine made the Nicene Creed law in an effort to homogenize Christianity in Rome. If one believed in Christ, then he also believed in the government that deemed that belief right and lawful. Thus, in Constantine's view, believing in Christ meant believing in Rome.

Section IV: Map Exercise

1. Using a black pencil, trace the rectangular outline of the frame for Map 1.1: The Empires of the Romans and Persians.

2. Using a blue pencil, trace the coastline of the Mediterranean Sea. Then trace the coastline of the Black Sea. Then, using your black pencil, trace the external limits of the two empires, Roman and Persian. Trace the dotted line that separates the two empires. Repeat these until the contours are familiar.

3. Using a new sheet of paper, trace the rectangular outline of the frame in black. Remove your tracing paper from the original. Using a regular pencil with an eraser, draw the coastline of the Mediterranean Sea, the limits of the two empires, and the coastline of the Black Sea, while looking at Map 1.1. Use the distance between the map and the rectangular frame as a guide.

4. When you are pleased with your map, lay it over the original. Erase and redraw any lines which are more than ¼ inch off of the original.

5. Look back at your map and study carefully the cities of Carthage, Rome, Athens, Alexandria, Ephesus, Nicea, Byzantium, and Antioch. When you are familiar with them, close the book. Use your regular pencil to locate and label these cities on your map. Check your map against the original. If you are more than ¼ of an inch off, erase and remark the cities while looking at the original.

Chapter Two

Seeking the Mandate of Heaven

The student may use her text when answering the questions in sections I and II.

Section I: Who, What, Where

Write a one or two-sentence answer explaining the significance of each item listed below.

280—**Pg. 15, ¶ 5—280 is the year the Jin army defeated the emperor of the Dong Wu, ending the era of the Three Kingdoms. In 280, all of China was united under the Jin.**

Amitabha—**Pg. 19, ¶ 5—Amitabha was the "Buddha of Shining Light" who lived in the Western Paradise, the Pure Land, a place where all those who believed in Buddha were to be reborn. The teachings of the Amitabha were first spread by the Chinese monk Hui-yuan and the Indian monk Kumarajiva.**

Battle of the Fei River—**Pg. 18, ¶ 5 & 6—The Battle of the Fei River was fought between the northern barbarian leader Fu Jian and the Jin emperor Jin Xiaowudi. Though Jin Xiaowudi's soldiers were outnumbered, the Jin triumphed over Fu Jian, and put an end to the northerner's campaign.**

Fu Jian—**Pg. 18, ¶ 3 to Pg. 19, ¶ 1—Fu Jian, chief of the barbarian state Qianqin, wanted to reunite all of China because he desperately wanted to be Chinese. He conquered most of the Sixteen Kingdoms, but after failing to conquer the Jin, he was strangled by his subordinate Tuoba Gui.**

Jin Huaidi—**Pg. 16, ¶ 2 and Pg. 17, ¶ 3 & 4—Jin Huaidi was the third emperor of the Jin dynasty, following Jin Wudi and the idiot emperor. After being captured by the Hanzhao invaders, Jin Huaidi was enslaved and made to serve officials of the Hanzhao before he was put to death by Hanzhao leader Liu Cong.**

Sima Rui/Jin Yuandi—**Pg. 17, ¶ 3—Sima Rui, the commander of a sizable Jin force quartered at the city of Jianye, took the imperial name Jin Yuandi. Although he had a short reign, he was**

succeeded by his son and grandsons in an unbroken imperial line that ruled from Jianye over a shrunken southeastern domain.

Sima Yan/Jin Wudi—**Pg. 15, ¶ 2 & 5—Sima Yan took the royal name Jin Wudi when he became emperor of the Cao Wei. Jin Wudi conquered the Dong Wu and united the Chinese into a single empire under the Jin dynasty.**

Sixteen Kingdoms—**Pg. 16, ¶ 2 & 3—Sixteen Kingdoms was the name for the numerous tiny states ruled by war lords to the north of that aspired to conquer the greater Jin kingdom below them. The Chinese to the south gave these states the collective name "Sixteen Kingdoms" even though their number was fluid.**

Sun En—**Pg. 19, ¶ 3—Sun En was a pirate who, around 400, recruited a navy and sailed along the shore raiding, burning, and stealing, earning the name "armies of demons" from the Jin shore-dwellers. Sun En's army was defeated by the Jin generals in 402.**

Three Kingdoms (territory)—**Pg. 13, ¶ 2—The Three Kingdoms were the pieces that resulted from the fracturing of the Han empire in 220 AD. The Cao Wei, the Shu Han and the Dong Wu made up the Three Kingdoms.**

Three Kingdoms (story)—**Pg. 14, ¶ 3 & 4—The *Three Kingdoms* is the most famous account of the years after the fall of the Han. Though the *Three Kingdoms* is a fictionalized account, it reflects the actual events surrounding the rise of the Jin dynasty.**

Tuoba Gui—**Pg. 19, ¶ 1 & 2—Tuoba Gui, Fu Jian's murderer, a barbarian descended from the Xianbei tribe, native of the Dai state, wanted to unify and conquer the north. In an effort to create a Chinese identity he changed his state's name from the Xianbei "Dai" to the Chinese "Bei Wei," and he changed his own family name from the Xianbei "Tuoba" to the Chinese "Yuan."**

Wei Yuandi—**Pg. 14, ¶ 3 & 4—Wei Yuandi was the seated emperor of the Cao Wei kingdom when Sima Yan demanded that he turn over the crown. Wei Yuandi handed over the seal of the state to Sima Yan and then returned to life an ordinary citizen.**

Section II: Comprehension

Write a two or three-sentence answer to each of the following questions.

1. What was Sima Yan's motivation to claim the Cao Wei crown for himself?

A1.—Pg. 14, ¶ 1 & 2—For his entire life, Sima Yan watched army men like his father and grandfather control the king. The commanders of the Cao Wei army led in the conquest of the Shu Han, but received no credit and remained crownless. Sima Yan craved legitimacy and the right power to command, so he decided to take the title that accompanied the sword.

2. How was the Cao Wei crown passed from Wei Yuandi to Sima Yan?

A2.—Pg. 14, ¶ 3 & 4—Sima Yan confronted Wei Yuandi in front of an audience of the army man's supporters, and asked the emperor "Whose efforts have preserved the Cao Wei empire?" to which the young emperor answered, "We owe everything to your father and grandfather." Sima Yan responded that it was clear that since Wei Yuandi could not defend the kingdom for himself, he should appoint someone who could. Wei Yuandi agreed to Sima Yan's plans; Sima Yan built an altar, and in a elaborate, formal ceremony, Wei Yuandi climbed to the top of the altar with the seal of state in his hands, gave it to his rival, and then descended to the ground a common citizen.

3. When Jin Wudi's armies arrived outside of Dong Wu territory and found the Jianye river blocked by barriers of iron chain, how did the Jin army break through? What happened after Jin Wudi's army broke through?

A3.—Pg. 15, ¶ 5—When the Jin armies found their passage through the Jianye river blocked by barriers of iron chain, they sent flaming rafts, piled high with pitch-covered logs, floating down into the barriers. As a result, the chains melted and snapped, the Jin flooded into Jianye and the tyrannical emperor of the Dong Wu surrendered.

4. What was the Rebellion of the Eight Princes? What caused the rebellion?

A4.—Pg. 15, ¶ 6 to Pg. 16, ¶ 1—The Rebellion of the Eight Princes was the chaos that swallowed up the Jin empire following Jin Wudi's death in 290. The heir to the throne was "more than half an idiot," and a fight to become regent for the idiot broke out between wife, father-in-law, step-grandfather, uncles, cousins, brothers and the twenty-four sons Jin Wudi left behind. Of the family members vying for control, eight royals managed to rise to the position of regent.

5. How did the Hanzhao take down Luoyang and begin the destruction of the Jin empire?

A5.—Pg. 16, ¶ 3 to Pg. 17, ¶ 1—The Hanzhao, one of the Sixteen Kingdoms, pushed constantly south, raiding Jin land and by 311, reaching the walls of the Jin capital Luoyang itself. While the Jin armies were fighting a dozen battles outside of Luoyang's walls, inside of the city the people were starving. The gates were finally opened and emperor Jin Huaidi was taken by the Hanzhao as a prisoner of war.

6. What happened to Jin Huaidi after he was taken prisoner by Liu Cong? What happened to the remaining Jin court?

A6.—Pg. 17, ¶ 2—Jin Huaidi spent two years as a palace slave, but visitors to the court were shocked to see the man who held the Mandate of Heaven forced into servitude. When the feeling that Jin Huaidi should be freed spread through Liu Cong's court, the Hanzhao ruler responded by killing the Jin emperor. Three years later, Liu Cong marched down to Chang'an, where the surviving Jin court had gathered, and conquered it.

7. What actions did Fu Jian take to make his barbarian kingdom more Chinese?

A7.—Pg. 18, ¶ 3–7—In order to make Qianqin more Chinese, Fu Jian founded Confucian academies in his state, reformed the government of his kingdom so that it was run along Chinese lines, his capital city was at the ancient Chinese capital of Chang'an and his chief minister was Chinese. Fu Jian also tried to reunite all of China, first by conquering most of the Sixteen Kingdoms and then by attempting to absorb the Jin.

8. Though joining a monastic community meant renouncing the world and giving up all ownership of private property, what benefits did joining the monastery offer?

A8.—Pg. 20, ¶ 1—Monasticism provided a refuge, which was particularly appealing in a world of the battling northern territories and the failing Jin. The followers of the Amitabha were exempt from the requirement of bowing to the emperor and from worrying about the battles in the north and south, because they existed in a different reality where they gained peace.

Section III: Critical Thinking

The student may not use her text to answer this question.

When Jin Wudi set about trying to reunify China, he knew he needed greater justification than force to bring together his empire. As written in our chapter, "Emperors ruled by the will of Heaven, but if they grew tyrannical and corrupt, the will of Heaven would raise up another dynasty to supplant them." Years after Jin Wudi's shortly reunified China fell apart, the Jin name managed to live on. Explain why neither the Hanzhao, nor any of the other Sixteen Kingdoms, did not try to bring a final end to the Jin. Then explain how the Jin were able to justify to themselves that the Mandate of Heaven was still alive and well in the *real* China.

The student needs to address two different questions in this answer: first, why didn't any kingdoms from the north try to finish the Jin off, and second, how did the Jin keep their court together?

The text explains on page 17 that "Neither the Hanzhao nor any of the other Sixteen Kingdoms tried to bring a final end to the Jin, possibly because the land south of the Yangtze didn't lend itself to fighting on horseback (the preferred method of northerners, inherited from their nomadic ancestors)." The Jin believed that the Yangtze marked the boundary between the real China and the northern realm of the barbarians. With a barrier firmly in place that demarcated the Chinese from the outside world, the Jin proved that the Mandate of Heaven still existed on their side of the Yangtze. By modeling itself on the old traditions of the Han, the torch of the ancient Chinese civilization was kept burning with the Jin. The Jin brought back rituals of ancestor worship and played host to Confucian scholars who taught, in the traditional manner, that the enlightened man was he who recognized his duties and carried them out faithfully. The Jin held on to the Confucian belief that a ruler will gain more and more authority over his people by ruling righteously. "Guide the people by virtue," the Analects had promised, "keep them in line by rites, and they will . . . reform themselves." The promise that virtuous government would always triumph held the Jin court together, and kept the belief in the Mandate of Heaven alive.

EXAMPLE ANSWER:

The Hanzhao, and the other barbarians in the Sixteen Kingdoms, left the Jin alone most likely because the land south of the Yangtze was difficult to traverse and fight in while riding a horse. This was how the northern barbarians preferred to fight. Since the barbarians left the Jin alone, the Jin were able to build up their morality by relying on ancient Chinese traditions. They believed the Mandate of Heaven lived on south of the Yangtze, in the "real" China. The Jin reinstated ancestor worship and the teachings of Confucius. Confucian scholars taught that the enlightened man recognized his duties and carried them out faithfully. The Jin held on to the belief that a ruler would gain more and more authority over his people by ruling righteously. A virtuous leader would be able to guide his people to reform themselves. The promise that a virtuous government would always triumph held the Jin court together, and kept the belief in the Mandate of Heaven alive.

Section IV: Map Exercise

1. Using a black pencil, trace the rectangular outline of the frame for Map 2.1: The Three Kingdoms.

2. Using a blue pencil, trace the outline of the Yellow Sea. Using your blue pencil, trace the line of the Yellow River. Then trace the line of the Yangtze River up to the perimeter. Using your black pencil, trace the lines delineating the Three Kingdoms, Cao Wei, Shu Han, and Dong Wu. Repeat until the contours are familiar.

3. Trace the rectangular outline of the frame in black. Remove your tracing paper from the original. Using a regular pencil with an eraser, draw the coastline of the Yellow Sea and the lines of the Three Kingdoms, while looking at Map 2.1. Use the distance between the map and the rectangular frame as a guide. Label the Yellow and Yangtze Rivers.

4. When you are pleased with your map, lay it over the original. Erase and redraw any lines which are more than ¼ inch off of the original.

5. Look back at your map and study carefully the cities of Jianye and Luoyang. When you are familiar with them, close the book. Use your regular pencil to locate and label these cities on your map. Check your map against the original. If you are more than ¼ of an inch off, erase and remark the cities while looking at the original.

Chapter Three

An Empire of the Mind

The student may use his text when answering the questions in sections I and II.

Section I: Who, What, Where

Write a one or two-sentence answer explaining the significance of each item listed below.

Asoka the Great—**Pg. 23, ¶ 1—Asoka the Great was the most powerful king of the Mauryan empire, four centuries before the Gupta rule. When he was king, the Mauryans had controlled almost the entire subcontinent.**

Brahmans—**Pg. 23, ¶ 5—The brahmans were the educated Hindu upper class of Gupta society, and the keepers of Sanskrit. Sanskrit's dominance shows that the brahmans, and not the Buddhists, were firmly at the top of the Gupta world.**

Chandragupta/ *maharajadhiraja*—**Pg. 21, ¶ 4 to Pg. 22, ¶ 1—Chandragupta, who inherited his father's throne and had the alliance of his wife's family, conquered his way from Magadha through the ancient territories of Kosola and Vatsa, building himself a small empire centered on the Ganges. He gave himself the title *maharajadhiraja*, which meant "Great King of Kings."**

Chandragupta II/Vikramaditya—**Pg. 25, ¶ 1 to Pg. 26, ¶ 1—Chandragupta II became king in 380 after he killed Prince Ramagupta. Through a marriage alliance between his daughter and the Vakataka dynasty, Chandragupta II grew his kingdom and gave himself the name Vikramaditya, or "Sun of Prowess."**

Ghatokacha—**Pg. 21, ¶ 3 & 4—Ghatokacha was a minor king of a small Indian state who passed his throne to his son, Chandragupta, in 319. Ghatokacha's most important accomplishment in life was making a match between Chandragupta and a royal princess from the Licchavi family.**

Kalabhra—**Pg. 21, ¶ 2—The Kalabhra were a line of kings that built a dynasty that lasted for over three hundred years and swallowed the entire southern tip of the Indian subcontinent. The Kalabhra kingdom left few inscriptions and no written history behind it, so we don't know much about it.**

Pataliputra—**Pg. 22, ¶ 3—Pataliputra was Samudragupta's capital city at the great fork in the Ganges river.**

Pillar Edicts—**Pg. 22, ¶ 3 and Pg. 24, ¶ 4—The Pillar Edicts were ancient stone pillars erected by Asoka the Great of the Mauryan empire, on which tales of Asoka's guilt were inscribed. He scattered these pillars around the empire in an act of penance for the death and destruction caused by his battles for territory.**

Prabhavati—**Pg. 25, ¶ 2—Prabhavati, daughter of Chandragupta II, married into the Vakataka dynasty of minor kings in the western Deccan. Her husband died not too long after their marriage and she became regent and queen, ruling the lands of the Vakataka under her father's direction.**

Samudragupta—**Pg. 22, ¶ 2 & 3—Samudragupta inherited the throne from his father Chandragupta in 335. He inscribed his victories on one of the ancient stone pillars erected by Asoka the Great.**

Satavahana—**Pg. 21, ¶ 2—The Satavahana were the last dynasty that managed to keep control over the Deccan, the desert south of the Narmada river. The Satavahana empire collapsed in the third century, giving way to a series of competing dynastic families.**

Section II: Comprehension

Write a two or three-sentence answer to each of the following questions.

1. What lands did Samudragupta conquer during his forty-five year reign?

A1.—Pg. 22, ¶ 2—During his forty-five year reign, Samudragupta conquered lands that encompassed almost all of the Ganges river. He also campaigned his way south, into the land of the Pallava on the southeastern coast, the Satavahana in the Deccan, and the Vakataka, just to the west, making each of these dynasties pay tribute to him.

2. Samudragupta may have called himself "conqueror of the four quarters of the earth," but he did not actually rule over all of India. How did Samudragupta justify this title?

A2.—Pg. 22, ¶ 5 to Pg. 23, ¶ 2—Even though most of the "conquered" land to the north and west of Samudragupta was not folded into his empire, he was able to wring tribute money out of the "conquered kings." If Samudragupta counted those who paid tribute to him with the lands that were actually conquered, his kingdom tripled in size, and so he justified

calling himself "conqueror of the four quarters of the earth" by ignoring the difference between empire and tributary land.

3. Why did Samudragupta inscribe his victories on an ancient stone pillar?

A3.—Pg. 22, ¶ 3 & 5 and Pg. 23, ¶ 3—Samudragupta inscribed his victories on an ancient stone pillar because it was erected by the powerful Mauryan king Asoka the Great. Samudragupta needed to connect himself with the past because he had to find a way to unite all the parts and people of his far-flung empire. By inscribing his victories on the ancient pillar, he used nostalgia to recreate the past core of Indian greatness to keep his empire together.

4. Where did Sanskrit come from? How are the prakrits related to Sanskrit? Who used Sanskrit during Samudragupta's time, and what important works were written in Sanskrit?

A4.—Pg. 23, ¶ 4—Sanskrit had come down into India long ago, trickling across the mountains from the central Asian war tribes that had seeped into India. The prakrits, or "common tongues," were mutations of Sanskrit that were used for the everyday, like Magadhi and Pali. During Samudragupta's time, Sanskrit was the preferred speech of philosophers and scholars, and the Hindu scriptures known as the Puranas, the law codes, and the epic tales of the Ramayana and the Mahabharata were all written in Sanskrit.

5. What is the general definition of a culture's golden age, and classical period? What must a historian do in order to identify a culture's golden age or classical period?

A5.—Pg. 24, ¶ 1—A golden age is when virtually every manifestation of life reached a peak of excellence, and a classic period implies a certain height from which a culture declines. Historians must first define excellence and the height of a culture before they can go back and discover when a culture went through one of these periods.

6. Describe both the Hindu and Buddhist elements of the Guptas.

A6.—Pg. 24, ¶ 2 & 3—The Guptas built Hindu temples and wrote their inscriptions in Sanskrit, but they also erected Buddhist stupas and supported Buddhist monasteries. Official inscriptions of the Gupta court were Sanskrit, and Samudragupta used Hindu rituals in victory as tools of his royal power. Sanskrit may have been more prominent, but the Guptas embraced both systems for understanding the world.

7. What do coins from the period after Samudragupta died tell us about the transfer of power that followed his rule?

A7.—Pg. 24, ¶ 6—Coins from the period show another royal name, Prince Ramagupta. This means there was not an orderly progression from father to son, but a battle for the throne sometime between 375 and 380.

8. Describe the plot of the play *Devi-Chandra-gupta.*

A8.—Pg. 24, ¶ 6 to Pg. 25, ¶ 1—The *Devi-Chandra-gupta* suggested that Prince Ramagupta schemed to kill his younger brother Chandragupta II. Chandragupta II had carried out

a daring offensive against the Shaka enemies to the west, infiltrating the Shaka court in woman's dress and assassinating the Shaka king, an act that made Chandragupta II so popular that Ramagupta decided to kill him. Chandragupta II discovered the plot, confronted his brother, and killed him.

Section III: Critical Thinking

The student may use his text to answer this question.

When Chandragupta began to grow his empire, he realized he could not actually conquer all of the far-flung Indian lands. Instead, he collected tribute from many smaller states and let the kings and tribal chiefs of these lands continue to rule per their own will. Chandragupta's son, Chandragupta II, followed in his father's footsteps and created an empire that was tied together through peace, an "empire of the mind." Using the Chinese monk Faxian's description of Indian lands, explain what life was like in Chandragupta II's empire. Then, describe how Chandragupta II's policies created an empire of the mind, and how that led to his remembrance as the wise king Vikramaditya.

The Chinese monk Faxian traveled to Indian to collect Buddhist scriptures for his monastery sometime between 400 and 412. The chapter provides us with a long excerpt from Faxian's writing that describes the peace and prosperity that resulted from Chandragupta II's laissez-faire style of government:

The people are numerous and happy; they have not to register their households, or attend to any magistrates and their rules; only those who cultivate the royal land have to pay (a portion of) the grain from it. If they want to go, they go; if they want to stay on, they stay. The king governs without decapitation or (other) corporal punishments. Criminals are simply fined, lightly or heavily, according to the circumstances (of each case). Even in cases of repeated attempts at wicked rebellion, they only have their right hands cut off. The king's body-guards and attendants all have salaries. Throughout the whole country the people do not kill any living creature, nor drink intoxicating liquor, nor eat onions or garlic.

Faxian found that in Pataliputra, the Gupta capital, "The inhabitants are rich and prosperous . . . and vie with one another in the practice of benevolence and righteousness." Faxian also praised Chandragupta II for his acceptance of Buddhism: "The Law of Buddha was widely made known, and the followers of other doctrines did not find it in their power to persecute the body of monks in any way." Ruling from the same city where King Asoka ruled, Chandragupta II, like his father, aligned himself with the glorious past in order to have a cohesive empire in the present.

Faxian's description, onion and garlic distaste aside, shows us how Chandragupta II created an empire of the mind, rather than an empire based on force or coercion. Chandragupta II paid his staff rather than forcing them into servitude, he didn't expect ridiculously large payments from his tributes, and he let the people who worked royal land keep most of the crops they grew. He treated his subjects fairly, and as a result they believed in his kingdom by choice. Ruling this way for nearly four decades, Chandragupta II became a legend for his wise rule. He was remembered as Vikramaditya, Sun of Prowess, subject of heroic tales and mythical songs.

EXAMPLE ANSWER:

When Chinese monk Faxian traveled through India, he was impressed by the peace and prosperity of the Indian people. He said "the people are numerous and happy." He thought it was good that they didn't have to register their households with the king, nor did they have to report to a magistrate. If you worked on royal farm land, you only had to give up a portion of the grain you grew, and if you were a criminal, your punishment was determined by the circumstances of the crime. Faxian saw happy government employees, and he saw that the inhabitants of the capital, Pataliputra, were rich, prosperous and treated each other with benevolence. Most importantly for the Buddhist monk, Faxian praised Chandragupta II for his acceptance of Buddhism; the Law of Buddha was widely known, and the followers of other religions did not persecute Buddhist monks. Ruling from the same city where King Asoka ruled, Chandragupta II, like his father, aligned himself with the glorious past in order to have a cohesive empire in the present. Chandragupta II treated his subjects fairly, and as a result they believed in his kingdom by choice, an empire of the mind. Ruling this way for nearly four decades, Chandragupta II became a legend for his wise rule. He was remembered as Vikramaditya, Sun of Prowess, subject of heroic tales and mythical songs.

Section IV: Map Exercise

1. Using a black pencil, trace the rectangular outline of the frame for Map 3.1: The Age of the Gupta.

2. Using a blue pencil, trace the coastline of the Arabian Sea and Bay of Bengal.

Use contrasting colors to designate the territories of Chandragupta, Samudragupta, Samudragupta's tributaries, and the tributaries of Chandragupta II. Use peaks to represent the mountains. Repeat until the contours are familiar.

3. Using a new sheet of paper, trace the black rectangular outline of the frame in black. Remove your tracing paper from the original. Using a regular pencil with an eraser, draw the coastline of the Arabian Sea and Bay of Bengal and the separate territories of Chandragupta, Samudragupta, Samudragupta's tributaries, and Chandragupta II, while looking at Map 3.1. Use the distance between the map and the rectangular frame as a guide. Label the Arabian Sea and Bay of Bengal.

4. When you are pleased with your map, place it over the original. Erase and redraw any lines which are more than ¼ inch off of the original.

Chapter Four

The Persian Threat

The student may use her text when answering the questions in sections I and II.

Section I: Who, What, Where

Write a one or two-sentence answer explaining the significance of each item listed below.

Ammianus Marcellinus—**Pg. 34, ¶ 4 and Pg. 35, ¶ 2—Ammianus Marcellinus, a Roman soldier that later wrote a history of the Roman wars with Persia, had been sent secretly into Persian-controlled Armenia by Constantius to spy on the Persian advance. Ammianus Marcellinus managed to survive several battles, and escaped from the ravaged city of Amida through a back gate, on a horse he found trapped in a thicket.**

Constans—**Pg. 32, ¶ 1 to Pg. 33, ¶ 1—Constans was Constantine's fourteen-year old son and heir, who ruled over the Prefecture of Italy, which included Rome and North Africa. Though he showed force by killing his brother Constantine II, and staunchly supported the church, Constans was very unpopular and was killed at age twenty-seven by one of his own generals.**

Constantine II—**Pg. 32, ¶ 1–3—Constantine II was Constantine's twenty-one-year old son and heir, who ruled over the Prefecture of Gaul. When he tried to take Italy away from his youngest brother, Constans, he was ambushed by Constans and killed.**

Constantius—**Pg. 33, ¶ 2, Pg. 34, ¶ 2 and Pg. 35, ¶ 4—Constantius, Constantine's oldest son and heir, became the sole ruler of the Roman empire after the death of his two brothers and the officer Magnentius. After creating much opposition to his rule by supporting Arianism, Constantius was demoted to co-emperor, a title he died defending against the Persians and his co-ruler, Julian.**

Ezana—**Pg. 29, ¶ 4 & 5—Ezana, king of the African kingdom of Axum, converted to Christianity and became Constantine's ally. This act was a threat against Shapur II's Persia.**

Hurmuz—**Pg. 28, ¶ 2—Hurmuz was the king of Persia, father of Shapur II. Hurmuz died before Shapur II was born, meaning Shapur II was made king before he was even born.**

Julian—**Pg. 33, ¶ 4, Pg. 34, ¶ 2 and Pg. 35, ¶ 4—Julian, nephew of Constantine, raised in Asia Minor survived the purges after his uncle's death and was later named heir to Constantius at twenty-three. Julian became co-emperor of the Roman empire after Constantius fell out of favor for making Arian Christology orthodox, and he became the sole emperor of Rome after Constantius's death in 361.**

Khosrov the Short—**Pg. 30, ¶ 5, Pg. 31, ¶ 5, and Pg. 32, ¶ 2—Khosrov the Short succeeded his father as a Christian king of Armenia. Khosrov the Short fled from his throne after Constantine's death, when Shapur II invaded Armenia, and was reinstated when Constantius took rule of the Roman Prefecture of the East.**

Magnentius—**Pg. 33, ¶ 2—Magnentius, an officer, was named co-emperor by the generals of Rome after Constans' death. Constantius marched against the usurper, and after two years of fighting Magnentius killed himself rather than falling into Constantius's hands.**

Shapur II/Shapur the Great—**Pg. 29, ¶ 2, Pg. 31, ¶ 1 & 5, and Pg. 35, ¶ 3—Shapur II, son of Shapur, made a name for himself early in his rule as being a shrewd and intelligent leader. Shapur II persecuted Christians in Persia, invaded Armenia after Constantine's death and successfully fought Constantius for control of Amida, some fortressed and fortified towns, and eastern land.**

Tiridates—**Pg. 30, ¶ 4 & 5—Tiridates, king of Armenia, baptized in 303, became an ally of the Romans when Constantine made Christianity the religion of his empire. Tiridates was poisoned in 330 because of Shapur II's handiwork, and became a martyr, and eventually a saint.**

Zoroastrianism—**Pg. 28, ¶ 2—Zoroastrianism was the state religion of the Persians.**

Section II: Comprehension

Write a two or three-sentence answer to each of the following questions.

1. Why didn't the Persians attack Constantine during his rise to power?

A1.—Pg. 28, ¶ 2—When Hurmuz died, his son and heir had not yet been born. The Persian noblemen and the priests of Zoroastrianism had crowned the queen's pregnant belly. The regents who controlled Persia until Shapur II was sixteen cared more about their own power than the greater good of Persia, distracting them from taking care of Constantine and his growing empire.

2. For what reason were the Arabs attacking Persia in the south? Why didn't Persia fight back?

A2.—Pg. 28, ¶ 3—The tribes of kingless and nomadic Arabs from the Arabian peninsula were driven northward by a sinking water table. Because of the harshness of their own native land, they attacked the cultivated land and cattle of the people in southern Persia. The Persians weren't able to fight back because their king was a child, and the regents were fighting amongst themselves.

3. When Shapur II was a boy, he could do nothing to help the Persians fight against the Arabs. How did he handle the problem when he attained his majority?

A3.—Pg. 28, ¶ 4 to Pg. 29, ¶ 1—When Shapur II gained his majority, he selected a thousand horsemen to act as a strike force against the Arab invaders, under his personal command. He slaughtered the invaders, took some into captivity, and pursued those that fled by sending a fleet of ships across the Persian Gulf to Bahrain. The fleet landed in eastern Arabia, where Shapur II shed more blood and then continued to take captives as far as the city of Medina.

4. What change did Shapur II make early in his career that showed he was intelligent, shrewd and a good administrator? Hint: think of the Tigris river.

A4.—Pg. 29, ¶ 2—Shapur II watched his people crossing a bridge over the Tigris, pushing against each other on the crowded span. To increase the efficiency of traffic flow, he gave orders for another bridge to be built, so that one of the bridges could be used for people crossing in one direction and the other bridge for people crossing from the opposite direction. Inventing a new traffic pattern was an innovation, and showed that Shapur II was a good administrator, as well as an intelligent and shrewd king.

5. Why did Constantine ask Shapur II to show mercy on the Christians living in Persia? How was this act contradicted by the conversion of the African king of Axum, Ezana, to Christianity?

Note to the parent—On page 29, ¶ 3, the text states, "Constantine's move to Byzantium was silent testimony that he intended to challenge Persia's hold on the east." Before attacking Persian land, Constantine first tried to make nice with Shapur II by asking that the Persian king refrain from persecuting Christians in Persia. However, when Ezana converted to Christianity, the act declared an alliance with the Roman empire, which was a threat against Persia.

A5.—Pg. 29, ¶ 3 & 4—Though Constantine's move to Byzantium was silent testimony that he intended to challenge Persia's hold on the east, he first approached his enemy politely. His request to Shapur II that he refrain from persecuting Christians was a sort-of act of diplomacy that did not reveal Constantine's true intentions. However, shortly after Shapur II agreed to Constantine's request, the African king of Axum, Ezana, converted to Christianity, which declared not only his religious faith but his political alliance to Constantine.

6. What does "Dhu al-Aktaf" mean? Why was Shapur II called "Dhu al-Aktaf"?

A6.—Pg. 30, ¶ 1 and note—"Dhu al-Aktaf" means "The Man of the Shoulders." Shapur II was called "Dhu al-Aktaf" because, as he continued to pursue the invading Arabs into the Arabian interior, he would either kill or tear out the shoulder-blades of their leaders. The act of tearing out the shoulder did not necessarily kill the victim; instead it left the sword-arm, used to fight against the Persian king, useless and dangling.

7. After the failed invasion of Armenia in 336, why did Shapur II crack down on Persian Christians?

A7.—Pg. 30, ¶ 7—Armenia, a buffer state between the Persian and Roman empires, had sided with the Romans by embracing Christianity. In his own empire, Shapur II saw Christians as likely double agents working for Rome, and so the systematic persecution of Persian Christians, mostly on the western frontier, began early in 337.

8. Why was Constantine buried in a mausoleum at the Church of the Holy Apostles?

A8.—Pg. 31, ¶ 4—Like the apostles, Constantine was a founder of the Christian faith. He was the first Roman emperor to honor God and honored the church like no Roman leader before him. He married Christianity and state politics, and in doing so had changed both forever.

9. How did Julian become co-emperor of the Roman empire?

A9.—Pg. 33, ¶ 5, and Pg. 34, ¶ 1 & 2—Constantius's declaration that Arian Christology was now orthodox made him very unpopular, while Julian was very popular because he was successful in his war campaigns and reduced taxes in the lands he governed. When Constantius fell into disfavor he demanded that Julian reduce his armed force by sending some of his troops eastward. Julian did no such thing and the army on the Rhine, backing him up, elevated him to the post of co-emperor.

10. Why was Constantius's displacement of Liberius, bishop of Rome, with a pro-Arian bishop, so offensive?

A10.—Pg. 33, ¶ 6 & 7—Constantius's displacement of the bishop of Rome, Liberius, with a pro-Arian bishop, was offensive for two reasons: first, Arianism was outlawed which made Constantius a heretic. Second, the bishops of Rome considered themselves the spiritual heirs of the apostle Peter, and they considered Peter to be the founder of the Christian church. The bishops believed they were the only ones who had the right to make decisions for the church, making Constantius's declaration even more insulting.

11. How did the Persians re-take control of Armenia? Describe how the Persians outsmarted the Romans who invaded Armenia at the Euphrates.

A11.—Pg. 33, ¶ 3–5 and Pg. 34, 4 & 5—While Constantius was dealing with the fallout from displacing the Roman bishop, Shapur invaded Armenia, captured the king, put out his eyes, and allowed his son to ascend the throne only on the condition that he remain subject to Persian wishes. When the Roman army attacked Armenia, they burned the fields and houses in front of the approaching enemy to prevent them from finding food, and made a

stand at the Euphrates river. The Persians, advised by a Roman traitor who had gone over to their side, made a detour north through untouched fields and orchards, outsmarting the Romans.

12. Describe the Roman defeat at the siege of Amida.

Pg. 35 ¶ 1–3—When the two Romans and Persians met at the walled city of Amida, the Romans found themselves attacked from two sides, so they hid in the city. The Persians attacked the walls of the city with archers and war elephants, and eventually climbed over the walls via mounds of dirt they had heaped up. The inhabitants were slaughtered and Constantius was forced to surrender not only Amida but also at least two other fortresses, a handful of fortified towns, and eastern land to the Persians.

Section III: Critical Thinking

The student may not use her text to answer this question.

Before he died, Constantine was preparing a crusade against Persia. This is not to be confused with the "Crusades" of the 11th, 12th and 13th centuries. Using a dictionary, look up the definition of crusade, and explain the different between "crusade" and "Crusade." Then, explain how Constantine's planned attack on Persia was a "crusade."

The Merriam-Webster Online Dictionary defines lower-case "c" crusade as: "a remedial enterprise undertaken with zeal and enthusiasm." Crusades, with a capital "C," refers to any military expedition undertaken by the Christians of Europe in the 11th, 12th and 13th centuries for the recovery of the Holy Land from the Muslims. Today, we often use the word "crusade" to refer to a religious war, but this should not be confused with capital-C "Crusade."

Constantine's "enterprise" was giving aid to the Christian Persians who were under attack in Shapur II's empire. The "zeal and enthusiasm" Constantine showed was apparent in the gear he planned to take with him in his fight against the Persians: a portable tabernacle, and a tent in which bishops who would accompany the army would lead regular worship. Constantine also planned to be baptized in the river Jordan as soon as he reached it. The details of Constantine's preparation to fight the Persians show his dedication to the cause of helping Persian Christians.

EXAMPLE ANSWER:

The Merriam-Webster Online Dictionary defines "crusade" as "a remedial enterprise undertaken with zeal and enthusiasm." "Crusades" refers to any military expedition undertaken by the Christians of Europe in the 11th, 12th and 13th centuries for the recovery of the Holy Land from the Muslims. Because the "Crusades" were wars based on religion, we often think of any holy war as a "crusade."

Constantine believed whole-heartedly in his effort to rescue the Christian Persians from their attackers. His "enterprise" was giving them aid. As he prepared for war, Constantine planned to take with him a portable tabernacle, and a tent in which bishops who would accompany the army would lead regular worship. Constantine also planned to be baptized in the river Jordan as soon as he reached it. The details of Constantine's preparation to fight the Persians show his dedication, or "zeal and enthusiasm," to the cause of helping Persian Christians. That is what made his plan to invade Persia a "crusade."

Section IV: Map Exercise

1. Using a black pencil, trace the rectangular outline of the frame for Map 4.1: The Romans and Persians.

2. Using a blue pencil, trace the coastal outline of the Mediterranean. Then trace the outline of the Black Sea, the Caspian Sea, the Red Sea, and the Persian Gulf.

3. Using your black pencil, trace the outlines of the Prefecture of Gaul, the Prefecture of Italy, and the Prefecture of the East. Using a contrasting color, trace the outline of the Persian Empire, including Axum. Use your black pencil to trace the outline of Armenia over the contrasted color you used to show the Persian Empire. Repeat until the contours are familiar.

4. Using a new sheet of paper, trace the black rectangular outline of the frame in black. Remove your tracing paper from the original. Using a regular pencil with an eraser as you look at Map 4.1, first draw the coastlines of the Mediterranean, the Black Sea, the Caspian Sea, the Persian Gulf, and the Red Sea. Then draw the outlines of the Persian Empire (again including Axum). Finally draw the outlines of the Prefecture of Gaul, the Prefecture of Italy, and the Prefecture of the East. Remember to use the distance between the map and the rectangular frame as a guide.

5. When you are pleased with your map, place it over the original. Erase and redraw any lines which are more than ¼ inch off of the original.

6. Looking at Map 4.1, study carefully the bodies of water (the Black Sea, the Caspian Sea, the Red Sea, and the Persian Gulf) and the locations of the Franks, North Africa, Italy, Rome, Asia Minor, Byzantium, Amida, Arabia, and Armenia. When you are familiar with them, close the book. Using your pencil, try to label each. Check your map against the original. If your labels are misplaced, erase and re-mark while looking at the original.

Chapter Five

The Apostate

The student may use his text when answering the questions in sections I and II.

Section I: Who, What, Where

Write a one or two-sentence answer explaining the significance of each item listed below.

Foederati—**Pg. 37, ¶ 5—The *foederati* were Roman allies with many of the rights of Roman citizens.**

Goths—**Pg. 37, ¶ 6—Goths were Germanic tribes who served as Roman allies with many privileges of Roman citizenship (*foederati*) since the days of Constantine.**

Jovian—**Pg. 38, ¶ 5 and Pg. 40, ¶ 2—Jovian, named emperor after the death of Julian, was a Christian and from his appointment on, Christian emperors would rule the empire. Jovian attempted to remove religion from the center of Roman politics but failed.**

Libanius—**Pg. 36, ¶ 1—Libanius was a famous teacher of rhetoric who guided Julian in his study of Greek literature and philosophy.**

Section II: Comprehension

Write a two or three-sentence answer to each of the following questions.

1. Why did Julian declare that no Christian could teach literature?

A1.—Pg. 36, ¶ 2—A literary education was required for all government officials. If he eliminated all Christians from education, then he guaranteed that all Roman officials had received a thoroughly Roman education.

2. What was the effect on the Christian community of Julian's ban on Christians teaching literature?

A2.—Pg. 36, ¶ 3 & 4—Julian's ban meant that the Christians in the empire were undereducated. Most Christians refused to send their children to schools where they would be indoctrinated in the ways of the old Roman religion. Instead, Christian writers began to try to create their own literature, to be used in their own schools, however most of this literature was so substandard that it disappeared almost at once.

3. How did Julian update the old Roman religion in order to compete with the unifying power of the Christian church?

A3.—Pg. 37, ¶ 2 & 3—Julian updated the Roman religion by reorganizing the Roman priesthood so it looked much like the hierarchy of the Christian church. He stole other Christian elements and added them to the Roman church as well, like adding sermons and singing into the old Roman rituals. Most importantly, he welcomed home all Christian churchmen banished by the Nicene-Arian debate, which meant chaos for the Christians, and stability for the Roman church.

4. How did Julian deal with the northern threat posed by the Germanic tribes of the Franks?

A4.—Pg. 37, ¶ 5—Julian wasn't able to fight the Persians and the Franks at the same time, so he made the Franks *foederati*. The Franks settled in northern Gaul and were treated as Roman allies with many of the rights of Roman citizens.

5. Who was part of Julian's 363 campaign against Persia? Were all the groups who accompanied Julian helpful? Why or why not?

A5.—Pg. 37, ¶ 6—In the campaign launched in 363 against Persia, Julian was backed by Romans, Goths, and Arabs. He also brought traditional soothsayers and Greek philosophers with him, who were less helpful than troublesome. The soothsayers insisted that the omens were bad and the army should withdraw, while the philosophers countered that such superstitions were illogical.

6. How did Julian plan on attacking the Persian capital of Ctesiphon?

A6.—Pg. 37, ¶ 6 to Pg. 38, ¶ 1—Julian gathered eighty-five thousand men, and at the Persian border, he divided his forces and sent thirty thousand of his men down the Tigris, himself leading the rest down the Euphrates by ship. The troops planned to reunite at the Persian capital of Ctesiphon and perform a pincer move on the Persians.

7. What did Shapur do when he saw Roman troops approaching Ctesiphon? How did Shapur get the Romans to retreat?

A7.—Pg. 38, ¶ 2—Shapur, alarmed by the size of the approaching army, left his capital city as a precaution, but the Romans laid siege to Ctesiphon anyway. Shapur rounded up additional men and allies from the far corners of his empire and returned to fight the besieging army.

Julian was forced to retreat back up the Tigris, fighting the whole way and struggling to keep his men alive because the Persians had burned all of the fields and storehouses in their path.

8. Describe the two versions of Julian's death, one Roman and one Christian, given to us in the chapter.

A8.—Pg. 38, ¶ 4—Ammianus Marcellinus described a beautiful, classic death, where Julian calmly discussed the nobility of the soul with two philosophers until he died. The Christian historian Theodoret insists that Julian died in agony, recognizing too late the power of Christ.

9. What were the terms of the treaty Jovian made with Shapur? How did the Roman public react to the treaty?

A9.—Pg. 38, ¶ 7 to Pg. 39, ¶ 2—The treaty Jovian made with Shapur allowed the Roman army to go home in peace. In exchange, Jovian agreed to hand over to the Persians all Roman land east of the Tigris, including the Roman fortress of Nisibis. Romans condemned the treaty as shameful, a disgrace to Rome, an unacceptable conclusion to Julian's bold and disastrous campaign.

10. After making peace with the Persians, how did Jovian deal with religious tensions in Rome? Were his new policies successful?

A10.—Pg. 39, ¶ 3 to Pg. 40, ¶ 2—On the way back to Rome, Jovian stopped at the city of Antioch where he revoked all of Julian's anti-Christian decrees, but rather than replacing them with equally restrictive decrees against the Roman religion, he declared religious toleration. Jovian's attempt to remove religion from the center of the empire's politics was unsuccessful. Jovian had no political authority after making an unpopular treaty with the Persians, and the only hope he had to have any control was through religion; his refusal to use religion to wield power meant he had no authority at all.

Section III: Critical Thinking

The student may use his text to answer this question.

What is an "apostate"? In this chapter, we learn that Julian earned the nickname "Julian the Apostate," for his renunciation of Christianity, and his renewed dedication to the old Roman religion. Write a paragraph that explains the meaning of "apostate," and then explain how Julian both was and was not an "apostate."

The student should start by looking up the definition of "apostate." An "apostate" is one who abandon's one's religious faith, political party, one's principles, or a cause. Julian was given the nickname "Julian the Apostate" because he turned his back on Christianity. However, while Julian may have abandoned the official religion of Rome, he did so in an effort to revive the old Roman religion he believed in. Julian believed in the glorious Roman past, and that past relied on Roman identity being tied to the Roman religion. Julian may have declared that no

Christian could teach literature, and allowed the return of Arian Christians into the empire, but he also reopened old Roman temples and updated the Roman church so it was more appealing to the contemporary Roman people. Julian may have been an apostate of the Christian church, but he was not an "apostate" of the old Roman faith—he was a champion of the old Roman religion.

EXAMPLE ANSWER:

An "apostate" is one who abandon's one's religious faith, political party, one's principles, or a cause. Julian was given the nickname "Julian the Apostate" because he turned his back on Christianity. However, while Julian may have abandoned the official religion of Rome, he did so because he believed in the glorious Roman past, and that past relied on Roman identity being tied to the Roman religion. Julian may have declared that no Christian could teach literature, and allowed the return of Arian Christians into the empire, but he also reopened old Roman temples and updated the Roman church so it was more appealing to the Roman people. Julian was an "apostate" of the Christian church, but he was not an "apostate" of the old Roman faith—he was a champion of the old Roman religion.

Chapter Six

Earthquake and Invasion

The student may use her text when answering the questions in sections I and II.

Section I: Who, What, Where

Write a one or two-sentence answer explaining the significance of each item listed below.

July 21, 365—**Pg. 42, ¶ 6 & 7—On July 21, 365, a massive earthquake hit Crete, Cyrenaica, Corinth, Italy, Sicily, Egypt and Syria. Shortly after the earthquake struck, a tsunami hit Alexandria.**

Alemanni—**Pg. 43, ¶ 4, Pg. 44, ¶ 4 and Pg. 46, ¶ 3—The Alemanni were a Germanic tribal federation that Valentinian fought in Gaul. Late in 367, the Alemanni attacked Valentinian, losing the battle but not retreating from Roman territory and in 375 the Alemanni king Macrianus made peace with Valentinian.**

Barbarica Conspirato—**Pg. 45, ¶ 4—The *Barbarica Conspirato,* or "Barbarian Conspiracy," was a coordinated attack on Roman Britain. Roman garrisons stationed at Hadrian's Wall allowed Pictish soldiers to cross over, while pirates from the western island landed on the coast, and Saxons invaded both southeast Britannia and northern Gaul, overwhelming the Dux Britanniarum and the Comes Litori.**

Britannia—**Pg. 44, ¶ 6—Britannia was the Roman province in Britain that existed south of the wall Hadrian built that divided civilization and wilderness. The largest of the cities to have been given the statutes of full Roman citizenship, Londinium, had twenty-five thousand inhabitants and shipping lines, baths and drainage, and military installations.**

Comes Litori—**Pg. 45, ¶ 3—The Comes Litori was a special commander that aided the Dux Britanniarum. His named meant "protector of the shore," and it was his job in particular to keep the Saxons away from the southeastern coast of Britannia.**

Dux Britanniarum—**Pg. 45, ¶ 2 & 3—The Dux Britanniarum was the Roman official who was in charge of defending Britannia from land invasions by the Picts, piratical raids launched by tribes on the western island, and sea attacks from the Saxons.**

Flavius Theodosius—**Pg. 47 ¶ 1 & 3—Flavius Theodosius, Theodosius the Elder's son, was exiled to Hispania after Valentinian put his father to death. Flavius Theodosius was recalled by Gratian to defend the Roman empire's northern frontier, and by 376, he was the highest ranking general in the entire central province.**

Gratian—**Pg. 47, ¶ 2—Gratian, Valentinian's son, was made co-emperor along with his little four-year-old brother Valentinian II, when his father died.**

The Huns—**Pg. 47, ¶ 4 to Pg. 49, ¶ 2—The Huns were nomads from the east who were fearless fighters that slaughtered and destroyed anything in their path, who were said to have no religion, no knowledge of right and wrong, not even a proper language. Roman historian Procopius insisted that they were the product of demons and witches mating, and church fathers believed they were the product of fallen angels (demons) and human women.**

Procopius—**Pg. 43, ¶ 4 & 5—Procopius, cousin to the dead emperor Julian, managed to convince the Gothic soldiers in Valens's army to support his claim to the eastern crown. Valens bribed Procopius's two chief generals and part of his army to turn against him, which led to his defeat by Valens in battle at the city of Thyatira.**

Quadi—**Pg. 46, ¶ 4 & 5—The Quadis, a Germanic tribe, asked that the Romans to stop building new forts north of the Danube, on Quadi land. When the Quadi king was killed by a Roman who did not know how to handle the constant requests to stop building the forts, the Quadis attacked the Romans on the other side of the Danube.**

Theodosius the Elder—**Pg. 45, ¶ 5 to Pg. 46, ¶ 1—Theodosius the Elder was sent over to Britain to try to retake the Roman provinces in 368. He waged a year-long war that finally restored Roman control of Britannia , and built new forts along the southeastern coast, with towers where guards could keep an eye out for the approach of Saxon ships.**

Valens—**Pg. 41, ¶ 5 to Pg. 42, ¶ 1—Valens, Valentinian's younger brother, was appointed co-emperor by his brother and took over rule of the eastern empire as far as the province of Thracia.**

Valentinian—**Pg. 41, ¶ 3—Valentinian, a lifelong soldier and zealous Christian, was named leader of the Roman empire after Jovian's death.**

Valentinian II—**Pg. 47, ¶ 2—Valentinian II was just four years old when his father died and he was made co-emperor along with his brother Gratian.**

Section II: Comprehension

Write a two or three-sentence answer to each of the following questions.

1. What military problems did the Roman empire face at the beginning of the co-rule of Valentinian and Valens?

A1.—Pg. 42, ¶ 2—The Roman empire faced a myriad of military problems after Jovian's death—Germanic tribes were invading Gaul and pushing across the Danube; the Roman holdings in Britannia were under attack by the natives; the North African territories were suffering from the hostility of the tribes to the south; and Shapur, claiming that his truce with Rome was null now that Jovian was dead, was ready to attack the east.

2. What was Valentinian's religious policy? Why did Valentinian reverse his law against sacrificing to the Roman gods?

A2.—Pg. 42, ¶ 3—Valentinian held to Nicene Christianity but was tolerant both of Arian Christians and of adherents to the traditional state religion. Valentinian reversed his law against sacrificing to the Roman gods because one of his proconsuls pointed out that many of his subjects held to these ancient customs as a way to define themselves as part of Roman society. Realizing that this new law did not support tolerance, Valentinian reversed it.

3. What was Valens's religious policy?

A3.—Pg. 42, ¶ 4—Valens belonged to the Arian branch of Christianity, and he was intolerant of any other form of doctrine. He began a war of extermination against the Nicene Christians in Antioch. He exiled their leader, drove out the followers, and drowned some of them in the Orontes.

4. How did the Goths and the Romans coexist before Valens declared war on the Goths?

A4.—Pg. 44, ¶ 3—Before Valens declared war on the Goths, the Goths provided soldiers for the Roman army, and in return were allowed to settle in Roman land with some of the privileges of Roman citizens. The Goths had become increasingly Christian, and their native bishop Ulfilas had invented an alphabet and had used it to translate the Bible into the Goths' own language.

5. Who were the tribes north of Hadrian's Wall and on the small island west of Britannia? How long had they been in Britannia, what were their names, and where did they live, respectively?

A5.—Pg. 44, ¶ 8 to Pg. 45, ¶ 1—The tribes who lived north of Hadrian's Wall, as well as on the island west of Britannia, had arrived on British shores around 500 BC. In the north, the strongest tribes were the Picts and Caledones. On the western island, the Venii dominated the south from their capital city of Tara, while the Uluti controlled much of the north.

6. Describe the state of Britannia after Theodosius the Elder squashed the participants of the Barbarian Conspiracy.

A6.—Pg. 46, ¶ 2—The barbarian invasion and the subsequent war led by Theodosius the Elder that followed had ravaged cities and burned settlements, wiped out entire garrisons, and destroyed the trade that had once existed between Britannia and the northern tribes. The Pictish villages near the Wall were burned, their people slaughtered, and along the border the Roman garrisons had shut themselves into crude and isolated fortresses. Things were not well in Britannia.

7. Meaning to censure the Roman commander that killed the Quadi king, what did Valentinian actually do when he got to the spot where Romans were attacked by the Quadis?

A7.—Pg. 46, ¶ 6—Valentinian had meant to punish the official that murdered the Quadi king, but when he saw the devastation of his frontier with his own eyes, he was horrified. Instead of punishing his general, Valentinian launched an invasion against the Quadi.

8. Why did the Goths ask Valens for permission to settle in Roman land? Why did he grant them permission?

A8.—Pg. 49, ¶ 2—The Goths asked Valens if they could settle in Roman land on the other side of the Danube because they were displaced from their own land by the ruthless Huns. Valens granted them permission to immigrate because he saw the opportunity for the Goths to farm the uncultivated land in Thracia and provide additional soldiers for the Roman army.

9. Why, even though Valens granted the Goths asylum in Roman territory, did another war between the Romans and the barbarians manage to break out?

A9.—Pg. 49, ¶ 3—Once Valens allowed Goths to move into Roman territory, he could not regulate the influx of Goths into the Roman empire. Roman officials in charge of the new settlers were quickly overwhelmed by the paperwork, taxes were mishandled, money was misappropriated, food supplies were wiped out and the newcomers began to go hungry. This led to angry Goths storming through Thracia in an act of war.

10. What were the circumstances of Valens' death?

A10.—Pg. 49, ¶ 4 & 5—Valens set out from Antioch to fight the Goths. He met them in battle at the city of Hadrianople where he plunged into battle and was killed. Valens was not wearing the imperial purple, and his body was so badly disfigured that it was never identified.

11. Why did the Goths withdraw from Hadrianople? From Constantinople? Though they withdrew, why were these Gothic battles so important to the fabric of Roman culture?

A11.—Pg. 49, ¶ 6—The Goths withdrew from Hadrianople because, though they tried to lay siege to the city, they had little experience with breaking down walls. The same happened at Constantinople, so they were forced to retreat. Though they withdrew, the invasion of the

Goths proved that the Roman empire was far from all-conquering, and that the emperor could be brought down by a band of refugees.

Section III: Critical Thinking

The student may use her text to answer this question.

Since the ancient world, different cultures have had different ways of remembering the same events. Often a lost war is glossed over by the wounded nation, or a small battle is made into an epic fight by a king looking to boost his reputation. In the past few chapters, we have seen several events interpreted differently by Roman and Christian historians. One of the most important events to affect the Roman empire was an unbiased act of nature, an earthquake followed by a tsunami. However, the event was interpreted differently by the Romans and Christians. Write a paragraph giving a brief overview of the damage done by earthquake and tsunami, and then explain how the event was rationalized differently by the Romans and the Christians. Despite the different explanations from two factions, what was the common link between their explanations?

The student can find the description of the earthquake that hit part of the Roman empire, and the tsunami that followed, from page 42, ¶ 6 to page 43 ¶ 3.

After the natural disasters, Roman chroniclers, like Ammianus, saw the attempt by Procopius to take Valens' throne as an explanation for the wave. However, Procopius's attempt to take the throne came after *the tsunami. Roman historians simply changed around the timing of events and suggested that rebellion and Procopius's challenge to Valens caused an upheaval in the natural order of things. Libanius, dead emperor Julian's philosophy teacher, suggested that the earth was mourning Julian's death. Both Roman explanations suggest that changes in the governing bodies of the empire upset the gods, which was reflected by the earthquake and tsunami. On the other side of things, the Christians were still smarting over Julian's offense to their religion. They believed the earthquake and tsunami were punishment for Julian's misdeeds, and his disavowal of Christianity. Despite their differences, both the Christians and the Romans needed an explanation for the natural disasters. As written in the chapter, "There was no place in either the Roman or the Christian world for an event that was not a direct response to human action—no place in either world for random evil."*

EXAMPLE ANSWER:

On July 21, 365, a massive earthquake hit the Roman territories of Crete, Cyrenaica, Corinth, Italy, Sicily, Egypt and Syria. In Crete buildings collapsed on top of their occupants, and in Cyrenaica, the cities crumbled. Then, in Alexandria, the water on the southern coast at the Nile Delta got sucked away from the shore. As people stared at the marvels of the ocean floor, a huge wave of water came in to land, crushing buildings and people alike. Roman chroniclers, like Ammianus, saw the attempt by Procopius to take Valens's throne as an explanation for the wave, changing the timeline of political events to fit with the natural disasters. Libanius, Julian's philosophy teacher, suggested that the earth was mourning Julian's death. Both Roman explanations suggest that changes in the governing bodies

of the empire upset the gods, which was reflected by the earthquake and tsunami. On the other side of things, Christians believed the earthquake and tsunami were punishment for Julian's misdeeds, and his disavowal of Christianity. Despite their differences, both the Christians and the Romans needed an explanation for the natural disasters because they both believed evil could be explained. Evil had to be a direct response to human action. If humans could act appropriately, then evil could be managed.

Section IV: Map Exercise

1. Using a black pencil, trace the rectangular outline of the frame for Map 6.2: The Barbarian Approach.

2. Using a blue pencil, trace the coastal outlines: the Mediterranean, the Black Sea, the Caspian Sea, the Persian Gulf, and the Red Sea. Repeat until the contours are familiar. Then, using your black pencil, trace the (bold) outline of the Roman Empire. Include the line separating east and west. Using a contrasting color, trace the outline of the Persian Empire. Repeat again until the contours are familiar.

3. Using a new sheet of paper, trace the black rectangular outline of the frame in black. Remove your tracing paper from the original. Using a regular pencil with an eraser, first draw the coastlines of the Mediterranean, the Black Sea, the Caspian Sea, the Persian Gulf, and the Red Sea. Now draw the outline of the Roman and Persian Empires, including the line separating east and west. Remember to use the distance between the map and the rectangular frame as a guide.

4. When you are pleased with your map, place it over the original. Erase and redraw any lines which are more than ¼ inch off of the original.

5. Using your regular pencil while looking at Map 6.2, label all the territories: Hispania, Gaul, Italy, Sicily, Crete, Dacia, Macedonia, Thracia, Asia, Syria, Egypt, North Africa, Armenia.

6. Now outside the perimeter of the Roman Empire, find different colors to denote the Saxons, Franks, Vandals, Bergundians, Alemanni, Quadi, Goths, and Huns. Use the color for the Huns to draw the big arrow associated with their movement.

7. Now study the cities: Rome, Milan, Corinth, Nicaea, Constantinople, Hadrianople, Thyatira, Antioch, and Alexandria. When you are familiar with them, close the book. Using your regular pencil while looking at Map 6.2, label all the cities. Check your map against the original. Erase and re-mark any misplaced labels.

Chapter Seven

Refounding the Kingdom

The student may use his text when answering the questions in sections I and II.

Section I: Who, What, Where

Write a one or two-sentence answer explaining the significance of each item listed below.

Chimnyu—**Pg. 54, ¶ 1 & 2—Chimnyu inherited the Baekje crown from his father, who inherited it from King Geunchogo. In 384, Chimnyu accepted the teachings of Buddhism spread by the Indian monk Malananda.**

Geunchogo—**Pg. 53, ¶ 6 to Pg. 54, ¶ 1—Geunchogo, king of the Baekje, attacked the Goguryeo kingdom and took Wanggomsong for Baekje. Geunchogo was the first Baekje king to establish a line of succession that passed from father to son, and when he died the crown went to his son and then to his grandson.**

Gogugwon—**Pg. 52, ¶ 3 & 4—Gogugwon, son of Micheon, inherited his father's powerful kingdom only to go into a period of inaction for thirty years. Gogugwon came out of hiding when the crown prince of Baekje attacked Wanggomsong, and subsequently died in battle.**

Goguryeo—**Pg. 51, ¶ 3—The kingdom of Goguryeo lay on the peninsula east of the Yellow Sea, and the ancestors of its people had probably come from the Yellow river valley long before. According to their own myths, the first kingdom in their land was Choson, created by the god Tan'gun in 2333 BC, which was the era of the oldest Chinese kingdoms.**

Guanggaeto—**Pg. 54, ¶ 4 & 7—Guanggaeto, Sosorim's nephew that came to the throne in 391, could attack neighboring kingdoms because Goguryeo was strong and ready for war. Guanggaeto's rule was spent in conquests so extensive that Guanggaeto earned himself the nickname "The Great Expander."**

Guanggaeto Stele—**Pg. 54, ¶ 7—The Guanggaeto Stele, the stone stele that stands at the tomb of Guanggaeto, was the first historical document of Korean history. The stele tells the story of Guanggaeto's successful leadership of Goguryeo.**

Malananda—**Pg. 54, ¶ 2—Malananda was an Indian monk who came to Baekje spreading the teachings of Buddha.**

Micheon—**Pg. 52, ¶ 2—Micheon, a past ruler of Goguryeo, captured the Chinese Lelang and added it to his own territory in 313. When King Micheon captured Lelang, he made Goguryeo the largest, most powerful and most dominant of the Three Kingdoms of Korea.**

Naemul—**Pg. 54, ¶ 5—Naemul, king of Silla, made an alliance with Guanggaeto against the powerful Baekje.**

Samskrita—**Pg. 53, ¶ 2—Samskrita was the philosophical idea that the conditions of the mind are non-existent. The enlightened student recognized that there was no discontent, no unhappiness, no fear; Sun-do taught Sosurim his court that unhappiness, ambition and fear were samskrita.**

Sosurim—**Pg. 51, ¶ 1, Pg. 52, ¶ 4 and Pg. 53, ¶ 5—Sosurim, son of Gogugwon, grandson of Micheon, inherited the crown of the fractured Goguryeo kingdom in 371. Sosurim adopted the policies of Buddhism and Confucianism to rebuild Goguryeo.**

Sun-do—**Pg. 52, ¶ 5—Sun-do, a Buddhist monk, brought gifts and Buddhist scriptures to Sosurim's court, and promised the king that the practice of Buddhism would help protect Goguryeo from its enemies.**

T'aehak—**Pg. 53, ¶ 1 & 2—T'aehak was formal name of the National Confucian Academy founded by Sosurim with the help of Sun-do in 372. T'aehak was patterned on Chinese principles of both Buddhism and Confucianism.**

Section II: Comprehension

Write a two or three-sentence answer to each of the following questions.

1. Who populated the north and south part of the Korean peninsula at the time when the Chinese dynasty of the Han was still in power?

A1.—Pg. 51, ¶ 4—When the Han were still in power, they captured the land in the north of the Korean peninsula and settled Chinese officials and their families there. In the south, three independent kingdoms formed: Silla, Goguryeo, and Baekje. The very southern tip of the peninsula was populated by the Gaya confederacy.

2. What were the Chinese holdings in Korea when the Han fell?

A2.—Pg. 52, ¶ 1—When the Han fell, its control over lands in the old Choson had shrunk to one district called Lelang, which was centered around the city of Wanggomsong.

3. What military disasters occurred while Gogugwon hid in his royal palace for thirty years?

A3.—Pg. 52, ¶ 3 & 4—During Gogugwon's time of inaction, Goguryeo was sacked twice. In 342, armies from the Sixteen Kingdoms took thousands of prisoners and broke down the walls of its capital city, Guknaesong. Later, in 371, the crown prince of Baekje led an invading army all the way up to Wanggomsong and then claimed much of Goguryeo's territory as his own.

4. Why did both the Goguryeo and the Baekje kings accept Buddhism into their kingdoms?

A4.—Pg. 54, ¶ 3—Both Goguryeo and Baekje were relatively new kingdoms. Buddhism had the weight of tradition behind it, a flavor of the ancient Chinese tradition, and in the new kingdoms all things Chinese were more desirable. Buddhism carried with it the resonance of centuries of inherited authority, and for both young kingdoms, a feeling of legitimacy.

5. How did the king of Baekje come to pay homage to King Guanggaeto of Goguryeo?

A5.—Pg. 54, ¶ 6—The armies of Goguryeo and Silla joined together and stormed through Baekje. Overwhelmed, Baekje could not resist for long and in 396, the king of Baekje handed over a thousand hostages to guarantee his good behavior. Giving up his own power, he agreed to pay homage to King Guanggaeto.

6. How did Guanggaeto earn himself the nickname "The Great Expander"?

A6.—Pg. 54, ¶ 7—Guanggaeto earned himself the nickname "The Great Expander" by conquering sixty-five walled cities and fourteen hundred villages for Goguryeo, recovering the northern land that had been taken away decades before, and making Baekje retreat to the south, all between 391 and 412.

Section III: Critical Thinking

The student may use his text to answer this question.

When King Sosurim came to Goguryeo's throne, his kingdom was a mess. The Buddhist and Confucian teachings of the monk Sun-do helped Sosurim shape the kingdom that would later become very powerful under the leadership of Sosurim's nephew, Guanggaeto. Write a paragraph explaining the Buddhist and Confucian teachings that fortified the weak Goguryeo, and how these ideas could exist together. Explain how these teachings promised future success for the kingdom while leaning on the past for support.

The main tenet of the Buddhism that Sosurim adopted was the idea of samskrita. *On page 53, the text reads: "Sun-do taught Sosurim and his court that discontent, unhappiness, ambition, and fear were* samskrita, *conditions of the mind that were nonexistent: the enlightened student recognized that in fact there was no discontent, no unhappiness, no ambition, no fear. The kingdom of Goguryeo was itself* samskrita, *a conception that had no ultimate reality." Truly understanding the philosophy of* samskrita *meant letting go of earthly desire, which, in politics, often translated into jockeying for control and power. Adopting this Buddhist philosophy quelled the greed and malice that was tearing apart Goguryeo.*

On the other hand, Confucianism taught its followers how to live properly. Confucianism stressed virtue and responsibility. The principles of Confucianism gave King Sosurim a tested framework for training new army officers, secretaries, accountants, and bureaucrats—everything a state needed to prosper. Since Buddhism did not demand its followers to relinquish opposing beliefs, King Sosurim could adopt Buddhism as his own faith without making it an official state religion. This allowed both Buddhist and Confucian ideals to exist together in Goguryeo.

For the third part of this answer, the student will want to think about how the blending of these two philosophies was innovative, and what it meant for the future of Goguryeo. The student should also consider how Buddhism and Confucianism tied Goguryeo to the past, and what that meant for the morale of Goguryeo's people. The combination of Buddhism and Confucianism was innovative because it relied on the right amount of each philosophy to create a formula that worked for ruling Goguryeo in particular. Taking a little from Buddhism and a little from Confucianism to make a peaceful and prosperous way of life for the people of Goguryeo was new. However, both Buddhism and Confucianism came from ancient Chinese ways, and for a young kingdom, each philosophy added an air of legitimacy to how the kingdom ran. In particular, Buddhism tied Goguryeo to a distant and glorious Chinese past, a past that the young kingdom hoped to recreate for itself.

EXAMPLE ANSWER:

The main tenet of the Buddhism that Sosurim adopted was the idea of *samskrita*. *Samskrita* were the conditions of the mind such as desire, fear, and ambition, which seemed real but actually did not exist. Truly understanding the philosophy of *samskrita* meant letting go of earthly desire, which, in politics, often translated into jockeying for control and power. Adopting this Buddhist philosophy quelled the greed and malice that was tearing Goguryeo apart. Applying Confucian beliefs to Goguryeo's management was more practical. Confucianism taught its followers how to live properly, and how to be virtuous and responsible. Confucianism gave King Sosurim a tested framework for training new army officers, secretaries, accountants, and bureaucrats—everything a state needed to prosper. Since Buddhism did not demand its followers to relinquish opposing beliefs, King Sosurim could adopt Buddhism as his own faith without making it an official state religion. This allowed both Buddhist and Confucian ideals to exist together in Goguryeo.

The combination of Buddhism and Confucianism was innovative because it relied on the right amount of each philosophy to create a formula that worked for ruling Goguryeo in particular. Taking a little from Buddhism and a little from Confucianism to make a peaceful and prosperous way of life for the people of Goguryeo was new. However, both Buddhism and Confucianism came from ancient Chinese ways, and for a young kingdom, each philosophy added an air of legitimacy to how the kingdom ran. In particular, Buddhism tied Goguryeo to a distant and glorious Chinese past, a past that the young kingdom hoped to recreate for itself.

Chapter Eight

The Catholic Church

The student may use her text when answering the questions in sections I and II.

Section I: Who, What, Where

Write a one or two-sentence answer explaining the significance of each item listed below.

Ardashir II—**Pg. 56, ¶ 2—Ardashir II succeeded Shapur the Great of Persia in 379. As the elderly brother of the great king, he was more concerned with holding on to his crown than invading foreign parts, diminishing the Persian threat to Rome.**

Emperor Theodosius I—**Pg. 56, ¶ 1—Emperor Theodosius I was the royal name for Flavius Theodosius, who was appointed co-emperor, ruler of the east, by Gratian after the death of Valens.**

Jerome—**Pg. 59, ¶ 5—Jerome, secretary of the bishop of Rome, recorded the bishop's 382 decision that he was to be the leader of all other bishops. Jerome was also called upon by the Roman council to work on a new Latin translation of the Scriptures—an act that declared that Latin, not Greek, was the proper language for the Scriptures.**

Section II: Comprehension

Write a two or three-sentence answer to each of the following questions.

1. What did Gratian, a devout Christian, do to show the Senate that he would not allow the Roman gods to undermine the empire's Christian faith?

A1.—Pg. 56, ¶ 3—In order to show the Senate that the Roman Gods would not undermine the Christian faith, Gratian removed the Altar of Victory from the Senate building in Rome in 382. He also removed the title pontifex maximus, high priest of the Roman state religion, from his list of titles and he refused to wear the sacred traditional robes of the emperor.

2. By rejecting the Roman gods and traditions, what else was Gratian rejecting?

A2.—Pg. 56, ¶ 3—When Gratian removed the Altar of Victory from the Senate building, an altar that had stood their since Augustus's defeat of Anthony and Cleopatra four hundred years before, he was not just rejecting the Roman gods but also the entire Roman past. Refusing to wear the imperial robes and doing away with the title pontifex maximus was like turning his back on over a thousand years of Roman history.

3. How did Theodosius deal with the destructive power of Christian division that had spread to even the lowest levels of Roman society?

A3.—Pg. 57, ¶ 3 & 4—Theodosius dealt with Christian divisions in Roman society by turning to the law. In 380, he declared that Nicene Christianity was the one true faith, and threatened dissenters with legal penalties.

4. What does "catholic" mean? What was the main tenet of the catholic Christian Church?

A4.—Pg. 57, ¶ 4—"Catholic" means universal, applying to all mankind. The main tenet of the catholic Christian Church was the Nicene Creed, the belief in the Holy Trinity.

5. After Theodosius's law declaring that Nicene Christianity was the one true faith of the Roman empire, what legally defined heresy? According to the law, how would heretics be punished?

A5.—Pg. 57 ¶ 5—Once Theodosius declared Nicene Christianity as the one true Roman faith, the legal definition of heretic meant someone who did not hold to the Nicene Creed. According to the law, anyone who practiced outside of the bounds of the catholic Christianity would "be subject to both divine and earthly retribution."

6. What actions did Theodosius take to enforce religious uniformity?

A6.—Pg. 58, ¶ 3—To enforce religious uniformity, Theodosius took all of the meeting places and churches of the non-Nicene Christians and handed them over to the Nicene bishops. Theodosius also threatened to expel heretics who insisted on preaching from the city of Constantinople and to confiscate their land.

7. Why did Gratian hand over part of his western empire to Theodosius?

A7.—Pg. 58, ¶ 5—Gratian gave up part of his western empire because it was flooded with Goths. By turning over the most Goth-infested part of his western empire—three dioceses in the central province of Pannonia—to Theodosius, Gratian was no longer responsible for driving the Goths out.

8. How did Theodosius beef up his army to fight against the Goths?

A8.—Pg. 59, ¶ 1—Theodosius used an innovative strategy to fight the Goths: he recruited barbarians from some regions to fight against barbarians in other regions. For example, he hired Goth mercenaries from Pannonia and then moved them over to Egypt where they were switched out for Roman soldiers. The Roman soldiers from Egypt would then fight the Goths in Pannonia, while the hired Goths did the work of the Roman soldiers in Egypt.

9. What were the terms of the treaty Theodosius made with the Goths in 382?

A9.—Pg. 59, ¶ 2—The treaty that Theodosius made with the Goths in 382 stated that the Goths could exist within the borders of the Roman empire, under their own king. The Gothic king would be subject to Theodosius as emperor, but the Goths themselves would not have to answer to any Roman official. Finally, the treaty stated that when the Goths fought for Rome, they would do so as allies, rather than as Roman soldiers.

10. Why was Theodosius's 381 declaration that the bishop of Constantinople would be equal to the bishop of Rome met with an uproar? How did the bishop of Rome react to this new law?

Note to the parent—The student learned in her previous reading that the bishop of Rome was the most powerful of all the bishops, and he led the decisions of the church.

A10.—Pg. 59, ¶ 4 & 5—Giving the bishop of Constantinople the same power as the bishop of Rome angered the clergy because traditionally the bishop of Rome was the highest of the bishops and gave the other bishops in the empire orders. The bishops of older cities that were the traditional centers of Christianity objected to the raising up of the bishop in Constantinople. In 382, the bishop of Rome called his own council and announced that the bishop of Rome was the leader of all other bishops, including the bishop at Constantinople, and the churchmen in Rome agreed.

Section III: Critical Thinking

The student may not use her text to answer this question.

While Constantine realized that Christianity could be the rope that tied his empire together, he did not do away with Roman custom. Rather, he added Christianity into the mix while continuing to honor Roman traditions. Both Gratian and Emperor Theodosius I followed in Constantine's footsteps, attempting to unify their kingdoms with Christianity. Explain how these two leaders attempted to make Christianity the highest belief in the Roman empire. Then explain how Theodosius I's laws backfired, and actually caused division instead of unity within his kingdom.

The student needs to address three different question in this critical thinking prompt. First, how did Gratian attempt to raise up Christianity; second, how did Theodosius I attempt to raise up Christianity; third, how did Theodosius I's plans backfire?

Gratian—Gratian, in an attempt to show the Senate that he would not allow the Roman gods to undermine the empire's Christian faith, removed the Altar of Victory from the Senate building in Rome. He also removed the title pontifex maximus, high priest of the Roman state religion, from his list of titles and he refused to don the sacred robes of the Roman emperor. Gratian rejected both the Roman religion and the Roman past in an effort to raise up Christianity.

Theodosius I—Theodosius I used the law to raise up Christianity in the Roman empire. Theodosius declared that Nicene Christianity was the one true faith, the universal religion of the Roman empire. He also made heresy illegal, and declared that anyone who did not believe in the Nicene Creed would be punished. He threatened to expel heretics who insisted on preaching from the city of Constantinople and to confiscate their land. He then took all of the meeting places and churches of the non-Nicene Christians and handed them over to the Nicene bishops. While he made strict sanctions, Theodosius I didn't always go through with his punishments; he wasn't interested in hurting his people, he only wanted everyone to believe in the same God. In an attempt to revamp Christianity further, Theodosius I declared the bishop of Constantinople equal to the bishop of Rome in authority. This is where Theodosius went too far—the bishop of Rome called his own council and announced that the bishop of Rome was the leader for all other bishops, including Constantinople. While Theodosius I's laws were meant to make all Christians one, he could not force it to happen. This was most clear in his inability to take power away from the bishop of Rome. Theodosius I would not unite Rome under his idea of Christinity.

EXAMPLE ANSWER:

Both co-emperors of the Roman empire, Gratian and Theodosius I, wanted to raise Christianity up to the highest belief in Rome. Gratian attempted to do this by turning his back on the old Roman religion, and on Roman tradition. He removed the Altar of Victory from the Senate building in Rome, he removed the title pontifex maximus, high priest of the Roman state religion, from his list of titles and he refused to don the sacred robes of the Roman emperor. Gratian might have taken a stand, but he did not unify his people under one God.

Theodosius I was slightly more successful in his use of the law to raise up Christianity. Theodosius declared that Nicene Christianity was the one true faith, the universal religion of the Roman empire. He also made heresy illegal, and declared that anyone who did not believe in the Nicene Creed would be punished. He threatened to expel heretics who insisted on preaching from the city of Constantinople and to confiscate their land. He then took all of the meeting places and churches of the non-Nicene Christians and handed them over to the Nicene bishops. It was clear that Theodosius did not want to harm his constituents, he only wanted them to believe in the same God; though he threatened to punish those that violated his sanctions, he didn't always follow through with his threats. Nevertheless, Theodosius took his cause to the top and declared the bishop of Constantinople equal to the bishop of Rome in authority. This is where Theodosius went too far—the bishop of Rome called his own council and announced that the bishop of Rome was the leader for all other bishops, including Constantinople. While Theodosius I's laws were meant to make all Christians one, he could not force it to happen. This was most clear in his inability to take power away from the bishop of Rome. Theodosius I would not unite Rome under his idea of Christianity.

Chapter Nine

Excommunicated

The student may use his text when answering the questions in sections I and II.

Section I: Who, What, Where

Write a one or two-sentence answer explaining the significance of each item listed below.

Ambrose—**Pg. 66, ¶ 4–6 and Pg. 69, ¶ 2—Ambrose, the bishop of Milan, refused to acknowledge Justina's request to turn over the New Basilica for Arian worship, which led to a massive protest, a show of power which threatened Valentinian II. Later, when Quintus Aurelius Symmachus suggested returning the Altar of Victory to the Senate, Ambrose made it clear that the Roman emperor was Christian, he worshipped Christ alone, and that any other practice went against the belief in God and the belief of the state.**

Note to the parent—The student might also include that Ambrose excommunicated the Roman emperor Theodosius from the church after the emperor put to death innocent bystanders involved in a riot in Pannonia (pg. 70, ¶ 2). This will be addressed in question 11 of Section II, so it is not necessary for the student to include it here.

Arbogast—**Pg. 67, ¶ 5—Arbogast, Theodosius's trusted general, murdered Magnus Maximus's son and heir to ensure no more trouble with the Britons, and then was appointed by Theodosius to be Valentinian II's right-hand man.**

Galla—**Pg. 67, ¶ 4—Galla, Valentinian II's sister, was offered to Theodosius by Justina in exchange for Theodosius driving Magnus Maximus out of Italy. A marriage to Galla meant an extra protection for Theodosius because he would now become part of the Valentinian dynasty.**

Justina—**Pg. 66, ¶ 4—Justina, Valentinian II's mother, caused a rift between her son, the emperor, and Ambrose, the bishop of Milan in 386 when she demanded first a church in Milan and then the New Basilica be made available to the Arians for worship.**

Macsen Wledgi—**Pg. 63, ¶ 2—Macsen Wledgi, the name for Magnus Maximus in Welsh legend, stars in the epic *Breuddwyd Macsen*, which is the tale of a Roman emperor that dreams of a beautiful maiden who must become his wife. After finding her in Britain, he marries her and then spends seven years building castles and roads in Britain—so long that a usurper back in Rome takes his throne from him.**

Magnus Maximus—**Pg. 63, ¶ 1–4, Pg. 65, ¶ 2 and Pg. 67, ¶ 5—Magnus Maximus, a Roman citizen and Spaniard by birth, was proclaimed the new emperor of Britain by the Roman army in 383. After Magnus Maximus conquered Gaul, he set his sights on conquering even more of the Roman empire, which led to his being put to death in Milan by Theodosius.**

Quintus Aurelius Symmachus—**Pg. 68, ¶ 3 to Pg. 69, ¶ 1—Quintus Aurelius Symmachus, the prefect, or chief administrative officer, of the city of Rome, made clear the three appeals of the senators to the imperial court in Milan to reinstall the traditional Altar of Victory in the Senate. He said it shouldn't matter what religion each man worshipped to seek the truth, and in the Roman empire, "Great is the love of custom."**

Note to the parent—The text gives us two different quotes from the appeal made by Quintus Aurelius Symmachus. The quotes are listed below. The student might use any part of either quote in defining Quintus Aurelius Symmachus's appeal to the imperial court.

Quote 1 (Pg. 68, ¶ 3): "We ask the restoration of that state of religion under which the Republic has so long prospered . . . Permit us, I beseech you, to transmit in our old age to our posterity what we ourselves received when boys. Great is the love of custom."

Quote 2 (Pg. 68 ¶ 4 to Pg. 69, ¶ 1): "Where shall we swear to observe your laws and statutes? by what sanction shall the deceitful mind be deterred from bearing false witness? All places indeed are full of God, nor is there any spot where the perjured can be safe, but it is of great efficacy in restraining crime to feel that we are in the presence of sacred things. That altar binds together the concord of all, that altar appeals to the faith of each man, nor does any thing give more weight to our decrees than that all our decisions are sanctioned, so to speak, by an oath . . . . We look on the same stars, the heaven is common to us all, the same world surrounds us. What matters it by what arts each of us seeks for truth?"

Shapur III—**Pg. 65, ¶ 5 and Pg. 66, ¶ 2—Shapur III, son of the great Shapur, took the Persian throne after the elderly Ardashir II was deposed by the Persian noblemen. Shapur III agreed to a treaty that split Armenia between the Persia and Rome, which kept the peace between the two empires.**

Stilicho—**Pg. 65, ¶ 6 to Pg. 66, ¶ 2—Stilicho, a Roman soldier of part-Vandal heritage, was sent as an ambassador of the Roman empire to negotiate a treaty with Shapur III about Armenia. His impressive negotiation between the Roman and Persian empires about Armenia lead Theodosius to appoint him to general and married him to the fourteen-year-old princess Serena, Theodosius's own niece and adopted daughter.**

Theodosian Decrees—**Pg. 68, ¶ 2—The Theodosian Decrees were a set of laws designed to bring the whole Roman realm into line with the orthodox Christian practice. The first decree was made in 389, and it stated that old Roman feast days, which had always been state holidays, would now be workdays instead.**

Vandal—**Pg. 65, ¶ 6—Vandals were barbarians, natives of the Germanic peoples who lived just north of the Carpathian Mountains. Unlike the Goths, the Vandals were not a present trouble to the Roman empire.**

Section II: Comprehension

Write a two or three-sentence answer to each of the following questions.

1. What hint of historical truth about Magnus Maximus's reign can we find in the epic *Breuddwyd Macsen*? Why would he appear in Welsh legend?

A1.—Pg. 63, ¶ 3—As in the tale *Breuddwyd Macsen*, Magnus Maximus did claim the title "Emperor of Rome" while still in Britain, and he did spend his time as a Roman commander building roads and developing the Roman infrastructure on the island. Magnus Maximus most likely appears in Welsh legend because he probably allowed tribes from the island west of Britain to settle on the western coast of Britain.

2. Geoffrey of Monmouth's *History of the Kings of Britain* includes a story inspired by Magnus Maximus's attack on Gaul, about King Arthur sailing into Gaul, laying waste to the countryside and setting up a royal court at the old Roman fortress town Lutetia Parisiorum, on the Seine. What is the real story of Magnus Maximus's attack on Gaul?

A2.—Pg. 65, ¶ 2—Unlike the Arthurian tale given to us by Geoffrey of Monmouth, Magnus Maximus marched into Gaul and arrived at Lutetia Parisiorum, where Gratian met him in battle. Gratian's army was divided, and part of the army wanted an emperor who, unlike the Christian Gratian, worshipped Jupiter and the Roman religion—this part of the army joined Magnus Maximus. The rest of Gratian's army was defeated and Gratian was killed either by Magnus Maximus's soldiers or by one of his own officers.

3. When Magnus Maximus took control of Gaul, how was the whole of the Roman empire divided?

A3.—Pg. 65, ¶ 3—When Magnus Maximus took control of Gaul, he became emperor of Gaul, Hispania, and Britannia, or, the far west of the Roman empire. Theodosius remained in control of the east, and in Gratian's younger brother and former co-emperor Valentinian II was in power in Italy and North Africa.

4. What were the circumstances of the alliance made between Magnus Maximus and Theodosius?

A4.—Pg. 65, ¶ 4—Magnus Maximus sent Theodosius an official message suggesting that they be allies and friends. Because the invasion had happened too quickly for Theodosius to block it, and now that it was done he could do nothing about it, he decided to accept

Maximus's offer. Maximus and Theodosius were old acquaintances that fought together in Britannia as young men and Theodosius agreed to recognize Magnus Maximus as a legitimate emperor, though Theodosius was secretly preparing for battle against his old war buddy.

5. What were the terms of the Armenian treaty made between Shapur III and Stilicho in 384?

A5.—Pg. 66, ¶ 2—The terms of the Armenian treaty made between Shapur III and Stilicho in 384 were that the western half of Armenia would be ruled by a Roman-supported king, and the eastern half by a king loyal to Persia.

6. What happened when Justina sent officials to the Basilica in Milan on the Friday before Palm Sunday to change the hanging in the church?

A6.—Pg. 66, ¶ 5 & 6—When the officials sent by Justina started to change the hangings in the Basilica while Ambrose was teaching, he ignored them. The invasion of the church by imperial officials infuriated the Nicene Christians in Milan; they gathered at the church to protest, the demonstrations spread, and with that came an influx of imperial soldiers to deal with the protesters. Ambrose could not leave the church because it was surrounded by soldiers, so he staged an involuntary sit-in with his congregants.

7. What did Ambrose preach while he was staging his sit-in at the Basilica? Why was this offensive to Justina, and the Arians?

A7.—Pg. 66, ¶ 6—During his sit-in, Ambrose preached that the church could never be controlled by the emperor because the church was in the image of God. The church was part of the body of Christ, and since Christ was fully God, the church was itself one with the Father. This was offensive to Justina, and the Arians, because they believed that God the Father was above Jesus Christ, that Christ was made from God but he was not God.

8. Even though Magnus Maximus had originally fought wars for territory in the name of the Roman god Jupiter, why did he decide to attack Valentinian II as a defender of the Nicene faith?

A8.—Pg. 67, ¶ 3—Though Magnus Maximus held Roman beliefs, he decided to call his attack on Valentinian in defense of Nicene Christianity because this gave him a sense of legitimacy. In order to be a real and lawful emperor of the Roman empire, he had to align himself with the Christian church.

9. Why did Theodosius surround himself with men like Arbogast?

A9.—Pg. 68, ¶ 1—Arbogast was of barbarian descent. His father was a Frank, which meant he could have a great military career, but he could never take the imperial throne. Theodosius's most trusted aides were men like Arbogast, half or more barbarian, because they could not challenge him for the crown.

10. What was the theoretical imperial answer to Quintus Aurelius Symmachus's question, "Why did all Romans have to practice the same faith?"

A10.—Pg. 69, ¶ 1 & 2—All Romans, the emperor believed, had to practice the same faith because without a common faith, they would have no single loyalty to hold them together. The Roman empire was already divided into three parts, so being a Roman citizen was not enough to create a single Roman identity. Christianity had to be the glue that held the Roman empire together.

11. Why was Theodosius excommunicated from the Christian church by Ambrose in 390?

A11.—Pg. 69, ¶ 3 to Pg. 70, ¶ 2—Theodosius was excommunicated from the Christian church because he ordered everyone involved in a riot caused by a drunken Pannonian governor to be put to death. Some of the people who were killed were innocent bystanders, and Ambrose was appalled by the injustice of Theodosius's punishment. Ambrose refused to allow him to enter the church either for prayer or for the celebration of the Eucharist for eight months.

12. After accepting several months of penance and being readmitted into the church, what did Theodosius do to assert his imperial power?

A12.—Pg. 70, ¶ 6 & 7—When his penance was over and Theodosius was readmitted to the church, he showed his imperial power by ordering all Roman temples closed and abandoned so that Christians could knock them down and build Christian churches instead. Then he put out the fire that was once guarded by the Vestal Virgins in the Roman Forum and he announced that the Olympic Games would be held one final time before their permanent cancellation. Finally he announced that any act of worship made in honor of the old Roman gods would be an act of treachery against the emperor himself, a declaration that showed Theodosius could still wield the power of the law.

Section III: Critical Thinking

The student may use his text to answer this question.

In order to use the Christian faith to unify the Roman empire, the church leaders had to be given significant power. Yet, how much was too much? If the church could make rules that trumped the law, who was really in control—the emperor, or the church? First, explain how Theodosius and Ambrose were able to work together to squelch Quintus Aurelius Symmachus and the senators of the imperial court's requests to reinstate the old Roman religion. Then explain how Theodosius's excommunication from the church showed that a bishop like Ambrose might have more power than the emperor of Rome.

In the first part of this question, the student needs to address how the Roman Senate, represented by Quintus Aurelius Symmachus, challenged the official faith of Rome by asking that the Altar of Victory be reinstalled in the Senate. Theodosius had just begun to issue the Theodosian Decrees, a set of laws designed to continue the unification of Romans under the Christian faith. Theodosius's insistence that everyone participate in the Christian church was supported by Ambrose, the bishop of Milan. On pages 68 and 69, we can read about Ambrose's official church response to Symmachus's request. Ambrose echoed Theodosius, "You ask the Emperors to grant peace to your gods, we pray for peace for the Emperors themselves from Christ. You worship the works of your own hands, we think it sacrilege that any thing which can be made should be called God. . . . A Christian Emperor has learned to honour the altar of Christ alone. . . . Let the voice of our Emperor speak of Christ alone, let him declare Him only Whom in heart he believes, for the king's heart is in the Hand of God." Ambrose reinforced the point that Romans only worship one God, and with that, they answer to only one emperor.

In the second part of the question, the student must explain how the power Ambrose was given as bishop challenged Theodosius's power as emperor. The governor of Pannonia was murdered by a mob after he jailed a popular charioteer. Theodosius put to death everyone involved in the riot, including those who were simply standing around and watching. Ambrose, appalled by Theodosius's handling of the matter, refused to allow Theodosius to enter the church when he was next in Milan. For the eight months that followed, Theodosius was not allowed to enter the church for either prayer or the celebration of the Eucharist. All Theodosius had to do was confess his sin, do his penance and then he could return to the church. However, Theodosius realized that in his excommunication, Ambrose and the church had more power than the emperor. If Theodosius refused Ambrose's punishment, he would be turning his back on the Eucharist, which would send him to hell. If Theodosius denied Ambrose's authority, he would have weakened the church and ruined the work of unification; if Theodosius didn't have to listen to the bishop, why would the people? Finally, recognizing that both his soul and the future of the Christian church in Rome relied on his confession, Theodosius went back to Milan, did his penance and was readmitted to the fellowship of the church.

EXAMPLE ANSWER:

A representative of the Senate, Quintus Aurelius Symmachus challenged the official faith of Rome by asking that the Altar of Victory be reinstalled in the Senate. Theodosius had just begun to issue the Theodosian Decrees, a set of laws designed to continue the unification of Romans under the Christian faith. Theodosius's insistence that everyone participate in the Christian church was supported by Ambrose, the bishop of Milan. Ambrose replied to Symmachus's request with a resounding "no." Ambrose stressed that Romans only worship one God, and with that, they answer to only one emperor. Together, Theodosius and Ambrose handled the unruly Senate.

It was Ambrose, however, that handled Theodosius after the emperor put to death anyone involved in the riot that caused the murder of the Pannonian governor. Ambrose, appalled that Theodosius included innocent bystanders in the Pannonian sweep, refused to allow Theodosius to enter the church when he was next in Milan. For the eight months that followed, Theodosius was not allowed to enter the church for either prayer or the celebration of the Eucharist. All Theodosius had to do was confess his sin, do his penance and then he could return to the church. However, Theodosius realized that in his excommunication, Ambrose and the church had more power than the emperor. If Theodosius didn't listen to Ambrose, why would the people of Rome listen to the bishop? Recognizing that both his

soul and the future of the Christian church in Rome relied on his confession, Theodosius went back to Milan, did his penance and was readmitted to the fellowship of the church.

Section IV: Map Exercise

1. Using a black pencil, trace the rectangular outline of the frame for Map 9.1: The Empire in Thirds.

2. Using a blue pencil, trace the outline of the Mediterranean while looking at Map 9.1. Using a black pencil, label the territories of Britannia, Hispania, Gaul, Italy, North Africa, Pannonia, Thracia, Egypt, and Syria. Then, using a contrasting color, trace the outline of the Persian Empire (including Armenia). Finally, using your black pencil, trace the territories of Magnus Maximus, Valentinian II, and Theodosius. Repeat until the contours are familiar.

3. Trace the rectangular outline of the frame in black. Remove your tracing paper from the original. Using a regular pencil with an eraser as you look at Map 9.1, draw the outline of the Mediterranean and the outlines of the territories of Magnus Maximus, Valentinian II, and Theodosius. Draw the outline of the Persian Empire as well. Erase and redraw as necessary as you look at the map.

4. When you are pleased with your map, lay it over the original. Erase and redraw any lines which are more than ¼ inch off of the original.

5. Using a blue pencil, trace the outlines of the Black Sea, the Red Sea, the Persian Gulf and the Caspian Sea.

6. Study the regions of Britannia, Hispania, Gaul, Italy, North Africa, Pannonia, Thracia, Egypt, and Syria. When you are familiar with them, close the book. Using your regular pencil, label all nine. Check your map against the original. Correct and replace any misplaced labels.

Chapter Ten

Cracked in Two

The student may use her text when answering the questions in sections I and II.

Section I: Who, What, Where

Write a one or two-sentence answer explaining the significance of each item listed below.

Alaric—**Pg. 72, ¶ 3; Pg. 74, ¶ 2 and 4—Alaric, leader of the Gothic foederati, fought with Theodosius and Stilicho against Eugenius, Arbogast and the Roman senators at the Battle of the Frigidus. He took control of the Gothic army and created a new kingdom (the Visigoths) with himself as their king.**

Arcadius—**Pg. 73, ¶ 3—Arcadius was eighteen when he became co-ruler of the Roman empire, taking the throne of Constantinople.**

Battle of the Frigidus—**Pg. 72, ¶ 3 to Pg. 73, ¶ 2—The Battle of the Frigidus was fought on September 5, 394 with Theodosius, his general and son-in-law Stilicho and Alaric, leading the foederati, triumphing over Eugenius, Arbogast and the Roman Senate. Stories of divine winds and demons that appeared during battle reflect the importance of the fight; it was the fight for how to understand the world.**

Ethnogenesis—**Pg. 74, ¶ 5—Ethnogenesis is when a confederacy, united together by necessity or geography, makes itself into a nation by giving itself a name, a history, and/or a royal lineage. The formation of the Visigoth nation by Alaric is an example of ethnogenesis.**

Eugenius—**Pg. 72, ¶ 2 to Pg. 73, ¶ 1—Eugenius, a Christian who was also supportive of the old Roman religion, was chosen by the senators and Arbogast to take Valentinian II's place as emperor of the western Roman empire. Eugenius was killed at the Battle of the Frigidus.**

Eutropius—**Pg. 75, ¶ 4—Eutropius, a eunuch, took the role of Arcadius's personal guard after Rufinus's death. Eutropius convinced Arcadius to call together the Senate and declare Stilicho an enemy of the state.**

Honorius—**Pg. 72, ¶ 3 and Pg. 73, ¶ 2 & 3—Honorius, son of Theodosius, was just eight years old when he was named by his father as Valentinian II's successor. When Theodosius died in 395, his two sons from his first marriage divided the rule as co-Augusti and Honorius, under the watch of Stilicho, inherited the west.**

Magister militum—**Pg. 74, ¶ 2—Magister militum is the title given to a regular Roman commander. The Gothic Alaric had hoped to become magister militum after Theodosius's death, but he was not offered the honor.**

Placida—**Pg. 73, ¶ 3—Placida, the daughter of Theodosius and Galla, was left in the care of Stilicho and his Roman wife Serena after Theodosius died.**

Rufinus—**Pg. 73, ¶ 4 and Pg. 75, ¶ 3—Rufinus, a Roman, was the head of Arcadius's personal guard, the highest military official in the east and the final decision-maker in the empire. Rufinus was murdered by a Gothic solider in the name of Stilicho.**

Visigoth—**Pg. 74, ¶ 3-5—Visigoth was the nation formed by Alaric, made of the Gothic army, which existed in the middle of Roman land. The Visigoths took their name from the land where many of the Goths had once lived—the western Gothic land—but they included west Goths and Goths from farther east, as well as members from other tribes farther north.**

Section II: Comprehension

Write a two or three-sentence answer to each of the following questions.

1. Why did Arbogast side with the Roman senate after Valentinian II's suicide?

A1.—Pg. 72, ¶ 2—Theodosius was prompted by his wife Galla to investigate Valentinian II's suicide, and Arbogast, Valentinian II's right hand man, realized that Theodosius's first action would most likely be to remove him from power. Acting on the offensive, Arbogast went to the Roman Senate and promised that he would help the senators restore the Altar of Victory and protect the Roman religion from extinction. Siding with the Roman Senate meant that Arbogast would have a defense against Theodosius.

2. What mystical things happened during the Battle of the Frigidus that predicted the defeat of Eugenius and Arbogast by Theodosius, Stilicho, and Alaric?

A2.—Pg. 72, ¶ 4 to Pg. 73, ¶ 1—During the Battle of the Frigidus, a diving wind supposedly blew up and rammed the arrows of the western army back into their own bodies. Also, Sozoman claimed that a demon appeared at the church where Theodosius prayed just before the battle, taunting the Christian cause and then fading away as Theodosius's army began to win the victory.

3. What might have caused the "divine wind" that blew up during the Battle of the Frigidus?

A3.—Pg. 72, ¶ 4 and note—The divine wind that blew up during the Battle of the Frigidus might actually have been a wind known as the "bora." The bora is formed when cold air is sucked into a low-pressure area over the Adriatic. The bora can gust up to 100 mph and can cause a rapid temperature drop of 40 degrees Fahrenheit.

4. Why did the Christian historian Orosius call the Battle of the Frigidus a battle of "pious necessity"?

A4.—Pg. 73, ¶ 1 & 2—Orosius called the Battle of the Frigidus a battle of "pious necessity" because the east and west parts of the Roman empire had two different ways of understanding the world. The fight was about the Christian faith versus the old Roman religion, and one had to win out over the other before both sides of the empire destroyed each other.

5. What were the signs that the great warrior Alaric was treated poorly by the Romans because of his barbarian blood?

A5.—Pg. 74, ¶ 2—Alaric hoped to become magister militum after Theodosius's death, in particular because the eastern victory at the Battle of the Frigidus was in large part due to his leadership. He was not offered the honor, and he believed this was because of his Gothic blood. Also, over ten thousand Goths, a disproportionate number of men, had fallen at the Battle of the Frigidus; being Goths, they were most likely used as human shields by the Romans, another sign of the Goths' mistreatment.

6. How did the historians of the late Roman empire, in particular Jordanes and Cassiodorus, define the Goths? Before Alaric, were the Goths a real nation?

A6.—Pg. 74, ¶ 4—The historians Jordanes and Cassiodorus divided the Goths into two separate groups: the Ostrogoths, who lived to the east, and the Visigoths, farther west. The names represented not nations but geographic locations, the Ostrogoths lived closer to the Black Sea and the Visigoths lived farther away. The Goths were not a nation before Alaric, they were a shifting collection of Germanic tribes that were sometimes allies and sometimes enemies.

7. How did Arcadius and Rufinus handle the Visigoth threat?

A7.—Pg. 75, ¶ 1—Arcadius and Rufinus did not have an army that could resist Alaric, so they asked Stilicho for help. Stilicho sent soldiers to the east to head off Alaric, and either because of the threat of Stilicho's army or because of some private negotiations made with the military leader of the west, Alaric left the eastern Roman empire alone.

8. What were the circumstances of Rufinus's death?

A8.—Pg. 75, ¶ 2—The Roman soldiers that were sent to help Arcadius and Rufinius out against Alaric were ordered by Stilicho to join the eastern army as a favor to the emperor of the east. When the troops arrived at Constantinople and were greeted by Arcadius and

Rufinius, they slowly encircled Rufinius and brutally stabbed him to death and tore his body apart.

9. Why was Rufinius murdered, and not Arcadius?

Note to the parent—To answer this question, it is important that the student remember Rufinius was a Roman, and so he could eventually become emperor. Stilicho, a barbarian, could never have that opportunity, so he had to get rid of this threat.

A9.—Pg. 75, ¶ 3 & 4—Rufinius, a Roman, could have become a powerful emperor. Arcadius was a weakling, and was given direction by his personal guard. Stilicho, who directed Honorius, needed to get rid of the threat Rufinius posed to his own ambitions.

10. Why did Eutropius have Stilicho declared an enemy to the empire?

A10.—Pg. 76, ¶ 1 & 2—Eutropius was pretty sure Stilicho was behind Rufinus's murder. If that was true, it meant that Stilicho had designs on ruling, in one way or another, the whole of the Roman empire. As the puppet-master for emperor Arcadius, Eutropius wanted to hold onto his own power in the east, so he used the law to attack Stilicho, declaring him via the Senate an enemy to the empire.

Section III: Critical Thinking

The student may not use her text to answer this question.

The trouble Theodosius faced trying to unite the Roman empire under Christianity could make it seem like bringing people together under one idea would be impossible. However, in the midst of Rome's turmoil, Alaric managed to create a new nation out of a motley group of people because of the very fact that they all did believe in the same thing. Write a paragraph explaining how Alaric was able to create a Visigoth nation. In your answer, make sure to explain how he was able to do this even though the Visigoths did not have a homeland.

As we know from past chapters, the Goths often allied themselves with the Romans, often times even receiving the same rights as Roman citizens (you can find a detailed explanation of the rights of the foederati on page 37, ¶ 5). However, the Goths were never seen as Roman. Alaric, seeing that his people deserved to be considered more than barbarians, decided to give up the struggle for Roman acknowledgement and make his own nation. He took control of his army, became supreme commander and leader, and in doing so created the Visigoth nation.

The Goths were made of a collection of tribes that moved and shifted, sometimes fighting together and sometimes fighting against one another. Historians divided the Goths into two main groups, the Ostrogoths, who lived to the east, and the Visigoths, farther west. Alaric brought together Goths from both sides, and from various tribes. Drawn together into a cohesive military unit, they fought for their pride together. Alaric was able to take this unit and turn it into a nation, bound together not by a single tribal heritage, but by a single purpose. When the Visigoth nation was formed, it did not have a homeland. So strong was the tie that bound these people together that they didn't even need a place to call their own. The were united by a single idea, something Constantine and Theodosius wanted so badly for Rome, but the Visigoths actually managed.

EXAMPLE ANSWER:

The Goths, while often allied with the Romans and given rights of citizenship at time, would always been seen by the Romans as barbarians. Alaric knew this, decided to give up the struggle for Roman acknowledgement and make his own nation. He took control of his army, became supreme commander and leader, and in doing so created the Visigoth nation. The people of his nation were Ostrogoths, Visigoths and people from other wandering tribes. Drawn together into a cohesive military unit, they fought for their pride together. Alaric was able to take this unit and turn it into a nation, bound together not by a single tribal heritage, but by a single purpose. When the Visigoth nation was formed, it did not have a homeland. So strong was the tie that bound these people together that they didn't even need a place to call their own. The were united by a single idea, something Constantine and Theodosius wanted so badly for Rome, but the Visigoths actually managed.

Chapter Eleven

The Sack of Rome

The student may use his text when answering the questions in sections I and II.

Section I: Who, What, Where

Write a one or two-sentence answer explaining the significance of each item listed below.

Aetius—**Pg. 83, ¶ 1—Aetius was the son of a high Roman official who was sent as a hostage to the Visigoths in order to guarantee an understanding between the Roman Senate and the Visigoth king Alaric.**

Attalus—**Pg. 82, ¶ 7—Attalus was elected emperor of Rome by the Roman Senate as a compromise to Alaric. Alaric was appointed Attalus's *magister militum*, making Attalus his puppet-king.**

Augustine—**Pg. 77, ¶ 2 to Pg. 78, ¶ 1 and Pg. 84, ¶ 1—After his conversion from Manichee to Christian, Augustine was appointed bishop of Hippo Regius in 396. Augustine was an author; the *Confessions* was his autobiography and his great work of history was the *City of God*.**

Battle of Pollentia—**Pg. 81, ¶ 3 & 4—The Battle of Pollentia was fought on April 6, 402 between Alaric and the Visigoths, and Stilicho and the Romans. April 6 fell on Easter weekend, so Alaric thought all fighting was off; however, Stilicho slyly attacked and defeated the Visigoths.**

Comes Africae—**Pg. 79, ¶ 3—The Comes Africae was the title of the officer in charge of the defense of the Roman territory in North Africa.**

Constantine III—**Pg. 81, ¶ 6 to Pg. 82, ¶ 1—Constantine III was declared emperor by the Roman army in Britannia in 407. Constantine III set out to rule Gaul and Hispania as well as Britannia.**

Donatists—**Pg. 78, ¶ 5—Donatists, named after their leader Donatus Magnus, believed that the church was a place where the grace of God was conveyed to believers through holy men. The Donatists, in their insistence that the church was supposed to be a gathering of holy and righteous people, and that the unrighteous and unworthy should be purged from its midst, were the first puritan Christians.**

Fravitta—**Pg. 80, ¶ 1—Fravitta was a Goth soldier that became consul and advisor to Arcadius after the third puppet-master of Arcadius, the Goth general Gainas, was put to death.**

Gildo—**Pg. 79, ¶ 3 & 5—Gildo, the Comes Africae, rebelled against Honorius and Stilicho in 397 and declared his loyalty to the eastern Roman empire and its ruler Eutropius. Gildo killed himself after his soldiers surrendered to Mascezel's army.**

Manichaeism—**Pg. 77, ¶ 3—Manichaeism taught that the universe was made up of two powerful forces, Good and Evil, which were eternally opposed. The Persian prophet Mani, for whom the religion is named, taught that matter was intrinsically Evil and that human beings could only return to the Good by withdrawing from as much contact with matter as possible.**

Mascezel—**Pg. 79, ¶ 4 & 5—Mascezel, Gildo's brother, commanded the army sent to attack North Africa. Mascezel's two sons were murdered by Gildo, so his triumph over his brother avenged not just Rome but his children's deaths.**

Theodosius II—**Pg 80, ¶ 4 to Pg. 81, ¶ 1—Theodosius II was the son of Arcadius and the future Roman emperor. He was kept safe from usurpers by Yazdegerd I of Persia.**

Yazdegerd I—**Pg. 81, ¶ 2—Yazdegerd I, son of Shapur III, inherited Persia's throne from his father. Yazdegerd swore peace with the Romans and acted as guardian to Arcadius's son, Theodosius II.**

Section II: Comprehension

Write a two or three-sentence answer to each of the following questions.

1. Briefly recap the story of Augustine's conversion from Manichee to Nicene Christian.

A1.—Pg. 73, ¶ 3 to Pg. 74, ¶ 1—In his thirties, Augustine lived in Milan and became friends with bishop Ambrose, whose teachings about Christianity prompted Augustine to reject his Manichee past and became a catechumen of Nicene Christianity. Augustine's new religion threw him into uncertainty and distress, and one day when he was reading in a garden weeping over the misery in his soul, he heard a child's voice chanting "Pick up and read." He interpreted this as a command to pick up St. Paul's Epistle to the Romans; reading from it, he was instantly converted to belief in Christ because all his anxieties and doubt were dispelled from his soul.

2. What was the dispute particular to the North African Christians that Augustine faced when he returned home from Milan?

A2.—Pg. 78, ¶ 3 & 4—When Diocletian was persecuting Christians in North Africa, a local Roman governor told the clergy that if Christians would just hand over their Scriptures as a symbol of recantation, they could go about their business and avoid slaughter. When Augustine returned home, there was a dispute over a newly appointed bishop in Carthage, a man that had chosen to avoid death and turn over his Scriptures. The Christians who had not turned over their Scriptures said this man had no right to be bishop, that any baptisms administered by this man would be a sham, and that his bishopric would contaminate the entire Christian church.

3. What is the fundamental difference between the Donatists and the Christians of Augustine's church?

A3.—Pg. 78, ¶ 5 & 6—Donatists believed baptisms were effective and Eucharists were real only when the priest who administered them was himself a holy man. Augustine, as the voice of the official position of the bishop in Rome, countered that the church was a place where the grace of God was conveyed to believers because God willed it to be so, not because of the character of the men who occupied its official positions. The Donatists were puritans who believed the church was supposed to be a gathering of holy and righteous people, whereas Augustine, and the bishop in Rome, were the orthodox, *catholic* thinkers of the church who said that it was impossible for men to attempt to purify the church of God.

4. Why might the Donatists have insisted on the purity of their members in the time of political turmoil faced by the Roman empire?

A4.—Pg. 79, ¶ 2—The Donatists' insistence on creating an identity they could control and a community that was well defined could have sprung from the uncertainty of what it meant to be a Roman. The political chaos of the Roman empire made it increasingly difficult to define Roman identity, where it was very clear what defined a Donatist. By proclaiming oneself a Donatist, one could be sure of one's identity and allegiances.

5. What was the most immediate problem for Stilicho caused by Gildo's rebellion? How did Stilicho decide to handle the problem?

A5.—Pg. 79, ¶ 4—The immediate problem Stilicho faced because of Gildo's rebellion was lack of access to the grain supplied by North Africa, and a subsequent corn shortage in Rome. When the people in Rome began to starve, Stilicho convinced the Senate to declare a war against Gildo.

6. What were the circumstances of Mascezel's victory against Gildo?

A6.—Pg. 75, ¶ 4 & 5—Mascezel and five thousand Roman soldiers sailed to Africa to meet Gildo and his seventy thousand men. Mascezel slashed at the first standard-bearer's arm with his sword, which caused the bearer to drop the standard, which caused all the

standard-bearers to drop their arms, which caused all of Gildo's soldiers to surrender. Gildo tried to flee but when his ship was blown back to African shores, he killed himself.

7. What do Rufinius, Eutropius, and Gainas have in common?

A7.—Pg. 80, ¶ 1—Rufinius, Eutropius and Gainas were all puppet-masters for Arcadius. Also, the tenure for all three men was short-lived; each man was killed not long into his service for Arcadius.

8. Why did the Visigoth king Alaric invade Italy in 400?

A8.—Pg. 80, ¶ 2—The Visigoth king Alaric invaded Italy in 400 because he was in search of a homeland for his new nation.

9. Why didn't Honorius launch an attack from Ravenna on the invading Visigoths? What was the result of Honorius's inaction?

A9.—Pg. 80, ¶ 3—Ravenna was a good place for Honorius and his court to take refuge because it was ringed with swampland and relatively easy to defend. However, it was an impossible place from which to launch a fight against the Visigoths because of the same environmental characteristics that made it safe for Honorius and his army to take refuge. Because Honorius didn't attack, the Visigoths continued to spread across the north of Italy for the next two years.

10. Explain why Arcadius bucked with tradition and did not name his son Theodosius II co-emperor when he was an infant. How did Yazdegerd I of Persia come to be the guardian of Theodosius II?

A10.—Pg. 81, ¶ 1—Though it had become tradition for emperors to appoint their infant sons as co-emperors, Arcadius was afraid that declaring his son co-emperor would sign the child's death-warrant. If Arcadius was to die and his son was already named co-emperor, there was no one that would protect his son's power, meaning there was no one that would protect his son's life. Knowing things were bad in Italy and Honorius could not be trusted, Arcadius turned to the Persian Yazdegerd I, king of the nation that had been at peace with the Roman empire for at least twenty years, for the protection of his baby son.

11. What were the terms of the treaty settled upon after the Battle of Pollentia?

A11.—Pg. 81, ¶ 5—The terms of the treaty settled after the Battle of Pollentia were that Alaric's wife, who had been captured by Stilicho's troops during fighting, be returned to the Visigoth king. In exchange, Alaric gave northern Italy back to Stilicho.

12. What were the circumstances of Stilicho's execution?

A12.—Pg. 82, ¶ 2—At twenty-three years old, Honorius decided to become independent and get rid of his puppet-master Stilicho. Honorius heard rumors that Stilicho was planning a match between his own son and Honorius's sister Placida, a marriage that would mean Stilicho's son could make a bid for the imperial throne. Honorius and the Roman officials at his court had Stilicho arrested and put to death for planning treason.

13. After being bribed out of Rome with gold, silk, leather and pepper, why did Alaric lay siege to Rome a second time?

A13.—Pg. 82, ¶ 4 & 5—Alaric didn't attack Rome for wealth; he was looking for a homeland. Alaric sent Honorius a message in 409 saying he'd attack Rome again if Honorius didn't give him land in Illyricum for his Visigoths to settle on. When Honorius refused, Alaric marched straight back to Rome and refused to leave, promising he would see the city starve to death unless he was given a place to settle his new nation.

14. After being named Attalus's *magister militum* and given a Roman hostage to ensure good faith between the Visigoths and the Romans, what caused Alaric to attack Rome a third time?

A14.—Pg. 83, ¶ 3—Alaric was incensed when Attalus refused to put an army of Visigoths and Romans together, claiming that putting a Visigoth commander in charge of Roman soldiers would be a disgrace. Alaric reacted to the anti-barbarian sentiment by taking Attalus's purple robe and diadem away by force, imprisoning him in his own camp, and attacking Rome for a third time. Angry that no matter what he did he would never receive the recognition he deserved because of his barbarian heritage, Alaric took what he thought he should have been given by right through force, including Placida.

15. How did Augustine react to Alaric's Sack of Rome?

A15.—Pg. 84, ¶ 1 & 2—Augustine's reaction to Alaric's Sack of Rome is recorded in his great work of history, the City of God. He explained in his book that Rome was a city of man that existed side by side with the city of God, and although the goals of the two cities may occasionally intersect, the ultimate purposes of their citizens diverged. The city of man seeks power; the citizens of God's city seek only the worship and glory of God.

Section III: Critical Thinking

The student may use his text to answer this question.

It took Visigoth king Alaric three attacks on Rome to get his point across—not only did he deserve recognition for his leadership, but also Rome was not all it was cracked up to be. Alaric might have wanted acceptance from Roman leaders, but his Sack of Rome also showed that it was not untouchable. In the chapter we learn that Alaric's Sack of Rome was not the most devastating attack the city had seen, but it was very damaging in terms of morale. Write a paragraph explaining why Alaric's Sack of Rome was so symbolically destructive.

Alaric's Sack of Rome caused the Roman world to question the esteem of the Eternal City. Alaric, a Visigoth, or barbarian, stormed into Rome three times. In the last of these sieges, he told his soldiers to take whatever they wanted and burn what they fancied. Alaric even took the emperor's sister as his hostage. The incident that spurred the Sack of Rome was an argument over the legitimacy of a barbarian commanding Roman soldiers. Romans thought they were above the barbarians, and Rome itself certainly was not expected to come under attack again and again by the barbarians. Rome, the symbol of political and religious power for the Roman empire, was now seen by the far-flung citizens of the empire, both east and west, as weak and broken. The text tells us, "not since 387 BC, when the city was not yet part of an empire," had a band of foreigners entered the city (pg. 83, ¶ 5). If the Visigoths could overrun the city with almost no effort, what did that mean for the power of the emperor? What did it mean for the power of the bishop of Rome, who commanded all other bishops? What did it mean for the power of the church? These questions show us just how damaging the Sack of Rome was for Roman morale. Without faith in the symbolic power of Rome, it was unclear what power the city, and the church, had left.

EXAMPLE ANSWER:

Alaric's Sack of Rome caused the Roman world to question the esteem of the Eternal City. Alaric, a Visigoth, stormed into Rome three times. In the last of these sieges, he told his soldiers to take whatever they wanted and burn whatever they wanted. Alaric even took the emperor's sister as his hostage. The incident that spurred the Sack of Rome was an argument over the legitimacy of a barbarian commanding Roman soldiers. Romans thought they were above the barbarians, and Rome itself certainly was not expected to come under attack again and again by the barbarians. Rome, the symbol of political and religious power for the Roman empire, was now seen by the far-flung citizens of the empire, both east and west, as weak and broken. No band of foreigners had attacked Rome in about 700 years. The citizens of the empire questioned the power of the emperor, the bishop and the church because a band of Visigoths, barbarians, ransacked the city. The Sack of Rome broke the symbolic power of the city and the church.

Section IV: Map Exercise:

1. Using a black pencil, trace the outlines of the rectangular frame of Map 11.1: The Visigoth Invasion.

2. Using a blue pencil, trace the coastline of the Mediterranean and the Black Sea. (You do not need to trace the outline of the Red Sea at this time.)

3. Using a black pencil, trace the outline of the Roman Empire, east and west. Include the dividing center line between east and west. Trace the mountain peaks of the Alps, simply using small peaks. Repeat until the contours are familiar.

4. Using a new sheet of paper, trace the rectangular frame of the map in black. Remove your tracing paper from the original. Using a regular pencil with an eraser as you look at Map 11.1, draw the outline of the Mediterranean and the Black Sea. Erase and redraw as necessary.

5. When you are pleased with your map, lay it over the original. Erase and redraw any lines which are more than ¼ of an inch off the original.

6. Now carefully study the locations of Gaul, North Africa, Italy, Sicily, Illyricum, Asia, Egypt, and Syria. When you are familiar with them, close the book. Using your regular pencil with the eraser,

label all eight locations. Check your map against the original. Erase and re-mark any misplaced labels.

7. Now carefully study the cities of Toulouse, Hippo Regius, Carthage, Ravenna, Milan, Jerusalem, and Bethlehem. When you are familiar with them, close the book. Using your regular pencil with the eraser, label all eight locations. Check your map against the original. Erase and re-mark any misplaced labels.

8. Now study the locations of the Franks (inside and outside the limits of the Roman Empire), the Visigoths, and the Ostrogoths. When you are familiar with them, close the book. Choose three different colors to represent the Franks, the Visigoths, and the Ostrogoths. Use these three colors to label the locations of each barbarian group. Use the color you used for the Visigoths to draw the arrows that show their movement. Check your map against the original, and erase and re-mark any misplaced labels.

9. Study the location of the Battle of Pollentia. When you are familiar with it, close the book, and mark the location on the map. Check your final map against the original. Erase and re-mark if necessary.

Chapter Twelve

One Nature versus Two

The student may use her text when answering the questions in sections I and II.

Section I: Who, What, Where

Write a one or two-sentence answer explaining the significance of each item listed below.

Avesta—**Pg. 87, ¶ 1—The Avesta, or divine 'aura' of the appointed king, showed Persians that a chosen king had the right to hold power. Bahram V was very handsome and was seen by Persians as possessing the Avesta, the will of the divine to rule.**

Bahram V—**Pg. 87, ¶ 1 & 2—Bahram V, the second son of Yazdegerd, returned from an exile imposed by his father in Arabia to take the Persian throne. Bahram attempted a war against Theodosius II, but ultimately decided to make peace with the Romans.**

Note to parent—The student might also include that Bahram V was very handsome, a quality that reflected the Avesta, or divine 'aura' of the appointed king. There is a separate "Who, What, Where" for Avesta—it does not necessarily have to be included in Bahram V's "Who, What, Where."

Codex Theodosianus—**Pg. 87, ¶ 4 and note—The Codex Theodosianus was a single coherent law code comprised of a synthesis of all the irregular and competing laws in the eastern empire. The Codex Theodosianus was started in 429 by Theodosius II and would be finished in 438.**

Council of Ephesus—**Pg. 88, ¶ 4—The Council of Ephesus was held to figure out which belief about the nature of God the Roman bishop would support. Nestorianism was ruled out, and monophysitism became the official stance on the matter from Rome.**

Monophysitism—**Pg. 88, ¶ 3 & 4—Monophysitism was the Christian belief that the two natures of God, God the Father and God the Son, had become mystically one, impossible to tease out by reason.**

Nestorianism—**Pg. 88, ¶ 3 & 4—Nestorianism was the Christian belief that the two natures of God, God the Father and God the Son, were two separate natures, divine and human, but mixed together. Nestorianism gets its name from Nestorius, the bishop of Constantinople and the belief's most ardent supporter.**

Pulcheria—**Pg. 86, ¶ 3—Pulcheria, Theodosius II's older sister, a devout Christian, talked the Roman Senate into naming her empress and co-ruler at the age of fifteen. In 420, Pulcheria convinced Theodosius II to declare war on Yazdegerd for his persecution of Persian Christians.**

Section II: Comprehension

Write a two or three-sentence answer to each of the following questions.

1. What measures did the Persian Yazdegerd I take to keep Roman Theodosius II safe during his guardianship of the young Roman heir?

A1.—Pg. 85, ¶ 2—Yazdegerd provided an accomplished Persian tutor for Theodosius II. Yazdegerd also sent the eastern Senate a letter detailing his intentions to keep Theodosius II safe and he threatened war on anyone who attacked the eastern Roman empire.

2. Why did Persians give Yazdegerd the nickname "Yazdegerd the Sinner"?

A2.—Pg. 85, ¶ 3 to Pg. 86, ¶ 1—Yazdegerd was given the nickname "Yazdegerd the Sinner" because of his loyalty to Theodosius II, which meant he was also loyal to Christians and to the Romans. Persians resisted Yazdegerd's policies, which mean he became more and more stringent with his own people, punishing them drastically for minor infractions. This only made the nickname seem more appropriate.

3. What spurred Yazdegerd to finally persecute Persian Christians?

A3.—Pg. 86, ¶ 2—Yazdegerd was pushed to persecute Persian Christians after a Christian priest in Ctesiphon tried to burn down the great Zoroastrian temple there. Yazdegerd could not tolerate this offense to the Persian religion.

4. How did Yazdegerd die? Explain the myth associated with Yazdegerd's death, and its meaning.

A4.—Pg. 86, ¶ 4—Yazdegerd died while struck by a sudden illness on his travels through Hyrcania, southeast of the Caspian Sea. An old Persian story says that while Yazdegerd was travelling a spirit-horse rose from a nearby stream, killed him, and then disappeared back into the water. The horse, a symbol of Persia's nobility, suggests the story means that someone watching out for Persia's well-being did Yazdegerd in.

5. How did the fight between the Persians and the Romans that began with Theodosius II's declaration of war against Yazdegerd end?

A5.—Pg. 87, ¶ 2—Though Yazdegerd died before he could meet Theodosius II on the battlefield, Bahram V took up the Persian cause against the Romans. Within a year of battle, a truce was called. Both sides agreed to refrain from building new frontier fortresses, and also to leave the Arab tribes on the edges of the desert, which each empire had been actively wooing to their respective side.

6. What civic acts did Theodosius II undertake during the Persian-enforced peace of his early years?

A6.—Pg. 87, ¶ 4—In the peaceful times of his early years, Theodosius appointed a commission to synthesize all the irregular and competing laws in his part of the empire into a single coherent law code which was called the Codex Theodosianus. Constantinople was now protected by new walls, which he called the Theodosian Walls. Finally, Theodosius II founded a school in Constantinople for the study of law, Latin, Greek, medicine, philosophy, and other advanced subjects—a school that would eventually be called the "University of Constantinople."

7. What was the purpose of creating the university in Constantinople?

A7.—Pg. 87, ¶ 5 to Pg. 88, ¶ 1—The university created in Constantinople was designed to take the place of the Roman university of Athens. The university in Athens represented the old state religion. In the University of Constantinople, there were a total of thirteen teachers of Latin and fifteen teachers of Greek, which showed the Greek language and philosophy was gaining some ground on traditional Latin.

8. Why was Arianism considered the religion of the barbarians?

Note to the parent—to answer this question, the student will have to remember that in 380, Theodosius declared the catholic Christian church was based on Nicene Christianity. This is found in Chapter Eight, on page 57, ¶ 4.

A8.—Pg. 88, ¶ 3—Arianism was considered the religion of the barbarians because Nicene Christianity was the official religion of Rome. If you were an Arian, you were not assimilated into Roman identity, meaning you must be a barbarian.

9. In the debate between monophysitism and Nestorianism, where did Mary fit in?

A9.—Pg. 88, ¶ 3, 4 and note—The monophysitists believed that God the Father and God the Son had become mystically one, and so if Jesus and God were one, then Mary was theotokos, or Mother of God. The Nestorians believed that God the Father and God the Son were separate but equal and mixed together, so Mary was understood as christotokos, the Mother of Christ.

10. In what way was the decision made at the Council of Ephesus a decision about power, rather than religion?

A10.—Pg. 88, ¶ 5 to Pg. 89, ¶ 1—The center of the Nestorian school was at Antioch, while the center of the monophysitists' school was in Alexandria, both of which were vying for

influence and importance. The same is true for the men who supported these causes; Cyril, the bishop of Alexandria, was a monophysitist like the Bishop in Rome, while the bishop of Constantinople, Nestorius, was a two-natured man. The condemnation of Nestorius's belief reflected the power of the Roman bishop, and gave more importance to the city of Alexandria.

11. Why did the bishops in the eastern empire suspect that Nestorius's two-natured beliefs were influenced by the Persians?

A11.—Pg. 89, ¶ 2—Persians practiced Zoroastrianism, a monotheistic religion that said earthly and divine substances could never be mixed. Since Nestorianism said God the Father and God the Son were separate, the bishops in the eastern empire believed Nestorius was influenced by the similar Persian philosophy.

12. If the arguments over Christology weren't just about monophysitism versus Nestorianism, what were they really about?

A12.—Pg. 89, ¶ 5—The arguments over Christology were about so much more than a one or two-natured God. The men who quarreled over Christology were fighting over the place of mysticism and the power of rationalism, the fear of Persian influence in the Roman empire, the rejection of all Persian culture, and the fear that one half of the empire might politically and practically overpower the other. Ultimately, the arguments over Christology were arguments about who, and what ideas, would dominate the Roman empire.

Section III: Critical Thinking

The student may use her text to answer this question.

Constantine thought belief in Christ would unite Rome. As we read more about the history of the medieval world, we see that not only would Christ *not* unite Rome, Christianity itself would be divided. Use this space to list all of the sects of Christianity we have read about up to this point, and explain the major belief of each sect. Start with the division between Arian and Nicene Christianity. You can use your text to go back and refresh your memory. Once you've made your list, explain why Constantine's idea that Rome could be united under Christianity could never last.

A) These are the different sects of Christianity that have been identified in our reading so far:

Nicene Christians (Chapter 1)—Nicene Christians believed in one God, the Father almighty. God the Father and God the Son are one in the same.

Arians (Chapter 1)—Arians believed in God the Father, who created God the Son. Jesus Christ might have been different from other created beings, but he was not Almighty God.

Ebionites (Chapter 1)—Ebionites believed that Christ was essentially human, and "divine" only in the sense that he had been selected to reign as the Jewish Messiah.

Docetists (Chapter 1)—Docetists believed that, because matter was impure, Christ could not have truly taken part in the corruption of the body, so he was a spirit who only appeared human.

Gnostics (Chapter 1)—Gnostics believed that the divine Christ and the human Jesus had formed a brief partnership in order to rescue mankind from the corrupting grasp of the material world.

*Catholics (Chapter 8)—Catholics were Romans who believed in Nicene Christianity as the state religion. [**NOTE**: Students might miss this because "catholic" refers to the declaration made by Theodosius that Nicene Christianity was the one true faith of his empire. While it is more a political designation than a religious designation, it is important to note nonetheless.]*

Donatists (Chapter 11)—Donatists believed the church was a gathering place of holy and righteous people. Donatists were puritans, and believed the unrighteous and unworthy should be purged from the church.

Monophysitists (Chapter 12)—Monophysitists believed God the Father and God the Son mystically came together into one single being, and could not be separated.

Nestorians (Chapter 12)—Nestorians believed God the Father and God the Son were both divine entities in the same being, equal but separate.

B) After listing all of these different variations of Christianity, it should be clear to the student that while Constantine might have thought God was the way to unite Rome, what God really became was another way for leaders to jockey for power, and for different groups of people to define themselves. Like debates on national identity, religious identity became another way for groups of people to distinguish themselves from one another, an act that had less to do with God and more to do with evolving cultures.

EXAMPLE ANSWER:

A) The listing of the variations of Christianity should look much like what is presented above.

B) Religion, like nationality, was a way for people to define themselves in the medieval world. Constantine thought God might have been the great leveler, something everyone could believe in, but as seen in the above list, the way people believed in God was very different. These differences led to conflict, and even war. Bringing Rome together under God might have worked for a little while, but it couldn't last long; instead of God being something that brought people together, He became another way for people to tear a nation apart.

Chapter Thirteen

Seeking a Homeland

The student may use his text when answering the questions in sections I and II.

Section I: Who, What, Where

Write a one or two-sentence answer explaining the significance of each item listed below.

Ataulf—**Pg. 91, ¶ 3—Ataulf, king of the Visigoths following Alaric, married Placida and thus bound the Visigoths with the Romans.**

Attila—**Pg. 93, ¶ 7—Attila, a twelve-year-old boy that was a relative of the Hun warleader Rua, was sent to live in western Rome in 418 as part of a hostage exchange between the Romans and the Huns.**

Constantius—**Pg. 93, ¶ 3, 4 & ¶ 6—Constantius was Honorius's right-hand general and *magister militum*. Constantius defeated Attalus and Ataulf, and helped with the treaty that ended fighting between the western Roman empire and the Visigoths; for this he was rewarded with marriage to Placida, the emperor's sister.**

Wallia—**Pg. 93, ¶ 3 & 4—Wallia killed the man who killed Ataulf in order to take the throne for himself. Wallia negotiated with Constantius and Honorius, and managed to get southwestern Gaul for the Visigoths, finally giving the kingdom a homeland.**

Section II: Comprehension

Write a two or three-sentence answer to each of the following questions.

1. Describe the burial Alaric was given by his men. Why was this type of burial significant to Alaric's memory?

A1.—Pg. 91, ¶ 2—When Alaric died, his men diverted the path of the river Busentus and put their captives to work digging a grave for Alaric in the riverbed. They buried Alaric with

many treasures, let the river run its natural course over the grave, and then put to death the digger-captives so that no one would ever know where he was buried. Alaric had sought recognition from the Romans all of his life and never truly received it; at his burial he was finally treated like a hero.

2. How did Ataulf join the Visigoth kingdom with the Roman empire without shedding any blood?

A2.—Pg. 91, ¶ 3—Ataulf married Placida, sister of emperor Honorius. By marrying a royal Roman, Ataulf joined together the two kingdoms without any bloodshed.

3. Why did Ataulf think Gaul would be a good place to vie for a Visigoth homeland?

A3.—Pg. 91, ¶ 4—Ataulf decided that Gaul would be a good place for a Visigoth homeland because it was in turmoil. Constantine III was fighting off the western emperor Honorius, who was trying to get his land back from the British pretender. The chaos would make it easier for the Visigoths to invade and take the land for themselves.

4. Why did Constantine ditch his position as leader of the British in Gaul to join the church? Was this move a smart one?

A4.—Pg. 92, ¶ 1 & 2—Constantine III had himself ordained as a priest because churches seemed to be off limits in Roman war. For example, even the Visigoth Alaric ordered his men to stay away from the churches when they sacked Rome. Constantine III's decision to join the church ultimately didn't matter; thought Constantine wasn't immediately killed by Honorius, he was taken captive and on the way back to Rome he was assassinated.

5. Where did Ataulf first settle the Visigoths in Gaul, in 413?

A5.—Pg. 92, ¶ 3—By 413, the Visigoths had conquered land in the old Roman territory of Narbonensis, in southern Gaul, and Ataulf made the city of Toulouse the capital of the small Visigoth kingdom.

6. How did Attalus manage to become, once again, a rival emperor to Honorius?

A6.—Pg. 93, ¶ 2—Ex-emperor Attalus had been made a prisoner of the Visigoths by Alaric. Ataulf, imagining himself the puppet-master for emperor Attalus, crowned the ex-emperor and set him up as Honorius's rival once again.

7. What happened when Honorius heard that Attalus and Ataulf were making a play for the Roman empire?

A7.—Pg. 93, ¶ 3—Soon after Attalus was re-crowned, Honorius sent Constantius to harass the Goths. Constantius captured and beheaded Attalus and reduced the new Visigoth kingdom to hunger and desperation.

8. What were the circumstances of Ataulf's death?

A8.—Pg. 93, ¶ 3—Ataulf was resented by the Visigoth people for putting them at the mercy of Constantius and the western Roman army. In 415, he was murdered by one of his own countrymen.

9. Explain the terms of the deal Wallia made with Constantius and Honorius to end the war between the Visigoths and the western Roman empire.

A9.—Pg. 93, ¶ 4—Wallia negotiated this deal with Constantius and Honorius: the Visigoths would help the western Roman army fight the Germanic tribes that had invaded Hispania, and he would send Placida, Aetius and other captives taken in Rome back to Ravenna if he could have southwestern Gaul for the Visigoths. Honorius agreed to the treaty.

10. What happened to Placida and Aetius when they returned to the western Roman empire?

A10.—Pg. 93, ¶ 6 & 7—Placida and Aetius were not free for long upon their return home. Placida was ordered by Honorius to marry Constantius. Aetius was sent off in another hostage exchange to guarantee good will between the western Roman empire and the Huns.

Section III: Critical Thinking

The student may use his text to answer this question.

Visions of grandeur are often paired with skewed visions of reality. Ataulf, after successfully campaigning for the Visigoths, believed he could become the emperor of Rome. Write a paragraph explaining how Ataulf's dream of being a great king of Rome ruined his chances at *actually* being a great king of the Visigoths.

This question has to do with greed, ambition and power. If Ataulf had only been happy with having secured himself a nation and growing that nation in Gaul, he could have been great. But instead he was seduced by visions of power, of ruling the whole Roman empire, and bit off more than he could chew. His image of himself was much greater than the reality, and in the end he got himself killed and put his kingdom through hell.

Ataulf was smart in his marriage to Placida, and he was smart to see that the unrest in Gaul would make for an easy fight, almost guaranteeing the Visigoths a homeland. He conquered land in the old Roman territory of Narbonensis, and made a capital for the Visigoths in Toulouse. Somehow, though, Ataulf's vision of his leadership wasn't of the new Visigoth nation, but of the entire Roman empire. He was seduced by the idea of reuniting and restoring Rome. The result of Ataulf's attempt to take the Roman crown, via the re-coronation of the ex-emperor Attalus, was an attack by Honorius that left the new Visigoth kingdom starving and desperate. Ataulf, resented by his people for his selfish actions, was hunted down and murdered by one of his own countrymen.

EXAMPLE ANSWER:

Ataulf did a lot for the young Visigoth kingdom, but it wasn't enough for him. Ataulf was smart in his marriage to Placida, and to see that the unrest in Gaul would make for an easy fight, almost guaranteeing the Visigoths a homeland. He conquered land in the old Roman territory of Narbonensis, and made a capital for the Visigoths in Toulouse. Somehow, though, Ataulf's vision of his leadership wasn't of the new Visigoth nation, but of the entire Roman empire. He was seduced by the idea of reuniting and restoring Rome. The result of Ataulf's attempt to take the Roman crown, via the re-coronation of the ex-emperor Attalus,

was an attack by Honorius that left the new Visigoth kingdom starving and desperate. Ataulf, resented by his people for his selfish actions, was hunted down and murdered by one of his own countrymen. If Ataulf had just focused on building up his new kingdom, his people would have loved him as they did Alaric.

Section IV: Map Exercise

1. Using a black pencil, trace the rectangular outline of the frame for Map 13.1: Visigoth Kingdom.

2. Using a blue pencil, trace the coastal outline present on the map: (the Atlantic) around Britannia and down along the shores of the Saxons and Franks and then Hispania. Continue to trace the coastline as it turns into the Mediterranean inside Hispania and North Africa and so forth. Now trace the perimeter of the Roman Empire, including the center line dividing east and west. Use a contrasting color to show the Kingdom of the Visigoths. Repeat until the contours are familiar.

3. Using a new sheet of paper, trace the rectangular frame of the map in black. Remove your tracing paper from the original. Using a regular pencil with an eraser as you look at Map 13.1, draw the complete coastal outline present on the map. Then draw the outline of the Roman Empire. Draw the outline of the Kingdom of the Visigoths and shade to delineate from the Roman Empire. Compare with the original, and erase and redraw as necessary.

4. When you are pleased with your map, lay it over the original. Erase and redraw any lines which are more than ¼ of an inch off the original.

5. Now study the locations of the barbarians: the Visigoths, the Vandals, and the Franks. Also study the locations of the cities of Toulouse, Milan, Ravenna, Rome, Hippo Regius, and Carthage. When you are familiar with them, close the book. Using your regular pencil, mark the locations of the barbarian regions, including the Kingdom of the Visigoths, and the cities. Check your map against the original. Correct any misplaced labels.

Chapter Fourteen

The Gupta Decline

The student may use her text when answering the questions in sections I and II.

Section I: **Who, What, Where**

Write a one or two-sentence answer explaining the significance of each item listed below.

Ajanta Caves—**Pg. 98, ¶ 3—The Ajanta Caves were a series of thirty or so caves that housed a series of temples that were carved into natural chambers. The construction of the caves took about 600 years.**

Budhagupta—**Pg. 97, ¶ 5—Budhagupta, second nephew to Skandagupta, became king of the Gupta empire after a brother and nephew of the dead king tried to claim the throne. He was the last Gupta king to reign over anything that resembled an empire.**

Harishena—**Pg. 98, ¶ 4—Harishena, king of the Vakataka, took the throne around 480. He celebrated his victories by carving at least two temples into natural caves in Ellora.**

Hephthalites—**Pg. 95, ¶ 2 & 3—The Hephthalites were nomads from central Asia and then spread out from their homeland during the fifth century, most likely a branch of Turkic peoples that descended from Asian tribes that had long ago shared a common language. The Hephthalites began to come down across the Kush mountains into India during Kumaragupta's rule.**

Kumaragupta—**Pg. 95, ¶ 2 and Pg. 96, ¶ 2—Kumaragupta, son and successor of Chandragupta II, battled internal contradictions and a Hephthalite invasion during his thirty-nine-year rule. Despite these upsets, Kumaragupta is remember as a great leader that brought the Gupta empire to its peak.**

Mahayana school of Buddhism—**Pg. 98, ¶ 7 to Pg. 99, ¶ 1—The Mahayana school of Buddhism, like the Theravada school, taught that all physical things were transient, and that only enlightenment could reveal the world as an impermanent and unreal place. Unlike the**

Theravada school, Mahayana Buddhism, which tended to dominate the Chinese experience, believed prayer, faith, divine revelations and emotion would lead to enlightenment.

Mekala—**Pg. 96, ¶ 3 to Pg. 97, ¶ 1—Mekala was the land of the Vakataka in the western Deccan, which had been folded into the Gupta empire during Chandragupta II's reign. Narendrasena made Mekala independent of India during his reign.**

Narendrasena—**Pg. 97, ¶ 1—Narendrasena, king of the Vakataka and great-nephew to the Gupta king Kumaragupta, rebelled against the Gupta and fought for Vakataka independence around the time of the Hephthalite invasions into Gupta.**

Skandagupta—**Pg. 97, ¶ 2, 4 & 5—Skandagupta, Kumaragupta's son and heir, led the battle against the foreigners that invaded the Gupta empire during the end of his father's reign. Skandagupta inherited the throne in 455, soon after fighting off the Hephthalites again, and continued to fight during his entire reign in order to keep the Gupta empire from disintegrating.**

Theravada school of Buddhism—**Pg. 98, ¶ 7 to Pg. 99, ¶ 1—The Theravada school of Buddhism, like the Mahayana school, taught that all physical things were transient, and that only enlightenment could reveal the world as an impermanent and unreal place. Unlike the Mahayana school, Theravada Buddhists believed reasoning, mindfulness and concentration would lead the mind to enlightenment.**

Viharas—**Pg. 98, ¶ 6—Viharas were networks of carved rooms in the cave-temples, monasteries complete with individual cells, common rooms, and refectories. The viharas offered monks a place to devote themselves to the practice of their beliefs without distraction.**

Section II: Comprehension

Write a two or three-sentence answer to each of the following questions.

1. Describe the contradictory composure of the India that Chandragupta II left for his son Kumaragupta when he died in 415.

A1.—Pg. 95, ¶ 1—When king Chandragupta II died in 415, the empire of India was based on the ancient glories of Asoka, but the means to get there was based on force, which Asoka renounced. The language of nomadic invaders, Sanskrit, had become the language of sophistication and education, and though India's territory seemed to be massive, it was really land that the king only ruled in name.

2. Why did the Indians call the Hephthalites *hunas* if they were not related to the Huns in the west? What two other designations were there for the Hephthalites?

A2.—Pg. 95, ¶ 3 and note—The Indians called the Hephthalites *hunas* because they used the general name "Huns" for all roaming nomadic groups north of the mountains. The Persians called the Hephthalites "Kushans" and other sources refer to the Hephthalites as "White Huns."

3. How do Roman historians describe the Hephthalites as different from other nomadic invaders? Where did Arab geographers stand on the matter? How did the Indians see the Hephthalites?

A3.—Pg. 95, ¶ 4 to Pg. 96, ¶ 1—Roman historians said that the Hephthalites were different from other nomadic invaders because they were ruled by a king, had a lawful government, and treated each other and their neighbors justly; they had all the characteristics of a civilized people. Later Arab geographers suggested that the Hephthalites were descended from Shem, the son of Noah, providing them with a legitimate biblical ancestry. The Indians, however, saw the Hephthalites as *mleccha*, which meant speakers of other tongues, ultimately meaning barbarian.

4. What does the royal inscription about Kumaragupta, that his fame "tasted the waters of the four oceans," mean? Why is he remembered as the "lord of the earth" and the "Moon in the firmament of the Gupta dynasty"?

A4.—Pg. 96, ¶ 2—Kumaragupta's empire stretched from Mount Kailasa on the north, to the forests on the slopes of the Vindhya Mountains in the south, and was bordered by the oceans on the east and west. This was the largest area ever claimed by the Guptas, and so Kumaragupta's fame was renowned over the known world, and "tasted the waters of the four oceans." In his expansion of the Gupta territory, Kumaragupta brought the empire to its peak, and so he is remembered and revered as "lord of the earth" and the "Moon in the firmament of the Gupta dynasty."

5. Though Kumaragupta was remembered as the "lord of the earth," what troubles did he face at the end of his reign? What do the coins from the end of Kumaragupta's reign tell us about these troubled times?

A5.—Pg. 97, ¶ 1–3—Towards the end of his reign, Kumaragupta had to fight off the Hephthalites, as well as a band of hostile invaders that were defeated. Despite his victories, the battles ultimately depleted the men and supplies of the Gupta army. Kumaragupta also had to watch Gupta control of Mekala slip as Narendrasena attempted to assert Vakataka independence. Coins from the end of Kumaragupta's reign were made from copper, not gold or silver, which tells us the Indian treasury was emptied as a result of the turmoil.

6. How do we know that religion flourished during the crumbling of the Gupta empire?

A6.—Pg. 98, ¶ 3—We know that religion flourished during the decline of the Guptas because Buddhist monuments called stupas were spread across the country, many carved with scenes of worshippers. In the west of India, a series of temples and monasteries were carved

into natural chambers, modeled after wooden buildings and complete with prayer rooms, staircases, pillars and great halls for the use of those who pursued knowledge rather than political power.

7. Why was the intersection between Harishena's victories and the cave-temples he built in Ellora a fluke?

A7.—Pg. 98, ¶ 4 & 5—The intersection between Harishena's victories and the cave-temples he built in Ellora were a fluke because most of the cave-temples were created simply to provide a place for worship, not to commemorate conquests. In general, the caves, and the men who lived in them, had nothing to do with politics.

8. Where did the monks who lived in the viharas get their food and clothing?

A8.—Pg. 98, ¶ 6—The monks who live and worshipped in the viharas did not live in isolation, and they stayed in touch with locals who they relied on for clothing and food.

9. What was the relationship between Theravada Buddhism and the monastic experience?

A9.—Pg. 99, ¶ 2—Theravada Buddhism emphasized thought and reasoning as the path to enlightenment, so the monastic experience was valued highly. By going into the monastery, and Theravada Buddhist could put all of his energies into study and meditation.

Section III: Critical Thinking 

The student may not use her text to answer this question.

As we have read about the political and religious turmoil in the Roman empire, we've seen that not only did religion shape the culture of the Romans, but it also played a role in dictating who was in power. In India, we also see religion shaping culture, but it was not a player in India's politics. Write a paragraph explaining how Theravada Buddhism was a model for the way the independent entities that made up India co-existed without struggling for power and dominance.

To answer this question, the student first needs to explain the tenets of Theravada Buddhism, and how the religion was practiced. Theravada Buddhism taught that all physical things were transient, and that only enlightenment could reveal the world as an impermanent and unreal place. Theravada Buddhists believed reasoning, mindfulness and concentration would lead the mind to enlightenment. The text explains on page 99 that Theravada Buddhism "placed a higher value on the monastic existence, which allowed the believer to put all of his energies into study and meditation. Certainly Theravada Buddhism gave no help to an army officer or minor king who wanted to conquer an empire. It was diametrically opposed to earthly conquest, and rather than binding its adherents together under one flag, it encouraged them to live side by side while seeking individual enlightenment."

The student then needs to consider what the chapter describes as the "nature" of the organization of Indian kingdoms. On page 98, the text reads, "In fact, it seems to have been the nature of Indian kingdoms to organize themselves as relatively small, independent entities with shifting borders. In the south, where the Gupta reach never extended, a multiplicity of dynasties claimed dominance over different parts of the subcontinent. Inscriptions and coins give us dozens of royal names, but no clear story emerges from the southern jostle. Towards the end of Budhagupta's reign, there was no political power that seemed capable of uniting even a small part of the subcontinent." Indian kingdoms seemed to exist naturally side by side, as their own independent nations, "each pursuing its own individual goals, none of them dominating the rest" (pg. 99, ¶ 3). Like the monks living in the viharas, smaller Indian kingdoms were not in isolation, but they were focused on their own individual goals. Like individual monks meditating together, the patchwork kingdoms of India existed independently but co-existed peacefully.

EXAMPLE ANSWER:

Theravada Buddhism taught that all physical things were transient, and that only enlightenment could reveal the world as an impermanent and unreal place. Theravada Buddhists believed reasoning, mindfulness and concentration would lead the mind to enlightenment. Monks practiced this concentration together in the viharas. They were not isolated, but the enlightenment they sought was individualized. Like the praying monks living together, the kingdoms in the south of India all claimed dominance over a part of the subcontinent, but not over each other. Indian kingdoms, like the monks, seemed to exist naturally side by side, as their own independent nations; the patchwork kingdoms of India governed themselves independently but co-existed peacefully.

Chapter Fifteen

Northern Ambitions

The student may use his text when answering the questions in sections I and II.

Section I: Who, What, Where

Write a one or two-sentence answer explaining the significance of each item listed below.

Ciu Hao—**Pg. 102, ¶ 6 and Pg. 103, ¶ 3—Cui Hao, Wei Taiwu's Chinese advisor, brought Chinese administration and Chinese law into the king's court. Cui Hao practiced a version of Taoism that taught its students to seek enlightenment through magical elixirs; Wei Taiwu adopted this type of Taoism as the state religion as a result of Cui Hao's advising.**

Ge Hong—**Pg. 103, ¶ 4 & 5—Ge Hong, a Chinese Taoist philosopher, preached a form of Taoism that emphasized the drinking of elixirs to attain enlightenment and bring eternal youth. Ge Hong claimed that his family had received three texts from a divine being, the "Scriptures of the Elixirs," or "Taiqing texts," with instructions on how to create these magical potions; because of his promotion of the practice of drinking elixirs, Ge Hong turned Taoism into something like a cult rather than a philosophy.**

Huang—**Pg. 104, ¶ 1—Huang, Wei Taiwu's son and the crown prince, was a Buddhist. After discovering Wei Taiwu's order to slaughter all of the Buddhist monks, Huang sent secret messages to all of the Buddhist priests he could reach, warning them to flee; he saved some lives, but many monks were captured and put to death, and their temples across the empire were reduced to rubble.**

Jiapu—**Pg. 100, ¶ 1—*Jiapu* were genealogical tables kept by the noble families of southern China in order to prove their connections to the oldest aristocratic Chinese families. Noble families kept these tables in order to be exempt from taxes and military service and to enjoy other advantages of the descendents of the oldest families that had fled from Luoyang.**

Jon Gongdi—**Pg. 100, ¶ 3 and Pg. 102, ¶ 1—Jon Gongdi was forced to give up his title as Jin emperor by Liu Yu in 420 in an official ceremony. After returning to private life, Jon Gongdi**

was murdered by one of Song Wudi (Liu Yu)'s officials, meaning the living memory of the Jin dynasty had been erased.

Kou Qianzhi—**Pg. 103, ¶ 5—Kou Qianzhi, a chief teacher of the new Taoism taught by Ge Hong, came to the Bei Wei in 415, and was built a temple by Wei Taiwu. In 442, Kou Qianzhi gave Wei Taiwu a book of charms that gave a magical bent to the emperor's claim to power.**

Liu Song—**Pg. 101, ¶ 1 & note—Liu Song was the dynasty started by Liu Yu that followed the Jin dynasty in southern China. The Liu Song ruled in the southeast of China from 420 to 479.**

Liu Yu/Song Wudi—**Pg. 100, ¶ 2, Pg. 101, ¶ 2 and Pg. 102, ¶ 1 & 2—Liu Yu, a general known for putting down the pirates of the "demon armies," forced Jin emperor Jin Gongdi to abdicate; when Liu Yu took the throne he changed his name to Song Wudi and founded the new dynasty, the Liu Song. Song Wudi removed all living traces of the Jin when he had Jin Gongdi murdered, but he only lived one year as the unquestioned emperor of the traditional Chinese realm.**

Shao—**Pg. 102, ¶ 2—Shao, Song Wudi's nineteen-year-old son, inherited the Liu Song throne after his father's death. Shao was a wild teenager and only ruled for a little over a year before the throne was taken by his older half-brother, Song Wendi.**

Song Wendi—**Pg. 102, ¶ 2 & 3—Song Wendi, Song Wudi's second son, took the Liu Song throne from his younger half-brother, Shao in 424. During his reign, Song Wendi brought the Liu Song to its high point, with successful war campaigns, a competent administration and the founding of four Confucian colleges.**

Song Xiaowu—**Pg. 104, ¶ 3—Song Xiaowu, Song Wendi's younger son, became emperor of the Liu Song in 454 and ruled for ten years. The Mandate of Heaven began to fade during Song Xiaowu's reign because of the emperor's frivolous and pleasure-seeking ways.**

Wei Taiwu—**Pg. 102, ¶ 4 and Pg. 103, ¶ 4 to Pg. 104, ¶ 1—Wei Taiwu, the Bei Wei king, conquered the remaining northern states to unify the north of China in 440. Wei Taiwu believed in a special kind of Taoism that used magical elixirs; threatened by the Buddhists, he ordered the slaughter of Buddhist monks in the Bei Wei empire in 446.**

Section II: Comprehension

Write a two or three-sentence answer to each of the following questions.

1. In what way did the power of the aristocrats finally bring an end to the Jin?

A1.—Pg. 100, ¶ 1 & 2—The aristocratic families of the Jin created *jiapu* to trace their physical connections to the oldest families in China. Being an aristocrat meant having certain privileges, like tax breaks and exemption from military service. As the tables got

more complex, and the estates of the aristocrats were threatened with piracy and pillage, Liu Yu was able to convince the aristocrats that he could help them with their problems; the backing of Liu Yu by the aristocrats gave him the power to depose Jin Gongdi and subsequently start a new dynasty.

2. Why did Liu Yu choose to make the abdication of the Jin throne legal?

A2.—Pg. 100, ¶ 3—Liu Yu chose to make the abdication of the Jin throne legal because he wanted to uphold the Mandate of Heaven. The myth of the Mandate demanded that Liu Yu gain the throne by virtue, not by force. Liu Yu made Jin Gongdi proclaim that since Liu Yu had preserved the empire, it was only just that its rule be handed over to him, thus upholding the Mandate.

3. How did Jin Gongdi die? How did Song Wudi react to the former Jin emperor's death?

A3.—Pg. 102, ¶ 1—Jin Gongdi was smothered to death by one of Song Wudi's officials. Song Wudi pretended he had nothing to do with the former emperor's death. According to tradition, he met with his officials the next day to receive news of the death and wept copiously, then he gave the murdered king a glorious royal funeral, with hundreds of mourners lamenting around the tomb.

4. What was the "Reign of Yuanjia"? What happened during the "Reign of Yuanjia"?

A4.—Pg. 102, ¶ 3—The "Reign of Yuanjia" were the twenty-nine years of Song Wendi's prosperous reign. During the "Reign of Yuanjia," the Liu Song saw successful war campaigns, mostly against the nomadic Xiongnu tribes, and the growth of a competent administration. Also during the "Reign of Yuanjia," Song Wendi established four Confucian colleges, each staffed by distinguished Confucian scholars, for the purpose of training the young men of his empire in the principles and precepts of Confucian literature—something that made them better officials and bureaucrats.

5. How was the Bei Wei kingdom under Wei Taiwu organized?

A5.—Pg. 102, ¶ 7 to Pg. 103, ¶ 1—Under Wei Taiwu, Bei Wei was organized into a strict hierarchy. The countryside was divided into communes, or *dang*, each one with its own administrator. Each *dang* was divided into five villages, or *li*, with a leader in each village reporting to the *dang* administrator; each *li* was made up of five *lin*, or neighborhoods; each *lin* consisted of five families.

6. What type of religion did Ciu Hao practice? What is the difference between traditional Taoism and the type of Taoism Ciu Hao practiced?

A6.—Pg. 103, ¶ 3 & 4—Cui Hao followed a weird and idiosyncratic version of Taoism. Traditional Taoism taught nonaction, withdrawal from the world of strife and politics in order to focus on personal enlightenment. The Taoism practiced by Cui Hao, spread by the Chinese philosopher Ge Hong, encouraged its followers to seek enlightenment through magical elixirs that would lift the drinker to a higher spiritual level and bring eternal youth.

7. Why did Wei Taiwu order the slaughtering of Buddhist monks in the Bei Wei empire?

A7.—Pg. 103, ¶ 5 to Pg. 104, ¶ 1—Wei Taiwu put down a rebellion in 446 led by a guerilla fighter who had stored weapons in the Buddhist temples. Convinced that Buddhist priests were starting a rebellion to overthrow him because he was magically appointed by the new Taoist religion, Wei Taiwu attempted to destroy every trace of Buddhism in his empire. He then ordered the slaughter of all Buddhist monks in his empire, starting in the capital of Chang'an.

8. Why did Song Wendi of the Liu Song deny Wei Taiwu's suggestion of a marriage alliance between the two empires? What did Song Wendi do after he refused the alliance?

A8.—Pg. 104, ¶ 2 & 3—Though Wei Taiwu thought the Bei Wei was just as Chinese as the southern Liu Song, Song Wendi did not. Song Wendi denied Wei Taiwu's suggestion of a marriage alliance between the two empires because he could not see Wei Taiwu's empire as anything other than barbarian. After refusing the alliance, Song Wendi invaded the Bei Wei territory, but only ended up damaging his own army.

9. How did Song Xiaowu's son react to his father's death? How does this reflect the fading of the Mandate of Heaven?

A9.—Pg. 104, ¶ 3 & 4—When Song Xiaowu died, his son showed no grief upon hearing the news. Like Song Xiaowu's use of undignified nicknames for his the officials and nobles in his court, the lack of sentiment from Song Xiaowu's son showed the warping of the natural order of things, including the Mandate of Heaven.

Section III: Critical Thinking

The student may use his text to answer this question.

Finish the sentence: "Money can't buy you . . ." There are many ways to conclude this thought; for Wei Taiwu, money couldn't buy him an authentic Chinese identity, or empire. Wei Taiwu did his best to infuse the Bei Wei with Chinese tradition—hiring a Chinese advisor, bringing Chinese administration to Bei Wei and ruling his empire with Chinese law. Write a paragraph explaining how Wei Taiwu's institution of a state religion, and the obtaining of the charm book, could also be understood as an effort to duplicate Chinese culture; in this case, the Mandate of Heaven.

To answer this question, the student should first explain what the state religions was, and the significance of obtaining a charm book. This can be found on page 103, ¶ 3–5. Wei Taiwu practiced a type of Taoism taught by Ge Hong, which encouraged its followers to seek enlightenment through magical elixirs that would lift the drinker to a higher spiritual level and bring eternal youth. Ge Hong claimed that his family had received three texts from a divine being, the "Scriptures of the Elixirs," or "Taiqing texts," with instructions on how to create these magical potions. In 415, one of the chief teachers of this new kind of Taoism, Kou Qianzhi, ended up in Wei Taiwu's court. Wei Taiwu welcomed Kou Qianzhi and built him a temple. In 442, Kou Qianzhi gave the emperor a book of charms, and every emperor of the Wei dynasty that followed Wei Taiwu also received a charm book at his accession. The state religion was sanctified by the magical powers of the Taoist charm book.

Next, the student should link the magical power of the charm book to the otherworldly power of the Mandate of Heaven. The traditional Chinese Mandate of Heaven gave the ruler the rightful power to command. The ruler was given control of his empire via the blessing of the heavens. The student should draw a parallel between the Chinese Mandate and the Bei Wei book of charms: receiving the Taoist book of charms at one's accession to the throne meant the Bei Wei king was blessed by the state's religion. The Bei Wei could not claim the Mandate of Heaven sanctified its rulers—they were not wholly Chinese—but they could claim that a divine Taoist power passed a charm book to the new ruler via the Taoist monk living in a temple in the Bei Wei court. The significance of the Bei Wei charm book ceremony echoed the passing of the traditional Chinese Mandate of Heaven.

EXAMPLE ANSWER:

Wei Taiwu practiced a type of Taoism taught by Ge Hong, which encouraged its followers to seek enlightenment through magical elixirs that would lift the drinker to a higher spiritual level and bring eternal youth. Ge Hong claimed that his family had received three texts from a divine being, the "Scriptures of the Elixirs," or "Taiqing texts," with instructions on how to create these magical potions. In 415, one of the chief teachers of this new kind of Taoism, Kou Qianzhi, ended up in Wei Taiwu's court. Wei Taiwu welcomed Kou Qianzhi and built him a temple. In 442, Kou Qianzhi gave the emperor a book of charms, and every emperor of the Wei dynasty that followed Wei Taiwu also received a charm book at his accession. The state religion was sanctified by the magical powers of the Taoist charm book. Wei Taiwu wanted the Bei Wei to be seen as Chinese, but he could not simply take the Mandate of Heaven from the traditional Chinese empire and apply it to his own rule. The traditional Chinese Mandate of Heaven gave the ruler the rightful power to command. The ruler was given control of his empire via the blessing of the heavens. The acquisition of the Taoist charm book acted for the Bei Wei like the traditional Mandate; receiving the Taoist book of charms at one's accession to the throne meant the Bei Wei king was blessed by the state's religion.

Chapter Sixteen

The Huns

The student may use her text when answering the questions in sections I and II.

Section I: Who, What, Where

Write a one or two-sentence answer explaining the significance of each item listed below.

Bleda—**Pg. 109, ¶ 4–6—Bleda, nephew of the Hun warrior chief Rua, succeeded his uncle as a joint chief of the expanding Huns with his brother, Attila, in 432. After attacking a Roman fort on the Danube and accepting tribute from the Romans twice, Bleda was killed by his brother Attila.**

Burgundians—**Pg. 107, ¶ 5—Burgundians were another Germanic tribe who had settled in the Rhine valley as *foederati*. During the time of their king Gundahar's rule, the Burgundians established a capital at Borbetomagus.**

Dioscorus—**Pg. 111, ¶ 1 & 2—Dioscorus, bishop of Alexandria, believed in a monophysitism that declared Christ's two natures became a single divine nature at the incarnation. At the Robber Council, Dioscorus proclaimed the bishop of Constantinople a heretic and he excommunicated Leo I from the church, an action which resulted in Dioscorus's excommunication.**

Eugenius—**Pg. 112, ¶ 4—Eugenius was Valentinian's sister Honoria's lover. When their affair was discovered, Eugenius was arrested and put to death on the charge of treason; if Honoria had married Eugenius, the pair could have become emperor and empress.**

Geiseric—**Pg. 106, ¶ 5 to Pg. 107, ¶ 3—Geiseric, king of the Vandals in Hispania, built a fleet of ships in 425 and sailed across the Mediterranean Sea, attacking Roman provinces on the North African coast, including Hippo Regius and Carthage. After his travels on the Mediterranean, Geiseric abandoned Hispania and concentrated on ruling as a North African pirate-king, headquartered at Carthage.**

Gundahar—**Pg. 107, ¶ 5 & 6—Gundahar, king of the Burgundians, built a capital for his tribe at Borbetomagus. In 437, the Romans and the Huns together destroyed Borbetomagus, crushed the Burgundians, and killed Gundahar.**

Leo I—**Pg. 110, ¶ 3 and Pg. 111, ¶ 2—Leo I, new bishop of Rome in 444, had Valentinian III decree that the bishop of Rome was the official head of the entire Christian church, which made Leo I the first Pope. After the Robber Council, where Dioscorus had Leo excommunicated, Leo I retaliated by excommunicating everyone who had been at the council.**

Nibelungenlied (Song of the Nibelungs)—**Pg. 107 ¶ 6—*Nibelungenlied* (Song of the Nibelungs) is a folk tale that describes the defeat of Gundahar by Aetius and the Huns. In the tale, king Gundahar, whose name is rendered Gunther, welcomes the dragon-slayer Siegfried to his court at the epic's beginning, and at the end travels to the land of the Huns and is murdered by treachery.**

Orestes—**Pg. 111, ¶ 4—Orestes was a Roman-born man of Germanic blood who was sent to Constantinople as a representative of Attila the Hun. Orestes carried a message from Attila, accusing the eastern empire of breaking the terms of its truce with him, and demanding that ambassadors of the highest rank meet with Attila at Sardica to resolve the issue.**

Suevi—**Pg. 107, ¶ 5—Suevi was the name of a Germanic tribe that captured parts of Hispania after Geiseric abandoned it for North Africa.**

Valentinian III—**Pg. 106, ¶ 2 and Pg. 113, ¶ 1 & 5—Valentinian III, son of Honorius's sister Placida and her second husband, the general Constantius, was crowned emperor after Honorius's death, and ruled with the help of his *magister militum* the Roman soldier Aetius. Valentinian III had his sister's lover Eugenius put to death in order to secure his throne; when he found out his sister had promised her hand to Attila the Hun, he had the messenger who delivered the news murdered.**

Section II: Comprehension

Write a two or three-sentence answer to each of the following questions.

1. What was the state of the western Roman empire at the time of Honorius's death?

A1.—Pg. 106, ¶ 1 & 2—At the time of Honorius's death in 423, the western Roman empire was struggling for survival. Britannia had been abandoned; the Visigoths prospered in southwestern Gaul, allies of Rome but a sovereign state in their own right; and despite the efforts of a combined Roman and Visigothic army, the Vandals had managed to take over much of Hispania, forming their own kingdom and shaking off all Roman attempts to retake the former province.

2. How did Aetius force his way into the role of Valentinian III's *magister militum*?

A2.—Pg. 106, ¶ 2 & 3—Aetius, a Roman soldier who had been sent as a hostage to the Visigoths and then to the Huns in his youth, was returned to Roman custody sometime before Honorius's death. After the emperor died, Aetius made it clear to Placida that his former hosts, the Huns, would attack Ravenna if he was not given the highest military post in the western Roman empire. Placida, forced to go along with Aetius's plan for fear of being attacked by the Huns, gave Aetius the title of *magister militum* and the power that went with it.

3. Before 434, why hadn't the Huns launched a sustained attack on the Romans?

A3.—Pg. 109, ¶ 2—The Huns had not launched a sustained attack on the Romans because they had never been a single unified force. Because they did not plant or tend crops, they remained in small nomadic knots, driving cows, goats and sheep in herds across the countryside. They were a coalition of tribes with no particular loyalty to each other, and no particular strategy for taking over the world.

4. Why was Leo I upset with the bishop of Thessalonica? What was Leo I's reasoning as to why the bishop of Thessalonica could not act the way that he did?

A4.—Pg. 110, ¶ 3—Leo I was upset with the bishop of Thessalonica because the bishop of Thessalonica brought up another bishop before the civil court in his province. In Leo I's mind, because he was the bishop of Rome, heir of Peter, only he had the right to exert authority over other bishops.

5. Why did Dioscorus, bishop of Alexandria, call together a hasty church council in Ephesus to affirm his version of monophysitism as orthodox? Why did Dioscorus excommunicate Leo I at the church council?

A5.—Pg. 111, ¶ 2—Dioscorus, bishop of Alexandria, called together a hasty church council in Ephesus to affirm his version of monophysitism as orthodox because he wanted to challenge Leo I's theological power. By excommunicating the absent bishop of Rome, now the Pope, Dioscorus attempted to usurp the power of Rome and transfer it to Alexandria.

6. Why was the council held in Ephesus by Dioscorus called the "Robber Council," or the Latrocinium?

A6.—Pg. 111, ¶ 2—At the council held in Ephesus by Dioscorus, the bishop of Alexandria had other bishops sign blank documents on which the theological content was filled in later. Other bishops who didn't sign simply found that their names mysteriously had appeared at the bottom of pro-monophysite statements. All of this earned the council the title "Robber Council," or the Latrocinium—a term condemning the council as illegitimate.

7. What was Honoria's motivation for sending a marriage proposal to Attila the Hun?

A7.—Pg. 113, ¶ 3—Honoria, Valentinian III's sister, hated her life in Rome, finding solace only in her lover Eugenius. When Valentinian put Eugenius to death, Honoria sent a letter

to Attila suggesting marriage. If Honoria were to marry Attila, he could become emperor of Rome, and she would be empress, and even if he failed to take Rome, she would still become queen of the Huns.

8. After Theodosius II's death, who did Pulcheria choose as a husband to help her rule the eastern empire? What were the terms of their marriage?

A8.—Pg. 113, ¶ 7—Pulcheria chose the soldier Marcian, who had been at Carthage when Geiseric took it from the Romans eighteen years earlier, as her husband. In order to marry Pulcheria, Marcian had to agree to maintain the fifty-one-year-old Pulcheria's virginity.

9. How did Pulcheria and Marcian manage to avoid an attack by the Huns after refusing to pay Attila the bribes Theodosius II had been shelling out to keep Constantinople safe?

A9.—Pg. 114, ¶ 2—Though it was a risk, Pulcheria and Marcian's refusal to continue giving tribute to Attila paid off. Honoria was waiting for Attila in Valentinian III's western empire, and that was the perfect excuse for the Huns to attack the west and leave the east alone.

Section III: Critical Thinking

The student may use her text to answer this question.

Until the rule of Rua, the Huns had not been able to sustain a prolonged attack on Rome because they were not a single unified force. Rua was able to extend his power to Hun tribes unrelated to his own, increasing the strength of the Huns and creating something like a nation. When Attila took over, he continued to grow the power, size and strength of the Huns. Write a paragraph describing Attila's headquarters, and then explain how the village he built as his temporary capital exemplified the rising force of the Huns.

On page 109, the text tells us the Huns could not sustain an attack on the Romans because they had never been a single, unified force. They were a coalition of tribes with no allegiance to one another. They did not work on the land together, nor were they invested in a single homestead. They remained in small nomadic knots which were easier to feed and support. They had no strategy for taking over the world. In fact, they were just trying to survive.

Around 432, Rua was able to extend his power over Hun tribes unrelated to his own, and his nephews Bleda and Attila followed in his footsteps. By the time Attila took the throne for himself in 445, "the Huns were mutating from a loose coalition into a ruthless conquering horde" (pg. 110, ¶ 1). On a mission to make peace with the Huns, the historian Priscus described Attila's headquarters, a village he built to be his temporary capital on the other side of the Danube. He wrote, it was more "like a great city" than a village, built of "wooden walls made of smooth-shining boards . . . dining halls of large extent and porticoes planned with great beauty, while the courtyard was bounded by so vast a circuit that its very size showed it was the royal palace." The student can use any part of Priscus's description in her explanation of Attila's headquarters.

For the second part of this question, the student must think about what it means to be able to build a grand palace with beautiful grounds. First, Attila was receiving tribute money from several cities afraid of Hun attacks.

Attila could invest some of this wealth into his city. Second, Attila had to be able to manage his men, having some dedicated to the building and upkeep of the city while others were out fighting. This exemplifies a group of orderly people who lived within a defined administration. Attila's capital showed that the Huns were no longer just trying to survive. They had a well-built city to return to, they had money to fund the city and the troops, and they had a leader to which they listened. Attila's city was not barbarian, it was a city that marked the nascent Hun nation.

EXAMPLE ANSWER:

Attila's capital city, located on the other side of the Danube, was built of wooden walls made of shining boards; it had large dining halls and beautiful well-planned porticoes. Attila's home was more like a palace because it was surrounded by a vast courtyard. For a long time the Huns were just trying to survive, moving from place to place in small groups looking for food and shelter. Now, Attila had built up a beautiful city, probably from the tribute money he was receiving from all of the scared Romans, that marked a Hun settlement. Not only were the Huns known for being wanderers, but also for being wild. Attila's city showed that they were somewhat tamed, able to listen to their leader and build and maintain a city. This exemplifies a group of orderly people who lived within a defined administration. Attila's capital showed that the Huns were no longer just trying to survive. They had a well-built city to return to, they had money to fund the city and the troops, and they had a leader to which they listened. Attila's city was not barbarian; it was a city that marked the nascent Hun nation.

Section IV: Map Exercise ★

1. Using a black pencil, trace the rectangular outline of the frame for Map 16.1: The Approach of the Huns.

2. Using a blue pencil, trace the coastlines of the Atlantic, the Mediterranean, the Black Sea, the Sea of Azov, the Caspian Sea, the Persian Gulf, and the Red Sea. Include the coastline of Britannia. Using your blue pencil, trace the path of the Danube along the perimeter of the Roman Empire. Using a black pencil, trace the perimeter of the Roman Empire, including the line dividing east and west. Then trace the outline of the Persian Empire. Repeat until the contours are familiar.

3. Using a new sheet of paper, trace the rectangular frame of the map in black. Remove your tracing paper from the original. Using a regular pencil with an eraser as you look at Map 16.1, draw the complete coastal outline present on the map: the Atlantic around Britannica, and above the region of the Saxons down through the Mediterranean. Include the Black Sea, the Sea of Azov, the Caspian Sea, the Persian Gulf, and the Red Sea. Then draw the outline of the Roman Empire and the outline of the Persian Empire. Draw the outline of the Kingdom of the Visigoths and shade to delineate from the Roman Empire. Using your blue pencil, draw the line of the Danube along the perimeter of the Roman Empire. Refer to the map as necessary as you draw. Compare with the original, and erase and redraw as necessary.

4. When you are pleased with your map, lay it over the original. Erase and redraw any lines which are more than ¼ of an inch off the original.

5. Study carefully the regions of Iberia, Gaul, Illyricum, and North Africa. When you are familiar with them, close the book. Using your regular pencil, mark all four on the map. Check your map with the original, and make any necessary corrections.

6. Study carefully the regions of the Huns, the Goths, the Vandals, the Visigoths, the Burgundians, the Alemanni, the Franks, and the Saxons, as well as the Suevi. Take especial note of the Kingdom of the Visigoths and the Kingdom of the Vandals. Note the movement in the map from the Huns to the left of the map down through Iberia, including the movement of the Vandals to their kingdom in North Africa. When you are familiar with these, close the book. Using your regular pencil, label each area with its barbarian inhabitants, and indicate the barbarian movement with arrows as is done on the original map. Check your map against the original. Correct any misplaced labels. When your map is complete, shade the Kingdoms of the Visigoths and the Vandals.

Chapter Seventeen

Attila

The student may use his text when answering the questions in sections I and II.

Section I: Who, What, Where

Write a one or two-sentence answer explaining the significance of each item listed below.

Ildico—**Pg. 117, ¶ 6—Ildico, the young and beautiful daughter of a Gothic chief, was chosen by Attila to be his bride. A marriage to Ildico gave Attila a closer tie with the Gothic allies he needed to rebuild his army.**

Merovech—**Pg. 115, ¶ 3—Merovech was the name that was assigned to the unknown chief of the Salians who led the entire Frankish coalition into the Roman camp to help fight against the Huns. Merovech was one of the earliest "long-haired kings" of the Franks.**

Salians—**Pg. 115, ¶ 3—The Salians were Franks, the strongest of the tribes who settled into northern Gaul as *foederati.* The Salians joined Aetius in the fight against Attila.**

Theodoric I—**Pg. 115, ¶ 2 and Pg. 116, ¶ 2—Theodoric I, king of the Visigoths of Hispania and southwestern Gaul, agreed to help Aetius in the battle against Attila. Though the Roman forces beat Attila at the battle of Châlons-sur-Marne, Theodoric I suffered a dismal fate, killed on the battlefield.**

Thorismund—**Pg. 116, ¶ 2—Thorismund was the son of the Visigoth king Theodoric I. After his father died, Thorismund led the shrunken Visigoth army back to Toulouse.**

Section II: Comprehension

Write a two or three-sentence answer to each of the following questions.

1. After Attila took Metz for the Huns, how far did his territory reach? Who did Aetius get to help him defend Rome's capitals against Attila?

A1.—Pg. 115, ¶ 1 & 2—After Attila took Metz for the Huns, his territory reached almost from the Black Sea to the north of Italy. Aetius, feeling the threat Attila imposed on both Roman capitals, enlisted the Visigoths of Hispania and southwestern Gaul and the Salians of northern Gaul to fight against the Hun leader.

2. Why did the Salian chiefs grow their hair long?

A2.—Pg. 115, ¶ 3—Salian chiefs wore their hair long to distinguish them from ordinary Franks, and to demonstrate their greater power.

3. What war strategy did Aetius use when he met Attila in June of 451 in battle at Châlons-sur-Marne?

A3.—Pg. 115, ¶ 5 to Pg. 116, ¶ 1—Knowing that the Huns put Attila and his strongest warriors in the center of their line, with the weaker and less reliable allies on each wing, Aetius and his Romans fought on one wing and Theodoric I and the Visigoths on the other. Then, they put the troops they thought might skip out on the fight in the middle, so that they could not easily flee in the midst of battle. With Rome's best fighters against the Hun's worst ones, the wings of the Hun forces disintegrated, the strategy was a success for the Romans, and Attila was forced to retreat with his core of warriors back across the Rhine.

4. Describe the losses suffered on the Roman side during and after the battle at Châlons-sur-Marne.

A4.—Pg. 116, ¶ 2—Though the Roman alliance saved Gaul, many men were killed in the fight. Over 150,000 soldiers fell in battle, and the chronicler Hydatius claimed that 300,000 men died. Jordanes claimed the slaughter was so great a brook flowing through the battle field turned into a river of blood. The Visigoths suffered badly: Theodoric I was killed, and his son Thorismund had to lead home the severely diminished troops kingless.

5. Describe Attila's attack on Italy after the Huns' defeat at Châlons-sur-Marne. What stopped Attila's ravaging of Italy?

A5.—Pg. 116, ¶ 4 to Pg. 117, ¶ 2—Attila's attack on Italy after his defeat at Châlons-sur-Marne began in early 452, and the north of Italy quickly fell to the Huns. Attila's army destroyed the city of Aquileia, sacked Milan and Ticinum, and laid waste to the countryside. Attila stopped attacking Italy and agreed to peace after a meeting with Leo the Great, bishop of Rome and pope of the Christian church.

6. What were some of the otherworldly explanations that the Romans came up with to explain Attila's agreement to a peace after meeting with Leo the Great?

A6.—Pg. 117, ¶ 3—Some Romans thought that Leo's success was caused by a magic spell. The historian Prosper of Aquitaine thought that Attila was overwhelmed by Leo's holiness. Paul the Deacon insisted that a huge supernatural warrior with a drawn sword stood beside Leo and terrified Attila into a truce.

7. What were the plausible reasons for Attila's agreement to a peace with Rome?

A7.—Pg. 117 ¶ 4—There were several possible reasons that Attila most likely agreed to peace with Rome. First, the Hun army was weakened after the battle at Châlons-sur-Marne, and while they could attack northern Italian towns, the Huns did not have enough manpower for a siege of Rome. Second, the Huns were already loaded down with riches so they weren't as eager to pillage as they were previously. Third, they were anxious to leave Italy; an episode of the plague was decimating their already thin troops.

8. How did Attila the Hun die?

A8.—Pg. 118, ¶ 2—Attila the Hun died after the celebration of his wedding. He probably drank an enormous amount of alcohol before passing out in the bridal chamber. He died after his nose started to bleed, asphyxiated by his own blood.

9. What happened to the Huns after Attila's death?

A9.—Pg. 118, ¶ 3-5—After Attila died, his sons tried to pick up where he left off, but they did not succeed. With Attila died the driving force behind the emergence of the new people. By 455, the Huns had been thoroughly defeated by the Romans; they scattered, and their chance to become a nation had passed.

Section III: Critical Thinking

The student may use his text to answer this question.

Leo the Great, the bishop of Rome and the first pope of the Catholic church, may seem like an unlikely candidate to make peace between the Roman Empire and Attila the Hun. But, he did just that. Write a paragraph explaining why Leo the Great was able, as a spiritual leader, to take such an active political role at the time of Attila's aggression.

To begin, ask the student to recall what he learned in Chapter 9, "Excommunicated," about the relationship between the church and the Roman emperor. He should recall that the bishop of Milan, Ambrose, excommunicated Theodosius. Theodosius was forced to subject himself to Ambrose's religious authority because the Roman empire relied on the peoples' belief in a single religion. Theodosius had to listen to the bishop because he had to reinforce the binding power of the church, even if it meant giving up some of his power as emperor.

Leo the Great, like Theodosius, knew that religion theoretically kept the empire together. As the pope, Leo was as invested as the emperor in keeping the empire safe. On page 117, the text explains, "For the first time in history, a bishop had taken on the emperor's job. Valentinian's decree, the six-year-old imperial pronouncement that made Leo head of the entire Christian church, had given the pope an extra dimension of power. He was the spiritual head of the church, but the spirit of the church could not survive if its adherents were wiped out. As spiritual leader, he could also claim the right to guarantee the church's physical survival."

In this case, Leo the Great needed to protect the Romans from more Hun attacks so that he continued to have a constituency in his church. If the Huns slaughtered the Romans, there would be no more churchgoers, and thus the church would not survive. Because Rome was not just bound together by land, but also by religion, Leo the Great saw Attila as a threat not to the empire but to the church. Leo's actions suggest that he had as much power as the emperor in the affairs of the state.

EXAMPLE ANSWER:

Over time, the Catholic church gained more and more power in the Roman empire. We saw just how much power the church had when bishop Ambrose of Milan excommunicated Theodosius, and the emperor was forced to subject himself to Ambrose's religious authority. Leo the Great, as pope of the Catholic church, was the spiritual counterpart to the Roman emperors. When the Huns threatened to take Rome, Leo saw that as a threat to the church. If the Romans were decimated, so would be his church. Because Rome was not just bound together by land, but also by religion, Leo the Great saw Attila as a threat to his own power. Invested in his place at the head of the Christian church, which put him on par with the Roman emperors, Leo was able to use his power as pope to negotiate a peace with Attila the Hun.

Chapter Eighteen

Orthodoxy

The student may use her text when answering the questions in sections I and II.

Section I: Who, What, Where

Write a one or two-sentence answer explaining the significance of each item listed below.

Battle of Vartanantz—**Pg. 123, ¶ 3 & 4—The Battle of Vartanantz took place in 451, when the Persians under Yazdegerd II invaded Armenia, led by Vartan, because they refused to give up their Christian faith and follow Yazdegerd II's decree that all Persians must follow Zoroastrianism. Though both sides suffered heavy losses, the Persians were victorious; Yazdegerd II imprisoned and tortured the surviving leaders, reduced Armenia to a Persian territory, and installed a new governor in charge of the country.**

Vartan—**Pg. 123, ¶ 3 & 4—Vartan was an Armenian general who fought against Yazdegerd II and his invading Persian army in order to defend the Armenians' freedoms and right to believe in Christianity. Vartan was killed defending his people and their beliefs in the Battle of Vartanantz.**

Yazdegerd II—**Pg. 122, ¶ 4 and Pg. 123, ¶ 1 & 4—Yazdegerd II, who succeeded his father Bahram V as emperor of Persia, welcomed Roman Christians into Persia that disagreed with the orthodoxy that Christ's two natures were separate but indivisible. Yazdegerd II then imposed his own orthodoxy when he declared that Zoroastrianism would be followed in all parts of his empire, a declaration that lead to war with Christian Armenia.**

Section II: Comprehension

Write a two or three-sentence answer to each of the following questions.

1. Describe the state of Christianity in the Roman empire when Marcian called a church council at Chalcedon in 451. For what religious reason did Marcian call the council?

A1.—Pg. 120, ¶ 3 and Pg. 121, ¶ 2—When Marcian called a church council at Chalcedon in 451, the Christian church was divided three ways. The bishops of Rome and Alexandria were excommunicated after the Robber Council, and the bishop of Constantinople was still declared a heretic. Marcian called the council to tackle the problem of how Christ's two natures, the human and the divine, related to one another.

2. What were Marcian's beliefs about Christ's two natures? Why did this complicate Marcian's dealings with the various bishops of the Roman empire?

A2.—Pg. 120, ¶ 4 and Pg. 121, ¶ 2—Marcian believed, like Pope Leo the Great, bishop of Rome, that the human and divine natures of Christ remained distinct. Though Marcian believed in Leo's doctrine, he did not want to admit to Leo's claim to ultimate spiritual power, which would diminish the power of Marcian's Constantinople.

3. For what political reason did Marcian call the 451 church council at Chalcedon? Why did Marcian want the council held at Chalcedon?

A3.—Pg. 121, ¶ 2—Marcian called the 451 church council at Chalcedon because he did not want to give more power to Pope Leo the Great, bishop of Rome. Leo suggested the council be held in Italy, but that would reinforce Leo's power. Instead, Marcian held the council at Chalcedon, right across from his home city of Constantinople.

4. What did Leo expect to happen after his statement on Christ's two natures was read at the Council of Chalcedon? What actually happened?

A4.—Pg. 121, ¶ 3—Leo expected the council to be a short one; since he was the heir of Peter, he expected that once his delegates read his statement, it would be acknowledged that Peter had spoken and no further discussion would be required. What actually happened was that the council agreed Leo's statement was in line with what they had already decided independently, theoretically diminishing Leo's power. They also agreed that the bishop of Constantinople, while second to the bishop of Rome, still had authority over other bishops, another challenge to Leo's supreme power.

5. How was the Syrian Orthodox Church formed?

A5.—Pg. 122, ¶ 4 and footnote—After the Council of Chalcedon had confirmed as orthodoxy that Christ's two natures were separate but indivisible, the Nestorians living in the Roman empire were upset because they felt that the Council did not make enough of a distinction between Christ's two natures. The Nestorians were welcomed into Persia by Yazdegerd II. The difference in doctrine ultimately split the Christians of Persia away from Rome and

Constantinople, and the branch of Nestorian Christianity formed in Persia became the Syrian Orthodox Church.

6. For how long did Yazdegerd II's welcome of Christians from Rome after the Council of Chalcedon last?

A6.—Pg. 123, ¶ 1—Though Yazdegerd II was at first willing to accept Christian refugees from the Roman empire after the Council of Chalcedon, he soon imposed his own orthodoxy when he decreed that Zoroastrianism would be followed in all parts of his empire, including the Persian half of Armenia, which had remained Christian.

7. Why did Yazdegerd II declare Zoroastrianism as the single faith of the Persian empire? How did the Armenians react to his decree?

A7.—Pg. 123, ¶ 2—Yazdegerd II was theologically and politically motivated when he declared Zoroastrianism the single faith of the Perisan empire. He was devout in his faith to Zoroastrianism, but he was also motivated to root out any sympathy with eastern Romans, particularly in the less loyal parts of his empire. The Armenians saw Yazdegerd II's decree as limiting their freedoms, and as religious persecution of their Christian faith.

8. After putting down rebellious Christians in Armenia at the Battle of Vartanantz, what further measures did Yazdegerd II take to prevent challenges to the orthodoxy of Zoroastrianism?

A8.—Pg. 123, ¶ 4—After reducing Armenia and is Christians to a Persian territory, Yazdegerd II continued to take preventative measures against religious dissidents. In 454, he began to enact a series of decrees that kept the Jews in Persia from observing the Sabbath and educating their children in Jewish schools.

Section III: Critical Thinking

The student may not use her text to answer this question.

This chapter is titled, "Orthodoxy." To be orthodox means to adhere to what is commonly accepted, what is customary or traditional. Yet, in our chapter, we did not read about people of the medieval world adhering to custom; we read about powerful figures establishing laws that were meant to create orthodoxy, and their subjects rebelling against these decrees. Write a paragraph explaining how the imposition of orthodoxy in the Roman empire actually created division instead of unity. In your answer, explain why the growing power of the clergy prompted Marcian to fight for the increased power of the bishop of Constantinople, and how that added to the divisions within the Roman empire.

The imposition of a single religious practice in eastern Rome had as much to do with theology and it did with political power. The battle over Christ's nature, and the authority of various church figures to enforce their particular beliefs, was "an argument over territory, over authority, over legitimacy" (pg. 122, ¶ 2). Wanting to claim the highest religious authority possible for his city of Constantinople, Marcian called the Council of

Chalcedon in order to challenge Leo the Great's power. The student learned in Chapter 17, "Attila," that Leo the Great was able to make peace with Attila because of his religious authority; the negotiations between Leo and Attila showed that Leo wasn't just a part of the church, he was a figure that could govern as well. Understanding that complete rule over the Roman people came from both the church and the state, Marcian had to show that his city had just as much theological power as it did imperial muscle. So, to show his might, Marcian had the bishops who met at the Council of Chalcedon, which was near Constantinople and not Rome, claim that they had decreed the orthodoxy of Christ's two natures as separate but indivisible, even though Leo was already making the same argument. Marcian also had the council proclaim that the bishop of Constantinople was "not merely a bishop but a patriarch: a churchman with authority over other bishops" (pg. 121, ¶ 2).

Marcian's imposition of orthodoxy for the purpose of raising up the status of Constantinople and its bishop caused widespread divisions within the Roman empire. In Egypt, the bishop of Alexandria resented being demoted to a place lower than the bishop of Constantinople. This resentment created a strong underground current against the emperor. Another consequence of the imposition of orthodoxy, a doctrine meant to bring Christians together, was the migration of Christians who didn't believe that Christ's two natures were separate but indivisible into Persia. Instead of tightening his control over his subjects and increasing his power in the church, Marcian created divisions between the major cities in the Roman empire and caused the movement of peoples away from his kingdom.

EXAMPLE ANSWER:

After Leo the Great made peace with Attila the Hun, it was clear the bishop of Rome, pope of the Christian church, had both major religious and political power. Marcian, threatened by the power of the Roman bishop, wanted to bolster his own city, Constantinople's, importance. The Council at Chalcedon was necessary not only to affirm Marcian's point of view about the separate but indivisible natures of Christ, but also to proclaim the bishop of Constantinople's power over other bishops. Marcian's imposition of orthodoxy for the purpose of raising up the status of Constantinople and its bishop caused widespread divisions within the Roman empire. In Egypt, the bishop of Alexandria resented being demoted to a place lower than the bishop of Constantinople. This resentment created a strong underground current against the emperor. Another consequence of the imposition of orthodoxy, a doctrine meant to bring Christians together, was the migration of Christians who didn't believe that Christ's two natures were separate but indivisible into Persia. Instead of tightening his control over his subjects and increasing his power in the church, Marcian created divisions between the major cities in the Roman empire and caused the movement of peoples away from his kingdom.

Section IV: Map Exercise

1. Using a black pencil, trace the rectangular outline of the frame for Map 18:1.

2. Using a blue pencil, trace the coastline of the Mediterranean, the Black Sea, and the small corner of the Red Sea visible towards the bottom of the map. Still using your blue pencil, trace the outline

of the Nile river. Then trace the outline of the Tigris and Euphrates. Repeat until the contours are familiar.

3. Using your black pencil, trace the dotted outline of the Eastern Roman Empire. Then, using a contrasting color, trace the outline of the Persian Empire. Use your black pencil to trace the outline of Armenia inside the Persian Empire. Repeat until the contours are familiar.

4. Using a new sheet of paper, trace the rectangular frame of the map in black. Remove your tracing paper from the original. Using your regular pencil with an eraser, trace the coastal outlines and the outlines of the Roman and Persian empire.

5. When you are pleased with your map, lay it over the original. Erase and redraw any lines that are more than ¼ inch off of the original.

6. Label the Eastern Roman Empire and the Persian Empire and then the regions of Thracia, Egypt, and Armenia.

7. Study carefully the locations of Rome, Constantinople, Chalcedon, Alexandria, and Ctesiphon. Study also the location of the Battle of Vartanantz. When you are familiar with their locations, close the book. Using your regular pencil, mark each location on your map. Check your map against the original and correct any locations that were mislabeled.

Chapter Nineteen

The High Kings

The student may use his text when answering the questions in sections I and II.

Section I: Who, What, Where

Write a one or two-sentence answer explaining the significance of each item listed below.

455—**Pg. 130, ¶ 4 & 5—455 was the year Vortigern finally managed to defeat the invaders of his country in a battle at the fords of the Medway river, in Kent. The victory did not last long; after Horsa's death, his son took up his father's fight and continued the attack on Britain for another fifteen years.**

Connachta—**Pg. 125, ¶ 2—The Connachta, in 451, were the strongest clan of the powerful Irish Venii/Feni tribe.**

Cunedda—**Pg. 128, ¶ 5 to Pg. 129, ¶ 1—Cunedda was a British warlord tasked by Vortigern to drive the Irish Laighin out of their new home in the area we now know as Wales. Cunedda, with his eight sons and soldiers, were successful in driving out the Laighin and founded a kingdom of their own, Gwynedd, in the conquered land.**

Hengest and Horsa—**Pg. 129, ¶ 6 and Pg. 130, ¶ 5—Hengest and Horsa were Saxon brothers that led the Jutes to occupy Britain's southern coast. Horsa was killed during battle, giving Vortigern a false sense of victory; soon after Horsa's death, his son took up his father's mantle, continuing the war against Vortigern for another fifteen years.**

Nennius—**Pg. 130, ¶ 2 & 3—Nennius, a Christian monk, wrote in the *History of the Britons* that a magical malice helped the invading Jutes, Angles and Saxons destroy Vortigern's Britain. Though Nennius reported that Vortigern would have to sacrifice a child born without a father in order to break the spell of the invaders, Nennius insists that the sacrifice did not happen, and instead the child prophesied future victory for Britain.**

Niall of the Nine Hostages—**Pg. 125, ¶ 2 and Pg. 126, ¶ 3—Niall of the Nine Hostages became the leader of the Connachta family after his father's death; the Connachta family was the strongest clan of the powerful Venii/Feni tribe. Niall earned his nickname by taking prisoners from nine of the tribes that lay around him, guaranteeing the loyalty of their leaders and his control over their kings.**

Patricius—**Pg. 126, ¶ 4 & 5—Patricius was a Romanized Briton that was taken to Ireland as a slave by Niall, where he served for six years before stowing away on an Irish raiding ship and escaping to Gaul. There, Patricius was converted to Christianity and had a vision calling him to return to Ireland to teach the Irish about Christ; his devotion to the spread of Christianity in Ireland earned him the name of Saint Patrick.**

Note to the parent—The student might also include that Patricius was credited with driving the snakes out of Ireland.

Venii/Feni—**Pg. 125, ¶ 2—The Venii or Feni were the strongest tribe in Ireland in 451, ruled by Niall of the Nine Hostages.**

Vortigern—**Pg. 128, ¶ 5 and Pg. 130, ¶ 4 & 5—Vortigern was elected high king by the minor kings and tribal chiefs of Britain sometime in the 450s. Vortigern had the unenviable job of defending his nation from invading Saxons, Angles and Jutes, a prolonged war he temporarily won in 455, but which then continued on for another fifteen years.**

Section II: Comprehension

Write a two or three-sentence answer to each of the following questions.

1. Though Ireland was never occupied by Roman soldiers, how was the island still touched by the Roman empire?

A1.—Pg. 125, ¶ 2 & 4—Though Ireland was never occupied by Roman soldiers, the island still felt Roman influence through the marriage between Niall of the Nine Hostages's father and his Roman bride, Eochaidh. Niall's father also took a Roman concubine during a raid on Britannia; this Roman woman was Niall of the Nine Hostages's mother.

2. What did Niall have to accomplish in Ireland before launching raids on Gaul and Britain? How did he build enough support to start his campaigns?

A2.—Pg. 125, ¶ 2 and Pg. 126, ¶ 3—Before launching raids on Gaul and Britain, Niall had to expand his control over the other tribes and clans that inhabited Ireland, each that had its own local power wielded by a warlord. Niall took prisoners from nine of the tribes that lay around him, guaranteeing the loyalty of their tribal leaders. Once he had the loyalty of these conquered tribes supporting him, he was able to begin campaigns against Gaul and Britain.

3. Saint Patrick is credited by Christian historians with driving the snakes out of Ireland, but the reality is that there were no snakes in Ireland. Explain what the Christian historians really meant when they said Saint Patrick rid Ireland of snakes.

A3.—Pg. 128, ¶ 1—For Christian historians a snake wasn't just a reptile, it was the shape Satan took in the Garden of Eden. Serpents were also sacred to the druids, the practitioners of the indigenous religion of Ireland, and symbolized the powers of darkness that were opposed to the Gospel of Christ. The spread of Christianity and the fading of the indigenous religion of Ireland is symbolized by the story of snakes being driven out of Ireland by the Christian Saint Patrick.

4. How was Ireland divided up by Niall's sons after Patricius's death, around 493? Though he is long dead and his kingdom was divided, in what way is Niall still with us in the modern world?

A4.—Pg. 128, ¶ 2—By the time of Patricius's death, sometime before 493, three sons of Niall held power over three kingdoms in the northern half of the island: Midhe, Ulaidh and Connachta. The descendants of Niall ruled as the Ui Neill dynasty for six hundred years, but the influence of Niall can still be found today. Niall's particular Y chromosome shows up in as many as three million men worldwide; one in twelve Irishmen are linked to the chromosome, and one in five in the part of Ireland that was once Connachta can claim Niall of the Nine Hostages as their ancestor.

5. What other Irish clans existed alongside the Ui Neill dynasty? How did one of these tribes end up in the area we now know as Wales?

A5.—**Pg. 128, ¶ 3—While the Ui Neill ruled in the north, the clan of the Eoghanach ruled in the southwest of Ireland. To the southeast, the Laighin tribe held onto its land as well. However, some of the Laighin left because of continued attacks from the Ui Neill, and settled on the coast of Britain. This is the area that came be to known as Wales.**

6. What happened to rule in Britain after the departure of Constantine III in 410? What enemies did Vortigern first face when he was elected warleader by the minor kings and tribal chiefs of Britain?

A6.—Pg. 128, ¶ 4—After the departure of Constantine III, Roman Britain was ruled by a collection of local warlords, and there also existed a few Saxon settlements which the Romans had allowed along the coast. When elected warleader, Vortigern faced raids from aggressive Irish pirates known as the Scoti. He also dealt with vicious attacks down across Hadrian's Wall by the northern Picts.

7. Having received no reply from the Roman *magister militum* Aetius in his request for help against the Picts, what strategy did Vortigern devise in an effort to squelch his northern opponents?

A7.—Pg. 129, ¶ 3—Receiving no reply from Rome for help against the northern invaders, Vortigern suggested that the remaining British soldiers bolster their ranks with Saxon allies. In exchange for tribute warriors who would help the British fight the Picts and the

Irish, the British would allow more Saxon and Angles settlements in the south, particularly in Essex and in Kent.

8. How did Vortigern's plan to allow Saxons and Angles to settle in the south of Britain in exchange for help fighting the Picts and the Irish backfire?

A8.—Pg. 129, ¶ 5—Vortigern's plan to use the Saxons and Angles to fight against the Picts and Irish in exchange for the right to settle in the south of Britain backfired because the new settlers started to spread farther than their designated settlement. Just a few months after settling in Kent, more Saxons, Angles and Jutes started arriving on the southeastern shores of Britain in longships with armed warriors, ready to invade the south.

9. Describe the prolonged invasion of Britain by the Saxons, Angles and Jutes.

A9.—Pg. 129, ¶ 6 to Pg. 130, ¶ 3 & ¶ 5—Two Saxon brothers, Hengest and Horsa, led the Jutes to occupy the southern coast of Britain, while the Saxons moved from Kent father inland to the south and southwest of Londinium, and the Angles invaded the southeastern coast just above the Thames. The British tribes remained allied behind Vortigern, fighting for six years against the overwhelmingly destructive influx. When Horsa died in battle, his son took up his father's mantle and continued the violent war against Vortigern for another fifteen years.

10. In what way does Nennius's *History of the Britons* suggest that Vortigern and his court were driven to drastic and ancient strategies to defend their country? Describe what sacrifice was to be made, and what course of action took place instead of the sacrifice.

A10.—Pg. 130, ¶ 2 & 3—Nennius, a Christian monk, echoes druidic rituals that were undertaken to beat the Angles, Jutes and Saxons in his *History of the Britons,* suggesting that the British were desperate enough to revert to drastic and ancient strategies to defend their country. Nennius wrote that because the invaders used magical malice against Britain, Vortigern was unable to build a fortress that would withstand them until he sacrificed a child born without a father and sprinkled his blood over the foundations of the building site. However, Nennius writes that what really took place was that the child avoided death by prophesying the future triumph of Britain; he showed Vortigern a pool beneath the proposed foundations of the fortress in which one white and one red serpent slept and told Vortigern, "The red serpent is your dragon, but the white serpent is the dragon of the people who occupy Britain from sea to sea; at length, however, our people shall rise and drive away the Saxon race from beyond the sea."

Section III: Critical Thinking

The student may use his text to answer this question.

As we know from our histories of both the Ancient and Medieval worlds, history and myth are often combined into powerful folklore that cannot be dismissed as mere fiction. Irish history is no different. Though we cannot be sure of the exact accomplishments of Niall of the Nine Hostages, we can surmise through a reading of "The Adventures of the Sons of Eochaid Mugmedon" that his rise to power was a bloody one. Write a paragraph that paraphrases "The Adventures of the Sons of Eochaid Mugmedon" and then write a paragraph that explains how the story showcases Niall's ambition to rule.

In the first paragraph, the student will rewrite, in his own words, the excerpt from "The Adventures of the Sons of Eochaid Mugmedon," which can be found on pages 125, ¶ 4 to Pg. 126, ¶ 2. The text reads:

"According to 'The Adventures of the Sons of Eochaid Mugmedon,' Eochaidh sends Niall and his four older brothers (all sons of his father's legitimate wife, unlike Niall) on a quest to determine which one of them deserved to inherit his power. On their journey, the sons grow thirsty and go in search of water. They find a well, but a horrible hag guards it: '[E]very joint and limb of her, from the top of her head to the earth, was as black as coal. Like the tail of a wild horse was the gray bristly mane that came through the upper part of her head-crown. The green branch of an oak in bearing would be severed by the sickle of green teeth that lay in her head and reached to her ears. Dark smoky eyes she had: a nose crooked and hollow. She had a middle fibrous, spotted with pustules, diseased, and shins distorted and awry. Her ankles were thick, her shoulder blades were broad, her knees were big, and her nails were green.' The hag demands that the brothers trade sex for access to the well. The four older brothers refuse, but Niall throws himself enthusiastically on her, ready to sleep with her for the sake of the water. Immediately she transforms into a beautiful maiden in a royal purple cloak. 'I am the Sovereignty of Erin,' she tells him, 'and as you have seen me, loathsome, bestial, horrible at first and beautiful at last, so is the sovereignty; for seldom it is gained without battles and conflicts; but at last to anyone it is beautiful and goodly.' In the tale, Niall's brothers then acclaim him as family leader of their own free will."

In the second paragraph, the student will explain how the story from "The Adventures of the Sons of Eochaid Mugmedon" showcases Niall's ambition to rule. The text tells us, "Niall's rise, first to power over his clan and then to the kingship of the Feni tribe, was undoubtedly accompanied with violence, forced possession, and bloodshed: bestial and horrible. Only with the crown in one hand and his sword in the other could he claim the beauty of legitimate kingship" (Pg. 126, ¶ 2). The gruesome description of the hag can be seen as the gruesome description of the acts Niall committed in order to gain power. Willing to do whatever was necessary—in the story he sleeps with the monstrous hag in order to quench his thirst, in real life he committed great acts of war to quench his thirst for power—Niall was eventually rewarded with kingship of the Feni tribe. Just as the hag revealed herself to be a beautiful maiden, the "beauty of legitimate kingship" was revealed to Niall after he outdid his brothers for the Feni throne.

EXAMPLE ANSWER:

In the "The Adventures of the Sons of Eochaid Mugmedon," Niall and his four brothers go on a quest to determine which brother will inherit his father's power. The boys grow thirsty on their journey. Luckily, they find a well. Unfortunately, the well is guarded by a disgusting hag that has green teeth, a crooked and hollow nose, and is covered in pustules. The hag demands sex in exchange for water from the well. Niall's four brothers refuse to sleep with the hag; Niall, however, is up for the challenge. Just as Niall throws himself on top of the hag, she transforms into a beautiful maiden in a royal purple cloak. The maiden tells Niall

that sovereignty is rarely gained without battles and conflict, but on the other side, like on the other side of her ugly appearance, beautiful things will come. The brothers then acclaim Niall their leader.

The story of Niall's rise to power via his willingness to have sex with the ugly hag suggests that Niall had to do gruesome things in order to become the leader of his clan. Willing to do whatever was necessary—in the story he sleeps with the monstrous hag in order to quench his thirst, in real life he committed great acts of war to quench his thirst for power—Niall was eventually rewarded with kingship of the Feni tribe. Just as the hag revealed herself to be a beautiful maiden, the "beauty of legitimate kingship" was revealed to Niall after he outdid his brothers for the Feni throne.

Section IV: Map Exercise

1. Using a black pencil, trace the rectangular outline of the frame for Map 19.1: Ireland and Britain.

2. Using a black pencil, trace the coastline in its entirety: around the continent, into the Baltic Sea, and around Britain and Ireland. You do not need to trace all the islands outside Scotland. With your blue pencil, trace the line of the Rhine on the continent and the line of the Thames in Britain. Repeat until the contours are familiar.

3. Trace the rectangular outline of the frame in black. Remove your tracing paper from the original. Using a regular pencil with an eraser, draw the coastline along the continent and around Britain. Remember to use the distance from the frame of the map as a guide.

4. When you are pleased with your map, lay it over the original. Erase and redraw any lines which are more than ¼ inch off of the original.

5. Study carefully the big regions of Ireland, Britain, and Gaul. Also study the regions of the Picts, Saxons, Angles, and Jutes. Be sure to study the locations of the Saxons, Angles, and Jutes in Britain as well as on the continent. When you are familiar with them, close the book. Mark the locations of Ireland, Britain, and Gaul on your map. Then mark the locations of the Saxons, Angles, and Jutes both on the continent and in Britain. Check your map with the original, and correct any misplaced labels.

6. Then study carefully the locations of the Eoghanach, the Connachta, the Ulaidh, the Midhe, and the Laighn. Also study the locations of Hadrian's Wall, Gwynedd, Essex, Kent, and Londinium. When you are familiar with them, close the book. Mark each location with your regular pencil. Check your map against the original, and erase and re-draw any misplaced labels.

7. Finally study and label the Irish Sea, the English Channel, the North Sea, and the Baltic Sea.

Chapter Twenty

The End of the Roman Myth

The student may use her text when answering the questions in sections I and II.

Section I: Who, What, Where

Write a one or two-sentence answer explaining the significance of each item listed below.

April 22, 455—**Pg. 134, ¶ 1 & 2—On April 22, 455, Vandals arrived in Rome and ransacked the city. For fourteen days, the North African barbarians roved through the city, plundering and wrecking it so thoroughly that their name became a new verb: to "vandalize," or, to ruin without purpose.**

Alypia—**Pg. 136, ¶ 3—Alypia, Anthemius's daughter, was married to Ricimer in 467 in order to create an extra layer of loyalty between the *magister militum* and the *imperator*. Alypia was not pleased with the marriage; Ricimer was in his sixties at the time of their union, fifteen years older than her own father.**

Anthemius—**Pg. 136, ¶ 2 and Pg. 137, ¶ 1 & 2—Anthemius, a Roman general married to the daughter of the eastern emperor Marcian, was appointed *imperator* by Ricimer and the Senate in 467 in order to be a figurehead in Ricimer's war against the Visigoths. Anthemius was murdered by Ricimer in 472 after the emperor started persecuting innocent men for supposedly using black magic against him.**

Avitus—**Pg. 133, ¶ 2, Pg. 134, ¶ 5 and Pg. 135, ¶ 1—Avitus, retired prefect of Gaul, was tasked by Petronius Maximus to negotiate an alliance between the Romans and the Visigoths against the Vandals. After the death of Petronius Maximus, Avitus declared himself emperor but his reign lasted barely a year; Avitus died after being taken prisoner by Ricimer.**

Eudocia—**Pg. 132, ¶ 2 and Pg. 134, ¶ 3—Eudocia, the daughter of Valentinian III that was engaged to the son of Aetius, was kidnapped by Geiseric, along with her mother and sister. Eudocia was then married to Geiseric's son, Honoric.**

Julius Nepos—**Pg. 137 ¶ 5 to Pg. 138, ¶ 1—Julius Nepos was the fourth emperor to succeed Anthemius. When various mercenary troops that were hired by Orestes marched on Ravenna to depose Julius Nepos, he fled without putting up a fight.**

Libius Severus—**Pg. 135, ¶ 5—Libius Severus became Ricimer's next puppet emperor of the western Roman empire after Majorian was beheaded. Libius Severus didn't seem to do much of anything, and died in 465, either of sickness or of poison.**

Majorian—**Pg. 135, ¶ 2 & 3—Majorian, a soldier, was appointed by Ricimer to be Ricimer's puppet emperor of the western Roman empire. Ricimer needed a puppet emperor to take the blame for faults in the Roman administration and failed battles; for example Majorian took the blame when Roman ships fell to Vandals on the coast of Hispania.**

Marcian—**Pg. 134, ¶ 4—Marcian, emperor of eastern Rome, refused to send his soldiers west to avenge the sack of Rome. Marcian had sworn, more than twenty years earlier, never again to fight against the Vandals; it had been a condition of his release after he had been taken prisoner at the capture of Carthage by Geiseric and his invading army.**

Odovacer—**Pg. 138, ¶ 3 & 5—Odovacer, a German and a Christian, leader of the Germanic mercenaries hired by Orestes to kick Julius Nepos off the throne, killed Orestes in battle after the Roman general refused to give Odovacer and his men more land in payment for their work against Julius Nepos. Odovacer gave up on the project of being Roman, and titled himself "King of Italy."**

Orestes—**Pg. 137, ¶ 4—Orestes, the Roman-born barbarian ambassador sent from Attila the Hun to Constantinople back in 449, took control of the Roman throne after several emperors failed to control it following Anthemius's death. Orestes put his ten-year-old less-barbarian-blooded son Romulus on the throne as puppet emperor.**

Petronius Maximus—**Pg. 132, ¶ 2 & 3 and Pg. 133 ¶ 1–3—Petronius Maximus, a Roman Senator who had been a prefect of Rome twice, convinced Valentinian III to murder Aetius, and then Petronius Maximus had Valentinian III killed, stole the dead emperor's crown, and declared himself emperor of the Western Roman empire. Petronius Maximus ruled for seven deadly and destructive years; his reign ended when he was struck and killed by a rock as he fled Rome, which was being attacked by the Vandals.**

Ricimer—**Pg. 134, ¶ 7, Pg. 135, ¶ 2 & 6—Ricimer, a half-German general and Avitus's *magister militum*, earned the respect of the Romans by driving the remaining Vandals back from the Italian coast. Ricimer took Avitus prisoner, and appointed Majorian as his puppet emperor; after Majorian's death Ricimer appointed two other puppets, cementing the myth of Roman imperial rule.**

Riotimus—**Pg. 136, ¶ 5—Riotimus, a Briton, had settled in the part of northwestern Gaul known as Brittany with over twelve thousand men. Feeling the threat of invaders, Riotimus agreed to supply twelve thousand men to Ricimer's cause against the Visigoths.**

Romulus—**Pg. 138, ¶ 1-4—Romulus, son of Orestes, emperor of Rome at ten years old, was placed on the throne because his barbarian father could not hold the title of *imperator*. Romulus, called "Augustulus," meaning "little Augustus," by his subjects, watched his empire fall apart in a year, and spent the rest of his days as a prisoner of Odovacer's in a castle in Campania called Castel dell'Ovo.**

Section II: Comprehension

Write a two or three-sentence answer to each of the following questions.

1. Why, in 454, did Aetius arrange for the engagement of his son to Valentinian III's daughter?

A1.—Pg. 132, ¶ 2—In 454, Aetius arranged for the engagement of his son to Valentinian III's daughter in an effort to put his family in line for the western throne.

2. What happened to Valentinian III's empire during the thirty years of his reign?

A2.—Pg. 132, ¶ 3—Valentinian III had lost a lot of his empire during his thirty-year reign; Hispania and much of Gaul were gone to the Suevi and the Visigoths. North Africa was lost to King Geiseric and the Vandals, who had already taken Sicily. The Huns had stormed through Italy, and now the Vandals had their eye on the peninsula; Valentinian III hid away while the chaos ensued.

3. What were the circumstances of Aetius's death?

A3.—Pg. 132, ¶ 4—In 455, Valentinian III was in Ravenna when Aetius came to court on a routine visit to discuss tax collection. As Aetius stood in front of Valentinian III, the emperor leaped up from his seat with his sword, shouting that he would no longer put up with treachery, and beheaded Aetius.

4. Why didn't Geiseric and his Vandal invaders try to hold Rome?

A4.—Pg. 134, ¶ 2—Geiseric didn't want to hold Rome; Geiseric only wanted the city's wealth. With the Vandals behind him, Geiseric stole all the gold and silver in Rome—even tearing the gold plating off the roof of the temple of Jupiter Capitolinus.

5. How did Avitus lose the support of both the Visigoth army that backed his takeover of the western throne, and the support of the Roman people?

A5.—Pg. 134, ¶ 6 & 7—After the Vandals' invasion, Avitus found himself grappling with a city devastated by famine and plunder. Because there was so little food, Avitus was forced to send the Visigothic army that backed him away. He had to pay the soldiers before they left, however, and since there was no money in the treasury, he stripped all the remaining bronze off the public buildings and handed it over to the Visigoths. This action infuriated the people of Rome, and so Avitus lost their support for his rule as well.

6. What trouble with the Visigoths inspired Ricimer to appoint a new emperor, after eighteen months of ruling without the myth of royalty?

A6.—Pg. 135, ¶ 7 to Pg. 136, ¶ 1—Though Ricimer had been happily ruling without an emperor since the death of Libius Severus, he felt he needed to appoint a new *imperator* in 467 because of trouble brewing with the Visigoths. Theodoric II of the Visigoths had been murdered by his brother Euric, who immediately took the Visigothic throne and began rapidly expanding his reign over land that had once been Roman. Ricimer had to fight back, and he needed a new emperor to be the face of the battle.

7. What happened in the battle between the Britons and the Visigoths?

A7.—Pg. 136, ¶ 6—Riotimus knew that the spread of Visigothic power threatened his new home, so he agreed when Ricimer asked for support that he would send twelve thousand men to fight against King Euric and his soldiers. King Euric cut the Britons off before they could reach Roman troops, ending the fight almost before it had begun.

8. What were the circumstances of Anthemius's death?

A8.—Pg. 137, ¶ 1 & 2—Anthemius believed the ill fortune of Rome, its losses against the Visigoths and the Vandals in North Africa, were all caused by black magic. He then began a witch hunt and started putting men to death for unproven sorcery. When Ricimer heard of Anthemius's irrational actions, he recalled six thousand solders from the North African front, marched into Rome and in 472 put Anthemius to death.

Section III: Critical Thinking

The student may not use her text to answer this question.

It finally happened . . . we have been waiting for this moment in our reading: the disintegration of the myth of the western Roman empire. As we read in the last paragraph of this chapter, the death warrant for the western empire was signed by Constantine over a century before Odovacer's declaration that he was the "King of Italy." The decline of the western empire has been dragging out over our chapters, and now we see how the myth of Roman greatness failed. Write a paragraph explaining how Ricimer's eighteen-month emperor-less rule was a sign of western Rome's imminent end. Make sure to explain why Ricimer did eventually decide to appoint Anthemius emperor after eighteen months of being without a figurehead. Then, write a paragraph explaining why Odovacer decided to call himself "King of Italy" rather than *imperator.*

In this first paragraph, the student should address the truth behind the Roman myth of power, that to be Roman was no longer exceptional, and that the divine kingdom of the past was no more. First the student should identify the last gossamer strings of tradition that held together the image of the Roman throne. On page 135, the text tells us that Ricimer "knew that his barbarian ancestry would prevent the Roman Senate from confirming his rule as emperor," so he had to appoint a puppet emperor, or "a public face." He first appointed Majorian. When

Majorian died, Ricimer appointed Libius Severus. When Libius Severus died, Ricimer did nothing. Ricimer ruled Rome, despite his barbarian blood, in all but name. The myth was revealed: Ricimer's present Rome had nothing to do with the glorious past, and to be Roman and barbarian were now one and the same. Ricimer was able to rule Rome for eighteen months without a puppet emperor because there was no higher office, bloodline or no bloodline, to challenge his rule. He only decided to take on a new emperor, Anthemius, so that if things went badly for him in battle against the Visigoths, there would be a different figurehead for the citizens of Rome to blame.

In the second paragraph, the student should identify what made Odovacer a suitable ruler by describing who ruled before him, and why he chose to call himself "King of Italy" rather than "emperor" of western Rome. On page 137, we learn that after defeating Orestes and taking Romulus prisoner, Odovacer took the title "King of Italy." Odovacer chose to call himself "King of Italy" because he wanted to separate himself from the old imperial past. As a Christian ruling over a largely Christian land, as a strong soldier and administrator, Odovacer's blood no longer mattered as a determinant of his worthiness to rule. Doing away with the title imperator meant blood was no longer the main qualifying factor to rule; it also meant the end of the Roman myth.

EXAMPLE ANSWER:

When Ricimer became *magister militum* of the western Roman empire, he knew his power also extended to the throne. However, because of his barbarian blood and the surviving myth that Roman emperors could not be barbarians, Ricimer knew he had to appoint a puppet-emperor, or a "public face." He first appointed Majorian. When Majorian died, Ricimer appointed Libius Severus. When Libius Severus died, Ricimer did nothing. Ricimer ruled Rome, despite his barbarian blood, in all but name. The myth was revealed: Ricimer's present Rome had nothing to do with the glorious past, and to be Roman and barbarian were now one and the same. Ricimer was able to rule Rome for eighteen months without a puppet emperor because there was no higher office, bloodline or no bloodline, to challenge his rule. Ricimer only decided to take on a new emperor, Anthemius, so that if things went badly for him in battle against the Visigoths, he would not be the one to take the blame.

After Anthemius followed four more emperors and then another barbarian soldier named Orestes. Sticking to tradition, Orestes appointed his son, Romulus, emperor. Romulus's mother was Roman, so he was less barbarian than his father. Orestes and his son Romulus were knocked off the throne by the Christian and German Odovacer. Instead of calling himself *imperator*, Odovacer chose to call himself "King of Italy." Odovacer took the title "King of Italy" because he wanted to separate himself from the old imperial past. As a Christian ruling over a largely Christian land, as a strong soldier and administrator, Odovacer's blood no longer mattered as a determinant of his worthiness to rule. Doing away with the title imperator meant blood was no longer the main qualifying factor to rule; it also meant the end of the Roman myth.

Chapter Twenty-One

The Ostrogoths

The student may use his text when answering the questions in sections I and II.

Section I: Who, What, Where

Write a one or two-sentence answer explaining the significance of each item listed below.

Alans—**Pg. 143, ¶ 2—Alans was the name of the tribe to which Aspar belonged. The Alans had once lived east of the Black Sea, but were driven out of their own lands by the Huns.**

Amalasuntha—**Pg. 147, ¶ 3—Amalasuntha, Theoderic's wife and Athalaric's mother and regent, wanted her son to go to school in Rome in order to receive the education "Roman princes" received. Her request was in opposition to the Ostrogoth nobles who believed a Roman education would make Athalaric a sissy.**

Ariadne—**Pg. 144, ¶ 2 & 3—Ariadne, daughter of Leo the Thracian, was married to Zeno, son of the Isaurian leader, in order to strengthen the alliance between the eastern Roman emperor and the Isaurians. Ariadne gave birth to Leo II, who followed Leo the Thracian as emperor of eastern Rome.**

Aspar—**Pg. 143, ¶ 2 and Pg. 144, ¶ 2—Aspar, an Alans barbarian, commander of the eastern Roman army when Marcian died, had designs on ruling eastern Rome, so he had Leo the Thracian elected in the hopes Leo could be easily manipulated. Aspar was executed by Leo the Thracian in 471, after the emperor made a strong alliance with the Isaurians.**

Athalaric—**Pg. 147, ¶ 3—Athalaric, Theoderic's son, was ten years old when his father died. Tensions between Athalaric's mother and the Ostrogoth nobles who wanted to control the kingdom came to a head over the possibility of Athalaric's Roman education.**

Basiliscus—**Pg. 144, ¶ 4—Basiliscus, brother-in-law of Leo the Thracian, ran Zeno out of Constantinople and crowned himself emperor of the eastern Roman empire. Basiliscus made himself unpopular because of heavy taxation policies; eighteen months after taking**

the throne, Basiliscus was himself kicked off the throne by Zeno and the unhappy public, and then left to starve to death in a dry cistern.

Benedict of Nursia—**Pg. 147, ¶ 4 and Pg. 148, ¶ 1 & 3—Benedict of Nursia, once a young man sent to school in Rome, became a pious hermit dedicated to the teachings of Christianity. After being asked to run a monastery and then leaving after learning of a plot to have him poisoned, Benedict formed the monastery Monte Cassino.**

Isaurians—**Pg. 143, ¶ 4 to Pg. 144, ¶ 1—The Isaurians, a mountain people of southern Asia Minor, were recruited by Leo the Thracian to be allies of the eastern Roman emperor. Despite their war-like characteristics, the Isaurians had been under Roman rule for 500 years; the Isaurians had the advantages of being barbarian, like their skill at war and self-directed purpose, but they were also indisputably Roman.**

Leo the Thracian—**Pg. 143, ¶ 3 & 4 and Pg. 144, ¶ 2 & 3—Leo the Thracian was chosen by Aspar to follow Marcian as emperor of eastern Rome. Leo made an alliance with the Isaurians, married his daughter to the son of the Isaurian leader, and in 471 had Aspar executed; he died three years later of dysentery.**

Leo II—**Pg. 144, ¶ 3—Leo II, the six year old son of Ariadne and Zeno, was crowned as emperor of eastern Rome after the death of Leo the Thracian. Leo II's regent was his father, and when Leo II died tenth months after ascending to the throne, his co-emperor was left to rule the empire.**

Theoderic the Ostrogoth (Theoderic the Great)—**Pg. 145, ¶ 2 & *, Pg. 146, ¶ 5—Theoderic, a former child hostage held in Constantinople, led the Ostrogoths in their pursuit of finding more food and land. After fighting for Italy for over three years, Theoderic the Ostrogoth became king of Italy after he killed Odovacer.**

Zeno—**Pg. 144, ¶ 2–4—Zeno, husband of Ariadne, father of Leo II, became emperor of eastern Rome following his son's death. Zeno was chased out of Constantinople by Basiliscus, Leo the Thracian's brother-in-law, but he returned with an army and retook his throne, locking away Basiliscus and leaving him to starve to death.**

Section II: **Comprehension**

Write a two or three-sentence answer to each of the following questions.

1. When and how did the Theodosian dynasty in eastern Rome end?

A1.—Pg. 143, ¶ 1—The Theodosian dynasty ended in 457. The dynasty ended when the eastern Roman emperor Marcian died at the age of sixty-five.

2. Why did Leo the Thracian ally himself with the Isaurians?

A2.—Pg. 143, ¶ 4—Leo the Thracian allied himself with the Isaurians because he did not want to be a puppet king. Aspar, the commanding general of the army, had great power in Rome. Leo the Thracian felt allying himself with the Isaurians would lessen Leo the Thracian's power.

3. Why did Odovacer, king of Italy, ask Zeno the Isaurian to be his overlord and emperor?

A3.—Pg. 144, ¶ 5—Odovacer, the Germanic general who took Ravenna by force and ruled over his people through terror, was in a precarious situation as king of Italy; he could not use fear to gain support from his people. To bolster his claim to power, Odovacer sent a message to Zeno saying he would acknowledge Zeno as overlord and emperor, and would rule Italy in submission to the eastern empire, if Zeno would in turn recognize him as rightful ruler of Italy.

4. What was Odovacer's new title after he became part of Zeno's empire? What happened after Odovacer received this new title?

A4.—Pg. 144, ¶ 6 to Pg. 145, ¶ 1—When Odovacer became a part of Zeno's empire, he was given the title patrician, not king, of Italy. Though Odovacer's title suggested he was subject to Zeno's authority, Odovacer continued to do as he pleased. Odovacer conquered Sicily, and made a treaty with the Visigoths and the Franks, acts that technically could only be done by a king or an emperor.

5. What are the differences between Theoderic the Ostrogoth and Theoderic the Squinter?

A5.—Pg. 145, *—Theoderic the Ostrogoth, or Theoderic the Great, commanded Ostrogoths from Pannonia. Theoderic the Squinter, named after his eyes, was a distant cousin of Theoderic the Ostrogoth, and ruled from Thracia. The two generals were not automatic allies since they were competing for the same scarce resources but they did act together against Zeno at least once. Theoderic the Squinter died around 481, after which Theoderic the Great dominated the Ostrogoths.

6. How did Zeno try to pacify Theoderic and the Ostrogoths as they advanced towards Constantinople in the years between 478 and 488?

A6.—Pg. 146, ¶ 1—Between 478 and 488, as Theoderic and the Ostrogoths advanced steadily towards Constantinople, Zeno tried to appease Theoderic with the title of *magister militum*. Zeno also awarded Theoderic land in the regions of Dacia and Moesia, and even paid Theoderic a substantial amount of money when he threatened to besiege Constantinople itself in 486. No solution seemed to work for long, however.

7. How did Theoderic the Ostrogoth come to attack Italy? Who went along with Theoderic in his pursuit of the peninsula?

A7.—Pg. 146, ¶ 2—Zeno, feeling the threat of Theoderic the Ostrogoth and worrying about the growing power of Odovacer, convinced Theoderic to get rid of Odovacer, and in exchange Zeno would name Theoderic king of Italy, giving the Ostrogoths a place to finally call home. Theoderic marched towards Italy with a mass of different supporters: Ostrogoths, Huns, Romans and displaced members of other Germanic tribes.

8. What were the circumstances of Odovacer's death?

A8.—Pg. 146, ¶ 4 & 5—After three years of fighting over Italy, Odovacer suggested a compromise with Theoderic the Ostrogoth in 491: Odovacer would sign a treaty making

the two of them co-rulers of Italy if Theoderic would lift his siege against Italy. Theoderic agreed to the compromise, but in 493 he put an end to the treaty by killing Odovacer.

9. Why did the monks at a monastery near Subiaco ask Benedict to come and live with them, and then try to poison him?

A9.—Pg. 147, ¶ 5 to Pg. 148, ¶ 1—After their abbot died, some monks that had heard of a pious hermit living in the wilderness asked Benedict to come and run their monastery. Benedict decided to run the community in a regulated, quiet and productive way, which included strict supervision. The monks, unhappy with Benedict's tightened rule, conspired to get rid of him and his strict ways by poisoning his wine.

10. What were the circumstances of the founding of Monte Cassino?

A10.—Pg. 148, ¶ 1 & 2—After leaving the monastery where the monks planned to poison his wine, Benedict went back into the forest and continued to teach the shepherds who came to see him, converting a number of them to the monastic lifestyle. Around 529, Benedict led his followers up a mountain near the town of Cassino where he and his monks burned the ruins of an old temple of Apollo and in its place built a monastery of their own—Monte Cassino.

11. What were the rules, or "the Rule of St. Benedict," by which the monks in Monte Cassino lived?

A11.—Pg. 148, ¶ 3 & 4—The rules by which the monks in Monte Cassino lived, or "The Rule of St. Benedict," revolved around the idea of bringing Christian practice back to the realm where the Indian and Chinese monks dwelt. The duties of the monks were to: relieve the poor, clothe the naked, visit the sick, bury the dead, to prefer nothing to the love of Christ, and to live life in silence. The monks also had to sleep with their clothes on so that they would always be prepared for worship and service. The monks followed the decisions of the abbot because his decisions were final, they were not allowed to own anything, and each monk spent a prescribed number of hours per day in manual labor.

12. If a monk broke one of Benedict's rules, what was the punishment? How did Benedict know that the rules were being broken?

A12.—Pg. 148, ¶ 4—If a monk broke one of Benedict's rules, the monk was to be barred from eating with the community or taking part in worship until he repented. The "spirit of prophecy" allowed Benedict to know when the monks were breaking the Rule even when they were away from the monastery.

Section III: Critical Thinking

The student may use his text to answer this question.

As the Roman empire crumbled, the myth of Roman superiority hung on tight. While the idea of Roman sophistication still lingered, there was no doubt that real power lay in the hands of cunning strategists and successful warriors. Write a paragraph explaining how Theoderic's actions after becoming king of Italy weakened the idea of Roman greatness. Then, explain how the argument over the education of his son, Athalaric, became symbolic of the struggle between real and imagined power.

In this critical thinking question, the student needs to differentiate between real power and the idea of power. Theoderic the Great, an Ostrogoth, managed to take the western Roman throne. When he became king of Italy, he declared that the only people who could claim Roman citizenship were those that supported him in his battle against Odovacer. Through this act, Roman citizenship was no longer a prized distinction; it was tied to the once-barbaric but now civilized and mighty Ostrogoths. Nothing Roman was sacred to Theoderic the Great: he did not prize Rome as did previous emperors; in fact, he went to Rome only once. In a dying effort to preserve some sense of old Roman ways, the Senate continued to meet in Rome, but the power of the law lay with the king. The Senate merely rubber-stamped Theoderic's decrees. And while the Goths adopted many Roman ways, including the use of Latin, Roman names, cultivating Roman estates and marrying Roman women, they did not believe that being Roman made them great. It was the warrior side of the Ostrogoths that gave them real power. Ask the student to consider who held the military offices under Theoderic's watch: it was the Goths, not the Romans. Romans were allowed to hold civil offices, but they were considered too weak for the military.

Athalaric's education became a central issue in the battle between brains and brawn. Education used to be a sign of greatness in Rome's heyday, but it was no longer celebrated in Theoderic's empire. Amalasuntha, Athalaric's mother, still held on to the belief that great leaders should be educated, and so she wanted her son to be sent to Rome for schooling. The Goths in power objected, arguing that "education would make him a sissy." Even Theoderic himself would never allow any of the Goths to send their boys to get educated, for they would lose their fearlessness. When Rome was a great and thriving empire, the life of the mind held as much power, if not more, as the sword. Amalasuntha was still under the impression that her son would rise in power because of his education. In Rome's present reality, it was military power that made a man a great leader. The debate between Amalasuntha and the Goths reiterated the tension between the old ways of Rome and the new. Amalasuntha, while benefitting from the strength of the Goths, still bought into the Roman myth of civilization and education as creating elite men. The truth was though, without power, those men could do nothing to protect and save their kingdom.

EXAMPLE ANSWER:

When Theoderic became king of Italy, he changed the terms of Roman citizenship. Theoderic declared that the only people who could claim Roman citizenship were those that supported him in his battle against Odovacer. Through this act, Roman citizenship was no longer an esteemed distinction. Nothing Roman was sacred to Theoderic the Great: he did not prize Rome as did previous emperors; in fact, he went to Rome only once. In a dying effort to preserve some sense of old Roman ways, the Senate continued to meet in Rome, but the power of the law lay with the king. The Goths adopted many Roman ways, including the use of Latin, Roman names, cultivating Roman estates and marrying Roman women, but they did not believe that being Roman made them great. It was the warrior side of the Ostrogoths that gave them real power. The only men who could hold military office were Goths; the Romans were considered too weak for the military.

The debate over education came to a head when Athalaric was old enough to be sent off to school. Amalasuntha, Athalaric's mother, still held on to the belief that great leaders should be educated, and so she wanted her son to be sent to Rome for schooling. The Goths in power objected, arguing that "education would make him a sissy." Amalasuntha was still under the impression that her son would rise in power because of his education. In Rome's present reality, it was military power that made a man a great leader. The debate between Amalasuntha and the Goths reiterated the tension between the old ways of Rome and the new. Amalasuntha, while benefitting from the strength of the Goths, still bought into the Roman myth of civilization and education as creating elite men. But actually, without power, those men could do nothing to protect and save their kingdom.

Section IV: Map Exercise

1. Using a black pencil, trace the rectangular outline of the frame for Map 21.1: Odovacer's Kingdom.

2. Using a blue pencil, trace the outline of the Mediterranean. At this time, you do not need to include the various islands except for Sicily. Be sure to include the coastline all the way up to the Black Sea. Trace the outline of the Black Sea as well. Repeat until the contours are familiar.

3. Using a black pencil, trace the dotted outline of the Eastern Roman Empire. Then trace the outline of Odovacer's kingdom. Trace the shading lines denoting the kingdom of the Vandals. Repeat until the contours are familiar.

4. Using a new sheet of paper, trace the rectangular frame of the map with a black pencil. Remove your tracing paper from the original. Using a regular pencil with an eraser as you look at the map, draw the coastlines of the Mediterranean and Black Sea. Then draw the outline of the Eastern Roman Empire and the outline of Odovacer's kingdom. Shade the Kingdom of the Vandals.

5. When you are pleased with your map, lay it over the original. Erase and redraw any lines which are more than ¼ inch off of the original.

5. Remove your map. Label Sicily, Dacia, and Asia Minor (if necessary, study first and then label). Then study carefully the regions of the Apennines, Moesia, and the Isaurians. When you are familiar with them, close the book. Mark the location of each. Check your map with the original, and correct any misplaced labels.

6. Now study carefully the cities of Carthage, Cassino, Subiaco, Rome, Nursia, Ravenna, Verona, and Constantinople. When you are familiar with them, close the book. Using your regular pencil, label all eight on your map. Compare with the original, and erase and re-mark your labels as necessary.

Chapter Twenty-Two

Byzantium

The student may use her text when answering the questions in sections I and II.

Section I: Who, What, Where

Write a one or two-sentence answer explaining the significance of each item listed below.

Anastasius—**Pg. 153, ¶ 6 and Pg. 156, ¶ 1—Anastasius, nicknamed "The Two-Eyed" because of his mismatched eyes, became the Roman emperor when he married Zeno's widow just a month after the former emperor's death. Anastasius dealt with several different outsider invasions which led to the building of the Long Wall, and with it, the Byzantine empire.**

Balash—**Pg. 151, ¶ 2—Balash, another of Peroz's sons, drove Kavadh out of Ctesiphon, took the throne for himself, and ended war with the Armenians. Balash was kicked off the throne by Kavadh and his Hephthalite friends.**

Mazdak—**Pg. 151, ¶ 3 to Pg. 152, ¶ 1—Mazdak, a Persian prophet, led a heretical cult that taught the ultimate power in the universe was a distant and uninvolved deity, and that two lesser but equal divine powers, good and evil, struggled over the universe. Mazdak believed that the primary way of aligning man with the good in the universe was to make all men equal, that everyone should share their resources equally, and that equality and brotherly love be man's priority.**

Na'man of al-Hirah—**Pg. 153, ¶ 7—Na'man of al-Hirah, the Arab king, was allied with Kavadh and the Persians in their fight against the Romans at Amida.**

Nevarsek Treaty—**Pg. 151, ¶ 2 & *—The Nevarsek Treaty granted Armenia independence from Persia, and as a result Armenia was able to preserve itself as a nation. Balash signed the treaty because the Persian treasury was bankrupt and he could not keep war going on multiple fronts.**

Justin—**Pg. 157, ¶ 3 & 4—Justin, seventy-year-old commander of the imperial guard and an ardent supporter of the Blues, was elected emperor after the death of Anastasius. He elected his nephew, Justinian, as his consul.**

Justinian—**Pg. 157, ¶ 4—Justinian, nephew of Justin, was made consul by his uncle in 521. Like Justin, Justinian supported the Blues, and did little to quell the growing violence of the chariot-racing fans in Constantinople.**

Kavadh—**Pg. 150, ¶ 3, Pg. 151, ¶ 2, Pg. 152, ¶ 3 and Pg. 153, ¶ 4—Kavadh, oldest son of Peroz, spent two years at the Hephthalite court as a hostage during his father's reign; the relationship Kavadh built with the Hephthalites helped him reclaim the Persian throne several times during his life. Kavadh was ousted from his throne by his brother Balash, then after he reclaimed it and started to make reforms based on the teachings of Mazdak he was ousted by his other brother Zamasb, and then he finally reclaimed the throne and held on to it for over thirty years.**

Peroz—**Pg. 150 ¶ 2—Peroz, the oldest son of Yazdegerd II, ruled Persia for a difficult twenty-seven years. Peroz spent much of his reign fighting against the Hephthalites, and was killed in battle against the invaders in 484.**

Zamasb—**Pg. 152, ¶ 3 & 4—Zamasb, another of Kavadh's brothers, took the Persian throne in 496 when Kavadh was ousted by the noblemen because of his social justice reforms. Kavadh, after breaking out of prison and once again getting support from the Hephthalites, took the throne back from Zamasb; consequently, Zamasb was blinded by a hot iron needle and imprisoned.**

Section II: Comprehension

Write a two or three-sentence answer to each of the following questions.

1. Describe the difficulties Persia faced during Peroz's twenty-seven year reign.

A1.—Pg. 150, ¶ 2—During Peroz's twenty-year reign, Persia suffered from a severe famine, an infestation of locusts, earthquakes, plague, and a solar eclipse. Soon after the famine, war between Persians and invading Hephthalites broke out.

2. Explain how Peroz was tricked by the Hephthalites in battle in both 471 *and* in 484.

A2.—Pg. 150, ¶ 3 to Pg. 151, ¶ 1—When Peroz marched into Hephthalite territory on the eastern side of the Persian empire, the Hephthalites retreated in front of Peroz's men and then circled around behind and trapped the Persian army. Peroz, forced to surrender, swore an oath that he would never attack again, and he also agreed to pay the Hephthalites an enormous tribute. Still angry about his first failure thirteen years before, Peroz attacked the Hephthalites again, this time falling into a giant pit dug by the enemy; Peroz was killed in the battle and Persia suffered a terrible defeat.

3. How did Persia become a subject of the Hephthalites?

A3.—Pg. 151, ¶ 1—In 484, Peroz decided to attack the Hephthalites despite a treaty he signed in 471 declaring he would never attack again. The Hephthalites brutally defeated the Persians. After their victory, the Hephthalites crossed the Oxus river, took control of Khorasan and the Persians became subject and tributary to the Hephthalites.

4. How did Kavadh's contemporaries react to his reforms based on Mazdak's ideas? What do their reactions suggest Kavadh was actually trying to achieve in his reforms?

A4.—Pg. 152, ¶ 2—Kavadh's contemporaries had different reactions to his reforms; al-Tabari says that he took "from the rich for the poor and [gave] to those possessing little out of the share of those possessing much" while Procopius writes that Kavadh wanted the Persians to have "communal intercourse with their women." We can understand from these disparate comments that Kavadh's ultimate goal was to redistribute some of the wealth held by the powerful Persian nobles and that he most likely lifted the restrictions that forced women to marry men of their own class.

5. In what way did Kavadh's reforms help his rule? Why did the Persian nobles resent Kavadh's reforms, and what did they do with their anger about the reforms?

A5.—Pg. 152, ¶ 2 & 3—Kavadh's reforms helped his rule because the reduction of the power and influence of noblemen meant an increase in the king's power. The nobles resented the reforms exactly because their power was reduced. The nobles, unable to handle the reduction of their power, removed Kavadh by force and placed his brother Zamasb on the Persian throne.

6. Who helped Kavadh escape from the "Fortress of Oblivion"?

A6.—Pg. 153, ¶ 2—There are two stories of how Kavadh escaped from the "Fortress of Oblivion," both of which revolve around a woman sleeping with the warden in exchange for visiting privileges. One story says that Kavadh's sister was the woman in question, and that she had her brother rolled up in a carpet and then had the carpet carried out of the prison. The other version is that his wife was the mystery woman, and when she saw her husband made him switch clothes with her so he could escape under cover of a woman's robe.

7. What were the conditions of Kavadh's return to the Persian throne after being locked away in the "Fortress of Oblivion"?

A7.—Pg. 153, ¶ 3 & 4—Kavadh could not return to the Persian throne on his own, so he once again pled for help from the Hephthalites. The Hephthalite king not only agreed but also gave Kavadh his own daughter as a wife to seal the bargain. After marching to Ctesiphon at the head of a Hephthalite army, Kavadh kicked his brother Zamasb off the throne and started his rule, aware that he could no longer make decisions that did not please the Persian noblemen—this time around he knew he needed their support in order to keep his rule.

8. Why did the war between the Romans and the Persians end? What were the terms of the treaty made between the two empires?

A8.—Pg. 154, ¶ 2 & 3—Though the Persians were doing very well against the Romans, the Persians were also dealing with another Hephthalite invasion despite Kavadh's alliance by marriage to his eastern enemies. Kavadh did not want to continue to fight on two fronts, so in 506 the Persians and Romans negotiated a treaty. Amida was given back to the Romans, and the Persians remained in control of the Caspian Gates, the narrow path through the Caucasus Mountains that had the power to let in or keep out invaders from the north.

9. Describe who fans rooted for in medieval Roman chariot-racing.

A9.—Pg. 156, ¶ 4—In chariot-racing, fans rooted not for drivers or horses, but for teams, and they hated fans of other teams irrationally. Teams were represented by colors—red, white, blue and green—each sponsored by different associations and companies. Several different horse-and-driver pairs might race under the same color, so spectators became fans of the colors and not the individual performers.

10. Explain how chariot-racing turned Constantinople into a city so dangerous its citizens raced home at sunset so they would be off the street before dark.

A10.—Pg. 157, ¶ 1, 2 & 5—Fans of chariot-racing were divided into two groups, the Blues and the Greens, and were so violent that thousands of fans died in bloody spectator riots. When Justin became emperor and elected Justinian as his consul, the men, both Blues supporters, did little to stop the growing violence in the city. Fans carried weapons all the time and they collected in gangs at nightfall robbing members of the upper class; the people of Constantinople stopped wearing jewelry in fear of being mugged and hurried home before dark in the hopes of staying safe.

Section III: Critical Thinking

The student may use her text to answer this question.

Tracking the developments of known civilizations during the medieval world can sometimes be mind-boggling: empires split up, nations absorbed one another, some barbarians found homelands and others were kicked out of what they thought was their own soil. In this chapter, we learned about the further disintegration of what was known as the Roman empire, and the formation of Byzantium. Write a paragraph or two, starting with the Slavs, that explains how barbarian invasions eventually led to the creation of Anastasius's Long Wall, and finally Byzantium. In your answer, make sure to explain the difference between the Slavs and Germanic peoples, why Anastasius uprooted the Isaurians, and how the Bulgars played into the formation of Byzantium.

This critical thinking question is meant to help the student sort out all the comings and goings of barbarians into Anastasius's empire, and how those meanderings led to the new formation called Byzantium. On page 154, ¶

5, we learn about the difference between the Slavs and the Germanic peoples. Just like the Romans could confuse any intruder from a northern territory, the student might be confused about who was coming from where and why. The Slavs came from north of the Danube, and they were moving south and west towards Rome's eastern borders. Though the Slaves came from the north, they were not "Germanic." Germanic peoples spoke languages with a common source, which suggests a shared origin. The Slavs, however, came from father east, and belonged to a different language family.

The Slavs that were moving towards the eastern Roman borers were coming from the Carpathian Mountains, north of the Danube. The Danube river valley wasn't big enough for them, and they were threatening to overflow into the old Roman provinces of Thracia and Illyricum. To deal with the problem, Anastasius uprooted the Isaurians and moved them to Thracia. Anastasius moved the Isaurians in order to weaken their sense of national identity—how could they feel like a real people when they were being moved from homeland to homeland—and to create a barrier between Constantinople and the Slavs. Anastasius's plan also worked because the Isaurians had to fight off the Slavs in order to keep their new homeland in Thracia.

While the Slavic invasion was taken care of, we learn on page 155 that another group of wanderers threatened Anastasius: the Bulgars. The Bulgars were from central Asia and they followed the Slavs west into their new territory. The Bulgars attacked the Slavs in 499, returned home, and then attacked again in 502. Because the Slavs were settled in Roman territory, the Bulgars counted their plunder of the Slavs as a "victory over a Roman army."

All of these outside invasions were chipping away at Anastasius's empire, and so he decided to build a wall against them. The Long Wall cut Thracia out of Anastasius's purview, but it kept Constantinople safe. As a result, the entire empire reoriented toward the east, becoming Byzantium.

EXAMPLE ANSWER:

As the medieval world grew more populated, several different groups wanted to settle in Roman territory. The Slavs, people who came from the north of the Danube, moved south and west toward Rome's eastern borders. Some Romans confused the Slavs for Germanic peoples. The Germanic peoples spoke languages with a common source, like the Slavs, but they were from a different language family. The Slavs had been living in the Danube river valley, but it wasn't big enough for them and they were threatening to overflow into the old Roman provinces of Thracia and Illyricum. To deal with the problem, Anastasius uprooted the Isaurians and moved them to Thracia. Anastasius moved the Isaurians in order to weaken their sense of national identity, which made them less of a threat to his empire, and to create a barrier between Constantinople and the Slavs. The Isaurians fought off the Slavs in order to keep their new homeland in Thracia, and Anastasius was protected from their invasion as well.

The Slavs might have been taken care of, but Anastasius could not relax—he had to deal with the invading Bulgars. The Bulgars were from central Asia and they followed the Slavs west into their new territory. The Bulgars attacked the Slavs in 499, returned home, and then attacked again in 502. Because the Slavs were settled in Roman territory, the Bulgars counted

their plunder of the Slavs as a "victory over a Roman army." All of these outside invasions were chipping away at Anastasius's empire, and so he decided to build a wall against them. The Long Wall cut Thracia out of Anastasius's purview, but it kept Constantinople safe. As a result, the entire empire reoriented toward the east, turning into Byzantium.

Section IV: Map Exercise

1. Using a black pencil, trace the rectangular outline of the frame for Map 22.1: Persia and the Hephthalites.

2. Using a blue pencil, trace the coastlines of the Mediterranean (the white portion inside the Byzantine Empire), the Red Sea, the Persian Gulf, the Caspian Sea, and the Black Sea. With the blue pencil, trace the line of the Nile, the Danube (what is visible), the Tigris, the Euphrates, and the Oxus. Repeat until the contours are familiar.

3. Using a black pencil, trace the outlines of the Persian Empire and the Byzantine empire. Use a contrasting color to show Armenia. Show the Carpathian mountains and the Caucasus mountains with simple peaks. Repeat until the contours are familiar.

4. Trace the rectangular outline of the frame in black. Remove your tracing paper from the original. Using a regular pencil with an eraser as you look at the map, draw the outlines of the Mediterranean, the Red Sea, the Persian Gulf, the Caspian Sea, and the Black Sea. Draw the lines of the Nile, the Danube, the Tigris, the Euphrates, and the Oxus. Draw the outlines of the Persian Empire, Armenia, and the Byzantine Empire. Show the Carpathian mountains and the Caucasus mountains with peaks as you did before.

5. When you are pleased with your map, lay it over the original. Erase and redraw any lines which are more than ¼ inch off of the original.

6. Remove your map. Study the regions of the Byzantine Empire, Arabia, the Persian Empire, Armenia, Khorasan, Bactria, and the Hephthalites. When you are familiar with them, close the book. Label them all, and then check your labels with the original. Erase and redraw any misplaced labels.

7. Then study carefully the locations of Constantinople, Amida, Edessa, Harran, Ctesiphon, the Fortress of Oblivion, and the Caspian Gates. When you are familiar with them, close the book, label each, and check your labels against the original. Erase and redraw any misplaced labels.

Chapter Twenty-Three

Aspirations

The student may use his text when answering the questions in sections I and II.

Section I: Who, What, Where

Write a one or two-sentence answer explaining the significance of each item listed below.

Ado—**Pg. 163, ¶ 5 & 6—Ado was the Indian monk that brought Buddhism to Silla. After Ado helped King Pophung out of an embarrassing situation in court, King Pophung endorsed the spread of Buddhism to the people of Silla.**

Chijung—**Pg. 162, ¶ 4 and Pg. 163, ¶ 3—Chijung came to Silla's throne in 500 and brought about a series of reforms that turned Silla into a strong nation. Chijung saw Chinese government, technology, dress and even Chinese names as the keys to bringing Silla strength, and he used these Chinese tools to turn Silla into a nation.**

Feng—**Pg. 159, ¶ 2 & 3—Feng, Chinese by blood, was the dowager empress, grandmother and regent to Wei Xiaowen. Feng shared power with her grandson, and together they transformed the Bei Wei court into a place that drew heavily from Chinese culture.**

Jangsu—**Pg. 161, ¶ 6 and Pg. 162, ¶ 1—Jangsu, son of the great Goguryeon king Guanggaeto the Expander, transformed Goguryeo from a collection of conquered territories into a state, and moved the capital city from Guknaesong to Pyongyang. Jangsu ruled for seventy-nine years, earning himself the nickname "The Long Lived."**

King Pophung—**Pg. 163, ¶ 4 & 6—King Pophung, Chijung's successor, came to the throne in 514. He solidified Silla's government into a true centralized state with a written code of law that was published in 520. He brought Buddhism to Silla, and soon after its introduction declared it the state religion.**

Wei Xiaowen—**Pg. 159, ¶ 2 and Pg. 161, ¶ 4—Wei Xiaowen, great-great-grandson of the Taoist emperor Wei Taiwu, emperor of the Bei Wei in 471 at the age of four, transformed Bei Wei**

into a Buddhist Chinese kingdom. Wei Xiaowen even moved the capital of Bei Wei away from its nomadic roots in Pingcheng to the old Jin capital of Luoyang.

Wei Xuanwu—**Pg. 161, ¶ 4—Wei Xuanwu, son of Wei Xiaowen, succeeded his father as ruler of the Bei Wei in 499. Wei Xuanwu oversaw the completion of the Bei Wei capital move from Pingcheng to Luoyang.**

Section II: Comprehension

Write a two or three-sentence answer to each of the following questions.

1. Why did the Tuoba clan decree that the mother of the crown prince be executed? How did Feng manage to escape this fate?

A1.—Pg. 159, ¶ 2—The ancient custom of the Tuoba clan decreed that the mother of each crown prince be put to death so that she could not influence the politics of the court. Feng, who was Chinese by blood, managed to maneuver herself out of this position.

2. How did Wei Xiaowen and Feng transform the Bei Wei court into an essentially Chinese court?

A2.—Pg. 160, ¶ 1—In order to transform the Bei Wei court into a more traditional Chinese court, Wei Xiaowen and Feng gave Chinese officials high places in government, the traditional nomadic dress of the Xianbei was banned, and they outlawed any use of the Xianbei language. The pair only allowed the court to speak Chinese, and they forced the great Bei Wei families to adopt Chinese surnames in place of their traditional clan names.

3. Why is Taoism so important to ancient Chinese medicine?

A3.—Pg. 160, ¶ 2—Taoism is important to ancient Chinese medicine because of the preparation of elixirs in the peculiarly magical form of the religion. This form, practiced by Wei Xiaowen's great-great-grandfather, was the bedrock on which medieval Chinese advances in pharmaceutical and chemical formulations were built.

4. In what way was Confucianism important for the formation of the Bei Wei government?

A4.—Pg. 160, ¶ 3—Confucianism was important for the formation of the Bei Wei government because it supplied a model of state hierarchy. Confucianism provided a picture of the world in which a properly ordered and properly structured government was an essential part of an orderly and moral universe.

5. Explain the legendary Buddhist origins of Kung Fu.

A5.—Pg. 160, ¶ 7 to Pg. 161, ¶ 1—One of the Buddhist monasteries that sprang up during the patronage of Wei Xiaowen was the Shaolin Monastery on the sacred mountain Song Shan, established by the Indian monk Batuo. As part of their prayer and meditation, the monks followed a set of physical exercises intended to focus the mind. According to legend, Bei Wei

generals who visited the monastery saw the monks carrying out their exercises, recognized the value of the systematic movements for fighting, and adopted them into the source material for the martial art of kung fu.

6. What did Wei Xiaowen tell his clan leaders when he suggested they move the Bei Wei capital from Pingcheng to Luoyang? Why did Wei Xiaowen want to move the capital?

A6.—Pg. 161, ¶ 3—When Wei Xiaowen halted a military party at Luoyang during what was supposed to be a reconnaissance mission into southern China, he told the party he wanted to move the Bei Wei capital to the old Jin capital. He said, "Pingcheng is a place from which to wage war, not one from which civilized rule can come." Wei Xiaowen's decision to move the capital was the pinnacle of his plan to turn the Bei Wei into a fully Chinese kingdom.

7. Describe the Bei Wei capital city of Luoyang at its peak.

A7.—Pg. 161, ¶ 4—At its peak, reconstructed Luoyang was home to over half a million people that were protected by eighty-foot-thick walls. There were five hundred Buddhist monasteries inside of the city, and only Chinese was spoken. Also, the Chinese classics had been gathered into a great city library for the education of the future officials of the Bei Wei.

8. Where was the Goguryeon capital when Guanggaeto ruled? Why did Jangsu move the capital to Pyongyang?

A8.—Pg. 161, ¶ 7 to Pg. 162, ¶ 1—Goguryeo's capital city was Guknaesong, on the Yalu river, when Guanggaeto was in power. As Goguryeo's territory expanded, Guknaesong proved to be too far north to act as a center of government, so Jangsu decided to move the capital to Pyongyang, which was on the plains of the Taedong river, farther south.

9. Why were Baekje and Silla alarmed by the move of the Goguryeon capital to Pyongyang? What happened to Baekje after the move?

A9.—Pg. 162, ¶ 2 & 3—Baekje and Silla were alarmed by the Goguryeon's capital move from Guknaesong to Pyongyang because that suggested a new focus on expanding to the south. Even though Baekje and Silla prepared for war with the Goguryeons, Jangsu was still able to attack the capital city of Baekje, capturing the king and beheading him. Jangsu also forced the remaining Baekje government south to the city of Ungjin.

10. What actions did Chijung take when he came to Silla's throne in 500 that turned Silla into a thriving nation?

A10.—Pg. 163, ¶ 2 & 3—When Chijung became leader of Silla, he took the Chinese title of king instead of the traditional title *maripkan*, which was less powerful, meaning something like "governing noble." Chijung outlawed ancient and unpleasant Silla customs, such as burying slaves along with their masters. He also improved industry by bringing in Chinese consultants to teach the people of Silla how to plow with oxen and to demonstrate how to construct an underground ice-cellar to preserve food in the hot summer months.

11. How did Buddhism come to Silla?

A11.—Pg. 163, ¶ 5 & 6—Buddhism came to Silla with the Indian monk Ado. Tradition has it that one day in court, the king of the Liu Song, in southern China, had sent an ambassador to Silla bringing gifts of incense, but neither the king of Silla nor his court knew what the incense was or how use it. Ado explained to the court how to burn incense, and in exchange King Pophung issued a decree supporting Buddhism.

Section III: Critical Thinking

The student may use his text to answer this question.

Taoism and Confucianism were both important to the transformation of the Bei Wei into a seemingly traditional Chinese culture. Buddhism, however, turned out to be key in moving the Bei Wei towards a more Chinese way of life. Buddhism also helped the young nation of Silla form its identity and become more Chinese. Write a paragraph that explains how Mahayana Buddhism shaped the Bei Wei during Wei Xiaowen's rule. Make sure to describe the structure of Mahayana Buddhism, and how the bodhisattvas provided a model of rule for Wei Xiaowen. Then, explain how King Pophung of Silla also used Buddhism to reinforce the strength of his small nation.

The text explains on page 160 that Mahayana Buddhism provided a model of kingship for Wei Xiaowen. In Mahayana Buddhism, there were several deities, each exercising a kinglike power, but not in a hierarchical fashion. Each deity was Buddha in a different manifestation; each manifestation was called a bodhisattva. The bodhisattvas had reached Nirvana but chose to remain in the world until all were saved. Mahayana Buddhism praised greater and more accomplished believers that worked on behalf of the less powerful. The bodhisattvas modeled kind leadership; they were above earthly men, but they were invested in the salvation of earthly man's soul. Wei Xiaowen translated Mahayana Buddhism into his own rule, presenting himself as a kind and benevolent ruler. Wei Xiaowen built lavish Buddhist temples, provided land and money and carved Buddhist sculptures into the cliffs near the northern Bei Wei capital of Pingcheng for all to see and enjoy. The student might note that when Wei Xiaowen moved the capital city of Bei Wei to Luoyang, he had more Buddhist sculptures carved into the side of cliffs so that "the divine eyes would still be watching the new capital city" (Pg. 161, ¶ 3).

Buddhism also helped Silla to establish itself as a nation. Silla invented its own tradition when King Pophung claimed that royal builders, while excavating for new foundations, had uncovered Buddhist stupas from long ago, as well as pillar bases, stone niches and steps. By claiming that the remains of an ancient Buddhist monastery were found in Silla, King Pophung refashioned Silla's history with the legitimacy of the Buddhist faith as support.

EXAMPLE ANSWER:

Buddhism helped both Bei Wei and Silla become greater nations. In Bei Wei, Mahayana Buddhism provided a model of kingship for Wei Xiaowen. There were several deities in Mahayana Buddhism, each exercising a kinglike power, but not in a hierarchical fashion. Each deity was Buddha in a different manifestation; each manifestation was called a

bodhisattva. The bodhisattvas had reached Nirvana but chose to remain in the world until all were saved. The bodhisattvas modeled kind leadership; they were above earthly men, but they were still invested in the salvation of earthly man's soul. Wei Xiaowen translated Mahayana Buddhism into his own rule, presenting himself as a kind and benevolent ruler. Wei Xiaowen built lavish Buddhist temples, provided land and money and carved Buddhist sculptures into the cliffs near the northern Bei Wei capital of Pingcheng and near the new capital city in Luoyang.

Buddhism also helped Silla to establish itself as a nation. Silla invented its own tradition when King Pophung claimed that royal builders, while excavating for new foundations, had uncovered Buddhist stupas from long ago, as well as pillar bases, stone niches and steps. By claiming that the remains of an ancient Buddhist monastery were found in Silla, King Pophung refashioned Silla's history with the legitimacy of the Buddhist faith as support.

Section IV: Map Exercise

1. Using a black pencil, trace the rectangular outline of the frame for Map 23.1: The East in the Era of King Jangsu.

2. Using a blue pencil, trace the outline of the East China Sea. You do not need to include islands at this time. Then trace the lines of the Yangtze and Yellow rivers. Using a black pencil, trace the outlines of the Bei Wei and the Liu Song. Repeat until the contours are familiar.

3. Using a new sheet of paper, trace the rectangular outline of the frame in black. Remove your tracing paper from the original. Using a regular pencil with an eraser as you look at Map 23.1, draw the coastline of the East China Sea, up through the Yellow Sea and into the bay above. Lightly draw the perimeters of the regions of the Bei Wei and the Liu Song.

4. When you are pleased with your map, lay it over the original. Erase and redraw any lines which are more than ¼ inch off of the original. When you are done, lightly shade the areas of the Bei Wei and the Liu Song inside their respective perimeters.

5. Remove your map. Study carefully the locations of Goguryeo, Silla, Baekje, and the Gaya Confederacy. When you are familiar with them, close the book. Label each on your map. Then check your map with the original, and erase and correct any misplaced labels.

6. Next study closely the locations of Chang'an, Pingcheng, Luoyang, Jianye, Ungjin, Pyongyang, and Guknaesong. Also study closely the location of Mount Song Shan. When they are familiar for you, close the book, and label each one. Then compare with the original. Erase and remark any misplaced labels.

Chapter Twenty-Four

Resentment

The student may use her text when answering the questions in sections I and II.

Section I: **Who, What, Where**

Write a one or two-sentence answer explaining the significance of each item listed below.

Erzhu Rong—**Pg. 169, ¶ 6 to Pg. 170, ¶ 2—Erzhu Rong, a general of the Bei Wei army, stormed Luoyang, sacked the city, killed the empress dowager and put Wei Xiaozhuang on the Bei Wei throne. Erzhu Rong was killed by Wei Xiaozhuang because the emperor feared the general would become more ambitious and try to take the throne for himself.**

Erzhu Zhao—**Pg. 170, ¶ 3—Erzhu Zhao, nephew of Erzhu Rong, captured Wei Xiaozhuang in battle in 531, murdered his infant son, and had the emperor strangled.**

"Inattentive Empress"—**Pg. 169, ¶ 4 and Pg. 170, ¶ 1—"Inattentive Empress" was the name given to Wei Xiaoming's mother, who was the empress dowager, because she had a habit of ignoring anything that was happening outside the city; she also had given her lover most of the power of the court and refused to grant any power to the young emperor Wei Xiaoming. The "Inattentive Empress" was drowned in the Yellow river by Erzhu Rong.**

Liang Wudi—**Pg. 166, ¶ 4 & 5 and Pg. 167, ¶ 2—Liang Wudi, the royal name for the general Xiao Yan, took the southern Chinese throne in 502 and began the Southern Liang dynasty. Liang Wudi made great bureaucratic strides for the Southern Liang, promoted Buddhism and hoped to earn the Mandate of Heaven by displaying his own virtue as ruler.**

Qi Gaodi—**Pg. 165, ¶ 2—Qi Gaodi was an official who was fed up with the Liu Song dynasty. He took the Liu Song throne by force, declared himself emperor, and started the new Southern Qi dynasty.**

Qi Hedi—**Pg. 165, ¶ 4 to Pg. 166, ¶ 1—Qi Hedi, or "the Idiot King," was the last emperor of the Qi dynasty and was disliked because he taxed his people heavily in order to build a beautiful palace. After poisoning an official that was the brother of the general Xiao Yan, a general that had the loyalty of the army, Qi Hedi was murdered and the Qi dynasty was finished.**

Qi Mingdi—**Pg. 165, ¶ 3—Qi Mingdi, brother of Qi Wudi, seized the throne in 494 after chaos broke out following Qi Wudi's death. Qi Mingdi ruled for only four years, and then he died.**

Qi Wudi—**Pg. 165, ¶ 3—Qi Wudi, Qi Gaodi's son, became emperor after his elderly father ruled for just three years. Qi Wudi ruled for ten years.**

Wei Xiaoming—**Pg. 169, ¶ 3-5—Wei Xiaoming, son of Wei Xuanwu, was granted no power by his regent, the "Inattentive Empress." When he was eighteen, Wei Xiaoming asked Erzhu Rong to remove the empress dowager from power, but she got to him first; Wei Xiaoming was poisoned by his mother before Erzhu Rong reached Luoyang.**

Wei Xiaozhuang—**Pg. 170, ¶ 2 & 3—Wei Xiaozhuang, cousin of Wei Xiaoming, was placed on the throne by Erzhu Rong. Wei Xiaozhuang had Erzhu Rong assassinated, which caused civil war; Wei Xiaozhuang was strangled on the order of Erzhu Rong's nephew Erzhu Zhao.**

Wei Xuanwu—**Pg. 168, ¶ 5 and Pg. 169, ¶ 2—Wei Xuanwu continued his father's campaign to Sinicize the northern kingdom into complete Chinese-ness by instituting the "equal-field" system. Wei Xuanwu also saw conflict during his rule between the primarily barbarian border guard in the north of his kingdom and the aristocratic noblemen at the capital of Luoyang.**

Section II: Comprehension

Write a two or three-sentence answer to each of the following questions.

1. List the emperors of the ill-fated Liu Song dynasty that ruled after Song Xiaowu. In your answer, include how long each emperor ruled and if possible, why his reign ended.

A1.—Pg. 165, ¶ 1 & 2—Song Ming, or "The Pig," followed Song Xiaowu as Liu Song emperor and ruled for seven years. Song Hou Fei followed Song Ming; known for his childish antics, Song Hou Fei was assassinated after three years of rule, replaced by his thirteen-year-old brother Song Shun. Song Shun was on the throne for only two years before an exasperated aristocrat took the throne by force, ending the Liu Song Dynasty.

2. Why did Xiao Yan act as prime minister, and support the rule of Qi Hedi's sixteen-year-old brother in his claim to the throne, after the Idiot King's death?

A2.—Pg. 166, ¶ 2—Xiao Yan acted as Qi Hedi's brother's prime minister because the Chinese people still believed in hereditary rule. China had never been a place where a general could

simply take power because of his strength, he had to fit into the dynastic system. Xiao Yan did not yet fit into the system, and thus he supported the emperor that did.

3. What bureaucratic and military accomplishments did Liang Wudi make during his reign as emperor of the Southern Liang dynasty?

A3.—Pg. 166, ¶ 5—During his reign, Liang Wudi built five new Confucian schools for the training of young officials and he declared that all heirs to the throne must be fully educated in Confucian ethics. Liang Wudi instituted a system for peasants and the poor to complain anonymously about the behavior of the rich so that the poor would not fear retaliation from the rich. Liang Wudi also made frontier defenses stronger and beat off an attack from the Bei Wei.

4. How did Buddhism shape Liang Wudi's China?

A4.—Pg. 167, ¶ 1—Liang Wudi, a devout Buddhist, sponsored the travels of monks from India so that they could come and preach in the capital city. He built Buddhist temples, and by the end of his reign there were almost thirteen thousand temples within the Southern Liang borders. He also ordered the gathering of the first Chinese Tripitaka, a comprehensive collection of Buddhist scriptures, and he did his best to make sure that Buddhist prohibitions against the taking of life were followed.

5. Why was being a virtuous ruler so important to Liang Wudi?

A5.—Pg. 167, ¶ 2—Chinese historians and philosophers believed, since the very first emperors had ruled in the Yellow river valley, that these men ruled because of their virtue. The Mandate of Heaven was the right to rule, a divine right given to emperors when they inherited the throne. Liang Wudi, the head of a new dynasty, was not technically given the Mandate of heaven and wanted to show that his virtuosity was worth the Mandate; he would earn his right to rule through displaying his virtue.

6. How did Liang Wudi's Buddhism conflict with his rule of the Southern Liang dynasty? What won out in the end, the temple or the throne?

A6.—Pg. 167, ¶ 3 & 4—As Liang Wudi developed his virtue, he became more and more convinced that Buddhism required him to renounce his ambitions to earthly power and in 527, he took off his royal robes, put on a monk's robe, and entered a monastery. However, when Liang Wudi resigned from the throne he did not designate an heir, and the remaining ministers had a difficult time running the country without the authority to make royal decrees. After a minister paid the head of the monastery a hefty sum to expel Liang Wudi from the monastery, the former emperor was kicked out of his religious haven and forced to reprise his role as head of the Southern Liang dynasty.

7. What is the *juntian*, or "equal-field" system? What was the purpose of the "equal-field" system?

A7.—Pg. 168, ¶ 4 & 5—The *juntian*, or "equal-field" system, is a system that claimed land in the Bei Wei kingdom belonged not to individual families or noblemen but to the

government. The government had the right to assign land to individuals, who would farm it, support their families with it, and pay taxes from it directly to the throne. When a farmer died, the government could then reassign his land to someone else. The purpose of the equal field system was to stop noblemen from collecting more and more land and passing it on to their sons, which could lead to independent hereditary kingdoms within the larger kingdom's borders.

8. How did the "equal-field" system redistribute private armies?

A8.—Pg. 168, ¶ 6—In the "equal-field" system, soldiers were given fields of their own, which they farmed in return for serving in the king's army for a certain number of months per year. In the old system, tribal leaders provided the throne with soldiers; these soldiers were first loyal to the tribal leaders or noblemen who owned their homes, and their second loyalty was to the king. The new system broke soldiers' ties to noblemen and reforged those ties directly to the king.

9. What was the Bei Wei strategy for dealing with nomads that attacked the kingdom's northern borders?

A9.—Pg. 169, ¶ 1—For many years, the Bei Wei strategy for dealing with nomads that attacked the kingdom's northern borders was to capture them and then integrate them into the garrisons posted along the northern frontier. The Bei Wei were able to control the threat of nomadic invasion by bringing the threat inside Bei Wei borders and turning it into part of the Bei Wei army.

10. Why was assignment to the northern frontier, once an honor, seen as a punishment during Wei Xuanwu's rule?

A10.—Pg. 169, ¶ 2—Bei Wei's northern frontier was primarily barbarian because of all the nomadic peoples that were captured and folded into the Bei Wei army. The northern garrison remained close to the nomadic roots of the Bei Wei people while the aristocrats at court moved further toward seeing themselves as fully Chinese. To be sent to the frontier was to regress in society, to turn back into a savage, and that was seen as a punishment for any man hoping to be viewed as Chinese.

11. Why did a proposal that did not pass—that soldiers would no longer be eligible to hold government offices—cause fighting between the Bei Wei and its own border guard?

A11.—Pg. 169, ¶ 2 & 3—Though the proposal that soldiers would no longer be eligible to hold government offices did not pass, it revealed the growing aristocratic scorn for a part-barbarian army. When the soldiers in Luoyang heard the proposal, they rioted; they were soldiers, but they were also part of the "Chinese" population living at the capital. The contempt of the proposal revealed deep hostility between the border and the court and in 523, the garrisons along the north began to revolt against the Bei Wei.

12. What were the circumstances of the Heyin Massacre?

A12.—Pg. 169, ¶ 6 to Pg. 170, ¶ 1—After Wei Xiaoming's death, the empress dowager and her lover appointed a two-year-old child to be the figurehead emperor. In response, Erzhu Rong and his army declared a cousin of the dead Wei Xiaoming to be the rightful emperor and crowned him in camp, which allowed Erzhu Rong and his men to sack Luoyang, capture the empress and drown both her and the child emperor in the Yellow river. The general then summoned two thousand of the empress dowager's officials and supporters to his headquarters and had them murdered, in an act that became known as the Heyin Massacre.

13. What was the cause of the Bei Wei civil war? What was the result of the civil war?

A13.—Pg. 170, ¶ 2–4—The Bei Wei civil war started after Wei Xiaozhuang, the cousin of the dead emperor Wei Xiaoming, was placed on the throne by the general Erzhu Rong. Wei Xiaozhuang married Erzhu Rong's daughter in order to strengthen the trust between the two men, but he could not get over his fear of the general and he had Erzhu Rong assassinated. This opened up a civil war between the general Erzhu Rong's relatives and his field army against the emperor and the army of the Luoyang. By 534, the civil war split the Bei Wei into two separate kingdoms: the Eastern Wei and the Western Wei.

Section III: Critical Thinking

The student may not use her text to answer this question.

The Bei Wei were in between two worlds: the nomadic and barbarian world of their past, and the aristocratic and refined Chinese world of their future. The transition between these two worlds was not smooth, as evidenced by the civil war that eventually split the Bei Wei in two. Explain how the conflict between the Bei Wei's past and present manifested itself in the land disputes of the Bei Wei tribal leaders. Write a paragraph that explains the plight of the "local aristocrats," how their desires conflicted with the desire of the emperor, and how their desire to be Chinese ultimately led to the sacrifice of their local power.

As explained in the chapter on page 168, "In the old nomadic clan system, tribal leaders held more or less equal authority, with one leader granted slightly greater power to oversee the joint efforts of the tribes." The tribal leaders "claimed the right to control their own portions of land, while collecting taxes from the peasants who lived on this land . . . and raising armies from the population they governed." In Wei Xuanwu's kingdom the taxes were supposed to be going to the royal treasury, and the armies were supposed to serve the interest of the royal family. The plight of the "local aristocrats" is that they wanted to continue to be independent petty rulers, but they also wanted to be part of a more traditional Chinese system where they were seen as powerful nobleman loyal to the throne.

The imposition of the juntian, or the "equal-field" system, in which land belonged to the government and was distributed by the government to noblemen and soldiers, kept noblemen from amassing land and handing it down to their sons, meaning no more independent hereditary kingdoms within the larger Bei Wei kingdom. Since soldiers were given land, noblemen were also deprived of their private army. Soldiers were now tied directly to the king because of the land they received from the government.

"Local aristocrats," or noblemen, went along with the juntian in the end because they longed to be Chinese. Though they had to give up their traditional powers, by going along with the emperor's wishes they were even closer to their new, Chinese, identities.

EXAMPLE ANSWER:

Under the rule of Wei Xuanwu, the plight of the "local aristocrats" had to do with the juntian. Under the "equal-land" system, noblemen had to give up their portions of land, the taxes they collected from it, and the private armies from the population they governed. The noblemen struggled with this law: they wanted to continue to be independent petty rulers, but they also wanted to be part of a more traditional Chinese system where they were seen as powerful noblemen loyal to the throne. "Local aristocrats," or noblemen, went along with the juntian in the end because they longed to be Chinese. Though they had to give up their traditional powers, by going along with the emperor's wishes, they were even closer to their new, Chinese identities.

Chapter Twenty-Five

Elected Kings

The student may use his text when answering the questions in sections I and II.

Section I: Who, What, Where

Write a one or two-sentence answer explaining the significance of each item listed below.

Aelle—**Pg. 176, ¶ 4 and Pg. 177, ¶ 2—Aelle was a Saxon leader that claimed land near the British fortress of Anderida as his own kingdom in 477: the Kingdom of the South Saxons, later shortened to Sussex. In 491, Aelle strengthened his grasp on his own kingdom by actually capturing Anderida and massacring all of its inhabitants.**

Amalaric—**Pg. 175, ¶ 1 & 2 and Pg. 179, ¶ 1—Amalaric, son of Alaric II, was the next in line for the Arian Visigothic throne. When Amalaric did become king, he was ultimately murdered in 531 by his own men because he could not prove himself as an effective warleader.**

Ambrosius Aurelianus—**Pg. 175, ¶ 7, Pg. 176, ¶ 3 and Pg. 177, ¶ 1 & 4—Ambrosius Aurelianus, most likely the son of one of the last Roman soldiers left in Britain, led the rulers of Britain in a great, victorious battle against Saxon invaders in 485. Thousands of Saxons were killed, hundreds more were driven out of England and as a result of this great victory, a score of legends grew around Aurelianus himself though they could not keep him safe from death; he was killed by another British king that had formerly been his ally.**

Childebert—**Pg. 178, ¶ 4 & 5—Childebert, one of the four sons designated leader after their father Clovis's death, chose to rule from Paris.**

Childeric—**Pg. 172, ¶ 2 & 3—Childeric, son of Merovech, became chief of the Salian Franks after his father's death sometime around 457. Though Childeric claimed the title "King of the Franks," he was king in name only; at the time of his death, he was merely chief of the Salians despite his royal title.**

Chlodomer—**Pg. 178, ¶ 4 & 5—Chlodomer, one of the four sons designated leader after their father Clovis's death, chose to rule from Orleans. Chlodomer was killed on an expedition against the Burgundians in 524.**

Chlothar—**Pg. 178, ¶ 4 & 5—Chlothar, one of the four sons designated leader after their father Clovis's death, took Soissons as his capital. After Chlodomer's death, Chlothar led his two brothers to Orleans to kill Chlodomer's sons before they could lay claim to their father's portion of the crown.**

Clotild—Pg. 172, ¶ 5 to Pg. 173, ¶ 1—**Clotild, the Christian daughter of the king of the Germanic tribe of Burgundy, married Clovis in order to forge a diplomatic alliance between her father and the "King of the Franks." Clotild evangelized her husband by convincing him that the Germanic gods he worshiped were no good, and that God would help Clovis defeat his enemies.**

Clovis—**Pg. 172, ¶ 4 and Pg. 175, ¶ 4 & 6—Clovis, Childeric's son, succeeded his father when he was fifteen, in 481, as "King of the Franks." After converting to Christianity and winning in battle against the Visigoths, Clovis took the title "Augustus, Consul of the West" and lived out his days as the first real king of all the Franks in his new capital of Paris.**

Theuderic—**Pg. 178, ¶ 4 & 5—Theuderic, the oldest of the four sons designated leader after their father Clovis's death, ruled from Reims.**

Theudis—**Pg. 179, ¶ 1 & 2—Theudis, an Ostrogothic soldier-official from Italy that was sent to the Visigoth court to watch over Amalaric as a child by Theoderic the Great of Italy, was elected to the Visigothic throne in 531 after the murder of Amalaric. From Theudis's rule on, ancestry played little part in the selection of Visigothic kings, and the nation had reverted to the old Germanic method of choosing their ruler.**

Section II: Comprehension

Write a two or three-sentence answer to each of the following questions.

1. Though he claimed to be "King of the Franks," who did Childeric truly rule over? Why didn't he rule over all of the Franks, and who did he have to fight with during his rule?

A1.—Pg. 172, ¶ 2 & 3—Though Childeric claimed the title "King of the Franks," he was really only one chief among many. The other Frankish tribes still kept their independence, even while acknowledging the long-haired Salians as leaders of the coalition. Frankish and Roman kings were scattered across the landscape, each with their own little domain and army. Childeric was forced to battle against these rival kings, against Odovacer of Italy, against Alemanni invaders to the east, and against Saxon pirates sailing into the Loire.

2. Describe Gregory's account of Clovis's conversion to Christianity.

A2.—Pg. 173, ¶ 2—Gregory explains that Clovis converted Christianity while on the battlefield: Clovis was losing against the Alemanni, and he raised his eyes to heaven, praying

"Jesus Christ, if you give me victory over my enemies I will believe in you. I have called upon my own gods, but, as I see only too clearly, they have no intention of helping me." Immediately following Clovis's prayer, the Alemanni men broke rank and surrendered. Clovis returned home a Christian and he and his wife Clotild summoned the bishop of Reims to come and baptize him.

3. What did Christianity offer to the Franks and that Roman-ness could not?

A3.—Pg. 173, ¶ 3 & 4—The Franks were a confederacy, not a nation, held together by custom, geography and necessity. Living within Rome's boundaries for over a century gave them Roman practices, Roman gods to worship and a Romanized army; these all created strong bonds, but Roman-ness was not enough to keep the Franks together. Christianity acted as a stronger bond than Roman-ness—with God on their side, the Franks were no longer a Romanized confederacy—they were now a Christian nation.

4. How did the Franks take the Arian Visigoths of Hispania? When the Visigothic court scattered from Toulouse, who did they take with them?

A4.—Pg. 173, ¶ 6 to Pg. 175, ¶ 1—Reinforced by soldiers lent to him by his father-in-law, the king of Burgundy, Clovis marched his army toward the Visigothic frontier, meeting his opponent in the Visigothic town of Vouille on the southwestern side of the Loire. With God on their side, the Franks were able to scatter the Visigothic army after their king, Alaric II, was killed in battle. Pressing southward, the Franks invaded Toulouse, and the remnants of the Visigothic court fled into Hispania, taking Alaric II's five-year-old son, Amalaric, with them.

5. How did the Italian Ostrogoths get into the fight between the Franks and the Arian Visigoths of Hispania? What was the end result of their battle?

A5.—Pg. 175, ¶ 2—The Italian Ostrogoths got involved in the fight between the Franks and the Arian Visigoths because Alaric II was married to the daughter of Theoderic the Great, meaning Amalaric was a member of the Ostrogothic royal family. In 508 Ostrogothic armies arrived at the Rhône river, forcing Clovis to withdraw from a small patch of Gaulish land called Septimania, keeping Clovis from establishing the Franks on the Mediterranean coast. This small defeat meant little; Toulouse was still controlled by the Franks, Septimania was now the only little patch of Visigothic land in all of Gaul, and the Visigoths had been driven almost entirely into Hispania.

6. How did Clovis become "Augustus, Consul of the West"? Even though this title was not meant for Clovis why did the eastern Roman emperor allow Clovis to continue to call himself as such?

A6.—Pg. 175, ¶ 3 & 4—Stopping in Tours on his way home from his victorious campaign against the Arian Visigoths, Clovis found a letter waiting there for him from Constantinople: the eastern Roman emperor wanted to give Clovis an honorary title that would recognize his success as a Christian monarch among barbarians. Clovis misinterpreted the letter and named himself "Augustus, Consul of the West." Though the eastern Roman emperor did not have such a high title in mind, he let Clovis keep the name

of Augustus because now Clovis would keep Theoderic the Great of Italy in check, who was a much greater problem for eastern Rome.

7. What did Clovis do after he became "Augustus," victorious Christian and Roman king?

A7.—Pg. 175, ¶ 5 & 6—After Clovis became "Augustus," victorious Christian and Roman king, he built a new capital called Paris in the place of the old Roman town Lutetia Parisiorum, on the Seine. He then issued a set of Latin laws for his domain, the Pactus Legis Salicae; the laws were very specific in forbidding the old Germanic traditions of blood revenge, instead substituting fines and penalties for clan-based revenge killings. To ensure his power Clovis/Augustus killed off the Frankish chiefs, one at a time, that might challenge him for sole power.

8. Even though Vortigern had managed to kill one of the invading Saxon generals in 455, why was he remembered so bitterly? What kinds of tales were spread about Vortigern?

A8.—Pg. 176, ¶ 1—Bitter memories of Vortigern lingered in British memory because he did not defeat the invading Saxons. Vortigern was later accused by British historians of killing the rightful king of all Britain and taking his place even though there was no rightful king of all Britain during Vortigern's time on earth. They also claimed he invited the Saxons in and handed the country over to them so that he could sleep with the Saxon women.

9. What are some of the stories that have circulated about the Battle of Mount Badon? Despite the contradictory accounts, what is the one constant among the different tales?

A9.—Pg. 176, ¶ 5—At the Battle of Mount Badon, the British, led by Ambrosius Aurelianus, won a great victory over the Saxons. Stories that circulated about the victory included the claim that Ambrosius's brother Uther Pendragon fought by his side; the duke of Cornwall lead a wing of the attack; they included Ambrosius's right-hand general, a soldier called Arthur, and finally a resurrected Vortigern appeared on the side of the opposition, fighting with the Saxons against his own people. The only constant among the different tales is that the British were victorious.

10. When King Clovis, Augustus, Consul of the West, died in 511, why did he leave his kingdom to his four sons?

A10.—Pg. 178, ¶ 4—When King Clovis died in 511, he left his kingdom to his four sons because in Frankish eyes it meant the same thing as leaving rule of the Franks to his clan. Clovis's realm was filled with warlike Franks who still carried with them the old Germanic ideal of kingship: that they had the right to choose their king. Because they would have resented any attempt to leave the kingship to a single designated heir, Clovis named his four sons rulers and the Franks, who were accustomed to recognizing the leadership of the Salian clan over the others, accepted their new rulers.

Section III: Critical Thinking

The student may use his text to answer this question.

The American poet Gertrude Stein once wrote, "A rose is a rose is a rose;" there is no variation, a rose is what it is: a rose. For the 5th century British, a king was a king was a king. Explain the difference between ideas of British kingship as described in the chapter and the ideas behind kingship in Rome. Then, explain how Geoffrey of Monmouth challenged the British idea that a king was a king was a king.

In the chapter we learn that Britain was held together not by what it was, but by what it was not—Saxon. As stated on page 177, ¶ 4, "There was no British kingdom and no British high king, no shared religion, no idea of nationhood. At the beginning of the sixth century, to be British was to be not Saxon, and the independent kings and tribal leaders were jealous of their power, no matter who threatened it." A result of this threat was the death of Ambrosius Aurelianus, who died in battle against another British king in 511.

In Britain, kingship ended with death. A king did not inherit his power, nor could he pass that power on to a successor. A British king earned his right to rule through successful leadership of his tribe in battle. His power was given to him by the men who followed him because he deserved it. When he died, his power died with him.

As we've seen throughout our history, Roman kingship was understood differently; for the Romans, the king represented something immortal that went on eternally. The idea of kingship for the Romans was bigger than the actual king, it was an idea that threaded all the kings together, the idea of a Roman state. Death did not mean a king lost his power, it meant it was time for the power to be passed on to his son, meaning there was a system of hereditary kinship. The thread of power that was passed on then led to a state held together by the eternal bond of the Roman king.

Because the same was not true for Britain, where power died with the king, Geoffrey of Monmouth wanted to find a way to create eternal life for the power of Ambrosius Aurelianus, who saved the British from the Saxons, through the alter ego Arthur. Like Ambrosius Aurelianus, Arthur is mortally wounded on the battlefield of Camlann, but he does not die. As written on page 178, ¶ 2, "he hands his crown to his cousin and is taken away to the Isle of Avalon to be healed. His kingdom survives because he survives, even though he is far away and mysteriously divided from his people. Arthur becomes the idea of the British state, in a time when the state and the king were the same. Like the idea of the state itself, he exists eternally." The British system did not allow for the immortal rule of the king, so Geoffrey of Monmouth created that immortality through his history of Arthur, hoping to keep the British state bound together.

EXAMPLE ANSWER:

British kingship was different from Roman kingship because a British king's power died with him. In Britain, a king did not inherit his power, nor could he pass that power on to a successor. A British king earned his right to rule through successful leadership of his tribe in battle. His power was given to him by the men who followed him because he deserved it. When he died, so did his power.

Roman kingship was based on something immortal and eternal, the Roman state, so a Roman king's power could be inherited and also passed on. The idea of kingship for the

Romans was bigger than the actual king, so death did not mean that a king lost his power, it only meant it was time for that power to be passed on to his son. The thread of power that was passed on then led to a state held together by the eternal bond of the Roman king.

Geoffrey of Monmouth challenged the idea that power died with the British king when he wrote the history of Arthur. It was his way of keeping British kingship alive. Like Ambrosius Aurelianus, Arthur is mortally wounded on the battlefield of Camlann, but he does not die. He hands his crown to his cousin, passing his power on, and then Arthur goes to the Isle of Avalon to be healed. Though he is divided from his people Arthur, and his power, live on. The British system did not allow for the immortal rule of the king, so Geoffrey of Monmouth created that immortality through his history of Arthur, hoping to keep the British state bound together.

Section IV: **Map Exercise**

1. Using a black pencil, trace the rectangular outline of the frame for Map 25.1: Clovis and His Neighbors.

2. Using a blue pencil, trace the coastline all the way down the coast to Hispania, into the Mediterranean, and up around Britain. You do not need to include islands at this time. Repeat until the contours are familiar.

3. Choose four contrasting colors. Use each to trace the territories of the Ostrogoths, the Franks, the Vandals, and the Visigoths. Use horizontal lines as the map-maker did to indicate the area conquered by Clovis. Repeat until the contours are familiar.

4. Trace the rectangular outline of the frame in black. Remove your tracing paper from the original. Using a regular pencil with an eraser, draw the coastal outline around Britain and down the continent and around the Mediterranean as you look at Map 25.1. As before, you need not draw islands at this time. Erase and redraw as necessary.

5. When you are satisfied with your map, lay it over the original. Erase and redraw any lines which are more than ¼ inch off of the original.

6. Remove your map. Mark (study first if necessary) the areas of England, Gaul, and Hispania on your map. Then study carefully the locations of the Saxons, Angles (on the continent and in Britain), Jutes, Thuringii, Burgundians, and Alemanni. When you are familiar with them, close the book, mark them on your map, and then check and make any needed corrections.

7. Now study the locations of Mount Baden, Camlann, Sussex, Anderida, Cambrai, Soissons, Reims, Paris, Orleans, Tours, Vouille, Toulouse, Rome, and Carthage. When you are familiar with them, close the book. Using your regular pencil, mark the location of each on your map. Then check your map against the original. If the city or the labels are more than ¼ inch off, erase and remark while looking at the original.

Chapter Twenty-Six

Invasion and Eruption

The student may use her text when answering the questions in sections I and II.

Section I: Who, What, Where

Write a one or two-sentence answer explaining the significance of each item listed below.

Aryabhata—**Pg. 182, ¶ 5 to Pg. 183, ¶ 1—Aryabhata was an Indian astronomer who had his home in the Gupta domain. By 499 he had calculated the value of pi, the exact length of the solar year, and suggested that perhaps the earth was a sphere that moved around the sun while rotating on its axis.**

Bhanugupta—**Pg. 180, ¶ 3—Bhanugupta, a man with royal blood that governed the area that included the city of Eran, mounted a great defense with his general Goparaja against the Hephthalites. The defense was fruitless; Goparaja died in the fighting, Bhanugupta disappeared from historical record and Eran was taken by the Hephthalite Toramana.**

Note to parent: Though each ID usually pertains to only one person or place, the text only mentions Goparaja briefly, and in conjunction with Bhanugupta. The student does not have to include Bhanugupta in her answer—for example: ***Bhanugupta, a man with royal blood that governed the area that included the city of Eran, mounted a great defense against the Hephthalites. The defense was fruitless; Bhanugupta disappeared from historical record and Eran was taken by the Hephthalite Toramana.***

King Candrawarman—**Pg. 183, ¶ 2 and Pg. 185, ¶ 6—King Candrawarman was the ruler of the kingdom of Tarumanagara, which was located on the northern end of Java. King Candrawarman was killed when Krakatoa exploded.**

Mihirakula—**Pg. 181, ¶ 3 and Pg. 182, ¶ 3—Mihirakula, son of Toramana, succeeded his father as king of India sometime between 515 and 520. Mihirakula tried to drive Buddhism out of India, but his cruel ways turned his people against him and in 528 he was driven into the northern reaches of the Punjab by the governor of Malwa, never able to return to the northern Indian lands he once ruled.**

Narasimha—**Pg. 180, ¶ 1 & 3—Narasimha, Budhagupta's brother, most likely took the Gupta throne after his brother's death in 497. Narasimha's fate is unknown following the taking of Eran by the Hephthalite Toramana.**

Toramana—**Pg. 180, ¶ 2–4 and Pg. 181, ¶ 2 & 3—Toramana, a Hephthalite warleader who conquered his way into northern India, took the city of Eran in 510 and declared himself king. Though Toramana's empire stretched from the eastern borders of Persia down across the mountains into India, he wasn't too concerned with defining his empire; he focused on building up his beautiful capital city of Sakala.**

Suryawarman—**Pg. 185, ¶ 2—Suryawarman succeeded King Candrawarman as leader of Tarumanagara after the explosion of Krakatoa. Despite moving the capital of his kingdom farther east, away from the site of the catastrophe, the once-thriving culture did not survive; all that is left now are a few inscriptions and the foundations of destroyed temples to the gods of Hinduism and the Buddha.**

Section II: **Comprehension**

Write a two or three-sentence answer to each of the following questions.

1. What happened to Chandragupta II's empire in the time since his passing to the reign of Narasimha?

A1.—Pg. 180, ¶ 1–3—After Chandragupta II's reign, his empire shrunk drastically. Tributaries had wandered away, minor kings had asserted their independence, and Hephthalites were pouring into the north of India. The Hephthalite Toramana conquered his way into India and in 510 attacked Eran, took the city for his own, forced Gupta power all the way back into its eastern cradle, and declared himself king.

2. How does *The Questions of King Milinda* describe Toramana's capital city of Sakala?

A2.—Pg. 180, ¶ 4 to Pg. 181, ¶ 1—*The Questions of King Milinda* says that Sakala was a great center of trade, full of gold, silver, copper and stone ware, with storehouses of corn and things of value like food, drinks, syrups and sweetmeats. The city was full of parks, gardens, groves, lakes and tanks, with rivers mountains and woods, and it was peaceful: all enemies and adversaries had been put down and the city was defended by strong towers, ramparts, superb gates and archways. Within the streets, squares, crossroads and marketplaces was the royal citadel, white walled and protected by a deep moat.

3. Despite Toramana's taste for the finer things in life, as evidenced by the upkeep of Sakala, what aspects of his empire still had nomadic qualities?

A3.—Pg. 181, ¶ 2—In parts of Toramana's kingdom, not in Sakala of course, Hephthalites overran vast tracts of land where they took tribute without establishing any definite terms with those they conquered. The Hephthalites did not attempt to enforce laws or have a tight

administration. Toramana's court accepted tribute from forty countries, but the payment of goods and money was the only hold Toramana had over the peoples on its edge.

4. Why did Mihirakula want to get rid of Buddhism in India?

A4.—Pg. 181, ¶ 4 & 5—Mihirakula, like his nomadic ancestors, was uncouth, rough, and hostile to Buddhism. The Hephthalites as a whole had been converted to Manichean and Nestorian Christianity that had filtered through Persia. Hoping to strengthen the borders of his kingdom, Mihirakula decided to rid Buddhism from his empire, firming up his religion and his territory. Mihirakula most likely also felt hostile toward Buddhism because it was the religion of the Guptas, the only threat left in India to Mihirakula's empire.

5. What is the difference between Manichaean, Chalcedonian and Nestorian Christianity?

A5.—Pg. 181, *—Manichean Christians saw good and evil as equally opposed. Chalcedonian Christians saw God as only good, and saw evil as ultimately subordinate to God. Nestorian Christians believed that Christ had two separate natures, human and divine, while Chalcedonian Christianity argued that the two natures were distinct but mystically combined into one in Jesus, who was thus both God and Man indivisibly. Manichaean and Nestorian Christianity tended toward dualism in Christ, while Chalcedonian Christianity tended towards unity.

6. How did Hinduism prosper under Mihirakula's rule?

A6.—Pg. 181, ¶ 5—Mihirakula only saw Buddhism as a threat, and so Hindu brahmans were able to gain power in Mihirakula's empire. They accepted grants of land from the king, and that made the Hindus more powerful than their Buddhist countrymen.

7. What land did the Guptas rule over during the reign of Mihirakula? Why was Mihirakula threated by a group with such a small domain?

A7.—Pg. 182, ¶ 1—When Mihirakula was king, the Gupta domain shrunk to the area of Magadha, in the Ganges valley. Though the Guptas were small, they were still the most powerful opponent to Mihirakula on the Indian frontier. Mihirakula was also threatened by their religion because he was against Buddhism.

8. Though Mihirakula was not targeting Hinduism in his religious battles, why were the Hindu Indians in his empire angered by Mihirakula's "high-handed" ways? How did his prosecution of Buddhism ultimately drive Mihirakula to control a diminished kingdom?

A8.—Pg. 182, ¶ 2 & 3—Though Mihirakula was not targeting Hinduism, the Indians he ruled were primarily Hindu and they had prized Buddhist teachings until Mihirakula came to power and began to destroy Buddhist temples, monasteries and books. Local rulers that were sick of Mihirakula's ways joined the Guptas in their fight against the king, and in 528 the governor of Malwa won a great battle against Mihirakula. Mihirakula was driven back up into the northern reaches of the Punjab where he lived for another fifteen years in his diminished kingdom, never able to return to the northern Indian lands he had once ruled.

9. What happened to power in northern India after Mihirakula was banished to the north of the Punjab?

A9.—Pg. 182, ¶ 4—Though the Guptas, with the help of the governor of Malwa, were successful in driving out Mihirakula, they were not able to fill the void in power after he was banished. Monasteries and cities had been destroyed in the Hephthalite wars and trade routes had been disrupted. As a result northern India returned to its patchwork condition, filled with little states ruled by independent kings, tribes who migrated from central Asia into the lands with no king, and small communities formed by farmers and shepherds who came down over the mountains and settled in the plains.

10. Where were Sumatra and Java located in relation to the southeastern Indian coast? What cities were found on these islands, and where was Krakatoa located in relation to the two islands?

A10.—Pg. 183, ¶ 2—Sumatra and Java were two islands that were to the east of the southeastern Indian coast, across the Indian Ocean. Sumatra was a large island, and the kingdom of Kantoli was located on the southern end of the island. Java was a smaller island, and the kingdom of Tarumanagara was located on the northern end of Java, ruled by King Candrawarman. Krakatoa, a mountain and a volcano, lay in between the two islands.

11. What piece of information from *The Book of Ancient Kings* suggests that Sumatra and Java may have been a single island at one time?

A11.—Pg. 183, ¶ 3—The description of the fallout from the eruption of Krakatoa in *The Book of Ancient Kings* says, "The inhabitants were drowned and swept away with all their property . . . and after the water subsided the mountain and the surrounding land became sea and the island [had been] divided into two parts." The description suggests that before the tidal wave caused by Krakatoa swept across Sumatra and Java, the two islands were one; it was only after the water settled that the islands were divided.

Section III: Critical Thinking

The student may use her text to answer this question.

While men with appetites for land, gold and power were very dangerous in the medieval world, sometimes there was nothing more treacherous than Mother Nature. Describe the explosion of Krakatoa and the fallout that came after the volcano's eruption. In your answer, make sure to explain how the aftermath of Krakatoa's eruption affected a much wider landscape than just Sumatra and Java.

The purpose of this critical thinking question is to reinforce the immense damage natural disasters can cause. For this reason, the student may use her text when answering the question in order to relay, in detail, the devastating and far-reaching effects of Krakatoa's explosion. The description of the eruption begins on page 183, ¶ 3 and continues through page 185, ¶ 1. This will also be a good exercise in paraphrase for the student. No sentence should look exactly like the one presented in the text, but the information relayed should be similar.

EXAMPLE ANSWER:

When Krakatoa erupted in 535, it changed the medieval world. Locally, pieces of mountain were thrown through the air and landed as far as seven miles away. A plume of ash and vaporized salt water rose thirty miles high, and the land around the volcano collapsed inward, forming a whirlpool of seawater that stretched thirty miles across. A tidal wave swept across Sumatra and Java, drowning the inhabitants. The islands were destroyed, and their culture lost.

Reports from far reaching lands described the treachery of the explosion. In China, yellow dust came down from the sky like snow. In Byzantium, the sun did not shine in a clear sky for somewhere between a year and eighteen months. The ash from the explosion created a dark sky that blocked the sun's heat and light. In Ravenna, it was recorded that the weather went haywire: "a winter without storms, a spring without mildness and a summer without heat." The consequence of the strange weather was missed harvests and crop failure. The effects spread even further: for four years following the explosion, acid snow fell in Antarctica and Greenland, and tree-ring data from modern Chile, California and Siberia show stunted summer growth from the time of the explosion until 540. Krakatoa's explosion darkened the sun, which mean plague, hunger and famine across the medieval world.

Section IV: Map Exercise

1. Using a black pencil, trace the rectangular outline of the frame for Map 26.1: India and Its Southeast Trading Partners.

2. Using a black pencil, trace the coastal outline in its entirety. You do not need to include all the islands at this time, but do include Sumatra and Java. Use your black pencil to outline the visible perimeter of the Persian Empire. Also use your black pencil to draw simple peaks to represent the mountains. Repeat until the contours are familiar.

3. Using a new sheet of paper as you look at the map, trace the rectangular outline of the frame in black. Remove your tracing paper from the original. Using a regular pencil with an eraser, draw the coastline of the mainland and the islands Sumatra and Java. Draw the perimeter of the Persian Empire and the mountain peaks.

4. When you are pleased with your map, lay it over the original. Erase and redraw any lines which are more than ¼ inch off of the original.

5. Remove your map. Study carefully the locations of the Hephthalites and the Guptas. Also study the locations of Sakala, Eran, Kantoli, and Tarumanagara. Study carefully also the location of Krakatoa. When you are familiar with them, close the book. Using your regular pencil with the eraser, mark the location of each on your map. Then check your map against the original. If the city or the labels are more than ¼ inch off, erase and remark while looking at the original.

Chapter Twenty-Seven

The Americas

The student may use his text when answering the questions in sections I and II.

Section I: Who, What, Where

Write a one or two-sentence answer explaining the significance of each item listed below.

The Maya—**Pg. 186, ¶ 3—The Maya were a group of tribal peoples related by language and culture that built cities and acted in alliance. The Maya were on the peninsula that jutted out from the central American land bridge into the Gulf of Mexico.**

Monte Alban—**Pg. 187, ¶ 1—Monte Alban was the capital city of the Zapotec Kingdom. Around 600 AD, there were over twenty thousand people in the city, extending for fifteen square miles across ridges and valleys.**

Sacred Round—**Pg. 187, ¶ 3 & 4—The Sacred Round was the 260-day cycle in the calendar of the Maya and the Zapotec. The calendar, which placed great importance on birth dates and auspicious days, was based on multiples of twenty; each of the twenty days had a different name, and occurred thirteen times during the central American year, each time paired with a number from 1 through 13.**

Teotihuacan—**Pg. 187, ¶ 5 and footnote—Teotihuacan was the city at the center of a powerful kingdom on the central American land bridge, which in 500 AD was the sixth largest city in the world, with a population of over 125,000. Teotihuacan is the name given to the city by the Aztecs—the city's ancient name is unknown.**

tonalli—**Pg. 189, ¶ 3—*Tonalli,* for the people of Teotihuacan, the Maya and the Zapotec, was a force, or radiance, or animating heat that brought life. *Tonalli* would come down to a human at the time of his/her birth linking the newborn with the ancestors, and in return, humans offered blood back to the sky in completion of the cycle.**

The Zapotec—**Pg. 187, ¶ 1—The Zapotec were a collection of small tribal territories united under the leadership of Monte Alban, the strongest city among them. The Zapotec territories were in the fertile plain known as the Valley of Oaxaca.**

Section II: Comprehension

Write a two or three-sentence answer to each of the following questions.

1. What is an "El Niño" event? What are some of the consequences of an "El Niño" event?

A1.—Pg. 186, footnote—An El Niño event occurs when the surface temperature of the Pacific Ocean near the South American coast warms significantly. The change shifts weather patterns, producing violent storms and flooding in some areas of South America. El Niño can also drastically reduce the fish population in heavily fished areas, causing difficulties for peoples who rely on them for food.

2. Why don't we know anything about the Americas before 600 AD?

A2.—Pg. 186, ¶ 2 & 3—We don't know much about the Americas before 600 AD because the people of the Americas did not write down the histories of their rulers. Though there are carvings and statues from before the sixth century, and even lists of dates and rulers, there are no stories written down to help us piece together the past of the Americas.

3. How was the writing in the Americas different from the writing across the ocean in the great urban civilizations of Rome and Egypt?

A3.—Pg. 187, ¶ 2—The written records of the Maya and the Zapotec were terse. In Rome and Egypt, writing developed to track goods and payments. For the Maya and the Zapotec, writing was used to keep track of time.

4. How long did it take for the cycle of the Sacred Round to match up to the Earth's rounding of the sun? How did the Maya and the Zapotec view all the days in between the matching up of the two calendars?

A4.—Pg. 187, ¶ 4—The 260-day cycle of the Sacred Round took 18,930 days, about fifty-two years, to match up again with day 1 of the 365-day calendar. The Maya and Zapotec viewed each day of the 52-year cycle with significance; each birth, death, marriage and conquest were placed within this framework.

5. How did the Maya and the Zapotec view the passage of time?

A5.—Pg. 187, ¶ 4—The Maya and the Zapotec viewed the passage of time as sacred. Each day had a sacred meaning, and this was at the center of each kingdom's history. For the Maya and the Zapotec, time was the firstborn of creation, it was around "before the awakening of the world," so every creative act, every god, and every human came into being already slotted into the intricate patterns of the calendar.

6. How did Teotihuacan grow to be such a big city?

A6.—Pg. 187, ¶ 5 to Pg. 188, ¶ 1—Teotihuacan grew to be so big because many of its inhabitants were forced to move within the city walls in an attempt by the kings of the city to prevent any nearby villages from growing into cities that might challenge their power.

7. Describe how the construction of Teotihuacan was a matrix in which sacred time met earthly existence; how its observation of sacred time was built directly into its streets and walls.

A7.—Pg. 188, ¶ 2 to Pg. 189, ¶ 1—Teotihuacan was oriented east to west, with the western horizon at the top of the compass; its map was shaped by sunrise and sunset, the phases of the moon, and the places of the stars. The Pyramid of the Sun stood at its center facing west, a channel dug through the city's center diverted water into an east-west flow and the city's major thoroughfare, the Avenue of the Dead, ran through the city from north to south, with the Pyramid of the Moon on the northern end. At the southern end of the Avenue of the Dead lay the Pyramid of the Feathered Serpent, built in honor of the god who protected mankind.

8. Explain how Quetzalcoatl restored life to humanity after all men and women had been destroyed in a battle between rival gods.

A8.—Pg. 189, ¶ 2—After all humanity had been destroyed, Quetzalcoatl went down into the Land of the Dead, ruled by the Bone Lord Mictlantecuhtli, and retrieved the bones of a man and a woman. Quetzalcoatl then slashed his own penis, dripped blood over the bones, and restored them to life.

9. What the did the cycle of droughts and storms that began in the 530s mean to the Teotihuacans? Why was the cycle so devastating for the city?

A9.—Pg. 190, ¶ 6 to Pg. 191, ¶ 1—The gods of the people of Teotihuacan were also gods of the elements, and if the elements were acting up it meant that the gods were angry with the people of Teotihuacan or they had given up on the city. Because of the vicious weather people were dying; by 540, people in Teotihuacan were dying of malnutrition and the death rate for people younger than twenty-five doubled.

10. What was the cause for the massive riot that broke out in Teotihuacan around 600? What damage was caused by the riot?

A10.—Pg. 191, ¶ 1—The bad weather that caused malnutrition and death in the people of Teotihuacan was the cause of the huge riot that broke out in the city. Majestic temples and royal residences were vandalized and burned; staircases leading up to the tops of the temples, where priests and kings met the gods, were broken apart; statues were smashed, reliefs and carvings slashed and damaged. Rulers, aristocrats and priests, the elite of the city that were connected to the gods but could not convince the gods to keep the city safe, were murdered—excavations reveal skeletons, skulls smashed and bones broken, lying in corridors and rooms of the royal palaces.

11. Why were the people of Teotihuacan ready to revolt against their rulers, in addition to fear and rage over deaths caused by the bad weather cycle?

A11.—Pg. 191, ¶ 3—The people of Teotihuacan were ready to revolt against their rulers because so many of them were forced to live in the city instead of the villages they once inhabited. Because the population of Teotihuacan was concentrated into a single urban area, they were particularly vulnerable to famine and disease when food sources faltered because of the erratic weather patterns. They had been living under an autocratic and heavy-handed government and when the famine struck, they were ready to revolt.

12. What happened to the population of Monte Alban between 550 and 650?

A12.—Pg. 191, ¶ 3 & 4—Between 550 and 650, the population of Monte Alban began to spread out from the city into the surrounding countryside. Reliefs in the remains of ceremonial buildings at Monte Alban show conquered tribal chiefs paraded naked and mutilated by Zapotec captors, telling us that the Zapotec rulers were not mild, nor gentle. When famine hit Monte Alban, the people moved away from the city, finding a way to survive outside the kingdom where their rulers were clearly not favored by the gods.

13. Who was Sky Witness, and Lord Water? Why is Cancuen important, and what is the significance of Chichen Itza? Why do all of these things mean little when considering 6th century Mayan history?

A13.—Pg. 191, ¶ 5 to Pg. 192, ¶ 2—Sky Witness was a Mayan king that ruled for ten years over the fifty thousand residents of Calakmul; Lord Water was the king of Caracol that defeated his neighbor, the king of Tikal, and offered him as a sacrifice around 562; Cancuen is important because of the enormous size of its royal palace; Chichen Itza is significant because it had one of the most elaborate ball courts of any Mayan city. All of these names and places mean little when considering Mayan history in the 6th century because most of the Mayan records break off at 534 and don't resurface for about a century.

Section III: Critical Thinking

The student may not use his text to answer this question.

The Sacred Round of the Maya and the Zapotec and the cycles of their calendar placed each day in the context of the past: a king in central America always ruled in the footprints of the king who had come before him in the previous cycle. As we read on page 190, ¶ 2, "each of the milestones of his rule—birth, marriage, coronation, conquest, death—occupied a particular slot on [the] elaborate calendar." Most importantly, each day according to the Sacred Round was a site of both past and present events. Write a paragraph explaining how the past and present affected the way the Maya and the Zapotec worshipped. In your answer, explain why the corners of the Pyramid of the Feathered Serpent were filled with sacrificial victims, and why a new king would cut himself on top of a pyramid at the beginning of his rule.

The creation myth of the people of central America revolved around Quetzalcoatl, whose greatest deed was to restore life to humanity after all men and women had been destroyed in a battle between rival gods. Quetzalcoatl went down into the Land of the Dead, ruled by the Bone Lord Mictlantecuhtli, and retrieved the bones of a man and a woman. He then slashed his own penis, dripped blood over the bones, and restored them to life.

For the central Americans, life came from death, as we see in the story of the retrieval of the dead bones that were brought back to life by Quetzalcoatl. The pyramid erected to worship Quetzalcoatl was called the Pyramid of the Feathered Serpent. Because the pyramid symbolized the beginning of life for the central Americans, it was also tied to death. At the corners of the Pyramid of the Feathered Serpent were mass graves filled with sacrificial victims, replicating the Land of the Dead, the place where life ended and also life began.

The central Americans believed bloodshed generated life, just as Quetzalcoatl shed blood to bring the bones he brought up from the Land of the Dead back to life. When a king cuts himself on top of a pyramid he sheds his blood as Quetzalcoatl did, acting alongside the god as his representative or perhaps his incarnation. Like the Sacred Round, the action of bloodletting was both a site of past and present events, an eternal circle worshipped by the central Americans.

EXAMPLE ANSWER:

For the people of central America, past and present affected the way they worshipped because their creation myth revolved around resurrection. Quetzalcoatl went down into the Land of the Dead, ruled by the Bone Lord Mictlantecuhtli, and retrieved the bones of a man and a woman. He then slashed his own penis, dripped blood over the bones, and restored them to life. Life came from death, meaning the present came from the past.

The intricate relationship between life and death is echoed in the foundations of the Pyramid of the Feathered Serpent. At the corners of the Pyramid of the Feathered Serpent were mass graves filled with sacrificial victims, replicating the Land of the Dead, the place where life ended and also life began. The importance of death in order to bring life is also seen when a new king cuts himself on top of a pyramid. There, he sheds his blood as Quetzalcoatl did, acting alongside the god as his representative or perhaps his incarnation. Like the Sacred Round, the action of bloodletting was both a site of past and present events, an eternal circle worshipped by the central Americans.

Chapter Twenty-Eight

Great and Holy Majesty

The student may use her text when answering the questions in sections I and II.

Section I: Who, What, Where

Write a one or two-sentence answer explaining the significance of each item listed below.

April 1, 527—**Pg. 199, ¶ 6 to Pg. 200, ¶ 1—April 1, 527 was the date of Justinian's coronation as co-emperor of Byzantium.**

Caleb—**Pg. 195, ¶ 4, Pg. 196, ¶ 3 & 4—Caleb, the Christian king of Axum, launched periodic raids towards Himyar, and when word of the massacre of the Christians at Najran got out, Caleb's army, backed by Justin and Justinian, attacked Dhu Nuwas and defeated him.**

Code of 529—**Pg. 200, ¶ 3 and Pg. 201, ¶ 3—The Code of 529 was the result of a committee appointed by Justinian in 528 to rewrite the unwieldy and often contradictory mass of laws passed by eastern emperors over several centuries into a single coherent code. The Code turned Justinian's word into law, and it did away with any competitors for authority: the Code of 529 forbade any adherents to the old Greek and Roman religions to teach in public.**

Dhu Nuwas—**Pg. 195, ¶ 2 & 3 and Pg. 196, ¶ 3 & 5—Dhu Nuwas, king of Himyar, converted to Judaism and declared Himyar to be a Jewish kingdom. The effort to preserve his kingdom backfired, and after word of his slaughter of Christians in Himyar and Najran got out to the Byzantine emperor, Dhu Nuwas was killed by the Byzantine-backed Caleb and his Axum army.**

Ghassanids—**Pg. 193, ¶ 5 to Pg. 195, ¶ 1—The Ghassanids, originally nomadic tribes from southern Arabia, were a people who settled as farmers just south of Syria where they converted to Christianity and in 502 had agreed to become *foederati* of Byzantium.**

Himyar—**Pg. 193, ¶ 2—Himyar was an Arabian kingdom that lay just on the other side of the Red Sea from Axum that had existed in southern Arabia for six hundred years. It expanded**

slowly until it controlled not only its ancient territory on the southwest corner of Arabia but also the central Arabian tribes known as Kindites.

Lakhmids—**Pg. 195, ¶ 2—The Lakhmids were Arab tribes who lived on the southern side of the Euphrates that served as the Persian arm into Arabia, and that dominated the tribes near them with the help of Persian cash and weapons.**

Macedonia—**Pg. 199, ¶ 2 & 3—Macedonia, a friend of Theodora's living in Antioch, was a former prostitute that found a new way to survive by acting as one of Justinian's secret police. Macedonia introduced Justinian to Theodora.**

Mecca—**Pg. 195, ¶ 1—Mecca was an Arabian city halfway between Himyar and the Mediterranean Sea that was home to the greatest shrine to traditional Arabian deities. The shrine was called Ka'aba and it housed the Black Stone, a sacred rock oriented towards the east that tribes came from the interior to worship; it was so sacred that war was banned for twenty miles around it.**

Mundir—**Pg. 196, ¶ 2 & 3—Mundir was the king of the Lakhmids. Dhu Nuwas tried to get Mundir to convert his people to Judaism in an effort to form an alliance of Arabic Jews who could unite against the Christians and drive Byzantine power entirely from the Arabian peninsula.**

Najran—**Pg. 195, ¶ 5—Najran was an oasis city at the intersection of caravan routes from Syria and Persia, and it was home to wealthy aristocrats that Dhu Nuwas targeted as enemies of his Judaic state. Between 518 and 520, Dhu Nuwas massacred the Christians of Najran.**

Theodora—**Pg. 197, ¶ 5 and Pg. 199, ¶ 4 to Pg. 200, ¶ 1—Theodora, a former actress and prostitute, as well as a monophysite, was Justinian's love. After the law that barred consuls from marrying actresses was repealed, Theodora became Justinian's wife, and empress of his kingdom.**

Section II: Comprehension

Write a two or three-sentence answer to each of the following questions.

1. Why were the people of Himyar, Axum and the Bedouins alike? Why were they different?

A1.—Pg. 193, ¶ 3 & 4 and Pg. 195, ¶ 1—The people of Himyar, Axum and the Bedouins were alike because their descendants migrated for centuries across the narrow strait between Africa and Arabia and had produced African-Arabian kingdoms on both sides of the water. The Bedouins descended from more-or-less the same tribal ancestors of the people of Himyar, though the nomadic peoples lived in competition with the people in cities for resources. The people differed in their choice of religion: while the people, in general, of the Arabian peninsula still followed traditional Arab ways and were loyal to the traditional

deities, the people of Axum were Christian, practicing for two hundred years since Ezana had converted, forged a friendship with Constantine, and made Axum an ally of Rome.

2. What threats did Dhu Nuwas see facing his kingdom? What action did Dhu Nuwas take in an effort to get ahead of these threats?

A2.—Pg. 195, ¶ 2 & 3—Dhu Nuwas saw Persia and Byzantium as great threats: the Persians loomed in the distance with the Lakhmids as their henchmen, dominating tribes near to them with Persian cash and weapons; to the northwest was Byzantium, which had ambitions to spread into Arabia with the help of its two allied kings, the rulers of the Axumites across the Red Sea and the Ghassanids south of Syria. Dhu Nuwas could not rely on the Kindites to buffer his kingdom from these threats, so he decided to convert to Judaism and declared Himyar to be a Jewish kingdom in an effort to get ahead of the threats in the north.

3. How did Dhu Nuwas think Judaism would help him to get ahead of Persia and Byzantium?

A3.—Pg. 195, ¶ 4—Dhu Nuwas wanted to distance himself from Byzantium and its Christian allies, and converting to Judaism was a good way to do so. He did not want to alienate his kingdom from Persia completely, and since the Persian king, Kavadh I, was kindly disposed towards Jews, Dhu Nuwas thought converting to Judaism would win him some grace from the Persians.

4. Who did Dhu Nuwas target as enemies of his state after his conversion to Judaism?

A4.—Pg. 195, ¶ 5—As a Jewish monarch, Dhu Nuwas pronounced the Byzantine and Axumite Christians in his kingdom to be his enemies. He also attacked aristocratic Himyarites because where Christianity did spread into Himyar, it had done so in the upper classes. Dhu Nuwas purged these Christians from his nation.

5. What was the source of hostility between the Persians and the people of Byzantium that came about when Justin became emperor?

A5.—Pg. 196, ¶ 1—When Anastasius was emperor of Byzantium, he paid a large yearly tribute to the Persian king Kavadh I, which kept the peace between the two empires. When Justin succeeded Anastasius as emperor, he decided not to renew the yearly payments. This angered Kavadh I, and in retaliation he sent an army of Lakhmid mercenaries to attack the Byzantine borders.

6. When the Lakhmids were negotiating with the Byzantine ambassador, a letter arrived describing the massacre in Himyar: what did it say? What did King Dhu Nuwas want from King Mundir?

A6.—Pg. 196, ¶ 2 & 3—The letter that arrived for King Mundir from King Dhu Nuwas told the tribal king that the Christians of Najran were dead. Dhu Nuwas had sent Jewish priests to the Christian churches in Najran bearing promises that if the Christians would surrender peacefully, he would send them all across the Red Sea to Caleb of Axum. Though he swore to keep them safe, when they surrendered, Dhu Nuwas ordered them slaughtered. The letter asked King Mundir to convert to Judaism, forming an alliance of Arabic Jews who could

unite against the Christians and drive Byzantine power entirely from the peninsula, for the weight of 3,000 dinari.

7. What happened to the Himyarite kingdom after Dhu Nuwas's massacre of the Christians of Najran?

A7.—Pg. 196, ¶ 5 to Pg. 197, ¶ 1—After Dhu Nuwas's massacre of the Christians of Najran, word got back to Justin and Justinian, who sent troops to back Caleb of Axum's army in their battles against the Himyarites. Caleb met Dhu Nuwas in battle and defeated him. Then Caleb of Axum installed a Christian lieutenant of his own as governor, folding the territory into his own, meaning the end of the Himyarite kingdom.

8. Explain the rumor that still lives on, started by the letter that Dhu Nuwas sent to King Mundir.

A8.—Pg. 196, ¶ 3 and Pg. 197, ¶ 2 & 3—Dhu Nuwas sent a letter to King Mundir that explained he was able to massacre the Christians of Najran by swearing an oath that he would not kill them if they surrendered peacefully; it is said that he swore his oath to the Christians on the Ark, or perhaps the Ark of the Covenant. The kingdom of Himyar had long ago spread across the old territory once governed by the Sabeans, whose queen had journeyed north to see the great Israelite king Solomon in his capital of Jerusalem, and it is possible that the Ark of the Covenant, lost long ago, had in fact been taken down into Sabea by descendants of the queen. Dhu Nuwas's oath on it meant that he had he Ark in his possession, and perhaps Caleb, plundering the capital city of Himyar after his victory, took the Ark back across the Red Sea into Axum. It is still rumored to rest there, in the Church of Our Lady Mary of Zion, in the ancient capital of the Axumites.

9. Why did Kavadh lose his Arab mercenaries after the fall of Himyar?

A9.—Pg. 197, ¶ 4—After the fall of Himyar, the Kindites were free from Himyarite dominance. They started a fight with the Lakhmids, which preoccupied the Lakhmid king Mundir for the next few years with the defense of his own people. If Mundir was defending his own people, he could not lend out is army to help the Persians.

10. How did Theodora end up working as an actress, and then end up in the company of an informant for Justinian's secret police?

A10.—Pg. 197, ¶ 5 & 7, Pg. 198, ¶ 1 and Pg. 199, ¶ 3—Theodora's father, a bear-trainer who worked in the half-time shows given by the Greens between chariot races, died of illness which left his wife to raise three small girls under the age of seven. In order to survive, the mother forced the girls to appear before the Blues as entertainers, which then led to prostitution, and by the time Theodora reached puberty she had already been in a brothel for years. When Theodora converted to Christianity, she had to give up her livelihood, so she went to stay with her friend Macedonia who happened to be an agent of the imperial secret police.

11. Why was Alexandria a welcome haven for those who found themselves out of step with the Chalcedonian Christianity of Constantinople and Rome? Why was it so important to the Christians in Alexandria that Jesus and God be seen as one person?

A11.—Pg. 198, ¶ 3 to Pg. 199, ¶ 1—The bishop of Alexandria was on the bottom of the holy ladder: he was placed below both the pope in Rome and the patriarch in Constantinople. Resentment over this ordering of church authority made Alexandria a welcome haven for Christians who found themselves out of step with the Chalcedonian Christianity of Constantinople and Rome because these Christians believed the Chalcedonian Creed had not gone far enough in condemning Nestorianism. Alexandrian Christians wanted no hint of two-ness in their theology because they wanted to be as distanced as possible from the pantheon of Persian deities; they did not want to practice any religion that resembled that of their enemies.

12. What obstacles did Theodora and Justinian have to overcome before they could be married?

A12.—Pg. 199, ¶ 4 & 5—Theodora and Justinian could not be married right away because there was a law that was passed by Constantine two hundred years earlier, meant to guard to morals of his officials, that said a consul could not marry an actress. Also, Justin's wife Euphemia announced that she would never approve the marriage between Theodora and Justinian because Theodora was a monophysite. Justin and Theodora had to wait for Euphemia to die before they could convince Justinian to pass a law revoking Constantine's ban—he agreed and as soon as it was done Justinian and Theodora were married at the Church of the Holy Wisdom in Constantinople.

13. What caused the shutdown of the academy at Athens? Where did the faculty go?

A13.—Pg. 201, ¶ 3—The academy at Athens was shut down by Justinian and the Code of 529, which forbade any adherents of the old Greek and Roman religions to teach in public. The faculty emigrated to Persia, with the intention of never returning to Byzantium.

Section III: Critical Thinking

The student may not use her text to answer this question.

Justinian's marriage to a former prostitute was not the only wild thing we read about concerning Constantinople's past in this chapter. Knowing Roman history and the inability of emperors to use the force of Christ to keep their empires together, it is just as wild that Justinian was able to make his word valid as secular *and* sacred law. Write a paragraph that explains how Justinian was able to make himself the arbiter of laws both secular and sacred.

Justinian took his duties as God's representative on earth as seriously as he did the protection of the borders of his empire. On page 528 we read about the committee Justinian gathered to collect and rewrite the old laws passed by eastern emperors over several centuries into a coherent code. The code was completed in 529, and Justinian added to the code: "What is greater or holier than the imperial majesty? . . . The emperors will rightly be considered as the sole maker and interpreter of laws." Using the language "greater and holier" allowed Justinian to claim the legitimacy of Roman custom as well as the legitimacy of Christian authority; "he was both the heir of Augustus Caesar and the representative of Christ on earth. His code regulated taxes, oaths, land ownership, and matters of belief." In fact, the first regulation in the first book of code was an acknowledgement from Justinian himself: "We acknowledge the only begotten Son of God, God of God, born of the Father, before the world and without time, coeternal with the Father, the Maker of all things." By aligning the ancient Roman power of imperium with one and only God, one and only Word, and one and only Son, the eastern emperor became the one and only man with the final authority to speak for both God and eastern Romans on earth.

EXAMPLE ANSWER:

Justinian took his duties as God's representative on earth as seriously as he did the protection of the borders of his empire. A single, coherent law was very important to Justinian, so in 528 he put together a committee to collect and rewrite the old laws passed by eastern emperors over several centuries into one law. The code was completed in 529, and Justinian made sure to add into the code that there was nothing greater or holier than imperial majesty, and only the emperor could make and interpret law. The greatness Justinian referred to was the legitimacy of Roman custom, and the holiness that he referred to was the legitimacy of Christian authority. His law reached taxes and landownership as well as matters of belief. Justinian also made sure the first regulation in the first book of code was an acknowledgement from the emperor himself of the only begotten Son of God, the God of God, Maker of all things. By aligning the ancient Roman power of imperium with one and only God, one and only Word, and one and only Son, the eastern emperor became the one and only man with the final authority to speak for both God and eastern Romans on earth.

Section IV: Map Exercise

1. Using a black pencil, trace the rectangular outline of the frame for Map 28.1: Arab Tribes and Kingdoms.

2. Using a blue pencil, trace the coastal outlines of the Mediterranean Sea, the Black Sea, the Red Sea, the Caspian Sea, and the Arabian Sea, including the Persian Gulf. You do not need to include islands at this time. With your blue pencil, trace the line of the Nile down from Alexandria parallel to the Red Sea. Use your blue pencil also to trace the line of the Oxus River. Use small peaks to represent the mountains. Repeat until the contours are familiar.

3. Using a new sheet of paper, trace the rectangular outline of the frame in black. Remove your tracing paper from the original. Using a regular pencil with an eraser as you look at the map, draw the coastlines of the Mediterranean, the Black Sea, the Red Sea, the Caspian Sea, and the Arabian Sea, including the Persian Gulf. Remember to use the distance from the rectangular frame as a

guide. Draw the line of the Nile and the line of the Oxus. Draw the mountains with small peaks. Erase and redraw as necessary. When you are done, label each body of water.

4. When you are pleased with your map, lay it over the original. Erase and redraw any lines which are more than ¼ inch off of the original.

5. Remove your map. Study carefully the locations of Byzantium, Arabia, Axum, Himyar, the Kindites, Syria, the Ghassanids, the Lakhmids, the Persian Empire, Khorasan, Bactria, and Kashmir. When you are familiar with them, close the book. Using your regular pencil, label Byzantium, Arabia, Axum, Himyar, Kindites, Syria, the Ghassanids, the Lakhmids, the Persian Empire, Khorasan, Bactria, and Kashmir. Check your map against the original. Correct any misplaced labels.

6. Now study closely the locations of Athens, Constantinople, Alexandria, Halikarnassos, Chalcedon, Edessa, Antioch, Amida, Mecca, Najran, Balkh, Sakala, and Eran. When you are familiar with them, close the book. Using your regular pencil, label each location. Check your map against the original, and correct any misplaced labels.

Chapter Twenty-Nine

Pestilence

The student may use his text when answering the questions in sections I and II.

Section I: Who, What, Where

Write a one or two-sentence answer explaining the significance of each item listed below.

al-Mada'in—**Pg. 210, ¶ 4—al-Mada'in was the territory where a Persian city was built as an exact street-by-street replica of the sacked city of Antioch, and where Khosru settled Byzantine prisoners. Persians called the city al-Rumiyyah, or "Town of the Greeks," but Khosru called it "Built Better than Antioch."**

Anthemius of Tralles—**Pg. 206, ¶ 2 and footnote—Anthemius of Tralles, Justinian's master-builder and mathematician of note, led the large building program instituted by Justinian after the destruction of the "Nika" revolt. Anthemius of Tralles built enormous glittering edifices on top of the ruins of the revolt, and he built the Church of the Holy Wisdom, the Hagia Sophia, which became the jewel of the restored city.**

Belisarius—**Pg. 204, ¶ 6, Pg. 207, ¶ 5 and Pg. 208, ¶ 4—Belisarius, Justinian's chief general, helped Justinian put down the 532 "Nika" rebellion. After the rebellion, Belisarius won back Carthage as well as, for a short while, all of Italy for Byzantium.**

Gelimer—**Pg. 206, ¶ 4 and Pg. 207, ¶ 2—Gelimer, the Vandal king ruling Carthage and distant relation to the kingdom's founder Geiseric, fled from his palace in Carthage as Belisarius approached in 533. After the city was occupied by Belisarius, Gelimer attacked his own city in an attempt to keep his throne, but his forces were wiped out, and the Vandal nation was destroyed.**

Hagia Sophia—**Pg. 206, ¶ 2—The Hagia Sophia, or the Church of the Holy Wisdom, built by Anthemius of Tralles, had a dome described by Procopius as both marvelous and terrifying "for it seems somehow to float in the air on no firm basis, but to be poised aloft to the peril of those inside it." The ceiling was overlaid with gold inset with stones, which added**

streaks of colored light to the shining yellow surface, the inner sanctuary was lined with forty thousand pounds of silver, and the church was filled with relics and treasures that Procopius described as being like "a meadow with its flowers in full bloom."

Hypatius—**Pg. 204, ¶ 4 and Pg. 205, ¶ 2—Hypatius, the nephew of the dead emperor Anastasius, was forced by the rioters of Constantinople to be their new ruler: he was dragged out of his house against his will, declared emperor and then placed on a throne in the Hippodrome. Hypatius was captured and assassinated the day after Belisarius put down the rebellion in the Hippodrome.**

Khosru—**Pg. 203, ¶ 2 and Pg. 213, ¶ 2—Khosru, Kavadh's third-eldest son, became king of Persia after his father's death. Khosru wanted to end the Eternal Peace with Byzantium and attacked Justinian's territory frequently, but after the plague hit Constantinople and his army was defeated at Edessa, Khosru agreed to a five-year treaty with Justinian.**

Theodahad—**Pg. 208, ¶ 1 and Pg. 208, ¶ 3—Theodahad became the Ostrogoth ruler after the young Athalaric drunk himself to death. After Belisarius defeated Sicily and Naples, Theodahad was dethroned and killed by the warrior Witigis.**

Totila—**Pg. 210, ¶ 1—Totila, an Ostrogoth soldier, was elected king by the Ostrogoths after Belisarius took Witigis prisoner and returned to Constantinople.**

Witigis—**Pg. 208, ¶ 3 & 4 and Pg. 210, 1—Witigis, an Ostrogothic warrior, dethroned and killed Theodahad after Belisarius took Sicily and Naples for Justinian and then claimed the Ostrogoth throne for himself. Witigis was captured by Belisarius in 540 and he eventually died in captivity after he was transported back to Constantinople.**

Section II: Comprehension

Write a two or three-sentence answer to each of the following questions.

1. What deal was made between the Persian and Byzantine emperors in 532? What was it called, and how long did it last?

A1.—Pg. 203, ¶ 1—In 532, the Persian and Byzantine emperors swore a truce with each other. The deal was called the Eternal Peace, and it lasted for eight years.

2. Why was it risky for Justinian to rely on the loyalty of the Blues in regards to the taxes he imposed for great building projects in Constantinople and reclamation of land lost in the west?

A2.—Pg. 203, ¶ 4 to Pg. 204, ¶ 1—It was risky for Justinian to rely on the loyalty of the Blues to support the imposition of more taxes because the factions were unstable, ambitious and inclined to pick fights whenever possible. Because faction support was irrational, the Blues could one day say they supported Justinian and then next be turned against him.

3. How did the Blues and Greens come to riot together against the government of Constantinople in 532?

A3.—Pg. 204, ¶ 2—In 532, two criminals, one Blue and one Green, were condemned to the gallows but twice in a row the ropes failed to function properly; the criminals did not die by hanging, each time they hit the ground alive. The ineptitude of the hangman infuriated the crowds and both Blues and Greens rioted together against the government of Constantinople.

4. Describe the rioting by the factionists in Constantinople in 532.

A4.—Pg. 204, ¶ 3—The rioting by the factionists in Constantinople in 532 was wild: city employees were indiscriminately slaughtered and the Church of the Holy Wisdom, part of the palace complex, the marketplace, and dozens of houses were set on fire. The rioters demanded that Justinian turn over two unpopular city officials so that the rioters could carry out their own executions. The rioters stormed through the streets shouting "*Nika!*"—"Victory!"—when the officials did not appear.

5. Why didn't Justinian flee Constantinople during the rebellion, even though he wanted to?

A5.—Pg. 204, ¶ 5—Justinian did not flee Constantinople during the rebellion, even though he wanted to, because his wife Theodora stopped him. She told him, "For one who has been an emperor, it is unendurable to be a fugitive . . . If you wish to save yourself, there is no difficulty. There is the sea, here are the boats. But consider: after you have been saved you may wish that you could exchange that safety for death. For myself, I accept the ancient saying that royalty is a good burial shroud." The speech persuaded Justinian to stay put in Constantinople.

6. How did Justinian and Belisarius put down the rebellion of 532, also known as the "Nika" revolt?

A6.—Pg. 205, ¶ 1 & 2—After Belisarius and the commander of the Illyricum army summoned reinforcement troops from nearby cities, Justinian sent one of his secretaries, posing as a traitor, into the Hippodrome to pass news to the leaders of the rebellion that Justinian had fled, while another official paid out bribes which produced disagreement between the Greens and the Blues. When the reinforcements arrived, Belisarius assembled his men at the small door right next to the throne where Hypatius sat, while the Illyricum commander went around to the entrance known as the Gate of Death. When the soldiers barged into the crowd, a panic erupted and Belisarius and his colleague mopped up the rebellion.

7. What were the circumstances of Justinian's reclamation of Carthage?

A7.—Pg. 206, ¶ 4 to Pg. 207, ¶ 2—Belisarius, the head of Justinian's campaign to retake Carthage, set sail from Constantinople with five thousand cavalry and ten thousand foot-soldiers. When Belisarius arrived at the coast of North Africa, half of the Vandal army was away from the city and the Vandal king Gelimer had fled the city with his bodyguard. As Justinian's men approached the city, the Carthaginians opened the gates and peacefully let Belisarius and his men occupy the city.

8. Describe how Belisarius was able to reclaim Italy, even if only for a moment, for Justinian?

A8.—Pg. 208, ¶ 2–4—In late 535, Belisarius conquered Sicily without difficulty, and then he moved on to the shores of Italy and captured Naples. From Naples, Belisarius advanced and in December of 536 he captured Rome itself. Belisarius fought for another four years, advancing towards Ravenna and finally, in 540, he captured the Ostrogoth king Witigis and Belisarius declared himself master of Italy.

9. What provisions did Justinian take to ensure that Italy would be reabsorbed into the Byzantine empire, rather than, say, being taken by Belisarius or by other wandering peoples?

A9.—Pg. 208, ¶ 5—To stop Belisarius from announcing himself king of Italy, Justinian ordered Belisarius to return to Constantinople. A skeleton force was left in Italy to assert Byzantine control. To protect the Byzantine garrisons, Justinian made treaties with the Gepids, the Lombards, and the Heruls, all northern tribal confederations, convincing them to settle along the Italian border northeast of the mountains and act as buffers, should any other wandering peoples attempt to invade.

10. What happened to control of Italy once Belisarius departed for Constantinople?

A10.—Pg. 210, ¶ 1—As soon as Belisarius departed for Constantinople after taking Ravenna, the remaining Ostrogoths elected Totila as their new king, and they began to fight back against the Byzantine occupation. For the next several decades, control of Italy seesawed back and forth between Ostrogoth and Byzantine forces. Justinian's tribal allies remained along the edges of the territory with their backs to the conflict, and war raged on because no one had enough men to bring the war to a decisive end.

11. Why did Khosru march into Syria and sack the ancient city of Antioch in June of 540? How did Justinian put Khosru off from doing further damage?

A11.—Pg. 210, ¶ 2 & 3—Khosru marched into Syria and sacked the ancient city of Antioch in June of 540 because Justinian was no longer paying the yearly tribute he owed to Persia as agreed upon in the Eternal Peace. After the wars in Italy and North Africa, and the enormous building projects in Constantinople, Justinian's treasury was drained. Justinian managed to put Khosru off from doing further damage by promising the Persian king he would send the tardy tribute as soon as he was able to raise it.

12. Before the bubonic plague hit the Byzantine empire, what actions did Khosru take that anticipated the end of the Eternal Peace and the beginning of war between Persia and Byzantium?

A.12—Pg. 210, ¶ 4 to Pg. 211, ¶ 1—Anticipating the end of the Eternal Peace and the beginning of war, Khosru built walls to fortify the city of Derbent, keeper of the Caspian Gates. He refused Justinian's requests for peace to be restored after his tardy tribute was paid, and he invaded Justinian's territory again in 541, capturing the fortress of Petra and the surrounding lands and defeating Belisarius's attempt to retake the fortress of Nisibis.

13. How did Khosru plan to take Edessa in 544? How did the people of Edessa defeat Khosru and his men?

A13.—Pg. 212, ¶ 4 to Pg. 213, ¶ 2—In 544, Khosru planned a siege against Edessa carefully; his men took their time, building a huge circular mound outside the city that would overtop the wall, so that besiegers could hurl their missiles at the same height as the defenders of the city. In a counter effort, the people of Edessa dug a chamber under the mound, lit a fire in it, and to distract the enemy from the smoke caused by the fire underneath, the soldiers on the walls of the city shot burning arrows into the top of the mound, using the smoke of the smaller fires to conceal the larger one underneath. After the pile of timber and earth went up in flames, and the mound came down, the entire population of the city—women and children included—formed chains up the walls, passing heated oil for those at the top to pour onto the attackers, which caused the Persian soldiers to retreat.

14. How was peace reached between Edessa and Khosru's Persian army, and then between Khosru and Justinian?

A14.—Pg. 213, ¶ 2—After Khosru's army began to retreat from the relentless defense of Edessa by its population, an interpreter came out on the walls to offer a treaty, and it was accepted. The city paid Khosru an enormous ransom in gold, and the Persian king lifted the siege on the city. Not long afterwards Justinian and Khosru concluded a five-year treaty that brought temporary peace to both empires.

15. What is the legend of the Mandylion?

A15.—Pg. 213, ¶ 3 & 4—According to the people of Edessa, a king named Abgar had ruled the city in AD 30, and when he fell ill he sent messengers to Jerusalem to ask the prophet Jesus to heal him. Jesus had written back, promising healing by means of the letter and the disciple who carried it; when the letter arrived in Edessa, Abgar was made well. In addition to the letter, the disciple was said to have also brought a miraculous cloth with the face of Jesus divinely imprinted on it. This cloth, the Mandylion, was treasured by the people of Edessa, who believed that the city could never be conquered as long as the Mandylion was inside it.

16. How did the Mandylion supposedly save Edessa from defeat by Khosru?

A16.—Pg. 213, ¶ 4—The historian Evagrius insists that the fire the citizens of Edessa set underneath the mound built by Khosru's men only caught after the Mandylion was washed in water and the water was sprinkled on the timber. Evagrius says the fire burned so hot that Khosru was forced to recognize "his disgraceful folly in having entertained an idea of prevailing over the God whom we worship."

Section III: Critical Thinking

The student may use his text to answer this question.

As we read in Chapter Twenty-Six, the effects of Krakatoa's eruption in 535 spread far and wide, both around the medieval world and forward through time. How is Krakatoa related to the pestilence that spread across Constantinople in 542? Write a paragraph explaining their connection; then, describe the plague, its cause and its eventual end.

Looking back at chapter Twenty-Six, we find on page 183, ¶ 4 Procopius's account of extreme weather following the eruption: "Procopius reports that in 536, all the way over in the Byzantine domain, 'the sun gave forth its light without brightness, like the moon, during this whole year, and it seemed exceedingly like the sun in eclipse, for the beams it shed were not clear.'" Further, Michael the Syrian wrote, "'The sun was dark and its darkness lasted for eighteen months; each day it shone for about four hours, and still this light was only a feeble shadow. . . . [T]he fruits did not ripen and the wine tasted like sour grapes.'" We also learn on page 183 that "The ash from the explosion was spreading across the sky, blocking the sun's heat." Krakatoa caused the cold dark summers that stopped a plentiful harvest in Byzantium. On page 211, ¶ 2, the text tells us that a ship docked on the Golden Horn, carrying much-needed grain from the mouth of the Nile because "the cold dark summers of the previous years had reduced food supplies, and the population of the eastern empire was already hungrier and weaker than normal." Fleas carrying the bubonic plague were also on the ship, and soon the people of Byzantium were falling to an illness that caused sudden fever, swellings in the groin and armpit, coma and death.

A detailed description of what the plague did to the bodies of those inflected can be found on page 211, ¶ 3 to page 212, ¶ 3. When physicians first dissected the bodies of the dead in an effort to find the cause of the plague, they were baffled when they found strange abscesses filled with pus and dead tissue at the center of the swellings. They did not know how to manage these swellings, nor how to stop the disease. As the sickness spread through Constantinople there were reports of five or ten thousand dead each day. Some victims broke out with black pustules, some died vomiting blood, some had high fevers and died screaming in pain when the swellings burst. Some healthy people went on about their business and then suddenly were hit with a high fever out of nowhere and simply laid down wherever they were to die. Death was so rampant and unexpected that people would wear nametags so that their remains could be identified in the case of sudden death.

The plague was caused by the fleas on the rats that lived in the ships that transported the grain to the Golden Horn. Because of the drop in temperature caused by the ash from Krakatoa, the bacterium Yersinia pestis *was able to grow, which is the active agent of the plague. The years of poor harvests after the eruption of Krakatoa necessitated an increase in imports of food to Constantinople. Finally, because they did not have enough food, the people of Byzantium were hungry, weak and vulnerable, making them perfect hosts for the vicious sickness.*

The spread of the plague died out in 543 because there were no more uninfected hosts for it to inhabit. Stories of survivors meant that some people were infected by the disease but did not die from it, meaning they carried the disease in their bodies without peril. People who hadn't come in contact with the disease were scarce—running out of infected hosts meant the plague began to decrease.

EXAMPLE ANSWER:

Krakatoa caused the world to darken for many years after its eruption. Even when the sun would shine, its light was feeble, darkened by the ash spreading across the sky. The sun's heat could not reach the earth, and so for years harvests in Constantinople were ruined by the cold and dark summers. As a result, the weak and hungry people of Byzantium had to rely on imports of food in order to survive. Ships carrying grain that came to port in the Golden Horn also carried rats; those rats carried fleas, and those fleas carried the plague.

The plague caused sudden fever, swellings in the groin and armpit, coma and death. Some victims broke out with black pustules, some died vomiting blood, some had high fevers and died screaming in pain when the swellings burst. Some healthy people went on about their business and then suddenly were hit with a high fever out of nowhere and simply laid down wherever they were to die. Death was so rampant and unexpected that people would wear nametags so that their remains could be identified in the case of sudden death.

Because of the drop in temperature caused by Krakatoa, the bacterium Yersinia pestis was able to grow, which is the active agent of the plague. The years of poor harvests after the eruption of Krakatoa necessitated an increase in imports of food to Constantinople. Finally, because they did not have enough food, the people of Byzantium were hungry, weak and vulnerable, making them perfect hosts for the vicious sickness. Thousands of people died each day because of the plague, and the people of Byzantium did not know how to stop its spread. The only reason the plague petered out is because, by 543, there were no more uninfected hosts for the sickness to inhabit. Stories of survivors meant that some people were infected by the disease but did not die from it, meaning they carried the disease in their bodies without peril. People who hadn't come in contact with the disease were scarce—running out of infected hosts meant the end of Constantinople's fight with the bubonic plague.

Section IV: Map Exercise

1. Using a black pencil, trace the rectangular outline of the frame for Map 29.1: Constantinople.

2. Using a blue pencil, trace the coastline of the Mediterranean (include the large islands of Sardinia, Corsica, Sicily, Crete, and Cyprus, but not the smaller islands), the Red Sea, the Black Sea, and the Caspian Sea. You do not need to trace the western coastline of the Atlantic at this time. With your blue pencil, trace the line of the Nile, the Tigris and Euphrates, and also the Danube, the Rhine, the Loire, and the Seine to the west. Show the Carpathian mountains with simple peaks. Repeat until the contours are familiar.

3. Now using your black pencil, trace the outline of the empire of Justinian. Trace the outline of the Persian Empire and the regions of the Franks as well. Use lines as the mapmaker did for the area of the Visigoths. Repeat until the contours are familiar.

4. Trace the rectangular outline of the frame in black. Remove your tracing paper from the original. Using a regular pencil with an eraser as you look at Map 29.2, draw the coastline of the Mediterranean (including only the islands which you traced), the Red Sea, the Black Sea, and the Caspian Sea. Draw the lines of the Nile, the Tigris and Euphrates, the Danube, the Rhine, the Loire, and the Seine. Draw simple peaks to represent the Carpathian mountains. Then draw the outline of the empire of Justinian, the outline of the Persian Empire, the region of the Franks, and the region of the Visigoths (use lines as you did while tracing). Erase and redraw as necessary as you look at the map.

5. When you are pleased with your map, lay it over the original. Erase and redraw any lines which are more than ¼ inch off of the original.

6. Remove your map from the original. Mark the regions of North Africa, Sicily, Egypt, Syria, and Asia Minor (study the map first if necessary). Mark the rivers and bodies of water. Then study carefully the locations of the Burgundians, the Alemanni, the Heruls, Gepids, Lombards, and Ghassanids. When you are familiar with them, close the book, mark them on your map, and then check and correct any misplaced labels.

7. Next study carefully the locations of the following cities: Tours, Paris, Arles, Carthage, Naples, Rome, Ravenna, Constantinople, Edessa, Antioch, Caesarea, Petra, al-Rumiyyah, Nisbis, Ctesiphon, and Derbent. When you are familiar with them, close the book. Using your regular pencil, mark the locations on your map. (If these are too many to learn at one time, first learn the cities up through Ravenna and then learn the remaining, starting with Constantinople.) When you are pleased with your map, check it against the original. Erase and replace any misplaced cities or labels.

Chapter Thirty

The Heavenly Sovereign

The student may use her text when answering the questions in sections I and II.

Section I: Who, What, Where

Write a one or two-sentence answer explaining the significance of each item listed below.

Bambetsu—**Pg. 218, ¶ 4—*Bambetsu*, or "foreign clans," were the clans that lived on the island Kyushu, which was located south of Yamato. The *bambetsu* were networks of families whose ancestors had migrated from the Korean peninsula or from the Chinese mainland and settled in a new home.**

Chinhung—**Pg. 216, ¶ 3 to Pg. 217, ¶ 1 and Pg. 219, ¶ 2 & 3—Chinhung, Pophung of Silla's successor, allied himself with the Baekje against the Goguryeo to regain land the Goguryeo had taken in the Han River Basin, but once the Goguryeo were driven out Chinhung turned against his ally and took the land for himself. Chinhung defeated Seong of the Baekje when the king attacked Chinhung's Kwansan Fortress; Chinhung kept fighting his way south until he held not only the land around the Han river but also the land along the Naktong river, all the way to the southern coast of the peninsula, making his country the largest and strongest on the peninsula.**

Ezo—**Pg. 218, ¶ 4—Ezo was the name given to the people who lived on the northern island Hokkaido by the Yamato. Ezo was a term meaning the barbarians; the people of Yamato looked at the Ezo as different, and other.**

Jomon—**Pg. 217, ¶ 4 and †—Jomon, meaning "cord marked," is the designation given to the first era of Japanese history by historians. It lasted from 10,000 to 400 BC. During the Jomon period, the inhabitants of the Japanese islands marked their clay by pressing braided cords into it, thus giving rise to the designation "Jomon."**

Jushichijo no Kempo—**Pg. 221, ¶ 2—The Jushichijo no Kempo, or the Seventeen-Article Constitution, issued in 602 by Shotoku Taishi, lists the principles by which the Yamato**

monarchs should be ruling their country—and by which the people should agree to be ruled. It reveals in every line the conviction that the monarch is the government, that the king is the law and that because the king is the law there is no need for a written law to restrict him, there is simply the need that the ruler be moral and virtuous.

Kimmei—**Pg. 218, ¶ 6 and Pg. 219, ¶ 2—Kimmei, the heavenly sovereign in charge when gifts related to Buddhism arrived in Japan in 552, decided to accept the Buddha into his culture and in return for the gifts help Baekje fight against Silla.**

Konwon—**Pg. 215, ¶ 1—Konwon, or the "Initiated Beginning," was the name declared by King Pophung for a new era for Silla beginning in 536. The new era marked the birth of Silla as a state just as important as its neighbors, the Baekje and Goguryeo.**

Ojin—**Pg. 218, ¶ 2—Ojin was the first ruler of the Yamato; a semi-mythical ruler, he ascended the throne in AD 270 when he was seventy and supposedly reigned for forty years. The real Ojin was probably a warrior-chief who was able to subdue his neighbors, not the entirety of the Japanese domain.**

Seong—**Pg. 215, ¶ 4 and Pg. 219, ¶ 2—Seong, king of the Baekje, moved the capital of his nation from Ungjin to Sabi around 540 in order to declare his kingdom's ambitions to rule the peninsula. Seong fought and died in battled against King Chinhung of Silla even though he had Japanese troops to reinforce his own.**

Shinto—**Pg. 219, ¶ 6—Shinto was the name given to the traditional faith of Japan. In its earliest forms, Shinto depended on rituals conducted at *kami*, sacred places where earthly existence and the sacred world were thought to intersect; clan leaders were charged with supervising the rituals and keeping the *kami* unpolluted.**

Shotoku Taishi—**Pg. 220, ¶ 6—Shotoku Taishi, a Buddhist scholar and Soga relative, became regent to Suiko when she was appointed to the Yamato throne in 539. Shotoku Taishi issued the Jushichijo no Kempo in 602, the Seventeen-Article Constitution, that stated the king is the law, and that as long as the king was moral and virtuous, there would be no need for a written law to restrict him.**

Sogo no Iname—**Pg. 219, ¶ 5—Soga no Iname, the Soga chief that was allowed by Kimmei to build a temple and begin following the ways of the Buddha, ignored a warning from the Nakatomi chief that the old gods of Japan would punish the foreign trespass of the Buddha on their territory. When an epidemic broke out in the capital, Soga no Iname heeded the Nakatomi advice, threw the statue into a canal, and burned down the temple.**

Soga no Umako—**Pg. 220, ¶ 5—Soga no Umako, chief of the Soga clan, responded to a death threat from his royal nephew Sushun by dispatching an assassin to kill the Yamato king. At the same time he led his clan in a successful attack on the most powerful rival to Soga power: the anti-Buddhist clan of the Mononobe, allies of the equally anti-Buddhist Nakatomi family.**

Suiko—**Pg. 220, ¶ 6—Suiko, daughter of Kimmei, half-sibling to the previous rulers of Yamato, daughter of a woman from the Soga clan and half-sister and wife of Bidatsu, was appointed to the throne by Soga no Umako after Sushun's death. She ruled along with the regent Shotoku Taishi, another Soga relative.**

Sushun—**Pg. 220, ¶ 4 & 5—Sushun, a descendant of Kimmei's dynasty, rebelled against Soga clan leaders and threatened clan leader Soga no Umako with death. Sushun was killed by an assassin dispatched by Soga no Umako.**

Tenno—**Pg. 218, ¶ 3—*Tenno*, or "heavenly sovereigns," was the designation given to the rulers of Yamato. Heavenly sovereigns were not rulers of their entire domain, they did not command world-conquering armies or control trade routes; they provided, instead, a nexus point where the divine could meet the earthly, where the presence of the sacred provided a stable center for the people of the Japanese islands.**

Uji—**Pg. 217, ¶ 6 to Pg. 218, ¶ 1—*Uji* was the name for the warrior clans that inhabited Japan; the geography of the country—four larger islands and several smaller ones and mountains chopping the larger islands into smaller self-contained areas—lent itself to multiple independent groups ruling themselves. The *uji* continued to exist while Japan moved towards monarchy and a royal family in AD 250.**

Wa—**Pg. 217, ¶ 3 & 4—Wa was the name of the first inhabitants of Japan. Though they did trade, buy and sometimes fight with the kingdoms on the Korean peninsula, little is known about the Wa; there is no written account from the ancient Japanese cultures, and the first written historical account, the *Kojiki*, was not written until the seventh century AD.**

Wideok—**Pg. 219, ¶ 3—Wideok, son of Seong, succeeded his father as king of Baekje after Seong was killed in the battle at the Kwansan fortress. Wideok made an alliance with the king of Goguryeo to protect himself against further aggression.**

Yamato—**Pg. 218, ¶ 1 & 2—Yamato is the first known dynasty that ruled in Japan, around AD 270. The Yamato ruled the flat and fertile Yamato plain, which gave its inhabitants easy passage to the Inland Sea.**

Yayoi—**Pg. 217, ¶ 5—Yayoi is the name given to the period in Japanese history spanning 300 BC to around AD 250. The new historical period was marked when the native culture combined with immigrant skills like new methods of farming and innovations in working bronze and copper, skills that most likely came with settlers from China and/or from the Korean peninsula.**

Section II: Comprehension

Write a two or three-sentence answer to each of the following questions.

1. Why were the Silla, Baekje and Goguryeo always at war?

A1.—Pg. 215, ¶ 2 & 3—The Silla, Baekje and Goguryeo were all alike—alike in language, in race, in custom, in shared culture, and in religion—and they all wanted to rule over the others. Unfortunately the three nations existed on a peninsula where there was little room to expand: sea to the south and east, Chinese to the west, and frigid temperatures to the north meant that the kingdoms had nowhere to else to go. The Silla, Baekje and Goguryeo were always at war because they were constantly fighting one another for more land and more power on their cramped peninsula.

2. For what reason, around 540, did King Seong of Baekje move his capital from Ungjin to Sabi?

A2.—Pg. 215, ¶ 4 to Pg. 216, ¶ 1—King Seong of Baekje moved his capital from Ungjin to Sabi around 540 in order to show the Silla and the Goguryeo that his nation had ambitions to take over the whole of the peninsula. Ungjin was in a safe, confined mountain-protected location, whereas Sabi, on the Kum river, was located in a broad central plain. By moving to an open space, Seong was showing his opponents that Baekje would no longer be a defensive state protecting its own territory, but an expansive country with ambitions to dominate the peninsula.

3. Why was Goguryeo a bitter enemy of the northern Chinese kingdoms? Why wasn't King Seong of Baekje afraid of making an alliance with the northern Chinese?

A3.—Pg. 216, ¶ 2—The kingdom of Goguryeo, located at the base of the Korean peninsula, was the biggest and most powerful of the three kingdoms. Goguryeo was a target for the northern Chinese kingdoms that were near enough to the upper reaches of the peninsula to attack. Baekje, located at the tip of the peninsula, had enough land and water between itself and China to make goodwill gestures without feeling the threat of invasion; making an alliance with the northern Chinese would also put Goguryeo at a disadvantage, a strategic move that only benefitted the Baekje.

4. Why did Seong of Baekje ally himself with Chinhung of Silla? How did the alliance backfire?

A4.—Pg. 216, ¶ 4 to Pg. 217, ¶ 2—Seong of Baekje allied himself with Chinhung of Silla in order to retake land in the Han river basin, currently occupied by the Goguryeo, that Seong believed rightfully belonged to the Baekje. The armies of the Baekje and the Silla were able to drive out the Goguryeo, but then, instead of letting Seong keep the land, Silla's army turned against the Baekje and Chinhung took the land for himself.

5. What were the two historical parts of the Yamato dynasty? Why were the parts named in this way?

A5.—Pg. 218, *—The two historical parts of the Yamato dynasty were the Kofun period (270-c. 538) and the Asuka period (538–715). The names come from designations for the types of burial mounds that were used during each time period.

6. What happened when the gifts—a statue of the Buddha made of gold and copper and books of Buddhist scriptures—sent by Seong arrived in Japan in 552? Why were some of the Japanese clans against keeping the gifts, while some were for it? What decision was made in the end?

A6.—Pg. 218, ¶ 5 to Pg. 219, ¶ 2—When the gifts sent by Seong arrived in Japan in 552, the heavenly sovereign Kimmei summoned the clan leaders loyal to him and asked them whether or not to accept the gifts; while Kimmei may have been the nexus of divine power on earth, the clan leaders held most of the political power in the land of Wa. The Nakatomi and Mononobe clans, were opposed—the Nakatomi because they controlled the worship of the traditional Japanese deities and the Mononobe because they objected to the gifts' foreignness. On the other hand, the leader of the powerful Soga clan argued that since every other kingdom followed the Buddha, Japan should too. Kimmei decided to keep the Buddha and in return dispatched an army to aid Seong in his battle against the Silla.

7. What was the result of King Seong's attack against the Kwansan Fortress, the keystone to the defense of the Silla frontier?

A7.—Pg. 219, ¶ 2—King Seong's attack against the Kwansan Fortress, even with the help of Japanese reinforcements, was a disaster. Seong was killed, the Baekje army was driven back, and Chinhung of Silla, elated by his success, kept fighting his way south until he held not only the land around the Han river but also the land along the Naktong river, all the way to the southern coast of the peninsula.

8. Describe the difference between the localized religious practice of the Shinto and the universal religious practice of Buddhism.

A8.—Pg. 219, ¶ 6 to Pg. 220, ¶ 1—Shinto was firmly connected to particular places: Shinto depended on rituals conducted at *kami*, sacred places where earthly existence and the sacred world were thought to intersect. Buddhism, with its global truths that extended beyond places and borders and its focus on vast all-encompassing realities, offered answers to questions that Shinto did not ask. The universalism of Buddhism meant that the faith did not collide with the local practices of Shinto.

9. How did Kimmei ensure that his legacy would keep the Soga clan close to the throne?

A9.—Pg. 220, ¶ 3—Kimmei had three royal wives, two of which were from the Soga family. Kimmei arranged the marriage of his son and heir Bidatsu to one of his own daughters, the prince's half-sister by a Soga wife, and when he died, the prince Bidatsu came peacefully to the crown. When Bidatsu died after a thirteen-year reign, he was followed by his half-brother Yomei and then his half-brother Sushun. All were children of Kimmei's Soga wives which kept the Soga clan close to the throne.

10. When Shotoku Taishi was in his thirties, he hit his ruling "stride." What actions did Shotoku take to increase Yamato power?

A10.—Pg. 221, ¶ 1—When he was in his thirties, Shotoku Taishi sent envoys to the Chinese kingdom, demanding that the Yamato ambassadors be received as representatives of an

equal and sovereign nation. In an attempt to diminish the power of the clan leaders, he instituted a Chinese-style set of government ranks, naming each rank after a cardinal virtue, such as fidelity, justice, and wisdom, in order to remind the officials that they were serving because of their character, not their birth. Finally, he took it upon himself to create a written statement of the principles by which the Yamato dynasty held power.

Section III: Critical Thinking

The student may not use her text to answer this question.

When a statue of the Buddha made of gold and copper and a book of Buddhist scriptures arrived in Japan in 552, the Yamato ruler had to decide whether or not to accept the Baekje's gifts. However, the decision was not the heavenly sovereign's to make: he had to ask the clan leaders what they thought. This check on the leader's power was meant to be ameliorated with the institution of the Jushichijo no Kempo in 602. Write a paragraph explaining the meaning of the Jushichijo no Kempo, and how even though it seemed to give the leader of the Yamato dynasty carte blanche, it also very much limited the sovereign's power.

The Jushichijo no Kempo, or Seventeen-Article Constitution, was issued in 602 by Shotoku Taishi. Shotoku Taishi wanted to move beyond the vague claim of divine sanction that gave him his power and lay out the principles by which the Yamato monarchs should be ruling their country, and by which the people should agree to be ruled. The Constitution was not a blueprint for the structure of the Yamato government, nor was it a list of what the ruler could and could not do. What the Constitution did do is make it very clear that the monarch is the government, that the king is the law. If the king was law, then what he said was law and there was no need to restrict him with written rules. Most importantly, the Constitution tried to define the moral character of the king, and also his people.

This is where there was a limit imposed upon the monarch's power. The Constitution said that the king should be virtuous and just, and as long as he was virtuous and just the rules he made would be accepted for the good of the kingdom. However, loss of virtue meant the ruler could be removed, in full compliance with the Constitution. If his people decided that he was no longer morally or spiritually pure, then his word would have no impact, and his laws would not be law anymore. While the Constitution gave the monarch power to make laws with just his words, it also gave the people power to declare that they did not think the king was virtuous, meaning he would be out of a job and the people would not have to obey his law. The Jushichijo no Kempo might make it seem like the power of the law was in the king's words, but really it was in the people's perception of the king, limiting his true power in the same way that it was limited by the clan leaders.

EXAMPLE ANSWER:

The Jushichijo no Kempo, or Seventeen-Article Constitution, was issued in 602 by Shotoku Taishi. The Constitution was not a blueprint for the structure of the Yamato government, nor was it a list of what the ruler could and could not do. What the Constitution did do is make it very clear that the monarch is the government, that the king is the law. If the king was law,

then what he said was law and there was no need to restrict him with written rules. Most importantly, the Constitution tried to define the moral character of the king, and also his people. This is where there was a limit imposed upon the monarch's power. The Constitution said that the king should be virtuous and just, and as long as he was virtuous and just the rules he made would be accepted for the good of the kingdom. However, loss of virtue meant the ruler could be removed, in full compliance with the Constitution. If his people decided that he was no longer morally or spiritually pure, then his word would have no impact, and his laws would not be law anymore. The Jushichijo no Kempo might make it seem like the power of the law was in the king's words, but really it was in the people's perception of the king, limiting his true power in the same way that it was limited by the clan leaders.

Section IV: Map Exercise

1. Using a black pencil, trace the rectangular outline of the frame for Map 30.1: The Far East in the Sixth Century.

2. Using a blue pencil, trace the coastline. You do not need to include all islands at this time; just include all the land down to Kyushu. Be sure to include the Inland Sea. Using your blue pencil, trace the line of the Yellow River and the Han River (in Silla). Repeat until the contours are familiar.

3. Using a black pencil, trace the line of the Great Wall. Then trace the outlines of Silla, Goguryeo, and Baekje. Repeat until the contours are familiar.

4. Using a new sheet of paper, trace the rectangular outline of the frame in black. Remove your tracing paper from the original. Using a regular pencil with an eraser as you look at Map 30.1, draw the coastline of China all the way around the Yellow Sea, up past Goguryeo, and down and around Kyushu and the Yamato Plain. Erase and redraw as necessary as you look at the map.

5. After completing the coastline, draw the Great Wall and Han and the Yellow Rivers, looking at the map and correcting as you go. Then draw the outlines of Goguryeo, Silla, and Baekje.

6. When you are satisfied with your map, lay it over the original. Erase and redraw any lines which are more than ¼ inch off of the original.

7. Remove your map from the original. Label the Great Wall, the Yellow River, the Yellow Sea, and the Goguryeo, Silla, and Baekje regions.

8. Now study carefully the areas of the Eastern Wei, the Southern Lang, Hokkaido, the Yamato Plain, and Kyushu. When you are familiar with them, close the book. Using your regular pencil, label each area on your map. Then study carefully the cities of Luoyang, Pyongyang, Sabi, and Unjin, as well as Kwanson Fortress. When you feel confident with them, close the book and label each city. Check your map against the original, and correct any misplaced labels. Then lay your map over the original and erase and redraw any cities which are more than ¼ inch off of the original.

Chapter Thirty-One

Reunification

The student may use his text when answering the questions in sections I and II.

Section I: Who, What, Where

Write a one or two-sentence answer explaining the significance of each item listed below.

Eulji Mundeok—**Pg. 229, ¶ 1 & 3—Eulji Mundeok, a great Goguryeon general, made his stand at the capital city Pyongyang in 612 when Sui Yandi took a Chinese army of more than a million men into Goguryeo. In a fierce, especially bloody battle, the Korean soldiers surrounded and obliterated the Chinese troops.**

Gao Huan—**Pg. 223, ¶ 1 & 2—Gao Huan, the general behind the Eastern Wei throne, died sometime around the same time that Liang Wudi of the Southern Liang tried to enter a monastery and was forced back on the throne for a third time. Gao Huan kept alive the fiction that a legitimate Wei ruler still sat on the throne by ruling from the shadows through a puppet-emperor with royal blood.**

Gao Ying—**Pg. 226, ¶ 7—Gao Ying was a general that was part of the inner circle that helped Yang Jian establish himself as emperor the Northern Zhou. Gao Ying helped Yang Jian wipe out opposition to his regency.**

Gaozu (Tang Gaozu)—**Pg. 229, ¶ 4—Gaozu, a rebel officer who declared himself emperor after Sui Yangdi's loss at Pyongyang, founded a new Chinese dynasty: the Tang.**

Hou Jing—**Pg. 224, ¶ 2 & 5—Hou Jing, a northerner, made his way into the government of the Southern Liang by offering Liang Wudi thirteen former Wei territories and a sizable army. After deposing Liang Wudi with the help of his son Jian, Hou Jin murdered Jian and took the throne for himself; his reign was cut short when the Jian's brother raised a rebellion and let the people of Nanjing (Jiankang) rip Hou Jing to pieces.**

Jian (Liang Jian Wendi)—**Pg. 224, ¶ 3 & 5—Jian, a son of Liang Wudi, attacked his father at Nanjing (Jianking) in alliance with Hou Jing. After deposing his father, Jian took the throne and became Liang Jian Wendi, but he was emperor for barely a year before Hou Jian murdered him.**

Li Delin—**Pg. 226, ¶ 7—Li Delin was a writer that was part of the inner circle that helped Yang Jian establish himself as emperor the Northern Zhou. Li Delin wrote beautifully convincing political rhetoric about Yang Jian's right to rule.**

Liang Yuandi—**Pg. 224, ¶ 6 to Pg. 225, ¶ 1—Liang Yuandi, a Taoist with over two hundred thousand books in his personal library, became king of the Southern Liang after the death of his older brother, Jian, and the slaughter of Hou Jing. Liang Yuandi's reign lasted barely three years; when one of his own nephews gathered a northern army, and came back south and threatened to besiege Nanjing (Jianking), Liang Yuandi turned on his books and burned them because he saw defeat was inevitable.**

Sui Yangdi—**Pg. 229, ¶ 2–4—Sui Yangdi, Sui Wendi's son and successor, continued to battle the problems left behind for him by Sui Wendi. An embarrassing and horrendous defeat by the Goguryeons at Pyongyang was the end for Sui Yangdi; a rebel officer declared himself emperor, Sui Yandi lost Luoyang to the revolt in 618 and he died in battle fighting for the city.**

Yang Jian (Sui Wendi)—**Pg. 226, ¶ 3 & 6, Pg. 227, ¶ 3 and Pg. 228, ¶ 2—Yang Jian, one of Zhou Wu's loyal followers and father of the crown prince's wife, was given the title "Duke of Sui" and helped Zhou Xuan ascend the throne of the north in 578. Yang Jian made himself regent for his seven-year-old grandson Zhou Jing after Zhou Xuan's death, and then eventually became emperor, reuniting all of China and then starting a war with Goguryeo in order to create cohesion within the newly reunified state.**

Zhou Jing—**Pg. 226, ¶ 6 and Pg. 227, ¶ 3—Zhou Jing, the seven-year-old grandson of Yang Jian, became the new emperor after the death of Zhou Xuan, ruling with Yang Jian as his regent. Eventually Yang Jian took away Zhou Jing's throne and declared himself emperor.**

Zhou Wu—**Pg. 226, ¶ 2—Zhou Wu, a young, ambitious, and sane Northern Zhou emperor, had ambitions to reunite the whole country under his throne. Unfortunately Zhou Wu grew ill, and while on campaign at the beginning of his plan of conquest, the sickness killed him at the age of thirty-five.**

Zhou Xuan—**Pg. 226, ¶ 3, 4 and 6—Zhou Xuan, son of Zhou Wu, married to the daughter of the Duke of Sui Yang Jian, and succeeded his father as emperor of the Northern Zhou in 578. Zhou Xuan was a terrible leader and even made his six-year-old son emperor in name, apparently to give himself more freedom to indulge in his pleasures; fortunately for the northern Chinese, Zhou Xuan died of a stroke in 579 at the age of twenty.**

Section II: Comprehension

Write a two or three-sentence answer to each of the following questions.

1. How did the Northern Qi dynasty come into existence?

A1.—Pg. 223, ¶ 2—Though Gao Huan kept alive the fiction that a legitimate Wei ruler still sat on the throne by ruling through a puppet-emperor, his son and successor had no desire to keep the myth going. In 550, he deposed the puppet-emperor and announced that he was emperor, founder of a new dynasty: the Northern Qi. Two years after he took the throne, he had the former puppet-emperor and his entire family murdered.

2. According to Yang Xuanzhi, who recounted a sixth-century dispute between a drunken Southerner and the palace master of the north, why should the Southern "Chinese" have stopped thinking of the Northerners as "barbarians"?

A2.—Pg. 233, ¶ 4 to Pg. 224, ¶ 1—According to Yan Xuanzhi's story, the Southern "Chinese" should have stopped thinking of the Northerners as "barbarians" because in every ancient tradition—ritual, law, custom, learning, and divine sanction—the North of China was the same as the South. The Wei dynasty had received the imperial regalia and set up its court in the region of Mount Sung and Loyang and it controlled the area of the five sacred mountains and made its home in the area within the four seas. The laws of the Wei dynasty on reforming customs were comparable to those of the five ancient sage rulers, while ritual, music, and laws flourished to an extent not even matched by the hundred kings.

3. What were the circumstances of Liang Wudi's death?

A3.—Pg. 224, ¶ 3 & 4—Jian, one of Liang Wudi's sons, joined forces with the government official Hou Jing and sieged Nanjing (Jianking). Liang Wudi was forced to surrender, deposed by his son, and imprisoned. The eighty-six year old Liang Wudi was allotted so little food and water while in prison that he weakened and died.

4. When did the Southern Chen dynasty come into existence?

A4.—Pg. 225, ¶ 2—The Southern Chen dynasty came into existence after three emperors claimed the Southern Liang crown in just three years, between 554 and 557. In 557, an army general named himself founder of the new Southern Chen dynasty.

5. How did the Northern Zhou dynasty come into existence? How did China move from having three ruling dynasties to two during this same period?

A5.—Pg. 225, ¶ 3—The Northern Zhou dynasty came into existence when an army officer deposed the king and named his son king of the new dynasty, the Northern Zhou. In 577, the Northern Zhou absorbed the Northern Qi, and China moved from having three ruling dynasties to two.

6. Who was Yan Zhitui and what can we learn about the prejudices of the Southern Chinese against the Northern Chinese from the rules he wrote down for his sons?

A6.—Pg. 225, ¶ 6 to Pg. 226, ¶ 1—Yan Zhitui, a southerner who served at the Southern Liang court that was forced to flee north when the Southern Chen deposed his employers, wrote down a set of rules for his sons to follow so that they would remember southern principles. Yan Zhitui told his sons to keep quiet about family matters; Southerners believed Northerners discussed family matters loudly in public, and even asked each other questions about it. He told his sons to embrace criticism (unlike Northerners who resented criticism) so that they could learn their failings and make improvements. Finally he told his sons that unlike Southern women, who conduct themselves in private, Northern women took charge of family affairs, actions that were most likely remnants of the customs of the barbarians which settled long ago in the north, the Tuoba.

7. What actions proved that Zhou Xuan was more interested in his own immediate power than reuniting all of China?

A7.—Pg. 226, ¶ 4—Zhou Xuan was a terrible leader: he began to call himself "The Heaven," designating his courtiers as "the earth"; he forced all of his officials to get rid of any ornaments or decorative clothing so that his own costume would stand out; he began to execute anyone who offended him; he went on lavish royal progresses through the countryside to demonstrate his power, leaving his father-in-law Yang Jian in charge at home. A year after his coronation, he made his own six-year-old son emperor in name, apparently to give himself more freedom to indulge in his pleasures, which included beating and raping the women of the court. Zhou Xuan's flagrant abuse of his kingly privileges showed that he was more interested in his immediate power than in reuniting all of China.

8. How did Yang Jian become regent for Zhou Jing?

A8.—Pg. 226, ¶ 6—When Zhou Xuan died, Yang Jian's seven-year-old grandson, Zhou Jing, became emperor. Yang Jian then forged a document making him regent for the new emperor.

9. What did the document say that was signed by Zhou Jing in September of 580? Why was this document important to Yang Jian's establishment of his own rule?

A9.—Pg. 226, ¶ 7 to Pg. 227, ¶ 2—In September of 580, Zhou Jing signed an edict giving official praise to Yang Jian's worthiness: it acknowledged him as "Supreme Pillar of State, Grand State Minister, responsive to the mountains and rivers, answering to the emanations of the stars and planets. His moral force elevates both the refined and the vulgar, his virtue brings together what is hidden and what is manifest, and harmonizes Heaven and Earth." Not only did the edict provide proof of Zhou Jing's worthiness to rule, the language of the edit also aligned him with the Mandate of Heaven.

10. What steps did Yang Jian take in order to make his role as emperor legitimate, and to eliminate any challenges to his power?

A10.—Pg. 227, ¶ 3 & ¶ 4—In order to make his role as emperor legitimate, Yang Jian put out a series of edicts that validated his worthiness to rule by creating for himself a royal lineage. One edict gave his grandfather, father, and great-grandfather posthumous royal titles; one made Yang Jian a prince, a higher rank than any other noble at court. The most important edict was Zhou Jing's abdication of the throne; Yang Jian customarily refused to accept the title of emperor three times, but eventually he ascended the throne as Sui Wendi, emperor of the north.

11. How was China reunited under the leadership of Sui Wendi?

A11.—Pg. 227, ¶ 6 & 7—Sui Wendi, over the course of seven years, sent agents into the south of China with a manifesto that detailed all the faults of the new southern emperor. Then, in 589, Sui Wendi marched towards the southern capital Nanjing; by the time his armies arrived at the city's walls, the power of the Southern Chen had crumbled. The Sui forces took control of the city and then all of the south, successfully reuniting China.

12. Why did Sui Wendi deprive everyone (except for the army) in newly reunited China of weapons? Why did he rebuild the Great Wall, and build canals between the Yellow and the Yangtze rivers?

A12.—Pg. 227, ¶ 8 to Pg. 228, ¶ 1—Sui Wendi deprived everyone but the army of weapons in order to reduce the possibility of rebellion and to eliminate tension between neighbors—without weapons there were fewer violent private feuds. Sui Wendi rebuilt the Great Wall to act as a barrier against northern invasion. Recognizing that the north and south would never hold together without free intercourse between them, he built a series of new canals linking the Yellow and Yangtze rivers, known collectively as the Grand Canal.

13. What did Sui Wendi do to the governments of North and South China upon reunification? What was his "New Code," and why was it created?

A13.—Pg. 227, ¶ 8 to Pg. 228, ¶ 1—Once China was reunified, Sui Wendi reorganized the governments of the north and the south into a single, rational, and efficient unit, that was highly structured and hierarchical, each office having its own rank, its own set of privileges, and even its own particular uniform. The new set of laws that were drawn up as part of the new government that would apply across the entire empire was called the New Code. The New Code was created to replace the messy and contradictory mass of local regulations.

14. Why did Sui Wendi start a war with the Korean kingdom of Goguryeo after reuniting China?

A14.—Pg. 228, ¶ 2—Sui Wendi started a war with the Korean kingdom of Goguryeo after reuniting China because he believed that a country gained cohesion while facing an outside enemy. Sui Wendi believed Goguryeo was close enough geographically to China to be considered a threat, but it was weak enough to pose no serious danger to Chinese power.

15. Describe the canals between the Yangtze and Yellow rivers. How were they built, and where did the money come for their construction?

A15.—Pg. 229, ¶ 1—The canals between the Yangtze and Yellow Rivers were a dazzling network of rivers and man-dug channels that ran for over a thousand miles from north to south, with roads and post stations and royal pavilions all along its banks. The canals were built with an enormous amount of manpower: over five million Chinese were forced to labor on the canal for part of the year, many dying of the hard labor, and many more were impoverished by the months spent away from their own crops and herds. The canals were paid for by massive amounts of tax money.

16. How did Sui Yangdi handle the problems he inherited with his Chinese crown?

A16.—Pg. 229, ¶ 2—Sui Yangdi handled the problems he inherited with his Chinese crown poorly, carrying on his father's attempt to build a country in less than one generation. He stepped up on the taxes and labor in order to complete the Grand Canal, and then took a victory sail on the completed waterway, celebrating the accomplishment without acknowledging the labor that went into the project. He also grew obsessed with completing the conquest of Goguryeo, pouring the remaining treasury into it and sending the remaining Sui troops—once the army had three hundred thousand soldiers but at the time it was reduced to less than three thousand—into the Korean peninsula over the bodies of their fallen comrades.

17. What was the state of China when Tang Gaozu began his rule, and his new dynasty?

A17.—Pg. 229, ¶ 5 & 6—China was a mess when Tang Gaozu began his rule. Sui Yangdi had just been defeated at Pyongyang, the army was weak and the treasury was empty from the Grand Canal project. When Tang Gaozu ascended the throne as the emperor, he founded a new dynasty: the Tang.

Section III: Critical Thinking

The student may not use his text to answer this question.

In the previous chapter we learned that there *isn't* much to learn about the history of ancient Japan because there are so few written records from that time. No matter how mighty their rulers may have been, we don't know about those leaders because we can't read about them. Stories influence what we know about the past and how we think of the future—Yang Jian certainly understood that. Write a paragraph or two explaining how Yang Jian took advantage of the power of words to become emperor and reunite China.

In the chapter we read that power was important to Yang Jian, but so was the Mandate of Heaven. If he wanted to have a lasting empire, he needed to take the throne in the most legitimate way possible. Yang Jian couldn't actually redo the past, but he could make it seem like his past was legitimate by creating a new past in writing.

Li Delin was employed by Yang Jian to write beautiful and convincing political rhetoric about Yang Jian's right to rule. Li Delin produced edict after edict that created a royal past for Yang Jian, creating layers of legitimacy with each document. First, Li Delin wrote an edict that gave official praise to Yang Jian's worthiness. The edict acknowledged him as "Supreme Pillar of State, Grand State Minister, responsive to the mountains and rivers, answering to the emanations of the stars and planets. His moral force elevates both the refined and the vulgar, his virtue brings together what is hidden and what is manifest, and harmonizes Heaven and Earth." The language of Li Delin's edict contextualized Yang Jian's worthiness within the greatness and power of the natural world, lining him up as a ruler to faithfully represent the Mandate of Heaven. Li Delin wrote edicts that gave Yang Jian's grandfather, father, and great-grandfather posthumous royal titles. This created a royal past for the hopeful emperor. One edict made Yang Jian a prince, a higher rank than any other noble at court, again affirming that was worthy of the throne. Li Delin also write the edict that declared Zhou Jing's abdication of the throne. This document made Yang Jian the official emperor.

Masterful stories were important for Yang Jian, known as Sui Wendi when he became emperor, after he ascended the throne, too. His goal was to reunite China, and he knew it would be a hard task to complete. In the seven years of preparation for physical war, Yang Jian used words to riddle and weaken the morale of southern China. Sui Wendi sent agents into the south with three hundred thousand copies of a manifesto listing all of the faults of the new southern emperor, and explaining that vice had deprived the southern dynasty of the Mandate of Heaven. With their faith in the south ruined because of Sui Wendi's propaganda campaign, the Southern Chen crumbled when Sui Wendi attacked. The sword may have conquered the people, but it was the words preceding the attack that made it easy.

EXAMPLE ANSWER:

In order to prove that he was worthy of the Mandate of Heaven, Yang Jian employed Li Delin to write beautiful and convincing political rhetoric about Yang Jian's right to rule. Li Delin produced edict after edict that created a royal past for Yang Jian, creating layers of legitimacy with each document. First, Li Delin wrote an edict that gave official praise to Yang Jian's worthiness. The edict acknowledged him as "Supreme Pillar of State, Grand State Minister, responsive to the mountains and rivers, answering to the emanations of the stars and planets." The edit also praised Yang Jian's morals and virtues, making him seem worthy of the Mandate of Heaven. Li Delin wrote edicts that gave Yang Jian's grandfather, father, and great-grandfather posthumous royal titles. This created a royal past for the hopeful emperor. One edict made Yang Jian a prince, a higher rank than any other noble at court, again affirming that was worthy of the throne. Li Delin also wrote the edict that declared Zhou Jing's abdication of the throne. This document made Yang Jian the official emperor.

Masterful stories were important for Yang Jian, or Sui Wendi, after he ascended the throne, too. His goal was to reunite China, and he knew it would be a hard task to complete. In the seven years of preparation for physical war, Yang Jian used words to riddle and weaken the morale of southern China. He sent agents into the south with three hundred thousand copies of a manifesto listing all of the faults of the new southern emperor, and explaining that vice had deprived the southern dynasty of the Mandate of Heaven. With their faith

in the south ruined because of Sui Wendi's propaganda campaign, the Southern Chen crumbled when Sui Wendi attacked. The sword may have conquered the people, but it was the words preceding the attack that made it easy.

Section IV: Map Exercise

1. Using a black pencil, trace the rectangular outline of the frame for Map 31.1: The Grand Canal.

2. Using a blue pencil, trace the coastline from Goguryeo down to the bottom of the frame. Using a black pencil, trace the outline of the shaded portion of the map. Repeat until the contours are familiar.

3. Using a new sheet of paper, trace the rectangular outline of the frame in black. Remove your tracing paper from the original. Using a regular pencil with an eraser as you look at Map 31.1, draw the coastline and then the shaded portion of the map. Erase and redraw as necessary.

4. When you are pleased with your map, lay it over the original. Erase and redraw any lines which are more than ¼ inch off of the original. Label Sui.

5. Remove your map from the original. Looking back at Map 31.1, study carefully the locations of Chang'an, Luoyang, and Nanjing. When you are familiar with them, close the book.

6. Looking back at Map 31.1, draw the lines of the Yellow River, the Yangtze River, and the approximate course of the Grand Canal. Label each. Draw the outline of the border of Goguryeo and label as well. Erase and redraw to be as correct as possible.

Chapter Thirty-Two

The South Indian Kings

The student may use her text when answering the questions in sections I and II.

Section I: Who, What, Where

Write a one or two-sentence answer explaining the significance of each item listed below.

Chalukya—**Pg. 231, ¶ 2—The Chalukya was a tribe of people that had probably come down from the area north of India. After living in the Deccan for many years, they became the natives of central India.**

Harsha Carita—**Pg. 233, ¶ 9 to Pg. 234, ¶ 1—The Harsha Carita was a eulogy praising the king of Thanesar's, Harsha Vardhana's, accomplishments. The Carita describes Harsha's royal ancestry when in fact Harsha's family was not particularly distinguished and had never ruled over much in the way of territory.**

Harsha Vardhana—**Pg. 233, ¶ 8 and Pg. 235, ¶ 1 & 4—Harsha Vardhana, ruler of Thanesar, defeated many chiefs in India, growing his kingdom slowly and moving his capital city eastward to Kannauj so he would be in the center of his expanding realm. Harsha tried to take Chalukya territory for his kingdom, but he was unable to defeat Pulakesi II.**

Kannauj—**Pg. 235, ¶ 1—Kannauj became Harsha Vardhana's capital as he defeated chief after chief in north India. Kannauj was united with Thanesar as Harsha Vardhana defeated the neighboring tribes in an ever-widening circle around him.**

Kirtivarman—**Pg. 232, ¶ 2—Kirtivarman, Pulakesi's son, succeeded his father as king of Chalukya in 566. He defeated the Mauryans, descendants of the ancient royal house that had once ruled much of India. He also built up the village of Vatapi, filling it with new temples and public buildings, beginning to turn it into a capital city.**

Mahendravarman—**Pg. 232, ¶ 6 and Pg. 233, ¶ 2—Mahendravarman, king of the Pallava, came to power around 600. He gave himself the nickname Vichitrachitta, meaning "the man with**

new-fangled ideas;" he was a polymathic king, a genius who happened to be born to the crown.

Mangalesa—**Pg. 232, ¶ 3 and Pg. 233, ¶ 3 & 5—Mangalesa, Kirtivarman's brother, served as regent for his nephew for thirteen years, controlling the kingdom even after Pulakesi II was of age. Though Mangalesa was an able leader and had royal blood, he was not in the direct line of succession for the throne; when he refused to give up his power Pulakesi II raised an army and Mangalesa was killed in the fighting.**

Pallava—**Pg. 232, ¶ 4 & 5—The Pallava, people who in ancient times lived in Vatapi, were driven out of their home city by the Chalukya to a territory known as the Vengi.**

Pulakesi—**Pg. 231, ¶ 2-4—Pulakesi, king of Chalukya, made conquests in 543 that pushed the Chalukya empire out from Vatapi against neighboring tribes. He conquered the Vakataka, took land on the western coast of India for his kingdom, and he performed the horse-sacrifice to assert his power and strength.**

Pulakesi II—**Pg. 232, ¶ 3, Pg. 233, ¶ 4 & 5 and Pg. 235, ¶ 5 & 6—Pulakesi II, Kirtivarman's son, took the throne when his father died in 597, but his brother and regent Mangalesa, actually controlled the kingdom. In 610 Pulakesi II raised an army, killed his uncle, claimed the throne and eventually beat off the invasion of Harsha Vardhana and captured the northern provinces once ruled by Mahendravarman.**

Rajyasri—**Pg. 234, ¶ 2 and Pg. 235, ¶ 1—Rajyasri, Harsha Vardhana's sister, was about to be killed after her husband, who was king, died. Rajyasri was saved by her brother and made co-ruler and empress of Harsha.**

Section II: Comprehension

Write a two or three-sentence answer to each of the following questions.

1. What did conquering land on the western coast of India do for Chalukya? What else did Pulakesi do to prove his worth as king of Chalukya?

A1.—Pg. 231, ¶ 3 & 4—Conquering land on the western coast of India meant that the Chalukya could trade unhindered with the Arabs. In addition to conquering other kingdoms, Pulakesi boasted of having fifty-nine royal ancestors, which gave his dynasty an impressive past. Pulakesi also performed the horse-sacrifice, the ancient Hindu ritual that brought health and strength to the people by channeling it through the king.

2. What made Mahendravarman, or "Vichitrachitta," the man with new-fangled ideas, stand out among the south Indian kings?

A2.—Pg. 232, ¶ 6 to Pg. 233, ¶ 2—Mahendravarman, or "Vichitrachitta," stood out among the south Indian kings because he managed to keep an interest in the arts alive, even while

directing constant military campaigns against bordering states. He was interested in architecture and pioneered a new method of carving out rock-temples; he was interested in painting and he commissioned a scholar at his court to write an instructional manual for painters, the Dakshinachitra; he was interested in town design and he built a number of new towns incorporating his own engineering techniques; he was interested in music and he is credited with inventing a method of musical notation; he was interested in writing and he wrote two plays in Sanskrit, one of them a satire skewering his own government.

3. Why do we know so little about Mahendravarman's accomplishments?

A3.—Pg. 233, ¶ 2—We know so little about Mahendravarman's accomplishments because they were chronicled only by single lines of inscriptions instead of with great stories written by courtiers and monks as would have been done in the west.

4. Why did Mangalesa believe he deserved to be king of the Chalukya?

A4.—Pg. 233, ¶ 3—Mangalesa had led the Chalukya to victory over one of their strongest enemies, the Kalachuri. He added buildings and cave-temples to the capital city of Vatapi. He had every quality of a king, including royal blood—except that he was not in the direct line of succession; nevertheless Mangalesa believed he deserved to be king.

5. What did Pulakesi II do once he came to the Chalukya throne?

A5.—Pg. 233, ¶ 6—Once Pulakesi II came to the Chalukya throne, he immediately started fighting. He defeated and forced into obedience a long list of chiefs: Gangas, Latas, Malavas, Gurjaras, and many more. He extended Chalukya power across much of the Deccan, clashing with the Pallava army in an ongoing struggle that would last for decades.

6. How did Harsha Vardhana come to claim the country of his sister's king for himself?

A6.—Pg. 234, ¶ 2 & 3—One day Harsha received a message from his sister Rajyasri, who had been married to a neighboring king for treaty-making purposes. She had been made a widow by her husband's sudden death, her adopted kingdom was about to be invaded by enemies, and she herself was facing death by fire on a funeral pyre honoring her husband. Harsha assembled an invasion force and went in to rescue her, and then he claimed the country for himself.

7. What was Pulakesi II's strategy to bolster his army when facing Harsha Vardhana's hundred thousand horsemen, hundred thousand foot soldiers and sixty thousand elephants?

A7.—Pg. 235, ¶ 3—Pulakesi II's court poet wrote that the king prepared for battle by getting both his soldiers and his war elephants drunk, which made them reckless, dangerous, and overwhelming. The drunk forces did not care who stood before them, they trampled everything down fearlessly.

8. While drunken courage may have helped Pulakesi II's army, what really helped the king defend Chalukya territory? After their battle, what became Harsha Vardhana's southern border?

A8.—Pg. 235, ¶ 4 & 5—Chalukya territory was cordoned off by mountains, river, and desert. The rough terrain stopped any king from sweeping both north and south India into the same kingdom, and that is what really helped Pulakesi II defend Chalukya territory. After the battle, Narmada became the southern border of Harsha.

9. How did Pulakesi II add Vengi to his territory?

A9.—Pg. 235, ¶ 6—Pulakesi II defeated the Pallava king Mahendravarman and took away the northern provinces—the Vengi—and added them to his own territory.

Section III: Critical Thinking

The student may use her text to answer this question.

The ancient Hindu ritual of the horse-sacrifice was intended to bring health and strength to the people by channeling it through the king. Write a paragraph explaining what the ritual entailed, and then explain how the horse-sacrifice gave Pulakesi II the power to defeat his various enemies and to grow a strong Chalukya kingdom.

The text describes the horse-sacrifice as follows:

The ancient Hindu ritual that was intended to bring health and strength to the people by channeling it through the king. The horse-sacrifice was, in the words of Indologist Hermann Oldenberg, the "highest sacral expression of royal might and splendor." It was an elaborate and time-consuming ritual. The consecrated horse was set to wander free for a full year, under guard, before it was brought back to the king. Priests covered the horse with a golden cloth, and the king killed it with his own right hand at the culmination of a three-day festival. The queen then lay down beside the dead horse, underneath the golden cloth, and acted out sexual congress with the corpse. The strength of the horse and the strength of the king became one; the power of the horse entered the queen and she gave birth to a royal heir, who would also bear the divine strength. Power and sex were interrelated. The crown, and the passing of the crown to a blood heir, were intertwined. It was the sacrifice of an emperor, not a minor king.

The student may use her text as reference when describing the horse-sacrifice ritual and may include as much detail as she sees fit.

What the student should understand is that the horse-sacrifice did not just benefit the king who ordered it; the horse-sacrifice gave power to bloodline. Pulakesi II was son of Kirtivarman, who was the son of Pulakesi, and it was Pulakesi who performed the sacrifice. When Pulakesi II was fighting his uncle and regent Mangalesa for power, he rationalized his fight for the throne by claiming rule "as the grandson, namesake, and rightful heir of Pulakesi I, the first of his family to rule the Chalukya as emperor. His grandfather had performed horse-sacrifice, and he alone had the right to rule." Though Mangalesa was a good leader and did have royal blood, he was not in direct succession for the throne. Performing the horse-sacrifice gave Pulakesi II the power to claim his rightful place on the Chalukya throne. Once king, Pulakesi II fulfilled his role as heir of the horse-sacrifice; he was a strong and courageous ruler that expanded his kingdom's size and wealth.

EXAMPLE ANSWER:

The ancient Hindu ritual of the horse-sacrifice was intended to bring health and strength to the people by channeling it through the king. In the horse sacrifice, the consecrated horse was set to wander free for a full year, under guard, before it was brought back to the king. Priests covered the horse with a golden cloth, and the king killed it with his own right hand at the end of a three-day festival. The queen then lay down beside the dead horse, underneath the golden cloth, and acted out sex with the corpse. The strength of the horse and the strength of the king became one; the power of the horse symbolically entered the queen and when she gave birth, the royal heir would also bear divine strength.

The horse-sacrifice did not just benefit the king who performed it, it also benefited the royals who were in line for the throne. Pulakesi's son was Kirtivarman, and Kirtivarman's son was Pulakesi II. This was the line of succession. Pulakesi II rationalized his fight for the throne against Mangalesa by claiming rule "as the grandson, namesake, and rightful heir of Pulakesi I, the first of his family to rule the Chalukya as emperor. His grandfather had performed horse-sacrifice, and he alone had the right to rule." Though Mangalesa was a good leader and did have royal blood, he was not in direct succession for the throne. Performing the horse-sacrifice gave Pulakesi II the power to claim his rightful place on the Chalukya throne. Once king, Pulakesi II fulfilled his role as heir of the horse-sacrifice; he was a strong and courageous ruler that expanded his kingdom's size and wealth.

Chapter Thirty-Three

Two Emperors

The student may use his text when answering the questions in sections I and II.

Section I: Who, What, Where

Write a one or two-sentence answer explaining the significance of each item listed below.

Alboin—**Pg. 242, ¶ 1 & 3—Alboin, the Lombard king at the time Italy faced the plague, conquered Milan in 569 and then moved southward, collapsing the Byzantine territory in central Italy.**

Athanagild—**Pg. 238, ¶ 2—Athanagild, a Visigothic nobleman, asked Justinian for help seizing the Visigoth throne in 552. With the Byzantine king's help, Athanagild became king.**

Bumin Khan—**Pg. 238, ¶ 5—Bumin Khan, a warchief of the T'u-chueh's, gathered his tribe and their allies in 552 at Ergenekon and declared himself their king. After marrying a Chinese princess from the former Western Wei royal family, Bumin Khan formed a new state called the Gokturk Khaghanate with its capital city at Otukan.**

Ergenekon—**Pg. 238, ¶ 5 & 6—Ergenekon was the place where Bumin Khan gathered his tribe and their allies when he announced that he would be their king. Ergenekon was the ancestral homeland of the Turks, and it was like the Turks' Garden of Eden, but within a living memory.**

Gokturk Khaghanate—**Pg. 238, ¶ 5 & 6—Gokturk Khaghanate was the first Turkish kingdom, founded by Bumin Khan.**

Justin II—**Pg. 241, ¶ 3 and Pg. 244, ¶ 1—Justin II, Justinian's nephew, succeeded his uncle as king of Byzantium. Justin II could not hold together his uncle's kingdom and ultimately he lost his mind: he used to bite people when he was angry with them, and he was only soothed when his courtiers let him sit in a little wagon and pulled him around the palace in it.**

Leovigild—**Pg. 242, ¶ 4—Leovigild, brother and successor to Athanagild the Visigothic king, had come to the throne of Hispania and reconquered the land his brother had lost. Justin II was unable to organize a decent defense against Leovigild, meaning the Byzantine attempt to claim the old Roman lands came to an end.**

Mukhan—**Pg. 238, ¶ 7 and Pg. 241, ¶ 1—Mukhan, son of and successor to Bumin Khan, expanded the Gokturk state and as a result he drove the Avars westward towards Persia and Byzantium. Mukhan also conquered the eastern tribes of the Bulgars, which agitated the remaining tribes who lived on the western shores of the Don river, sending some into Byzantine land.**

Narses—**Pg. 237, ¶ 2 & 4—Narses, a soldier-eunuch, was assigned by Justinian to hire mercenaries from the Gepids and the Lombards in order to help the Byzantine cause in Italy. Narses attacked Rome, killed the Ostrogoth king Totila, and then recaptured Ravenna for Justinian.**

Quraysh—**Pg. 243, ¶ 1—The Quraysh was the strongest tribe in Mecca, with three clans within it but not one which was dominant over the other.**

Sophia—**Pg. 244, ¶ 2—Sophia, Justin II's wife and niece of Theodora, convinced Justin to name courtier Tiberius to be his Caesar. When Tiberius was crowned emperor after Justin II's death in 578, Sophia offered to marry him if he would divorce his wife, but he declined.**

T'u-chueh—**Pg. 238, ¶ 5—T'u-chueh, nomads from northern China, moved westward and settled into central Asia.**

Tiberius—**Pg. 244, ¶ 2—Tiberius, a courtier, was named the mad Justin II's Caesar and he controlled the empire with Sophia, Justin II's wife, until the emperor died in 578. At Justin II's funeral, Tiberius was crowned emperor.**

Section II: Comprehension

Write a two or three-sentence answer to each of the following questions.

1. Where might the Lombards have come from? What evidence is there that they might have come from this place?

A1.—Pg. 237, ¶ 3—The Lombards may have come from the cold northern lands on the far side of the Baltic Sea, known to ancient historians as Scandia. Their own oral history testifies to this origin: "The peoples [of Scandinavia] . . . had grown to so great a multitude that they could not now dwell together . . . so they divided their whole troop into three parts" and from there figured out who would forsake their country and find a new place to live. The Lombards were one of those bands of people that were forced to find a new home.

2. Who helped Narses attack Rome in 551? What happened at Rome, and then at Ravenna, with Narses leading the Byzantine army?

A2.—Pg. 237, ¶ 4 to Pg. 238, ¶ 1—The Lombards helped Narses attack Rome, as well as a few Gepids and some Huns. Totila, king of the Ostrogoths, had recaptured Rome and mounted his defense there, but Narses and his thirty thousand men attacked Rome and killed Totila as well as six thousand other Ostrogoths. Then Narses and his mercenaries recaptured Ravenna and re-established a Byzantine capital there.

3. What was an exarch, and what was his job when it came to Italy?

A3.—Pg. 238, ¶ 1—An exarch was a general who also had authority to administer civilian affairs. In terms of Italy, the exarch ruled on behalf of the emperor Justinian.

4. What price did Justinian pay for regaining the heart of the Roman empire?

A4.—Pg. 238, ¶ 1—Justinian paid to regain the heart of the Roman empire with years of war that had destroyed the countryside, wrecked the cities, and impoverished the people.

5. How did Justinian recapture southern Hispania by 554?

A5.—Pg. 238, ¶ 2—In 552, the Visigothic king that controlled southern Hispania had been murdered, the court was in disarray and one of the nobles, Athanagild, sent a message to Constantinople, appealing for help in seizing the throne. Byzantine ships arrived to support him and Athanagild got his throne. By 554, however, Byzantine armies had captured ports and fortresses all along the southern coast, and Justinian was able to establish a Byzantine province there with Cartagena as its capital.

6. How did Belisarius end up in jail, rather than in retirement, in the years before he died? What was the state of Justinian and Belisarius's relationship when both men died in 565?

A6.—Pg. 241, ¶ 1 & 2—When Mukhan began to conquer the Bulgars, other tribes who lived on the western shores of the Don river breached Byzantine land. Justinian recalled Belisarius from his retirement to drive them away. Belisarius did a fantastic job which flared up Justinian's old insecurities about the security of his throne; in 562 the emperor accused Belisarius of corruption and jailed him. A year after jailing his old friend, Justinian pardoned Belisarius—this was the last fight between them before they both died in 565.

7. What threatened Byzantine domination in Italy after Justin II's accession to the throne?

A7.—Pg. 241, ¶ 4—The plague arrived in Italy just after Justin II's accession to the throne. The plague made Italy vulnerable and emptied it of subjects, threatening Byzantium's domination.

8. Why did the Lombards want to expand into Italy?

A8.—Pg. 242, ¶ 2—The Lombards wanted to expand into Italy because they needed more space. Their numbers had grown because Alboin had conquered the Heruls and the Gepids.

With over a quarter of a million in their kingdom, the Lombards needed more land for their people.

9. What was left of Byzantium's hold in Italy after the Lombards moved in en masse in 568?

A9.—Pg. 242, ¶ 3—After the Lombards moved en masse into Italy, capturing Milan and moving southward, the Byzantine territory in central Italy fell. Only the southern coasts and a strip of land from Ravenna down the coast, cutting across to Rome, remained in Byzantine hands.

10. What is the difference between Sasanian Persia and the ancient Persian empire?

A10.—Pg. 242, †—Sasanian Persia refers to medieval Persia, which lay in the same general area as ancient Persia. Ancient Persia lost its independence to Alexander the Great. Persia did not regain its existence as an independent kingdom until a man from the Sasanian clan declared himself Ardashir, emperor of a revived Persia, in AD 224.

11. How did Khosru reorganize the vast expanse of land that he controlled after many successful campaigns?

A11.—Pg. 242, ¶ 5—Khosru reorganized his vast expanse of land by dividing it into quadrants and placing a military commander over each. The quadrants were divided as such: one was the far eastern land won from the Hephthalites, one was the central area of the kingdom; one was the lands to the west near the Byzantine border; and the last was the southern Arabian territories.

12. Why did Axum want to attack Mecca?

A12.—Pg. 243, ¶ 1—The king of Axum, Abraha, was Christian. Mecca was the center of the traditional Arabic religion. If Axum attacked and conquered Mecca, then Abraha would be able to spread Christianity throughout Arabia.

13. While God may have stopped Abraha of Axum from invading Mecca once, what stopped a repeat attack against the city?

A13.—Pg. 243, ¶ 3—After Axum's first attempt at attacking Mecca, the tribes of southern Arabia asked Khosru of Persia for aid. In 575, he came south with both foot-soldiers and a fleet of ships into the land Abraha had hoped to conquer. The Persian intervention halted Abraha's attempts to organize a second invasion.

14. Describe the good Khosru did for Persia before his death in 579, during his forty-eight-year reign.

A14.—Pg. 244, ¶ 3—During his forty-eight year reign, Khosru made several reforms to make sure his empire was just: children with questioned paternity were given their fair inheritance; women that were married against their will could choose to leave their husbands if they wished; convicted thieves were encouraged to make restitution, not merely suffer punishment; widows and orphans were provided for by relatives and by the state. He had also conquered new territory and equipped Persia with a strong infrastructure of canals

and irrigation conduits, he rebuilt bridges and restored villages, he kept the roads well-maintained, he trained tax officials and administrators well, and he built a strong army.

Section III: Critical Thinking

The student may not use his text to answer this question.

We have all heard the phrase "God works in mysterious ways." According to the Qur'an, it was God that stopped Abraha of Axum from conquering Mecca by blighting his forces with the plague. The presence of God also affected how things were run in Mecca. Write a paragraph describing how the government in Mecca was structured. In your answer, explain why, in a religious center such as Mecca, all of the tribes were bound together even if there was no common law and no central authority.

On page 243 of the text, we learn that there was no king in Mecca. The text continues, "Arabs were loyal to the tribe of their birth; the tribe was their ethical center, which meant that loyalty did not extend outside of tribal boundaries. Raiding another tribe for food, animals, and women was a constant that bore no stigma of moral wrong. Arabia was a dry land of ever-colliding micro-nations." Even the strongest tribe in Mecca, the Quraysh, was divided, with three clans within it struggling for dominance.

Mecca, the religious center of these tribes, was governed by a council made up of heads of the leading families, all of whom had equal authority. All of the tribes abided by the rule that no one was to draw a weapon in the sacred territory of the Ka'aba. While there was no common law, no central authority, and no acknowledged warleader, the tribes were tied together by something bigger, and it was centered in Mecca. As a religious center, Mecca was theoretically protected by God, so no central figure was needed to rule over the Arabian tribes.

EXAMPLE ANSWER:

Arabian tribes were loyal to themselves, and their loyalty did not extend outside of tribal boundaries. At Mecca, the religious center of all of these tribes, governance came from a council made up of heads of the leading families, all of whom had equal authority. Despite any differences, all of the tribes abided by the rule that no one was to draw a weapon in the sacred territory of the Ka'aba. There was an acknowledgement that the tribes centered at Mecca were tied together and ultimately governed by something unseen: God.

Section IV: Map Exercise

1. Using a black pencil, trace the rectangular outline of the frame for Map 33.2: The Gokturk Khaghanate.

2. Using a blue pencil, trace all the coastline visible on the map (the areas shaded with horizontal lines). Include Lake Baikal. Using your black pencil, trace the perimeters of the Northern Zhou,

the Southern Chen, and the Northern Qi. Then trace the outline of the shaded area showing the approximate extent of the Gokturk Khaghanate. Trace the Himalaya mountains and the Altay mountains with simple peaks. Repeat these tracings until the contours are familiar.

3. Take a new sheet of paper. Using a black pencil, trace the rectangular frame of the map in black. Remove your tracing paper from the original. Using a regular pencil with an eraser as you look at the map, draw the visible coastline, including Lake Baikal. Then draw the perimeters of the Northern Zhou, the Southern Chen, and the Northern Qi. Draw the outlines of the approximate extent of the Gokturk Khaganate. Finally draw the mountain peaks of the Himalaya and the Altay mountains.

4. When you are pleased with your map, place it over the original. Erase and redraw any lines which are more than ¼ inch off of the original.

5. Remove your map from the original. Study the locations of the Gokturk Khaganate and also Northern Zhou, the Southern Chen, and the Northern Qi. Also study carefully the locations of the Great Wall, the possible location of Ergenekon, and the area of the T'u-hueh. When you are familiar with them, close the book. Using your regular pencil, draw and label the Great Wall and label the locations of the Gokturk Khaganate and also Northern Zhou, the Southern Chen, and the Northern Qi. Also mark and label the possible location of Ergenekon and the area of the T'u-hueh. Check your map against the original. If your labels are misplaced, erase and remark while looking at the original.

Chapter Thirty-Four

The Mayors of the Palaces

The student may use her text when answering the questions in sections I and II.

Section I: Who, What, Where

Write a one or two-sentence answer explaining the significance of each item listed below.

Aquitaine—**Pg. 252, ¶ 3—Aquitaine was a small territory where the younger half-brother of Dagobert was sent when he tried to claim the throne of Neustria. Once Charibert the half-brother was in Aquitaine, Dagobert supervised his assassination and claimed the whole kingdom for himself.**

Brunhilda—**Pg. 247, ¶ 1, Pg. 248, ¶ 6, Pg. 249, ¶ 6, Pg. 250, ¶ 5 and Pg. 251, ¶ 2—Brunhilda, daughter of King Athanagild and a Visigothic princess, married Sigebert of Austrasia and served as a very competent and strong regent for her son Childebert II. Not willing to give up her own power, Brunhilda was kicked out of court by her grandson Theudebert II (who she later had murdered), taken in by her other grandson Theuderic where she took control of his court and finally in 613 she was deposed, captured and killed by her nephew Chlothar II.**

Charibert—**Pg. 246, ¶ 5—Charibert, the second oldest son of Chlothar I, died in 567. When he died, his territory was divided between his brothers and the Frankish kingdom assumed a three-way division that would dictate its politics for the next century.**

Childebert II—**Pg. 248, ¶ 4 and Pg. 249, ¶ 4—Childebert II, son of Childebert, became heir to his father's throne at age five, with his mother Brunhilda serving as his regent. Childebert II died in 595 with he was in his mid-twenties, leaving his mother to serve as regent to his two young sons.**

Childebert the Adopted—**Pg. 253, ¶ 3 & 4—Childebert the Adopted, Grimoald's son, was placed on the Austrasian throne by his father after Sigebert III died and Sigebert's son and heir was sent off to a monastery. When Clovis II heard of this appointment, he invaded Austrasia and put Childebert the Adopted and his father to death.**

Chilperic—**Pg. 246, ¶ 5, Pg. 247, ¶ 4 and Pg. 248, ¶ 3 & 7—Chilperic, one of Chlothar I's sons, controlled the central and southern Frankish lands known as Neustria, which contained the cities of Soissons and Paris. Chilperic married Visigothic princess Galswintha who was most likely murdered by Chilperic's most important wife Fredegund, he fought for years for more power with his brother Sigebert, and was murdered in 584 by a man with a personal grudge.**

Chlothar II—**Pg. 249, ¶ 2, Pg. 251, ¶ 2–5—Chlothar II, son of Fredegund and supposedly the son of Chilperic, king of Neustria, tried to attack his cousins and get their land in 599 and was defeated; however, he became the single ruler of the Franks after he was invited to invade Burgundy so that he could do away with Brunhilda. Chlothar II was responsible for giving the mayors of the palaces great power when he issued the Edict of Paris in 615 and when he declared that a mayor of a palace had a lifetime appointment.**

Clovis II—**Pg. 252, ¶ 6 and Pg. 253, ¶ 5 & 6—Clovis II, Dagobert's younger son, was crowned king of Neustria and Burgundy after his father's death, and he ruled his realm with help from the mayors of each territory's palace. After Grimoald tried to put his own son on the Austrasian throne, Clovis II invaded and became king of all the Franks, but he died after being king for barely a year.**

Dagobert—**Pg. 252, ¶ 2, 4 & 5—Dagobert was made ruler of Austrasia in 617 by his father Chlothar II. Dagobert reunited the Franks under his rule, but then made his son Sigebert III ruler of Austrasia in order to appease the Frankish noblemen.**

Dagobert II—**Pg. 253, ¶ 3—Dagobert II, Sigebert III's six-year-old heir, was tonsured and sent off to a monastery in England by Grimoald.**

Edict of Paris—**Pg. 251, ¶ 4—The Edict of Paris, issued by Chlothar II in 615, promised that the king of the Franks would not try to overrule the authority of the local palaces of Austrasia, Neustria, and Burgundy. The three Frankish kingdoms would be united under Chlothar II, but there would be no single centralized government, the offices of mayor would not be combined into one and each mayor of the palace would continue to administer his own realm.**

Erchinoald—**Pg. 253, ¶ 5—Erchinoald, one of Clovis II's officials, declared Clovis II king of the entire Frankish realm after Childebert the Adopted's death. Erchinoald also became mayor of the palace for Neustria, Burgundy and Austrasia simultaneously when Clovis II became the single king.**

Fredegund—**Pg. 247, ¶ 4, Pg. 248, ¶ 2 and Pg. 249, ¶ 1 & 5—Fredegund, one of Chilperic's former wives that refused to leave her husband's side when his new wife Galswintha arrived at his palace, became queen of Chilperic's court after Galswintha was found strangled in her bed. Fredegund gave birth to a son after Chilperic's death that she claimed was the king's son; Fredegund and her son Chlothar II tried to seize Paris, failed, and in the following year Fredegund died.**

Galswintha—**Pg. 247, ¶ 2-4—Galswintha, daughter of the Visigothic King Athanagild and sister of Brunhilda, was married to Chilperic of Neustria. After complaining about the presence of Fredegund, Galswintha was found strangled in her bed.**

Grimoald—**Pg. 252, ¶ 8 to Pg. 253, ¶ 4—Grimoald, son of Pippin the Elder, tonsured the rightful heir of the Austrasian throne and had him sent to a monastery in England in order to put his son Childebert the Adopted on the throne. When Clovis II heard of this appointment, he invaded Austrasia and put Grimoald and his son to death.**

Guntram—**Pg. 246, ¶ 5 and Pg. 249, ¶ 2 & 3—Guntram, one of Chlothar I's sons, ruler of Burgundy, supported Fredegund and her claim that Chlothar II was actually the son of Chilperic after three bishops swore an oath that King Chilperic was his father. When he died in 592, Guntram left his part of Frankish rule to Childebert II of Austrasia.**

Pippin the Elder—**Pg. 252, ¶ 2, 7 & 8—Pippin the Elder, mayor of the Austrasian palace, held great power over Dagobert. When Pippin the Elder died, he had managed to subsume the mayoralties of Burgundy and Neustria and to pass them on to his son Grimoald.**

Rado—Pg. 250, ¶ 6 and Pg. 251, ¶ 2—**Rado, mayor of the palace for Burgundy, stopped Brunhilda from taking over Burgundy after Theuderic's death by inviting Chlothar II to invade.**

Sigebert—**Pg. 246, ¶ 5 and Pg. 248, ¶ 3 & 4—Sigebert, one of Chlothar I's sons, ruled the northern territory of the Franks, known as Austrasia and moved the capital of Austrasia from Reims to Metz, which was closer to the border and allowed him to guard against wandering Avars. Sigebert, who was always fighting with Chilperic, died in 575 when Chilperic's wife Fredegund had the Austrasian king poisoned.**

Sigebert III—**Pg. 252, ¶ 5 and Pg. 253, ¶ 2 & 3—Sigebert III, Dagobert's son, was made king of Austrasia at age three. Sigebert left an heir to his throne before he died at an unexpectedly young age in 656.**

Song of the Nibelungs—**Pg. 248, ¶ 6—The Song of the Nibelungs was a Germanic epic that chronicled hostility towards the Austrasian queen Brunhilda. The epic says the queen was brought from Iceland to be the wife of the German king, and that she was a "thing of terror."**

Theudebert II—**Pg. 249, ¶ 6 and Pg. 250, ¶ 4 & 5—Theudebert II, Childebert II's older son, ruler of Austrasia, kicked his grandmother Brunhilda out of her regent role and decided to rule alone. Theuderic II and Chlothar II attacked Theudebert II in 612; Theudebert II was captured, imprisoned, and while in prison he was murdered at the command of Brunhilda.**

Theuderic II—**Pg. 249, ¶ 6 and Pg. 250, ¶ 4 & 5—Theuderic II, Childebert II's younger son and ruler of Burgundy, welcomed his grandmother Brunhilda after she was kicked out of Theudebert II's court in Austrasia. Theuderic joined forces with his cousin Chlothar II of Neustria against Theudebert II of Austrasia and was successful; Theuderic claimed**

Austrasia as his own but did not enjoy his rule for long—he died of dysentery less than a year later.

Warnachar—**Pg. 250, ¶ 6 and Pg. 251, ¶ 2—Warnachar, mayor of the palace for Austrasia, stopped Brunhilda from taking over Austrasia after Theuderic's death by inviting Chlothar II to invade.**

Section II: **Comprehension**

Write a two or three-sentence answer to each of the following questions.

1. How long did Chlothar I's rule of the unified Franks last? Why did the Frankish nation split again after Chlothar I's death?

A1.—Pg. 246, ¶ 2 & 3—Chlothar I's rule of the unified Franks lasted only three years. After his death, Chlothar I left the crown to all four of his surviving sons, splitting the nation up once again. Chlothar I believed the king should earn his right to rule, not merely inherit it, meaning he felt his sons should battle for power.

2. Why did Sigebert marry the Visigothic princess Brunhilda?

A2.—Pg. 247, ¶ 1—Sigebert wanted to hold the high king's seat and rule over his brothers, so in an effort to gain more power he decided to ally himself with the Visigoths via a marriage to the princess Brunhilda.

3. What deal did Chilperic of Neustria make with King Athanagild in order to gain the hand of Galswintha? What happened once Galswintha arrived in Neustria?

A3.—Pg. 247, ¶ 2–4—Chilperic, who had several wives, promised King Athanagild that he would put all his other wives away if he was given the hand of Galswintha, a promise he kept when Galswintha arrived at his court. Soon, however, Galswintha noticed that a woman named Fredegund kept showing up in the royal bedchamber. After complaining about Fredegund's presence and insisting she go away, Galswintha was found strangled in bed.

4. What were the circumstances of Sigebert's death in 575?

A4.—Pg. 248, ¶ 3 & 4—After seven years of inconclusive war between Austrasia and Neustria, Fredegund sent two assassins to kill Sigebert in his palace in 575. They pretended to be traitors from Chilperic's court, willing to change sides and recognize Sigebert as king, but when they got into Sigebert's presence they attacked him with poisoned scramasaxes—long Scandinavian knives normally used as eating tools. Sigebert died in agony.

5. How did Childebert II become the heir of Burgundy?

A5.—Pg. 248, ¶ 5—Brunhilda convinced Childebert's brother Guntram, who was childless, to adopt Childebert II as his own. This made young Childebert II both the king of Austrasia and the heir of Burgundy.

6. Why did Fredegund need three bishops and three hundred of the more important leaders in Neustria to assure the public that Fredegund's baby was fathered by Chilperic?

A6.—Pg. 248, ¶ 7 to Pg. 249, ¶ 1—When Chilperic was murdered in 584, he died childless, but after the funeral Fredegund announced that she was pregnant with her husband's heir. The announcement was greeted with skepticism, and when the baby was born Guntram suggested that the child's father was a Frankish courtier. To prove the baby was actually Chilperic's son, Fredegund rounded up three bishops and three hundred of the more important leaders and they all swore an oath that King Chilperic of Neustria was the baby's father.

7. How did the Frankish nation come to be ruled by two women that hated each other?

A7.—Pg. 249, ¶ 3—In 592, Guntram of Burgundy died and left his part of the Frankish rule to Childebert II of Austrasia, his nephew and adopted son. This meant that Brunhilda, who had kept her power after her son reached his majority, was helping her son to rule over both Austrasia and Burgundy. Fredegund acted as regent for Chlothar II, meaning she ruled Neustria. Brunhilda blamed Fredegund for the death of both her sister and her husband and loathed her deeply; this is how the Frankish nation came to be ruled by two women that hated each other.

8. Why did Fredegund and Chlothar II decide to seize Paris? What stopped the consummation of full-fledged war between Fredegund and Brunhilda?

A8.—Pg. 249, ¶ 4 & 5—When Childebert II died, his kingdom was divided between his two young sons, one taking Austrasia and one taking Burgundy. Seeing this as an opportune moment for attack, Fredegund and Chlothar II attempted to seize Paris. The battle didn't accomplish much, and war seemed to be on the horizon; however, a year later Fredegund died and war was averted.

9. Why did Theuderic II plan to marry the Visigothic princess Ermenberga? How did the arrangement fall apart?

A9.—Pg. 250, ¶ 1–3—Theuderic II planned to marry the Visigothic princess Ermenberga because he needed a way to lessen his grandmother Brunhilda's power. He didn't want to ask his brother in Austrasia or his cousin in Neustria for help because he was afraid they'd see him as weak and he'd end up losing his throne, so he sought a new ally and asked the Visigothic king Witteric for the hand of his daughter Ermenberga in 607. Though Witteric agreed, Brunhilda poisoned Theuderic II's mind against Ermenberga, and by the time the princess arrived, Theuderic II was uninterested, the marriage was never consummated and a year later he sent his wife back to her father.

10. Describe the events that led to Theudebert II's murder in prison at the request of Brunhilda.

A10.—Pg. 250, ¶ 4–6—To gain power, Theuderic II made an alliance with Chlothar II of Neustria against his brother, Theudebert II of Austrasia, and in 612, the joint force attacked Theudebert II's army on the edge of the Forest of Ardennes. The carnage was terrible and

after the attack Theuderic II and Chlothar II marched to Cologne, took Theudebert II's treasure, and captured Theudebert II. After being captured, Theudebert II was taken back to Chlothar II's court, imprisoned and then ordered murdered in prison by Brunhilda.

11. What does the term "mayor of the palace" mean?

A11.—Pg. 250, ¶ 7—The term "mayor of the palace" was the Frankish title for the king's right-hand man, the official who took care of the royal estates, supervised the other government offices, and generally acted as prime minister and household steward combined. When the king was a child, or weak, or dead, his mayor ran the realm.

12. How did the Franks come to be united under Chlothar II?

A12.—Pg. 250, ¶ 5 and Pg. 251, ¶ 2 & 3—After uniting with Clothar II, Theuderic II claimed Austrasia for his own, but then he died of dysentery not a year later; he did not leave a legitimate heir, meaning power was in Brunhilda's hands. Mayors Warnachar and Rado did not want to see their domains taken over by Brunhilda, so they invited Chlothar II to invade. In 613, he marched into Brunhilda's territory, put her to death, and then claimed single rule of the Franks.

13. Explain these terms, found on page 252: *Francia, Austrasia, Neustria.* How did these terms come to be?

A13.—Pg. 252, ¶ 1—*Francia* was the name the western Franks called their land and they referred to the eastern half as *Austrasia,* or "East Land." The Austrasians refused to acknowledge the name *Francia;* they used the term *Neustria,* or "New West Land" instead. These terms came to be because the eastern and western halves of the Frankish kingdom wanted to separate their interests, maybe because of ancient tribal differences, or obscure clan hostilities.

14. Why did Dagobert make his three-year-old son, Sigebert III, king of Austrasia?

A14.—**Pg. 252, ¶ 5—In an effort to appease the nobles of Austrasia, Dagobert made his three-year-old son Sigebert III king, which once again gave the mayor of the palace real power in the Austrasian realm. Dagobert was trying to balance the power of the king, the rights of the royal family, and the intense desire of the previous Frankish clan chiefs who were now noblemen to rule themselves. The rule of an infant king under the power of a local mayor of the palace was a workable solution.**

15. What does it mean to be "tonsured"?

A15.—To be tonsured was to have the top of one's head shaved to indicate one's intentions to become a priest. To be tonsured was a sacred version of mutilation, rendering the user unfit for rule by dedicating him to the service of God.

Section III: Critical Thinking

The student may not use her text to answer this question.

The chronicle of the rise of the Merovingian *rois faineants*, or "do-nothing kings," is a complicated one. Yet, the premise behind why these "do-nothing kings" came about is simple: the mayors of the palaces wanted more power. Explain how putting a single king on the throne of the united Franks actually made it very easy for the majors of the palaces to decentralize royal rule and claim more power for themselves. In your answer, first write a paragraph describing how Chlothar II became king of all the Franks. Then explain the Edict of Paris, the 617 declaration that followed, and finally how these two laws rendered the Frankish king essentially powerless.

Uniting a kingdom under a single ruler is usually, as we have seen in our reading, the ultimate declaration of power. This was not the case for the Merovingian Franks, however. After chronicling the change in power that resulted in a single king of the Franks under Chlothar II, the student should explain how getting a single king on the throne meant the whole of the Franks had to abide by the Edict of Paris and the declaration that a mayor would rule for a lifetime. The student should then explain how these two laws rendered the king essentially useless and gave power to the mayors.

Chlothar II of Neustria became king of all the Franks after first uniting with Theuderic II of Burgundy against Theudebert II of Austrasia. The cousins successfully defeated Theudebert II, and then Theuderic II took Austrasia as his own, making him king of both Burgundy and Austrasia. Two mayors of the palace—Warnachar of Austrasia and Rado of Burgundy—saw this union as an opportunity to finally get rid of strong-willed Brunhilda. Warnachar and Rado invited Chlothar II of Neustria to invade the newly united Burgundy and Austrasia, and he did so without much opposition. Chlothar II took Burgundy and Austria, added the realms to his rule of Neustria, and became king of all the Franks.

In 615, Chlothar II issued the Edict of Paris, which promised that the king of the Franks would not try to overrule the authority of the local palaces of Austrasia, Neustria, and Burgundy. The three Frankish kingdoms would be united under Chlothar II, but there would be no single centralized government, the offices of mayor would not be combined into one, and each mayor of the palace would continue to administer his own realm. This meant that power was in the hands of the mayors, not in the hands of the king.

Chlothar II then agreed, two years after the Edict of Paris, to declare that to be mayor of the palace was a lifetime appointment. This meant that the independent mayors could not be removed from office. Chlothar II may have had the crown of the Franks, but most of his country was ruled by the mayors. The mayors could not be terminated, they had the authority to legislate for their own realms, and they were able to act independently of the Frankish king. When Warnachar and Rado invited Chlothar II to invade, they probably made a deal with the future king, levying mayoral power for the title of "King of all the Franks." The deal was a losing one for Chlothar II, and for the Frankish kings that followed.

EXAMPLE ANSWER:

Chlothar II of Neustria became king of all the Franks after first uniting with Theuderic II of Burgundy against Theudebert II of Austrasia. The cousins successfully defeated Theudebert

II, and then Theuderic II took Austrasia as his own, making him king of both Burgundy and Austrasia. Two mayors of the palace—Warnachar of Austrasia and Rado of Burgundy—saw this union as an opportunity to finally get rid of strong-willed Brunhilda. Warnachar and Rado invited Chlothar II of Neustria to invade the newly united Burgundy and Austrasia, and he did so without much opposition. Chlothar II took Burgundy and Austria, added the realms to his rule of Neustria, and he became king of all the Franks.

In 615, Chlothar II issued the Edict of Paris, which promised that the king of the Franks would not try to overrule the authority of the local palaces of Austrasia, Neustria, and Burgundy. The three Frankish kingdoms would be united under Chlothar II, but there would be no single centralized government, the offices of mayor would not be combined into one, and each mayor of the palace would continue to administer his own realm. This meant that power was in the hands of the mayors, not in the hands of the king.

Chlothar II then agreed, two years after the Edict of Paris, to declare that to be mayor of the palace was a lifetime appointment. This meant that the independent mayors could not be removed from office. Chlothar II may have had the crown of the Franks, but most of his country was ruled by the mayors. The mayors could not be terminated, they had the authority to legislate for their own realms, and they were able to act independently of the Frankish king. When Warnachar and Rado invited Chlothar II to invade, they probably made a deal with the future king, levying mayoral power for the title of "King of all the Franks." The deal was a losing one for Chlothar II, and for the Frankish kings that followed.

Section IV: Map Exercise

1. Using a black pencil, trace the rectangular outline of the frame for Map 34.1: Territories of the Franks.

2. Using a blue pencil, trace the coastline around Britannia and up the coastline of the continent. You do not need to include any islands at this time. Then trace the lines of the Loire, the Seine, the Rhine, the Rhone, and the Danube. Trace the mountains with simple peaks. Using your black pencil, trace the perimeter of the approximate extent of Frankish rule. Repeat until the contours are familiar.

3. Trace the rectangular outline of the frame in black. Remove your tracing paper from the original. Using a regular pencil with an eraser as you look at the map, draw the coastline and then the approximate extent of Frankish rule. Draw the mountain peaks as well. Erase and redraw as necessary.

4. When you are pleased with your map, lay it over the original. Erase and redraw any lines which are more than ¼ inch off of the original.

5. Remove your map from the original, and label the different rivers.

6. Now study carefully the locations of Aquitaine, Neustria, Burgundy, and Austrasia. When you are familiar with them, close the book, and mark them on your map. Check your map against the original, and correct if necessary.

7. Now study carefully the locations of the cities of Tours, Orleans, Paris, Soissons, Reims, Metz, Cologne, and Mainz. When you are familiar with them, close the book. Using your regular pencil, mark each city on your map and label it. When you are done, lay your map over the original. Correct any misplaced labels, and erase and redraw any cities which are more than ¼ inch off of the original.

Chapter Thirty-Five

Gregory the Great

The student may use his text when answering the questions in sections I and II.

Section I: Who, What, Where

Write a one or two-sentence answer explaining the significance of each item listed below.

Agilulf—**Pg. 256, ¶ 1 and Pg. 257, ¶ 5—Agilulf, a Lombard duke, took the job of overseeing Lombard borders in 590, after Authari's death. Agilulf attempted to take Rome for the Lombards, but he negotiated a peace with Gregory the Great and withdrew his troops for the sum of five hundred pounds of gold.**

Augustine—**Pg. 258, ¶ 4 and Pg. 259, ¶ 4 & 5—Augustine, a monk who had served in Gregory's former monastery, was chosen by Gregory to bring Christianity back to Britain. Though Augustine tried to abandon the mission in 596, he eventually succeeded in baptizing Ethelbert, was made bishop of the Angles at Canterbury by Gregory, and ended up living in Britain with his converts.**

Authari—**Pg. 255, ¶ 5—Authari, a Lombard duke, was elected to oversee Lombard resistance to any invasion in 584. His election came after the decision that the separate Lombard kingdoms would benefit from a shared defense.**

Bertha—**Pg. 259, ¶ 2—Bertha was the Christian wife of Ethelbert, king of Kent. Bertha's Christianity suggested to Augustine that the king might be an easier target for conversion.**

Ethelbert—**Pg. 259, ¶ 4 & 6—Ethelbert, king of Kent, agreed to be baptized by the monk Augustine. Ethelbert did not force conversion on his subjects, but he did show greater favor and affection to those who did become Christians, which meant that those with political and social ambitions tended to convert.**

Gregory the Great—**Pg. 256, ¶ 5, Pg. 257, ¶ 6 and Pg. 259, ¶ 4—Gregory, a monk elected to become pope after the death of Pope Pelagius II, earned himself the name "Gregory the**

Great" after he saved Rome from a Lombard invasion. Gregory the Great sent the monk Augustine to bring Christianity to Britain, a task that was completed successfully and led to Gregory naming Augustine bishop of the Angles at Canterbury.

Rosemund—**Pg. 255, ¶ 2 & 3—Rosemund, daughter of the Gepid king killed at the hands of Alboin, blackmailed a court official into assassinating the Lombard king. Though she escaped punishment and was welcomed by the exarch in Ravenna, she poisoned herself and died anyway.**

Section II: Comprehension

Write a two or three-sentence answer to each of the following questions.

1. What were the circumstances of the Lombard king Alboin's death? How did Alboin's death lead to Rosemund's death?

A1.—Pg. 255, ¶ 2 & 3—After taking the Gepids into his realm by force, killing their king and marrying the king's daughter Rosemund, Alboin held a feast and handed Rosemund a goblet made from her father's skull and invited her to drink merrily. Rosemund's hatred boiled over and she blackmailed a court official into assassinating Alboin while he slept. Rosemund and her accomplice fled to Ravenna, where they were welcomed, but the two fugitives poisoned each other not long after arriving and both died on the same day.

2. What happened to the Lombard kingship after Alboin's death? How were "duchies" and the "Rule of the Dukes" related to the disintegration of the Lombard kingship?

A2.—Pg. 255, ¶ 4—After Alboin's death, the Germanic nature of the Lombards reasserted itself. Warleaders took control of the army, conquered a series of cities, and each warlord established his own little kingdom, known as a "duchy." The time period where the Lombards did not have a single king and the land was divided into duchies was called the "Rule of the Dukes."

3. How did the areas of Lombard territory in the south of Italy come to be known as Duchy of Spoleto and Duchy of Benevento?

A3.—Pg. 256, ¶ 2—When Agilulf was elected Lombard overlord, two dukes that governed Lombard land in the south of Italy refused to recognize his leadership. After a few clashes Agilulf forced both to acknowledge him. After this, the two Lombard kingdoms in the south were known as the Duchy of Spoleto and the Duchy of Benevento, seemingly loyal to Agilulf but actually continuing on as rulers of two small independent kingdoms.

4. Describe the state of Rome at the time of Pope Pelagius II's death.

A4.—Pg. 256, ¶ 4—At the time of Pope Pelagius II's death, Rome was a mess. The Lombards had cut the city off from Ravenna and from Constantinople, the plague made a sweep

through the city, and the Tiber flooded so severely that its waters flowed in over the walls of the city and filled great regions in it.

5. How did the monk Gregory become the pope after Pelagius II, even though he did not want to be pope?

A5.—Pg. 256, ¶ 3–5—Twelve years before the death of Pelagius II, Gregory had been sent to Constantinople on a diplomatic mission for the pope, but he happily returned to his monastery when his mission was complete. In the years after, Gregory rose to be the abbot of his monastery and when he was asked by the priests of Rome to be the next pope, he wrote to the emperor at Constantinople begging not to be confirmed. A chief official of Rome intercepted the letter and instead forged another one that begged the emperor to make the appointment official as soon as possible, meaning Gregory found himself as pope.

6. Why did everyone in Rome—the people, priests and officials—turn to Gregory for guidance after he was made pope?

A6.—Pg. 256, ¶ 6 to Pg. 257, ¶ 1—Though Gregory was supposed to be Rome's spiritual leader, he became the leader everyone turned to. The civil authority of Rome was cut off from easy communication with its superiors, and Gregory theoretically had continual communication with God, so he found that the people, priests, prefects and officials of Rome all turned to him for guidance.

7. Explain the Lombard threat that faced Rome in 593. How did Gregory handle the threat?

A7.—Pg. 257, ¶ 2, 4 & 5—Hoping to take Rome from Byzantine control, Agilulf moved south towards the city while the dukes of Spoleto and Benevento were moving west to complete the pincer move. Gregory asked for help in the form of soldiers or money from the new emperor of Constantinople, Maurice, but none came. Gregory decided to pay the troops out of church funds and went out to negotiate with Agilulf on his own authority. He agreed to pay the Lombard king five hundred pounds of gold, also from the church treasury, and Agilulf withdrew, meaning Gregory saved Rome.

8. Why wouldn't the exarch at Ravenna agree to a truce with Agilulf? How was peace negotiated between the Byzantines and Lombards when Callinicus came into power?

A8.—Pg. 257, ¶ 6 & 7—The exarch at Ravenna believed that Gregory had overstepped his authority as pope. Because of his wounded pride, the exarch would not agree to a treaty with Agilulf that would create a general peace between the Lombards and all Byzantine territories. When the exarch died in 596 he was replaced by Callinicus; Callinicus agreed to sign a treaty with Agilulf and for a time there was peace between the Lombards and the Byzantine territories.

9. What happened to Christianity in Britain after the collapse of the Roman empire?

A9.—Pg. 258, ¶ 2—The Romans that had come to Britain when the late empire was in full swing were Christian in name and they built a few churches. But after the collapse of Rome,

there was no organized Christian presence on the island. Churches in the south and east had crumbled as the unconverted Saxons had pushed in; the British churches that remained, mostly in the north and west, had been separated from the mother church at Rome for over a century.

10. What was the cultural makeup of Britain at the end of the sixth century, when Gregory took it upon himself to bring the island back into the kingdom of God?

A10.—Pg. 258, ¶ 3—At the end of the sixth century, Saxons ruled along the eastern coast and in much of the southeast. The descendants of the general Aelle ruled in Sussex, the kingdom of the South Saxons; another royal line had established itself in the kingdom for the West Saxons; the descendants of Hengest ruled the southern kingdom of Kent; and small kingdoms ruled by Saxons and Angles bracketed the remaining British kingdoms, which still held the west and north of the island.

11. How did Augustine end up with the title "bishop of the Angles at Canterbury"? How did he end up living in Britain?

A11.—Pg. 259, ¶ 4 & 5—Augustine was successful in his conversion of the king of Kent, Ethelbert. More priests were sent to Britain, Ethelbert turned over a wrecked sanctuary in Canterbury to Augustine to act as his headquarters, and Gregory consecrated Augustine as the bishop of the Angles at Canterbury.

12. Why did Augustine express concern about living with his monks in Britain? How did Gregory convince Augustine to stay and live with his converts?

A12.—Pg. 259, ¶ 4—Augustine wasn't sure if he should have to stay and live with the converts, which showed a low opinion of the Romans on the mission of the Saxon people. Gregory scolded him and said of course he should live with his new clergy in the church of Angli. In Gregory's eyes, the Saxon converts had become one with the believers in Rome, part of the common Christian cause, and it was Augustine's duty to stay and guide the new believers.

Section III: Critical Thinking

The student may not use his text to answer this question.

Gregory the Great did not ask to become pope, but it happened anyway. As pope, he was tasked with not only the religious protection of Rome, but also with the safety of its people. Protecting Rome against the Lombards was a victory, but Gregory longed to get back to the work of God. Explain how, through his guidance of Augustine, Gregory the Great was able to fulfill his spiritual responsibilities by spreading Christianity in Britain. In your answer, make it clear how Ethelbert had a hand in making sure the Saxons under his rule also found salvation in Christ.

The student should start by explaining how Gregory the Great was able to convince Augustine to go back to Britain, despite the monk's hesitance. Gregory's letter of exhortation to Augustine read: "Let neither the toil of the journey nor the tongues of evil-speaking men deter you. . . . May Almighty God grant to me to see the fruit of your labour in the eternal country; that so, even though I cannot labour with you, I may be found together with you in the joy of the reward; for in truth I desire to labour." Gregory the Great was stuck in Rome fulfilling his duties as pope, so he looked to Augustine to act as his surrogate and fulfill his duties of spreading Christianity. When Augustine expressed reluctance, Gregory made Augustine see that the task was not just about his missionary work, but about the work desired to be done by Gregory himself. Augustine would be letting both God and Gregory down if he did not try to convert the Saxons in Britain.

Augustine and his men took Gregory's words to heart and in 597 arrived on Thanet Island, just off the coast of Kent. Kent's king Ethelbert, who also ruled Thanet Island, told the men to stay put while he decided if they were a threat. Once he realized they were not a threat, Ethelbert allowed the men to come onto the mainland to convert as many Saxons as they could, though Ethelbert said he would not forsake the beliefs he had long held. Eventually though, Ethelbert was baptized. After Ethelbert's conversion, Augustine was told to say in Britain, and was made bishop of the Angles at Canterbury.

Unlike Clovis, Ethelbert did not force anyone's conversion, but he did show greater favor and affection to those who did. Inevitably, the politically ambitious in the higher classes of society tended to convert. Ethelbert's nephew, king of the East Saxons, accepted Christianity in 604, and the faith began to ripple out into Saxon society. Augustine brought Christianity back to Britain, and by favoring those who converted, Ethelbert made sure the religion spread across the island.

EXAMPLE ANSWER:

After his victory over the Lombards, Gregory the Great sent the monk Augustine to Britain in an effort to bring Christianity to the island. Augustine left for the mission, but he turned back before arriving, scared. Gregory wrote a letter to Augustine saying it was his duty, to both God and to Gregory, to teach Christianity to the Saxons. Augustine acquiesced, and arrived on Thanet Island in 597 ready to do God's work.

Augustine and his men were greeted by Ethelbert, the king of Kent, who also ruled over Thanet Island. Ethelbert let Augustine work to convert as many Saxons as he could, but said he himself would not be swayed from his long held religious beliefs. Eventually though, Ethelbert was baptized. Augustine continued to do God and Gregory's work in Britain, making a permanent residence there and serving as the bishop of the Angles at Canterbury.

Christianity continued to spread in part because of Ethelbert. While he did not force anyone's conversion, Ethelbert did show greater favor and affection to those who did. Inevitably, the politically ambitious in the higher classes of society tended to convert. Ethelbert's nephew, king of the East Saxons, accepted Christianity in 604, and the faith began to ripple out into Saxon society. Augustine brought Christianity back to Britain, and by favoring those who converted, Ethelbert made sure the religion spread across the island.

Section IV: Map Exercise

1. Using a black pencil, trace the rectangular outline of the frame for Map 35.2: Saxon Kingdoms.

2. Using a black pencil, trace the coastline all around Britannia and what is visible of Ireland. You do not need to include any islands at this time. Then, with your black pencil, trace the outline of the British (the shaded area). Repeat until the contours are familiar.

3. Trace the rectangular outline of the frame in black. Remove your tracing paper from the original. Using a regular pencil with an eraser as you look at the map, draw the coastline. Erase and redraw as necessary.

4. When you are pleased with your map, lay it over the original. Erase and redraw any lines which are more than ¼ inch off of the original.

5. Label the Irish Sea, the North Sea, and the English Channel. Draw and label Hadrian's Wall. Draw and label the Thames River.

6. Remove your map from the original. Looking back at Map 35.2, study the areas of the British, the Angles, the West Saxons, and the East Saxons. Also study the locations of Sussex, Kent, Canterbury, London, and Thanet Island. When you are familiar with them, close the book. Using your regular pencil, label the areas of the British, the Angles, the West Saxons, and the East Saxons and the locations of Sussex, Kent, Canterbury, London, and Thanet Island. Check your map against the original and correct any misplaced labels or cities.

Chapter Thirty-Six

The Persian Crusade

The student may use her text when answering the questions in sections I and II.

Section I: Who, What, Where

Write a one or two-sentence answer explaining the significance of each item listed below.

Bahram Chobin—**Pg. 261, ¶ 3 & 4 and Pg. 262, ¶ 2—Bahram Chobin, a Persian general who had earned himself a great reputation by beating off a Turkish invasion on the far eastern border, revolted again Hurmuz after the king ordered him to leave his post on the Byzantine frontier. Bahram Chobin took the Persian throne from Khosru II, only to flee east to the Turks, where he was eventually killed, when Khosru II came back to Ctesiphon backed by Byzantine troops.**

Bonus—**Pg. 268, ¶ 4—Bonus, a city of official, was left in charge of Constantinople when Heraclius headed into battle against the Persians on Easter Monday, 622. Bonus, along with Sergius, acted as a regent for Heraclius's ten-year-old son Constantine.**

Heraclius—**Pg. 266, ¶ 1 & 3 and Pg. 271, ¶ 4—Heraclius, son of the exarch of Carthage, was crowned emperor after the death of Phocas. Heraclius defended the Byzantine empire against Khosru II's Persian crusade; he saved the empire.**

Hurmuz—**Pg. 261, ¶ 2–4—Hurmuz, successor to Khosru and the Persian throne, made himself unpopular with the Persians because of the drawn out war with Byzantium, and because of his kindness to Christian Persians. After Bahram Chobin revolted against Hurmuz, the king was seized by nobles, blinded, and killed in prison not long after his capture.**

Kavadh II—**Pg. 270, ¶ 9 and Pg. 271, ¶ 2—Kavadh II, son of Khosru II, took the Persian throne in 628 and immediately offered to make peace with Heraclius. Kavadh II ruled only for a few weeks before dying of unknown causes.**

Khosru II—**Pg. 261, ¶ 4 and Pg. 270, ¶ 8—Khosru II, son of Hurmuz, led Persia in a religious crusade against Byzantium. Khosru II was unable to keep Persia strong, and after many years of war the people of Ctesiphon turned on Khosru II when the Byzantine army invaded, and crucified him.**

Kubrat—**Pg. 271, ¶ 3—Kubrat, chief of the Bulgars, asked to negotiate with Heraclius as an independent sovereign. Heraclius agreed to recognize Kubrat's kingship, and from 632 on the Bulgarian chief reigned as king of the first Bulgarian kingdom: Old Great Bulgaria.**

Narses—**Pg. 264, ¶ 5—Narses was the Byzantine general that was responsible for defeating the Persians. Persian children shivered when they heard Narses's name, and while the Romans mourned Narses after he was put to death by Phocas, the Persians celebrated the death of the ruthless general.**

Phocas—**Pg. 263, ¶ 4, Pg. 264, ¶ 1 and Pg. 266, ¶ 2—Phocas, an officer of the Byzantine army, won the favor of the Byzantine army as general, and then the Byzantine people as emperor, because of Maurice's mistreatment of the Byzantine army. Phocas was not in favor for long, and ultimately he was burned alive in the Forum.**

Samo—**Pg. 269, ¶ 5 & 6—Samo, a Frankish merchant turned general, united a number of Slavic tribes that were unhappy with Avar domination. Samo, who had twelve Slavic wives, led his kingdom into battle against the Avar overlords.**

Sergius—**Pg. 267, ¶ 4 and Pg. 270, ¶ 2—Sergius, bishop of Constantinople, convinced Heraclius that the defense of New Rome against the Persians was his sacred duty. Left in charge of Constantinople while Heraclius was at war with Persia, Sergius whipped the city of Constantinople into a religious fervor when Khosru II attacked the city, thus saving Constantinople.**

Sisebut—**Pg. 266, ¶ 4—Sisebut, a Visigothic noble, seized the crown of the Visigothic kingdom by force in 612 and then began to drive the Byzantines out of the lands they held along the coast of Hispania, capturing the imperial cities along the seaboard, razing them to the ground. He recaptured the peninsula and brought the Visigothic kingdom to the height of its power.**

Theodosius—**Pg. 263, ¶ 5 and Pg. 263, ¶ 1 & 2—Theodosius, son of Maurice, refused to take the reins of power away from his father when the army revolted and made Phocas general. Theodosius was murdered by an assassin sent by Phocas, but because his head was so disfigured by the time it made it back to Constantinople, rumors continued to circulate that Theodosius had actually made it to the Persian court and that the head staked out for the people to see was actually the head of someone else.**

Section II: Comprehension

Write a two or three-sentence answer to each of the following questions.

1. Why did Hurmuz send Bahram Chobin a dress?

A1.—Pg. 261, ¶ 3—Bahram Chobin had earned a great reputation for himself by beating off a Turkish invasion on the far eastern border of Persia. Expecting Bahram to repeat his success, Hurmuz sent him to the Byzantine frontier, but in 589 Bahram lost a battle on the banks of the Araxes river to Byzantine forces. Hurmuz was furious: he sent his general a dress to wear, along with an insulting letter dismissing him from command.

2. Why did Khosru II flee into Byzantine territory after he was threatened by Bahram Chobin? What were the results of Khosru II's negotiations with Maurice?

A2.—Pg. 262, ¶ 1–3—When Bahram Chobin threatened to kill Khosru II unless the young man relinquished the throne, Khosru fled into Byzantine territory because Maurice was the only other king strong enough to fight Bahram. Maurice agreed to help Khosru II, sending a Byzantine army back to Ctesiphon with the displaced king, and after a protracted battle Bahram was forced out of the city. In exchange for the help, Khosru II agreed to a truce with Maurice that gave the Byzantine king back some of the frontier cities that had been captured decades earlier by the Persians, and he sealed the truce with a marriage to one of Maurice's daughters.

3. Why did Maurice decide to head back to Constantinople, rather than face the Slavs invading the Danube with his soldiers? What did Maurice give his soldiers in his place?

A3.—Pg. 262, ¶ 5 to Pg. 263, ¶ 1—Maurice, hearing rumors that the Slavs were turning into frightening warriors like the Huns, "refusing to be enslaved or governed" and "bearing readily heat, cold, rain, nakedness, and scarcity of provisions," decided it would be best if he returned to Constantinople rather than face this treacherous enemy himself. He did, however, write a handbook for his men, the *Strategikon*, that described everything that contemporary generals knew about the Slavs. He warned his men to attack in winter, if possible, when the trees were bare, since the Slavs were expert at guerilla tactics and preferred to fight in the deep woods; he told them to look out for clusters of reeds in the river, since the Slavs might be lying on the bottom, breathing through the hollow stems; and he suggested that since the Slavs had multiple chiefs instead of one king, it might be worthwhile trying to bribe some of them to turn against the others.

4. What happened in 599 that made Maurice very unpopular with his troops? What made him even more unpopular in 602?

A4.—Pg. 263, ¶ 2 & 3—In 599, the Avars that were invading in the wake of the Slavs offered to return twelve thousand Byzantine prisoners of war in return for a generous payment. Maurice refused to agree to the deal made by the Avar leader, so the Avars executed all twelve thousand Byzantine men. Then, in 602, Maurice declared that troops would not be

returning home over the winter in order to save travel costs and supplies, and instead they would camp across the Danube, foraging in enemy territory for enough food to sustain them. These two decisions made Maurice very unpopular with his troops.

5. Why did Maurice arm the Blues and the Greens when he heard that Phocas had been declared general of the Byzantine army? What was the result of arming the gangs?

A5.—Pg. 263, ¶ 5—Maurice decided to arm the Blues and the Greens when he heard that Phocas had been declared general of the Byzantine army because he thought Phocas was going to march into the city and take the throne. Phocas wasn't coming for the throne, but Maurice's arming of the gangs created a new problem. After staying on the walls of the city like a garrison for a day and a half, the Blues and Greens started fighting each other, a mob set fire to the house of one of the senators, and rioting spread throughout the city.

6. Explain the circumstances of Maurice's death, and his son Theodosius's death.

A6.—Pg. 263, ¶ 6 to Pg. 264, ¶ 1—With riots spreading in Constantinople because of armed Blues and Greens, Maurice decided to flee to the city of Chalcedon with his wife and sons. When Phocas arrived at the city, he could not be declared emperor because Maurice was still alive, so Phocas sent a trusted officer to Chalcedon, where he caught up with Maurice and murdered him and his four sons. Theodosius had been sent to find shelter in Persia, but he was caught by another assassin in Nicaea and was killed as well.

7. Describe the killing spree Phocas embarked upon at the start of war with Persia in 605, and his political ban on the Greens.

A7.—Pg. 264, ¶ 5—Worried about the security of his crown at the start of the war with Persia in 605, Phocas began executing possible challengers to the throne left and right. He burned alive the general Narses; he executed all of Maurice's male relatives, killed the commander of his bodyguard for plotting against him, and then sanctioned the deaths of Maurice's widow and her three daughters. The Greens turned against him, and he reacted by forbidding anyone with Green affiliations to take part in politics.

8. How did Heraclius come to be elected emperor of Byzantium?

A8.—Pg. 264, ¶ 7 to Pg. 266, ¶ 3—Heraclius's father, the exarch of Carthage, led a rebellion against Constantinople and in 610, he assembled a fleet under the command of Heraclius. When the Byzantine commander at Alexandria in Egypt heard of the expedition, he too joined and the combined forces sailed into the harbor at Constantinople to find the gates open, the people waiting for them, and Phocas already under citizen's arrest. As Heraclius entered the city, Phocas was burned alive in the Forum and Heraclius was crowned emperor.

9. Describe the state of Byzantium when Heraclius was crowned emperor. In your answer, make sure to include the state of Byzantine relations with Persia and the Visigoths at the start of Heraclius's rule.

A9.—Pg. 266, ¶ 3 & 4—When Heraclius was crowned emperor, Byzantium was a mess: the Roman state was exhausted, the Avars were devastating Europe and the Persians had

destroyed the Roman army. In addition, the Persians conquered Edessa and took the Mandylion off to some archive in Ctesiphon, and then Caesarea fell into Persian hands as well. Sisebut, king of the Visigoths, captured Byzantine land on the coast of Hispania and then he recaptured the peninsula, bringing the Visigothic kingdom to the height of its power.

10. What happened when Heraclius asked Khosru II to bring an end to the war in exchange for a tribute? What did Khosru and his Persian army do next to solidify his empire's warring stance?

A10.—Pg. 266, ¶ 5 to Pg. 267, ¶ 1—Khosru II refused to stop fighting in exchange for a tribute from Heraclius—he had already consolidated his power on the Arabian peninsula and in 614 he marched across to the northwest of Arabia and destroyed the Arab Ghassanids, who had helped protect Syria on behalf of Constantinople. Next, Khosru II besieged Jerusalem and the city fell, with Persians storming into the city and massacring the population. Not only did the Persians kill nearly sixty-seven thousand people in Jerusalem, they also stole the most precious relic of Jerusalem, a fragment of the True Cross, and added it to the Persian archives.

11. Why did Heraclius think his empire was doomed, and what did he do with all of Constantinople's treasures? What happened to these treasures?

A11.—Pg. 267, ¶ 3 & 4—With the Persians advancing on Constantinople from the east, the Avars and Slavs approaching from the northwest, the Byzantine army exhausted and no more grain supplies from North Africa and Egypt, Heraclius saw no way to save his empire. In an attempt to save some of Byzantine culture, he loaded all of Constantinople's treasures onto ships, sent them to North Africa for safekeeping, and began to make plans to abandon the city for Carthage. Even more bad news came to Heraclius when he found out the ships holding all of the Byzantine treasure sank in a storm not too long after leaving the Golden Horn in 618.

12. What made Heraclius recommit to war with Khosru II? How was the war funded?

A12.—Pg. 267, ¶ 4 and Pg. 268, ¶ 1—When the people of Constantinople found out that Heraclius lost all of the city's treasures and planned to flee to Carthage, they expressed horror to the bishop Sergius. Sergius convinced Heraclius that the defense of New Rome was his sacred duty and so Heraclius took a vow before God at the altar of the Hagia Sophia to stay in the city. When Khosru II framed the war as Zoroastrianism versus Christianity, the people of Constantinople were fired with indignation, men began to join the army in increasing numbers, and Sergius melted the treasures of Constantinople's churches into coins and presented the money to Heraclius so he could pay for the war.

13. What was Heraclius able to buy with the church's money?

A13.—Pg. 268, ¶ 3—Heraclius used the church's money to pay and provision new troops, outfit the army with new weapons, and build ships. He also bought a temporary peace with the Avars, protecting his western flank from attack and preventing the necessity of

carrying on a two-front war. Heraclius was able to pay sailors to man ships that guarded the Bosphorus Strait, stalling the Persians at Chalcedon because they were not quite ready to launch a full naval assault across the water.

14. Why did Heraclius sail to Asia Minor, to the Cilician Gates, instead of meeting the Persians straight on at Chalcedon?

A14.—Pg. 268, ¶ 5 & 6—Heraclius sailed to the Cilician Gates so he could pass through the Taurus Mountains, which would protect the troops from immediate attack when meeting the Persians. Landing in Asia Minor also gave refugees from Syria the opportunity to land on the shore and join the fight against the Persians. Landing in Asia Minor also gave Heraclius a place to train his army, which was full of men that had never fought before.

15. Describe the progress of the war between Heraclius and Khosru II after the Byzantine army successfully defeated the Persians in their first meeting outside of Armenia. What drastic move did Khosru II make in 626 in order to bring the war to an end?

A15.—Pg. 268, ¶ 7 to Pg. 269, ¶ 3—After the Byzantine army successfully broke the Persian line when the enemies met outside of Armenia, they continued to defeat Persian advances. For the next three years, Heraclius and his men drove the Persians backwards towards Nineveh, reclaiming Asia Minor and parts of Armenia and Syria. In 626, fed up with defeat, Khosru II decided it was necessary to besiege Constantinople.

16. Describe Khosru II's attack on Constantinople in July of 626.

A16.—Pg. 269, ¶ 6 to Pg. 270, ¶ 1—Khosru II attacked Constantinople from all sides: Slavs and Avars marched on the city while Persian ships prepared to sail from the opposite shore. Khosru II chose to attack the city with his eighty thousand troops when Heraclius and the bulk of the army were far from Constantinople, on the northern shore of Persia. On the first day of the attack, the city was completely surrounded, all of the buildings outside the walls were set on fire, siege engines and catapults surrounded the city and archers kept up a hail of arrows over the city wall.

17. What tactical mistake did the Persian general in charge of the attack on Constantinople make during the siege on the city? How did this mistake cost the Persians victory?

A17.—Pg. 270, ¶ 3 & 4—The general in charge of the Persian attack sent his entire fleet into the Bosphorus Strait, planning for the Avars and Slavs to occupy the garrison so that his ships could approach by water without much opposition. This was a mistake because the Byzantine navy was strong and they drove back the Persian fleet, sinking ships and drowning their crews. Once the attack from the east was over, Byzantine troops focused on beating off the Avar and Slav assault from the west, killing thousands of Avars and Slavs until the allies began to retreat, ending the siege.

18. Who were the Khazars, and why were they important to Heraclius?

A18.—Pg. 270, ¶ 6 & 7—The Khazars were a nomadic tribe driven west to the Byzantine borders by the Turks, and they had made a home for themselves in the mountains north of the Black Sea. The Khazars agreed to ally themselves with Heraclius and joined in the fight against Persia. With the help of the Khazars, the Byzantine army was able to fight their way south into Persian territory, sacking the city of Derbent and Nineveh as Heraclius made his way to Ctesiphon.

19. What were the terms of the peace made between Kavadh II and Heraclius in 628? When was the True Cross returned to Jerusalem?

A19.—Pg. 270, ¶ 9 to Pg. 271, ¶ 1—When Kavadh II took the throne in 628, he immediately sent to Heraclius, offering to make peace. The treaty gave back to Heraclius all of the land that Khosru II had conquered; it also returned to Heraclius the fragment of the True Cross the Persians had taken from Jerusalem. Heraclius proceeded from Ctesiphon to Jerusalem and on March 21 of 630, he returned the True Cross to the city with his own hands.

Section III: Critical Thinking

The student may not use her text to answer this question.

Khosru II had mighty ambitions for Persia, and for his own power. Khosru II's early victories against Edessa, Caesarea and Jerusalem suggested the gods were on his side. He was even able to take two precious Christian relics—the Mandylion and a fragment of the True Cross—into Persian possession. But claiming divine intervention as the reason for his success was a misstep on Khosru II's part. Explain why turning the Persian war against the Byzantine empire into a crusade was a mistake, and how religious fervor was actually exactly what Persia's opponent—Byzantium—needed in order to defeat Khosru II.

For this answer, the student should identify two key factors: first, the Zoroastrians in Persia were largely aristocrats, not the people who were in the trenches fighting. When Khosru II wrote a letter to Heraclius demanding his surrender, telling him he should not "deceive [himself] with a vain hope in that Christ who was not able to save himself from the Jews, that killed him by nailing him to a cross," Khosru II turned the war into a religious battle. But using Zoroastrianism as a carrot for his soldiers created little motivation since most of them were not Zoroastrians. The second key factor was that Heraclius's soldiers were Christians. When Khosru II made the conflict about faith, the Byzantine soldiers were fired up, believing they weren't just defending Heraclius's empire, but God's land. On page 268, ¶ 1, the text tells us: "But when Heraclius told the people of Constantinople that the Persians were blaspheming Christ, they were fired with indignation. Men began to join the army in increasing numbers. Sergius, the bishop of Constantinople, melted the treasures of Constantinople's churches, turned them into coins, and presented the money to Heraclius." All of Constantinople's treasures had been lost at sea, and Heraclius's treasury was bankrupt. But because this was now a crusade, the church found money to fund the war.

The student should also describe how religious fervor saved Constantinople from Khosru II's siege on Constantinople, and ultimately won the war for Byzantium. While Constantinople was ringed with fire and surrounded on all sides by Persians, Avars and Slavs, the bishop Sergius held regular sermons, vigils, services, and sacred processions, reminding the people that they were suffering through a war of religion. As a result the entire city was seized with a fervor that would have carried the people through a much longer siege, and helped to create enough energy for the Byzantine people to drive the Persians out of Constantinople. After they were driven out of Constantinople, the Persians continued to retreat to Ctesiphon. When the Byzantine army reached Ctesiphon, the citizens turned on Khosru II and crucified him. If Khosru II had not initially turned the war into a crusade, the Byzantine people would not have been unified under the task of defending their God. When Khosru II pitted Zoroastrianism against Christianity, he made a mistake that cost him the war, and his life.

EXAMPLE ANSWER:

Khosru II made a big mistake when he turned his war against Byzantium into a religious crusade. The people of Byzantium were unified in their devotion to Christ, but the people of Persia were divided in their religious beliefs. Khosru II tried to make the war a conflict between Zoroastrianism and Christianity, but the soldiers he led weren't moved by fighting for Zoroastrianism since it was the aristocracy of Persia that mostly practiced that religion. However, the men that fought for Heraclius were all Christian, so when Khosru II made the conflict about faith, the Byzantine soldiers were fired up, believing they weren't just defending Heraclius's empire, but God's land. Men signed up left and right to fight for Heraclius, and the church found money to fund the war after Heraclius lost all of the city's money and treasures.

Christianity won the war for the Byzantine empire. Khosru II felt he had to attack Constantinople in order to take control of the war. But even with the city ringed in fire, and surrounded on all sides by Persians, Avars and Slavs, the religious spirit of the Byzantine people could not be broken. The bishop Sergius held regular sermons, vigils, services, and sacred processions, reminding the people that they were suffering through a war of religion. As a result the entire city was seized with a fervor that would have carried the people through a much longer siege, and helped to create enough energy for the Byzantine people to drive the Persians out of Constantinople. After they were driven out of Constantinople, the Persians continued to retreat to Ctesiphon. When the Byzantine army reached Ctesiphon, the citizens turned on Khosru II and crucified him. If Khosru II had not initially turned the war into a crusade, the Byzantine people would not have been unified under the task of defending their God. When Khosru II pitted Zoroastrianism against Christianity, he made a mistake that cost him the war, and his life.

Chapter Thirty-Seven

The Prophet

The student may use his text when answering the questions in sections I and II.

Section I: Who, What, Where

Write a one or two-sentence answer explaining the significance of each item listed below.

Abu Bakr—**Pg. 277, ¶ 4 to Pg. 278, ¶ 1 and Pg. 279, ¶ 4—Abu Bakr, Muhammad's close friend, was one of Muhammad's first followers. Abu Bakr helped Muhammad escape from his house in Mecca, which was being watched, to flee to Medina.**

Abu Talib—**Pg. 276, ¶ 3 and Pg. 278, ¶ 3 & 5—Abu Talib, an ambitious man who had fought for the Quraysh in the Sacrilegious War, raised his nephew Muhammad. When the clan leaders in Mecca threatened Muhammad, Abu Talib stuck by his nephew, and he died under the wretched conditions created by the upper classes in Mecca for the followers of Muhammad.**

Ali—**Pg. 277, ¶ 4 and Pg. 279, ¶ 4—Ali, Muhammad's cousin, son of Muhammad's uncle Abu Talib, was one of Muhammad's first followers. Ali helped Muhammad escape Mecca, and stayed behind to make sure that all the prophet's debts were settled.**

Ansar—**Pg. 279, ¶ 1—Ansar, or "Helpers," was a name given to the followers of Allah who were not from the city of Mecca and not part of Muhammad's own tribe. The name came about when Muhammad spoke to a delegation of people that had fled Mecca and come to Medina and some of those people converted.**

The Hijra—**Pg. 279, ¶ 4—The Hijra was the day of Muhammad's flight from Mecca, on September 24, 622. Afterwards, all dates for the followers of Muhammad were counted as "after the Hijra."**

Khadija—**Pg. 276, ¶ 4 and Pg. 278, ¶ 5—Khadija, a Quraysh merchant and widow, married Muhammad when she was forty years old and when he was twenty-five, bearing his three**

children and remaining his only wife during her lifetime. Khadija died under the wretched conditions created by the upper classes in Mecca for the followers of Muhammad.

Muhammad—**Pg. 276, ¶ 3, Pg. 277, ¶ 2 and Pg. 280, ¶ 2—Muhammad, born into the clan of Banu Hashim, orphaned at the age of six, had a vision of the angel Gabriel and understood that he was the prophet of God. Muhammad left Mecca for Medina, where he was not just the prophet to his believers but also the civil authority over the non-believers, and he achieved political power not through conquest but through his reputation for wisdom.**

Muslim—**Pg. 279, ¶ 4—Muslim was the name given to the followers of Muhammad.**

Sacrilegious War—**Pg. 275, ¶ 4—The Sacrilegious War was fought between the Quraysh tribe and the Qays tribe to keep their power in Mecca. The war was called the "Sacrilegious War" because it was fought during a sacred month.**

Umma—**Pg. 279, ¶ 5 & 6—Umma was the name given to the tribe of people that followed the words of Muhammad, and they were the most powerful group in Medina.**

Zaid—**Pg. 277, ¶ 4—Zaid, a servant taken captive in a tribal battle, who had married and stayed with the Quraysh clan and fathered four daughters, was one of Muhammad's first followers. Zaid's four daughters also followed Muhammad.**

Section II: Comprehension

Write a two or three-sentence answer to each of the following questions.

1. What is a *wadi*? Why was the dam at the Wadi Dhana so important to the people of Marib?

A1.—Pg. 273, * and ¶ 3—A wadi is valley whose floor becomes a river or stream during times of rain. A dam closed off the Wadi Dhana, which meant the rainwater and runoff from nearby mountains during wet seasons was collected and able to be channeled, irrigated and connected to Marib's cultivated fields. The dam at the Wadi Dhana was so important to the people of Marib because it supplied food and water to its fifty thousand residents.

2. Why was the third breach of the dam at the Wadi Dhana in 590 so significant to the history of medieval southern Arabia?

A2.—Pg. 274, ¶ 2 & 3—The third breach of the dam at the Wadi Dhana in 590 caused a flood so catastrophic that villages downstream from the damn were wiped out for good and Marib, already shrunken from its former size after the two previous breaches, was basically deserted. The breach was so significant because it divided the history of medieval southern Arabia; the time before the breach was remembered as a mythically glorious time, the height of southern Arabian civilization, and the time after the breach was known as the end of the civilization's glory. We also know the breaking of the dam was significant because it is remembered in the Qur'an.

3. How was Medina affected by third dam breach at the Wadi Dhana? Why was Medina already an important city on the Arabian peninsula?

A3.—Pg. 275, ¶ 2—When the dam was breached for the third time at the Wadi Dhana, many of the inhabitants of villages downstream from the dam, and the inhabitants of Marib, ended up in the city of Medina. Medina was already an important city on the Arabian peninsula because it was a mixed town, made up of Jews who had migrated into Arabia long before and native Arabs. In Medina, intermarriage eased the racial distinction between the two groups.

4. Explain the social divisions of clans (*banu*) and tribes in Arabian culture, using the clans and tribes of Mecca as your example.

A4.—Pg. 275, ¶ 3—The Arabs of Mecca were first and foremost members of clans (*banu*) linked together by blood and marriage, and the clans themselves were loosely associated into larger groups, or tribes. Mecca was governed by a council made up of the patriarchs of the most powerful clans. Among these were the clans of the Banu Hashim, the Banu Taim, and the Banu Makhzum, all of them belonging to the Quraysh tribe; the Quraysh tribe was dominant in Mecca, and its clan members controlled the Mecca council.

5. What four sacred months of the year were the Arabic tribes supposed to observe? Were these months of observation fixed?

A5.—Pg. 275, † continued on Pg. 276—The Arabic tribes were supposed to observe four sacred months per year. They were supposed to observe the eleventh (Dhu al-Qi'dah), twelfth (Dhu al-Hijjah), and first (Muharram) in a row, which provided a three-month break from any fighting. The seventh (Rajab) was also supposed to be observed. The months of observation were not fixed because the old Arabic calendar was lunar and the months moved from year to year, meaning the tribal chiefs could change the beginning of sacred times if they weren't finished with an ongoing war.

6. How did Muhammad come to work in the caravan business?

A6.—Pg. 276, ¶ 3 & 4—An orphan at the age of six, Muhammad was raised by his uncle Abu Talib. Muhammad entered the caravan business as a way to survive: he earned his keep by accompanying his uncle's merchant caravans on their journeys to other cities. At twenty-five, Muhammad led a caravan for Khadija which went all the way to Syria, and doubled in value because of Muhammad's management.

7. Why did the wall around Ka'aba have to be rebuilt? Why did Muhammad take part in the rebuilding?

A7.—Pg. 276, ¶ 5 to Pg. 277, ¶ 1—The wall around Ka'aba had to be rebuilt because men had stolen part of the treasure, showing that even shrines were not exempt from the greed of people in Mecca. Muhammad took part in the rebuilding because he was disturbed by the growing distance between the rich and poor in his city, and the rampant materialism of his tribesmen.

8. What was Muhammad doing when he was given a vision of the angel Gabriel in 610?

A8.—Pg. 277, ¶ 2—For one month each year, Muhammad provided for the poor: he would pray, give food to all the poverty-stricken residents of Mecca who came to him, and then walk around the Ka'aba seven times. It was during his month of service in the year 610 that Muhammad was given a vision of the angel Gabriel.

9. What did Gabriel say to Muhammad during his vision? What words did Muhammad read in his vision?

A9.—Pg. 277, ¶ 2 & 3—When Muhammad had his vision of Gabriel, Gabriel told Muhammad to "Read!" a coverlet of brocade whereon there was some writing, and he repeated this command three times. After Muhammad read the cloth, he was told by Gabriel that he was the prophet of God, appointed to take the messages of the angel to the rest of the people. However, the account does not say exactly what Muhammad read in his visions, and for the rest of his life Muhammad struggled to receive, interpret and pass on the revelations of God.

10. Describe the basic tenets of the religion that was given to Muhammad in his vision of 610. What is *al-mar'ruf* and how did this relate to Muhammad's new religion?

A10.—Pg. 277, ¶ 3—The basic tenets of the religion given to Muhammad in his vision of 610 were to worship the one God, the creator Allah. Muhammad was assigned to pursue personal purity, piety, and morality, all of which were already prescribed by Arab sacred practice. *Al-mar'ruf,* meaning "that which is known," was the word used for Muhammad's righteous behavior, and was the behavior that Meccan tribesman knew to be right but did not themselves follow.

11. Explain the core of the message Muhammad received from Allah in 613. Who followed Muhammad when he started to proclaim his message in public? Who resented Muhammad's faith?

A11.—Pg. 278, ¶ 1–3—The core of the message Muhammad received from Allah in 613 was simple: worship Allah, care for the orphan, give to the poor, and share the wealth that had been divinely granted. When he started to proclaim his message in public, the weak, poor and disinherited followed Muhammad. The newly prosperous upper classes of Mecca and the clan leaders of the Quraysh resented Muhammad's faith, complaining to Muhammad's uncle Abu Talib that he was insulting them, mocking their way of life, and that if he wasn't stopped, they would get rid of both Muhammad and his uncle.

12. What happened to the followers of Muhammad in Mecca? Where did they go when conditions in Mecca worsened?

A12.—Pg. 278, ¶ 4—A campaign of terror was launched by the clan leaders against the followers of Muhammad that resided in Mecca: they were attacked in the alleyways, imprisoned on false charges, refused food and drink, and pushed outside the city walls. Afraid for their lives, followers of Muhammad fled across the Red Sea to Axum, where they were welcomed by the Christian king Armah because they were also worshippers of one God, and others fled north to Medina. The followers of Muhammad that stayed in Mecca were

forced into a ghetto, a ban was declared on them, and no one could trade with them, which cut off their food and water supply.

13. What revelation was Muhammad given while surviving in the wretched conditions in Mecca, during which time his wife and uncle died?

A13.—Pg. 278, ¶ 5—While surviving in the wretched conditions created by the clan leaders in Mecca, during which time his wife and uncle died, Muhammad was given a new revelation: God permitted those who were wronged and driven from their homes to fight back.

14. When was Muhammad given permission by God to leave Mecca?

A14.—Pg. 279, ¶ 2 & 3—When the clan leaders of the Quraysh found out that Muhammad had a revelation that his followers were allowed to fight back against their oppressors, they became fearful of Muhammad. The Quraysh planned that one representative of each clan would join in a group assassination of Muhammad and that way, no single family would bear responsibility for his death. When the assassination of Muhammad was planned, God finally gave permission to his prophet to migrate.

15. When did Muslim identity truly take shape? What was the Muslim identity based on?

A15.—Pg. 279, ¶ 5—Muslim identity truly began to take shape when Muhammad left Mecca, the day known as the Hijra. When Muhammad came to Medina he was able to shape his followers based on their bond of belief in one Creator, commitment to a life of justice and purity in His name. The tribe Muhammad created were called *umma*, "one community to the exclusion of all men."

Section III: Critical Thinking

The student may use his text to answer this question.

In this chapter we read about several visions received by Muhammad that were directly related to the conditions of living in Mecca. For example, when he was being persecuted by the Quraysh clan leaders, he was given the vision that those who were wronged and driven from their home could fight back. When Muhammad found out his assassination was being planned, he had a revelation that God gave him permission to migrate. Write a paragraph explaining how the system of Arabic clans in Mecca was related to Muhammad's first revelation. Then explain how Muhammad's first vision influenced his own leadership in Medina.

The student may use the text to answer this question. Referencing pages 275 and 276 would be helpful in describing the corruption of the Quraysh tribe. Muhammad's original vision is described on pages 277 and 278, and details about Muhammad's rule of Medina can be found on page 280.

To answer this question fully, the student must first explain the corrupt clan system in Mecca. The three ruling clans in Mecca were all part of the Quraysh tribe, and the Quraysh tribe controlled the Mecca council. Clans within the Quraysh tribe were hostile to one another. When the tribes were roaming the desert before settling in Mecca, they shared the common goal of food, water, and staying alive. Such extreme conditions no longer existed, so the clans fought about money and power. Because the Arabs were constitutionally anti-king, several men fought for more power, greed triumphed, and those in need, like widows and orphans, were pushed aside.

Next, the student must explain the core of the first message received by Muhammad and how it related to current political conditions in Mecca. The message was to worship Allah, and pursue personal purity, piety, and morality. As Muhammad thought about the vision and what it meant, he understood the larger message was to care for the orphan, give to the poor and share the wealth that had been divinely granted. Everything Muhammad was supposed to do in the name of Allah was the opposite of how the clans treated the citizens of Mecca. Instead of fighting for power and money, Muhammad was supposed to teach his followers to care for those weaker than themselves, and to share their wealth rather than hoard it.

The student should then explain how Muhammad's original vision affected his leadership in Medina. Not all residents of Medina were members of Muhammad's tribe, the umma. Muhammad provided protection for these groups like theoretical orphans. They were not part of his tribe, but he cared for them anyway. Muhammad became known as a great leader and achieved political power not through fighting and conquest, but through his reputation for wisdom.

Finally, he should connect Muhammad's first vision, and his later leadership in Medina, back to the corruption of the Quraysh tribe. Muhammad lived in a corrupt city where the leaders valued wealth and power over the welfare of their people. Muhammad's first vision, the vision that told him he was God's messenger, showed him that he and his followers were to give to the poor and share the wealth that was divinely granted. By doing so, Muhammad gained great political power in Medina. Unlike the clans within the Quraysh that fought their way to importance in Mecca, Muhammad was given power by the people of Medina by acting out the principles of his vision from God.

EXAMPLE ANSWER:

Muhammad lived in a city that was ruled by the corrupt. The three ruling clans in Mecca were all part of the Quraysh tribe, and the Quraysh tribe controlled the Mecca council. Clans within the Quraysh tribe were hostile to one another. When the tribes were roaming the desert before settling in Mecca, they shared the common goal of food, water, and staying alive. Such extreme conditions no longer existed, so the clans fought about money and power. Because the Arabs were constitutionally anti-king, several men fought for more power, greed triumphed, and those in need, like widows and orphans, were pushed aside. Muhammad received a message from the angel Gabriel that told him he was God's prophet. Muhammad understood the message from God to mean: worship Allah, care for the orphan, give to the poor and share the wealth that had been divinely granted. Everything Muhammad was supposed to do in the name of Allah was the opposite of how the clans treated the citizens of Mecca. Instead of fighting for power and money, Muhammad was supposed to teach his followers to care for those weaker than themselves, and to share their wealth rather than hoard it.

When Muhammad left Mecca for Medina, he took with him his message of rights for all. Not all residents of Medina were members of Muhammad's tribe, the umma. Muhammad provided protection for these groups like theoretical orphans. They were not part of his tribe, but he cared for them anyway. Muhammad became known as a great leader and achieved political power not through fighting and conquest, but through his reputation for wisdom. Muhammad lived in a corrupt city where the leaders valued wealth and power over the welfare of their people. Muhammad's first vision, the vision that told him he was God's messenger, showed him that he and his followers were to give to the poor and share the wealth that was divinely granted. By doing so, Muhammad gained great political power in Medina. Unlike the clans within the Quraysh that fought their way to importance in Mecca, Muhammad was given power by the people of Medina by acting out the principles of his vision from God.

Section IV: Map Exercise

1. Using a black pencil, trace the rectangular outline of the frame for Map 37.1: Muhammad's Arabia.

2. Using a blue pencil, trace the coastline along Arabia and the outline of the Black Sea, the Caspian Sea, the Red Sea, and the visible portion of the Mediterranean. Then select four contrasting colors. Use these respectively to trace the Persian Empire, the Byzantine Empire, Himyar, and Axum. Repeat until the contours are familiar.

3. Using a new sheet of paper, trace the rectangular outline of the frame in black. Using your regular pencil with an eraser as you look at Map 37.1, draw the coastline along Arabia. Then draw the outlines of the Black Sea, the Caspian Sea, the Red Sea, and the visible portion of the Mediterranean. Then trace the outlines of the Persian Empire, the Byzantine Empire, Himyar, and Axum. Erase and redraw as necessary while looking at the map.

4. When you are pleased with your map, lay it over the original. Erase and redraw any lines which are more than ¼ inch off of the original. When your map is correct, shade each area as the map maker does. Shade Axum and cross with diagonal lines. Shade Himyar very lightly. Shade the Byzantine Empire less lightly and the Persian Empire most heavily of all. If you have trouble making your shading tones distinct, you can substitute horizontal or hatched lines to distinguish each area.

5. Remove your map from the original. Study closely the locations of Jerusalem, Damascus, Medina, Mecca, Marib, Ctesiphon, Wadi Dhana, and Marib Dam. When you are familiar with them, close your book. Mark each on your map, and label it. Then check your map against the original. If your locations or labels are misplaced, erase and remark while looking at the map.

Chapter Thirty-Eight

Tang Dominance

The student may use her text when answering the questions in sections I and II.

Section I: Who, What, Where

Write a one or two-sentence answer explaining the significance of each item listed below.

Battle of Baekgang—**Pg. 289, ¶ 4—The Battle of Baekgang, fought at the same place as the Battle of Hwang San Beol, took place in 663, between the Baekje-Japan alliance, led by Prince Naka no Oe of Japan and Buyeo Pung of Baekje, and the Tang-Silla forces. The Tang-Silla alliance was triumphant; Prince Naka no Oe returned to Japan to shore up his defenses against invasion, Buyeo Pung escaped into Goguryeo and the nation of Baekje ceased to exist.**

Battle of Hwang San Beol—**Pg. 287, ¶ 4—The Battle of Hwang San Beol was great fight between Silla, aided by 130,000 Chinese troops, and the Baekje. The Baekje army was devastated, the Baekje king Uija surrendered and was taken to China as a prisoner.**

Buyeo Pung—**Pg. 289, ¶ 2, 4 & 5—Buyeo Pung, the Baekje prince that was formerly exiled as a Japanese hostage, was proclaimed by the Japanese via Naka no Oe to be the rightful king of Baekje after Muyeol the Great proclaimed himself king of Silla and Baekje. After the Japanese-Baekje alliance lost to the Tang-Silla alliance, Buyeo Pung escaped into Goguryeo only to be later captured and taken off as a prisoner to Tang China.**

Gaozong (Tang Gaozong)—**Pg. 286, ¶ 4 and Pg. 287, ¶ 2—Gaozong, Tang Taizong's favorite son, who fasted and wept at the dead emperor's bed, was rewarded with the Tang crown, becoming Tang Gaozong when he was acclaimed emperor. When Tang Gaozong fell ill, he relied on his wife Wu Zetian to read his state paper and make decisions in his name.**

Gar Tongtsen—**Pg. 286, ¶ 3—Gar Tongtsen was the regent to Mangson Mangtsen, who inherited the Tibetan throne when he was just an infant.**

Hsieh-li—**Pg. 282, ¶ 4 and Pg. 283, ¶ 6—Hsieh-li took control of the Eastern Khaghanate after the Turkish kingdom fractured following Bumin Khan's death. Hsieh-li was sent into exile by his nephew when his nephew staged a coup d'état with the backing of Tang Taizong.**

Kotoku—**Pg. 288, ¶ 4—Kotoku, uncle of Naka no Oe and younger brother of Saimei, took the throne as Japan's Heavenly Sovereign after Soga power was dismantled.**

Li Shimin (Tang Taizong)—**Pg. 282, ¶ 4, Pg. 285, ¶ 2 and Pg. 286, ¶ 1—Li Shimin, the second son of Tang emperor Tang Gaozu, became the second emperor of the Tang dynasty in 626, taking the name Tang Taizong. Emphasizing his northern methods of fighting and emphasizing strength over scholarship, Tang Taizong extended the Tang empire into the Eastern and part of the Western Turkish Khaghanate, and he made a marriage alliance with the Tibetan Songtsen Gampo when he sent his niece Wen-ch'eng to the Tibetan ruler's court.**

Mangson Mangtsen—**Pg. 286, ¶ 3—Mangson Mangtsen, Songtsen Gampo's grandson and heir, inherited the throne when he was just an infant so his power went to his regent Gar Tongtsen.**

Munmu—**Pg. 289, ¶ 3-6—Munmu, son of Muyeol the Great, took Silla's throne just as Japanese forces were invading but he was able to beat the Japanese-Baekje alliance with the help of Tang China. Munmu, still reinforced by the Tang, then successfully invaded Goguryeo, bringing the Three Kingdoms period in Korean history to an end and starting the Unified Silla period.**

Muyeol the Great—**Pg. 287, ¶ 3-5—Muyeol the Great, king of Silla, threatened by the triple alliance of Goguryeo, Baekje and Japan, made an alliance with Wu Zetian and with China's help defeated the Baekje at Hwang San Beol. After Uija was taken prisoner, Muyeol the Great declared himself king of Silla and Baekje.**

Naka no Oe—**Pg. 287, ¶ 6, Pg. 288, ¶ 3 & 6 and Pg. 289, ¶ 2—Naka no Oe, crown prince of the Yamato dynasty, took down the Soga empire, but never became Heavenly Sovereign of Japan himself. Though he never took the sacred title, Naka no Oe remained commander in chief of Japan's forces.**

Nakatomi no Kamatari—**Pg. 287, ¶ 8—Nakatomi no Kamatari, a senior member of the Nakatomi clan, rival to the Soga clan, worked with Naka no Oe to get rid of the Soga influence on the Japanese throne.**

Namri Songtsen—**Pg. 285, ¶ 3—Namri Songtsen, father of Songtsen Gampo, was the leader of one of the Tibetan tribes. He had taken the first tentative steps towards dominating the neighboring tribes when he died, sometime between 618 and 620, and then Songtsen Gampo inherited his title.**

Saimei—**Pg. 287, ¶ 7 and Pg. 288, ¶ 3—Saimei, the empress of Japan, had taken the throne in 642 after her husband's death; though her son was a better choice for ruler, the Soga clan chose to put Saimei on the throne because they could control her from behind the scenes.**

When leaders of the Soga clan were being attacked by her son in her court, Saimei walked away so she could not see nor hear what was happening.

Soga no Emishi—**Pg. 288, ¶ 1 & 3—Soga no Emishi worked with his son Soga no Iruka to raise Saimei to the Japanese throne because together they stood to gain more power by controlling the heavenly sovereign. When Emishi heard the news that his son had been murdered, he took his own life.**

Soga no Iruka—**Pg. 288, ¶ 1—Soga no Iruka, a leader of the Soga clan, was the primary target of Naka no Oe's plot to get rid of Soga power, because with his father Soga no Emishi, Soga no Iruka raised Saimei to empress in order to gain power. Soga no Iruka was murdered by Naka no Oe in his mother's court.**

Songtsen Gampo—**Pg. 285, ¶ 3 & 4 and Pg. 286, ¶ 1 & 2—Songtsen Gampo, leader of the Tibetan tribes, strengthened his territory by attacking the Tuyu-hun nomads, sending armies out to the Tang border and the Indian border and making a marriage alliance with the Tang. Through his marriage to Wen-ch'eng, Tibetan culture became infused with northern Chinese culture, and developed a script based on Indian Sanskrit.**

Su Dingfang—**Pg. 286, ¶ 6 to Pg. 287, ¶ 1—Su Dingfang, the Chinese general in charge of the western front, took advantage of the civil war in the Western Turkish Khaghanate and in 657 sent his men to attack the Turks through a blizzard and two feet of snow. The surprise attack worked, the unprepared soldiers of the Western Turks were defeated, and the land of the Khaghanate was reduced to a Tang protectorate.**

Uija—**Pg. 287, ¶ 4—Uija, the king of Baekje, was taken prisoner by the Chinese after the Baekje defeat at Hwang San Beol.**

Wen-ch'eng—**Pg. 286, ¶ 1—Wen-ch'eng, niece of Tang Taizong, was married to the Tibetan leader Songtsen Gampo as a way to ally China and Tibet.**

Wu Zetian—**Pg. 286, ¶ 5 and Pg. 287, ¶ 2—We Zetian, one of Tang Taizong's concubines, rescued from the Buddhist monastery where she had been sent after Taizong's death, became the first wife of Tang Gaozong and empress in 656, and her three-year-old son was named crown prince. We Zetian became the decision maker in the Tang dynasty when her husband became too ill to rule.**

Section II: Comprehension

Write a two or three-sentence answer to each of the following questions.

1. In what ways did Tang Gaozu relate to his neighbors in the Eastern Khaghanate?

A1.—Pg. 282, ¶ 3—Tang Gaozu related to his neighbors in the Eastern Khaghanate in several ways: Tang Gaozu had grown up in the northern reaches of China, where the Turks and

Chinese mingled along the border. Gaozu's mother and grandmother had been of nomadic blood, and Gaozu himself had raised his sons as hunters and warriors, more interested in horses and hunting dogs like the Turks than in Confucian classics like the Chinese.

2. How did Li Shimin stop a full Eastern Khaghanate invasion of Tang territory?

A2.—Pg. 282, ¶ 4 to Pg. 283, ¶ 1—When Hsieh-li started attacking northern Chinese lands every two or three months, and then in 624 when Hsieh-li sent the army of the Eastern Khaghanate down to cross the Yellow River, Tang troops panicked. But then Li Shimin rode out and offered to challenge Hsieh-li to single combat which struck the Turkish khan as the act of a man confident of victory. The khan began to suspect that his own men were in league with Li Shimin and that the duel was a trap, so he refused to fight and instead accepted another huge payment from the Tang and withdrew.

3. Describe Li Shimin's rise to the Tang throne as Tang Taizong.

A3.—Pg. 283, ¶ 3—Li Shimin had fought for his father in the wars that brought Tang Gaozu to the throne, and had earned a loyal following of his own through his bravery against the Turks. In 626, he murdered his older brother, the crown prince of the new dynasty, and asked his father to appoint him heir instead, to which Tang Gaozu agreed. A few months later Tang Gaozu abdicated his throne, giving it to his son, and Li Shimin became Tang Taizong.

4. After his coronation, how did Tang Taizong once again stop the invading Eastern Turks?

A4.—Pg. 283, ¶ 4 & 5—As the Eastern Turks invaded again, Tang Taizong rode out to meet their forces at the Wei river, north of Chang'an, with just six men. Tan Taizong kept his small number of troops far off in the distance, so that Hsieh-li and his men could not count the number in Tang Taizong's army. When they met, Tang Taizong offered to go through a brotherhood ceremony with Hsieh-li, and the Turkish khan accepted, meaning Tang Taizong avoided another Turkish invasion.

5. How did Tang Taizong become "Heavenly Khan of the Eastern Turks"? How did Tang Taizong make himself popular with his new subjects?

A5.—Pg. 283, ¶ 6 to Pg. 285, ¶ 1—After going through the brotherhood ceremony with Hsieh-li, Tang Taizong convinced the Turkish khan's subjects to revolt against him, and he encouraged Hsieh-li's nephew to lead a coup d'état. Civil war between uncle and nephew began in 629; the Tang armies marched up to "help," and by 630, Tang Taizong had driven Hsieh-li into exile, accepted his nephew's surrender, and named himself "Heavenly Khan of the Eastern Turks" as well as Tang emperor. Tang Taizong made himself popular with his new subjects by making Turkish tribal leaders into Tang court officials.

6. Where did the Tibetan tribes come from? Where did the Tibetan tribes reside during Tang Taizong's rule?

A6.—Pg. 285, ¶ 3—Thousands of years before, the Tibetan tribes had come from the same area as the Chinese, but continued in a nomadic lifestyle long after the Chinese had started

on the road to farming and town-building. At the time of Tang Taizong's rule the Tibetan tribes were located on the high central Asian land known as the Tibetan plateau.

7. How did Songtsen Gampo use both war and alliance to bring coherence to the Tibetan tribes?

A7.—Pg. 285, ¶ 4 to Pg. 286, ¶ 1—Songtsen Gampo brought the nearby tribes under his authority in 620 and then launched campaigns against the Tuyu-hun nomads to the northeast. Then he sent armies west toward India and east toward the Tang border, as a way to distract the other tribal chiefs from the fact that they were now under his domination. In 640, he sent an ambassador to the Tang court with a message: he wanted to make a marriage alliance with the ruling family. At first Tang Taizong refused to send a princess to the Tibetan leader, but after Songtsen Gampo invaded the Sichuan, Tang Taizong saw the strength of the leader and sent one of his nieces, Wen-ch'eng, to Songtsen Gampo's court and the two were married in 641.

8. How did northern Chinese culture and Indian culture infiltrate Songtsen Gampo's Tibetan empire?

A8.—Pg. 286, ¶ 2—When the Chinese Wen-ch'eng was married to Songtsen Gampo and sent to live on the Tibetan plain, she brought with her Buddhist monks, Buddhist scriptures, and the Chinese habits of eating butter and cheese, drinking tea and wine, and consulting the stars. Later, she brought over Chinese craftsmen who could teach the Tibetans how to make wine and paper, how to cultivate silkworms and build mills to grind grain, and how to treat patients according to Chinese medical principles. Discovering the Tibetans had no written language, Wen-ch'eng suggested that her husband send one of his officials into northern India to bring back principles of written Sanskrit, and by the end of Songtsen Gampo's reign, a Tibetan script based on Sanskrit was in use.

9. Where did Baekje rebels go for help after Muyeol the Great of Silla proclaimed himself king of Silla and Baekje?

A9.—Pg. 287, ¶ 5 & 6—After Muyeol the Great declared himself king of Silla and Baekje, Baekje rebels fled to Japan, where one of the captive king Uija's sons already lived. The rebels appealed to the crown prince of the Japanese Yamato dynasty, Prince Naka no Oe, for help.

10. Why did the Japanese Soga clan want to keep Saimei on the throne?

A10.—Pg. 287, ¶ 7—After the death of the emperor, the Soga clan threw its weight behind Saimei as empress instead of Naka no Oe, who was of age to rule and the natural choice for succession, because she was less independent-minded than her son. The Soga could influence Saimei's choices, and make her dependent upon their power.

11. Despite King Munmu's bringing Silla into dominance on the Korean peninsula, why was Silla still not fully sovereign after entering the Unified Silla period?

A11.—Pg. 289, ¶ 7—Wu Zetian had always intended to extend Tang rule into Korea, so Silla's successes were secondary to China's dominance. Wu Zetian and Tang Gaozong organized the peninsula into a set of administrative districts under Tang control. They declared King Munmu of Silla the governor-general of the Tang rulership, named the "Protectorate General to Pacify the East."

12. How did King Munmu manage to regain some Tang-controlled land for Silla? What happened to Tang's Protectorate General in Silla?

A12.—Pg. 289, ¶ 8 & 9—Angered by his nation's role as subordinate to the Tang, Munmu appealed to Goguryeo's freedom fighters and formed an alliance with the rebels against the Tang. For five years, the rebels fought against Tang troops in all three of the former Three Kingdoms. In 676, after a series of losses in the Han river basin, Wu Zetian and Tang Gaozong decided to yield a good chunk of the Tang-controlled land to Munmu's rule, and moved the Office of the Protectorate General northwest to the city of Liaodung Cheng, outside the peninsula.

Section III: Critical Thinking

The student may not use her text to answer this question.

Japan's powerful Soga clan was the only thing that stood between Naka no Oe and the throne. When Naka no Oe managed to get rid of Soga power, the result was not what he expected. Explain the "Isshi Incident," and how, by taking command and doing what had to be done, Naka no Oe actually lost his right to take the title of Heavenly Sovereign.

Naka no Oe resented the Soga for putting his mother on the throne after the death of his father. Naka no Oe was old enough and capable enough to rule, but the Soga wanted to put Saimei on the throne so that they could influence her decisions. Naka no Oe knew he had to get rid of Soga power in order to claim the throne. He conspired with Nakatomi no Kamatari and they came up with a way to get rid of the family's two most powerful members, Soga no Iruka and his father Soga no Emishi. The plan and its aftermath is called The "Isshi Incident." The "Isshi Incident" is described on page 288:

"In 645, the year Isshi, on the twelfth day of the sixth month, it came to fruition. Soga no Iruka had come to court wearing his sword, as usual (he was, says the Japanese chronicle Nihongi, "of a very suspicious nature"), but Nakatomi no Kamatari had hired actors to put on an elaborate performance that would convince him to disarm. Soga no Iruka's suspicious nature deserted him when he most needed it; he laughed at the actors, took off the sword, and went into the empress's presence. The nineteen-year-old Naka no Oe quietly ordered the Guards of the Gates to lock all twelve entrances to the palace. He had given the task of carrying out the assassination of Soga no Iruka to three other members of the conspiracy, but as they stood in the throne room listening to the business of the day being read out, it became increasingly clear that the three swordsmen had lost their nerve.

When none of them made a move towards their victim, Naka no Oe leaped forward and struck the first blow against Soga no Iruka. Wounded, the statesman staggered to the empress and begged for mercy; but Saimei stood and left the throne room, going farther into the palace so that she could no longer hear or see what was happening. The prince's three allies, spurred into action, finished the injured man off. When his father Emishi heard the news, he took his own life."

The student does not have to recapture all of what happened during the debacle at Saimei's court. The main points to be highlighted are that the men hired to kill Soga no Iruka failed to do so, and that Naka no Oe had to kill Soga no Iruka himself.

Once the Soga clan's power was diminished, Naka no Oe was free to take the throne after his mother stepped down. But he did not. Instead, his uncle took the throne as Heavenly Sovereign Kotoku and ruled for nine years. When he died, Saimei returned from her retirement and again governed as heavenly sovereign from 655 until 661. When Saimei died, Naka no Oe still did not rise to be heavenly sovereign. Because Naka no Oe was the one to kill Soga no Iruka, which led to the suicide of his father Soga no Emishi, Naka no Oe felt he was polluted by the blood of both men. Naka no Oe felt he was sullied and thus could never be the heavenly sovereign. Getting rid of the obstacle that stood between himself and the throne did not free him to be ruler, it chained him to his crimes and kept him away from the throne forever.

EXAMPLE ANSWER:

Naka no Oe resented the Soga for putting his mother on the throne after the death of his father. Naka no Oe was old enough and capable enough to rule, but the Soga wanted to put Saimei on the throne so that they could influence her decisions. Naka no Oe knew he had to get rid of Soga power in order to claim the throne. He conspired with Nakatomi no Kamatari and they came up with a way to get rid of the family's two most powerful members, Soga no Iruka and his father Soga no Emishi. The plan and its aftermath is called The "Isshi Incident." Nakatomi no Kamatari would trick Soga no Iruka into letting down his guard while visiting Saimei's court. Then, three men that were hired by Naka no Oe would assassinate Soga no Iruka. But as the plan went forward, Naka no Oe realized the assassins were not going to do their jobs, and that he had to kill Soga no Iruka. After Soga no Iruka's death was reported, Soga no Emishi took his own life.

Once the Soga clan's power was diminished, Naka no Oe was free to take the throne after his mother stepped down. But he did not. Instead, his uncle took the throne and when he died, Saimei once again took the title. When Saimei died, Naka no Oe still did not rise to be heavenly sovereign. Because Naka no Oe was the one to kill Soga no Iruka, which led to the suicide of his father Soga no Emishi, Naka no Oe felt he was polluted by the blood of both men. Naka no Oe felt he was sullied and thus could never be the heavenly sovereign. Getting rid of the obstacle that stood between himself and the throne did not free him to be ruler, it chained him to his crimes and kept him away from the throne forever.

Section IV: Map Exercise

1. Using a black pencil, trace the rectangular outline of the frame for Map 38.1: The East in the Seventh Century.

2. Using a blue pencil, trace the coastline. You do not need to include any islands at this time other than Japan; be sure to include the entirety of Japan. Then with your blue pencil trace the outline of the Caspian Sea. Trace the line of the Yellow River and the Yangtze River. Trace the mountain peaks of the Himalaya mountains and the Altay mountains. Repeat until the contours are familiar.

3. Now with your black pencil trace the areas of Western Khaganate, of Eastern Khaganate, of Tang, and of the Persian Empire. Lightly trace the perimeter of the shaded area of Tibet. Trace the areas of Goguryeo, Baekje, and Silla. Repeat until the contours are familiar.

4. Trace the outline of the course of the Grand Canal until familiar. Trace the outline of the Great Wall repeatedly until it is familiar.

5. Using a new sheet of paper, trace the rectangular frame of the map in black. Using a regular pencil with an eraser as you look at the map, draw the coastline up and around through Japan. Draw the Caspian Sea, the Yellow River, the Yangtze River, the Great Wall, the Grand Canal, and the Himalaya and Altay mountains. Then draw the areas of the Western Khaganate, the Eastern Khaganate, Tang, and the Persian Empire. Lightly draw Tibet. Then draw the areas of Goguryeo, Baekje, and Silla.

6. Finally, check your map against the original. Erase and redraw as necessary as you look at the map.

Chapter Thirty-Nine

The Tribe of Faith

The student may use his text when answering the questions in sections I and II.

Section I: Who, What, Where

Write a one or two-sentence answer explaining the significance of each item listed below.

Abu Sufian—**Pg. 293, ¶ 5 & 6, Pg. 294, ¶ 4 and Pg. 295, ¶ 1—Abu Sufian, an old enemy of Muhammad's, expected trouble as he transported a large caravan of goods from Syria past Medina, so he sent to Mecca asking for reinforcements and a thousand men came to help him, with representatives from every Quraysh clan; the reinforcement didn't help the Quraysh, and Abu Sufian managed to escape with some of the booty from the caravan back to Mecca. When Muhammad was coming to attack Mecca with an army of ten thousand, Abu Sufian favored a truce between the two cities and when Muhammad did enter Mecca, Abu Sufian agreed to convert to Islam.**

Aishah—**Pg. 291, ¶ 2 and Pg. 296, ¶ 4—Aishah, daughter of Abu Bakr, was betrothed to Muhammad after the death of Khadija. Aishah was only six when the union was set up, but the marriage ceremony was not celebrated until she was older.**

Ali ibn Abu Talib—**Pg. 296, ¶ 4 & 5—Ali ibn Abu Talib was Muhammad's son-in-law, and many Muslims felt he should have been elected as Muhammad's successor instead of Abu Bakr. Some accounts say Ali ibn Abu Talib offered Abu Bakr his support, and others say that Ali ibn Abu Talib believed he should have succeeded Muhammad.**

Battle of the Trench—**Pg. 294, ¶ 1—The Battle of the Trench was the second battle to take place between Mecca and Medina between 625 and 627, and was named "The Battle of the Trench" because the people at Medina dug a moat in front of their city to protect it from invasion. The battle was a draw, with the attackers from Mecca forced to withdraw because of the cold, but the Muslims of Medina also blamed the non-participation of the Jews for their inability to beat the Meccans.**

Constans II—**Pg. 299, ¶ 5 & 6—Constans II, son of Constantine III, was made emperor at the age of eleven. Too young to rule, Constans II asked the Senate to advise him, a statement that was most likely provided to him by the Senate so they could keep the symbol of God's presence in the palace at Constantinople while they kept the governing power for themselves.**

Constantine III—**Pg. 299, ¶ 2 & 3—Constantine III, son of Heraclius, was made emperor after his father's death. Constantine III was in constant poor health, and so his rulership was shared with half-brother Heraklonas just in case Constantine III died suddenly, which he did just a few months after his coronation.**

Heraklonas—**Pg. 299, ¶ 2 & 3—Heraklonas, Constantine III's half-brother and co-emperor, became sole emperor at fifteen when Constantine III died suddenly, with his mother Martina ruling as his regent. Heraklonas was kicked off the throne by Valentinus because he was the product of an unholy marriage.**

Khalid—**Pg. 297, ¶ 3—Khalid was Abu Bakr's general and right-hand man, and he helped the caliph conquer all of the Arabian peninsula.**

Khalifat ar-rasul Allah—**Pg. 297, ¶ 2—Khalifat ar-rasul Allah was the title given to Abu Bakr, the sole heir of Muhammad's power. It meant the caliph, the representative of the message of the prophet of God.**

Martina—**Pg. 299, ¶ 2 & 3—Martina, Heraclius's niece and wife, mother to Heraklonas, became regent for her fifteen-year old son when he became sole emperor after Constantine III's death. Because Martina was Heraclius's niece, the Romans thought the marriage was a breach of biblical law, so when she became regent the army revolted, her tongue was cut out and she was sent into exile.**

Muhajirun—**Pg. 291, ¶ 2—Muhajirun was the name given to the Arabs who had followed Muhammad to Medina from Mecca. Muhajirun means the "Emigrants."**

Ridda—**Pg. 297, ¶ 3—Ridda, or the "apostasy," was the name given to the resistance to Abu Bakr's rule.**

Rothari—**Pg. 299, ¶ 7 to Pg. 300, ¶ 1—Rothari, the Lombard king at the time of Constans II's reign, took the remaining Byzantine lands in Italy from the shrinking empire in 642.**

S'ad—**Pg. 294, ¶ 2—S'ad, a Jewish convert to Islam, was appointed by Muhammad to pronounce the fate of all Jews in Medina: the men would be executed and the women and children would be made into slaves.**

Umar—**Pg. 298, ¶ 2 & 3—Umar, Abu Bakr's son-in-law, inherited the power of the caliph without chaos. Umar changed his title to "Commander of the Faithful," which showed the caliph was no longer a messenger, or Muhammad's successor—he was a leader in his own right, the commander in chief of the Muslim empire.**

Yazdegerd III—**Pg. 297, ¶ 6 and Pg. 298, ¶ 6—Yazdegerd III, grandson of Khosru II, took the Persian throne with the help of the Eastern Roman emperor Heraclius. When Khalid marched towards Persia, Yazdegerd III was able to survive, but he lost his capital city.**

Section II: Comprehension

Write a two or three-sentence answer to each of the following questions.

1. What did Muhammad expect from non-Muslims in the city of Medina?

A1.—Pg. 291, ¶ 3—Muhammad had expected that he would enfold the whole of Medina into the *umma*. His protection of the rights of non-Muslims was sincere, but he always expected them to see the light and become followers of Allah. Muhammad's expectations were let down when he realized the Jews of Medina were always going to hold themselves apart.

2. What is the content of the revelation Muhammad received that appears as Surah 2 in the Qu'ran? How did this revelation relate to Muhammad's frustration with those outside the *umma*?

A2.—Pg. 292, ¶ 1—The revelation that appears as Surah 2 in the Qu'ran states that Abraham worshipped the same God as the Christians, and that Jews, Christians and Muslims would all enter paradise if they submit to Allah and do good. The revelation related to Muhammad's frustration with those outside the *umma* because Jews and Christians worshipped the same God as the Muslims, so they were practically part of the *umma* but they continued to hold themselves apart.

3. How did the *umma* become the most powerful "tribe" in Medina? What was one disingenuous reason some Arabs were converting to the Muslim faith?

A3.—Pg. 292, ¶ 2—Medina was a city that operated around the Muslim faith: the city's schedule had been reorganized around the five daily prayers that Muhammad prescribed for faithful believers, fasting and the giving of alms to the poor had been written into city law, and the mosque Muhammad had built was the city's center. Because everything about the city was based on being a Muslim, the *umma*, Muhammad's faithful tribe, had the most power. It was politically advantageous to be Muslim, and the result was that some of the Arabs were converting just to get ahead.

4. What message was Muhammad sending to Mecca by raiding the caravans that passed between Mecca and destinations to the north?

A4.—Pg. 292, ¶ 4—The caravans that passed Medina on their way from Mecca to destinations in the north were usually owned by the Quraysh. Raiding these caravans sent a message to Mecca: loyalty to the *umma* had replaced the old tribal loyalties, and the ties of birth had been broken and supplanted with ties of faith. Old tribal connections meant nothing to the followers of Muhammad, and they were willing to fight in order to prove it.

5. Why was Muhammad upset by the death of a Quraysh merchant during a raid on a passing caravan?

A5.—Pg. 292, ¶ 6 to Pg. 293, ¶ 1—Muhammad was upset by the death of a Quraysh merchant during a raid on a passing caravan because his death happened during the sacred month in which fighting was forbidden. The corruption in Mecca started with a disregard for ancient traditions, and Muhammad felt that death during the sacred month was repeating that behavior.

6. What was the revelation that Muhammad received after the death of the Quraysh tradesman during the sacred month? What was the implied meaning of that revelation?

A6.—Pg. 293, ¶ 2 & 3—The revelation that Muhammad received after the death of the Quraysh tradesman during the sacred month was that while fighting during the sacred month was bad, the sins of the Meccans were much worse. The implication of this revelation was that not only was fighting back when wronged okay in the eyes of Allah, but it was also okay to fight back against those who continued to wrong you.

7. How did Muhammad manage to win the fight against the Meccans at the Wells of Badr on March 17, 624?

A7.—Pg. 293, ¶ 6—When Muhammad's men met the Quraysh army from Mecca at the Wells of Badr on March 17, 624, Muhammad called out that any man who was killed fighting with steadfast courage would certainly enter Paradise. The combination of religious fervor, guaranteed entry into Paradise, hatred for their enemies and the fear of losing everything they gained in Medina, made Muhammad's men fight with such vigor that they were able to drive back the Quraysh army.

8. Why were the Jews driven out of Medina? What happened to them?

A8.—Pg. 294, ¶ 1 & 2—The *umma* drove out two Jewish tribes that refused to recognize Muhammad's authority. The final tribe of Jews were exiled from the city after they refused to fight in the Battle of the Trench, which was a violation of Muhammad's declaration that Jews and Arabs support each other both in peace and in war. The exiled Jews were given the choice to either convert to Islam or choose death and slavery—and the Jews chose the latter.

9. How was Muhammad able to justify his large attack on Medina? What kind of troops did he assemble for the fight by 630?

A9.—Pg. 294, ¶ 3—Nomadic allies of the Quraysh had attacked nomadic allies of the Muslims: this was a hostile act against the people of the faith, and Muhammad was able to justify his attack on Mecca by saying the Muslims were simply fighting back. By 630, Muhammad was able to assemble an army of ten thousand made up of Helpers, Emigrants, and numerous soldiers from outlying tribes who either had accepted Islam or were willing to make common cause with it.

10. What happened when Muhammad arrived at the walls of Mecca with his massive army?

A10.—Pg. 295, ¶ 1—When Muhammad arrived at the walls of Mecca with his massive army, he was met by Abu Sufian, who extracted a promise that the Muslims would enter the city without bloodshed: a truce was reached between Muhammad and Mecca, and that truce meant Mecca's surrender to the prophet. When Muhammad's army entered the city the only violence done was to the idols of various deities around the city, which were smashed and thrown down. Muhammad himself worshipped Allah at the Ka'aba and he was joined by Abu Sufian, who had agreed to convert to Islam.

11. When did Mecca become the core of Islam? How was Muhammad's influence spreading?

A11.—Pg. 295, ¶ 2—Mecca became the core of Islam after Abu Sufian surrendered the city to Muhammad. Muhammad moved his headquarters to Mecca and directed various campaigns from the city, converting more Arab tribes. His conquests reached so far down into the south that Himyar became part of the *umma*.

12. Where does the division between Sunni Muslims and Shi'ite Muslims stem from?

A12.—Pg. 296 and 297, *—The division between Sunni and Shi'ite Muslims stems from the controversy over Ali ibn Abu Talib's reaction to Abu Bakr's legitimacy. Sunni Muslims believe that the passing of the caliphate to Abu Bakr was legitimate, and that the line of caliphs who follow him is thus also legitimate. Those who disagree and support Ali as the divinely chosen successor of Muhammad were known as Shi'at Ali, "The Party of Ali" and today they are known as Shi'ite Muslims.

13. How did Abu Bakr deal with the resistance to his leadership? How did this lead to a united Arabian peninsula?

A13—Pg. 297, ¶ 1—Abu Bakr reacted to resistance to his leadership with force. He divided his own followers into eleven armed groups under eleven competent commanders, and assigned each one the task of subduing, by force, the areas where resistance to his leadership was making itself known. The eleven columns of leadership fanned out across the Islamic kingdom by conquering nearby tribes, the rest of the peninsula fell steadily, and in about a year, the peninsula was united behind Abu Bakr.

14. Why did Abu Bakr start wars with Persia and Byzantium in 633?

A14.—Pg. 297, ¶ 4–6—When Abu Bakr became caliph, he became the head of an enormous group of people that were not all sold on the truth of Islam. In order to create a bond between the people in his empire, he decided to target an outside enemy because nothing welded people together like war.

15. What made Abu Bakr take troops away from the Persian front and send them to the Byzantine front? What was the result of this military move?

A15.—Pg. 298, ¶ 1—Abu Bakr called Khalid away from the Persian front to help out the forces attacking Palestine and Syria because the Byzantine troops put up a stronger

resistance than expected. The result was success for Abu Bakr: the combined Arab troops defeated the Byzantine army, capturing Damascus and moving through Palestine into Syria.

16. What title was Umar given when he took Abu Bakr's role as leader of the Arabs? Why was his title changed, what was it changed to, and why was this change significant?

A16.—Pg. 298, ¶ 3—When Umar took Abu Bakr's place, he was called "Caliph of the Caliph of the Messenger of God." Umar said the title was too long, and questioned what the next caliph would be called: "Caliph of the Caliph of the Caliph of the Messenger of God?" Instead Umar insisted that his people were faithful and he was their commander, so he would be called "Commander of the Faithful." The change was significant because Umar was no longer a messenger, or Muhammad's successor—he was a leader in his own right, the commander in chief of the new Muslim empire.

17. Despite gathering an army of 150,000, what happened to Heraclius and his Byzantine holdings in the battle with the Arabic forces at the Yarmuk river in Syria? What was Heraclius's one victory?

A17.—Pg. 298, ¶ 5—When Heraclius met Arabic forces at the Yarmuk river in Syria, his troops fought for six days before realizing they were defeated. Heraclius was forced to give up the provinces of Syria and Palestine, which he had just gotten back from the Persians and in 637 he also gave up Jerusalem. Heraclius's one victory was in managing to get the fragment of the True Cross back to Constantinople before Jerusalem was forced to surrender to occupying Arab forces.

18. What was the symbolic purpose of slitting Heraklonas's nose? What did the mutilation of Heraklonas suggest about the emperor's role in Byzantium?

A18.—Pg. 299, ¶ 4—Mutilating a claimant to royal power was a ritual method of making him ineligible for rule. While Heraklonas could still technically rule with a split nose, the symbol of his split nose meant that he was not fit to be a king. The splitting of the nose played on the Old Testament regulation which stipulated that deformed priests could not minister in the temple, which suggested that the emperor's role had become greater than just being a king: he was also some sort of guarantor of God's favor, the channel of God's grace. The people of Constantinople believed the incestuous marriage that brought Heraklonas into the world was damned and it was bringing judgment upon them as a people.

Section III: Critical Thinking

The student may not use his text to answer this question.

When Muhammad became a religious leader, he preached inclusivity and rights for all. But by the time Muhammad became the political leader of Medina, one had to be part of the *umma* in order to be protected by Muhammad. Write a paragraph explaining what happened to the Jews that were living in Medina. Then, explain how their treatment contradicted Muhammad's basic message of equality as espoused in his farewell sermon.

The student already answered a question about the fate of the Jews in Medina in the "Comprehension" section, so it should be easy for him to recap what happened. The Jews were driven out of Medina because they refused to convert to Islam, or they refused to fight on behalf of Islam. After the Battle of the Trench, Jews that refused to convert were either killed or made slaves.

Muhammad's farewell sermon said "Allah has forbidden you to charge interest.
Your women have the right to be fed and clothed in kindness.
Worship Allah.
Say your five daily prayers.
Fast during the month of Ramadan.
Give your wealth in charity.
Perform Hajj [pilgrimage to Mecca] if you can afford to.
An Arab has no superiority over a non-Arab.
A white has no superiority over black.
No prophet or apostle will come after me and no new faith will be born." Muhammad had said the Jews were being punished for violating the declaration that Arabs and Jews support each other in both peace and in war, but two Jewish tribes that refused to convert had already been forced out of Medina, thus suggesting their slaughter was not just about their failure to fight. Muhammad's treatment of the Jews contradicted this message because in killing those that refused to convert, Muhammad was showing that Arabs had superiority over the non-Arab Jews.

EXAMPLE ANSWER:

The Jews in Medina suffered a terrible fate: they were exiled from the city. After the Battle of the Trench, Jews that refused to convert to Islam were either killed or made slaves. In his farewell sermon, Muhammad said "An Arab has no superiority over a non-Arab.
A white has no superiority over black,"
yet the slaughter of the Jews in Medina suggested that the truth was otherwise. Muhammad had said the Jews were being punished for violating the declaration that Arabs and Jews support each other in both peace and in war, but two Jewish tribes that refused to convert had already been forced out of Medina, thus suggesting their death and enslavement was not just about their failure to fight. Muhammad's treatment of the Jews contradicted his message of equality because in killing those that refused to convert, Muhammad was showing that Arabs had superiority over the non-Arab Jews.

Section IV: Map Exercise

1. Using a black pencil, trace the rectangular outline of the frame for Map 39.1: The Conquests of Muhammad and Abu Bakr.

2. Using a blue pencil, trace the visible portion of the Mediterranean, the Black Sea, the Caspian Sea, the Red Sea, and the coastline around Arabia. Also trace the lines of the Tigris and Euphrates. Select four contrasting colors. Use each respectively to trace the Persian Empire, the Byzantine Empire, Muhammad's conquests, and Abu Bakr's conquests.

Repeat until the contours are familiar.

3. Using a new sheet of paper, trace the rectangular outline of the frame in black. Remove your tracing paper from the original. Using a regular pencil with an eraser, draw the visible portion of the Mediterranean, the Black Sea, the Caspian Sea, the Red Sea, and the coastline around Arabia. Also draw the lines of the Tigris and Euphrates. Then draw the Persian Empire, the Byzantine Empire, Muhammad's conquests, and Abu Bakr's conquests. Erase and redraw as necessary.

4. When you are pleased with your map, lay it over the original. Erase and redraw any lines which are more than ¼ inch off of the original. When your map is correct, shade the areas of the Persian Empire, the Byzantine Empire, Muhammad's conquests, and Abu Bakr's conquests as the mapmaker has done: darker for the Persian Empire, lighter for the Byzantine Empire, and contrasting lines for Muhammad and Abu Bakr's conquests.

5. Remove your map. Label the Black Sea and the Caspian Sea. Study carefully the locations of Egypt, Palestine, Syria, Yemen, Oman, and Banu Hanifa. When you are familiar with them, close the book, and label each. Check your map against the original, and correct any misplaced labels.

6. Then study closely the locations of Alexandria, Damascus, Yarmuk, Jerusalem, Medina, Mecca, and Ctesiphon. Also study the location of the Battle at Wells of Badr. When you are familiar with them, close the book. Mark each location on your map, and label it. Then lay your map over the original. Correct any misplaced labels, and erase and redraw any cities which are more than ¼ inch off of the original.

Chapter Forty

Intersection

The student may use her text when answering the questions in sections I and II.

Section I: Who, What, Where

Write a one or two-sentence answer explaining the significance of each item listed below.

al-Hakam—**Pg. 302 ¶ 3 and Pg. 303, ¶ 1—al-Hakam, the commander of the Arabian army that attacked the Makran and Sindh, was forbidden to cross the Indus further into Indian territory by Umar because the caliph declared the land was not worth fighting over.**

Kannauj—**Pg. 304, ¶ 1—Kannauj, Harsha's capital, was the premier city of northern India when Harsha's rule had reached its strength and maturity.**

Makran—**Pg. 302, ¶ 2 and Pg. 303, ¶ 1—Makran was a local Hindu kingdom that existed independently of the huge realm ruled by Harsha. Makran was invaded by the Arabs under the command of al-Hakam, and it became the eastern border of the growing Islamic realm.**

Manavamma—**Pg. 305, ¶ 7—Manavamma, a warrior, made himself the king of Sri Lanka in 684 with the help of Pallava soldiers. As payment for the reinforcements, Manavamma was forced to pay tribute to the Pallava, which meant Manavamma's power was second to Pallava power.**

Pandya—**Pg. 305, ¶ 3—Pandya was an ancient kingdom in the far southwest of India that experienced a revival during the time of Vikramaditya's reign. Though their ancient power had dwindled, they began to reestablish themselves in the decades before Vikramaditya's rule, first as governors of the city of Madurai, then as rulers of the surrounding countryside.**

Paramesvaravarman I—**Pg. 305, ¶ 5—Paramesvaravarman I was the Pallava king at the time of Vikramaditya's attack in 670. Paramesvaravarman I was defeated by Vikramaditya, but four years later Paramesvaravarman I successfully retaliated and defeated Chalukya soldiers.**

Rasil—**Pg. 302, ¶ 1—Rasil, king of the Makrans, gathered an army on the bank of the Indus river in an attempt to stop Arab armies from crossing the water. Rasil was aided by the king of Sindh.**

Sangam—**Pg. 305, ¶ 4—Sangam, located in Madurai, was an academy where poets and their patrons gathered to write and read. The academy met at Madurai for a century and a half, from around 600 until 750, and it is where poems and epics written in Tamil, the language of the south Indians, were joined by a translation of the Mahabharata into Tamil.**

Shahi—**Pg. 302, ¶ 2—Shahi, a local Hindu kingdom that existed independently of the huge realm ruled by Harsha, was a Buddhist kingdom that had existed in the northern mountains for a hundred years, in control of the Khyber Pass, its capital city at Kabul. They had adopted the Persian title "king of kings" (*shahi-in-shahi*).**

Sindh—**Pg. 302, ¶ 2—Sindh was a local Hindu kingdom that existed independently of the huge realm ruled by Harsha.**

Vikramaditya—**Pg. 304, ¶ 6 and pg. 305, ¶ 1, 2 & 5—Vikramaditya, the third son of Pulakesi II, claimed the Chalukya throne in 655 after thirteen years of civil war with his brothers. Vikramaditya had lost some of his father's conquests for the Chalukya, so he spent his kingship fighting to take back the land that had been lost to the Pallava.**

Vinayaditya—**Pg. 305, ¶ 6—Vinayaditya, son of Vikramaditya, inherited his father's rule of the Western Chalukya in 680, when his father died. Vinayaditya managed to avoid major confrontations during his sixteen-year reign, stretching Chalukya power across the center of the Indian subcontinent.**

Section II: Comprehension

Write a two or three-sentence answer to each of the following questions.

1. How were the kingdoms of Makran, Sindh and Shahi related?

A1.—Pg. 302, ¶ 2—The kingdoms of Makran, Sindh and Shahi were local Hindu kingdoms in the north of India that existed independently of the huge realm ruled by Harsha.

2. Why didn't the Shahi assist the Makran and Sindh when the Arabs attacked? What was the result of the attack?

A2.—Pg. 302, ¶ 3—The Shahi did not feel threatened by the Arabs, so they did not send troops to help the Makran and the Sindh. The result was Indian defeat: the Arabs pursued them back to the Indus river and drove the Makran and Sindh across it.

3. What stopped Umar from expanding the edge of his kingdom from the Makran further into India?

A3.—Pg. 302, ¶ 4 to Pg. 303, ¶ 1—After al-Hakam had defeated the Makrans, he asked Umar what to do next, and wrote a report to the Caliph that said Makran land was mountainous,

only produced poor quality dates, was not prosperous, and had little else going for it. Umar decided that neither the Makran nor the Sindh were worth expending any more energy on, so he forbid al-Hakam form crossing the Indus. The result was that the Arab armies turned back, and the eastern border of the growing Islamic realm remained, for the time being, in the Makran.

4. In what way did the kingdoms of the Shahi and the Sindh protect Harsha's northern Indian kingdom from Arab invasion?

A4.—Pg. 303, ¶ 2—Harsha had continued his wars of conquest until the entire north and northeast were under his control, and the king of the Sindh and the ruler of the Shahi were probably his tributaries. That meant that the two independent kingdoms acted as buffers between Harsha's kingdom and outside invasion. Had Umar known that Harsha's kingdom lay beyond the wasted Sindh, he most likely would have continued his expansion, but the buffer did its job and the Arabian army returned home.

5. What was Harsha's relationship like with the Chinese, and why were the Chinese (via Xuan Zang) impressed with his ruling style?

A5.—Pg. 304, ¶ 1—Harsha had a friendly relationship with the Chinese, and sent at least one diplomat from his court to the east. The Chinese, as reported by the pilgrim Xuan Zang, were impressed with Harsha's reasonable taxes, and with the fact that if Harsha forced people to work on roads or canals, he paid them for their time.

6. What happened to Harsha's Northern Indian kingdom after his death in 647?

A6.—Pg. 304, ¶ 4—When Harsha died in 647, he left no sons to take his throne. His prime minister took the throne but his reign lasted for only a few weeks. The empire fell back into minor battling kingdoms, disintegrating into chaos over time.

7. Despite taking the throne in 655, what losses did Vikramaditya suffer at the start of his reign? How did these losses divide the Chalukya kingdom?

A7.—Pg. 304, ¶ 6 to Pg. 305, ¶ 2—Vikramaditya might have won out over his brothers for the throne of Chalukya after thirteen years of civil war, but by the time the brothers started fighting, the Vengi territory taken by Pulakesi II had been taken back by Pallava armies. Vikramaditya also lost the eastern part of his kingdom to his uncle, who had been viceroy of the eastern territories while Pulakesi II was alive. This split divided Chalukya into two: the Western Chalukya, where the king governed from Vatapi, and the Eastern Chalukya where the king ruled over the coastal area.

8. How did the Pandya get involved in the fight between the Western Chalukya and Pallava?

A8.—Pg. 305, ¶ 5—The Pandya had been forced to pay tribute to the Pallava king, so when Vikramaditya attacked Pallava in 670, they were dragged into the conflict as Pallava allies.

Section III: Critical Thinking

The student may not use her text to answer this question.

Political and religious practices were rarely separated in the medieval world. Similarly, the personal beliefs of rulers usually influenced the beliefs and rituals of their realms. This was no different in Harsha's northern Indian kingdom. Write a paragraph explaining how Harsha's personal history with his sister affected the kingdom's Hindu religious beliefs. Make sure to explain the meaning of shakti, and to recap the play written by Harsha, *Nagananda*. Then write a few sentences explaining how Harsha's Buddhist beliefs affected the laws of his kingdom.

In this chapter we revisit Harsha's past. When Harsha was young, he rescued his sister from death by funeral pyre, and as a result Harsha eventually made his sister co-ruler of his kingdom. During Harsha's reign, a particular form of Hinduism that highlighted female power, or shakti, became more prominent. The worshippers who pursued this stream of Hinduism were called Shaivas, followers of the god Shiva and of his consort, the Goddess. Wisdom flowed from Shiva through the Goddess, and then from the Goddess to the human world. Harsha's devotion to his sister is connected to shakti worship. His rescue of his sister from the funeral pyre is echoed in the rescue of the king's son from death. Harsha's play, Nagananda, *is about how Shiva's goddess resurrects the dead son and heir of a grief-struck king and bestows upon him royal powers. Again, Harsha's past is seen in the events of his play. Harsha's devotion to his sister is then reflected in the Hindu worship of female power popular during Harsha's reign.*

Harsha's personal beliefs did not just affect his kingdom's religious practice, but also its law. Harsha practiced Hinduism and Buddhism. As he grew older, he turned more and more towards Mahayana Buddhism and channeled more of the royal funds towards Buddhist monasteries. Towards the end of his life, adopting non-violence in his heart, Harsha decreed that no living thing should be killed in his domain and that no one could eat meat for food. It was in this way that Harsha's Buddhist beliefs changed the laws of his kingdom.

EXAMPLE ANSWER:

When Harsha was young, he saved his sister from death on a funeral pyre. When Harsha had a kingdom to rule, he made his sister co-ruler. In that kingdom, a form of Hinduism that worshipped female power, or shakti, was popular. The worshippers in this type of Hinduism were called Shaivas and they followed the god Shiva and his consort, the Goddess. Harsha's devotion to his sister is connected to shakti worship. His rescue of his sister from the funeral pyre is echoed in the rescue of the king's son from death. Harsha's play, *Nagananda*, is about how Shiva's goddess resurrects the dead son and heir of a grief-struck king and gives him royal powers. Again, Harsha's past is seen in the events of his play. In addition to his Hindu beliefs, Harsha also practiced Buddhism. He put a lot of his kingdom's money into building Buddhist monasteries. Towards the end of his life, Harsha decreed that no living thing should be killed in his domain and that no one could eat meat for food. It was in this way that Harsha's Buddhist beliefs changed the law of his kingdom. Shakti worship and non-violence were both ways that we can see Harsha's beliefs affecting the beliefs and laws of his kingdom.

Chapter Forty-One

The Troubles of Empire

The student may use his text when answering the questions in sections I and II.

Section I: Who, What, Where

Write a one or two-sentence answer explaining the significance of each item listed below.

Abn 'Amir—**Pg. 312, ¶ 1—Abn 'Amir, a relative of Uthman but a man unpopular with many, was appointed by Uthman to a high government position in Kufa. In 655 the people of Kufa deposed Abn 'Amir.**

Battle of the Camel—**Pg. 313, ¶ 5—The Battle of the Camel, which took place in December of 656 six months after Ali became caliph, took place between Aishah and her supports and Ali, his army, and supporters from Kufa. When the armies met just outside of Basra, Ali won quickly, Aishah's supporters were killed and she was forced to return to private life.**

Berbers—**Pg. 308, ¶ 6—"Berbers" was the name given to the native northern Africans from the west of Egypt by the Arabs. Berbers were made slaves and were used to pay tribute to the Arab conquerors as they marched across Egypt; Berber slaves became involuntary recruits to the Arab army.**

Fitna—**Pg. 313, ¶ 6 and Pg. 315, ¶ 4—The *fitna*, or the "Trials," was the name given to the civil war that started over the caliphate after Ali defeated Aishah and her followers at the Battle of the Camel. The *fitna* ended after Ali's murder and Muawiyah's appointment to the caliphate.**

Fostat—**Pg. 308, ¶ 6—Fostat, known today as Cairo, was made the new capital of Egypt by the Arab appointed governor.**

Hasan—**Pg. 313, ¶ 3—Hasan, Ali's son and Muhammad's grandson, was put up for the caliphate by Ali's supporters after his father's death. Hasan agreed to a settlement with Muawiyah, who far more Arabs wanted to be caliph; Hasan would retire peacefully to**

Medina as a private person; in return Muawiyah promised that the caliphate would pass back to Hasan should Muawiyah die before him.

Kharijis—**Pg. 315, ¶ 2 & 3—Kharijis, or "Seceders," was the name given to those who rebelled against Ali's rule by the men loyal to Ali. It was a *Khariji* that killed Ali.**

Muawiyah—**Pg. 308, ¶ 4 & 5, Pg. 314, ¶ 1 and Pg. 315, ¶ 3—Muawiyah, the Arab governor of Syria, created a naval force made up of volunteers and became admiral of the Arab navy. When Ali became the caliph, Muawiyah opposed his leadership and when Ali was murdered, Muawiyah was named caliph, putting the Banu Umayya in power once again.**

Saqiba—**Pg. 307, ¶ 4 to Pg. 308, ¶ 1—*Saqiba* meant "priority in Islam." At the time of his death, Umar had been using *saqiba* to build a hierarchy based on one's length of service; the earlier you became a Muslim, the higher position you received.**

Uthman—**Pg. 307, ¶ 2 and Pg. 310, ¶ 1—Uthman, a Meccan of the Quraysh tribe, was named caliph by the council of six Muslims appointed to find Umar's successor. Under Uthman Arabia grew, but after he lost the signet ring of the Prophet, he experienced many difficulties in his reign, and both his legitimacy as the proper successor and his ability as the Arabic leader were called into question.**

Section II: Comprehension

Write a two or three-sentence answer to each of the following questions.

1. What were the circumstance of Umar's death, and the naming of his successor?

A1.—Pg. 307, ¶ 1—Umar died in 644 when he was stabbed to death by a Persian captive slave as he led morning prayers in Medina. Umar died slowly, over several days, which made it possible for him to arrange a successor. Yet, instead of electing a successor himself, he appointed a council of six Muslims from Mecca to pick the next caliph.

2. Why did the council of six Muslims choose to name Uthman the next caliph rather than Muhammad's son-in-law Ali ibn Abu Talib?

A2.—Pg. 307, ¶ 2—The council of six Muslims chose to name Uthman the next caliph rather than Ali ibn Abu Talib because Uthman was Meccan and of the Quraysh tribe. In the years since Muhammad's death, Ali had spent most of his time with non-Quraysh Muslims, and the council wanted to ensure that the Quraysh stayed in control. Tribal loyalties were still important in the *umma*.

3. What was Uthman's vision for the organization of the entire Arabic conquered realm? How did he enact this vision?

A3.—Pg. 308, ¶ 2—Uthman envisioned the entire Arabic conquered realm to be organized like a mirror of Mecca, with the Quraysh clan in power. To enact this vision, he governed

from Medina and appointed governors to supervise the outer reaches of the empire. He kept tight hold of the chief governors and military officials, appointing and removing them himself, and they were responsible only to him.

4. In what way did occupying Alexandria benefit the Arabic empire, other than increasing its size? What was the first conquest of Muawiyah's navy?

A4.—Pg. 308, ¶ 3, 5 & 7—When Arabic forces occupied Alexandria, they gained an important new power: the use of the sea. The first conquest of Muawiyah's navy was Cyprus. In 649 Muawiyah launched a fleet of seventeen hundred ships and landed on the island of Cyprus, which was still in Byzantine hands, and it fell almost at once.

5. Describe what happened to Yazdegerd III's court in Khorasan, and the Persian king's murder on the banks of the Murghab river. What did this mean for the Persian empire?

A5.—Pg. 309, ¶ 4–6—Yazdegerd III traveled to Khorasan, demanding shelter for the winter, bringing with him the remnants of his royal court—four thousand or so secretaries, displaced officials, palace staff, and their women and children. There was no way to support that many idle people during winter, in the mountains, in a province cut off from its former trade partners, so the Khorasan governor hired a couple of assassins to do away with Yazdegerd III's bodyguard. Yazdegerd III fled eastward to the banks of the Murghab river, where he was murdered by the stonecutter than had given him shelter. With Yazdegerd III's death came the end of the Persian empire.

6. What relation did the signet ring of the Prophet have to do with the difficulties in Uthman's rule? In your answer, make sure to describe the signet ring and its significance.

A6.—Pg. 310, ¶ 1—The signet ring of the Prophet, made from silver with "Muhammad, the Messenger of God" engraved on it, was used by Muhammad to seal his correspondence with non-Arabs. The ring was passed from Muhammad to Abu Bakr to Umar to Uthman. Uthman lost the ring in a well; he had a new one made, but it was too late. Arab historians say that the turn in his fortunes came when he lost the signet ring.

7. What territorial problems did Uthman face in the second part of his reign?

A7.—Pg. 311, ¶ 1—In the second part of his reign, Uthman was unable to halt the continual rebellions of the conquered cities in Persia. Despite being ruled by the Arabs, Persian aristocracy, religion, language and practice continued to thrive. In North Africa, Arab power existed in separated, highly reinforced areas along the coast, and communication between those enclaves required that Arab troops keep on conquering and reconquering the connecting areas, meaning the fighting was endless and coherence was not achieved.

8. Why did Uthman create a definitive version of Muhammad's teachings?

A8.—Pg. 311, ¶ 2 & 3—Muhammad did not write; his revelations (*surahs*) were recorded by his followers, sometimes in several different forms. With the expansion of the empire, Muslims widely separated in geography were beginning to compile their own collections and there

were differences among these local anthologies. Creating one unified sacred book, the Qur'an, would hopefully create religious cohesion in the empire.

9. How was the stage for revolt against Uthman set in the city of Kufa?

A9.—Pg. 311, ¶ 5—The city of Kufa, a large and bustling Muslim city on the western bank of the Euphrates, was filled with Arabs that had emigrated from all over Arabia. But under Uthman's policies, only Quraysh were promoted into positions of power, with particular preference for members of Uthman's own clan, the Banu Umayya. Resentment deepened when Uthman ordered the city to send all of its surplus revenue to Medina, for use by the Arabs there, and the stage for revolt was set.

10. Describe the circumstances of Uthman's death.

A10.—Pg. 312, ¶ 2–4—Uthman was besieged in his house by rebels from Kufa that were upset about the appointment of Abn 'Amir, and the general treatment of Kufa by Uthman. Ali gave Uthman a three-day grace period to meet all of the complaints made by the people, but during his three-day grace, Uthman did nothing to alter what made the people unhappy and instead prepared for war and gathered arms. When the three days were up, Uthman's enemies surrounded his house again, broke in, and stabbed him to death.

11. What happened to Uthman's body after he died?

A11.—Pg. 312, ¶ 5—After Uthman was stabbed to death, his body was left in a courtyard for three days even though Muslim custom dictated a body be buried at once. Once his family got permission to take the body, Uthman was buried in a Jewish cemetery because no Muslim cemetery would accept his corpse.

12. Why did Aishah oppose Ali as the next caliph? Why was her argument flawed?

A12.—Pg. 313, ¶ 1 & 2—Aishah did not want Ali to be the next caliph because she claimed that Ali had no right to rule since the leadership of the Muslim community should stay within the clan of the Umayyad, with its blood tie to Muhammad himself. But the Banu Umayya clan was only related to Muhammad distantly through a common ancestor that linked the Banu Umayya to Muhammad's actual clan the Banu Hashim. Ali, however, was Banu Hashim, and he was not only Muhammad's son-in-law but also his cousin. His son Hasan was the grandson of the Prophet, child of Muhammad's daughter Fatima. Ali was more connected to the Prophet than any previous caliph.

13. What was Aishah's real purpose in trying to keep Ali out of the seat of Arab power?

A13.—Pg. 313, ¶ 4—Aishah's real purpose in trying to keep Ali out of the seat of Arab power was to keep the Quraysh in power, since she knew he didn't intend to. Aishah insistence's that Uthman's clan, rather than Muhammad's own, was part of the "royal" family was an effort to preserve Quraysh dominance.

14. Why did Ali move the seat of his caliphate from Medina to Kufa? Who did not support Ali?

A14.—Pg. 313, ¶ 6 to Pg. 314, ¶ 1—Ali moved the seat of his caliphate from Medina to Kufa because Kufa was solidly behind his rule, and Kufa was also more central to all parts of the newly conquered empire. When Ali sent new governors to take over the administration of rebellious provinces, Muawiyah refused to support Ali until Uthman's murderers were put to death.

15. What happened when Muawiyah and Ali met for battle on the upper Euphrates in July of 657? What was the result of their truce?

A15.—Pg. 314, ¶ 3 & 4—When Muawiyah and Ali met for battle, neither was very comfortable with battle between Muslims, and their soldiers knew it; Muawiyah's men pulled back, impaled leaves of the Qur'an on the tips of their spears, and insisted that the two leaders work out their differences according to the laws of Islam. The result of the truce was that Ali would remain caliph, ruling from Kufa and Muawiyah would remain in Syria with no title but ruling independently. Unity under one caliphate was now a myth for the Arabic empire.

16. In what way did Uthman's murder haunt Ali's time as ruler? How did Ali die?

A16.—Pg. 315, ¶ 1–3—In 658, a segment of Ali's army broke away accusing Ali of injustice because he had not avenged Uthman's death, and that injustice invalidated Ali's right to rule. Ali attacked these rebels, the *Kharijis,* but Ali's own soldiers did not want to continue to fight with their own kin. In 661, a *Khariji* assassin murdered Ali in his camp.

Section III: Critical Thinking

The student may not use his text to answer this question.

Like all the charismatic and engaging rulers we've read about before him, Muhammad was able to keep his rapidly expanding empire together largely because of his personality. The caliphs that followed Muhammad barely held the empire together, and by the time Ali ibn Abu Talib was caliph, a piece of the empire had essentially split itself off from the whole. Write a paragraph that explains all the ways the different caliphs tried to keep the Arabic empire together. Then explain why it was so difficult to create cohesion. Make sure to include how issues of both nationality and religion upset Arab unity.

First the student will explain the different ways the caliphs tried to keep the Arab empire together. Abu Bakr warred with provinces outside of the Arabian peninsula, so those within the "tribe" would stick together to defeat the outside enemy. Umar came up with saqiba, *which gave the highest positions of power to those who had become Muslim the earliest. His system had potential because converts who persisted would eventually rise to power—there was hope for everyone. Uthman did away with* saqiba *in order to keep his clan, the Banu Umayya, in power. He kept a tight grip on the governors and military officials he appointed and managed their roles himself. In addition to force, Uthman tried to bond his empire together by creating a standard version of the Qur'an to be adopted across his land. Ali didn't have a lot of time to create cohesion, but he did hold steady to the claim that he was part of Muhammad's true clan, the Banu Hashim. Muawiyah tried to keep the empire together by constantly fighting rebels who resented his power.*

Next, the student will address why it was so difficult to create unity in the Islamic empire. The student should weave in how nationality and religion affected unity in this section. The Arab empire was huge, encompassing several conquered peoples that had their own cultures. For example, the Arabs may have conquered Persia, but Persian aristocracy, language and customs were still thriving. The many different conquered peoples did want to submit themselves to Arab rule. The student might also use the tension on the North African coast as an example. Arab power was concentrated in pockets, and in between those pockets groups constantly rebelled against their subjugators, so the Arabs were always fighting to stay in power. Within the faith itself, two groups had formed. After Ali and Muawiyah met to battle in 657, a compromise was made where Ali would remain caliph and rule from Kufa, while Muawiyah would rule from Syria, though he had no title. This split the empire apart because different groups believed the religious right to rule belonged to different men. Though Muawiyah eventually became caliph, clan rivalries and conquest continued to tear the Arab empire apart.

EXAMPLE ANSWER:

The caliphs that followed Muhammad tried to keep the empire together in myriad ways. Abu Bakr warred with provinces outside of the Arabian peninsula, so those within the "tribe" would stick together to defeat the outside enemy. Umar came up with saqiba, which gave the highest positions of power to those who had become Muslim the earliest and that gave hope to everyone—if you stuck it out, you might rise up. Uthman did away with saqiba in order to keep his clan, the Banu Umayya, in power. He kept a tight grip on the governors and military officials he appointed and managed their roles himself. In addition to force, Uthman tried to bond his empire together by creating a standard version of the Qur'an to be adopted across his land. Ali didn't have a lot of time to create cohesion, but he did hold steady to the claim that he was part of Muhammad's true clan, the Banu Hashim. Muawiyah tried to keep the empire together by constantly fighting rebels who resented his power.

The Arab empire was huge, encompassing several conquered peoples that had their own cultures. For example, the Arabs may have conquered Persia, but Persian aristocracy, language and customs were still thriving. The many different conquered peoples did want to submit themselves to Arab rule. Within the faith itself, two groups had formed. After Ali and Muawiyah met to battle in 657, a compromise was made where Ali would remain caliph and rule from Kufa, while Muawiyah would remain and rule from Syria, though he had no title. This split the empire apart because different groups believed the religious right to rule belonged to different men. Though Muawiyah eventually became caliph, clan rivalries and conquest continued to tear the Arab empire apart.

Chapter Forty-Two

Law and Language

The student may use her text when answering the questions in sections I and II.

Section I: Who, What, Where

Write a one or two-sentence answer explaining the significance of each item listed below.

Abd al-Malik ibn Marwan—**Pg. 322, ¶ 7 and Pg. 325, ¶ 1, 3 5 & 6—Abd al-Malik ibn Marwan was made caliph in 685 and he spent the first part of his rule fighting with those who opposed his leadership. Once his leadership was safe, Abd al-Malik ibn Marwan raided the Byzantine coast, conquered North Africa, built a center of worship in Jerusalem and decreed that the Arabic language would be the official language of the empire.**

Alcek—**Pg. 322, ¶ 2—Alcek, the fifth son of Kubrat, took his followers all the way to Italy and formed a little Bulgarian enclave there.**

Aripert—**Pg. 320, ¶ 2 & 3—Aripert, Rothari's successor, was the first Catholic king of Lombardy. When Aripert died in 661, a war erupted between his sons for the throne.**

Asparukh—**Pg. 322, ¶ 2-5—Asparukh, the third son of Kubrat, settled between the Dniester and the Prut river with over thirty thousand followers of his own. After Constantine IV failed to take over Asparukh's holdings, the two leaders made a peace treaty in 681, with Constantine IV agreeing to pay the Bulgars yearly tribute; Asparukh's conquests and Constantine IV's tribute payments turned Asparukh's land into the First Bulgarian Empire.**

Bayan—**Pg. 322, ¶ 2—Bayan, the oldest son of Kubrat, remained in his homeland, ruling over the diminished population that remained once his brothers had left with their followers. As soon as his brothers left, the Khazars attacked Bayan, reduced his kingdom to rubble, and swallowed his territory, bringing an end to the original Old Great Bulgarian kingdom.**

Constantine IV—**Pg. 321, ¶ 3—Constantine IV, son of Constans II, became emperor of Byzantium from his throne in Constantinople after his father's death.**

Dome of the Rock—**Pg. 325, ¶ 5 & 6—The Dome of the Rock was a mosque built in Jerusalem that provided a central place of worship and pilgrimage for Islam. The Dome of the Rock was built on the site of the destroyed Second Temple of the Jews; it protected the rock from which Muhammad was said to have ascended into heaven.**

Grimoald of Benevento—**Pg. 320, ¶ 3—Grimoald of Benevento, formerly a duke and semi-independent Lombard chief who was supposed to be loyal to the Lombard king, ended up as king of the Lombards after a feud between Aripert's sons over the crown ended with one of them dead and the other in flight.**

Justinian II—**Pg. 324, ¶ 3 and Pg. 325, ¶ 2—Justinian II, son of Constantine IV, became the ruler of the Byzantine empire after his father's death. After massacring the wives and children of the Bulgarian mercenaries that deserted Byzantine forces at the Battle of Sebastopolis, Justinian II's army rebelled against him, took him captive, and mutilated him by cutting off his nose, slitting his tongue, and sending him in chains to the military prison of Cherson.**

Kotrag—**Pg. 322, ¶ 2—Kotrag, the second son of Kubrat, went north to the Volga and settled with his followers, where they became known as the Silver Bulgars.**

Kouber—**Pg. 322, ¶ 2—Kouber, the fourth son of Kubrat, led a little band of Bulgarians first into Pannonia and then back toward Macedonia.**

Kubrat—**Pg. 321, ¶ 7—Kubrat, a Bulgarian chief, was recognized by Heraclius as king thirty years before the attack of Constantinople by the Arabs. When Kubrat died in 669, after a long reign during which he pushed the boundaries of Old Great Bulgaria up to the Donets and down to the Danube, he left the kingdom to his five sons jointly.**

Leontios—**Pg. 325, ¶ 2 & 3—Leontios, a general from the Byzantine army, was made emperor after Justinian II was dethroned. It was during Leontios's rule that Byzantium lost Carthage, and the empire's eight hundred years of settlement in North Africa came to an end; as a result Leontios was taken prisoner in 698, mutilated, and sent to a monastery.**

Musa bin Nusair—**Pg. 325, ¶ 3—Musa bin Nusair was appointed by Abd al-Malik ibn Marwan to rule the new Muslim province in North Africa, Ifriqiya.**

Section II: Comprehension

Write a two or three-sentence answer to each of the following questions.

1. How did the Arab invasions affect the Lombards of Italy?

A1.—Pg. 319, ¶ 1—The Lombards of Italy benefited from the Arab invasions. The wars to the east of Italy allowed the Lombard king Rothari to throw off all remaining vestiges of Byzantine control. Rothari was able to wipe out the Byzantine emperor's claim on all Italian lands except for Ravenna and Rome.

2. What did Rothari hope to do by creating a set of laws for the Lombards in 643? What was his code called? What are some examples of the laws Rothari came up with?

A2.—Pg. 319, ¶ 3 & 4—Rothari hoped to create cohesion for the Lombards via statehood by creating a set of laws for his people to follow. The code he came up with was called the Edict of Rothari. A few of the laws in the Edict were: you would be fined if you pulled a man's beard, you would be sentenced to death if you deserted a comrade in battle, and you had the right to transfer property to another if you did it in the presence of the assembly of freemen, known as "the thing."

3. According to the Edict of Rothari, how were outsiders supposed to act once they entered the Lombard kingdom? Why was this law important for the realization of Lombard Italy as a nation?

A3.—Pg. 319, ¶ 5 to Pg. 320, ¶ 1—Outsiders that entered the Lombard kingdom were supposed to live according to Lombard laws. This law was important for the realization of Lombard Italy as a nation because it created firm borders for the kingdom. Once wanderers or foreign warriors settled on Lombard land, they were expected to abide by the rules of the new nation.

4. Describe the medley of religions that existed within the Lombard kingdom, and how the Lombard religious mix moved towards Catholicism.

A4.—Pg. 319, ¶ 3 and Pg. 320, ¶ 2—The Lombard kingdom was made up of those who worshipped the old Germanic gods, some Arian Christians and some Catholic Christians. Aripert, Rothari's successor, became the first Catholic king of Lombardy, moving the nation away from the Arian Christianity left over from its Germanic days and moving it toward the political mainstream.

5. Why did Constans II move his headquarters to Tarentum in 661?

A5.—Pg. 320, ¶ 4—Constans II decided to move his headquarters to Tarentum in 661 because he was planned to reconquer Italy for the Byzantine empire.

6. Who was in charge of Benevento at the time of Constans II's approach? What happened to Constans II's planned attack of Benevento once Grimoald was summoned?

A6.—Pg. 320, ¶ 6 & 7—Benevento was governed by one of Grimoald's sons. When he heard of Constans II's approach, he summoned his father. Constans II was alarmed by Grimoald's large army, so he retreated first to Naples, and then to Rome.

7. How long did Constans II stay in Rome? What did he do while he was in Rome? Where did he go next and what did he do from there?

A7.—Pg. 321, ¶ 1 & 2—Constans II stayed in Rome for twelve days, and while he was there he attended divine services conducted by the pope and then he raided the city for any remaining gold or copper ornaments he could melt down and use to fund his war against the Lombards. He left Rome for Sicily, went to Syracuse, and declared it to be his new

capital. From Syracuse he launched attacks against the south of Italy; these attacks kept the southern Italian coast under Byzantium's control.

8. What happened to the Shahi kingdom as the Arabs moved east into India in 670?

A8.—Pg. 321, ¶ 4—As the Arab spread continued into the east, the king of Shahi was driven out of his capital at Kabul. The Shahi kingdom kept control of the Khyber Pass, but was forced to move its capital city east to Udabhandapura.

9. How was Constantine IV able to defend Constantinople against the Arab attacks that started in 674? In your answer, make sure to explain "Greek fire," and how it caused Arab troops to withdraw from the city.

A9.—Pg. 321, ¶ 5—Arab armies first laid siege to Constantinople in 674, and though the attacks lasted four years, Constantinople was able to continually refresh its supplies by sea, and fend off the invaders. The Arab navy launched a final sea attack in 678, but the Byzantine ships made use of their famous "Greek fire," a chemical concoction launched through tubes that kept burning even when it met the water, and finally the Arab ships withdrew—followed shortly after by the land forces.

10. What did Kubrat tell his sons on his deathbed, according to Nicephorus in the *Chronographikon syntomon*? How did his prophecy come true?

A10.—Pg. 322, ¶ 1—According to Nicephorus, in the history the *Chronographikon syntomon*, Kubrat brought his sons around him in his deathbed and challenged each to break a bundle of sticks with his bare hands. When they all failed, he undid the bundle and broke the sticks easily, one by one. "Stay united," he told them, "for a bundle is not easily broken." When Kubrat died his five sons split apart, and the eldest was immediately attacked by the Khazars, bringing an end to the original Old Great Bulgarian kingdom.

11. How did Constantine IV come to make a peace treaty with Asparukh? What were the terms of the treaty, and what was the outcome of the treaty for the Bulgarians?

A11.—Pg. 322, ¶ 3 & 4—In 679, Constantine IV marched against Asparukh and the thirty thousand Bulgarians that were with him on Byzantium's western border. Constantine IV had to withdraw because he was suffering from gout, his troops fled, and then Asparukh made an alliance with the Slavic tribes nearby, fighting his way down into Thracia and annoying the Byzantine troops on the northwestern border. By 681, Constantine IV realized that peace was the only option and he made a truce with Asparukh, agreeing to pay the Bulgars a yearly tribute, which resulted in Asparukh forming the first Bulgarian empire.

12. How did Abd al-Malik ibn Marwan spend the first years of his caliphate? How did the circumstances of Abd al-Malik ibn Marwan's first years of rule lead to peace with the Byzantines?

A12.—Pg. 322, ¶ 7 to Pg. 323, ¶ 2—Abd al-Malik ibn Marwan spent the first years of his caliphate ruthlessly squelching the Arabs who supported other candidates to the caliphate. He fought against the opposition for six years, while also dealing with famine and sickness

(which might have been the plague) in Syria. Because Abd al-Malik ibn Marwan was so busy dealing with internal troubles, he decided to make peace with Constantine IV, offering to pay tribute in order to confirm their treaty.

13. Describe the organization of Byzantium as it existed when Justinian II came to power. In your answer, make sure to explain how the military was organized as well.

A13.—Pg. 324, ¶ 3 & 4—When Justinian II came to the throne, Byzantium was organized into "themes" defended by native soldiers. Soldiers were awarded land in the themes in return for lifelong military service, and taxes were paid directly to the local troops, which gave soldiers strong motivation to protect their land. There were four themes in Asia Minor, one in Thracia, and two in Greece and Sicily.

14. Why were Abd al-Malik ibn Marwan and Justinian II so eager to go to war? What was the cause of their war, and how did Justinian II plan on defending Byzantine land?

A14.—Pg. 324, ¶ 6 & 7—Abd al-Malik ibn Marwan was eager to go to war against Justinian II because he was no longer fighting other Arabs over his appointment as caliph, and Justinian II was eager to prove his worth as emperor. Abd al-Malik ibn Marwan had been working to create a standard Arabic coinage and in late 692, Abd al-Malik ibn Marwan paid his tribute to Justinian II with Arab coins rather than Byzantine currency, which caused Justinian II to announce the coins counterfeit and declare war. Justinian II planned on defending Byzantine land with a "special army" made up of his own army reinforced by thirty thousand mercenary Bulgarian troops.

15. Why did the Bulgarian mercenaries abandon Byzantine troops at the Battle of Sebastopolis in 694? What was the result of the battle?

A15.—Pg. 324, ¶ 8 to Pg. 325, ¶ 1—The Bulgarian mercenaries hired by Justinian II abandoned Byzantine troops at the Battle of Sebastopolis because they were bribed by the Arabs. Abd al-Malik ibn Marwan had sent them money behind the scenes and promised them more if they would retreat once the battle began. The Byzantine troops were unable to hold the front without their allies and retreated. Abd al-Malik ibn Marwan then began a series of raids on the Byzantine coast.

16. How did the tribal structure of the Berbers help hasten the Islamic conquest of North Africa?

A16.—Pg. 325, ¶ 4—The tribal structure of the Berbers made conversion to Islam a mass event rather than an individual decision; when the leaders of a tribe converted, the rest of the tribe followed. The result was that the Berbers converted in remarkable numbers, aiding in the Islamic conquest of North Africa.

17. What did Abd al-Malik ibn Marwan do during his rule to create a more coherent Arab nation?

A17.—Pg. 325, ¶ 5 & 6—Abd al-Malik ibn Marwan introduced standard currency into the Arab nation; he put his brothers, whom he trusted, into the most important governors' offices; and he began to construct a new mosque in Jerusalem, called the Dome of the Rock,

that provided a central place of worship and pilgrimage. He also decreed that the Arabic language would be the official language of the empire, which glued together the widely scattered realm.

Section III: Critical Thinking

The student may not use her text to answer this question.

The idea of Rome's greatness has done more harm to its various leaders than actually bringing them any kind of glory or triumph. Constans II was seduced by the image of Rome in his mind, and it was his ultimate undoing. Write a paragraph explaining why Constans II left Constantinople, what he hoped to find in Rome, and what he actually found there. How was Constans II's end perfectly suited to the kind of ruler he turned out to be?

The student will answer this question successfully if she pits Constans II's idea of Rome against what he actually found there. Constans II was unpopular in Constantinople, so he fantasized about reviving his greatness in the glorious city of Rome. The old idea of being Roman still pulsed through the Byzantine kingdom. But the truth was, as stated on page 320, "few of them had ever been to the Eternal City; no emperor had visited Rome in generations; Italy itself had long been out of Byzantine hands." The text goes on, "Yet somehow Rome still occupied a place in the imagination. Constans II, heading for Rome, was out to recapture the glorious past."

Constans II left for Rome when he heard that King Grimoald and his large Lombard army were approaching Tarentum. Instead of fighting the Lombard king, Constans fled. When Constans II got to Rome, he only spent twelve days there. He attended divine services conducted by the pope, raided the city for any remaining gold or copper ornaments he could melt down and use to fund his war, and then departed for Sicily. Constans II couldn't stay in the broke, dirty and demoralized city of Rome—it was not the Rome of his dreams.

Though Constans II managed to keep control of the southern Italian coast for Byzantium by launching endless attacks from Syracuse, he never became the great emperor he envisioned himself to be. Unwanted in Constantinople, disgusted by Rome, Constans II sent for his wife and sons, ruling from Syracuse as a despot. Constans II couldn't see himself ruling in his time; he could only romanticize what his leadership would have been like during Rome's days of glory. As a result, he ended up far from Rome in Syracuse, where he was eventually killed by a house servant that battered him on the head with a soap box. Death by soap box seems fitting for a king who touted an outdated idea of a glorious city long gone.

EXAMPLE ANSWER:

Constans II was unpopular in Constantinople, so he fantasized about reviving his greatness in the glorious city of Rome. The old idea of being Roman still pulsed through the Byzantine kingdom, but few had been to Rome, no emperor had visited Rome in years and Italy wasn't even part of Byzantium anymore.

When Constans II heard King Grimoald and his large Lombard army were coming for him, he fled to Rome. When he got there, he only stayed for twelve days. He attended divine services

conducted by the pope, raided the city for any remaining gold or copper ornaments he could melt down and use to fund his war, and then departed for Sicily. Constans II couldn't stay in the broke, dirty and demoralized city of Rome—it was not the Rome of his dreams.

Though Constans II managed to keep control of the southern Italian coast for Byzantium by launching endless attacks from Syracuse, he never became the great emperor he envisioned himself to be. Unwanted in Constantinople, disgusted by Rome, Constans II sent for his wife and sons, ruling from Syracuse as a despot. Constans II couldn't see himself ruling in his time; he could only romanticize what his leadership would have been like during Rome's days of glory. As a result, he ended up far from Rome in Syracuse, where he was eventually killed by a house servant that battered him on the head with a soap box. Death by soap box seems fitting for a king who touted an outdated idea of a glorious city long gone.

Section IV: Map Exercise

1. Using a black pencil, trace the rectangular outline of the frame for Map 42.1: Byzantium, the Arabs, and the Bulgars.

2. Using a blue pencil, trace the coastline of the Atlantic around the continent and then the Mediterranean. You do not need to include Britain or islands other than Sardinia, Corsica, Sicily, Crete, and Cyprus at this time. Also with your blue pencil, trace the outline of the Black Sea, the Azov Sea, and the Caspian Sea. Trace the lines of the Danube, the Prut, the Dniester, the Donets, the Don, and the Volga. Then trace the lines of the Tigris and Euphrates. Repeat until the contours are familiar.

3. Select three contrasting colors (or seven if you have them). Use these respectively to trace the areas of the Visigoths, the Franks, Lombardy, Byzantium, the Khazars, the First Bulgarian Empire, and the Arab Empire. Either use seven contrasting colors to distinguish the regions, or use three contrasting colors for the different shaded areas and then draw different lines across the areas as the mapmaker did for the remaining four regions. Be sure to include the islands of Sardinia, Corsica, Sicily, Crete, and Cyprus, showing which territory each belongs in. Repeat until the contours are familiar.

4. Using a new sheet of paper, trace the rectangular outline of the frame in black. Remove your paper from the original. Using a regular pencil with an eraser as you look at Map 42.1, draw the entire coastline, again including only the islands of Sardinia, Corsica, Sicily, Crete, and Cyprus. Then draw the Black Sea, the Azov Sea, and the Caspian Sea. Draw the Danube, the Prut, the Dniester, the Donets, the Don, and the Volga. Draw also the Tigris and Euphrates. Now draw the outlines of the territories of the Visigoths, the Franks, Lombardy, Byzantium, Khazars, the First Bulgarian Empire, and the Arab Empire. Erase and redraw as necessary while looking at the map.

5. When you are pleased with your map, lay it over the original. Erase and redraw any lines which are more than ¼ inch off of the original.

6. Finally draw the arrows showing the Bulgar movements.

Chapter Forty-Three

Creating the Past

The student may use his text when answering the questions in sections I and II.

Section I: Who, What, Where

Write a one or two-sentence answer explaining the significance of each item listed below.

Fujiwara—**Pg. 327, ¶ 4—Fujiwara was the name Tenji gave to his longtime friend and ally Nakatomi no Kamatari for his lifelong loyalty. The name Fujiwara gave Nakatomi no Kamatari the place of patriarch of a new clan; he became the founder of a new family that would rise steadily in power, one day becoming more powerful than the Soga clan.**

Gemmei—**Pg. 329, ¶ 5 to Pg. 330, ¶ 1—Gemmei, daughter of Tenji and mother of Mommu, followed her grandson as heavenly sovereign. Gemmei moved her capital city to Nara, known as Heijo, the City of Peace, and it became the capital city for the next eighty years.**

Gensho—**Pg. 331, ¶ 1—Gensho, daughter of Gemmei, was made heavenly sovereign in 714 when her mother abdicated the throne. Gensho presided over the publication of the Yoro Code, a code that stated that the heavenly sovereign not only touched the divine but was herself godlike.**

Jimmu—**Pg. 331, ¶ 3—Jimmu, as stated in the *Kojiki* and the *Nihon shoki*, was the first Yamato king, the grandson of the sea god and the great-great-grandson of the son goddess. Jimmu rose to rule his people, telling them after the world had descended into darkness the gods gave man the gift of the imperial house, and under the heavenly sovereign the darkness gave way to beauty and order.**

Mommu—**Pg. 329, ¶ 3 & 5—Mommu, Tenji's grandson, took the role of heavenly sovereign in 697 and completed the first surviving set of laws from Japan, the *Taiho ritsu-ryo*, or Great Treasure, in 701. Mommu died at the age of twenty-five, not long after issuing the Great Treasure.**

Shomu—**Pg. 331, ¶ 2—Shomu, brother of Gensho, son of Gemmei, followed his sister as heavenly sovereign, during which time he ruled with grandeur, had an elaborate court, and**

a government filled with bureaucrats. Shomu commissioned an ancient past for the Yamato kings called the *Kojiki* and the *Nihon shoki.*

Tenji—**Pg. 327, ¶ 3 and Pg. 329, ¶ 2—Tenji was named Naka no Oe took when he accepted the title of Heavenly Sovereign in 668, at the age of forty-two. After reorganizing the Yamato domain via the Taika reforms, and bringing culture to the Japanese people, Tenji grew ill after four years of official rule and died in severe, unrelieved pain.**

Section II: Comprehension

Write a two or three-sentence answer to each of the following questions.

1. How did Tenji's (then Naka no Oe) attempt to help the Baekje against the Tang-Silla alliance end up reinforcing Japan's isolationist policy?

A1.—Pg. 327, ¶ 5—When Tenji was still Naka no Oe, he attempted to help the Baekje king regain his throne by fighting the Tang-Silla alliance. The battle was disastrous and Japan suffered a great defeat. Japan's defeat reinforced its desire to focus on its own affairs and not meddle in the affairs of other nations.

2. Why did then crown prince Naka no Oe and Nakatomi No Kamatari create the Great Reform, or "Taika reforms"?

A2.—Pg. 328, ¶ 1—Naka no Oe and Nakatomi no Kamatari created the Great Reform, or the Taika reforms, because they wanted to transform the Yamato domain from divided to unified. When Naka no Oe was still crown prince, the Yamato domain remained divided between a series of linked clans that were dominated by clan leaders who fiercely guarded their own authority. Naka no Oe and Nakatomi no Kamatari envisioned the Yamato domain as a single royal realm, governed by a single monarch, and so they created the reforms.

3. What did the first Reform Edict declare, and how did this reform change the law associated with titles and land ownership?

A 3.—Pg. 328, ¶ 1—The first of the Reform Edicts declared that all of the Yamato domain was to be a single public realm, held by the crown on behalf of the people. Private estates and hereditary clan rights over them were abolished, as was the old system of titles. Instead of owning their land and claiming the titles of nobility, the former clan leaders and village chiefs were granted the right to govern the land, which theoretically belonged to the Yamato ruler, and instead of claiming their noble titles, they were awarded ranks in the newly formed bureaucracy.

4. From where did the idea of the Great Reform come? What model was it based on?

A4.—Pg. 328, ¶ 2—The idea of the Great Reform came from China, modeled after the ancient Chinese map of the world, a set of concentric rings with the emperor's power all-encompassing at the center and executed by proxy at the distant edges. Some of the edicts

of the Great Reform quote, word for word, from the Chinese histories that Naka no Oe's emissaries brought back from their travels in China, where they learned the long history of Chinese emperorship. The Japanese wanted to claim, like the Chinese, to belong to a tradition of royal authority that flowed down from the beginnings of time.

5. What is a "polestar monarchy"? How did Tenji try and influence the culture of Japan in his role as "polestar monarch"?

A5.—Pg. 328, ¶ 3—Historian Joan Piggott, borrowing the term from Confucius, calls a polestar monarch one that "exercises government by means of his virtue and thus may be compared to the north polar star, which keeps its place and all the stars turn towards it." Tenji, wanting to be more than a chief general and war leader, brought historians and poets to his court and founded a university. He and his court read the Chinese classics, which had arrived in the hands of a traveling Buddhist monk in 660, and he led his court in celebrating Chinese rites that linked heavenly order to earthly tranquility.

6. Why did Tenji attempt to set down a written legal code for all of Japan?

A6.—Pg. 329, ¶ 1—Tenji, in part because of contact with the governments of Tang China and United Silla, and in part because he felt that the heavenly sovereign should have more earthly power, felt that it was time for Japan to have a set of written laws. The written legal code would be distinct from the Great Reforms, and it would make the theoretical power of the heavenly sovereign more concrete.

7. How was the rule of Japan laid out in the *Taiho ritsu-ryo* different from the reality of how Japan was governed?

A7.—Pg. 329, ¶ 3 & 4—The rule of Japan laid out in the *Taiho ritsu-ryo* seemed thorough and well-controlled, with one authority that spread out in an elaborate series of branching bureaucracies, each with its own set of ranks and offices. It was a beautifully structured set of laws, and the world it envisioned was just as orderly as the concentric rings of authority laid out in the edicts of the Great Reform. However, beneath the template of the *Taiho ritsu-ryo* vast swathes of the country ran along just as they had before, with clan leaders holding bureaucratic ranks instead of noble titles while still exercising the same authority as they did before the Great Treasure. Similarly, the land might belong to the crown in name, but it was still farmed and divided, plowed and shaped, by the same men who had owned it before the reforms.

8. Why was Gemmei's capital city special? What new name was the city given, and what changes were made to enhance the city?

A8.—Gemmei's capital city, Nara, was special because it would remain the capital city for the next eighty years, during the time known as the "Nara period" of Japan. The city, called Heijo, the City of Peace, was enlarged and glorified, based on the layout of the Tang capital of Chang'an.

9. How did the capital at Nara help to extend the heavenly sovereign's power from the divine to the real world?

A9.—Pg. 330, ¶ 2—By settling the capital of the heavenly sovereign in one place for several decades, it suggested a locus of power that was both divine and earthly. In the past, the dwelling place of the heavenly sovereign had been a minor matter because the sovereign was a locus of heavenly power, not earthly power. But at Nara, with a stone Senate building, a royal court, and a throne, the heavenly sovereign's power was more strongly connected to the real world.

10. What was the Yoro Code?

A9.—Pg. 331, ¶ 1—The Yoro Code, presided over by Heavenly Sovereign Gensho, put into words the idea that the heavenly sovereign not only touched the divine but was herself godlike. The polestar did not just relay the message of the gods, she was the source of the message itself.

Section III: Critical Thinking

The student may not use his text to answer this question.

External conquest was *de rigueur* in the medieval world. In this chapter, however, we see the infiltration of Chinese ideas into isolated Japan, and rather than breaking Japan apart, this infiltration actually strengthened the multiple-island nation. Write a paragraph explaining the historical myth that was produced to give a foundation to Japanese kingship. In the second part of your answer, explain how the myth justified internal conflict for the sake of a united Japan.

In the first part of his answer, the student will explain the mythical history of Japanese kingship as described on page 331, ¶ 3. The Kojiki and the Nihon shoki tell us that the first Yamato king, Jimmu, had been the grandson of the sea god and the great-great-grandson of the sun goddess. As a grown man, he gathered his sons together and gave them a charter, telling them that long ago the world was gloomy and dark. But then the gods had given man a gift—the leadership of the imperial house, and under the heavenly sovereign, darkness and chaos had given way to beauty and order, and the land had become a place of fertility and light, good crops and peaceful days and nights.

The accounts go on to explain how internal conquest was approved by the gods because the places in Japan outside of the blessings of Imperial rule were "suitable for the extension of the heavenly task." In the second part of his answer, the student will explain that Jimmu told his people that remote regions did not enjoy the blessings of Imperial rule, so "every town had always been allowed to have its lord, and every village its chief, who, each one for himself, makes division of territory and practices mutual aggression and conflict." Jimmu continued to explain that these far reaching lands were suitable for extending the heavenly task, meaning these lands needed to be subsumed under the heavenly sovereign in order to bring light to the darkness, and beauty to the chaos. When Jimmu asks "Why should we not proceed there?" he is asking "Why shouldn't we bring the light of the heavenly sovereign to these people?" This story acts as justification for warfare between the Japanese people. Internal conquest for the sake of unity under the heavenly sovereign theoretically turned any bitterness between old divisions into a united Japan founded on "heroism, legendary feats of strength, and the favor of the gods."

EXAMPLE ANSWER:

The Kojiki and the Nihon shoki tell us that the first Yamato king, Jimmu, had been the grandson of the sea god and the great-great-grandson of the sun goddess. As a grown man, he gathered his sons together and gave them a charter, telling them that long ago the world was gloomy and dark. But then the gods had given man a gift—the leadership of the imperial house, and under the heavenly sovereign, darkness and chaos had given way to beauty and order, and the land had become a place of fertility and light, good crops and peaceful days and nights.

As the account goes on, Jimmu explains to his people that because the remote regions of Japan did not enjoy Imperial rule, towns had their own lords, villages had their own chiefs, and these leaders divided territory, and fought for their territory, on their own. These areas, Jimmu claimed, were perfect places to extend the rule of the heavenly sovereign, to be brought light and divine blessings, so he asked his people "Why should we not proceed there?" This story acts as justification for warfare between the Japanese people. Internal conquest for the sake of unity under the heavenly sovereign theoretically turned any bitterness between old divisions into a united Japan founded on heroism and the favor of the gods. As independent villages were subsumed into the larger nation, they were told they were being given the blessing of the divine, their chaos was turning into beauty, and the darkness of their pasts was now giving way to the light of a united Japanese future.

Section IV: Map Exercise

1. Using a black pencil, trace the rectangular outline of the frame for Map 43.1: The Nara Period.

2. Using a blue pencil, trace the coastal outline up the coast of China and around the coast of Japan. You need not include any islands other than Japan at this time, but do include the Inland Sea. Using your blue pencil, trace the line of the Yellow River. Then, using a black pencil, trace the line of the Great Wall. Repeat until the contours are familiar.

3. Using a new sheet of paper, trace the rectangular outline of the frame for Map 43.1 in black. Remove your tracing paper from the original. Using a regular pencil with an eraser, draw the coastal outline around China and Japan, including the Inland Sea. Draw the line of the Yellow River and the Great Wall.

4. When you are pleased with your map, lay it over the original. Erase and redraw any lines which are more than ¼ inch off of the original.

5. Now study carefully the locations of the Yellow Sea, Hokkaido, Nara, the Yamato Plain, Kyushu, and the Inland Sea. When they are familiar to you, close the book. Label each location, and then check your map against the original. Erase and remark any misplaced locations.

Chapter Forty-Four

The Days of the Empress

The student may use her text when answering the questions in sections I and II.

Section I: Who, What, Where

Write a one or two-sentence answer explaining the significance of each item listed below.

Empress Wei—**Pg. 338, ¶ 5-7—Empress Wei, wife of Zhongzong, ran the Tang court during her husband's five-year reign. After she poisoned her husband in 710 and tried to install her husband's young son as emperor so that she could be regent, the court led a palace rebellion and Empress Wei was killed.**

Khitan—**Pg. 336, ¶ 2 & 4—The Khitan, nomadic tribes from north of China, moved south toward the Tang border near Beijing during Wu Zetian's reign as emperor and rebelled against her in 695. The Khitan were defeated by Mo-ch'o, the same man who encouraged them to attack China in the first place.**

Khri-'bring—**Pg. 336, ¶ 3 and Pg. 337, ¶ 1—Khri-'bring, Gar Tongtsen's son, controlled Tibet in his role as regent for Tridu Songtsen, and continued the conquests begun by Songtsen Gampo by attacking Tang land in the Tarim Basin. Khri-'bring extended Tibetan holdings two hundred miles west of Chang'an and then agreed to retreat after a buyout offer from Wu Zetian.**

Li Chongzhao—**Pg. 333, ¶ 2—Li Chongzhao, the son of Zhongzong, was made "Heir Apparent Grandson" by the dying Tang Gaozong in order to ensure the continuance of the Tang dynasty.**

Mo-ch'o—**Pg. 336, ¶ 2 and Pg. 337, ¶ 1—Mo-ch'o, a descendent of the royal family of the Eastern Turkish Khaghanate, led the Eastern Turks in a rebellion against Wu Zetian's northwestern frontier in 695. After beating the Khitan on behalf of the Tang, Mo-ch'o continued to attack the Tang, managing to rebuild the power of the Eastern Khaghanate in just a few years.**

Ruizong—**Pg. 333, ¶ 4, Pg. 335, ¶ 2 and Pg. 339, ¶ 1—Ruizong, the younger brother of Zhongzong and son of Wu Zetian, asked his mother to do him the favor of removing him from the throne from which he ruled as a puppet-emperor. He lived in peaceful obscurity until his brother's murder in 710, at which time he was asked by the Tang court to become emperor once again; this time his reign lasted for only two years before he abdicated.**

Tang Xuanzong—**Pg. 339, ¶ 2 & 3—Tang Xuanzong, son of Ruizong, was made emperor by his father in 712. He made great reforms in China and brought the Tang dynasty to the height of its glory, which earned him the name "Brilliant Emperor."**

Tridu Songtsen—**Pg. 336, ¶ 3—Tridu Songtsen, Mangson Mangtsen's son, was the next emperor of Tibet but his rule was enforced by his regent Khri-'bring.**

Xue Huaiyi—**Pg. 336, ¶ 1—Xue Huaiyi, a salesman of medical herbs and Wu Zetian's lover, became troublesome and burned down one of the great Buddhist temples in the city in a fit of rage. In response, the emperor picked the strongest ladies-in-waiting at court and sent them to surround Huaiyi and strangle him.**

Zhongzong—**Pg. 333, ¶ 2 & 4, Pg. 337, ¶ 2 and Pg. 338, ¶ 6—Zhongzong was chosen by the dying Tan Gaozong to be emperor in 683, but then was kicked off the throne by Wu Zetian after ruling for only two months, and then he was reinstalled as Heir Apparent when he was nearly fifty. After his mother's death, Zhongzong ruled for five years until he was murdered by his ambitious wife in 710.**

Zhou—**Pg. 335, ¶ 4 and Pg. 338, ¶ 4—Zhou was the name of the dynasty created by Wu Zetian when she became emperor in 690. When the emperor died, the court records almost unanimously ignored her attempts to create a new dynasty.**

Section II: Comprehension

Write a two or three-sentence answer to each of the following questions.

1. In addition to naming his heir apparent, and heir apparent grandson, what else did Tang Gaozong order before his death? How did Wu Zetian take advantage of this decree?

A1.—Pg. 333, ¶ 3–5—The last order Tang Gaozong issued was that the new emperor had to consult Empress Wu Zetian whenever important matters of defense and administration could not be decided. Wu Zetian believed her husband's last order meant she had the power to make final decisions, so she ousted Zhongzong from the throne and installed her younger son, a shy young man with a stutter, as emperor. Because of his ailments, Ruizong had no choice but to let his mother rule on his behalf.

2. How did the decree, the "Act of Grace," affect the royal court in Tang China? What did the decree symbolize?

A2.—Pg. 334, ¶ 2—The "Act of Grace" changed the colors of imperial banners, the styles of dress at court, and the insignia of court officials. The decree symbolized change, and the possibility that a new ruler was going to found a new dynasty.

3. Why was it relatively easy for Wu Zetian to make so many changes within Tang China?

A3.—Pg. 334, ¶ 3—It was relatively easy for Wu Zetian to make so many changes within Tang China because her people were happy. The people were temporarily prosperous and peaceful, the farmers and peasants were well fed and well supplied, and the general agitation needed for mass revolt was missing. The one revolt that did break out, led by a nobleman whose family had been exiled, was put down quickly and without much fuss by the empress's soldiers.

4. How did Wu Zetian solve the problem of resentment felt by aristocrats of the court over a former concubine rising to the power of empress and leader?

A4.—Pg. 334, ¶ 5—Wu Zetian solved the problem of aristocrats of the court resenting her power by replacing them with officials from the lower classes. Wu Zetian was from the lower classes herself, so the people she appointed were thankful that they were able to rise in society because of their talent rather than aristocratic blood. By making common people officials of the court, Wu Zetian guaranteed that she would be surrounded by loyal supporters.

5. In addition to making common people officials, what else did Wu Zetian do to ensure support of her rule?

A5.—Pg. 334, ¶ 6—In addition to making common people officials, Wu Zetian created a secret police headed by two notorious officials, Zhou Xing and Lai Junchen. The secret police composed a book of instructions and elaborated many new and frightful tortures to extract confessions. Dissidents were too frightened by the pain of torture to object to Wu Zetian's rule.

6. How did Wu Zetian come to accept the title "Emperor, Son of Heaven"?

A6.—Pg. 335, ¶ 1 & 2—In 690, one of Wu Zetian's officials asked her to assume the title "Emperor, Son of Heaven," and she declined. A second petition signed by sixty thousand of her subjects was presented and again she refused. Finally, the puppet emperor Ruizong presented the third and final petition himself, asking that his mother do him the favor of removing him from the throne. The empress Wu agreed and she was crowned on September 24, 690.

7. How did Mo-ch'o most likely orchestrate and use the triple uprising in the north against Wu Zetian to his advantage?

A7.—Pg. 336, ¶ 4—Mo-ch'o most likely suggested to the Khitan that they attack Wu Zetian, causing one of the three uprisings against Wu Zetian. Then Mo-ch'o offered his help to the Chinese emperor, saying he would attack the Khitan on behalf of the Tang, in return for very large payments. Once the plan was set, Mo-ch'o defeated the Khitan in 696, and then after collecting his fee he continued to attack the Tang, managing to rebuild the power of the Eastern Khaghanate in the following years.

8. How did Zhongzong become heir apparent to the Chinese throne, after once being emperor, and then how did he become emperor once again?

A8.—Pg. 337, ¶ 2 to Pg. 338, ¶ 2—When Wu Zetian began an affair with two brothers with the family name of Zhang, court officials worried they were going to talk her into making them her successors. In response, they suggested Zhongzong be brought back out of obscurity and restored to the throne; Wu Zetian did the next best thing and named him her Heir Apparent, even though he had once been emperor. In 699, Emperor Wu went through her first major illness and by 705, at eighty years old, she was ready for retirement. She abdicated and handed over her crown to Zhongzong, who was then made emperor once again.

9. What happened to the Zhou dynasty after Wu Zetian's passing?

A9.—Pg. 338, ¶ 4—After Wu Zetian's death, court records almost unanimously ignored her attempts to found a new dynasty, and went right back to chronicling the years of the Tang. The Zhou dynasty basically disappeared.

10. What caused Ruizong to give up his role as Tang emperor?

A10.—Pg. 338, ¶ 9 to Pg. 339, ¶ 1—Ruizong, made emperor at forty-eight after the death of his brother, was reluctant to re-enter the palace fray. He lasted for just two years. In 712, after seeing a comet appear in the sky, he hailed it as an omen and abdicated.

11. How did Tang Xuanzong fix the mess made by the emperors before him?

A11.—Pg. 339, ¶ 2 & 3—Tang Xuanzong increased revenue from taxes by cutting government tax breaks for Buddhist monasteries—meaning monks and nuns had to return to civilian life. He broke the power of aristocratic families by reinstituting the Confucian system of choosing officials through a series of examinations, he stabilized the frontiers by setting up a series of command zones along the trouble spots and giving a military governor vast powers to deal with any difficulties, and he drove back the Tibetans, making them sue for peace. Because of the relative peace on the frontiers and the money coming from his new tax policies, Tang Xuanzong was able to move the capital back to Chang'an, where trade recommenced and brought caravans from as far away as Constantinople. He brought the Tang dynasty from ruin to the height of its glory.

Section III: Critical Thinking

The student may not use her text to answer this question.

In this chapter we read about two brilliant emperors, though only one was given that nickname. Tang Xuanzong may have brought the Tang dynasty to greatness, but Wu Zetian, once a concubine, managed to convince the empire that she could be a masculine emperor even though she was a woman. Explain how Wu Zetian was able to manipulate the system and turn herself into an emperor. Why were the Chinese people able to accept her in this role?

Wu Zetian's rise from concubine to emperor is brilliant indeed. Her final transformation, from empress to emperor, relied on the acceptance of the myth of the Mandate of Heaven. The Mandate had been stretched by previous rulers, but never before had a woman become a Son of Heaven.

The student should explain how Wu Zetian put on a masculine persona for the purposes of court ceremonies. She did not change her dress or appearance, she did not even try to appear male, but she still created a male persona through her power, a power that the entire country accepted. By starting the new Zhou dynasty, to which she was the patriarch, Wu Zetian made all of China players in her theater. Emperor Wu moved her court to Luoyang, which detached her from her role as empress—she had a new city from which to rule as emperor.

The fiction was captivating in part because Wu Zetian was a great ruler: she built a strong administration full of talented and well-trained men, and Tang China was prosperous during her reign. By shrouding herself in the aura of masculinity, Emperor Wu convinced her public to accept her as a Son of Heaven, worthy of the Mandate. The Chinese people were able to accept her in this role because they were already so removed from the reality of the Mandate. But, perhaps more importantly, the willingness of the population to accept her as Emperor Wu is proof of her brilliance.

EXAMPLE ANSWER:

Wu Zetian, once a concubine, managed to become an empress and then emperor of Tang China. Her final transformation relied on the acceptance of the myth of the Mandate of Heaven. The Mandate had been stretched by previous rulers, but never before had a woman become a Son of Heaven. When Wu Zetian became emperor, she put on a masculine persona for the purposes of court ceremonies. She did not change her dress or appearance, she did not even try to appear male, but she still created a male persona through her power, a power that the entire country accepted. By starting the new Zhou dynasty, to which she was the patriarch, Wu Zetian made all of China players in her theater. Emperor Wu moved her court to Luoyang, which detached her from her role as empress—she had a new city from which to rule as emperor.

The fiction was captivating in part because Wu Zetian was a great ruler: she built a strong administration full of talented and well-trained men, and Tang China was prosperous during her reign. By shrouding herself in the aura of masculinity, Emperor Wu convinced her public to accept her as a Son of Heaven, worthy of the Mandate. The Chinese people were able to accept her in this role because they were already so removed from the reality of the Mandate. Wu Zetian's maneuvering from concubine to emperor surely makes her worth of the label "brilliant."

Chapter Forty-Five

Paths in Europe

The student may use his text when answering the questions in sections I and II.

Section I: Who, What, Where

Write a one or two-sentence answer explaining the significance of each item listed below.

Al-Andalus—**Pg. 344, ¶ 4—Al-Andalus was the name of the Islamic province carved out of Hispania from the old Visigoth territory. Al-Andalus was placed under the control of the command of the governor of North Africa.**

Al-Ghafiqi—**Pg. 348, ¶ 6 & 7 and Pg. 349, ¶ 3—Al-Ghafiqi, the new governor of al-Andalus after Odo's murder of the previous governor, led an army back towards the northeast in 732, beating Odo of Aquitaine at the Battle of the River Garonne and then continuing into Bordeaux, then to Poitiers. Al-Ghafiqi was killed in battle when the Arabs met the Franks near Poitiers.**

Al-Samh—**Pg. 347, ¶ 1 and Pg. 348, ¶ 5—Al-Samh, governor of al-Andalus, brought the Islamic army through the old Visigothic land to the Frankish land known as Aquitaine.**

Alpaida—**Pg. 347, ¶ 6—Alpaida, mistress of Pippin the Fat, bore the mayor two illegitimate sons, one of which was Charles Martel.**

Busir Glavan—**Pg. 341, ¶ 2 & 3—Busir Glavan, khan of the Khazars after they had driven back the Arabs and conquered Old Great Bulgaria, agreed to let his sister marry Justinian the Noseless in exchange for his help getting Byzantium back for the dethroned emperor. Busir Glavan broke his agreement with Justinian the Noseless when he was paid by Tiberios to murder the mutilated emperor.**

Charles Martel—**Pg. 348, ¶ 1 & 2 and Pg. 349, ¶ 4—Charles Martel, the ambitious and older son of Alpaida and Pippin the Fat, escaped from the prison he was placed in by Plectrude, returned to Neustria, fought Plectrude and various claimants to the office of mayor of**

the palace for two years until 717 when he made himself mayor of the palace of Austrasia. Martel was called "The Hammer" because he supposedly hammered away at his enemies and ground them to dust, a nickname he earned after beating the Arab army at the Battle of Tours.

Egica—**Pg. 343, ¶ 4—Egica, king of the Visigoths, appointed as co-ruler his eight-year-old son, Wittiza, as an attempt to introduce dynastic right to the throne into the Visigothic succession. Egica was unpopular because he had claimed some of the land designated for the use of the king as his own personal property, but before anyone could revolt against him the plague broke in Toledo and Egica died shortly afterwards.**

Leo III—**Pg. 346, ¶ 1, 3 & 5—Leo III, a Syrian soldier, became emperor when Theodosius III abdicated after the armies at Nicaea proclaimed Leo to be the new leader. Leo III kept Constantinople safe from Arab attack when he drove Arab ships out of the Golden Horn and when he beat Arab land troops in battle by creating an alliance with the Bulgarians.**

Odo—Pg. 348, ¶ 4 & 5 and Pg. 348, ¶ 9—**Odo, ruler of Aquitaine, beat the invading Arabs at the Battle of Toulouse on June 9, 721, killing the governor of al-Andalus and halting the Arab advance into Europe. After being defeated by al-Ghafiqi, Odo swore his loyalty to Charles Martel, was made a commander in the army and given authority over the Aquitaine wing of the Frankish army.**

Pelayo—**Pg. 346, ¶ 7 to Pg. 347, ¶ 1—Pelayo, a Visigoth noble, retreated into the northern mountains with his followers in 718 and declared himself king of a Christian kingdom called Asturias. Pelayo and his kingdom of Asturias survived repeated Arab attacks because of its mountain defenses.**

Pippin the Fat—**Pg. 347, ¶ 3–5—Pippin the Fat, also known as Pippin the Middle, grandson of Pippin the Elder, ruled as the de facto king of Austrasia, and after beating Theuderic III in battle, was named mayor of the Austrasian, Neustrian and Burgundian palaces. Pippin the Fat called himself "Duke and Prince of the Franks," ruling for nearly thirty years and dying in 714 at the age of eighty.**

Plectrude—**Pg. 347, ¶ 6 to Pg. 348, ¶ 2—Plectrude, wife of Pippin the Fat, insisted that her grandsons were the rightful heirs to her husband's throne, and in an attempt to stop Alpaida and her sons from getting power she locked up Alpaida's older son Charles Martel. When Charles Martel escaped from prison he beat Plectrude in battle and installed himself as mayor of the Austrasian palace.**

Ruderic—**Pg. 344, ¶ 1 & 2—Ruderic, who followed the disappeared Wittiza as Visigoth king in 711, fought in a civil war caused by opposition to his kingship. Ruderic faced the invading Arab army at the Battle of Guadalete where his defense was shattered and he was killed.**

Suleiman—**Pg. 344, ¶ 5 and Pg. 346, ¶ 4—Suleiman, younger brother of Walid I and his successor to the caliphate, started his rule by strategizing the Islamic attack on Byzantine**

borders. Suleiman died from sickness while his forces were regrouping after retreating from an attack on the harbor at Constantinople.

Tariq bin Ziyad—**Pg. 342, ¶ 7 and Pg. 344, ¶ 2—Tariq bin Ziyad, a Berber soldier that was once a slave but earned his freedom through military service, was appointed military commander by the governor of the Islamic province of North Africa Musa ibn Nusair. Tariq bin Ziyad led an army of Arabs and Berbers against the Visigoths, wiping out the Visigoth kingdom in Spain.**

Tervel—**Pg. 342, ¶ 2—Tervel, Asparukh's son and ruler of the Bulgarians, agreed to an alliance with Justinian the Noseless because the Bulgarians were an enemy of the Khazars and because Justinian promised Tervel cash and the eventual marriage of his own daughter to the Bulgarian king.**

Theodosius III—**Pg. 344, ¶ 6 to Pg. 346, ¶ 1—Theodosius III, the third of three temporary emperors that followed Justinian II, was a tax official who had been elevated against his will; when he found out that his soldiers were planning on putting him on the throne, he hid in the woods. When the Syrian Leo was proclaimed emperor by the armies at Nicaea in response to the pending Arab attack, Theodosius III happily abdicated, went to a monastery, trained for the priesthood, and eventually became bishop of Ephesus.**

Theuderic III—**Pg. 347, ¶ 4—Theuderic III, the youngest son of Clovis II, attacked Austrasia in 687 but was beaten so badly he had to agree to make Pippin the Fat the joint mayor of all three Frankish palaces: Austrasia, Neustria and Burgundy.**

Tiberios III—**Pg. 341, ¶ 1 and Pg. 342, ¶ 3—Tiberios III, general-turned-emperor of Constantinople, was murdered by Justinian the Noseless in 705 when the ex-emperor stormed Constantinople with the help of the Bulgarian king Tervel.**

Umar II—**Pg. 346, ¶ 5—Umar II, Suleiman's cousin and successor to the caliphate, had to withdraw his troops from their attack on Constantinople in August 15, 718 after Leo III enlisted the help of the Bulgarians to beat the invaders.**

Walid I—**Pg. 342, ¶ 6 and Pg. 344, ¶ 5—Walid I, son of Abd al-Malik, succeeded his father as caliph. Walid I left as his legacy the Arab entrance into Europe via the defeat of the Visigoths.**

Wittiza—**Pg. 343, ¶ 4 to Pg. 344, ¶ 1—Wittiza, son of Visigoth king Egica, was appointed as co-ruler when he was eight years old in 694, and around 700, when he had reached adulthood, he was given a coronation ceremony. After his father's death, Wittiza returned the land his father had taken for himself, but this did not save him because by 711 he disappears from the historical record.**

Section II: Comprehension

Write a two or three-sentence answer to each of the following questions.

1. What was Justinian the Noseless's first plan to get back the Byzantine throne? How was that plan derailed?

A1.—Pg. 341, ¶ 2 to Pg. 342, ¶ 1—Justinian the Noseless tried to make an alliance with Busir Glavan, offering the Khazar king a connection to the Byzantine throne via a marriage alliance to Justinian's sister. Busir Glavan agreed to the alliance, but then he received a bribe from Tiberios III that would be paid if Busir Glavan agreed to assassinate Justinian the Noseless. The Khazar king said yes to Tiberios III's bribe, but Justinian was tipped off by his wife, after which he murdered the men that were supposed to murder him and then fled Khazar territory.

2. How did Justinian manage to get back onto the throne at Constantinople? What were the consequences of his siege?

A2.—Pg. 342, ¶ 2 & 3—Justinian the Noseless convinced the Bulgarian king Tervel to support his attack on Constantinople by offering him cash and a marriage alliance to his own daughter. Tervel accepted and in 705 Justinian was able to lead a Bulgarian army to the walls of Constantinople, where they spent three days trying to negotiate their way into the city before the ex-emperor led the army into the city through a water main. They stormed the palace, Tiberios was murdered, and the patriarch that supported Tiberios's rule was blinded—payback for the mutilation suffered by Justinian.

3. What special appendage did Justinian the Noseless wear during his second reign? What was his main objective during his second reign, and how did it end?

A3.—Pg. 342, ¶ 4 & 5—During his second reign, Justinian wore a special silver nose that was used to cover the hole in his face where his real nose used to be. His second reign was a reign of terror, with his main objective being to hunt down those that had betrayed him during his first reign. The brutality came to an end in 711 when the army rose up and murdered Justinian II.

4. Why did Musa ibn Nusair and Tariq bin Ziyad want to take Tangiers for the Islamic holdings in North Africa?

A4.—Pg. 342, ¶ 7—Musa ibn Nusair and Tariq bin Ziyad wanted to take Tangiers for the Islamic holdings in North Africa because they hoped that Tangiers could serve as a staging point for the Arab armies to cross the mouth of the Mediterranean Sea and move into the Visigothic kingdom of Hispania.

5. What rules were made about Visigoth kingship at the Fifth and Eighth Councils of Toledo? What do the Toledo decrees tells us about where the Visigoths hoped to find stability?

A5.—Pg. 343, ¶ 1-3—At the Fifth Council of Toledo, the priests, scholars, and officials that made Visigoth laws decreed that only a Gothic noble, of Gothic blood, could ever be king.

At the Eighth Council of Toledo, the stipulation was added that the Visigoth king had to be chosen by the "great nobility," or the Goths of the powerful families. The Toledo decrees tell us that the Visigoths hoped to find stability in the assurance that the king would be of Gothic blood.

6. What caused civil war amongst the Visigoths during Ruderic's rule?

A6.—Pg. 344, ¶ 1—Ruderic's rule was supported by the Gothic nobles, but some accounts mention two other kings in other parts of Hispania, which suggest that support for Ruderic was not unanimous amongst all of the nobles. As a result, civil war broke out.

7. What might have made it easier for Tariq bin Ziyad to fight against the Visigoths led by Ruderic? What was the result of the Battle of Guadalete on July 19, 711?

A7.—Pg. 344, ¶ 2—Some sources say that those opposed to Ruderic's rule sided with Tariq bin Ziyad, making it easier for the Arabian general to move through Visigothic land. When Tariq bin Ziyad and his troops met Ruderic at the Battle of Guadalete on July 19, 711, they wiped out the Visigoths and killed Ruderic.

8. How did the Battle of Guadalete bring an end to the Visigothic kingdom in Spain?

A8.—Pg. 344, ¶ 3—The Battle of Guadalete brought an abrupt end to the Visigothic kingdom in Spain because almost the entire stratum of aristocrats, the men who held the right to elect the monarch, was wiped out. There was no more king and no one who could claim the right to appoint one. Because of the Toledo decrees, no one had the authority to organize a resistance or to negotiate a treaty with the invaders.

9. How did Leo III drive back the first round of Arab ships that tried to attack the entrance into the Golden Horn?

A9.—Pg. 346, ¶ 3 & 4—Leo III launched an attack force of ships burning with Greek fire into the first approaching Arab fleet. The wind was with him and as a result hundreds of Arab ships were set on fire and they sunk or were grounded. Then Leo III unhooked the chain that protected the entrance into the Golden Horn, playing a mind game with the Arabs: Suleiman thought Leo III would stretch the chain out again once the Arab ships were in the harbor, so instead of going in they retreated; after docking at a nearby inlet the Arab troops were struck by a severe winter and the death of Suleiman.

10. What happened when Umar II took up the siege against Constantinople started by his cousin Suleiman?

A10.—Pg. 346, ¶ 5 & 6—When Umar II was made caliph, he sent a new admiral from Egypt to lead the Arab troops in an attack on Constantinople. However, Leo III had made an alliance with the Bulgarians, and the Arabs were not able to defeat the combined Byzantine and Bulgarian forces. After twenty-two thousand Arabs died in battle outside of Constantinople, Umar II sent word that the siege should be abandoned; on August 15, 718 the Arabs left Byzantine territory in disgrace and returned home.

11. Why did Pippin the Fat start calling himself *dux et princeps Francorum*, "Duke and Prince of the Franks"? What did the label mean?

A11.—Pg. 347, ¶ 5—Pippin the Fat started calling himself *dux et princeps Francorum*, "Duke and Prince of the Franks," after he was made mayor of all three Frankish palaces. Neither a king, nor a servant of the king, he had returned to an older Germanic description of his power, calling himself the principal leader (*princeps*) among many leaders (*duces*, dukes).

12. How does Fredegar's account of what happened at the battle between the Arabs and the Franks at Poitiers differ from what really happened?

A12.—Pg. 349, ¶ 3—Fredegar says that after defeating the Arabs, Charles Martel pursued them in retreat to grind them small, utterly destroy them, and scatter them like stubble. What really happened was that while the Arabs had lost the battle, they were not entirely defeated. Charles Martel followed behind them as they burned and looted their way back into al-Andalus.

13. How did Charles Martel earn the nickname "The Hammer"? Why was this a misnomer?

A13.—Pg. 349, ¶ 4—Charles Martel earned the nickname "The Hammer" after the Franks beat the Arabian armies in 732 at the Battle of Tours. Martel supposedly hammered away at his enemies and ground them to dust. While Martel was at the head of the Franks when the Arabs turned back to al-Andalus, it was Odo that fought fiercely against the Arabs at Toulouse, the River Garonne and Poitiers; Odo was the real hammer.

Section III: Critical Thinking

The student may not use his text to answer this question.

Great and loyal leaders are not always remembered as such, especially if historical accounts decide to leave their bravery out of the chronicles. Fredegar did a good job of glorifying Charles Martel, "The Hammer," in his history of the Franks, but he did not give Odo the attention he was due. Now is the chance for Odo to get the recognition Fredegar denied him. Write a paragraph that praises Odo and all that he did for the survival of Aquitaine and the Frankish nation.

The student's answer can be written in a boastful style; since this is the time for Odo to shine, exaggeration and creativity are okay. We learn about Odo's fighting skills on page 348, starting in paragraph 3. Odo made his small region of Aquitaine pretty much independent during Charles Martel's civil war. Odo was suspicious of Martel's ambition, and wanted to keep his distance. The student could suggest here that Odo was of higher moral character than Martel, choosing to protect his people instead of manipulating the court, as Martel sought to do. Of course, we can't be sure of Odo's, or Martel's, motives, but this is the student's chance to embellish in favor of Odo.

When Arab forces showed up on the southern border of Aquitaine, Odo had no reinforcements. On June 9, 721, the tiny army of Aquitaine—reinforced by only a few resistance fighters from the mountains of Asturias—met the Arab armies at the Battle of Toulouse, under Odo's command. Odo defeated the Arabs at the Battle of Toulouse, killing the governor of al-Andalus in the fighting, and halting the Arab advance into Europe. By making the Islamic army suffer a devastating defeat, Odo was able to preserve the culture of the Franks.

When the Arab forces attacked again under the lead of al-Ghafiqi, Odo courageously went out to meet the invaders again. He was not so fortunate this time and he was defeated at the Battle of the River Garonne. After this Odo gave up his pride and went to Charles Martel. The student might suggest that only a great leader full of love for his people could make a decision that was so self-effacing. Odo swore his loyalty to Charles Martel, giving up Aquitaine's sovereignty, in exchange for the help of the Franks against the invaders.

Odo fought against the expanding Muslim empire again, this time as one of Charles Martel's commanders and the leader of the Aquitaine wing of the army. In 732, the Arabs and the Franks fought viciously at Poitiers. After the Arab leader was killed, his troops began to retreat. Charles Martel claimed to have crushed the Arabs, but in reality he followed the trail they made themselves as they burned and looted their way back home. The student might end by praising Odo over Charles Martel. Charles Martel may have been given the name "The Hammer," immortalized by Fredegar, but it was Odo, the brave leader, that truly saved the Franks from being subsumed into the Muslim empire.

EXAMPLE ANSWER:

Odo stood out as a great leader when he decided to take advantage of the civil war started by the manipulative Charles Martel to make his small region of Aquitaine pretty much independent. Odo was suspicious of Martel's ambition, and wanted to keep his distance. Clearly Odo was of higher moral character than Martel, choosing to protect his people instead of manipulating the court, as Martel sought to do.

When Arab forces showed up on the southern border of Aquitaine, Odo had no major reinforcements because he wouldn't ally himself with the wily Martel. On June 9, 721, the tiny army of Aquitaine—reinforced by only a few resistance fighters from the mountains of Asturias—met the Arab armies at the Battle of Toulouse, under Odo's masterful command. Odo defeated the Arabs at the Battle of Toulouse, killing the governor of al-Andalus in the fighting, and halting the Arab advance into Europe. By making the Islamic army suffer a devastating defeat, Odo was able to preserve the culture of the Franks.

When the Arab forces attacked again under the lead of al-Ghafiqi, Odo courageously went out to meet the invaders again. He was not so fortunate this time and he was defeated at the Battle of the River Garonne. After this Odo gave up his pride and went to Charles Martel. Only a great leader full of love for his people could make a decision that was so self-effacing. Odo swore his loyalty to Charles Martel, giving up Aquitaine's sovereignty in exchange for the help of the Franks against the invaders.

Odo fought against the expanding Muslim empire again, this time as one of Charles Martel's commanders and the leader of the Aquitaine wing of the army. In 732, the Arabs and the Franks fought viciously at Poitiers. After the Arab leader was killed, his troops began to retreat. Charles Martel claimed to have crushed the Arabs, but in reality he meekly followed the trail they made themselves as they burned and looted their way back home.

Charles Martel may have been given the name "The Hammer," immortalized by Fredegar, but it was Odo, the brave leader, that truly saved the Franks from being subsumed into the Muslim empire.

Section IV: Map Exercise

1. Using a black pencil, trace the rectangular outline of the frame for Map 45.1: The Arab Advance.

2. Using a blue pencil, trace the coastline from the Atlantic on the west into the Mediterranean. You do not need to trace the coastline of Britain at this time. Trace the coastline of Sardinia, Corsica, Sicily, Crete, and Cyprus, but you do not need to trace any other islands. Trace the coastline of the Black Sea, the Caspian Sea, and the Azov Sea. Trace the lines of the Danube, the Prut, the Dniester, the Donets, the Don, and the Volga. Then trace the lines of the Tigris and Euphrates. Repeat until the contours are familiar.

3. Select six contrasting colors (or use lines and shading to distinguish the regions) to trace the Franks, Lombardy, Byzantium, Khazars, the First Bulgarian Empire, and the Arab Empire. Trace the different regions with a corresponding color for each, or use lines and shading like the mapmaker to distinguish the regions. Repeat until the contours are familiar.

4. Using a new sheet of paper, trace the rectangular outline of the frame in black. Remove your tracing paper from the original. Using a regular pencil with an eraser as you look at the map, draw the coastline around the continent and through the Mediterranean. (Again, do not draw the coastline of Britain, but do draw that of Sardinia, Corsica, Sicily, Crete, and Cyprus. Do not draw any other islands.) Draw the coastline of the Black Sea, the Caspian Sea, and the Azov Sea. Draw the lines of the Danube, the Prut, the Dniester, the Donets, the Don, the Volga, the Tigris, and the Euphrates. Erase and redraw as necessary. Then lay your map over the original and correct any lines which are more than ¼ inch off of the original.

5. Next, using a regular pencil as you look at the map, draw the perimeters of the territories of the Visigoths, Franks, Lombardy, Byzantium, Khazars, First Bulgarian Empire, and the Arab Empire. Erase and redraw as necessary.

6. When you are pleased with your map, lay it over the original. Erase and redraw any lines which are more than ¼ inch off of the original.

7. Next, create a coding system similar to what the mapmaker did on the original map to show which color (or shading or lines, depending on what you used) corresponds to which region. Provide labels to identify each color (or shading/lines).

8. Next, as you look at your map, label the regions of Ifriqiya, Libya, Egypt, Syria, Armenia, Asia Minor, Thracia, Macedonia, Greece, Pannonia, Austrasia, Neustria, Aquitaine, Asturias, and Al-Andalus. Then label the locations of Tangiers, Toledo, Toulouse, Bourdeaux, Poitiers, Tours, Cologne, Pavia, Ravenna, Rome, Benevento, Naples, Syracuse, Carthage, Tarentum, Constantinople,

Jerusalem, Damascus, Kufa, Medina, and Mecca. (Because there are so many locations on this map, you will be studying the battle locations instead of the city locations. You are marking city locations here for reference.)

9. Study carefully the locations of the Battle of Guadalete, the Battle of Toulouse, the Battle of the River Garonne, and the Battle of Tours. When you are familiar with them, close the book. Using your regular pencil, label the location of each battle. Check your map against the original, and correct any misplaced labels.

10. Mark the location of the Dardanelles and the Sea of Marmara.

Chapter Forty-Six

The Kailasa of the South

The student may use her text when answering the questions in sections I and II.

Section I: Who, What, Where

Write a one or two-sentence answer explaining the significance of each item listed below.

Al-Hajjaj—**Pg. 351, ¶ 2—Al-Hajjaj, the governor of the eastern reaches of the Islamic empire, used his son Muhammad bin Qasim to conquer the Sindh.**

Brahmanabad—**Pg. 352, ¶ 5—Brahmanabad, a city in the northeast of India, was used as a safe haven for Dahir's troops. Brahmanabad became bin Qasim's capital after he conquered a swath of land across the Indus, claiming a new Indian province for the Arab nation.**

Dahir—**Pg. 351, ¶ 3 and Pg. 352, ¶ 4—Dahir, a tribal leader, controlled Debal at the time of Muhammad bin Qasim's attack in 712, and he stood as a barrier between the Arabs in Makran and the lands further east. Dahir was chased out of Debal by bin Qasim, over the Indus, and was eventually beheaded in battle against the Arabs.**

Dantidurga—**Pg. 353, ¶ 3 to Pg. 354, ¶ 5—Dantidurga, a man with Chalukya blood who became leader of his tribe in 745, successfully attacked Kirtivarman II in 753, claiming most Chalukya land for himself. Dantidurga carved out the borders of the next great Indian power, the kingdom of Rashtrakuta, but he did not get to see it grow because he died just two years after taking tribute from Nagabhata.**

Dhruva—**Pg. 355, ¶ 2 & 4—Dhruva, son and heir of Krishna I, seized Mandore in 786 and fought his way to Kannauj. Even though Dhruva was not able to take Kannauj, he did bring north and south India together over the Ganges and under the Rashtrakuta throne.**

Howdah—**Pg. 352, ¶ 4—Howdah is the name for the reinforced carriage that sits on an elephant's back.**

Kailasa (Krishnesvara)—**Pg. 354, ¶ 7 & 8—The Kailasa, or Krishnesvara, was a new temple commissioned by Krishna I to join the caves at Ellora. The cave was a mirror of the northern landscape of the peak in the northern Himalaya where the Ganges river sprung.**

Kirtivarman II—**Pg. 353, ¶ 3 to Pg. 354, ¶ 1—Kirtivarman II, son and heir of the Western Chalukya king Vikramaditya II, lost most of his kingdom to Dantidurga in a devastating battle, keeping only a small remnant of his father's previous domain.**

Krishna I—**Pg. 354, ¶ 6 to Pg. 355, ¶ 1—Krishna I, uncle and successor to Dantidurga, warred for nearly eighteen years, filling in the outlines of Dantidurga's kingdom, bringing down the Western Chalukya king and seizing the remaining Western Chalukya lands for his own. Krishna I commissioned the Kailasa, a beautiful temple that made the Vindhya mountains into a new sacred border.**

Muhammad bin Qasim—**Pg. 351, ¶ 2 and 352, ¶ 5—Muhammad bin Qasim, son of al-Hajjaj, was sent by his father to conquer the Sindh, starting with the port city of Debal. Muhammad bin Qasim conquered a swath of land across the Indus, including Debal and Brahmanabad, which turned out to be very lucrative for the Arab nation.**

Nagabhata—**Pg. 354, ¶ 3 & 4—Nagabhata, king of the Pratihara, was forced to pay tribute to Dantidurga after he occupied the city of Mandore. After Dantidurga returned south, Nagabhata recaptured all the northern territory.**

Vikramaditya II—**Pg. 352, ¶ 7 to Pg. 353, ¶ 1—Vikramaditya II, a Chalukya king, brought his kingdom to dominance over the south central plain in the 8th century, pushing the kingdom's boundaries to the same borders ruled by Pulakesi II one hundred years earlier.**

Section II: Comprehension

Write a two or three-sentence answer to each of the following questions.

1. How did al-Hajjaj and his son Muhammad bin Qasim trick Dahir into a fight? Why did they need a reason to attack Debal?

A1.—Pg. 351, ¶ 4—Al-Hajjaj and Muhammad bin Qasim insisted Dahir punish the pirates that attacked Arab ships setting off from the coast of the Makran. Dahir thought this request was ridiculous because he had no authority over the pirates, and the Arabs took this retort as hostile, thus authorizing an attack against Debal. al-Hajjaj and Muhammad bin Qasim's attack against Debal might not have been authorized by the caliph, so by claiming Dahir was hostile they were able to justify their invasion without the caliph's permission.

2. Describe the Arabs' attack on Debal. What were the results of the attack?

A2.—Pg. 352, ¶ 1 & 2—Muhammad bin Qasim approached Debal by land, while other Arab troops arrived by sea, and al-Hajjaj managed the attack by sending three letters every day

with battle instructions. After a long siege, Debal was taken by bin Qasim. Dahir withdrew and fled, bin Qasim slaughtered any remaining defenders, and ordered a mosque to be built before leaving a garrison behind and marching eastward.

3. How did bin Qasim move the battle at Debal so that it followed Dahir over the Indus? What was the result of the battle?

A3.—Pg. 352, ¶ 3 & 4—When Dahir fled to the other side of the Indus, bin Qasim ordered a pontoon bridge laid across the river, stationing a boat full of archers at the head of the bridge and thrusting it forward a little farther as each boat was added behind. Bin Qasim then marched his men across the bridge and attacked Dahir's men, who were mounted on elephants, with flaming arrows. Dahir was knocked from his elephant and beheaded by an axman when he fell on the ground, and his men retreated to Brahmanabad.

4. Though conquest of the Sindh was once abandoned because the land seemed barren, how did its eventual conquest benefit the Arabs?

A4.—Pg. 352, ¶ 5—The Arabs' new Indian province proved to be a treasure trove rather than a desolate area, as Umar once thought. The conquered tribes paid regular and expensive tribute to the occupiers: when al-Hajjaj tallied up the tribute paid during the first year of occupation, his profit was double the cost of the conquest.

5. How was it that Dantidurga had Chalukya blood in his veins?

A5.—Pg. 353, ¶ 3—Dantidurga's father had kidnapped his mother. She was a Chalukya noblewoman, and was forced to marry Dantidurga's father. While the marriage may not have been a happy one, Dantidurga ended up being part Chalukya.

6. What three groups had a stake in protecting the northern city of Kannauj?

A6.—Pg. 355, ¶ 3—The three groups that had a stake in protecting Kannauj were the Rashtrakuta, the Pratihara, and the Pala. Dhruva wanted the city for his kingdom of the Rashtrakuta, which reached up from the south of India. The Pratihara, who were in the north and east, had extended their rule over into the Ganges valley and wanted to keep Kannauj for themselves. The Pala, with a capital city in the east at Gaur, advanced their territory west towards Kannauj and wanted the city for their holdings.

Section III: Critical Thinking

The student may not use her text to answer this question.

Power and conquest often mean more when they are backed by the gods. The creation of the Rashtrakuta kingdom was incomplete when Dantidurga died, not only because he wasn't able to fill out the borders he'd carved, but also because he did not declare a spiritual center for his kingdom. Write a paragraph explaining how Krishna I fortified the Rashtrakuta kingdom through both conquest and spiritual grounding.

The answer to this question is very straightforward and comes right from the text on pages 354–55. The student should remember the answer clearly from her reading.

Krishna I fought for eighteen years straight, filling in the outlines of the border created by Dantidurga. This is how he bolstered the kingdom through conquest.

Krishna I had a new temple built to join the caves at Ellora, the Kailasa, or Krishnesvara. Kailasa was the name of a peak in the northern Himalaya where the Ganges river originated. The Indians believed that that the Ganges river was the source of life, so the place of its origin was especially sacred. Kailasa was the highest and holiest place in the Himalaya, and it was believed to be the spot from which all creation sprang.

When Krishna I created a reflection of the Kailasa in the south, he was proclaiming himself to be equal to the godlike rulers of ancient India. He was declaring that the south was sacred, tied to the creation of life just as the Kailasa in the north. The building of the temple gave the Rashtrakuta kingdom a spiritual grounding that matched its expanding conquests.

EXAMPLE ANSWER:

Krishna I continued the work of his nephew Dantidurga by fighting for eighteen years straight, filling in the outlines of the Rashtrakuta kingdom. He created a spiritual center for the kingdom when he built a temple near the caves of Ellora that he called the Kailasa, or Krishnesvara. Kailasa is the name for the peak in the northern Himalaya where the Ganges river, believed to be the source of life, originated. To name the southern temple the same name as the highest and holiest place in the Himalaya was to declare the sacred importance of southern India. Krishna I, with the building of the temple, proclaimed himself to be equivalent to the godlike rulers of ancient India, building a new kingdom that was blessed and protected by its sacred border.

Chapter Forty-Seven

Purifications

The student may use his text when answering the questions in sections I and II.

Section I: Who, What, Where

Write a one or two-sentence answer explaining the significance of each item listed below.

Eutychius—**Pg. 361, ¶ 2—Eutychius, working with Leo III to get rid of Pope Gregory II, arrived in Naples with a series of gifts and bribes for King Liutprand, promising the Lombard leader more if he would help Eutychius assassinate the pope. Liutprand did not cooperate.**

Constantine V—**Pg. 361, ¶ 6—Constantine V was Leo III's son and successor. When he came to the throne in 741, he continued the iconoclastic work started by his father.**

Germanos—**Pg. 361, ¶ 4—Germanos, the patriarch of Byzantium, refused to support Leo III's January 730 edict to destroy all icons across the empire. He was deposed for his beliefs.**

Hodegetria—**Pg. 359, ¶ 3—The hodegetria was a portrait of Mary that was rumored to have been painted by the gospel-writer Luke. The people of Constantinople believed the hodegetria saved Constantinople from the Arab siege.**

Liutprand—**Pg. 360, 7 and Pg. 361, ¶ 3—Liutprand, king of the Lombards, took advantage of the turmoil in Byzantium over icons and extended his kingdom to the port at Ravenna. Liutprand refused to work with Eutychius and assassinate Pope Gregory II; instead he took control of Sutri and in 728 gave the land to the church in exchange for a large sum of money.**

Mo-chi-lien—**Pg. 358, ¶ 1—Mo-chi-lien, Mo-ch'o's nephew and successor to the Eastern Khaghanate throne, conquered the land known as the Western Khaghanate and re-established a unified Turkish empire.**

Pope Gregory II—**Pg. 360, ¶ 4 and Pg. 361, ¶ 3—Pope Gregory II reacted to Leo III's declaration to destroy icons in the church by ignoring him, and telling the king he had no right to make**

religious rules. Working with Liutprand, Pope Gregory II received the Sutri Donation in 728 resulting in the creation of the first of the Papal State.

Pope Gregory III—**Pg. 361, ¶ 5—Pope Gregory III called a church council in 731 and excommunicated all icon-destroyers.**

Yazid II—**Pg. 357, ¶ 4 to Pg. 358, ¶ 1—Yazid II, Umar II's successor, was made immediately unpopular in his rule because he reinstated the "head tax" repealed by Umar II. The reinstatement of the tax caused Khorasan to rebel, resulting in a ten year struggle with Yazid II's army.**

Section II: Comprehension

Write a two or three-sentence answer to each of the following questions.

1. What was the "head tax" Muhammad instituted during his reign? How did later officials take advantage of the "head tax"?

A1.—Pg. 357, ¶ 2—The "head tax," a fee paid by Christians and Jews that lived within the Muslim community, was instituted by Muhammad in return for accepting the protection of the Muslim state. Later officials often conveniently forgot to exempt new converts from the tax because they did want to give up the revenue brought in by the tax.

2. Why did Umar II do away with the "head tax"? What was the result of its repeal?

A2.—Pg. 357, ¶ 3 & 4—Umar II was trying to rule by the exact prescriptions of the Prophet Muhammad, and felt that converts paying the head tax was corrupt. He declared that all Muslims, no matter their race or length of commitment to Islam, should be exempt from the tax. While the repeal of the tax made Umar II very popular, it ruined the empire's tax base, especially because many conquered people were converting now that they didn't have to pay the tax.

3. What was the reason for the non-Arab tribes in Khorasan to rebel against Yazid II? Who did they go to for help in their rebellion?

A3.—Pg. 357, ¶ 5 to Pg. 356, ¶ 1—The non-Arab tribes in Khorasan rebelled against Yazid II because he reinstated the "head tax," and they did not want to pay. The people in Khorasan asked Mo-chi-lien of the rebuilt Turkish empire for aid against the Islamic armies; Mo-chi-lien was pleased with the excuse to push father southwest, so he agreed to help Khorasan.

4. Why did the Jews leave Byzantium around the time of the fight between Khorasan and the Arab empire?

A4.—Pg. 358, ¶ 2—The Jews left Byzantium around the time of the fight between Khorasan and the Arab empire because Leo III commanded that all Jews in his empire be baptized as

Christians. While some did convert, many Jews left Byzantium for Arabic lands or for the lands of the Khazars.

5. What is the meaning of the Greek word *eikon*? What was the purpose of an icon, for example, a painting of the Virgin Mary?

A5.—Pg. 358, ¶ 3—The meaning of the Greek word *eikon* is "image" or "likeness." The purpose of an icon was to act as a symbol of the divine. An icon was a window into the sacred world, where a worshipper could pray or meditate and feel closer to God.

6. Why was Leo III opposed to icon worship? After the eruption of the volcano on Thera in 726, how were Leo III's fears about his people's overreliance on icons justified?

A6.—Pg. 359, ¶ 3, 5 & 6—Leo III was opposed to icon worship because he did not want the people in his empire to treat icons as though they were magic. After the eruption of the volcano on Thera, Leo III thought God was angry with him because of the icon worship; in response, Leo III ordered the icon of Christ that hung over the Bronze Gate to be taken down. A mob rioted when they found out what was happening, a soldier was killed, and Leo III's fears about his people's overreliance on icons became a reality.

7. What resulted from Leo III's taking down of the icon of Christ that hung over the Bronze Gate?

A7.—Pg. 359, ¶ 6 to Pg. 360, ¶ 2—Leo III retaliated against the mob at the Bronze gate with arrests, floggings, and fines. The conflict spread to the administrative theme of Hellas, and they set up their own emperor, declaring that they would not follow a man who attacked the holy icons. The rebellion in Hellas did not last long: the new emperor was captured and beheaded.

8. Explain the difference between iconoclasts and iconodules. How did iconodules twist Leo III's ban of icons into a political battle?

A8.—Pg. 360, ¶ 2—An iconoclast, an icon-smasher, did not believe in icons. An iconodule, an icon-slave, meaning icon-lover, believed in the worship of icons. Some iconodules accused Leo III of having too much sympathy for Muslims, who refused to make images of living things, making the debate over the icons political.

9. What was Pope Gregory II's reaction to Leo III's ban on the use of icons?

A9.—Pg. 360, ¶ 4 & 5—Pope Gregory II reacted to Leo III's ban on the use of icons by telling the king he did not have the right to make theological pronouncements. The pope ordered his people to ignore the imperial commands to destroy icons.

10. How did the Byzantine cities in Italy react to Leo III's declaration that banned the use of icons?

A10.—Pg. 360, ¶ 5 & 6—The Italian cities still under Byzantium's umbrella were ready for an excuse to revolt, fed up with paying higher and higher imperial taxes. The duke of Naples tried to carry out the emperor's command but he was killed by a mob in the process. The exarch of Ravenna was killed by his own subjects. In Rome, the pope pretty much stopped listening to Leo III.

11. What was the Sutri Donation, and why was it so important to the papacy?

A11.—Pg. 361, ¶ 3—The Sutri Donation was a gift of land made up of the city of Sutri and the territory nearby, given to Pope Gregory II by King Liutprand of the Lombards. It wasn't really a gift—Pope Gregory II gave Liutprand an enormous payment from the church treasury for the land. The Sutri Donation was important to the papacy because the pope now had a little kingdom of his own, the first extension of papal rule outside of Rome, the first of the Papal States.

12. How did Leo III react to Pope Gregory III's 731 excommunication of all icon-destroyers?

A12.—Pg. 361, ¶ 5—Leo III reacted to Pope Gregory III's excommunication of icon-destroyers by announcing that the Byzantine possessions left in Italy were no longer subject to the authority of the pope. Instead, they would answer to the patriarch.

Section III: Critical Thinking

The student may use his text to answer this question.

The debate over the worship of icons in Christianity has its roots in the separation of Christianity from the old Roman religion. The debate is also an echo of Nestorianism versus monophysitism. Explain why the worship of icons was frowned upon at first, at the beginning of Christianity, and then explain how the use of icons reflected different views about the true nature of Christ. You may go back to *Chapter 12: One Nature versus Two* for help.

The first part of the student's answer will come straight from Chapter 47. On page 359, the text states "In the earliest years of apostolic teaching, Christians had been distinguished from followers of the old Roman religion primarily because they refused to worship images, and for the second- and third-century theologians the use of icons veered perilously close to idolatry. Once the ancient Roman customs had died out, so did the risk that Christians would be drawn back into them, and the use of icons became much less fraught with danger."

The second part of the student's answer is also referenced in the chapter. On page 359 we find out that "a strong subset of Christian theologians continued to oppose the use of icons . . . because painting an image of Christ suggested that the son of God was characterized by his human nature, not his divinity. God, Who was Spirit, could not be pictured; if Christ could *be, didn't that imply that he was not truly God? Couldn't it be argued that an image of Christ 'separates the flesh from the Godhead' and gives it a separate existence? Arguments over the use of icons became a subset of the arguments over the exact nature of Christ as God-man." These questions echo the debate over God and his humanity.*

In Chapter 12: One Nature versus Two *the student learned about Nestorianism and monophysitism. Nestorianism was the Christian belief that the two natures of God, God the Father and God the Son, were two separate natures, divine and human, but mixed together. Monophysitism was the Christian belief that the two natures of God, God the Father and God the Son, had become mystically one, impossible to tease out by reason. By representing God as human, the question of whether or not God was human, divine, or both resurfaced. The argument over God's true nature was replayed in the debate over whether or not he could be depicted as human, and whether or not that picture could be worshipped as a symbol of a non-human power.*

EXAMPLE ANSWER:

Icon worship was frowned upon in the beginning of Christianity because idolatry was practiced in the old Roman religion. In an effort to distance themselves from that religion, believers in Christ turned away from idolatry. Once ancient Roman customs died out, the argument over the worship of icons began to reflect the argument that started in the 5th century over God's true nature. Nestorians believed that the two natures of God, God the Father and God the Son, were two separate natures, divine and human, but mixed together. Those who subscribed to monophysitism believed that the two natures of God, God the Father and God the Son, had become mystically one. The debate over God's true nature was replayed in the debate over whether or not he could be depicted as human, and whether or not that picture could be worshipped as a symbol of a non-human power.

Section IV: **Map Exercise**

1. Using a black pencil, trace the rectangular outline of the frame for Map 47. 2: The First Papal State.

2. Using a black pencil, trace the coastline around Italy, Sicily, Sardinia, and Corsica. Repeat until the contours are familiar.

3. Select three contrasting colors. Use each respectively to trace the regions of the Lombard Kingdom, Byzantium, and the first papal state. Repeat until the contours are familiar.

4. Using a new sheet of paper, trace the rectangular frame of the map in black. Remove your tracing paper from the original. Using a regular pencil with an eraser as you look at the map, draw Italy, Sicily, Sardinia, and Corsica. Then draw the regions of the Lombard Kingdom, Byzantium, and the First Papal State. Erase and redraw as necessary.

5. When you are pleased with your map, lay it over the original. Erase and redraw any lines which are more than ¼ inch off of the original.

6. Study carefully the locations of Milan, Venice, Ravenna, Sutri, Rome, and Naples. Then study the locations of the Duchy of Spoleto and the Duchy of Benevento. When you are familiar with them, close the book. Using your regular pencil, label each city and the Duchy of Spoleto and of Benevento. When you are done, lay your map over the original. Erase and redraw any cities that are more than ¼ inch off of the original. Correct any misplaced labels.

Chapter Forty-Eight

The Abbasids

The student may use her text when answering the questions in sections I and II.

Section I: Who, What, Where

Write a one or two-sentence answer explaining the significance of each item listed below.

Abd ar-Rahman—**Pg. 365, ¶ 6 to Pg. 366, ¶ 2 and Pg. 367, ¶ 3 to Pg. 369, ¶ 1—Abd ar-Rahman, Hisham's grandson and the heir apparent to the caliphate, escaped Abu al-Abbas's mass murder of the remaining Umayyads by fleeing to Ifriqiya. In 756 Abd ar-Rahman arrived in al-Andalus claiming it as his rightful territory, beheading the governor Yusuf al-Fihri and in 763 defeating the Abbasid army, keeping his land and his throne.**

Abu al-Abbas—**Pg. 365, ¶ 4 and Pg. 366, ¶ 2—Abu al-Abbas, a man who could trace his lineage back to Muhammad's uncle, was elected by the Hashimites to be their caliph in 749. He earned the nickname *al-Saffah*, "The Slaughterer," for his slaughter of Umayyads.**

Al-Mansur—**Pg. 366, ¶ 7 and Pg. 369, ¶ 3—Al-Mansur, brother of al-Abbas and successor to the caliphate, moved the capital of the Arab empire to Baghdad. Al-Mansur was a ruthless leader who murdered all those opposed to his rule.**

Gao Xianzhi—**Pg. 366, ¶ 5 & 6—Gao Xianzhi, Tang general under emperor Xuanzong, pushed the boundaries of China across the Asian plateau all the way to the eastern reaches of the Islamic empire in Sogdiana. Gao Xianzhi's troops were wiped out by the Abbasids at the Battle of Talas in 751, and the general returned for home.**

Hashimites—**Pg. 365, ¶ 3—Hashimites were a group of people who opposed Umayyad rule and argued that the caliphate should go to a member of Muhammad's clan, the Banu Hashim.**

Hisham—**Pg. 363, ¶ 1 and Pg. 364, ¶ 2 & 3—Hisham, Yazid II's brother and successor the caliphate, started his rule by sending strike forces to Khorasan, Armenia and north**

against the Khazars. By 743, the year he died of diphtheria, Hisham had tamed the various rebellions plaguing his empire, though at great financial cost.

Khan Bihar—**Pg. 363, ¶ 2-4—Khan Bihar, khan of the Khazars, ruled over one of the largest empires in the medieval world, the borders of which stretched from the Black Sea to the Caspian Sea and far up north. After making an alliance with Constantine V, Khan Bihar decided to convert his empire to Judaism.**

Marwan II—**Pg. 364, ¶ 3 and Pg. 366, ¶ 2—Marwan, a general, took the caliphate by force in 744, named himself Marwan II and then moved the capital city of the Umayyad caliphate to Harran. After losing to Abu al-Abbas's rebel army, Marwan II fled to Egypt to try and raise an army against the Hashimite leader; he was found sleeping in a church by Abbasid soldiers, was murdered, and his head was sent back to Abd al-Abbas.**

Qadi—**Pg. 364, ¶ 1—A qadi is a specialist in Islamic law.**

Shi'at Ali—**Pg. 365, ¶ 3—Shi'at Ali, or "The Party of Ali," was the name for the group of people that believed only a man of Ali's blood could be a worthy caliph. The Shi'at Ali believed a successor of Ali would be spiritually and supernaturally fit to rule.**

Tzitzak—**Pg. 363, ¶ 3—Tzitzak, daughter of Khan Bihar, was a critical component of an alliance between the Khazars and Constantine V of Constantinople. In 732 the alliance was sealed when Tzitzak agreed to be baptized as a Christian, changed her name to Irene, and married Constantine V.**

Yusuf al-Fihri—**Pg. 367, ¶ 3 & 4—Yusuf al-Fihri, governor of al-Andalus, was running the territory as an independent Umayyad ruler, and he did not want to give up his power to Abd ar-Rahman, a man with a better claim to the throne than he did. Yusuf al-Fihri met Abd ar-Rahman in battle just outside of Cordoba, where his forces were defeated and he was beheaded.**

Section II: **Comprehension**

Write a two or three-sentence answer to each of the following questions.

1. What caused aggression between the Khazars and the Arabs? When Hisham came to power, what were the two empires fighting over?

A1.—Pg. 363, ¶ 2—The aggression between the Khazars and the Arabs started when the Khazars took Ardabil out of Arab hands. The Arabs then invaded Khazar land along the Volga river. When Hisham came to power, the Arabs and the Khazars were fighting over control of Derbent, the port city that lay on the Caspian coast right between the two empires.

2. According to the account of one of the Jewish kings of the Khazars, how did Khan Bihar come to the conclusion that he should convert his empire to Judaism? In what way was this a very smart political decision?

Note to the parent—The student's answer may be four or five sentences in order to accommodate the story of Khan Bihar's decision.

A2.—Pg. 363, ¶ 4 to Pg. 364, ¶ 2—According to the account of one of the Jewish kings of the Khazars, Khan Bihar brought together a priest, a rabbi and a *qadi* so that they could argue about their different religions. To put a stop to the arguing, Khan Bihar asked the Christian priest which of the religions he preferred of the Jews and the Muslims, to which the priest answered the religion of the Israelites. He asked the *qadi* if he preferred Christianity or Judaism and the *qadi* said that he preferred the religion of the Israelites. Hearing from both that the religion of the Israelites was better, he chose to convert his people to Judaism. By choosing Judaism for his empire, and not one of the religions of powerful neighbors, Khan Bihar managed to find a way to keep his realm independent and out of the affairs of the Byzantine and Arab empires.

3. List the caliphs that followed Hisham, the length of their leadership, and the circumstances of their death or their loss of the caliphate.

A3.—Pg. 364, ¶ 3—Walid II, an alcoholic poet and Hisham's nephew, followed his uncle as caliph, and was murdered in less than a year by his cousin, Yazid III. Yazid III's caliphate lasted for six months, and then he grew ill and died. Ibrahim, Yazid III's brother, was named as his successor, but he was driven out of power by the general Marwan; Ibrahim surrendered to Marwan and joined the general's men.

4. How did Constantine V's defeat of the Arab navy in a 747 sea battle near Syria affect Marwan II's rule? What was the cause of the main opposition to Marwan II's leadership?

A4.—Pg. 364, ¶ 4 to Pg. 365, ¶ 2—Marwan II was working hard to bring internal order to his Umayyad empire, but when Constantine defeated the Arab navy in a 747 sea battle near Syria, internal opposition to Marwan II's rule intensified. Detractors were opposed to Marwan II's rule because they were opposed to the power of the Umayyad clan—they claimed that the Muslim empire would only grow strong again if the leader was from the Holy Family, a member of Muhammad's own clan.

5. What happened when Marwan II's hundred thousand men met Abu al-Abbas's troops just east of the Tigris in early 750?

A5.—Pg. 365, ¶ 5—When Marwan II's hundred thousand men met Abu al-Abbas and his rebel troops in early 750, the will of the rebels outdid the Umayyad forces. The rebels were fighting for a cause important to them, and Marwan II's men were largely unwilling recruits, who were driven back and scattered by the men fighting with conviction. Marwan II fled, first into Syria, then Palestine and then into Egypt, hoping to raise another force against Abu al-Abbas.

6. Why did Abd ar-Rahman flee from Damascus? Describe his escape with his brother and Greek servant.

A6.—Pg. 365, ¶ 6 to Pg. 366, ¶ 2—Abu al-Abbas sent men out on horseback with a mission to find and kill any remaining Umayyads; Abd ar-Rahman, heir apparent to the Umayyad caliphate, had to flee in order to survive. He left Damascus with his brother and his Greek servant, hoping to hide out in old Persian lands, but Abu al-Abbas's men caught up with the trio on the banks of the Euphrates. While Abd ar-Rahman and his Greek servant attempted to swim across the river, his brother hesitated and was beheaded by the Abbasid soldiers. Abd ar-Rahman and his servant made it across, seeking safe haven first in Egypt and then when they found it wasn't safe, moving to Ifriqiya.

7. How did al-Abbas deal with the Umayyads that remained in his realm?

A7.—Pg. 366, ¶ 3—Al-Abbas promised that all remaining members of the Umayyad family would be granted amnesty and given back their family property if they would come and swear allegiance to him. He invited the Umayyads to a welcome banquet in Kufa, where instead of actually welcoming them, he had them all killed.

8. Why was Gao Xianzhi's army able to get as close to the Islamic empire as Sogdiana? What happened at the Battle of Talas in 751?

A8.—Pg. 366, ¶ 5 & 6—Gao Xianzhi's army was able to get as close to the Islamic empire as Sogdiana because Umayyad caliphs, weak and disorganized, could not get it together to halt his advance. Under al-Abbas, the Arab army was powerful and strong. The Abbasid army of one hundred thousand met Gao Xianzhi's thirty thousand men in 751 at the Battle of Talas, where the Tang forces were nearly wiped out, forcing Gao Xianzhi to return for home.

9. Why did al-Mansur move the capital of the Arab empire to Baghdad?

A9.—Pg. 366, ¶ 7 to Pg. 367, ¶ 1—Al-Mansur moved the capital of the Arab empire to Baghdad in order to strategically build the empire's wealth. The Tigris and the Euphrates were used for major trade, and by placing the capital at Baghdad, al-Mansur had access to both.

10. What did Abd ar-Rahman call himself when he became ruler of al-Andalus? Why was his rule of al-Andalus so significant?

A10.—Pg. 367, ¶ 4 to Pg. 369, ¶ 1—When Abd ar-Rahman defeated Yusuf al-Fihri he took the title "Emir of Cordoba." His rule of al-Andalus was significant because he was the ruler of the first Muslim kingdom to be entirely independent of the caliphate. He also proved his strength and significance when he beat an Abbasid army sent in 763 to bring the territory back into the Abbasid empire; Abd ar-Rahman fought back and won, and after that al-Mansur left him alone.

11. How did al-Mansur begin his caliphate? For what reason did people believe he had a magic mirror that told him who was loyal and who was planning revolt?

A11.—Pg. 369, ¶ 3—Al-Mansur began his caliphate with murder: he murdered a number of prominent Shi'a leaders who had refused to support the Abbasid claim to power. He used a

network of spies to root out his enemies, ordering them beaten, imprisoned and executed. People believed he had a magic mirror because of his frightful intelligence and his ability to tease out dissenters.

Section III: Critical Thinking

The student may not use her text to answer this question.

Before Muhammad was given a vision of the angel Gabriel, he was already disconcerted by the growing divide between the rich and poor in Mecca. Once he received his vision, Muhammad preached purity, piety and morality. In the decades after his rule, the caliphate moved further and further away from Muhammad's original teachings. Write a paragraph explaining how the break from the Umayyad caliphate was meant to be a return to Muhammad's original role as spiritual ruler, but ended up being even further from Muhammad's teachings by the time of al-Mansur's rule.

To start, you might want to ask the student about the caliphs that reigned prior to Marwan II. Last chapter we read about Umar II's attempts to bring Muhammad's teachings back to the Umayyad caliphate. His major reform was to stop the corrupt practice of continuing to charge converts a "head tax." His spiritual work was undone as soon as leadership passed on to Yazid II, who reinstated the tax. Hisham followed Yazid II and quelled rebellions in the empire, but he almost bankrupt it at the same time. The caliphs that followed Hisham turned over quickly, proving to many that the Umayyad caliphate was no longer effective.

Then you might ask the student, why were there so many people against Umayyad rule? In the chapter we learn doubt related to the Umayyad caliphate had much to do with the political bent of the clan. While worship of Allah was supposed to be the way of life for the Arab culture, it became secondary to politics and war. As written on page 365, "the Umayyad caliphs were, in the last analysis, politicians more than prophets, soldiers more than worshippers."

What happens next? How can a government leader be more spiritual than political? The answer, in the Arab empire, was that the leader should be from the clan of Muhammad, a member of the Holy Family. If a ruler could be connected to Ali, Muhammad's son-in-law, or to Muhammad himself, through the Banu Hashim clan, then it would be assumed that he would reinvigorate the spiritual aspect of the caliphate.

In fact, the opposite seemed to happen. Abu al-Abbas, a member of Muhammad's clan, took over the caliphate and set out to slaughter all remaining Umayyads. Al-Mansur, Abu al-Abbas's brother, continued the murderous streak and put down any dissent to his rule. Al-Mansur moved the capital of the Arab empire to Baghdad, where he built a royal residence, full of ornate buildings. The text states on page 369, "In the hands of al-Mansur, the spiritual authority of the caliph took a definite second place to political ambitions." A member of Muhammad's own clan was now the caliph, but instead of reinforcing the worship of Allah, purity, piety and morality, murder, taxes and fear were the norm.

EXAMPLE ANSWER:

The Umayyad caliphate seemed to be falling apart by the time of Marwan II's rule. While Umar II tried to reinstall the righteous teachings of the Prophet into the government, the

caliphs that followed him were interested in power and money. By the time of Marwan II, Arab defeat by Constantinople was blamed on the Umayyads' being too political. The spiritual center of the caliphate was missing and thus fortune was turned against the Arab empire. Those opposed to Umayyad rule claimed that a member of the Holy Family would be able to fix things, to reinvigorate the spiritual aspect of the caliphate and bring strength back to the empire. Yet, the opposite seemed to happen. Abu al-Abbas, a member of Muhammad's clan, took over the caliphate and set out to slaughter all remaining Umayyads. Al-Mansur, Abu al-Abbas's brother, continued the murderous streak and put down any dissent to his rule. Strength via mass murder did not seem to follow the teachings of the prophet. Al-Mansur moved the capital of the Arab empire to Baghdad, where he built a royal residence, full of ornate buildings. Instead of giving to the people, like Muhammad, al-Mansur was amassing wealth for himself and his family. At the time of al-Mansur's rule, a member of Muhammad's own clan was the caliph, but instead of reinforcing the worship of Allah, purity, piety and morality, murder, taxes and fear were the norm.

Section IV: **Map Exercise**

1. Using a black pencil, trace the rectangular outline of the frame for Map 48.1: The Battle of Talas.

2. Using a blue pencil, trace the coastline along Persia. Using a black pencil, trace the mountain peaks. Using your blue pencil, trace the line of the Jaxartes, Oxus, and Indus rivers. Using a black pencil, trace the outline of the Abbasid Caliphate. Using a contrasting color, trace the area which is the approximate extent of the eastern Khaghanate. Repeat until the contours are familiar.

3. Using a new sheet of paper, trace the rectangular outline of the frame in black. Remove your tracing paper from the original. Using a regular pencil with an eraser, draw all the visible coastline. Draw the mountain peaks and the three rivers. Then draw the perimeters for the Abbasid Caliphate and the approximate extent of eastern Khaghanate. Erase and redraw as necessary.

4. When you are pleased with your map, lay it over the original. Erase and redraw any lines which are more than ¼ inch off of the original.

5. Looking at your map, label the Khyber Pass. Label all three rivers.

6. Study carefully the regions of Persia, Makran, Khorasan, Pratihara, Rashtrakuta, Pala, Tibet, and Tang. When you are familiar with them, close the book and mark each on your map. Check your map against the original, and make any needed corrections.

7. Now study carefully the locations of the cities of Debal and Kannauj. Then study the location of the Battle of Talas. When you are familiar with them, close the book. Mark each on your map. Then lay your map over the original. Erase and redraw any locations which are more than ¼ inch off of the original.

Chapter Forty-Nine

Charlemagne

The student may use his text when answering the questions in sections I and II.

Section I: **Who, What, Where**

Write a one or two-sentence answer explaining the significance of each item listed below.

Aistulf—**Pg. 372, ¶ 3 and Pg. 373, ¶ 4—Aistulf followed Liutprand as king of the Lombards, and in 751 he captured Ravenna and took the last of the exarchs captive. Aistulf was driven out of papal lands and the lands once governed by the exarch by King Pippin the Younger, and his bad fortune continued when in 756 he was thrown from his horse while hunting and killed.**

Carloman (of Charles Martel)—**Pg. 372, ¶ 5 & 6—Carloman, one of Charles Martel's sons, became mayor of the palace in Austrasia after his father's death. In 747 Carloman left his wife and children in his brother's care in order to become a monk; he ended up at Monte Cassino, the monastery established by Benedict himself, and lived out his life in silence and isolation.**

Carloman (of Pippin the Younger)—**Pg. 374, ¶ 5 & 6—Carloman, Pippin the Younger's younger son, ruled over the southern territories of the Frankish nation after the death of his father. After his brother dismissed his Lombard wife, the Lombard king suggested to Carloman that they destroy Charles together, but just as the plan was being formed Carloman died.**

Charles/Charlemagne—**Pg. 374, ¶ 5 & 6, Pg. 377, ¶ 2 and Pg. 378, ¶ 3—Charles, the older son of Pippin the Younger, became ruler of the whole Frankish kingdom after his brother's death in 771, and king of Lombard Italy after his defeat of Desiderius and claiming the Iron Crown in 774. Charles became known as Charles the Great, or "Charlemagne," because of victories like the one he achieved against the Lombards, however even Charlemagne could not break into al-Andalus.**

Childeric III—**Pg. 372, ¶ 5 and Pg. 373, ¶ 2—Childeric III was made king of the Franks, a figurehead king with no real power, by Carloman and Pippin the Younger. After getting permission from Pope Zachary to take the throne, Pippin the Younger had Childeric III tonsured and sent to a monastery, where he died five years later.**

Desiderius—**Pg. 373, ¶ 4 and Pg. 377, ¶ 2—Desiderius, a Lombard nobleman, was chosen by Pippin the Younger to be the king of Italy following Aistulf's death. Desiderius was sent to a monastery in northern Francia by king Charles of the Franks after Charles laid siege to the Lombard capital city of Pavia.**

Donation of Constantine—**Pg. 374, ¶ 1 & 2—The Donation of Constantine, a letter forged by a talented cleric, stated the fourth-century pope Sylvester had healed Constantine of a secret case of leprosy, and in exchange for his help, Constantine declared that the pope would have power over Antioch, Alexandria, Constantinople and Jerusalem, as well as all of the churches of God in the whole world, and that all of Rome's possessions and power were to be ruled over by the pope. While King Pippin knew the Donation of Constantine was a forgery, he was willing to give the pope power over Rome and the surrounding lands because the popes had given him the authority he craved.**

Hildegard—**Pg. 374, ¶ 6—Hildegard, an Alemanni girl, was married to Charles when she was just thirteen years old. Her marriage to the Frankish king connected him to eastern region of his lands where the sometimes-troublesome Alemanni people lived.**

Irminsul—**Pg. 376, ¶ 2—The Irminsul was a Saxon shrine made of a great wooden pillar; it represented a tree trunk which symbolized the sacred tree that supported the vault of the heavens. Charles ordered the Irminsul to be destroyed during his 772 venture into Saxon land.**

Iron Crown of the Lombards—**Pg. 377, ¶ 2—The Iron Crown of the Lombards was so named because the Lombards believed that the iron band inside it was beaten from one of the nails from Christ's cross. When Charles claimed the Iron Crown, the Lombard kingdom ceased to exist.**

Pippin the Younger—**Pg. 372, ¶ 5, Pg. 373, ¶ 2 & 4—Pippin the Younger, one of Charles Martel's sons, became mayor of the palace in Neustria after his father's death and then king of the Franks, the first king of the Carolingian dynasty, after being given permission to take the throne by Pope Zachary. After making Aistulf recognize him as overlord, and then appointing a new king of Italy after Aistulf's death, King Pippin was not only king of the Franks, but also the *de facto* ruler of Italy.**

Pope Stephen II—**Pg. 373, ¶ 3 to Pg. 374, ¶ 1—Pope Stephen II followed Pope Zachary and continued to build the relationship started by Zachary between the pope and king of the Franks by re-anointing Pippin the Younger in an elaborate ceremony and then convincing King Pippin to reclaim the papal lands taken by the Lombards. Pope Stephen II justified his possession of Rome and the old imperial center of Ravenna by having the Donation of**

Constantine forged, a document that gave the pope the right to rule over the city of Rome and all the provinces, districts and cities of Italy.

Pope Zachary—**Pg. 373, ¶ 1—Pope Zachary granted Pippin the Younger the right to rule as king of the Franks in exchange for protection against the Lombards.**

Song of Roland—**Pg. 378, ¶ 2—The Song of Roland, written in the twelfth-century, was the first French epic. The subject of the Song of Roland was Roland, Lord of the Breton Marches, a victim of the Vascones' attack on Charlemagne's army after he sacked Pamplona in the 8th century.**

Sulayman al-Arabi—**Pg. 377, ¶ 4—Sulayman al-Arabi, a chief administrator of the northeastern part of al-Andalus, invited Charlemagne to help get rid of the Umayyad rule in the Emirate of Cordoba. Sulayman al-Arabi promised Charlemagne use of the city of Zaragoza as a base for his military operations, but when Charlemagne arrived at the gates of the city, the governor of the city would not let him in.**

Section II: Comprehension

Write a two or three-sentence answer to each of the following questions.

1. Why didn't Charles Martel appoint a new king of the Franks after Theuderic IV's death in 737?

A1.—Pg. 371, ¶ 1—Charles Martel did not appoint a new king of the Franks after Theuderic IV's death in 737 because he was just as powerful without a king of the Franks as he was with one. Martel was mayor of the palaces of the Franks, *dux et princeps Francorum*, the most prominent Christian warrior in all of the old Roman lands, and except for the Lombard king Liutprand, he had more power than anyone else in the western landscape.

2. What was the cause of tension between Pope Gregory III and Liutprand in 738? Who did Pope Gregory III go to for help and what did he promise in exchange for aid?

A2.—Pg. 371, ¶ 2 & 3—In 738, the duke of Spoleto defied Liutprand and fled to Rome for sanctuary. When Pope Gregory III refused to turn the duke back over to Liutprand, the Lombard king began to take back bits of the brand-new Papal State, occupying that land himself. Cut off from Constantinople, Gregory III asked Charles Martel for help, promising Martel lasting fame on earth and eternal life in heaven (salvation).

3. Why did Charles Martel refuse to help Pope Gregory III in his battle against Liutprand?

A3.—Pg. 371, ¶ 3 to Pg. 372, ¶ 1—Charles Martel was not swayed by Pope Gregory III's promise of salvation if he would help the religious leader against the king of the Lombards. Martel had fought by the side of Liutprand at least once, and he knew that making enemies of the Lombards would gain the Franks nothing.

4. What was the significance of Pope Gregory III's appeal to Charles Martel for help in the fight against Liutprand?

A4.—Pg. 372, ¶ 2—Pope Gregory III's appeal to Charles Martel for help in the fight against Liutprand was significant because it revealed a shift in the political landscape. The pope could no longer ask the Byzantine emperor for aid, so the religious leaders in Rome now had to make alliances on their own with whatever power might be willing to protect them.

5. Why did Pippin the Younger need Pope Zachary's permission to take the Frankish throne?

A5.—Pg. 372, ¶ 7 to Pg. 373, ¶ 1—Pippin the Younger needed Pope Zachary's permission to take the Frankish throne because of his lingering regard for royal blood lines. Pippin the Younger needed a higher power, and there was no higher power than the pope, to tell him it was all right to take the throne from Childeric III and become king himself.

6. How did Pippin the Younger become the *de facto* ruler of Italy?

A6.—Pg. 373, ¶ 4—After he was re-anointed by Pope Stephen II, King Pippin marched into Italy prepared to defend papal lands. He defeated Aistulf and forced the Lombard king to recognize him as his overlord. When Aistulf died, King Pippin chose the Lombard nobleman Desiderius to be the next king of Italy, making Pippin not only the king of the Franks but the *de facto* king of Italy as well.

7. Why did Desiderius want to destroy Charles? Despite the threat from the Lombard king, how was Charles's marriage to Hildegard advantageous for the Frankish king?

A7.—Pg. 374, ¶ 6—Desiderius wanted to destroy Charles because he had given the young man his daughter's hand in marriage, and after just one year the Frankish leader decided to dismiss his wife. Charles then married a thirteen-year-old Alemanni girl called Hildegard. The marriage was advantageous to Charles because it gave him a useful connection with the eastern region of his empire where the sometimes-troublesome Alemanni people lived.

8. What made Charles head for Saxon territory in 772? Why did Charles want to make sure his men destroyed the Irminsul?

A8.—Pg. 376, ¶ 1 & 2—Charles headed for Saxon territory in 772 because he wanted to enlarge his kingdom, and the Saxons were a relatively easy target because they were divided into three main factions: the central Saxons on the Weser river, the Eastphalians on the Elbe, and the Westphalians closer to the coast. Charles ordered his men to destroy the Irminsul because it was the most sacred shrine of the Saxons, and it symbolized the sacred tree that supported the vault of the heavens. He wanted to show the Saxons that he was the God-appointed Christian king, and as such he dominated both the Saxons and their gods.

9. Describe Charles's conquest of the Lombards. What was his "crowning" achievement?

A9.—Pg. 376, ¶ 3 to Pg. 377, ¶ 2—When Charles crossed the Alps, Desiderius and the Lombard army were waiting for him in the north of Italy, but Charles pushed Desiderius back into his capital city of Pavia and laid siege for the following year, stopping only when

Desiderius surrendered. Desiderius was sent by Charles to a monastery in northern Francia and Desiderius's son and heir fled to Constantinople, where he took refuge at the imperial court. Charles's "crowning" achievement as king of all the Franks and Lombard Italy was to claim the traditional Iron Crown of the Lombards.

10. What was supposed to happen when Charlemagne arrived at the city of Zaragoza in al-Andalus, and what really happened? After leaving Zaragoza, why did Charlemagne sack Pamplona?

A10.—Pg. 377, ¶ 4 & 5—Charlemagne was supposed to be welcomed at the city of Zaragoza, and was told by Sulayman al-Arabi that he could use the city as the base of his operations against the Umayyad rule. However, when Charlemagne arrived at the city, the governor refused to let him in. After camping outside of the city for weeks, being refused entry, Charlemagne angrily withdrew and sacked the fortress of Pamplona in his rage.

11. Why was Charlemagne's sacking of Pamplona a miscalculation? How did the Vascones get their revenge on the Frankish king?

A11.—Pg. 377, ¶ 6 to Pg. 378, ¶ 1—Charlemagne's sacking of Pamplona was a miscalculation because the fortress was not firmly in the control of the emir of Cordoba; it was the home of the Vascones, a tribe that had been in Hispania before the Romans arrived and had survived in the mountains through the Roman occupation, the Visigoth takeover, and the arrival of the Arabs. At the Pass of Roncesvalles, the Vascones attacked the end of the Frankish column, wiping out the baggage train and killing every last man in the rear guard. Because they were lightly armed and experienced in the mountains, the Vascones were able to disappear into the rough terrain after the slaughter, leaving the Franks, weighed down by their own weapons and armor, unable to pursue them.

12. Why was the Vascones' ambush on Charlemagne's men so devastating to the Frankish king? In what way did time and distance theoretically heal Charlemagne's wounds?

A12.—Pg. 378, ¶ 2 & 3—The Vascones' ambush on Charlemagne's men was so devastating because a number of his officers and personal friends were killed, including Roland, Lord of the Breton Marches. Over time, as stories were told about the minor ambush, it turned into a pivotal battle and became the subject of the first French epic, the twelfth-century *Song of Roland*. In the epic, Charlemagne takes vengeance on the Arabs with the help of God, running the Arabs into the Valley of Shadows just as they had killed those close to him.

Section III: Critical Thinking

The student may not use his text to answer this question.

We know from our readings that kings and emperors will invoke the power of the heavens to justify their rule on earth. In this chapter, we read about two popes that took advantage of earthly power to ensure their place as religious leaders. Explain how the power of the pope and the power of the Frankish king merged, and how this merge benefitted both parties.

After the protection of the Byzantine emperor was taken away from Rome, the pope and his constituents had to rely on men rather than God for their earthly safety. As the student has seen previously, an earthly ruler needed to justify his power via heavenly sanction; Pippin the Younger needed a power greater than force to sanction his rise to the throne, so he made a deal with Pope Zachary. In exchange for protection against Aistulf and the Lombards, Pope Zachary blessed Pippin the Younger's rise to the throne. The papacy was now protected by the Franks, and the Frankish king's rule was blessed.

Pope Stephen II wanted to secure the pope's power on earth even further, so in 754, he travelled north into the lands of the Franks and re-anointed Pippin the Younger as king in an even more elaborate ceremony than the one given by Pope Zachary, which also included the anointing of his sons, Charles and Carloman, as his heirs. Pope Stephen then told the Franks that no future Frankish king could take the throne without being confirmed and consecrated by the pope himself. This bound the pope to the power of the king, and vice versa.

After being re-anointed by Pope Stephen II, King Pippin attacked the Lombards and forced the Lombard king to acknowledge him as his overlord. In turn, Pope Stephen II's power extended over a much larger kingdom, which included Rome and the old imperial center of Ravenna. Pope Stephen II justified his possession of these lands with the forged document called the Donation of Constantine. The document, which said that the pope ruled over Antioch, Alexandria, Constantinople, and Jerusalem, and also over all the churches of God in the whole world, and finally that Constantine himself handed over the city of Rome and all the provinces, districts and cities of Italy to the pope, gave Pope Stephen II's growth in power the semblance of legitimacy. King Pippin was willing to award the pope power over Rome and the surrounding lands because the pope had given him the permission he needed to take the Frankish throne.

EXAMPLE ANSWER:

When Pippin the Younger wanted to become king of the Franks, he needed permission from God to take the throne. That kind of transaction was nothing new. What was new was that the pope and his constituents needed to rely on man rather than God for protection after separating from the Byzantine empire. Pippin the Younger needed a power greater than force to sanction his rise to the throne, so he made a deal with Pope Zachary. In exchange for protection against Aistulf and the Lombards, Pope Zachary blessed Pippin the Younger's rise to the throne. The papacy was now protected by the Franks, and the Frankish king's rule was blessed.

Pope Stephen II wanted to secure the pope's power on earth even further, so in 754, he travelled north into the lands of the Franks and re-anointed Pippin the Younger as king in an even more elaborate ceremony than the one given by Pope Zachary, which also included the anointing of his sons, Charles and Carloman, as his heirs. Pope Stephen then told the Franks that no future Frankish king could take the throne without being confirmed and consecrated by the pope himself. This bound the pope to the power of the king, and vice versa.

After being re-anointed by Pope Stephen II, King Pippin attacked the Lombards and forced the Lombard king to acknowledge him as his overlord. In turn, Pope Stephen II's power extended over a much larger kingdom, which included Rome and the old imperial center of Ravenna. Pope Stephen II justified his possession of these lands with the forged document called the Donation of Constantine which gave his growth in power the semblance of legitimacy. King Pippin was willing to award the pope power over Rome and the surrounding lands because the pope had given him the permission he needed to take the Frankish throne.

Section IV: Map Exercise

1. Using a black pencil, trace the rectangular outline of the frame for Map 49.1: Charlemagne's Kingdom.

2. Using a blue pencil, trace the coastline of the Atlantic and the Mediterranean. Include the coastline of Britain and the islands of Sardinia, Corsica, and Sicily, but do not include any other islands. Trace the Alps and the Pyrenees mountains with simple peaks with a black pencil. With your blue pencil, draw the lines of the Loire, Seine, Rhone, Rhine, Elbe, and Danube. Repeat until the contours are familiar.

3. Using a new sheet of paper, trace the rectangular outline of the frame in black. Remove your tracing paper from the original. Using a regular pencil, draw the coastline as you traced it while you look at Map 49.1. Show the Alps and the Pyrenees mountains with simple peaks, and draw the lines of the rivers Loire, Seine, Rhone, Rhine, Elbe, and Danube. Erase and redraw as necessary.

4. When you are pleased with your map, lay it over the original. Erase and redraw any lines which are more than ¼ inch off of the original.

5. Remove your map. Study carefully the areas of Asturias, the Emirate of Cordoba, Aquitaine, Neustria, and Austrasia. When you are familiar with them, close the book and label them on your map. Check your map against the original, and correct any misplaced labels.

6. Then study carefully the locations of Cordoba, Zaragoza, Pamplona, and Soissons. Also study the locations of Milan, Venice, Pavia, Ravenna, Sutri, Rome, and Naples. Study the locations of the Duchy of Spoleto and the Duchy of Benevento. When you are familiar with them, close the book. Using your regular pencil, mark the cities of Cordoba, Zaragoza, Pamplona, Soissons, Milan, Venice, Pavia, Ravenna, Sutri, Rome, and Naples. Then mark the Duchy of Spoleto and the Duchy of Benevento. Check your map against the original. Correct any misplaced labels.

7. Mark the locations of the Pass of Roncesvalles and the Breton Marches.

Chapter Fifty

The An Lushan Rebellion

The student may use her text when answering the questions in sections I and II.

Section I: Who, What, Where

Write a one or two-sentence answer explaining the significance of each item listed below.

An Lushan—**Pg. 381, ¶ 1, Pg. 383, ¶ 2 and Pg. 384, ¶ 2—An Lushan, an army officer, was awarded greater authority by Tang Xuanzong because Yang Guifei demanded it, and eventually this power grew to the point where An Lushan was able to declare rebellion against Tang Xuanzong. Though An Lushan made it as far as occupying Chang'an and declaring himself emperor, he contracted a terrible disease that made him short-tempered and paranoid, and in 757 he was murdered by one of his house servants.**

Geluofeng—**Pg. 382, ¶ 1—Geluofeng, Piluoge's successor as leader of the Nanzhao kingdom, took advantage of Tang weakness and successfully attacked the Tang border instead of working with the Tang as Piluoge had.**

Gyeongdeok—**Pg. 385, ¶ 2—Gyeongdeok was king of Unified Silla at the time of the end of the An Lushan rebellion. His kingdom suffered because of the Tang civil war, and Unified Silla became second in power to the new Balhae kingdom.**

Li Bai—**Pg. 380, ¶ 2—Li Bai was a Tang poet writing during Tang Xuanzong's rule whose reputation had spread empire-wide because he wrote in the new "regulated" style which was orderly and metered. One of his versus was "Cut water with a sword, the water flows on;/ Quench sorrow with wine, the sorrow increases,/ In our lifetime, our wishes are unfulfilled."**

Note to the parent—The student should include that Li Bai was famous for writing in the "regulated" style, but the student does not have to include Li Bai's verse in her answer. If she does want to include some verses, another example of Li Bai's writing is found on Pg. 381, ¶ 2—"There seems no end to the fighting./ In the wilderness men hack one another to pieces,/ Riderless horses neigh madly to the sky. . . . /

The blood of soldiers smears grass and brambles;/ What use is a commander without his troops?/ War is a fearful thing—
And the wise prince resorts to it only if he must."

Li Linfu—**Pg. 381, ¶ 1—Li Linfu, a dictatorial, privileged aristocrat, became chancellor because of the influence of Yang Guifei after Zhang Jiuling was dismissed by Tang Xuanzong.**

Mun—**Pg. 385, ¶ 2—Mun, the king of Balhae, took advantage of the weakness on the Korean peninsula caused by the Tang civil war. He conquered the surrounding territory until his kingdom was even larger than Unified Silla.**

Piluoge—**Pg. 381, ¶ 4—Piluoge, a Bai chief, rose to power by claiming the rulership of all six Bai tribes and burning the chiefs of the other tribes alive. His rise as leader of the Nanzhao kingdom was so quick and powerful that barely a decade after seizing power he was able to match is grandson to a princess of Tang descent.**

Tang Daizong—**Pg. 384, ¶ 3 and Pg. 385, ¶ 3—Tang Daizong, son of Tang Suzong, managed to put out the last fights of the An Lushan rebellion in 763. By the time of Tang Daizong's death in 776, the Tang had lost all of its holdings in central Asia.**

Tang Suzong—**Pg. 384, ¶ 2 & 3—Tang Suzong, Tang Xuanzong's son, and the heir apparent, forced his father to abdicate in 756, and then he took the throne for himself, even though he was in exile. After An Lushan's death, Tang Suzong managed to drive the rebels out of Chang'an, but the fighting with rebels continued even after Tang Suzong's death in 762.**

Wang Wei—**Pg. 380, ¶ 2—Wang Wei was a Tang poet and painter working during Tang Xuanzong's rule known for writing *jueju*, "cut-short" quatrains that glanced at a truth and then away, leaving the reader to seek the deeper meaning. An example of Wang Wei's writing was "A morning shower in Weicheng has settled the light dust;/ The willows by the hostel are fresh and green;/Come, drink one more cup of wine,/West of the pass you will meet no more old friends."**

Note to the parent—The student should include that Wang Wei was famous for writing jueju, but she does not have to include an example of Wang Wei's writing in her answer.

Wu Daozi—**Pg. 380, ¶ 2—Wu Daozi was a Tang painter working during Tang Xuanzong's rule that created murals and portraits so breathtaking that he was rumored to have opened a painted door in one of his landscapes and stepped through.**

Yang Guifei—**Pg. 381, ¶ 1 and Pg. 383, ¶ 6—Yang Guifei, Tang Xuanzong's son's young wife, was divorced from her husband and made the Brilliant Emperor's consort, even though she was fond of the army officer An Lushan. After the rebellion of An Lushan, the royal court wanted Yang Guifei killed because she had helped him rise to power; instead, Yang Guifei was mercifully killed by a court eunuch ordered by the Brilliant Emperor to commit the deed.**

Yang Guozhong—**Pg. 381, ¶ 1, Pg. 382, ¶ 2 and Pg. 383, ¶ 5—Yang Guozhong, cousin of Yang Guifei, was given great power in the court because of his cousin's influence, and after the death of Li Linfu, he was made the next chancellor of the Tang. After leading the Tang army to a great defeat against An Lushan, Yang Guozhong was murdered by the Brilliant Emperor's royal guard.**

Zhang Jiuling—**Pg. 381, ¶ 1—Zhang Jiuling, a man who was famous for his wisdom, asceticism and stern moral compass, was dismissed as chancellor by Tang Xuanzong because he wanted to put someone in Zhang Jiuling's place approved by Yang Guifei.**

Section II: Comprehension

Write a two or three-sentence answer to each of the following questions.

1. Describe the greatness of the Tang empire as it thrived under the leadership of Tang Xuanzong.

A1.—Pg. 380, ¶ 2—Under Tang Xuanzong the Tang empire reached its most brilliant era. The arts flourished with brilliant painters and poets creating breathtaking works and verses that would endure for centuries, and Tang porcelain, as clear and thin as glass, was prized by every country that bought goods from the Silk Road. The Tang empire was at the height of its creativity, power and size under Tang Xuanzong.

2. What was the cost of China's expanding empire, according to the poet Li Bai? How was this cost affected by Tang Xuanzong's preoccupation with Yang Guifei?

A2.—Pg. 381, ¶ 2 & 3—China's expansion came with great human cost, which was recorded by the poet Li Bai who wrote, "White bones are the only crop in these yellow sands . . . There seems no end to the fighting./
In the wilderness men hack one another to pieces,/ Riderless horses neigh madly to the sky. . . ./
The blood of soldiers smears grass and brambles;/ What use is a commander without his troops?/ War is a fearful thing—And the wise prince resorts to it only if he must." While Tang Xuanzong was preoccupied with his personal life, Gao Xianzhi continued to struggle with the Arabs to the far west, the generals on the frontiers took more and more authority themselves, the Khitan invaded the north and Tibetan attacks and raids on the central Asian frontier intensified.

3. How did the Nanzhao kingdom come to be? How did Tang Xuanzong view Piluoge's strengthening domain?

A3.—Pg. 381, ¶ 4 to Pg. 382, ¶ 1—The Nanzhao kingdom was formed when Piluoge brought together six tribes that centered around Lake Erhai, known to the Chinese as the Bai. Piluoge claimed the rulership of all six tribes and burnt the chiefs of the other tribes alive to show his power. Tang Xuanzong saw Piluoge's strengthening domain as a useful buffer

between the Tang border and the hostile soldiers of Tibet, and had bestowed a title on Piluoge; he even invited the new king and his grandson to come to Chang'an and celebrate the marriage between Piluoge's grandson and a Tang princess.

4. In what way did the Tang conflict with Nanzhao allow An Lushan to declare his challenge to the emperor's power?

A4.—Pg. 382, ¶ 1 & 3 and Pg. 383, ¶ 1 & 2—When the army of the southwestern Tang territories first fought against the rebellious Nanzhao they suffered an unexpected and embarrassing defeat. In 754, the Nanzhao were again victorious against the Tang at the Battle of Xiaguan, where the Tang army was massacred and then almost all of the survivors were killed by the plague as they headed home. Taking advantage of the anger and discontent of the Tang army, An Lushan declared himself an open rival to Tang Xuanzong.

5. Describe the beginning of An Lushan's advances against The Brilliant Emperor. How did Gao Xianzhi suffer as a result of An Lushan's uprising?

A5.—Pg. 383, ¶ 2 & 3—After the second defeat of the Tang army by the Nanzhao, An Lushan declared himself in 755 to be a rival to the Brilliant Emperor, and he made a royal capital of his own at Fanyang. He commanded over a hundred thousand men, a mixture of well-trained soldiers and northern horsemen recruited from the Khitan that followed him south along to Luoyang, where they rested and prepared for an attack on Chang'an itself. The Brilliant Emperor was furious, and when Gao Xianzhi did not act fast enough after being commanded to campaign against An Lushan, the Brilliant Emperor had him beheaded.

6. What was Yang Guozhong's plan to fight An Lushan? What was the result of his plan?

A6.—Pg. 383, ¶ 3 & 4—Yang Guozhong planned an enormous frontal assault against An Lushan even though military advisors said it was not a good idea. In July 756 the Tang royal army met the rebels and the Tang troops were decimated, with one hundred thousand men killed, and no one left to defend Chang'an. As a result, An Lushan easily occupied the capital and Tang Xuanzong and Yang Guozhong fled to the west.

7. How did the An Lushan rebellion end?

A7.—Pg. 384, ¶ 2 & 3—While in Chang'an, An Lushan declared himself emperor Yan, but his reign was short-lived because he contracted some disease that caused him to suffer from large and excruciatingly painful boils on his face, and as a result he became paranoid and short-tempered, behavior that led to his murder in 757 by one of his fed-up house servants. An Lushan's son tried to continue the rebellion, but Tang Suzong managed to re-enter Chang'an with his own soldiers later in the same year and drive the remaining rebels out. Resistance continued for the next six years, and in 763, Tan Daizong finally managed to put down the last remnants of the An Lushan rebellion.

8. Who were the Uighur people, and where did they come from? What was the relationship between the Uighur and Tang China like before the An Lushan rebellion?

A8.—Pg. 384, ¶ 5 to Pg. 385, ¶ 1—The Uighurs had been a vassal tribe of the Eastern Turkish Khaghanate, but they had broken away from their overlords and established their own kingdom, with its capital at Ordu-Baliq. Uighur mercenaries were routinely hired by Tang Suzong and Tang Daizong, and the heavy payments that the emperors handed over boosted Uighur wealth. The Uighur even adopted some knowledge of Chinese writing, and this became the basis of a Uighur writing system which sparked a transformation that gradually turned the tribes of warrior nomads into a more stable kingdom.

9. How did the Balhae form? Why was the Balhae a threat to Unified Silla?

A9.—Pg. 385, ¶ 2—The Balhae formed when the survivors of the destroyed Korean kingdom of Goguryeo gathered in the north, where they had settled and intermarried with the semi-nomadic tribes of the Malgal. The Balhae king Mun took advantage of the lessened Tang presence on the peninsula to conquer the surrounding territory, making Balhae even bigger than, and threatening to, Unified Silla.

Section III: Critical Thinking

The student may not use her text to answer this question.

Often when we think of singular events reshaping the ancient or medieval world, we think of great natural disasters that forced peoples to rethink their way of life. The An Lushan rebellion was a singular event that altered life for many peoples in the same way that the Great Flood, or the explosion of Mount Vesuvius, altered the lives and customs of people in the past. Write a paragraph or two explaining how the one An Lushan rebellion ended up reshaping an entire system of political relations. In your answer, make sure to explain the concrete effects of the rebellion on the relationship between Tang China and its surrounding peoples.

The most important thing for the student to know about the An Lushan rebellion is that it showed the far eastern medieval world that the power of the Tang was broken. Because the surrounding peoples were no longer afraid of the Tang, and more concretely because all the border guards were recalled to fight in the civil war, the borders of the empire were, for all intents and purposes, open. The first negative effect of the rebellion on Tang China's relations with its surrounding peoples was evident in its relationship with Tibet. In late 763, while Tang Daizong was occupied in Luoyang, Tibetan troops crossed the border all the way into Chang'an and looted it before withdrawing. For the next decade, Tibetan troops would attack from the southwest annually.

To the north and the northwest, the Tang border was infiltrated by the Uighur tribes. To the northeast, Unified Silla suffered greatly because of the Tang civil war. The kings of Silla had gained their unified empire with the help of Tang forces, and they needed Tang support because of constant challenges to their power. The biggest threat to

Unified Silla was the Balhae, whose king Mun took advantage of the lessened Tang presence on the peninsula to conquer the surrounding territory until Balhae had grown even bigger than Unified Silla.

The effects of the rebellion were felt most strongly in Tang China itself. The population shifted away from the north and west, and the ancient cities of the north fell into decline. By the time of Tang Daizong's death in 779, the Tang had lost all of its holdings in central Asia. The trade routes to the west had been disrupted and blocked. The generals who were tasked with protecting the shrunken outer reaches of the empire gained more and more power and neither the Tang emperor nor his ministers were able to check their growing independence. With the shifting of power within Tang China, Tibet, Nanzhao, the Uighurs, Balhae and Unified Silla, it is clear that the An Lushan rebellion changed the political landscape of the entire continent.

EXAMPLE ANSWER:

The An Lushan rebellion showed the far eastern medieval world that the power of the Tang was broken. Within Tang China, the population shifted away from the north and west, the ancient cities of the north fell into decline, and by 779 the Tang had lost all of its holdings in central Asia. The trade routes to the west had been disrupted and blocked. Generals on the edges of the empire were growing more and more independent, and neither the emperor nor the ministers were able to stop them.

The Nanzhao were already taking advantage of Tang weakness before the An Lushan rebellion even started. After the rebellion, Tibetan troops crossed the border in 763 and went all the way into Chang'an and looted it before withdrawing. For the next decade, Tibetan troops would attack from the southwest annually. To the north and the northwest, the Tang border was infiltrated by the Uighur tribes. To the northeast, Unified Silla suffered without the help of the Tang to keep their dominance on the peninsula. King Mun of the Balhae took advantage of the lessened Tang presence on the peninsula to conquer the surrounding territory until Balhae had grown even bigger than Unified Silla. Though the effects of the rebellion were felt most strongly within Tang China itself, the changes in Nanzhao, Tibet, the Uighurs, Balhae and Unified Silla, made it clear that the An Lushan rebellion changed the political landscape of the entire continent.

Section IV: Map Exercise

1. Using a black pencil, trace the rectangular outline of the frame for Map 50.1: New Kingdoms and the Tang.

2. Using a blue pencil, trace the coastline as far as it is visible. You do not need to include any islands at this time. Trace the line of the Yangtze River and the Yellow River. Mark Lake Erhai and Lake Kokonor. Using your black pencil, trace the Himalaya mountains with simple peaks. Repeat until the contours are familiar. Then trace the regions of the Tang, the land lost by the Tang, Tibet, and Balhae. Repeat until the contours are familiar.

3. Trace the rectangular outline of the frame in black. Remove your tracing paper from the original. Using a regular pencil with an eraser as you look at Map 50.1, draw the coastline, the Yangtze River, the Yellow River, and the mountains. Draw the perimeters of the regions of the Tang, the land lost by the Tang, Tibet, and Balhae. Mark and label Lake Erhai and Lake Kokonor. Erase and redraw as necessary.

4. When you are pleased with your map, lay it over the original. Erase and redraw any lines which are more than ¼ inch off of the original.

5. Remove your map. Study carefully the regions of Uighur, Fanyang, Khitan, and Unified Silla. Also study the locations of Nanzhao and Weicheng. When you are familiar with them, close the book, and mark the locations on your map. Check your map with the original, and make any necessary corrections.

6. Now study the locations of Ordu-Baliq, Fanyang, Chang'an, Luoyang, and Beijing. Also study the locations of the Battle of Talas and the Battle of Xiaguan. When you are familiar with them, close the book. Mark the locations on your map. Check your map with the original, and correct any misplaced locations or labels.

7. Mark the locations of Lake Erhai and Lake Kokonor as you look at the map. Then draw and mark the Silk Road and the Great Wall.

Chapter Fifty-One

Imperator et Augustus

The student may use his text when answering the questions in sections I and II.

Section I: Who, What, Where

Write a one or two-sentence answer explaining the significance of each item listed below.

Alcuin—**Pg. 389, ¶ 3—Alcuin, Charlemagne's personal tutor, was a British churchman whom Charlemagne had recruited to teach his sons. Under Alcuin's guidance, Charlemagne developed a stronger and stronger sense of mission, believing his conquests brought the Gospel to stubborn unbelievers who needed to be saved not just from their sins but from their own unwillingness to hear.**

Alfonso II—**Pg. 391, ¶ 3—Alfonso II, Asturian king, wanted recognition from Charlemagne, the greatest Christian king of the west, for the legitimacy of his own throne. In 798, Charlemagne recognized Alfonso II as a legitimate king.**

Al-Mahdi—**Pg. 388, ¶ 3—Al-Mahdi, son of al-Mansur, took advantage of Byzantine weakness and launched a new offensive into Asia Minor, drove the Byzantine defenders away and set up camp at the port city of Chrysopolis, demanding a huge ransom and yearly tribute from Irene in order for him to withdraw from Chrysopolis.**

Charles the Younger—**Pg. 388, ¶ 5—Charles the Younger, Charlemagne's second son, was designated to inherit the job of king of the Franks.**

Constantine VI—**Pg. 388, ¶ 2, Pg. 390, ¶ 3 and Pg. 391, ¶ 1—Constantine VI, Leo IV's son, succeeded his father as the Byzantine emperor when he was just nine years hold, and his mother Irene served as his regent. In 790 Constantine VI became the ruler of Byzantium, after the army forced his mother to hand over her authority, but he turned out to be a tyrannical ruler that was eventually shut up to die in the imperial chamber where he was born.**

Irene—**Pg. 388, ¶ 2, Pg. 390, ¶ 2 & 3, Pg. 391, ¶ 1 and Pg. 394, ¶ 4—Irene, mother of Constantine VI, served as her nine-year-old son's regent and kept the power of the throne**

long after her son was old enough to rule, until she was forced out in 790. After Constantine VI proved to be a terrible leader, Irene managed to take back the throne, and in 802 she lost the throne for good, forced out by her finance minister.

Kardam—**Pg. 390, ¶ 3 & 5—Kardam, the Bulgarian khan in power during Constantine VI's reign, twice defeated Constantine VI during his attempted attacks on the Bulgars. After he was sent horse-turds by Constantine VI, Kardam successfully received tribute from the Byzantine king, and he pledged not to invade Thracia.**

Leo IV—**Pg. 387, ¶ 5 to Pg. 388, ¶ 2—Leo IV, Constantine V's half-Khazar son, succeeded his father as ruler of Byzantium. Instead of attacking the First Bulgarian Empire, Leo IV concentrated on defending his throne, exiling two of his five brothers that were a threat, and then planning an attack on the Arabs in Syria—a plan that was cut short because he died in 780 after only five years on the throne.**

Louis the Pious—**Pg. 388, ¶ 5—Louis the Pious, Charlemagne's fourth son, was king of the Frankish territory Aquitaine.**

Nikephorus—**Pg. 390, ¶ 3 & 4—Nikephorus, Constantine VI's uncle and Constantine V's half-brother, was supposed to be placed on the throne after the imperial guard revolted against Constantine VI. The plan did not work, and Nikephorus was caught by Constantine VI and blinded.**

Nikephoros I—**Pg. 394, ¶ 4–6—Nikephoros I, Irene's finance minister, led a coup against Irene in 802, removed her from the throne, and was crowned emperor in her place. In 803, Nikephoros I made a treaty with Charlemagne called the *Pax Nicephori*, but when he signed the treaty, he would not acknowledge Charlemagne as "Emperor."**

Pippin—**Pg. 388, ¶ 5 and *—Charlemagne's son, formerly known as Carloman, was renamed Pippin after Charlemagne's oldest son, Pippin the Hunchback, was disinherited. Pippin was crowned by his father as king of Italy.**

Rotrude—**Pg. 388, ¶ 7 to Pg. 389, ¶ 2—Rotrude, Charlemagne's third-oldest daughter, was married to Constantine VI of Byzantium but since she was only eight years old, the betrothal took place in name only while both children remained with their parents. Rotrude never ended up marrying Constantine VI; Irene broke the engagement when Rotrude was thirteen years old.**

Widukind—**Pg. 389, ¶ 4—Widukind, leader of the Saxons, fled Charlemagne's attack on Saxon resistance in 782, but was captured and forced to surrender three years later. As part of his surrender, Widukind agreed to a Christian baptism.**

Section II: Comprehension

Write a two or three-sentence answer to each of the following questions.

1. Why was Constantine V planning to go to war against the First Bulgarian Empire in 775? What stopped him from attacking?

A1.—Pg. 387, ¶ 3 & 4—As Constantine V captured various peoples, many of which were from his battles with the Arabs, he resettled them in Thracia. This settling of captive peoples along Bulgarian borders annoyed the Bulgarian khans, and in retaliation, Bulgarian troops had begun to raid Byzantine land. Constantine decided that the Bulgarians needed to be put in their place, but as he was preparing to start out on his campaign, he fell ill with an infection that caused severe fever and ultimately his death.

2. Why did Irene ask Charlemagne to betroth one of his daughters to the eleven-year-old Byzantine king Constantine VI?

A2.—Pg. 388, ¶ 4—Irene was embarrassed by her inability to defend Byzantium against al-Mahdi. After he drove through Asia Minor and set up camp at Chrysopolis, directly across the water from Constantinople, Irene was forced to pay him an enormous ransom and agree to a yearly tribute in order to get him to withdraw. Irene needed a strong alliance to back her up against the Arabs, so in 782 she sent two messengers to the kingdom of the Franks, and asked Charlemagne to betroth one of his daughters to the eleven-year-old emperor.

3. Describe the reach of Charlemagne and his family's power when he received the request from Irene to marry one of his daughters to the young Constantine VI.

A3.—Pg. 388, ¶ 5 & 6—When Charlemagne received the request from Irene to betroth one of his daughters to her young son, he was equal in stature to the regent of Constantinople. He controlled the lands of the Franks and Italians, and he was creating a dynasty; his second son, Charles the younger, was designated to inherit the job of king of the Franks, he had crowned his third son Pippin as king of Italy, his fourth son Louis the Pious was king of the Frankish territory Aquitaine, and he ruled over them as an emperor rules over vassal kings. Also, Charlemagne had taken on the responsibility as defender of the Christian faith, protecting and defining the Papal States.

4. Why would an alliance between the Carolingians and the Byzantine emperors be a real challenge to the power of the Arabs?

A4—Pg. 388, ¶ 6—An alliance between the Carolingians and the Byzantine emperors would not only create a united front against the Arabs, but it alliance would also create an empire of the spirit. The alliance would be a western mirror for the eastern empire, a Christian counterpart to the ever-advancing Islamic kingdom.

5. Why did Irene break the engagement between Constantine VI and Rotrude?

A5.—Pg. 389, ¶ 2—Irene broke the engagement between Constantine VI and Rotrude because her position as ruler of Byzantium was more secure and she no longer needed an alliance

with Charlemagne. Further, Charlemagne's growing power was a threat to the remaining enclaves of Byzantine-loyal land on the Italian peninsula.

6. How did Charlemagne come to be called "King David" by his royal circle of scholars and clerics? How did King David spark the "Carolingian renaissance"?

A6.—Pg. 389, ¶ 3 and *—Charlemagne had gathered around him a royal circle of scholars and clerics who were filling in the gaps from his early education. They not only discussed with him theology, philosophy, and grammar, but also called him "King David," after the Old Testament monarch who was handpicked by God to lead the chosen people. Charlemagne's intellectual curiosity and Alcuin's teaching combined to spark a revival of learning often called the "Carolingian renaissance," which produced innovations in art, music, architecture, and calligraphy.

7. Why did Charlemagne attack the Saxons in 782? What rules did the Saxons have to abide by after Widukind's capture?

A7.—Pg. 389, ¶ 3 & 4—Charlemagne's attack against the Saxons was a result of Saxon resistance to his rule. In 782, he ordered forty-five hundred Saxon prisoners to be massacred, though their leader Widukind managed escape surrender for three years; when he was finally caught he had to agree to Christian baptism. Afterward Charlemagne decreed that any "unbaptized Saxon who conceals himself among his people and refuses to seek baptism, but rather chooses to remain a pagan shall die," that a Saxon who stole from a church, or did violence to a priest, or indulged himself in the old Saxon rites instead of Christian worship, would be put to death, and that any Saxon who did not observe Lent properly would be executed.

8. How were the religious rules imposed upon the Saxons part of Charlemagne's forceful evangelism? In what way did Alcuin suggest Charlemagne be a little less forceful?

A8.—Pg. 389, ¶ 4 to Pg. 390, ¶ 1—The religious rules imposed upon the Saxons were part of Charlemagne's forceful Evangelism because he did everything possible to make stubborn unbelievers follow the gospel. Alcuin suggested that Charlemagne ease up on the Saxons by revoking the death penalty for aberrations against the gospel.

9. What actions did Irene of Byzantium take to prove she held the highest God-sanctioned position of authority in the known world?

A9.—Pg. 390, ¶ 2—Irene of Byzantium felt she held the highest God-sanctioned authority in the known world. After she broke Constantine VI's engagement, she refused to yield the throne to her son even though he was old enough to rule in his own name. She named herself not just regent, but empress; and on that authority, she summoned a church council—the Second Council of Nicaea—to reverse all of the icon-condemning pronouncements made during the reigns of Leo III and his successors.

10. How did Constantine VI react when he found out there was a plot to take him off of the throne?

A10.—Pg. 390, ¶ 4—When Constantine VI found out there was a plot to take him off of the throne, he cruelly punished everyone involved. He had all five of his uncles arrested and

brought to court. He blinded Nikephorus, who was supposed to replace him on the throne, and had the other four brothers de-tongued.

11. What happened when Kardam threatened to invade Thracia unless Constantine VI paid him tribute? How did Kardam eventually get his tribute?

A11.—Pg. 390, ¶ 5—When Kardam demanded tribute, Constantine VI put horse-turds into a towel and sent him this message, "I have sent you such tribute as is appropriate for you." However, after insulting Kardam, Constantine VI lost his nerve. When Kardam approached at the head of his army, Constantine VI went out to meet him and agreed to send him tribute after all.

12. Why did Charlemagne consider the throne of Constantinople to be empty? How did Charlemagne respond to the Second Council of Nicaea?

A12.—Pg. 391, ¶ 2—Charlemagne believed the throne of Constantinople to be empty because it was filled by a woman with no legitimate claim to the throne. On top of that, Charlemagne believed Irene to be an idol-worshiper, proven by her putting together of the Second Council of Nicaea. Charlemagne responded to Irene's Second Council of Nicaea by putting together a theological committee of his own to study the report of the Second Council and write a rebuttal called the *Libri Carolini*.

13. What did the title *imperator et augustus* mean to Charlemagne? How was the crowning of Charlemagne viewed in Constantinople?

A13.—Pg. 394, ¶ 3 & 4—The title *imperator et augustus* meant to Charlemagne that he had the authority to stand as the protector of faith, guarantor of civilization and the highest power in the Christian world. In Constantinople, the coronation was scorned as meaningless.

14. What were the terms of the agreement made between Nikephoros I and Charlemagne called the *Pax Nicephori*? Why wouldn't Nikephoros I acknowledge Charlemagne as "Emperor" when he signed the treaty?

A14.—Pg. 394, ¶ 5 & 6—The *Pax Nicephori* protected the Byzantine-loyal city of Venice from Frankish occupation. The agreement stated Nikephoros I and Byzantium would keep control of Venice and its important port and in return, Charlemagne would receive a generous annual payment. While the terms of the treaty made it clear that it was an agreement between equals, Nikephoros would not acknowledge Charlemagne as "Emperor" because he was holding on to the imperial title himself.

Section III: Critical Thinking

The student may not use his text to answer this question.

In 799, Pope Leo III was attacked by a band of his enemies, who tried to cut out his eyes and tongue. Pope Leo III managed to escape his attackers, and he went immediately to Charlemagne, asking the Frankish king to help him drive out his enemies from Rome. Write a paragraph explaining why Charlemagne had to think hard about his decision to send soldiers to Rome. Then write a paragraph explaining what Charlemagne decided to do, and the unexpected reward he received for helping Pope Leo III.

When Leo was consecrated as pope, Charlemagne had promised to defend him. It might seem to the student that Charlemagne had no choice but to send soldiers to Rome. However, the language of the agreement did not specify that Charlemagne would do any actual fighting at home: "My task, assisted by the divine piety, is everywhere to defend the Church of Christ, abroad, by arms, against pagan incursions and the devastations of such as break faith; at home, by protecting the Church in the spreading of the Catholic faith." Defending the church at home with arms was not specifically in the contract, and also many of the Frankish officials believed that Pope Leo III, who was not an aristocrat, was immoral and dishonest.

However, Charlemagne decided that whether or not Pope Leo III was rightly attacked by enemies or not, it was the position of the pope that he had sworn to defend. If the pope spoke for God, he could not be removed by a military coup. However, in order to protect the office of the papacy from being another throne that could be contested and won by force, Constantine would have to use force to keep it safe. Ultimately Charlemagne decided to fight for Rome and Pope Leo III, convinced by his advisor Alcuin that he was the only remaining representative of God in the known world who still had any power to right wrongs. Alcuin told him, "On you alone the whole safety of the churches of Christ depends."

As a result, Charlemagne decided in 800 to send the pope back to Rome with an armed bodyguard. He followed the guard, and when he arrived he made Pope Leo III put his hand on the copy of the Gospels in St. Peter's Cathedral and swear, in the presence of onlookers, that he was guiltless of any wrongdoing. Then, worshipping on Christmas Day, Leo III came forward and put a gold crown on Charlemagne's head. This was an unexpected reward for Charlemagne: to be crowned imperator et augustus.

EXAMPLE ANSWER:

Charlemagne promised to defend Leo when he was consecrated as pope. He swore that he would defend the Church of Christ abroad by arms and at home by spreading the Catholic faith. He did not say he would defend the Church of Christ at home with arms, which was what Pope Leo III was asking him to do: bring soldiers to Rome in order to protect him from his enemies. This was a hard decision for Charlemagne, and it wasn't made any easier by his officials, who believed that Leo was immoral and dishonest.

While the pope's character was challenged, Charlemagne decided he was charged to protect the position of the pope, rather than the pope himself. He needed to protect the papacy from usurpation so that it would not become another throne to be contested. Charlemagne decided in 800 to send the pope back to Rome with an armed bodyguard. He followed the guard, and when he arrived he made Pope Leo III put his hand on the copy of the Gospels in St. Peter's Cathedral and swear, in the presence of onlookers, that he was guiltless of any wrongdoing. Then, worshipping on Christmas Day, Leo III came forward and put a gold crown on Charlemagne's head. As a reward for his service to Rome, Charlemagne was crowned *imperator et augustus*.

Chapter Fifty-Two

The New Sennacherib

The student may use her text when answering the questions in sections I and II.

Section I: Who, What, Where

Write a one or two-sentence answer explaining the significance of each item listed below.

Abu'l-Abbas—**Pg. 397, ¶ 2—Abu'l-Abbas was the name of the albino war elephant sent to Charlemagne from Harun al-Rashid. Charlemagne liked the idea of having a war elephant, and took it on campaign with him when he had to fight against invading Scandinavians.**

Harun al-Rashid—**Pg. 396, ¶ 2 and Pg. 398, ¶ 1—Harun al-Rashid, son of al-Mahdi, was made caliph in 786 and was nicknamed "The Righteous" because during his first time leading the annual pilgrimage to Mecca and Medina he gave the leaders of both cities enormous gifts. Harun al-Rashid amassed great wealth in part because of thriving Arabian trade routes, leading him to be memorialized in the *Arabian Nights*.**

Michael Rangabe—**Pg. 401, ¶ 5 and Pg. 402, ¶ 2 & 5—Michael Rangabe, Staurakios's brother-in-law and successor to the Byzantine throne, made a treaty with Charlemagne that gave Rangabe the confidence to attack the Bulgarians. Krum managed to wipe out the Byzantine troops once again; as a result, Michael Rangabe abdicated, fearing his own assassination.**

King Offa—**Pg. 397, ¶ 3 & 4—King Offa, Christian ruler of the English kingdom Mercia, made the blunder of thinking he was almost equal to Charlemagne in dignity; when Offa suggested his son and heir marry one of Charlemagne's daughters, Charlemagne temporarily closed Frankish ports to Mercian ships. Another blunder of Offa's was to okay a new design of English coins based on one of al-Rashid's gold dinars, which resulted in pretty coins with the words "There is no God but Allah, and Muhammad is the prophet" written in Arabic text upside down on one side of the new coins.**

Krum—**Pg. 400, ¶ 4, Pg. 401, ¶ 4 and Pg. 402, ¶ 7—Krum, the Bulgarian khan that followed Kardam (who might have been his uncle), brought Bulgaria up into a major power,**

slaughtering Byzantine troops and drinking out of Nikephoros I's silver-coated skull while expanding his territory. Krum earned the name "the new Sennacherib" because, like the Assyrian king of ancient times that tried to wipe out the people of God when he attacked Jerusalem, Krum was relentless in his attacks against Constantinople and Byzantium.

Leo V—**Pg. 402, ¶ 5 & 6 and Pg. 403, ¶ 1 & 3—Leo V, formerly Leo the Armenian, military governor of Byzantine lands in Asia Minor, was made emperor after Michael Rangabe's disastrous campaign against the Bulgarians. Though Leo V botched Krum's assassination, he was finally able to make a thirty-year peace with Krum's successor, Omurtag.**

Omurtag—**Pg. 403, ¶ 3—Omurtag, Krum's successor, agreed to thirty-year peace with Leo V after the Byzantine ruler began to have some military successes against the Bulgarians.**

Staurakios—**Pg. 401, ¶ 5—Staurakios, Nikephoros I's son and second-in-command, was badly injured in battle against Krum but was crowned emperor after his father's death nonetheless. Just months later, his wound incurable, Staurakios had to give up his crown to his brother-in-law Michael Rangabe.**

Section II: **Comprehension**

Write a two or three-sentence answer to each of the following questions.

1. Why did Harun al-Rashid pursue a friendly relationship with Charlemagne?

A1.—Pg. 396, ¶ 1—Harun al-Rashid pursued a friendly relationship with Charlemagne because as an Abbasid ally, Charlemagne could halt Byzantine expansion to the west and help guard Abbasid interests against the breakaway Umayyad realm, the Emirate of Cordoba.

2. Why did Harun al-Rashid move his court from Baghdad to Ar Raqqah?

A2.—Pg. 396, ¶ 3—Harun al-Rashid was more interested in security and prosperity than he was with conquest. As a result, he moved his court from Baghdad to Ar Raqqah because it was closer to the northern trade routes from the Abbasid empire into Khazar territory.

3. How was it that Arab merchants were able to trade with Scandinavian merchants? What did the Scandinavian merchants have to offer, and what did they want from Arab merchants?

A3.—Pg. 396, ¶ 3 to Pg. 397, ¶ 1—Arab merchants were able to trade with Scandinavian merchants because, as a result of semi-peace with the Khazars, they were able to travel north through the Caspian Gates to the Volga river. Scandinavian adventurers had previously crossed the Baltic Sea and built trading posts southward along the rivers that reached down into Europe. Scandinavian merchants offered furs, which were exotic and luxurious to the Arabs, and they wanted gold and silver coins, which were scarce in their own lands.

4. Describe how peace with Charlemagne allowed the Arabs unhindered access to trade routes via water. In what way did peace and healthy trade with the Arabs benefit Charlemagne?

A4.—Pg. 397, ¶ 2—Because of the peace between Harun al-Rashid and Charlemagne, Arab ambassadors were able to take the sea route from the Mediterranean coast, south around Italy and up to the port city of Genoa, then north to Charlemagne's court at Aachen. Peace and healthy trade with the Arabs benefited Charlemagne because al-Rashid sent the king many gifts, including a water-driven clock, a chess set, spices, and an albino elephant named Abu'l-Abbas, which had been captured from an Indian king.

5. How did Harun al-Rashid keep his Abbasid empire safe during his reign?

A5.—Pg. 398, ¶ 2—Harun al-Rashid kept his empire safe by allying himself with the Chinese emperor Tang Shunzong, which kept the Tibetans in check and fortified the kingdom's eastern borders. On the other side of the empire he authorized ongoing raids into Byzantine land, which forced Nikephoros I to pay a yearly tribute of three hundred thousand dinars, which was about a ton and a quarter of gold.

6. What important declaration did al-Rashid make in 807 regarding Christian holy sites in Jerusalem? What is the significance of al-Rashid directing this declaration towards Charlemagne, and not the pope?

A6.—Pg. 398, ¶ 3 to Pg. 400, ¶ 2—In 807, al-Rashid made a decree that protected the Christian holy sites in Jerusalem, which was under Arab governance: Christian pilgrims would be allowed, without restriction, to visit the Church of the Holy Sepulchre (to which Charlemagne was given the key by the bishop of Jerusalem), Via Dolorosa, and the other landmarks of their faith. Directing the declaration towards Charlemagne instead of the pope reinforced Charlemagne's high place in the Christian hierarchy—al-Rashid even guaranteed special treatment of Frankish pilgrims.

7. Why did Nikephoros I declare war on the Bulgars? What happened when Nikephoros I finally got his troops on the road?

A7.—Pg. 400, ¶ 4–6—Nikephoros I declared war on the Bulgars because Krum was growing increasingly powerful, and the Byzantine king was threatened by Bulgarian southern territories that lay against his border. In 805, Krum invaded the territory of the Avars and folded it into his own, so Nikephoros I decided to declare war before Krum grew even stronger. When Nikephoros I finally got his troops on the road in 808, they were driven back by Krum's men in the Strymon river valley, a number of soldiers and officers were killed, and all the money Nikephoros I had sent along with the generals—eleven hundred pounds of gold—was captured.

8. What happened to Nikephoros I and his army in his second siege against Krum?

A8.—Pg. 400, ¶ 8 to Pg. 401, ¶ 3—When Nikephoros I set out for a second time against Krum, he decided he was going to wipe out the khan entirely, so he imported soldiers from Thracia and Asia Minor to beef up his forces. Nikephoros I and his troops were successful at first,

forcing Krum out of his headquarters at Pliska, slaughtering the population, taking the goods and burning everything down, but this success did not last long. On the journey home, Byzantine troops came across a wooden wall built by Krum's forces, on the other side of which was a ditch filled with burning logs; the Bulgarians attacked the trapped officers, Nikephoros I died fighting, and any man that managed to climb the wall fell into the burning pit.

9. Why wouldn't Michael Rangabe make a truce with Krum?

A9.—Pg. 401, ¶ 6—Michael Rangabe refused to make a truce with Krum because he believed Krum was a barbarian. Even though Krum was the second or third most powerful sovereign in Europe for a time, his skull-goblet represented a world of savagery. In Michael Rangabe's eyes, Krum was a khan, not a king; a wild man, not an equal; a barbarian, not the ruler of a western kingdom, and so he would not make a treaty with such a beast.

10. What were the terms of the treaty between Michael Rangabe and Charlemagne?

A10.—Pg. 402, ¶ 2—Though Michael Rangabe had to acknowledge Charlemagne's claim as emperor in order to secure an alliance with the Frankish king, the language of the treaty between the two men revealed Michael Rangabe's hesitancy. Michael Rangabe hailed Charlemagne as emperor of the Franks and praised him for the establishment of his Roman empire; but nowhere, at any time, did he call him emperor of the Romans. In exchange, Charlemagne agreed to stop contesting Byzantine possession of the Italian city of Venice and its port.

11. What happened to Michael Rangabe and his family after his failed 813 campaign against the Bulgarians?

A11.—Pg. 402, ¶ 5 & 6—After fleeing back to Constantinople from the front, Michael Rangabe abdicated because he was certain he would be assassinated if he remained on the throne. Michael Rangabe and his sons took refuge in a church and put on monks' clothes to demonstrate their willingness to give up power. This saved their lives but not their manhood; Leo V's first act was to castrate Michael's sons before sending them off into monastic exile, wiping out any chance that they might later claim the legitimate rule of Byzantium.

12. How did Krum react after Leo V failed to kill him under the flag of truce?

A12.—Pg. 403, ¶ 1–3—After Leo V's fake truce and failed assassination attempt, Krum ordered his army to sack the land around Constantinople before he retreated to recover from the attempt. On the way home, he burned a good part of Thracia and took scores of captives, whom he settled in Bulgaria as exiles and constant reminders of the Byzantine treachery. Once recovered, Krum began to plan a final assault on Constantinople, but he died in 814 while he was still preparing for the attack.

Section III: Critical Thinking

The student may use her text to answer this question.

The Abbasid caliph Harun al-Rashid did not expand the borders of his kingdom through conquest. Yet the reach of his empire penetrated several borders, and even transcended time. Explain how healthy trade routes allowed Harun al-Rashid's empire to grown in space and in time. In your answer, make sure to include the stories of the "OFFA REX" coin and the *Arabian Nights.*

Early in the chapter we learn that Harun al-Rashid was "more interested in trading than raiding." Al-Rashid moved his court from Baghdad to Ar Raqqah, closer to the northern trade routes leading into Khazar territory. The semi-peace with the Khazars meant that Arab merchants could travel north through the Caspian Gates to the Volga river, trading with the Khazars and also with Scandinavian merchants. Al-Rashid's attention to the trade routes gave him access to waterways without fear of attack, and it also meant that there was a healthy exchange between his empire and Charlemagne's court—Harun al-Rashid was even able to send Charlemagne an albino elephant named Abu'l-Abbas.

The story of the "OFFA REX" coin demonstrates how far al-Rashid's influence stretched without conquest. One of al-Rashid's merchants paid a gold dinar to a Scandinavian trader, who took the coin north to buy goods from an Anglo-Saxon merchant. The merchant then sailed home with the coin and landed at a port in the English kingdom of Mercia. As described in the chapter, "Once in Mercia, the merchant used the coin to buy a night's lodging from an innkeeper, who later that year used it to pay the king's tax collector. And so it came into the hands of Offa's silversmith, who was mulling over the designs for the next year's English coinage. He liked the pretty patterns on al-Rashid's gold dinar and decided to copy them." The result was that when the coins came out the following year, on one side of the coins was written "OFFA REX," for the English monarch. On the other side of the coin were the Arabic words for "There is no God but Allah, and Muhammad is his prophet." Not only were these words on the back, but they were also upside down. The silversmith, just thinking the pattern was pretty, had no idea what he had put on the coins. Harun al-Rashid's influence was now part of the everyday exchange of buyers and sellers in Christian Southeast England.

The story of Arabian Nights *is not so much about the reach of Harun al-Rashid's empire in space, but in time. Al-Rashid managed to get very rich because of his empire's thriving trade with far-flung lands, and also because he would confiscate the goods of his wealthy subjects when they died. His riches became legendary, becoming myth less than two generations after his death, and within a century taking shape as the* Arabian Nights. Arabian Nights is *a collection of stories about a thousand and one nights of thievery and heroism, the antics of courtesans and queens, and at the center of the tales is Harun al-Rashid and his court jester. Now famous,* Arabian Nights *shows us the reach of Harun al-Rashid's empire into other nations and future times.*

EXAMPLE ANSWER:

Harun al-Rashid's empire stretched out in space and time not through conquest, but through the successes of his kingdom's trade. With his court centered in Ar Raqqah, close to the northern trade routes leading into Khazar territory, and with a semi-peace with the Khazars enabling Arab merchants to trade with both the Khazars and Scandinavians,

Abbasid riches just grew and grew. Al-Rashid was also friendly with Charlemagne; one of the gifts al-Rashid sent the Frankish king was a war elephant named Abu'l-Abbas. Abbasid culture even shaped English culture because of the kingdom's thriving trade. One of al-Rashid's merchants paid a gold dinar to a Scandinavian trader, who took the coin north to buy goods from an Anglo-Saxon merchant. The merchant then used the coin to pay for lodging in Mercia, an English kingdom. The owner of the inn where the merchant stayed then used the coin to pay his taxes to Mercia's King Offa. From there the coin made its way to King Offa's silversmith, who was looking for new designs for English coins. Liking the designs on al-Rashid's coin, but having no idea that what was written on the coin actually meant "There is no God but Allah, and Muhammad is his prophet," the silversmith copied the pattern upside on the back of a coin that read "OFFA REX," or King Offa, on the front. Harun al-Rashid's influence was now part of the everyday exchange of buyers and sellers in Christian Southeast England.

Like the reach of Harun al-Rashid's currency, the stories of the Arabian nights extend al-Rashid's influence far from its point of origin. Al-Rashid managed to get very rich because of his empire's thriving trade with far-flung lands, and also because he would confiscate the goods of his wealthy subjects when they died. His riches became legendary, becoming myth less than two generations after his death, and within a century taking shape as the Arabian Nights. Arabian Nights is a collection of stories about a thousand and one nights of thievery and heroism, the antics of courtesans and queens, and at the center of the tales is Harun al-Rashid and his court jester. Now famous, Arabian Nights shows us the reach of Harun al-Rashid's empire into other nations and future times.

Section IV: Map Exercise

1. Using a black pencil, trace the rectangular outline of the frame for Map 52.1: Expansion of the First Bulgarian Empire.

2. Using a blue pencil, trace the coastline from the Baltic Sea down the Atlantic around Britain and into the Mediterranean. Include as usual the islands of Sardinia, Corsica, Sicily, Crete, and Cyprus, but you do not need to include any other islands at this time. Then draw the coastline of the Black Sea, the Azov Sea, the Caspian Sea, the Red Sea, and what is visible of the Persian Gulf on the far right of the map. Repeat until the contours are familiar.

3. Now try to find six contrasting colors to delineate the Empire of Charlemagne, the Papal States, Byzantium, Khazars, the First Bulgarian Empire, and the Abbasid Empire. Trace each with its respective color until the contours are familiar.

4. Using a new sheet of paper, trace the rectangular outline of the frame in black. Remove your tracing paper from the original. Using a regular pencil with an eraser as you look at Map 52.1, draw the coastline from the Baltic Sea around Britain and down the continent through the

Mediterranean, including the five major islands. Draw the Black Sea, the Azov Sea, the Caspian Sea, the Red Sea, and the Persian Gulf. Then draw the six different territories of the Empire of Charlemagne, the Papal States, Byzantium, Khazars, the First Bulgarian Empire, and the Abbasid Empire. Erase and redraw as necessary.

5. When you are pleased with your map, lay it over the original. Erase and redraw any lines which are more than ¼ inch off of the original.

6. Looking at your map, label the regions of Ifriqiya, Libya, Egypt, Syria, Armenia, Asia Minor, Khazars, Thracia, Macedonia, Pannonia, Scandinavian traders, Saxons, Austrasia, Burgundy, Neustria, Aquitaine, Asturias, Al-Andalus, and Mercia.

7. Study carefully the locations of Pliska and Serdica. When you are familiar with them, close the book. Using your regular pencil, label both cities. Check your map against the original, and correct if necessary.

8. Finally trace the lines of the Dniester, Prut, and Danube rivers. Label each.

Chapter Fifty-Three

Castle Lords and Regents

The student may use his text when answering the questions in sections I and II.

Section I: Who, What, Where

Write a one or two-sentence answer explaining the significance of each item listed below.

Aejang—**Pg. 406, ¶ 6 to Pg. 407, ¶ 1—Aejang, son of Soseong, became king of Silla before he was thirteen, meaning the power of the crown went to his uncle, who served as his regent. In 809, King Aejang was murdered by his uncle.**

Akira Keiko—**Pg. 411, ¶ 2—Akira Keiko, Montoku's primary consort, daughter of Fujiwara nobleman Fujiwara no Yoshifusa, was eventually married to Montoku and with the heavenly sovereign she gave birth to a son and heir to the throne.**

Chang Pogo—**Pg. 407, ¶ 3 to Pg. 408, ¶ 1—Chang Pogo, Heungdeok's young commander, received permission to establish a coastal garrison on the southwestern island of Wando, which both drove the pirates out of Silla's waters and also gave him the opportunity to grow powerful as the ruler of a little private kingdom of his own. Chang Pogo was assassinated in 846 by nobles fearing his power, after he suggested to King Munseong that the king marry his daughter.**

Fujiwara no Mototsune—**Pg. 411, ¶ 5—Fujiwara no Mototsune, the adopted son of Fujiwara no Yoshifusa, gained his father's office after his father's death. He convinced Seiwa to abdicate, and became Sessho for Yozei, the five-year-old Heavenly Sovereign.**

Fujiwara no Yoshifusa—**Pg. 411, ¶ 2—Fujiwara no Yoshifusa, an ambitious Fujiwara nobleman, engineered a marriage between his daughter and the heavenly sovereign Montoku, was then appointed Chief Minister in 857, and he moved up in stature again when he became his grandson Seiwa's regent.**

Heian Period—**Pg. 410, *—The Heian period in Japanese history was marked by the move of the capital from Nagaoka to Heian. The Nara period ended in 794, and the Heian period lasted until 1185.**

Heizei—**Pg. 410, ¶ 2 & *—Heizei, one of Kammu's thirty-two children, succeeded his father as Heavenly Sovereign, but only ruled for three years before growing sick and abdicating in favor of his brother Saga. When Heizei recovered he attempted to get the throne back but failed; his accomplices were arrested or committed suicide, and Heizei was forced to enter a Buddhist monastery, where he remained until his death.**

Heondeok—**Pg. 407, ¶ 1–3—Heondeok was the name Aejang's uncle took when he murdered his nephew and became king. The mandate of the monarch lost power during Heondeok's reign, and by the time he died in 826, bone rank was becoming second to the size of one's private army.**

Heungdeok—**Pg. 407, ¶ 3—Heungdeok, Heondeok's brother and successor, struggled to keep control of the Sillan countryside, where lawlessness reigned because the king's forces had moved inwards towards the capital and pirates from China blocked trade routes and kidnapped Sillans to sell them as slaves.**

Kammu—**Pg. 409, ¶ 1, 3 & 5—Kammu, Japan's heavenly sovereign, broke with tradition and moved the capital from Nara to Nagaoka in large part to get away from the power of the Fujiwara clan. Kammu did not escape the Fujiwara in Nagaoka, nor did he have a successful time in his new capital city, so he moved the capital a second time to Yamashiro-no-kuni, renaming the city Heian-kyo meaning "Capital of Peace."**

Junna—**Pg. 410, ¶ 2—Junna, one of Kammu's thirty-two children, became Heavenly Sovereign after his brother Saga abdicated in his favor. He reigned for ten years before handing the crown to his nephew Ninmyo, Saga's twenty-three-year-old son, in 833.**

Kim Ujing—**Pg. 408, ¶ 2—Kim Ujing, Chang Pogo's ally, was installed by the commander as the king of Silla, usurping the throne from Heungdeok's successor. Kim Ujing took the name King Sinmu when he became king, but his reign only lasted four months because he died from an illness.**

Montoku—**Pg. 410, ¶ 5 to Pg. 411, ¶ 2—Montoku, Ninmyo's half-Fujiwara son, became Heavenly Sovereign at twenty-three, and with little to do because of his lack of power, he spent most of his time fathering children: by his early thirties he had twenty-seven offspring. Montoku died at thirty-two, leaving his son with Akira Keiko, Seiwa, as his heir.**

Munseong—**Pg. 408, ¶ 3—Munseong, Kim Ujing's son, followed his father as king of Silla, but unlike his father, he managed to reign for almost two decades. Munseong was able to rule for so long because Sillan nobility started to create their own little kingdoms, which greatly diminished the power of the king.**

Ninmyo—**Pg. 410, ¶ 2 & 4—Ninmyo, Saga's son, became Heavenly Sovereign in 833 when his uncle Junna abdicated in his favor, and he later abdicated in favor of his half-Fujiwara son, Montoku. During Ninmyo's reign, Fujiwara power grew as did great poverty throughout the countryside.**

Saga—**Pg. 410, ¶ 2—Saga, one of Kammu's thirty-two children, became Heavenly Sovereign after his brother Heizei abdicated in his favor. After fourteen years Saga abdicated in favor of his brother Junna.**

Seiwa—**Pg. 411, ¶ 2 & 5—Seiwa, son of Montoku and Akira Keiko, became heavenly sovereign when he was eight years old, and his grandfather Fujiwara no Yoshifusa acted as his Sessho, or regent. After Yoshifusa's death, Seiwa's new regent, Fujiwara no Mototsune convinced the heavenly sovereign to abdicate at twenty-six in favor of the heir-apparent, Seiwa's five-year-old son Yozei.**

Seol Chong—**Pg. 406, ¶ 4 & 5—Seol Chong, a Confucian monk, was famous for his ability to take Chinese classics and transcribe them into the language spoken by the people. Because the language of Silla had no writing system of its own, Seol Chong was forced to invent a new system that used Chinese characters to represent Sillan words; the match between characters was not perfect, and it left thousands of Sillan words with no text equivalent, but Seol Chong's system survived for seven hundred years and was a first step in separating Korean culture from Chinese culture.**

Soseong—**Pg. 406, ¶ 6—Soseong, King Wonseong's grandson and successor, ruled for only two years before he died.**

Takaiko—**Pg. 411, ¶ 4—Takaiko, Fujiwara no Yoshifusa's niece, was married to Seiwa in an arranged union. She had a lover of her own, but he was exiled from court and forced into a monastery; they did not see each other again until her lover had grown old and feeble.**

Wonseong—**Pg. 406, ¶ 2, 3 & 6—Wonseong, king of Silla, True Bone by birth but given his royal power because he was the successor to his royal cousin Seondeok, worked to break down bone rank by instituting a new state examination system. Wonseong's reforms were unpopular with the True Bone aristocrats, and as a result the minister of state led a resistance against Wonseong's efforts.**

Yozei—**Pg. 411, ¶ 5—Yozei, son of Seiwa, became the heavenly sovereign at five years old, with Fujiwara no Mototsune ruling as his Sessho.**

Section II: Comprehension

Write a two or three-sentence answer to each of the following questions.

1. In eighth century Sillan culture, what did "bone rank" mean? What were the various ranks within bone rank, and what rank was currently in power?

A1.—Pg. 405, ¶ 2 & 3—In eighth century Sillan culture, power was based on bone rank, which was another term for bloodline, and only people with bone rank could be privileged or employed. An aristocrat whose parents were both of royal descent was of "Hallowed Bone" status; if only one parent was royal, the child was "True Bone;" "head ranks" were held by

nobles, with the privilege level dependent upon the purity of their family descent. Until the middle of the seventh century, only Hallowed Bone aristocrats had ruled in Silla, but after the time of King Muyeol the Great, True Bone aristocrats had held the Sillan throne.

2. Why was one able to move up in status in Chinese society, but not in eighth century Sillan society?

A2.—Pg. 405, ¶ 4 to Pg. 406, ¶ 1—In eighth century China, Confucian academies allowed diligent students to work their way up through the ranks by demonstrating virtue and mastery of the orderly rituals that gave Confucian society its framework. However, in eighth century Silla, the bone rank system meant that there was no social mobility, no hope for capable commoners, with power only in the hands of the aristocrats.

3. What did candidates have to do in order to pass King Wonseong's new examinations? What did King Wonseong want the candidates to prove during these examinations?

A3.—Pg. 406, ¶ 3—In order to pass King Wonseong's new examination, candidates would have to show understanding of the Chinese texts and principles taught in the National Confucian Academy, which had been founded in Goguryeo in the fourth century. King Wonseong built his new examination system based on Confucian teachings of virtue and intelligence, which he wanted future Sillan leaders to prove they had.

4. When did Silla's Late Period start? What was the defining characteristic of the Late Period? Use the beginning of King Heondeok's reign as an example.

A4.—Pg. 406, ¶ 7 to Pg. 407, ¶ 1—The Late Period in Unified Silla's history began around the time Aejang came to power. The Late Period was defined by frequent and violent turnovers between leaders, beginning with King Aejang's murder in 809 by his uncle, who took the throne as King Heondeok. The characteristics of the Late Period could be seen not just in the way King Heondeok took the throne, but also in the resistance to his rule: immediately Heondeok had to put down two subsequent rebellions caused by descendants of King Muyol that claimed they had the right to rule.

5. In the Late Period turmoil in Silla, how was it that Munseong was able to hold onto the throne for almost two decades?

A5.—Pg. 408, ¶ 3—Munseong was able to hold on to the Sillan throne for almost two decades in large part because the Sillan nobility and their private armies were beginning to work out a satisfactory division of power, and that division of power rendered the king increasingly irrelevant. Rather than fighting for control of the capital city and the crown, they turned outwards and built themselves little private enclaves in outlying areas, where they reigned supreme. From their personal kingdoms, they traded with the merchants of Tang China and with Japan, building their wealth as well as their power.

6. Describe the state of Silla after the death of Chang Pogo. What were "castle lords," who was managing the Buddhist monasteries, and what did farmers and tradesmen do for protection?

A6.—Pg. 408, ¶ 5—At the time of Chang Pogo's death, the most powerful aristocrats with the largest private armies erected fortresses at the center of their domains; they were called "castle lords" and exercised the right to collect taxes for themselves, without passing any of the money on to the government in Kyongju. Buddhist monasteries were no longer managed

by the weak king, collecting land and tax revenues on their own account. Farmers and tradesmen, with no armies and no protection from the king, increasingly began to turn outlaw, like the robbers that roamed through Silla's hills.

7. Why was the Fujiwara clan such a threat to Kammu?

A7.—Pg. 409, ¶ 3—The Fujiwara clan was a threat to Kammu because they had become more powerful than all of the other aristocratic clans in Japan. The Fujiwara clan had inherited from Nakatomi no Kamatari the privilege of overseeing court rites and rituals, a responsibility that gave Fujiwara officials control over the center of the palace. By the beginning of Kammu's rule, there were no fewer than four major branches of the family living in and around the capital city.

8. Describe Kammu's move to Nagaoka. Was the move successful in distancing the Heavenly Sovereign from the Fujiwara?

A8.—Pg. 409, ¶ 4—Kammu's move to Nagaoka was fast and desperate; three hundred thousand men, working around the clock, built an entire royal complex in less than six months. Even though he moved, Fujiwara power followed him via his chief consort, the daughter of a Fujiwara nobleman. Also, the posts of "Great Minister of the Right" and "Great Minister of the East" were held by Fujiwaras and he was forced to appoint a Fujiwara official as overseer of his new capital city.

9. Why did Kammu move the capital a second time? Where was the new capital city, and what was it renamed?

A8.—Pg. 409, ¶ 5—While in Nagaoka, Kammu was plagued by bad luck, illness, death in his family, and bloody infighting among his court officials. In 794 he had decided that a curse hung over the city. He moved the capital a second time to the city of Yamashiro-no-kuni and he ordered it renamed Heian-kyo which meant "Capital of Peace."

10. How did the two moves of the capital and the corrupt tax practices of the Fujiwara affect the peasants who lived along the Kamo river?

A10.—Pg. 410, ¶ 4—The farmers and small tradesmen of Japan were financially strained because each change of Kammu's capital cities required a raise in taxes to pay for the new construction, and the farmers were preoccupied with building these new residences instead of tending to their own land. In addition, Fujiwara officials raised taxes so they could take more money for themselves, which left the Japanese poor even more destitute. The peasants who lived along the Kamo river were so poor that they could not afford tombs or deep graves for their dead; instead they scratched holes in the sand for the bodies, and as the river wore the sand away, the bones were flung up onto the shore.

Section III: Critical Thinking

The student may not use his text to answer this question.

In this chapter we learned that by the middle of the 9th century, United Silla was not united at all. Power had moved away from the king to nobles that ruled over small enclaves, creating their own mini-kingdoms, and the Buddhist monasteries took government accounting into their own hands, collecting land and revenues taxes for themselves. The shift away from a concentrated center of power in United Silla was mirrored in Japan. Explain the dimming light of the polestar, and connect it to the shifts in power in United Silla.

The student should notice how this chapter is about the loss of centralized power in both United Silla and Japan. Just as Munseong was "on the throne but not in control," the heavenly sovereign's connection with the divine and his role as the guarantor of order and law was "rapidly becoming symbolic." Like the bone-ranked nobles of United Silla, clan leaders in Japan created their own pockets of power through the countryside. Taking advantage of the heavenly sovereign's weakness, both Buddhist monasteries and wealthy aristocrats were lending money to the poor and then claiming the land of those who could not pay back the money that was borrowed.

The series of abdications following Kammu's reign shows us that the heavenly sovereign's power was weak, and he no longer had the ability to protect his people. Fujiwara officials had taken over, running the court and its rituals. Fujiwara governors controlled provinces father away from the city. Like the corruption of taxes by the aristocrats and monasteries in United Silla, Fujiwara governors collected taxes that were quite often used for their own purposes rather than passing them on to the capital. Because the heavenly sovereign exercised no real power, he could not protect his people from the unjust practices of these noblemen.

By the time of Seiwa's rule, the polestar was only a symbol. An outsider, someone not from the royal line, ruled as his regent. The royal line and the Fujiwara clan had become so intertwined that the idea of a separate royal line was just as symbolic as the idea of the heavenly sovereign. Seiwa might have been the polestar, but his Sessho Fujiwara no Yoshifusa had all the power. This mirrored the position of the Sillan king and his relationship to the Sillan castle lords. The lack of the polestar's power was further magnified when Fujiwara no Yoshifusa's son, Fujiwara no Mototsune, convinced Seiwa to abdicate in favor of his five-year-old son, Yozei. As written in the last paragraph in the chapter, "to abdicate *in favor of a child shows one thing clearly: the heavenly sovereign no longer needed to rule. The Sessho, refracting his glory, would rule for him. The sovereign himself needed merely to exist: a necessary, but passive, node of connection with the divine order." In both United Silla and Japan, the ruler had become a symbol: he may have sat on a throne, but the power of rule was located elsewhere.*

EXAMPLE ANSWER:

Kammu may have moved his capital from Nara, to Nagaoka, to Heian-kyo, but he could not outrun his fading power. Like the bone-ranked nobles of United Silla, clan leaders in Japan created their own pockets of power through the countryside. Taking advantage of the heavenly sovereign's weakness, both Buddhist monasteries and wealthy aristocrats were lending money to the poor and then claiming the land of those who could not pay back the money that was borrowed. After Kammu's death, a series of abdications followed, meaning

the heavenly sovereign was weak. Fujiwara officials had taken over, running the court and its rituals. Fujiwara governors controlled provinces father away from the city. Like the corruption of taxes by the aristocrats and monasteries in United Silla, Fujiwara governors collected taxes that were quite often used for their own purposes rather than passing them on to the capital. Because the heavenly sovereign exercised no real power, he could not protect his people from the unjust practices of these noblemen.

By the time of Seiwa's rule, the polestar was only a symbol. An outsider, someone not from the royal line, ruled as his regent. The royal line and the Fujiwara clan had become so intertwined that the idea of a separate royal line was just as symbolic as the idea of the heavenly sovereign. Seiwa might have been the polestar, but his Sessho Fujiwara no Yoshifusa had all the power. This mirrored the position of the Sillan king and his relationship to the Sillan castle lords. The lack of the polestar's power was further magnified when Fujiwara no Yoshifusa's son, Fujiwara no Mototsune, convinced Seiwa to abdicate in favor of his five-year-old son, Yozei. Abdicating in favor of a child showed that they heavenly sovereign no longer needed to rule. In both United Silla and Japan, the ruler had become a symbol: he may have sat on a throne, but the power of rule was located elsewhere.

Section IV: Map Exercise

1. Using a black pencil, trace the rectangular outline of the frame for Map 53.1: Unified Silla and Japan.

2. Using a blue pencil, trace the coastal outline around the Yellow Sea and up and around Japan. You do not need to include any islands at this time other than the main islands of Japan, but do include the Inland Sea. Then trace the line of the Yellow River. Repeat until the contours are familiar.

3. Using four contrasting colors, trace the perimeters of the regions of Unified Silla, Japan, Balhae, and Tang. Repeat until the contours are familiar.

4. Using a new sheet of paper, trace the rectangular outline of the frame in black. Remove your tracing paper from the original. Using a regular pencil with an eraser, draw the coastline, including the Inland Sea, and the Yellow River. Then draw the outlines of the four regions. Erase and redraw as necessary.

5. When you are pleased with your map, lay it over the original. Erase and redraw any lines which are more than ¼ inch off of the original.

6. Remove your map. Study carefully the locations of Ch'ungju, Kyongju, Wando, Hokkaido, and Kyushu. When you are familiar with them, close the book. Using your regular pencil, label each location. Check your map against the original. Correct any misplaced labels.

7. Draw the line of the Great Wall. Draw the arrows showing the Khitan.

Chapter Fifty-Four

The Triumph of the Outsiders

The student may use her text when answering the questions in sections I and II.

Section I: Who, What, Where

Write a one or two-sentence answer explaining the significance of each item listed below.

Abaoji—**Pg. 418, ¶ 4—Abaoji was a northern Khitan warchief that made an alliance with the Shatuo and began a series of conquests that would eventually create an enormous Khitan realm.**

Ch'oe Chi'won—**Pg. 419, ¶ 4 & 5 and Pg. 420, ¶ 5—Ch'oe Chi'won applied for a post in Heonggang's government in 885 but he was not given the position because his ideas about reform did not fit with the king's decadence. After attempting to help Queen Jinseong reform her government and being rejected once again, Ch'oe Chi'won left the Sillan government for monastic life.**

Fanzhen—**Pg. 413, ¶ 2—*Fanzhen* was the Chinese name for the military governors appointed over time by earlier emperors. The *fanzhen*, made up of military commanders of Chinese ancestry, and some leaders of "barbarian" descent, were supposed to manage the outlying Tang provinces in the name of the emperor.**

Gyeongmun—**Pg. 418, ¶ 6 to Pg. 419, ¶ 2—Gyeongmun, king of Unified Silla, married a noblewoman that couldn't have children, then married her sister, who also couldn't have children, and when he finally did sire an heir the sisters murdered his mother and attempted to murder the baby. Later, Gyeongmun had a child with another concubine, protected him, named him crown prince, and sent him to China to learn the principles of Confucian government.**

Heonggang—**Pg. 419, ¶ 2 & 3—Heonggang, Gyeongmun's son, was sent to China to learn the principles of Confucian government and when he returned to Silla he became King**

Heonggang after his father's death. Heonggang spent his rule ignoring Silla's problems and spending money, which made it look to outsiders like the country was doing well.

Huang Chao—**Pg. 415, ¶ 3, 4 & 7 and Pg. 416, ¶ 4—Huang Chao was a young man that did not pass China's civil service examination, got mad, and started a rebellion by selling salt illegally in the northeast of China. When Huang Chao's rebellion reached Chang'an, he declared himself king of a new dynasty, but his reign did not last long: Tang Xizong fought back with the help of the Shatuo and after being defeated at the bank of the Yellow river, Huang Chao committed suicide.**

Hyogong—**Pg. 420, ¶ 6 to Pg. 421, ¶ 1 & 5—Hyogong, a boy that courtiers claimed was a son of Heonggang, became King Hyogong in 897 at fourteen when Queen Jinseong was forced to abdicate in his favor. After the days of United Silla ended, Hyogong took comfort in alcohol.**

Jinseong—**Pg. 419, ¶ 7 and Pg. 420, ¶ 6—Jinseong, sister of Heonggang, became Queen Jinseong in 887 and in many ways her sexuality was blamed for the collapse of Silla rather than the real reason for its demise: corrupt castle lords. Queen Jinseong was forced to give up her throne after rebellion broke out because of raised taxes, and as Kyonhwon, Yanggil and Kungye gained power.**

Kungye—**Pg. 418, ¶ 7 to Pg. 419, ¶ 1, Pg. 420, ¶ 3, Pg. 421, ¶ 3—Kungye, the son of Heonggang that escaped an attempt on his life but lost an eye in the process, was the rebel leader Yanggil's second in command. Kungye murdered Yanggil and then proclaimed himself king in the old lands of Goguryeo and named his kingdom Later Goguryeo.**

Kyonhwon—**Pg. 420, ¶ 1 & 2 and Pg. 421, ¶ 3—Kyonhwon, farmer-turned-soldier rebel leader of an army in the southwest of China, was given the title "Duke of the Southwest" by Queen Jinseong after he emerged as the strongest of leaders in the rebellions caused by her tax hike. By 900, Kyonhwon proclaimed himself king in the old lands of Baekje, so he named his new state Later Baekje.**

Later Three Kingdoms—**Pg. 421, ¶ 3 & 4—Later Three Kingdoms was the name of the period in Korean history that started after the fall of United Silla, and it corresponded to the three kingdoms that occupied the peninsula: Silla, Later Baekje and Later Goguryeo. The period began with war and famine.**

Li Keyong—**Pg. 416, ¶ 2, 5 & 6 and Pg. 417, ¶ 1—Li Keyong, a Turk from the Shatuo tribe, helped Tang Xizong put down Huang Chao's rebellion and was rewarded by being made military governor of most of the north. Le Keyong grew his military governorship into a minor kingship where he installed his own Shatuo allies in official positions and no longer acknowledged the rule of the Tang emperor.**

Muzong—**Pg. 414, ¶ 1—Muzong, Tang Xianzong's son and heir, was rumored to have had a hand in his father's sudden death. As emperor, Muzong preferred banquets and ball games to war, and he left his father's conquests of the *fanzhen* slip away.**

Shatuo—**Pg. 413, ¶ 3 and Pg. 415, ¶ 8—Shatuo was the name of a Turkish tribe taken in by the Tang. The Shatuo, who were interested in transforming themselves from Turkish to Chinese, remained loyal to the emperor and helped Tang Xizong defeat the rebel Huang Chao.**

Tang Aidi—**Pg. 418, ¶ 1–3—Tang Aidi, Tang Zhaozong's son, was made Zhu Wen's puppet-king at the age of thirteen. Tang Aidi was forced by Zhu Wen to decree the murder of his nine remaining brothers and all the ministers who were still loyal to the royal family. He was then forced to abdicate when he was sixteen and then he was murdered by Zhu Wen the following year.**

Tang Jingzong—**Pg. 414, ¶ 1 & 2—Tang Jingzong, son of Muzong, preferred partying to politics and left the running of his palace to the court eunuchs. The same court eunuchs that Jingzong trusted to run his state had the emperor murdered when he was eighteen, not even three years into his rule.**

Tang Wenzong—**Pg. 414, ¶ 2 & 3—Tang Wenzong, Jingzong's younger brother, was put on the throne as a puppet emperor by the court eunuchs after they murdered his brother. Tang Wenzong remained alive and on the throne for fourteen years because he was willing to relinquish his power to the *fanzhen* and the officials in his palace.**

Tang Xianzong—**Pg. 413, ¶ 4 to Pg. 414, ¶ 1—Tang Xianzong sought to bring order to his empire through a series of wars between 806 and 817 that brought the *fanzhen* back into his imperial fold. By 820 Tang Xianzong was close to restoring the emperor's control over old Tang land, but he died unexpectedly, supposedly poisoned by two court eunuchs on behalf of his son and heir Muzong, before unity was achieved.**

Tang Xizong—**Pg. 415, ¶ 7 and Pg. 416, ¶ 5—Tang Xizong, Tang Yizong's successor, fled from Chang'an to Chengdu and managed to defeat Huang Chao with the help of Li Keyong and Zhu Wen. Though Tang Xizong kept his title, his kingdom was destroyed, and his power was gone.**

Tang Zhaozong—**Pg. 416, ¶ 6 and Pg. 417, ¶ 4—Tang Zhaozong, son of Tang Xizong, came to the throne in 888. After giving Zhu Wen a royal title, Tang Zhaozong was isolated from his supporters by the general, and he was ultimately murdered by Zhu Wen's men.**

Wang Kon—**Pg. 421, ¶ 4 & 6—Wang Kon, a competent naval officer who fought in the forces of Kungye, was elevated to the kingship of Later Goguryeo after Kungye's murder.**

Yanggil—**Pg. 420, ¶ 1 & 3 and Pg. 421, ¶ 2—Yanggil, a robber leader that led the resistance against Queen Jinseong in the northeast with Kungye as his second-in-command, made a deal with the "Duke of the Southwest" that put him and Kungye in charge of an area in the north of China. Yanggil met his end when he was murdered by the vengeful Kungye.**

Zhu Wen—**Pg. 416, ¶ 3, Pg. 417, ¶ 3 & 4 and Pg. 418, ¶ 2—Zhu Wen, a former ally of Huang Chao, helped Tang Xizong and Li Keyong defeat Huang Chao. After manipulating his way**

into a royal title, murdering Tang Zhaozong, putting the young Tang Aidi onto the throne and then forcing him to abdicate and then murdering him, Zhu Wen declared himself the head of the new Later Liang dynasty.

Section II: Comprehension

Write a two or three-sentence answer to each of the following questions.

1. Despite a healthy salt trade and an effective system of tax collection, why was Tang rule still shaky after the An Lushan rebellion?

A1.—Pg. 413, ¶ 2 & 3—Though thriving salt trade and effective tax collection were filling the royal treasury, the outlying provinces ruled by the *fanzhen* were out of the emperor's control because the *fanzhen* had turned into mini-monarchs controlling their own lands. The loyalty of the *fanzhen* to the Tang varied widely, making the borders of the Tan empire indistinct; the farther from Chang'an a traveller got, the harder it was to figure out if he was still in Tang land.

2. Who really ran China during the reign of Tang Wenzong? What stroke of luck kept China prosperous?

A2.—Pg. 414, ¶ 3 to Pg. 415, ¶ 1—Though Tang Wenzong was emperor, China was actually run by *fanzhen* and court officials that were efficient and supported a thriving economy. The reason this was possible was that, by chance, there were no invasions or wars threatening China. With no military conflict to worry about, the eunuchs running the empire could focus on trade, the salt monopoly, careful tax collection and on literary pursuits.

3. Why was Huang Chao so upset after he took the civil service examination in 874? How did he make up for his failure?

A3.—Pg. 415, ¶ 3 & 4—Huang Chao was known for his intelligence and literary ability, so when he found out he failed his civil service examination he was furious; he proclaimed that the exam system was exclusionary, used by the government to block the unwanted from official positions. He then turned outlaw, breaking the government monopoly by selling salt illegally in the northeast of China, near the coast and just south of the Yellow river. He was soon joined by other people unhappy with Chinese government and they turned into a band of smugglers that would rob rich merchants on the nearby roads, raid wealthy towns, and attack and kill foreign traders along the coast.

4. What happened when Tang troops were dispatched from Chang'an to put down Huang Chao and his gang?

A4—Pg. 415, ¶ 5 & 6—When Tang troops were finally dispatched from Chang'an to arrest Huang Chao and his gang, the troublemakers fought back, with more and more farmers and

peasants joining the cause. The group soon had over half a million followers, turning the fight into a full-fledged rebellion that would last for four years.

5. How were Tang Xizong, Li Keyong and Zhu Wen able to defeat Huang Chao and his rebel army?

A5.—Pg. 416, ¶ 2–4—Li Keyong led forty thousand horsemen to Chang'an, which had been captured by Huang Chao, and helped Tang Xizong lay siege to the city. In 882, outside Chang'an's walls, the Tang army and the Turkish mercenaries defeated an enormous rebel army commanded by Huang Chao at the Battle of Liangtianpo. Huang Chao was driven northwards towards the territory of the Shatuo, and there Zhu Wen helped the royal army defeat Huang Chao on the banks of the Yellow River in 884.

6. Using the words of poet Wei Zhuang, describe the state of Chang'an after the fighting between Huang Chao and Tang Xizong.

Note to the parent: The student may use any part of the poet's words that appear on page 416, ¶ 5. The lines found in the text are "Chang'an lies in mournful stillness: what does it now contain? / Ruined markets and desolate streets, in which ears of wheat are sprouting. / Fuel-gatherers have hacked down every flowering plant in the Apricot Gardens, /
Builders of barricades have destroyed the willows along the Imperial Canal. . . .
/ All the pomp and magnificence of the olden days are buried and passed away; /
Only a dreary waste meets the eye. . . .
/ All along the Street of Heaven one treads on the bones of State officials."

A6.—Pg. 416, ¶ 5—Chang'an was destroyed because of the fighting between Huang Chao's rebel army and the royal army. As Wei Zhuang described, the city was in "mournful stillness," with "ruined markets and desolate streets" covered in the "bones of State officials." The city was no longer glorious, as Zhuang writes, "All the pomp and magnificence of the olden days are buried and passed away."

7. Explain how both Li Keyong and Zhu Wen gained more power in the years after putting down Huang Chao's rebellion through the time of Tang Zhaozong's death.

A7.—Pg. 416, ¶ 5 to Pg. 418, ¶ 1—After Huang Chao's rebellion, Li Keyong was made military governor of most of the north by Tang Xizong, and then during the reign of Tan Zhaozong, Li Keyong extended his military governorship of the north into a minor kingship. Though he had slowly been taking more and more land for himself between Chang'an and the borders of Li Keyong's province, Zhu Wen was not satisfied and managed to convince Tang Zhaozong to give him a royal title. After being given this title, Zhu Wen started a campaign against the emperor. He had Tang Zhaozong murdered while proclaiming his loyalty, and then finally installed Tang Zhaozong's thirteen-year-old son Tang Aidi as his puppet-king.

8. What period did the abdication of the last Tang emperor mark in Chinese history? Why was the period given this name?

A8.—Pg. 418, ¶ 3—When the last Tang emperor abdicated the Later Liang was formed, and the period in Chinese history known as the Five Dynasties and Ten Kingdoms started. The

fifty year period was given this name because it was a time of struggle between the *fanzhen* that were creating and then losing a slew of minor kingdoms. Five ruling dynasties rose and fell in the north and more than ten separate kingdoms appeared and disappeared in the south.

9. Why did King Gyeongmun's two queens want to murder Kungye and his mother? Were they successful?

A9.—Pg. 418, ¶ 7 to Pg. 419, ¶ 1—King Gyeongmun's two queens wanted to murder Kungye and his mother because they were resentful of the woman's ability to bear a child, and fearful of that child's role as heir to the throne. While the women were able to murder the concubine that produced Kungye, they were not successful in killing the child. Saved by his wet-nurse and given refuge at a monastery, Kungye grew up safely but constantly reminded of the treachery because he had lost an eye in the assassination attempt.

10. What kinds of things did Heonggang do during his reign to make it seem like all was well in Silla? What was the reality of the state of Silla outside of the capital city?

A10.—Pg. 419, ¶ 3—During his reign, Heonggang spent money like water in order to show the public that all was well in Silla. He also made sure his capital city looked beautiful and rich, putting a tile roof on every house and making sure that instead of firewood people burned charcoal so that the skies would remain clear. However, outside of the capital city, Silla was in disarray: the countryside seethed with thieves and bandits, private armies and ambitious warlords.

11. How was Queen Jinseong described in contemporary accounts of her rule? Why was she described in this way?

A11.—Pg. 419, ¶ 7—Queen Jinseong is described negatively in contemporary accounts of her rule. One account calls her build "manly" while another accuses her of bringing "pretty young men" to court and installing them in paper positions. She was described this way because she was a woman and her kingdom was falling apart; instead of blaming the corrupt castle lords that continued to shake down the peasants and farmers, the accounts make it seem like the problems were caused because a female was on the throne.

12. In what way did Queen Jinseong's crackdown on taxpayers to fund her government backfire?

A12.—Pg. 419, ¶ 8 to Pg. 420, ¶ 1—Queen Jinseong's crackdown on taxpayers backfired because farmers and craftsmen had been paying taxes, but the funds weren't reaching the capital; they were going into the pockets of the castle lords. Forced to pay double taxes—to the castle lords and to the queen—men were driven into banditry, and the bandits then organized themselves into small and powerful anti-government armies under capable rebel leaders. Queen Jinseong wanted to fund her government, but she ended up starting a massive rebellion.

13. What happened to Kungye after he formed Later Goguryeo?

A13.—Pg. 421, ¶ 5 & 6—After Kungye formed Later Goguryeo, he continued to work on completely destroying the remnants of Silla, spending the first years as king pushing deeper and deeper into Sillan territory. Kungye's resentment made him crazy and when he was not fighting he was riding a white horse around his kingdom in a purple robe and gold crown, with a choir of two hundred monks following behind to sing his praises. He became even more cruel, paranoid and tyrannical, ordering his wife and sons put to death for treachery, heavily taxing the people and spending money to make his palace grand; in 918, fed up with his treachery, Kungye's own officers murdered him.

Section III: Critical Thinking

The student may use her text to answer this question.

This chapter is full of usurpation and murder, a reflection of the chaotic leadership in 9th century China and Korea. The Confucian scholar-poet Ch'oe Chi'won was so distraught by the turmoil that he decided to trade in doomed palace life for the monastery. Using what you learned about Ch'oe Chi'won's life, and some of the words from the verse below, explain why Ch'oe Chi'won decided to leave politics to practice a life of peace.

> The frenzied rush through the rocks roars at the peaks,
> and drowns out the human voices close by.
>
> Because I always fear disputes between right and wrong
> I have arranged the waters to cage in these mountains.

After the long list of names in "Who, What, Where," and the questions about the numerous turns in Chinese and Korean 9th century power, this "Critical Thinking" question should serve as a little break for the student. On page 419, ¶ 4, we learn that Ch'oe Chi'won, son of a Sillan aristocrat, had spent his school years in Tang China where he absorbed the principles of Confucian government. He passed the civil service exam in China on his first try and was appointed "Chief of Personnel" for a Tang province. When Tang China began to spin into chaos, Ch'oe Chi'won decided to return home to Silla. In 885, Ch'oe Chi'won applied for a post in Heonggang's government. He wanted to reform Silla before it collapsed like Tang China. However, Heonggang, as the Samguk sagi says, lived in "decadent times." Ch'oe Chi'won's conservative views caused him to be looked at as an "object of suspicion and envy" and so he did not receive a post in Heonggang's government.

When Queen Jinseong was on the throne, Ch'oe Chi'won tried again to bring stability to Silla. He submitted a ten-point proposal for reform meant to steady Sillan government. But again, he was rejected. He would not try a third time. We learn on page 420, ¶ 5 that "Ch'oe Chi'won left the doomed palace and retreated to a distant mountain monastery, where he devoted himself instead to the pursuits of the spirit and the composition of mournful lyrics in Chinese." The lyrics presented above are reprinted from the chapter. The student may use the lyrics in any way she desires as long as she presents the verse in support of Ch'oe Chi'won's frustration, and his decision to isolate himself from Sillan politics.

EXAMPLE ANSWER:

Ch'oe Chi'won had a knack for the principles of Confucian government. He passed the civil service exam in China on his first try and was appointed "Chief of Personnel" for a Tang province. When Tang China began to spin into chaos, Ch'oe Chi'won decided to return home to Silla. In 885, Ch'oe Chi'won applied for a post in Heonggang's government. He wanted to reform Silla before it collapsed like Tang China. Unfortunately, Heonggang and his court were more interested in decadence than reform, so Ch'oe Chi'won was not given the position. Later, when Queen Jinseong was on the throne, Ch'oe Chi'won tried again to bring stability to Silla. He submitted a ten-point proposal for reform meant to steady Sillan government. But once more, he was rejected. He would not try a third time. Retreating to a mountain monastery, Ch'oe Chi'won devoted himself to the pursuits of the spirit and the composition of mournful lyrics. For example in one verse he writes, "The frenzied rush through the rocks roars at the peaks, and drowns out the human voices close by." The mountains gave Ch'oe Chi'won the distance he needed from the noise and chaos of the Sillan court. He continues, "Because I always fear disputes between right and wrong I have arranged the waters to cage in these mountains." Not wanting to continue to fight for the "right" way to run a country, Ch'oe Chi'won found solace and protection in the mountains.

Chapter Fifty-Five

The Third Dynasty

The student may use his text when answering the questions in sections I and II.

Section I: Who, What, Where

Write a one or two-sentence answer explaining the significance of each item listed below.

Al-Amin—**Pg. 423, ¶ 2–4 and Pg. 425, ¶ 1—Al-Amin, al-Rashid's oldest son, was deemed his father's successor as caliph but he had to fight his brother al-Mamun who would not give up what he thought was his right to the throne. Al-Mamun ended up winning, which resulted in al-Amin's capture and decapitation.**

Al-Mamun—**Pg. 423, ¶ 2 and Pg. 425, ¶ 5—Al-Mamun, al Rashid's younger son with a concubine, was made governor of Khorasan by his father, and he was also named as the heir to the caliphate. Al-Mamun fought in a civil war with his brother and won, holding on to the caliphate until he died in 833 from typhoid.**

Al-Mutasim—**Pg. 425, ¶ 5—Al-Mutasim was al-Mamun's half-brother and his successor as caliph of the Abbasid empire.**

Tahir—**Pg. 424, ¶ 1 and Pg. 425, ¶ 2 & 3—Tahir, al-Mamun's chief general, was given governorship of Khorasan after al-Mamun defeated his brother, and from this position Tahir declared his own independence. Before he could go to war against al-Mamun, Tahir died.**

Talhah—**Pg. 425, ¶ 4 & 5—Talhah, son of Tahir, took up his father's quest for independence and declared himself ruler of Khorasan. Tahir created a new dynasty that would rule in the east of the Muslim empire: the Tahirids.**

Section II: Comprehension

Write a two or three-sentence answer to each of the following questions.

1. How did Harun al-Rashid die? What did he leave behind?

A1.—Pg. 423, ¶ 1—Harun al-Rashid died when he was on his way to Khorasan with an army, ready to put down a rebellion in the province. He left behind a fortune, with close to three thousand tons of silver in his possession.

2. Why was al-Rashid torn between who to appoint as heir? How did he solve the problem?

A2.—Pg. 423, ¶ 2—Though al-Rashid's older son al-Amin was the obvious choice to follow al-Rashid as caliph, the ruler was fond of his younger son al-Mamun, the product of an affair with a concubine, because he believed al-Mamun had a greater talent for governing. He solved the problem by announcing that while al-Amin would succeed him as caliph, al-Mamun would become governor of Khorasan and his brother's heir.

3. Why did al-Amin want al-Mamun to come to Baghdad? What did al-Mamun do instead?

A3.—Pg. 423, ¶ 3—Al-Amin had children of his own, so he wanted al-Mamun to come to Baghdad and recognize al-Amin's oldest son as the heir to the caliphate. Al-Mamun refused to go to Baghdad, and instead he stopped sending any reports to Baghdad and removed al-Amin's name from its place in the official mottoes embroidered on the robes of state used at Khorasan. Al-Mamun wanted him to give up his claim to the throne, but what happened was that al-Mamun started to act independently.

4. What were the circumstances that led to war between al-Amin and al-Mamun?

A4.—Pg. 423, ¶ 4—After al-Mamun refused to give up his claim to the throne and started to act independently in Khorasan, al-Amin retaliated by ordering that no one was to pray for al-Mamun during the Friday sermons. When al-Mamun received word of this, he realized that his brother was preparing to depose him as governor of Khorasan, and he began to prepare for war. Al-Amin was also preparing for war, and in 811, the two brothers met in battle.

5. Describe what happened to Baghdad and its surrounding cities while it was under siege during the Abbasid civil war.

A5.—Pg. 424, ¶ 3—When al-Mamun arrived at Baghdad, Al-Amin and his men barricaded the city's gates, and for the next year the city was under siege. The walls of the city began to crumble because they were being pounded by siege engines. Merchants sailing into the city were dodging rocks hurled by al-Mamun's catapults, and the surrounding cities were forced to surrender—if they did not they were burned to the ground. Tahir promised that anyone who left the city and came over to the attackers' side would be treated well and given gifts; hungry, tired and fed up, the defenders finally gave up in 813.

6. How did Tahir claim his own independence? Why was this independence so short lived?

A6.—Pg. 425, ¶ 2 & 3—Tahir was given the governorship of Khorasan by al-Mamun out of gratitude for his service, but instead of remaining loyal to his master, Tahir paid less and less attention to al-Mamun's commands. One Friday evening, Tahir did not pray for the caliph during his Friday sermon, which was a clear declaration of his own independence. Tahir's independence was short lived because, on the night word was sent to Baghdad of Tahir's defiance, the general died suddenly.

7. How did the Tahirids come to be?

A7.—Pg. 425, ¶ 4 & 5—After Tahir's death, his son Talhah picked up where his father left off and declared himself ruler of Khorasan. From his place in the east, Tahir formed the Tahirids, a new dynasty that would pay empty respect to the authority of the caliph but act independently. When Talhah died, he passed his authority on to his brother, which meant the power of the Tahirids was growing in the east.

Section III: Critical Thinking

The student may use his text to answer this question.

The Muslim empire, created by Muhammad with unity in mind, was by the beginning of the 9th century fractured in three. Squabbles over rightful heirs were at the root of both divisions. Explain how fighting over the right to rule caused the first break in the Muslim empire, and then explain how warring over the right to rule was also the cause of the second split.

The student should remember that the first split in the Muslim empire was a result of fighting over who had the right to rule: Abu Bakr, Muhammad's old friend and father of Muhammad's wife Aishah, or Ali ibn Abu Talib, Muhammad's son-in-law. If needed, the student can revisit Chapter 39. In Chapter 41, we learned more about the clash between the Banu Umayya, which had the blood tie to Muhammad, and the Banu Hashim, Muhammad's actual clan. The result was that Ali ibn Abu Talib was given the title of caliph, and Muawiyah, of the Umayyads, ruled independently from Syria but without a title.

In this chapter, we read about al-Amin's anger over his brother al-Mamun being named as his heir. Al-Amin believed his own sons had the right to rule. Demanding that al-Mamun give up his title caused war between the two brothers, a war that was won by al-Mamun only with the help of the general Tahir. Once the war was over and Tahir was given governorship of Khorasan as thanks for his service, the general was able to garner more and more power, eventually defying the caliph and declaring his independence. Talhah, Tahir's son, continued his father's push for independence and declared himself ruler of Khorasan. A new dynasty was formed, the Tahirids, which existed independently within the empire, acknowledging but not bowing down to the caliph. It was the fight between al-Amin and al-Mamun over the lineage of the caliphate that gave Tahir his opening to break away and Talhah the opportunity to declare himself ruler of Khorasan, head of the new Tahirid dynasty.

EXAMPLE ANSWER:

Abu Bakr, Muhammad's old friend and father of Muhammad's wife Aishah, and Ali ibn Abu Talib, Muhammad's son-in-law, were both believed to have claims to the caliphate, but it was Abu Bakr that was given power. The quarrel continued between the Banu Umayya, which had the blood tie to Muhammad, and the Banu Hashim, Muhammad's actual clan. A few Umayyad rulers followed Abu Bakr, but eventually Ali ibn Abu Talib was given the caliphate and the Umayyad leader Muawiyah was given power over Syria. Though Muawiyah was not given a title, he ruled Syria independently—the first break in the Muslim empire.

The second break happened because of the fight between al-Amin and al-Mamun over the lineage of the caliphate. Al-Mamun was named by his father as al-Amin's successor, but al-Amin believed his own sons had the right to rule. Demanding that al-Mamun give up his title caused war between the two brothers, a war that was won by al-Mamun only with the help of the general Tahir. Once the war was over and Tahir was given governorship of Khorasan as thanks for his service, the general was able to garner more and more power, eventually defying the caliph and declaring his independence. Talhah, Tahir's son, continued his father's push for independence and declared himself ruler of Khorasan. A new dynasty was formed, the Tahirids, which existed independently within the empire, acknowledging but not bowing down to the caliph. It was the fight between al-Amin and al-Mamun over the lineage of the caliphate that gave Tahir his opening to break away and Talhah the opportunity to declare himself ruler of Khorasan, head of the new Tahirid dynasty.

Section IV: Map Exercise

1. Using a black pencil, trace the rectangular outline of the frame for Map 55.1: The Tahirids.

2. Using a blue pencil, trace the visible coastline: the Mediterranean Sea (you do not need to trace any islands), the Black Sea, the Caspian Sea, the Red Sea, and the Persian Gulf. Then trace the line of the Nile, the Tigris and Euphrates, and the Oxus rivers. Show the Caucasus mountains with simple peaks. Repeat until the contours are familiar.

3. Select three contrasting colors. Use them to trace respectively the perimeters of Byzantium, the Abbasid Empire, and the Tahirids. Repeat until the contours are familiar.

4. Using a new sheet of paper, trace the rectangular outline of the frame in black. Remove your tracing paper from the original. Using a regular pencil with an eraser, draw the coastline of the Mediterranean, the Black Sea, the Caspian Sea, the Red Sea, and the Persian Gulf. Draw the Nile, Tigris and Euphrates, and the Oxus. Draw the Caucasus mountains. Then draw the perimeters of Byzantium, the Abbasid Empire, and the Tahirids. Erase and redraw as necessary.

5. When you are pleased with your map, lay it over the original. Erase and redraw any lines which are more than ¼ inch off of the original.

6. Remove your map. Study carefully the locations of Alexandria, Fostat, Antioch, Constantinople, Chalcedon, Antioch, Edessa, Amida, Baghdad, Kufa, Basra, Medina, Mecca, Hamadan, Tus, and Balkh. When you are familiar with them, close the book. Using your regular pencil, label each location. Then check your map against the original. Erase and remark any misplaced labels.

7. Label the areas of Fars, Mirman, and Khorasan.

Chapter Fifty-Six

The Vikings

The student may use her text when answering the questions in sections I and II.

Section I: Who, What, Where

Write a one or two-sentence answer explaining the significance of each item listed below.

Abd ar-Rahman II—**Pg. 431, ¶ 6—Abd ar-Rahman II, emir of Cordoba, started to built a fleet of defensive ships after facing a Viking attack in 844.**

Charles—**Pg. 429, ¶ 1 & 8—Charles, Louis the Pious's son with his second wife, was nicknamed "Charles the Landless" (sometimes translated "Charles the Bald") because he lost his rule over both Alemannia and Aquitaine. Charles was made king of Neustria by his father, and in 840 he became king of the Franks when his father died.**

Garcia I—**Pg. 433, ¶ 2—Garcia I, Inigo I's son and former Viking hostage, was able to turn back most of the Viking invasion that hit Pamplona in 859. He was able to do this with the help of Ordono I of Asturias.**

Inigo I—**Pg. 431, ¶ 5—Inigo I, king of Pamplona, had his son kidnapped by the Vikings, who demanded a sizeable amount of money for the king's son's release.**

Lothair—**Pg. 428, ¶ 4 and Pg. 429, ¶ 3 & 6—Lothair, Louis the Pious's oldest son, co-emperor and king of Italy, declared war on his father after Louis the Pious took part of Lothair's land to give to his youngest son Charles. Lothair's plan to take power from his father failed, and he ended up ruling just Italy after swearing in front of the public assembly that he would be content with his original kingdom.**

Louis—**Pg. 428, ¶ 4 and Pg. 429, ¶ 3—Louis, Louis the Pious's second son and king of Bavaria, was known as Louis the German because of the Germanic flavor of his kingdom.**

Michael III—**Pg. 434, ¶ 6 to Pg. 435, ¶ 1—Michael III, grandson of Michael II, inherited the Byzantine crown in 842 at the age of two, and his mother and uncles served as his regents.**

Michael III and his regents faced a terrible Viking attack on Constantinople, but the raiders did not manage to break through the walls of the city.

Ordono I—**Pg. 433, ¶ 2—Ordono I, king of Asturias, helped Garcia I turn back a Viking invasion in 859.**

Pippin—**Pg. 428, ¶ 4—Pippin was Louis the Pious's youngest son. He was king of Aquitaine and died unexpectedly in 838.**

Pippin II—**Pg. 429, ¶ 7—Pippin II, son of Pippin of Aquitaine, was crowned king of Aquitaine by the people of his country after Louis the Pious tried to install Charles as their leader following the death of Pippin.**

Ragnar Lodbrok—**Pg. 431, ¶ 7 to Pg. 433, ¶ 1—Ragnar Lodbrok, pirate leader of the Vikings that invaded Charles the Landless's kingdom in 845, stopped his invasion of Paris for seven thousand pounds of gold. However, even after his ships retreated, Viking raids on the city continued.**

Rhos/Rus—**Pg. 434, ¶ 1-3—Rhos, or Rus, was the name given to Scandinavian travelers moving through the villages of the Finno-Ugrian tribes. Some of the travellers also adopted this word to describe themselves, and they eventually settled down and intermarried with the Finno-Ugrian natives, creating a new state ruled by a king, or khagan, centered around the village of Gorodishche on Lake Ilmen, at the southern end of the Volkhov river.**

Rurik—**Pg. 435, ¶ 3—Rurik, a Viking warrior, built a kingdom in Europe among the native Slavs with his capital at Novgorod. The *Russian Primary Chronicle*, written 250 years later, tells us that he had to fight other Vikings for control of the subject Slavs, and though Rurik is probably a legend, his tale tells us that a real struggle may have happened between the Rus and Viking newcomers.**

Section II: Comprehension

Write a two or three-sentence answer to each of the following questions.

1. Describe the reach of Charlemagne's imperial power and kingdom by 813.

A1.—Pg. 427, ¶ 1—By 813, Charlemagne's imperial power had been recognized by both Byzantium and Baghdad. He claimed to rule lands as far north as Scandinavia, he had extended his empire down into the Spanish Marches, the land between the Emirate of Cordoba and the Frankish border, and he controlled the northern part of Italy, the old Lombard kingdom. He acted as the protector of the Papal States in the middle of the peninsula and he was the master of the dukes who ruled the Italian territories of Spoleto and Benevento.

2. What were the terms of Charlemagne's 806 will?

A2.—Pg. 427, ¶ 2—The will Charlemagne had drawn up in 806 divided his kingdom between his three sons in the traditional Frankish manner. Though he was the emperor of the Romans, Charlemagne did not believe that he now ruled a Roman empire that should be passed on whole to his successor. His heirs would rule each part of their kingdom independently and were expected to cooperate only in "the defense of the Church of St. Peter."

3. Why was Charlemagne's 806 will thrown out?

A3.—Pg. 427, ¶ 3 and *—Charlemagne's 806 will was thrown out because by 813 only one of his sons was still alive. Pippin the Hunchback, Charlemagne's oldest son, had long ago been disinherited and sent to a monastery; Pippin, subject king in Italy, died in 810; Charles the Younger, his heir apparent, suffered a fatal stroke the following year. His only remaining heir was his youngest son Louis the Pious, who ruled as a sub-king to his father in the Frankish territory of Aquitaine.

4. With what long title did Charlemagne refer to himself? How did Louis the Pious change this title, and what did the change signify?

A4.—Pg. 428, ¶ 3—Charlemagne referred to himself as "Charles, serene Augustus governing the Roman Empire, at the same time king of the Franks and of the Lombards." The year after his accession, Louis the Pious shorted the title to "Emperor Augustus." The change signified Louis the Pious's thinking that all the different realms under his control were merging together.

5. How did Louis the Pious treat his sons once they were all crowned as kings of their various domains? How did the sons react to his treatment?

A5.—Pg. 4 & 5—Louis the Pious treated his sons more as governors than as kings, using the title "emperor" in order to tighten his grasp over the imperial realm. His sons did not take well to this heavy oversight; they viewed their kingdoms as peculiarly their own. In 829, the two different points of view clashed and threw the empire into civil war.

6. Why was Lothair upset when Louis the Pious made Charles the king of Alemannia? How was Lothair able to convince his brothers to go to war against their father?

A6.—Pg. 429, ¶ 2 & 3—Lothair was upset when Louis the Pious made Charles king of Alemannia because Alemannia was a part of Lothair's territory, and Lothair did not believe his father had a right to take over part of his kingdom. Lothair convinced his two younger brothers that Louis the Pious would next take part of their kingdoms in order to give some territory to Charles. By 830, Lothair, Pippin of Aquitaine and Louis of Bavaria had declared war on their father.

7. What happened during the third year of the civil war between Louis the Pious and his sons?

A7.—Pg. 429, ¶ 4–6—In the third year of fighting between Louis the Pious and his sons, Louis the Pious and Charles were caught and put under guard, and Charles was supposed to be trained for monastic life. However, Louis the Pious was able to convince Pippin and Louis that he would make both of their realms larger if they would join together against Lothair and help him get his throne back. When Lothair found himself standing alone against his father and all of his brothers at a public assembly, he conceded the fight, was forced to return to Italy and he had to swear an oath to be content with his own kingdom for the rest of his life.

8. Why were Louis the Pious's sons forced to make a treaty in the middle of their very bloody civil war? What was the name of the treaty, and what were its terms?

A8.—Pg. 430, ¶ 3 & 4—Louis the Pious's sons were forced to make a treaty in the middle of their very bloody civil war because they needed to ensure that their kingdoms would survive: in addition to the thousands of Franks that died because of the war, and the crops that were destroyed because of battle, pirates from Scandinavia and al-Andalus had sailed down the Seine and burned Rouen, destroyed trading posts, raided the coast, and generally produced terror across the countryside. In 843 the brothers agreed to the Treaty of Verdun, which divided the empire into three parts: Charles the Landless got Neustria and the rest of the old western Frankish kingdom; Louis the German took Bavaria and the eastern Frankish lands; and Lothair added the lands between the Rhine and Rhône rivers to his holdings in Italy. Burgundy was divided into two; Lothair claimed the larger part of it, the southeastern portion, and Charles the Landless got the smaller portion to the north.

9. What was the Medieval Warm Period, also known as the Medieval Climactic Anomaly? How did the Medieval Warm Period contribute to Viking exploration?

A9.—Pg. 431, ¶ 3 & 4—The Medieval Warm Period, also known as the Medieval Climactic Anomaly, was the time period in medieval history, beginning around 800, when temperatures in Europe rose a few degrees—just enough to melt ice away from northern sea routes that had been impassable. The change in weather set the Vikings free to sail to lands that they had previously been unable to get to.

10. Who did the Vikings attack between 844 and 860?

A10.—Pg. 431, ¶ 6 to Pg. 433, 2—In 844, the Vikings attacked the emir of Cordoba, and in the next year they went after Charles the Landless's kingdom, in particular Paris. They continued attacks on the city after Ragnar Lodbrok was bought off by the king. Between 858 and 860, Viking fleets made continual raids on the southern and eastern coasts of Hispania, and tried to invade Pamplona. Other Viking ships sailed into the Mediterranean and harassed the Italian coast, with some even making it all the way across the Mediterranean to Alexandria.

11. What did Charles the Landless start to built in 860 to fortify his land against the Viking invaders? Did his plan work?

A11.—Pg. 433, ¶ 4—Charles the Landless began to build fortified bridges at the rivers to block Viking invaders in 860, and the bridges proved very useful in slowing down the Viking longboats. In fact, the bridges were so successful that flimsy barriers were soon going up all around the country, and Charles had to issue an edict forbidding such "unauthorized strongholds" to be built. And while Charles's bridges were a good defense, it took years for them to be complete, which left the farms on the lowland near the mouths of the rivers vulnerable to Viking attacks.

12. Who made up the people that spoke Finno-Ugrian? What did they call the later Scandinavian travellers who came through their villages?

A12.—Pg. 433, ¶ 6 to Pg. 434, ¶ 1—The people that spoke Finno-Ugrian were Scandinavian merchants that had struck out from their homes, sailed across the Baltic Sea, and built settlements along the opposite coast even before the Medieval Warm Period. The settlements had remained small, the Finno-Ugrian villagers didn't trade far away, nor did they use the rivers as roads as the Scandinavians did. They called the travellers who came through their villages *Rhos*, or Rus—the word may mean "red," referring to the foreigners' ruddy coloring.

13. How did Michael III's regents explain the retreat of the Vikings after their vicious attack on the area outside of the walls of Constantinople? What was most likely the real reason for the Vikings's retreat?

A13.—Pg. 435, ¶ 1—When the Vikings sailed away from Constantinople, Michael III's regents claimed that fear of Byzantine reprisals had driven the enemy away. The more plausible reason for their retreat was that the Vikings's natural pattern was to arrive, plunder and leave. They retreated because raiding and retreating was what they did best.

Section III: Critical Thinking

The student may not use her text to answer this question.

The Rus were an adaptable people. They made their way down from Scandinavia, adopted their name from the Finno-Ugrians, with whom they intermarried, and formed a new state centered around Gorodishche with its own khagan. The khagan was easy going, exercising loose and informal control over the mix of Scandinavian newcomers and Finno-Ugrian natives who lived around him. Write a paragraph explaining how the Rus khagan avoided Viking attack around 860. Then write a paragraph explaining how the flexibility of the Rus saved them from being destroyed by the Vikings in 862.

The Rus seem to have come together as a state in a very natural way, with people flowing together from different lands, settling, intermarrying, and then choosing to have some sort of ruler. Though the Rus khagan had loose and informal control over his people, he had enough grasp of his role and his power to fend off a Viking invasion in 860. When the Vikings appeared in the land of the Rus, finding their distant cousins settled and prospering in trade, they could have made a mess. But the khagan adapted and instead of fighting suggested that if they continued downriver they would find richer lands to raid. The Vikings went on their way, leaving the Rus state alone.

After the Viking attack on Constantinople, it seems there was a tussle between the Vikings and the Rus. Ruins along the Volkhov river show that a year or two after the attack on Constantinople, fires destroyed part of Gorodishche and all of the nearby village of Staraia Ladoga. The Russian Primary Chronicle, *written 250 years later, says that in 862 the Viking warrior Rurik settled in Europe, and that he had to fight other Vikings for control of his Slavic subjects. While Rurik's tale may be legend, the story does tell us that there was most likely a struggle between the Vikings and the Rus. However, after the attack, the Rus population grew, the wooden buildings of Gorodishche were repaired and Staraia Ladoga was rebuilt in stone. This tells us that while there was some resistance, a few of the Viking newcomers settled down, and the Rus came out on top. The Rus adapted and found a way to incorporate the invaders into their lives instead of losing their land altogether.*

EXAMPLE ANSWER:

The Rus khagan may have had loose and informal control over his people, but he had enough grasp of his role and his power to fend off a Viking invasion in 860. When the Vikings appeared in the settled and prosperous land of the Rus, they could have attacked. But the khagan adapted and instead of fighting suggested that if they continued downriver they would find richer lands to raid. The Vikings went on their way, leaving the Rus state alone.

After the Viking attack on Constantinople, it seems there was a tussle between the Vikings and the Rus. Ruins along the Volkhov river show that a year or two after the attack on Constantinople, fires destroyed part of Gorodishche and all of the nearby village of Staraia Ladoga. The *Russian Primary Chronicle* says that in 862 Viking warrior Rurik settled in Europe, and that he had to fight other Vikings for control of his Slavic subjects. While Rurik's tale may be legend, the story does tell us that there was most likely a struggle between the Vikings and the Rus. This could have been the end of the Rus. However, after the attack, the Rus population grew, the wooden buildings of Gorodishche were repaired and Staraia Ladoga was rebuilt in stone. This tells us that while there was some resistance, a few of the Viking newcomers settled down, and the Rus came out on top. The Rus adapted and found a way to incorporate the invaders into their lives instead of losing their land altogether.

Chapter Fifty-Seven

Long-Lived Kings

The student may use his text when answering the questions in sections I and II.

Section I: Who, What, Where

Write a one or two-sentence answer explaining the significance of each item listed below.

Aditya—**Pg. 440, ¶ 3—Aditya, son of the Chola warlord Vijayala, ruled for nearly forty years, during which time the Chola domain grew stronger and richer. By the end of the ninth century, Aditya had killed the Pallava king and claimed his land, he had begun to chip away at the southern border of the Rashtrakuta, and his long life allowed him to form a new dynasty.**

Amoghavarsha—**Pg. 437, ¶ 1, Pg. 438, ¶ 3 & 5 and Pg. 439, ¶ 3—Amoghavarsha, who followed his father Govinda III as ruler of Rashtrakuta in 814, spent the first ten years of his reign putting down rebellions, even fleeing his own country in 818, leaving his cousin Karka to deal with Rashtrakuta's problems. During Amoghavarsha's sixty-four year reign, he built a beautiful new cave-temple in the city of Ellora, wrote poetry, dabbled in art, and gave his kingdom stability that resisted conquest.**

Chola—**Pg. 440, ¶ 3 & 5—The Chola was a clan subject to the Pallava. The Chola warlord Vijayala took advantage of fighting between the Pallava and the Pandya to conquer the Pandya. Later, Vijayala's son Aditya conquered the Pallava, forming the new Chola dynasty.**

Devapala—**Pg. 437, ¶ 1 & 3 and Pg. 439, ¶ 1—Devapala, who followed his father Dharmapala as ruler of Pala, was in control of Kannauj in 814 but was driven out of the city by Nagabhata II. Devapala was able to regain control of lands taken away by the Pratihara during Mihirbhoj's reign, taking back land from the Himalaya down to the Vindhya range.**

Dhruva—**Pg. 438, ¶ 4—Dhruva, son of Karka but not loyal to the king like his father, declared independence from Amoghavarsha and Rashtrakuta after his father died. The fight between Dhruva and Amoghavarsha went on for twenty years.**

Karka—**Pg. 438, ¶ 3 & 4—Karka, the elderly cousin of Amoghavarsha, ruled Rashtrakuta when his king-cousin fled in 818. Karka was very loyal, retiring to his family lands once the empire was under control and the king returned to rule Rashtrakuta.**

Krishna II—**Pg. 440, ¶ 1—Krishna II, Amoghavarsha's son and successor, faced attacks in the north from the Eastern Chalukya and the Pratihara almost as soon as he started his reign, and he had to fight off the Chola king Aditya in the south.**

Mihirbhoj—**Pg. 438, ¶ 6 and Pg. 439, ¶ 2—Mihirbhoj, grandson of Nagabhata II, lost some of his land to the seasoned Pala king Devapala, but when Devapala died Mihirbhoj was able to regain the land he lost and subdue the Pala, reducing the kingdom to a minor tributary.**

Nagabhata II—**Pg. 437, ¶ 1 and Pg. 438, ¶ 2—Nagabhata II, who followed his father Vatsaraja as ruler of Pratihara, drove the Pala out of Kannauj and by 820 was holding court in the city. He also took part of Rashtrakuta's domain in his conquest of the Kannauj.**

Vijayala—**Pg. 440, ¶ 3—Vijayala, a Chola warlord, had been permitted by the Pallava king to attack the city of Thanjavur and take it as his headquarters. Vijayala then took advantage of the conflict between the Pallava and Pandya kings and conquered Pandya for himself.**

Section II: Comprehension

Write a two or three-sentence answer to each of the following questions.

1. What is another name for the Pratihara? Where did this name come from?

A1.—Pg. 437, *—The Pratihara are also known as the Gurjara Pratihara. The name most likely came from their ancestry. The word "Gurjara" probably refers their descendants, the people of the central Asian Gurjaras, who came down through the northern mountains just after the fall of the Guptas.

2. Why was Kannauj a special city? What happened each time Kannauj was taken over by a different Indian king?

A2.—Pg. 437, ¶ 1 & 2—Kannauj, the great king Harsha's capital filled with Hindu temples and Buddhist monasteries, touched the edges of all three kingdoms in India. The city had grown into a great metropolis, and its location and wealth made each king want Kannauj as part of his kingdom. When control of the city passed between Indian kings, the citizens of the city had to flee for cover whenever a new army stormed through the gates, making it very uncomfortable to live there.

3. What previous successes occurred in Nagabhata II's reign that made him believe he could take Kannauj away from Devapala?

A3.—Pg. 437, ¶ 3 to Pg. 438, ¶ 1—Nagabhata II, who was in his ninth year of reigning when he decided he should have control of Kannauj, had already successfully campaigned against

Devapala, who was in control of Kannauj. Nagabhata had previously annexed some of the northern Pala lands for his own. He had also driven off a Muslim attempt to storm across the Sindh into his land and capture his capital city of Ujjain, giving him more reason to believe he should have control over Kannauj.

4. How do we know that Nagabhata II had taken some of Amoghavarsha's territory when he took control of Kannauj? Why wasn't Amoghavarsha able to protect Rashtrakuta from Pratihara attacks in the beginning of his reign?

A4.—Pg. 438, ¶ 2–4—We know that Nagabhata II had taken some of Amoghavarsha's territory when he took control of Kannauj because of the inscriptions the king left behind claiming he rose to be the most powerful ruler of the three Indian worlds. Amoghavarsha wasn't able to protect his kingdom from Pratihara attacks because for the first decade of his reign he dealt with continuous internal rebellions, struggling so much that at one point he fled his kingdom and put his cousin Karka in charge. When Amoghavarsha returned, Karka gave the throne back to the king, but when Karka died his son Dhruva declared independence from Amoghavarsha and the Rashtrakuta king had to fight him for twenty years, putting him in no position to fight the Pratihara.

5. How did Mihirbhoj get the Pala back for taking away land from the Pratihara kingdom early in his reign?

A5.—Pg. 439, ¶ 2—Mihirbhoj was able to pay back the Pala for taking away land from the Pratihara kingdom early in his reign by living a long life that gave him the opportunity to continue to fight and grow in power. Mihirbhoj remained on his throne for thirty-six years following Devapala's death. During this time he pushed back and regained his lost territory and more: by the time of Mihirbhoj's death, the Pala were reduced to a minor tributary in the east.

6. How did the Srivijayan empire come to be? What was the relationship between the Srivijayan empire and the Chola?

A6.—Pg. 440, ¶ 4—After the eruption of Krakatoa in 535, the people of Sumatra slowly returned to rebuild their villages and replow their fields. The Sumatran village of Jambi had grown into a city and spread its authority across the water to the eastern parts of Java, and by the ninth century, Java, Sumatra, and the peninsula that jutted down from the Asian mainland were all part of the Srivijayan empire. The Srivijayan empire was a wealthy and powerful trading partner for the Chola that could help the new kingdom rise to dominance in the south.

Section III: Critical Thinking

The student may not use his text to answer this question.

At some point in your secondary education it has most likely been pointed out to you that, while you are wonderful and unique, in many ways you are very much like everyone else completing *their* secondary education (and we may be referring in particular here to looming college applications. . .). How can you distinguish yourself? What makes you *more* wonderful and unique than someone else in your same shoes? This is an ancient question, and one that was particularly important for the long-lived kings of 9th century India. Explain why the Indian kingdoms were all very much alike, and how it was possible for those kingdoms to set themselves apart from the others. In your answer, use at least two specific examples of how individual kings were able to set their kingdoms apart from the others on the Indian subcontinent.

As explained on page 438, ¶ 5, Indian kingdoms across the subcontinent were essentially alike. They had, more or less, the same governments, armies and military strategies. The two things that each kingdom had to set themselves apart were their kings, and how long those kings could stay on the throne. If a king was ambitious, he could make great strides for his kingdom, but only if he was alive long enough to see those ambitious goals through.

There are several different examples a student can use from the chapter to demonstrate how individual kings, either because of ambition or longevity, were able to set their kingdoms apart from the others.

- *Nagabhata II was able to take Kannauj from the Pala, and parts of the Rashtrakuta kingdom for himself.*
- *Amoghavarsha, while not warlike, was able to stay on the throne long enough—sixty-four years—to give his kingdom stability that resisted complete conquest.*
- *Devapala was driven out of Kannauj by Nagabhata II, but when Mihirbhoj came to the Pratihara throne, Devapala had thirty years of experience on the young king and was able to reconquer lands from the Himalaya down to the Vindhya range.*
- *Mihirbhoj lost some of his land to Devapala, but the Pala king died and Mihirbhoj lived on and ruled for another thirty-six years. The length of Mihirbhoj's reign gave him the opportunity to take back the land that was lost to Devapala and more: by the time of Mihirbhoj's death, he had reduced Pala to a minor tributary in the easy.*
- *Aditya came to his father's throne in 871 and ruled for nearly forty years. Aditya killed the Pallava king and claimed his land, and chipped away at the southern border of the Rashtrakuta. His long life allowed him to create a new dynasty.*

EXAMPLE ANSWER:

Indian kingdoms across the subcontinent were all very similar, with more or less the same governments, armies and military tactics. An Indian kingdom could distinguish itself from the others by having an ambitious king. But ambition wasn't enough—the king also had to live long enough to see his ambitions come to fruition. The combination of determination and longevity can been seen in the Pratihara king Mihirbhoj and the Chola king Aditya. Mihirbhoj had a rough start to his reign, losing some of his land to Devapala. But while the Pala king died, Mihirbhoj lived on and ruled for another thirty-six years. The length of Mihirbhoj's reign gave him the opportunity to take back the land that was lost to Devapala and more: by the time of Mihirbhoj's death, he had reduced Pala to a minor tributary in the easy. Aditya came to power before his kingdom was fully formed. His father had conquered the Pandya for the Pallava, to which the Chola clan belonged. Aditya's rule lasted for nearly forty years, and in that time he was able to take advantage of trade with the Srivijayan

empire to become more wealthy and powerful. He was then able to kill the Pallava king, claim his land, and chip away at the southern border of the Rashtrakuta. Aditya's ambition and long rule led to the formation of the Chola dynasty.

Section IV: **Map Exercise**

1. Trace the rectangular outline of the frame for Map 57.1: The Rise of the Chola in black.

2. Using a blue pencil, trace the coastal outline of the Indian Ocean. You need only include islands which are part of the Rashtrakuta territory, as well as Sri Lanka. Trace the Sindh and the Punjab. Using a black pencil, trace the mountain peaks. Repeat until the contours are familiar.

3. Now trace the outlines of the Rashtrakuta territory, the Srivijaya Empire, and the Pratihara territory. Repeat until the contours are familiar.

4. Using a new sheet of paper, trace the rectangular outline of the frame in black. Remove your tracing paper from the original. Using a regular pencil with an eraser, draw the coastline, rivers, and mountains as you look at Map 57.1. Then draw the outlines of the Rashtrakuta territory, the Srivijaya Empire, and the Pratihara territory. Erase and redraw as necessary.

5. Remove your map. Study closely the areas of Makran, Central Asia, the Tibetan Plateau, the Himalaya mountains, Sri Lanka, Sumatra, and Java. Then study closely the locations of Ujjain, Kannauj, Ellora, Thanjavur, and Jambi. When you are familiar with them, close the book. Using your regular pencil, mark the location of each place on your map. Check your map against the original. Correct any misplaced labels while looking at the original.

7. Mark the location of Krakatoa. Mark the direction of Chola expansion and trade routes with arrows as the mapmaker did.

Chapter Fifty-Eight

Foreign and Domestic Relations

The student may use her text when answering the questions in sections I and II.

Section I: Who, What, Where

Write a one or two-sentence answer explaining the significance of each item listed below.

Basil—**Pg. 447, ¶ 6 & 7 and Pg. 448, ¶ 2—Basil, a horse-trainer from Macedonia and Michael III's best friend, was named co-emperor and heir, and in 867 he was also adopted as Michael III's son. Basil had Michael III murdered in 867, after which Basil claimed the crown for himself as Basil I, founder of the new Macedonian dynasty.**

Boris—**Pg. 446, ¶ 2 & 3—Boris, king of Bulgaria, was thinking of joining the Roman church, but the Bulgarian aristocracy was not crazy about the idea. When Michael III's troops showed up at Bulgaria's door, Boris made a deal with Michael III: he would convert and be baptized in Constantinople, taking the baptismal name "Michael" in honor of the emperor, and in return, the Byzantine forces would withdraw.**

Cyril—**Pg. 443, ¶ 3 and Pg. 444, ¶ 2—Cyril, a native of Thessalonica that spoke a Slavic language from birth, was sent to Moravia with his brother Methodius by Michael III as a missionary. Cyril and Methodius created a new alphabet for the spoken Slavonic language, and spent years translating the liturgy and gospel in Moravian.**

Cyrillic—**Pg. 447, ¶ 2—Cyrillic was a new script based on Greek uncials meant especially for the Bavarian tongue. Cyrillic was named for Cyril, and a decade after its creation, the Bulgarian church declared that it would only worship in its own language.**

Eudokia Dekapolitissa—**Pg. 447, ¶ 5—Eudokia Dekapolitissa, Michael III's wife, was ignored by her husband in favor of Eudokia Ingerina.**

Eudokia Ingerina—**Pg. 447, ¶ 5, 6 & 8—Eudokia Ingerina, Michael III's mistress since he was fifteen, was married off by Michael III to his best friend Basil. Eudokia Ingerina continued**

to sleep with Michael III, and when she gave birth to Leo he was most likely the Byzantine king's son.

Glagolitic—**Pg. 444, ¶ 2—Glagolitic was a new alphabet for the spoken Slavonic language created by Cyril, which was based on Greek letters called uncials. Glagolitic came from the Slavic word for "speak."**

Leo—**Pg. 448, ¶ 1, 6 & 7—Leo was the son of Eudokia Ingerina, most likely fathered by Michael III. After Basil's hunting accident, rumors flew that Leo had Basil assassinated; he was crowned emperor after Basil's death.**

Methodius—**Pg. 443, ¶ 3, Pg. 444, ¶ 2 and Pg. 446, ¶ 6 to Pg. 447, ¶ 1—Methodius, a native of Thessalonica that spoke a Slavic language from birth, was sent to Moravia with his brother Cyril by Michael III as a missionary. After working for years on translating the Scriptures into Slavonic, Methodius was arrested and thrown into jail by Louis the German; Methodius tried to salvage his work when he was released from jail, but when he died in 885 his work was in tatters.**

Mojmir—**Pg. 442, ¶ 5—Mojmir was the leader of a Slavic tribe north of Bulgaria that conquered a neighboring tribe to form the kingdom of Moravia. Mojmir ruled from 833 until 846.**

Rastislav—**Pg. 442, ¶ 3 & 5, Pg. 443, ¶ 2 and Pg. 446, ¶ 5—Rastislav, nephew of Mojmir and king of Moravia, asked Michael III to send missionaries to Moravia in order to teach his people the meaning of the Scripture. Rastislav believed that aligning himself with Michael III would stop Moravia from being swallowed up by the Franks but this alliance only worked for so long; in 870 Rastislav lost his throne to his nephew, was jailed by Louis the German and died in prison not long after.**

Svatopluk—**Pg. 446, ¶ 5—Svatopluk, King Rastislav's nephew, usurped the Moravian throne in 870 with Louis the German's help. This arrangement put Svatopluk, and Moravia, under Louis the German's control.**

Section II: **Comprehension**

Write a two or three-sentence answer to each of the following questions.

1. Describe the state of Constantinople in 856, when Michael III assumed power.

A1.—Pg. 442, ¶ 2—When Michael III assumed power, Constantinople was relatively stable because his regents—his mother and his uncle—had presided over a council that restored icon-use to Byzantium and brought a final end to over a century of theological struggle. But the empire's encounters with outside powers had been disastrous. The Rus had raided

Byzantine land at will, Abbasid armies had beaten its troops in battle, and the Khazars had refused offers of closer alliance.

2. Why did Louis the German ensure that Rastislav was placed on the Moravian throne following his uncle Mojmir's death?

A2.—Pg. 442, ¶ 5 to Pg. 443, ¶ 1—Louis the German wanted Moravia's king to be dependent on him, and for Moravia itself to be under Frankish supervision. Guaranteeing Rastislav's inheritance of his uncle's throne gave Louis the German power over the Moravian king.

3. For what political reason did Rastislav ask Michael III of Byzantium for help with his country's religious practice?

A3.—Pg. 443, ¶ 1 & 2—Rastislav saw that Louis the German wanted to take Moravia for the Franks; he had already dispatched his own Frankish missionaries to evangelize the Moravians, hoping to convert them into the Roman church, which would have given him even more control over Moravia's people. Instead, Rastislav decided that his people would be better off submitting themselves to the patriarch of Constantinople. Asking Louis the German for help aligned Moravia with Byzantium and took power away from the Franks.

4. What major obstacle did Cyril and Methodius face when they arrived as missionaries in Moravia?

A4.—Pg. 443, ¶ 4 to Pg. 444, ¶ 1 & 2—Cyril and Methodius arrived at Rastislav's court in 863, bearing gifts from Michael III and copies of the sacred liturgy used in the churches of Constantinople. However, before the Moravians could be taught the traditions of the eastern church, the liturgies had to be translated into Slavonic. The problem was that Slavonic had no written form, so a new alphabet needed to be created.

5. Why did Michael III decide to invade Bulgaria?

A5.—Pg. 445, ¶ 2 to Pg. 446, ¶ 1—While Michael III was working to pull Moravia under Constantinople's wing, Louis the German was doing the same thing in Bulgaria with his own Frankish missionaries. Michael III believed Bulgaria was too big, too close, and too well armed to risk a Frankish-Bulgarian alliance. Michael III thought the fate of Bulgaria's alliance was too important to leave to missionaries, so he assembled his army and prepared to invade.

6. Explain Boris/Michael I of Bulgaria's wavering faith after his conversion and baptism in Constantinople.

A6.—Pg. 446, ¶ 4—Boris/Michael I of Bulgaria remained Christian but in 866 he announced that he would submit himself to the pope. Then in 870 he reversed himself again and resubmitted Bulgaria to the patriarch of Constantinople. Then he decided that what Bulgaria really needed was its own state church, neither Roman nor Byzantine, in order to preserve Bulgarian independence.

7. Why would twenty-seven year old Michael III adopt fifty-six year old Basil as his son?

A7.—Pg. 447, ¶ 8 to Pg. 448, ¶ 1—Michael III continued to sleep with his mistress Eudokia Ingerina after she became Basil's wife, so when she found out she was pregnant her son was most likely fathered by the Byzantine king. By adopting Basil, Michael became his illegitimate son's legitimate grandfather. This meant that the baby now had a legitimate path to claim the throne.

8. What was the low point in the conflict between Byzantium and the Abbasid empire during Basil's reign? What was Basil's greatest project as emperor?

A8.—Pg. 448, ¶ 3—Continued fighting with the Abbasid empire reached a low point for Byzantium when the Arabs captured Syracuse in 878. Basil's greatest project as emperor was an attempt to revise and update the laws of Justinian. He intended to publish the updated laws in an enormous collection that would be called "Purification of the Old Law."

9. How did Basil die?

A9.—Pg. 448, ¶ 5 & 6—In 886, Basil was hunting when a stag turned on him which caused his horse to bolt and throw him onto the stag's antlers. The stag dragged him through the woods until one of his guards caught up with him and cut him loose; instead of being grateful Basil accused the guard of trying to kill him with the drawn sword the man had used to free him. Basil died shortly after ordering the guard put to death, but what did not die were the rumors that Basil's son Leo had somehow assassinated his father.

10. To where did Leo move Michael III's final resting place? Why was this move significant?

A10.—Pg. 448, ¶ 7—Shortly after he was crowned emperor, Leo had Michael III's body exhumed from its burial place in a monastery outside of Constantinople and reburied in Constantine the Great's own mausoleum. Moving Michael III's body suggests that he really was Leo's father.

Section III: Critical Thinking

The student may not use her text to answer this question.

Going to earthly battle in the name of a heavenly power was commonplace in the Medieval world. In 862, Michael III had an opportunity to strengthen his kingdom in the name of God, but without the conflict. Write a paragraph explaining how Michael III's mission in Moravia had more to do with power than with God. Then explain how religious freedom ended up being bestowed on Bulgaria, rather than greater political power on Byzantium.

In this chapter the student read about Michael III's attempt to grow Byzantine power by taking Moravia under its religious wing. When King Rastislav arrived at his court asking for help translating the Scripture into Moravian, Michael III saw an opportunity to change the political landscape. Louis the German had made sure that Rastislav followed his uncle Mojmir as the leader of Moravia. This gave the Franks power over the Moravians, and Louis the German wanted to increase his hold by converting the Moravians to Roman Catholicism. If Michael III could get his missionaries into Moravia, then Louis the German would lose his grasp on the young country. By translating the Scripture into Moravian with the new alphabet Glagolitic, the Slavs would then be using a language tied to the Greek of the east, rather than the Latin of the west.

In 870 Louis the German managed to reassert himself in Moravia, kicking Rastislav off the throne and installing his nephew Svatopluk—who was loyal to the Franks—as king. Moravians that fled to Bulgaria after the change in power passed their liturgy and Scriptures on to the Bulgarian clerics. The Bulgarian churches began to use Methodius's works in preference to the Greek rituals, distancing themselves from the eastern church hierarchy. Methodius's disciples began to create a new script as he did, based on Greek uncials meant especially for the Bulgarian tongue. They named this script "Cyrillic," after the missionary Cyril, and it took root and grew. A decade later, the Bulgarian church forbade its clerics to use any Greek in the liturgy. The Bulgarian church would now worship only in its own native language. While Moravia was not free of the Franks, as Methodius and Cyril had hoped, Bulgaria was freed from both Rome and Constantinople because of the work of the two missionaries. Michael III had used Methodius and Cyril to gain power in Moravia, but Bulgaria found religious freedom instead.

EXAMPLE ANSWER:

When King Rastislav arrived at his court asking for help translating the Scripture into Moravian, Michael III saw an opportunity to change the political landscape. Louis the German had made sure that Rastislav followed his uncle Mojmir as the leader of Moravia. This gave the Franks power over the Moravians, and the Louis the German wanted to increase his hold by converting the Moravians to Roman Catholicism. If Michael III could get his missionaries into Moravia, then Louis the German would lose his grasp on the young country. By translating the Scripture into Moravian with the new alphabet Glagolitic, the Slavs would then be using a language tied to the Greek of the east, rather than the Latin of the west.

However, in 870, Louis the German managed to reassert himself in Moravia by placing Svatopluk—who was loyal to the Franks—on the throne. Moravians that fled to Bulgaria after the change in power passed their liturgy and Scriptures on to the Bulgarian clerics. The Bulgarian churches began to use Methodius's works in preference to the Greek rituals, which gave them some religious independence. Then, Methodius's disciples began to create a new script as he did, based on Greek uncials meant especially for the Bulgarian tongue. They called the script Cyrillic, and it took root and grew. A decade later, the Bulgarian church forbade its clerics to use any Greek in the liturgy. The Bulgarian church would now worship only in its own native language. While Moravia was not free of the Franks, as Methodius and Cyril had hoped, Bulgaria was freed from both Rome and Constantinople because of the work of the two missionaries. Michael III had used Methodius and Cyril to gain power in Moravia, but Bulgaria found religious freedom instead.

Section IV: Map Exercise

1. Using a black pencil, trace the rectangular outline of the frame for Map 58.1: Moravia.

2. Using a blue pencil, trace the coastline of the Mediterranean. Include Sardinia, Corsica, and Sicily, but no other islands at this time. Include the coastline of Britain and the coastline up and around the North Sea. Then trace the outline of the Black Sea.

3. Using a new sheet of paper, trace the rectangular outline of the frame in black. Remove your tracing paper from the original. Using a regular pencil with an eraser, draw the coastlines of the Mediterranean, Atlantic, North Sea, and Black Sea as you look at Map 58.1. Erase and redraw as necessary.

4. When you are pleased with your map, lay it over the original. Erase and redraw any lines which are more than ¼ inch off of the original.

5. Remove your map. Study carefully the regions of Mercia, Western Francia, the Kingdom of Italy, Eastern Francia, Moravia, the Rus, the Slavs, the Khazars, the First Bulgarian Empire, Byzantium, the Papal States, Sicily, and the Abbasid Empire. When you are familiar with them, close the book. Using your regular pencil, label each region. Check your map against the original, and correct any misplaced labels.

6. Next, study closely the locations of Rome, Spoleto, Benevento, Syracuse, Thessalonica, and Constantinople. When you are familiar with them, close the book, mark each location on your map, and label. When you are done, lay your map over the original. Erase and redraw any locations which are more than ¼ inch off of the original.

7. Draw and label the Loire and the Rhine.

Chapter Fifty-Nine

The Second Caliphate

The student may use his text when answering the questions in sections I and II.

Section I: Who, What, Where

Write a one or two-sentence answer explaining the significance of each item listed below.

Al-Muntasir—**Pg. 453, ¶ 1 & 2—Al-Muntasir, son of al-Mutawakkil, went to the Turks after his father threatened to disinherit him and persuaded them that they would prosper better under his rule rather than under the rule of any of his brothers. The Turks murdered al-Mutawakkil and saw that al-Muntasir was made caliph, but he died of illness shortly after his ascension.**

Al-Mutamid—**Pg. 454, ¶ 1—Al-Mutamid was the Turk-appointed caliph that ruled for twenty-two years by allowing his official and army to control the palace.**

Al-Mutasim—**Pg. 451, ¶ 2 and Pg. 452, ¶ 4 & 6—Al-Mutasim, al-Mamun's half-brother and heir, raised an army of Turks to fight off enemies of the caliphate. He moved his capital to Samarra and created special isolated quarters for his Turks, resulting in a tightly knit and powerful Turkish community that had no allegiance to Muslim doctrine.**

Al-Mutawakkil—**Pg. 452, ¶ 6 to Pg. 453, ¶ 1—Al-Mutawakkil, al-Mutasim's younger son, followed his older brother as caliph after his father's passing. Al-Mutawakkil was murdered by the Turkish guard after he threatened to disinherit his son al-Muntasir.**

Al-Mutazz—**Pg. 453, ¶ 3—Al-Mutazz, the caliph that followed the ousted caliph (that followed al-Muntasir) in Baghdad, ruled only for three years because he spent too much money on his court and ran out of cash to pay his army. The Turks beat and starved al-Mutazz, and he finally died after being sealed into a vault with heavy plaster.**

Imams—**Pg. 451, ¶ 5 to Pg. 452, ¶ 1—*Imams* were the leaders in the Shi'a party: their followers were willing to obey them without question because imams could not make mistakes as they**

were filled with the wisdom of the Divine. Shi'ites believed that the Prophet himself had designated his successor, and that each *imam* had the God-given, infallible knowledge that allowed him to designate the next successor.

Ismail—**Pg. 454, ¶ 4 and Pg. 455, ¶ 3—Ismail, brother of Nasr, led the Samanid forces against Ya'qub-i Laith Saffari and then he took control of the Samanids when Nasr died. He established his own military headquarters in the city of Bukhara and began to expand his control across Khorasan, growing the Samanid territory and chiseling away at the Abbasid empire.**

Ja'far al-Sadiq—**Pg. 455, ¶ 6 to Pg. 456, ¶ 1—Ja'far al-Sadiq was Ali's great-great-grandson. Shi'a Muslims were divided over which of Ja'far al-Sadiq's sons, Musa or Ismail, had been heir to his power.**

The Maghreb—**Pg. 455, ¶ 6 to Pg. 456, ¶ 1—The Maghreb was the name Muslims gave to the westward lands of northern Africa. During the time of Ya'qub-i Laith Saffari's attacks on Baghdad, the faction of Shi'a Muslims known as Ismailis had been gathering in the Maghreb, forming an aggressive and militant community.**

The *mihna*—**Pg. 451, ¶ 1—The *mihna*, or the ordeal, was the inquisition led by al-Mamun to stamp out wrong belief and evil practice. Teachers, scholars, and leaders were subjected to intense questioning, which sometimes involved quite forceful persuasion, until the interrogated were "convinced" that Mu'tazilite ideas were true.**

Mu'tazilism—**Pg. 450, ¶ 4—Mu'tazilism was the Muslim belief that God held Divine Logic, that his judgment was perfect, and that there was no uncertainly about his intentions. The Mu'tazilites believed there was no need to appeal for mercy because mercy required the giver to change his mind about the severity of an offence, and God did not share in such human qualities as changing one's mind: his original judgments were always right.**

Muhammad—**Pg. 455, ¶ 2—Muhammad was the young Tahirid ruler captured by Ya'qub-i Laith Saffari. He was rescued by the Turks and Abbasids and sent back to Khorasan so that he could try to take up the governorship again, but his power was shattered, and he was unable, even with the help of Turkish forces, to recapture the land he had lost to Ya'qub-i Laith Saffari.**

Nasr—**Pg. 454, ¶ 3 & 4—Nasr, governor of Samarkand, agreed to fight against Ya'qub-i Laith Saffari at the request of al-Mutamid in exchange for the title "Ruler of Transoxania."**

Ubaydallah al-Mahdi—**Pg. 456, ¶ 1 & 2—Ubaydallah al-Mahdi, who claimed to be a descendent of Ismail and of Ismail's great-great-great-grandmother Fatima, the Prophet's daughter, was proclaimed caliph in 909 by the Ismailis in Maghreb. His caliphate was known as the "Fatimid" caliphate and this declaration of power split the Islamic empire into two.**

Ya'qub-i Laith Saffari—**Pg. 453, ¶ 5 and Pg. 455, ¶ 1 & 2—Ya'qub-i Laith Saffari, a coppersmith turned bandit, began conquering territory ruled by the Tahirids of Khorasan and by 873 he took the Tahirid capital city of Nishapur where he captured the young Tahirid ruler, ending the Tahirid dynasty. Ya'qub-i Laith Saffari had to fight against the Samanids and the Abbasids, and he suffered a loss in 876 that halted his advances towards Baghdad.**

Section II: Comprehension

Write a two or three-sentence answer to each of the following questions.

1. What were the five foundational principles of Mu'tazilism?

A1.—Pg. 450 to 451, *—The five foundational principles of Mu'tazilism were unity (God's nature as a single transcendent being), justice (God's judgment governed by rational principle), the "promise and the threat" (those who obey will be given rewards, while those who fail to repent will suffer eternal torment), the "in-between position" in relation to Muslims who commit sins (they are in the moment of sinning neither believers nor infidels, but something "in between"), and the leader's responsibility to exhort the community to do good and forbid them to do evil.

2. What were the duties of a Mu'tazilite leader?

A2.—Pg. 450, ¶ 5 to Pg. 451, ¶ 1—Mu'tazilite leaders were charged with guiding the community in right belief and right practice. Though men have the ability to reason and thus are able to predict what God's judgment on their acts will be, they do not always choose the righteous act. In addition to guiding the community, it was also the leader's job to stamp out wrong belief and evil practice.

3. What was the difference between the authority of a Sunni caliph and a Shi'a imam?

A3.—Pg. 451, ¶ 5 to 452, ¶ 2—A Sunni caliph was chosen by the people, and so his power was limited because the people could decide that they had chosen the wrong caliph. A Shi'a imam's power was irrefutable because the imam was filled with the divine wisdom that allowed him to designate the next successor to the caliph—a successor designated by the Prophet. The caliph was a man that represented the divine, where the imam was in contact with the divine, the living version of God's voice.

4. Why did al-Mutasim decide to go to war against his own people?

A4.—Pg. 451, ¶ 2 & 3 and Pg. 452, ¶ 2—Al-Mutasim was a follower of Mu'tazilite doctrine, and Mu'tazilite doctrine told him that as caliph he had the right to define good and evil and punish his people respectively. But Al-Mutasim ruled over divided Muslims, so he had to fight a war in order to get his people to follow his doctrine. He had to force them to follow his doctrine because he was an elected caliph.

5. From where did al-Mutasim find the men for his army?

A5.—Pg. 452, ¶ 4 & 5—Al-Mutasim formed his army around the core of his own personal guard—captives who had been brought back to Baghdad after wars with the Western Turkish Khaghanate and the other Turkish tribes across the Oxus river. Before he was even caliph, al-Mutasim had a personal guard of four thousand Turkish slave-soldiers. Within a few years of the start of his caliphate, he had expanded his force until he had seventy thousand men under his control—mostly Turks, but also a few Slavs and North Africans who had been captured in battle and brought to the capital as slaves.

6. What was al-Mutasim's reason for moving his capital to Samarra? Why did he isolate his Turks from the rest of the population, and what was the result?

A6.—Pg. 452, ¶ 6—Al-Mutasim moved his capital to Samarra because continual fighting broke out between al-Mutasim's Turks—who were now in the inner circle—and the Arab and Persian officials they had replaced. In Samarra al-Mutasim constructed separate quarters for his Turks and kept them isolated from the population to prevent street riots, but it also resulted in the Turks turning into a highly cohesive, self-contained community that had no particular loyalty to Muslim doctrine.

7. How was the caliph that followed al-Muntasir chosen? What happened to this caliph, and how did the political center of the caliphate move back to Baghdad?

A7.—Pg. 453, ¶ 2—The caliph that followed al-Muntasir was chosen by the Turkish army. When the caliph displeased the Turks, they tried to depose him so he fled to Baghdad and barricaded himself inside the city. Baghdad once again became the center of the caliphate after the Turks laid siege to the old capital, forced the powerless caliph to abdicate, and picked a new caliph to rule from the Turkish-controlled Baghdad.

8. What was the significance of al-Mutazz's brutal murder by the Turks?

A8.—Pg. 453, ¶ 3—Al-Mutazz's brutal murder by the Turks signified the weakness of the caliphate. The Turks had been brought in to protect the caliph, but now they were deciding who had the right to be caliph. While the Abbasid caliph might claim to be God's spokesman, God could not protect him from the Turks.

9. Why did Ya'qub-i Laith Saffari want to storm Baghdad? Why did he want the caliph's approval?

A9.—Pg. 454, ¶ 1—Ya'qub-i Laith Saffari wanted to storm Baghdad because he planned to force the caliph to grant him official recognition as a legitimate Muslim ruler. Even though the caliph had no real power—al-Mutamid lasted as long as he did only because he let his officials and army make all of the decisions—the idea of a God-ordained caliph was still functioning and Ya'qub-i Laith Saffari wanted his approval.

10. Describe the succession of caliphs that followed al-Mutamid. Who had power during this succession of caliphs?

A10.—Pg. 455, ¶ 4—Al-Mutamid was succeeded by his nephew, who was followed by al-Mutamid's nephew's half-Turkish son, and then the son's son. Power during this succession of caliphs was held by the royal guard and the court officials. The senior vizier, who was supposed to be the helper to the caliph, accumulated more and more power until his power was as great as that of any previous caliph.

11. What did all Shi'a Muslims agree upon as far as where the designated line of *imams* began? At what point did the Shi'a Muslims disagree?

A11.—455, ¶ 6—All Shi'a Muslims agreed that there should be a designated *imam* leading the Prophet's people, and that the designated line of Shi'a *imams* began with Ali himself and continued on with his sons, his grandson, his great-grandson, and his great-great-grandson, Ja'far al-Sadiq. After Ja'far al-Sadiq, the Shi'a had an internal argument. The largest group of Shi'a Muslims insisted that the rightful *imams* were descended from Ja'far al-Sadiq's younger son, Musa, and a smaller group claimed that Ja'far al-Sadiq's older son Ismail had instead been the heir to his power.

12. What did Ubaydallah al-Mahdi's role as the Fatimid caliph mean for the Islamic empire?

A12.—Pg. 456, ¶ 2—When Ubaydallah al-Mahdi was proclaimed to be the North African, or Fatimid, caliph, he was directly challenging the power of the Abbasids. Until this point, no other faction within the Islamic empire had a leader that called himself caliph; instead he was emir or imam. With Ubaydallah al-Mahdi as the Fatimid caliph, the Islamic empire was split into two.

Section III: Critical Thinking

The student may not use his text to answer this question.

On June 29, 2014, the militant group known as the "Islamic State of Iraq and Syria" (ISIS) proclaimed Abu Bakr al-Baghdadi to be its caliph. The caliph took a new name, Amir al-Mu'minin Caliph Ibrahim, and the group renamed itself the "Islamic State." The group's aim is to establish a ruling caliphate where the Sunni majority resides in both Iraq and Syria. The names of the ISIS caliph, and the fighting over Muslim majority/minority beliefs must seem familiar to you: the fighting that goes on in the Middle East over the Muslim faith started so long ago, with the arguments over who was Muhammad's true successor. Though we have been reading about this fight over the course of several chapters of our history, understanding it is perplexing. Do your best to write a paragraph—without looking at the text—that explains the differences within the Muslim factions up to this point in our medieval history. First, write a shorthand answer for each listed question. If you need to reference the text after you've taken a stab at answering the questions, then you may do so. Once you have a brief answer for each question, write your paragraph.

While the student has read about the arguments over Muslim rule before, the differences in leadership ideologies are most likely still confusing. This critical thinking question is meant to help the student understand better the differences in Muslim leadership and the various factions that grew out of the quarrels over who had the right to rule. Below each question you will find an example of the shorthand answer the student will prepare. The example essay follows.

- What were the main beliefs of the Sunnis? What clan ruled the Sunni starting in 750?
    - **Sunni caliph elected by the community**
    - **Abbasids (descendants of Muhammad's uncle) took over rule in 750**
- What were the main beliefs of the Shi'a? What leader did they follow?
    - **Muslims should be led by a direct descendent of the Prophet Muhammad**
    - **the direct descendent of the Prophet would be a descendent of Fatima, the Prophet's daughter, and her husband Ali**
    - **followed imams: the Prophet designated a successor, and the imam had the God-given knowledge to designate the next successor**
    - **the majority of Shi'a's believed the rightful imams descended from the younger son, Musa, of Ali's great-great-grandson, Ja'far al-Sadi**
- Who were the Ismailis and what were their main beliefs? Who was their leader?
    - **a faction of the Shi'ites**
    - **believed the rightful imams descended from the older son, Ismail, of Ali's great-great-grandson, Ja'far al-Sadi**
    - **In 909, Ismailis made their own caliphate in North Africa (the Fatimid caliphate), led by Ubaydallah al-Mahdi, who claimed to be a descendant of Ismail and Fatima**

EXAMPLE ANSWER:

The fight over who has the God-given right to rule the Muslim people is long and confusing. Sunni Muslims elect a caliph, and in the time of the Abbasid rule that caliph had to come from a pool of men that could claim to be the descendant of Muhammad's uncle. Shi'a Muslims believed the Sunni caliph was a farce because he was not a direct descendant of Muhammad. This descendent would be related to Fatima, the Prophet's daughter, and her husband Ali. Instead of following the false caliph, Shi'ites followed the word of their imams, men who were in direct contact with the divine and had the power to designate the next successor to the caliphate. However, there was also a division within the Shi'ites over the successions of imams. Most Shi'ites believed that rightful imams descended from the younger son, Musa, of Ali's great-great-grandson, Ja'far al-Sadi. A smaller faction, called Ismailis, believed that the rightful imams descended from Sadi's older son, Ismail. In 909, the Ismailis decided to declare their own caliph, sick of the squabbling between the pretenders put in power by the Sunnis and the Shi'ite majority. This is how the Fatimid caliphate was formed in North Africa, with Ubaydallah al-Mahdi, who claimed to be a descendant of Ismail and Fatima, the Prophet's daughter, at its head.

Chapter Sixty

The Great Army of the Vikings

The student may use her text when answering the questions in sections I and II.

Section I: Who, What, Where

Write a one or two-sentence answer explaining the significance of each item listed below.

Alfred—**Pg. 461, ¶ 2, Pg. 462, ¶ 2 and Pg. 464, ¶ 1, 2 & 5—Alfred, brother of King Ethelred of Wessex, husband to the daughter of the king of Mercia, went into hiding with his men in 878 because he could not see the point of fighting a losing war against the Vikings. Alfred came out of hiding to defeat the Vikings at Edington, after which they agreed to convert to Christianity and to divide England up via the Treaty of Wedmore.**

Cinaed mac Ailpin—**Pg. 458, ¶ 3 to Pg. 459, ¶ 1—Cinaed mac Ailpin, ruler of the Scoti kingdom Dal Riata on the northwestern coast in about 845, attacked the Picts to the east and folded their land into his own. Cinaed mac Ailpin was later known as Kenneth MacAlpin or Kenneth I, the first king of Scotland and his dynasty, the House of Alpin, ruled over this united northern kingdom from the city of Scone.**

Edward—**Pg. 464, ¶ 4—Edward was Alfred's son and the heir to his southern Anglo-Saxon kingdom.**

Ethelred—**Pg. 461, ¶ 2 & 4—Ethelred was the king of Wessex at the time of the Viking Invasion in the 9th century. Ethelred, with the assistance of his younger brother Alfred, helped the king of Mercia avoid total war with the Vikings, though he lost many of his own men in battle against the Great Army.**

Guthrum—**Pg. 462, ¶ 1 & 4 and Pg. 464, ¶ 2—Guthrum, Ubbe's warrior-chief lieutenant, helped lead the Great Army after Ivar the Boneless's death, and he became the sole leader of the army after Ubbe's death in 878. After defeat at Edington, Guthrum agreed to sign the Treaty of Wedmore which divided England in two, and he agreed to convert to Christianity.**

Halfdan—**Pg. 459, ¶ 4, Pg. 461, ¶ 5 and Pg. 462, ¶ 1—Halfdan was one of three sons of Ragnar Lodbrok that commanded the invading Vikings in 865. After making steady headway into Ethelred's kingdom, he took control of London in 871 but then he fell out of favor with his brothers because of his ruthlessness.**

Ivar—**Pg. 459, ¶ 4 and Pg. 461, ¶ 3—Ivar, the oldest of three sons of Ragnar Lodbrok commanding the invading Vikings in 865, was known as Ivar the Boneless; while he most likely suffered from a bone disease that weakened his legs, we know for sure that he was often carried on a shield into battle, where he fought with a long spear. Ivar the Boneless led the Great Army as it captured the north and west of England.**

Odda—**Pg. 462, ¶ 3—Odda, a Saxon ealdorman who governed in the king's name, killed Ubbe in the Battle of Cynuit in 878 and captured the Raven banner, which was the sign of Odin's power.**

Odin—**Pg. 459, ¶ 4 & 5—Odin, the Viking god known to be the king of battles, was said to be able to blind and deafen his foes, still the sea and turn winds to give victory, awaken the dead, and his two ravens that flew over the land could bring him intelligence of his enemies. Odin appeared on the Raven Banner that Ivar and his brothers took into battle.**

Oswiu—**Pg. 460, ¶ 2—Oswiu, king of Northumbria in 664, called a council at the monastery of Whitby and announced that his kingdom would join the rest of the Christian world. When Oswiu made this declaration at Whitby, England was officially Christian, but the actual spread of the Christian faith was uneven.**

The Scoti—**Pg. 458, ¶ 2—The Scoti were pirates from Ireland that landed on Britain's northern coast. As they tried to root themselves into the area, they fought constantly with the already settled Pictish tribes.**

Treaty of Wedmore—**Pg. 464, ¶ 2—The Treaty of Wedmore was signed by Alfred and Guthrum after the Viking defeat at Edington in 878. The treaty divided England in two, with the south and southwest in Anglo-Saxon hands and with Northumbria, the eastern coast and the eastern half of Mercia in Viking hands.**

Ubbe—**Pg. 459, ¶ 4 and Pg. 462, ¶ 1 & 3—Ubbe, one of three sons of Ragnar Lodbrok commanding the invading Vikings in 865, took over control of the Great Army with the help of Guthrum after Ivar the Boneless's death. Ubbe was killed in 878 in the Battle of Cynuit.**

Section II: Comprehension

Write a two or three-sentence answer to each of the following questions.

1. Name the seven English kingdoms that existed in ninth century Britain. Who ruled in the north? Who ruled on the southwestern coasts?

A1.—Pg. 458, ¶ 2 & *—The seven English kingdoms that existed in ninth century Britain were Northumbria, Mercia, East Anglia, Essex, Kent, Sussex, and Wessex. The north was ruled by a mix of Pictish tribes and Scoti pirates. The Welsh ruled on the southwestern coasts.

2. What physical separation existed between Mercia and Wales, and how did it come about?

A2.—Pg. 458, ¶ 2—Between Mercia and Wales lay a massive fortification built by the eighth-century Mercian king Offa. Offa built a great ditch in front of a twenty-foot wall of earth because the Welsh continued to devastate his territory. Offa built the fortification so that there would be a boundary between his kingdom and Wales.

3. How did the southeast of England come to be united under the king of Wessex?

A3.—Pg. 459, ¶ 2—After King Offa's reign, Mercia continued to dominate over the eastern kingdoms of Kent and East Anglia, but that domination did not last. By 860, Mercia had declined in power and this allowed for the king of Wessex to annex both Kent and Sussex, making the southeast of England united under his throne.

4. Explain the significance of Ivar's Raven Banner.

A4.—Pg. 459, ¶ 4 to Pg. 460, ¶ 1—The Raven Banner was a symbol for the Viking god Odin, who was known to be the king of battles, and it was carried by Ivar into battle. Legend has it that three sisters of Ivar wove the banner in one day, and that in every battle the raven in the middle of the design seemed to flutter as if it were alive if the fortune of the Vikings were good. If the Vikings were facing defeat, the raven would droop down without moving.

5. Describe the religious fabric of England in the ninth century.

A5.—Pg. 460, ¶ 2—England was labeled as officially Christian in 664 after Oswiu called a council at Whitby and announced that his kingdom would join the rest of the Christian world, but Christianity did not spread evenly across the country. The country was not united, different political allegiances kept people separate, and religious practice was dependent each peoples' preference. Christianity was practiced in some places, while the old British religions stayed alive in between villages and outside of struggling churches.

6. What happened when the Vikings first landed in East Anglia in 865? What happened at the end of 867 between the Vikings and the king of East Anglia?

A6.—Pg. 460, ¶ 5 and Pg. 461, ¶ 3—When Ivar the Boneless and his Viking troops first landed in East Anglia, they forced the East Anglian king to provide them with food and shelter over the winter and horses in the spring in exchange for keeping his throne. At the end of 865, after the Vikings had fought their way through much of England, the invaders returned to East Anglia, killed the king who provided them with shelter and took it for themselves.

7. How did the Vikings come to control the north and part of the east of England? How did Mercia and Wessex manage to circumvent Viking control through 867?

A7.—Pg. 461, ¶ 1–3—By the end of 867, the Vikings had overrun Northumbria, taken York, and laid waste to the monastery at Whitby. The king of Mercia made a deal with King Ethelred of Wessex and his younger brother Alfred, and Ethelred was able to make temporary peace with the Vikings that spared Mercia and Wessex. East Anglia was not

so lucky, and at the end of 867, the Vikings killed their king and took the territory for themselves.

8. Describe the battles between the Vikings and the English during the year of 871.

A8.—Pg. 461, ¶ 4–6—The Vikings marched into Wessex in January of 871, and though Ethelred and Alfred braced themselves for the attack, the Vikings moved steadily westward into Ethelred's kingdom. On January 4, the Anglo-Saxon army was defeated at Reading in Sussex but four days later they were able to push the Vikings back during battle at Ashdown. Two weeks later, the Vikings had a great victory at Basing, Halfdan took over London, and more Vikings showed up, increasing the Great Army's power. Ethelred died in April, Alfred took over and promptly lost another fight against the Vikings and was forced to make a temporary peace treaty.

9. How did Alfred react to the seemingly inevitable takeover of England by the Vikings? Why did he react this way?

A9.—Pg. 462, ¶ 2—Alfred reacted to the seemingly inevitable takeover of England by the Vikings by going in to hiding. Alfred had watched Ethelred fight battle after battle at the cost of thousands of lives, and could see no future in continuing such a bloody war. While Anglo-Saxon refugees sailed away from the island, and the Vikings were camped firmly on the Avon, Alfred and his men were far out of sight, living hidden in the swamps of Athelney in Alfred's Wessex kingdom.

10. What happened after the Viking defeat at Edington in 878?

A10.—Pg. 464, ¶ 2—After the Viking defeat at Edington, the Viking chief Guthrum agreed to sign the Treaty of Wedmore, which divided England into two, and to convert to Christianity. He brought thirty of his strongest warriors with him, and all of them were baptized on the same day. Afterwards the Vikings retreated to their own land, which now consisted of Northumbria, the eastern coast and the eastern half of Mercia. Alfred returned to rule in the southern lands, and Alfred's daughter and son-in-law ruled over Mercia under Alfred's supervision.

11. What was the more plausible reason for the Viking concession to sign a treaty other than their defeat at Edington?

A11.—Pg. 464, ¶ 3—While the Vikings may have been defeated at Edington, Guthrum most likely agreed to peace with the Anglo-Saxons for other reasons. The Vikings had been in England for almost fifteen years, rooting themselves into the countryside, marrying Anglo-Saxon women, fathering children, and planting farms: this made them feel like they were at home, not like they were tyrannical invaders. The Vikings were ready to accept the treaty so they could live peacefully with their new families on their new farms.

12. Though the Treaty of Wedmore divided England between the Anglo-Saxons and the Vikings, how was it an unprecedented win for Alfred?

A12.—Pg. 464, ¶ 4—Before the Great Army arrived, England was divided up into small kingships. Though the Treaty of Wedmore divided England between the Vikings and the Anglo-Saxons, Alfred still managed to become king of a united area that was bigger than any previous king.

Section III: Critical Thinking

The student may not use her text to answer this question.

Myths and legends that are passed down through time often tell us as much, or more, about history than the actual history books themselves. In this chapter you read about two interesting tales that have survived the test of time. Write a short recap of the story of *Beowulf* and then explain how the story reflected ninth-century religious anxiety. Then, write a short recap of the story about Alfred, the housewife, and the burnt cakes, and explain how the story shows how Alfred was viewed by contemporaries despite constant defeat by the Vikings.

The story of Beowulf *is found on page 460, ¶ 3: In* Beowulf *"a Christian king and his warriors live on top of a well-lit hill, but a monster prowls through the tangled swamps below: a demon, a kinsman of Cain, an enemy of God. He haunts 'the glittering hall,' attacking at night to drag the warriors away into the heathen darkness. 'These were hard times,' the poet [that wrote* Beowulf*] says; the threat of the monster's attack even drove the warriors back to pagan shrines, where they made offerings to the old gods in hopes of deliverance. 'That was their way,' the poet writes, 'their heathenish hope; deep in their hearts they remembered hell.'" The student learned in the chapter that even thought England was on the books as a Christian land, the actual spread of Christianity was uneven, and the old British religions were still practiced. The story of* Beowulf *relays the fear the people of England felt at the Viking attackers, and the reversion to their old faith in order to find some protection. Their new God was not helping them to defeat the invading monsters, the representation of Cain on earth, so they reverted to their ancient religions for comfort.*

The story of Alfred, the housewife and the burnt cakes is found on page 462, ¶ 4. While Alfred was hiding out from the Vikings, he found himself in the hut of an Athelney cowherd and "was told by the housewife to watch the cakes baking on the hearth. Preoccupied with thoughts of his war against the Vikings, he ignored the cakes when they began to burn, and the housewife came storming back into the hut. 'You're anxious enough to eat them when they're hot!' she scolded, "why can't you turn them when they're burning?'" The rest of the story goes that he "humbly turned the cakes" and did not "reveal to the housewife that she [had] just told off the king of England." Instead of being remembered for hiding out while the Vikings attacked, Alfred was remembered for his kindness and grace. This shows us that Alfred's contemporaries saw him as a virtuous man, and no matter how it happened, as the savior of the kingdom.

EXAMPLE ANSWER:

***Beowulf* is an old English epic poem about a monster that prowls through the swamps at the bottom of the mountain where a Christian king and his warriors live. The monster attacks**

at night, and drags the soldiers away into his swamp. The warriors, afraid of the monster, prayed to their old gods for help. The story reflects the anxieties ninth-century English people had about the Viking invasions and their new Christian religion. The monster is representative of the Vikings and the terror they brought to England. Warriors reverting to their pagan gods, instead of praying to the new God, shows the difficult transition to Christianity England faced.

The story of Alfred, the housewife and the burnt cakes shows us that he was looked at as a virtuous ruler by his contemporaries. While Alfred was hiding out from the Vikings, he found himself in the hut of an Athelney cowherd and was told by the housewife to watch the cakes that were baking. He was distracted by his own thoughts, let the cakes burn, and was then scolded by the housewife. He took his scolding, never telling her she had just yelled at the king of England. Instead of being remembered for hiding out while the Vikings attacked, Alfred was remembered for his kindness and grace. His people remembered him as a gracious and kind man, and as the savior of the kingdom.

Section IV: Map Exercise

1. Using a black pencil, trace the rectangular outline of the frame for Map 60.1: The Treaty of Wedmore.

2. Using a black pencil, trace the coastline around Ireland, Britain, and the continent. You do not need to trace any minor islands at this time. Using your blue pencil, trace the lines of the Loire and the Seine in Western Francia. Repeat until the contours are familiar.

3. Place a new sheet of paper over the map, and trace the rectangular outline of the frame in black. Remove your tracing paper from the original. Using a regular pencil with an eraser, draw the coast all around Ireland, Britain, and the continent. Draw the lines of the Loire and the Seine on the continent. Erase and redraw as necessary.

4. Study the regions of Ireland, the Picts, Northumbria, Mercia, Wales, Wessex, Sussex, Kent, Essex, East Anglia, Britanny, Western Francia, and the Kingdom of Italy. When you are familiar with them, close the book. Using your regular pencil, label Ireland, the Picts, Northumbria, Mercia, Wales, Wessex, Sussex, Kent, Essex, East Anglia, Britanny, Western Francia, and the Kingdom of Italy. Now study the locations of Scone, York, Nottingham, Edington, Basing, Ashdown, Reading, London, Rouen, and Paris. When you are familiar with them, close the book. Then, on your own map, label Scone, York, Nottingham, Edington, Basing, Ashdown, Reading, London, Rouen, and Paris. When you are done, lay your map over the original. Correct any misplaced labels. Erase and redraw any locations that are more than ¼ inch off of the original.

5. Mark the locations of Offa's Dike, the Battle of Cynuit, and the Monastery of Whitby.

Chapter Sixty-One

Struggle for the Iron Crown

The student may use his text when answering the questions in sections I and II.

Section I: Who, What, Where

Write a one or two-sentence answer explaining the significance of each item listed below.

Adalbert—**Pg. 471, ¶ 1—Adalbert, a northern Italian duke, suffered greatly because of the Magyar attacks on Italy. He organized resistance against Berengar of Friuli by inviting Louis of Provence to come to Italy and take up the Iron Crown.**

Arnulf of Carinthia—**Pg. 468, ¶ 3 & 5 and Pg. 469, ¶ 3 & 4—Arnulf of Carinthia, Charles the Fat's nephew, removed his uncle from the throne, then took over rule of Eastern Francia after his uncle's death and in 806 had Formosus declare him not only king of Eastern Francia but also king of Italy and emperor of the Romans. He did not keep his titles for long: after leaving Rome he suffered a stroke which paralyzed him and made him give up his plans to confirm his title by fighting against Lambert, the intended king of Italy.**

Arpad—**Pg. 470, ¶ 1 & 2—Arpad was the first king of an alliance of Finno-Ugrian tribes called the Magyars. Under Arpad the Magyars attacked Italy, encouraged by Arnulf of Carinthia.**

Berengar of Friuli—**Pg. 469, ¶ 1, 6 & 7—Berengar of Friuli, an Italian nobleman, challenged Guy of Spoleto and Guy of Spoleto's son Lambert for the title of king of Italy. After Arnulf of Carinthia's stroke, Berengar of Friuli made a deal with Lambert, where Lambert would marry Berengar's daughter Gisela and rule the southern lands of Italy while Berengar would rule the north. Berengar became king of all Italy after Lambert's death at the age of eighteen.**

Carloman—**Pg. 466, ¶ 4—Carloman, one of Louis the German's sons, took possession of a part of the eastern Frankish realm but when he had a stroke his lands were passed on to his younger brother Charles the Fat.**

Charles the Fat—**Pg. 466, ¶ 4 & 5, Pg. 467, ¶ 2 and Pg. 468, ¶ 4—Charles the Fat, son of Louis the German, was given control of part of the eastern Frankish realms in addition to his rule of Italy after his brother Carloman's stroke, and in 881 he was crowned emperor of the Romans by the pope. After two Frankish kings died of separate natural causes in 882 and the third Frankish king was killed in 884 while hunting, Charles the Fat became the most powerful monarch in the west; his reign was cut short in 887 after he failed to stop the Viking invasion and he died in 888.**

Formosus—**Pg. 469, ¶ 2 & 5—Formosus, pope Stephen V's successor, promised Arnulf of Carinthia the title of emperor if he would restore peace between Lambert and Berengar of Friuli. After his death, Formosus's body was exhumed and thrown into the Tiber by Lambert as punishment for making Arnulf of Carinthia emperor.**

Gisela—**Pg. 469, ¶ 6—Gisela, daughter of Berengar of Friuli, was married to Lambert of Spoleto as a sign of good faith between the two rulers of Italy. Gisela's marriage to Lambert secured his place as the ruler of the southern lands of Italy while her father ruled in the north.**

Guy of Spoleto—**Pg. 467, ¶ 1 & 2 and Pg. 468, ¶ 6 & 7—Guy was the ambitious duke of Spoleto, and even though he raided the Papal States during Charles the Fat's rule as emperor, he was made king of Italy and emperor in 891 by Pope Stephen V after Charles the Fat's death. He was given the title of king and emperor as long as he agreed to leave the Papal States alone; his reign was cut short when he died unexpectedly three years later.**

Lambert—**Pg. 468, ¶ 7 and Pg. 469, ¶ 5 & 6—Lambert, son and heir to Guy of Spoleto, reclaimed the title of King of Italy after Arnulf of Carinthia suffered a stroke, and he used his royal power to defrock Pope Formosus's dead body. Six months after agreeing to split the rule of Italy with Berengar, and marrying his daughter Gisela to seal the deal, Lambert broke his neck while hunting.**

Louis of Provence—**Pg. 471, ¶ 1—Louis of Provence, a Carolingian prince (great-great-great-grandson of Charlemagne on his mother's side) came to Italy at the request of Adalbert to take the Iron Crown from Berengar of Friuli. Louis of Provence had many supporters, and Berengar was forced to flee from northern Italy.**

Louis the Stammerer—**Pg. 466, ¶ 4—Louis the Stammerer, Charles the Landless's son and heir, succeeded his father as king of the Franks. His reign lasted barely two years.**

Louis the Younger (Louis III)—**Pg. 466, ¶ 4—Louis the Younger (Louis III), one of Louis the German's sons, divided up the eastern Frankish realms between himself and Carloman after Louis the Stammerer's death.**

Louis II the Younger—**Pg. 466, ¶ 2—Louis II the Younger, son of Lothair, became king of Italy and emperor of the Romans after his father's death in 855. Louis II the Younger died in 875, and Louis the German expected to inherit Louis II the Younger's title.**

Stephen V—**Pg. 468, ¶ 6—Stephen V, pope at the time of Charles the Fat's death, declared Guy of Spoleto king of Italy and crowned him as Roman Emperor in 891.**

Section II: Comprehension

Write a two or three-sentence answer to each of the following questions.

1. How did Charles the Landless become emperor of the Romans?

A1.—Pg. 466, ¶ 1—Charles the Landless became emperor of the Romans by offering Pope John VIII a huge bribe in exchange for the title.

2. Why was Louis the German so upset when Charles the Landless was named emperor? Did he get his revenge on Charles the Landless?

A2.—Pg. 466, ¶ 2 & 3—After his older brother Lothair's son Louis II the Younger died, Louis the German, who was the oldest Frankish king remaining, expected to become the next emperor. When Charles the Landless paid for the title, Louis the German was left angry and ready for revenge. He stormed into Charles the Landless's western Frankish lands, burning them in fury, but before he could face his enemy and get revenge, Louis the German died.

3. How were the Frankish kingdoms divided after Louis the Stammerer's death?

A3.—Pg. 466, ¶ 4—After Louis the Stammerer's short time on the throne, the Frankish kingdoms were divided up among living heirs. Louis the German's two sons Carloman and Louis the Younger (Louis III) divided the eastern Frankish realms between them, but when Carloman had a stroke, his lands passed on to his younger brother Charles the Fat, who was already ruling in Italy. The western Frankish kingdom was ruled jointly by Charles the Landless's two grandsons.

4. Why did the pope crown Charles the Fat emperor of the Romans in 881? What came of the pope's plan?

A4.—Pg. 466, ¶ 5 to Pg. 467, ¶ 2—The pope crowned Charles the Fat emperor of the Romans because he was worried that the papal states might come under attack by the duke of Spoleto. The pope was worried that if the king of Italy was not made emperor, then he might now allow the named emperor to come into his kingdom to protect the papal states. Even though Charles the Fat was made emperor, he never returned to southern Italy after his coronation, and sent no help to the Papal States during Guy of Spoleto's raids: the pope's plan failed.

5. Describe the major threat to Charles the Fat's reign that began just a year after he became king of his enormous empire in 885. How did he deal with the threat?

A5.—Pg. 467, ¶ 3 to Pg. 468, ¶ 1—In 885, the major threat Charles the Fat faced was a Viking invasion. The Vikings were storming Frankish territory on horseback, seemingly raiding

every town and killing every person they came across. At first Charles the Fat tried to buy the Vikings off with silver, and occasionally hostages, but when this did not stop the raids he assembled an army that marched against the Vikings at Louvain; the Franks were defeated, the Vikings captured the city of Rouen, and then sent a mass of seven hundred ships up the Seine to the walls of Paris to lay siege to the city.

6. How did Charles the Fat manage to lift the Viking siege on Paris? How did this strategy affect his rule?

A6.—Pg. 468, ¶ 2–4—After failing to lift the siege on Paris by sending an army to fight the Vikings, Charles the Fat offered the invaders seven hundred pounds of silver and winter quarters in Burgundy in exchange for their retreat. Charles the Fat's people were furious at him for the way he handled the Vikings, and the Burgundians in particular were so mad that they revolted, with Arnulf of Carinthia marching into Frankish territory to remove his uncle by force. Charles the Fat agreed to give up his titles as king and emperor because of all of this hostility.

7. For what reason did Pope Formosus want Arnulf of Carinthia to be named the Roman Emperor?

A7.—Pg. 469, ¶ 2—Arnulf of Carinthia was part of the Carolingian bloodline. Pope Formosus felt that Stephen V had made a mistake by granting the title of emperor to an Italian warrior rather than to a king from the family of Charlemagne. For this reason, Pope Formosus wanted Arnulf of Carinthia to be the next Roman emperor.

8. According to Liudprand of Cremona, what were the circumstances of Lambert's death?

A8.—Pg. 469, ¶ 6—According to Liudprand of Cremona's first account, Lambert died when he was just eighteen, breaking his neck after falling off his horse while out hunting boars. However, Liudprand of Cremona revised his history and in his second account he added that Lambert may have been murdered by a young man from Milan whose father had been executed. It was supposed that the assassin arranged the body so that rather than it looking like murder, it looked like the king died by accident.

9. What did Arnulf of Carinthia have to do with the Magyar attacks on Italy?

A9.—Pg. 470, ¶ 2—Arnulf of Carinthia was forced to give up his conquest of Italy because of his stroke, but he did not give up hope of ruining his kingdom's competitors. The new Magyar alliance was moving through Moravia towards Italy, and Arnulf of Carinthia encouraged them to do so. He gave them clothing and money in exchange for their attacks on northern Italy.

10. How did Berengar of Friuli lose his title as "King of Italy"?

A10.—Pg. 470, ¶ 3 to Pg. 471, ¶ 1—Berengar of Friuli fought hard against the attacking Magyars, but they were difficult to defeat. Berengar began to lose the backing of the Italian noblemen who had been willing to support his rule and soon the northern Italian duke Adalbert, whose land was hit hard by the Magyars, invited a minor Carolingian prince,

Louis of Provence, to take the Iron Crown. Berengar continued to fight, but ultimately he was forced to flee from northern Italy and give up his crown.

Section III: Critical Thinking

The student may not use his text to answer this question.

There is a fine line between justice and revenge. Lambert could not punish Pope Formosus for naming Arnulf of Carinthia king of Italy and emperor of the Romans while he was alive, so he found a way to do it after his death. Explain how Lambert enacted justice (or revenge) on Pope Formosus during the "Trial of the Cadaver." In your answer, define "synod." You may use a dictionary to look up its definition.

The general definition of "synod" is "a formal meeting of church leaders."

On page 469, we learn that Lambert was outraged that Pope Formosus had named Arnulf of Carinthia king of Italy and emperor of the Romans. Lucky for Lambert, Arnulf of Carinthia suffered from a stroke shortly after getting all of these new titles, and he was forced to give them up. Though Arnulf of Carinthia was no longer a threat to the title "king of Italy," Lambert still had to punish someone. However, Pope Formosus died before Lambert could castigate him. The ordeal could have ended there, but Lambert needed justice—or revenge.

Lambert ordered Formosus's dead body exhumed, dressed in vestments and set behind a table. Then Pope Stephen VI's synod was convened to condemn and defrock the body. Next, Lambert ordered the corpse to be stripped of its holy vestments and the three fingers Formosus had used to bless the people of Rome to be cut off. These actions defiled any religious power the former pope may have had. Finally, Formosus's body was tossed into the Tiber. The "Trial of the Cadaver" gave Lambert an outlet for his rage . . . but could one really find justice putting a dead body on trial? It seems revenge was served.

EXAMPLE ANSWER:

Lambert was outraged that Pope Formosus had named Arnulf of Carinthia king of Italy and emperor of the Romans. Lucky for Lambert, Arnulf of Carinthia suffered from a stroke shortly after getting all of these new titles, and he was forced to give them up. Though Arnulf of Carinthia was no longer a threat to the title "king of Italy," Lambert still had to punish someone. However, Pope Formosus died before Lambert could castigate him. Needing justice, Lambert ordered Formosus's dead body exhumed, dressed in vestments and set behind a table. Then a gathering of church leaders—a synod—was convened by Pope Stephen VI to condemn and defrock the body. Next, Lambert ordered the corpse to be stripped of its holy vestments and the three fingers Formosus had used to bless the people of Rome to be cut off. These actions defiled any religious power the former pope may have had. Finally, Formosus's body was tossed into the Tiber. For Lambert, the "Trial of the Cadaver," where he put a dead body on the stand, gave the king of Italy the justice (or revenge) that he needed.

Chapter Sixty-Two

Kampaku

The student may use her text when answering the questions in sections I and II.

Section I: Who, What, Where

Write a one or two-sentence answer explaining the significance of each item listed below.

Ariwara no Narihira—**Pg. 474, ¶ 2—Ariwara no Narihira was a distant relative of the heavenly sovereign Kammu that became a poet after he had run afoul of the Fujiwara. In his poetry, he voiced the hopes of Mototsune's enemies that old age and death would bring an end to Mototsune's lifelong grab for more power.**

Daigo—**Pg. 475, ¶ 1 & 3—Daigo, Uda's oldest son, was crowned as heavenly sovereign when his father abdicated. Daigo was convinced by Tokihira that his father was working with Michizane to remove him from the throne, so Daigo had Michizane removed from the court and exiled.**

Fujiwara no Tadahira—**Pg. 475, ¶ 6 to Pg. 476, ¶ 1—Fujiwara no Tadahira, Mototsune's younger son, took his brother's powerful position after his death, and then he was elected Sessho for Daigo's seven-year-old son Suzaku when the heavenly sovereign died. When Suzaku reached the age of responsibility, Tadahira was made his Kampaku, regaining his father's position and reinforcing Fujiwara power in Heian.**

Hiromi—**Pg. 473, ¶ 7 to Pg. 474, ¶ 1—Hiromi, Uda's secretary, was blamed for the offering of the post of Ako instead of Kampaku to Mototsune. Uda said that Hiromi had misunderstood his intentions and written the wrong title in the offer letter to Mototsune, basically ending Hiromi's political career.**

Koko—**Pg. 472, ¶ 2 and Pg. 473, ¶ 1 & 2—Koko, Yozei's great-uncle, was made heavenly sovereign by Mototsune at the age of fifty-four. Koko paid no attention to politics, and let Mototsune, the Kampaku, rule for him.**

Suzaku—**Pg. 476, ¶ 1—Suzaku, Daigo's son, followed his father as heavenly sovereign. Tadahira served as Suzaku's Sessho, and when he reached the age of responsibility, Tadahira was made his Kampaku.**

Sugawara no Michizane—**Pg. 474, ¶ 3 and Pg. 475, ¶ 5—Sugawara no Michizane, a poet and scholar in his fifties, was Uda's most trusted advisor. When Daigo became the heavenly sovereign, Michizane tried to resign from his position in government but was unable to; he died in exile after Daigo was convinced by Tokihira that Michizane was plotting to dethrone him.**

Taira no Masakado—**Pg. 476, ¶ 4 and Pg. 477, ¶ 3 & 5—Taira no Masakado, a skilled and ambitious fighter related to emperor Kammu, declared himself the "New Emperor" after having some success in conquering other provinces in the north of Japan. Hearing of this threat to his own power, Tadahira banded together with two other great landowners to put Masakado down, wiping out his forces and killing the "New Emperor."**

Tokihira—**Pg. 474, ¶ 3 and Pg. 475, ¶ 4—Tokihira, Mototsune's son, was given a junior post in Uda's court when he was around twenty-one, and over the course of ten years was promoted steadily until he held one of the two highest positions in Uda's government. After Uda's abdication and Daigo's placement as heavenly sovereign, Tokihira convinced Daigo that Sugawara no Michizane was plotting against him, and that he should be exiled from Heian.**

Uda—**Pg. 473, ¶ 3 and Pg. 475, ¶ 1—Uda, the twenty-one-year-old son and successor to Koko, tried to break Fujiwara power in his court by refusing to reinstate Mototsune as Kampaku. Uda came to be known as "the Cloistered Emperor" because though he abdicated this throne and went through the motions of moving towards monastic life, he kept a heavy hand in politics.**

Section II: Comprehension

Write a two or three-sentence answer to each of the following questions.

1. What power was held by the *Kampaku*? Why was this position invented?

A1.—Pg. 472, ¶ 1—The Kampaku, or Civil Dictator, was given the power of being a super-advisor to the crown, it was almost the same power given to a Sessho over an underage ruler, but for an adult ruler. The position was invented by Mototsune so that he could keep his power even though Yozei was old enough to rule for himself.

2. Describe Yozei's psychopathic tendencies. How was Mototsune able to get Yozei off the throne?

A2.—Pg. 472, ¶ 2—Yozei liked to watch dogs killing monkeys and feeding frogs to snakes; he had also begun to suggest that he should carry out the execution of criminals with his own hands. Mototsune called a council of palace officials, all of whom agreed with him that the young emperor should be dethroned because he was crazy. Mototsune then lured Yozei into

a carriage, promising him a visit to the races, but instead taking him out of the city and off of his throne.

3. What happened to Yozei after he was dethroned?

A3.—Pg. 472, ¶ 3—Though Yozei was supposedly responsible for two murders, he was never jailed and he was allowed to roam the mountains on horseback, hunting and sleeping outside and sometimes even appearing at the gates of great landowners demanding to be let in. He fell in love at least once, and wrote a poem about the woman he desired based on images of the Mina river plunging three thousand feet off Mount Tsukuba into a boiling pool.

4. Why did Mototsune resign from his position as Kampaku after Koko's death? Why did he expect to get his position back?

A4.—Pg. 473, ¶ 3—Mototsune resigned from his position as Kampaku as ceremony; it was a political gesture that had become standard practice, but it was not supposed to be a real resignation from his duties. Uda was supposed to accept the resignation and then reappoint Mototsune, which was also a standard gesture.

5. What position did Uda offer to Mototsune in his new administration? How did Mototsune react to the offer of this new role?

A5.—Pg. 473, ¶ 4–6—Uda offered Mototsune the position of Ako, or "Supreme Minister," which was an old and respected role, but it was largely ceremonial, meaning Mototsune would not have the same power he had as Kampaku. Mototsune was furious, and in his continuing role as prime minister, he refused to sign papers or answer petitions, which brought the business of the court to a standstill. Mototsune's standoff went on for nearly a year.

6. Describe the circumstances of Mototsune's reinstatement as Kampaku. What did Mototsune's reinstatement prove about the distribution of power in Japan?

A6.—Pg. 473, ¶ 7 to Pg. 474, ¶ 2—Uda was forced to reinstate Mototsune because nothing was getting done in his government. He blamed the offer of the post of Ako on his secretary Hiromi, saying he had misunderstood Uda's intentions and written the wrong title in the appointment letter; Mototsune accepted the position of Kampaku after Uda's apology. Mototsune's reinstatement proved that he, the Kampaku of the Fujiwara clan, had the last word at court—not the heavenly sovereign.

7. What major reforms did Uda make before abdicating his throne?

A7.—Pg. 474, ¶ 5—Uda made major reforms in the relationship between the court at Heian and the outer provinces. Uda knew that noblemen in the outer reaches of the kingdom were collecting taxes for the crown and keeping them for themselves. Uda passed a series of reforms that prevented those noblemen from seizing the land of the peasants under their power.

8. Why did Sugawara no Michizane want to resign from his position in Daigo's court? How was his plea answered?

A8.—Pg. 475, ¶ 1 & 2—After Uda abdicated, Sugawara no Michizane was left to deal with the battle started by Uda against the Fujiwara and their political ambitions. This position made Sugawara no Michizane uncomfortable, and when he heard of a plot against him, led by Fujiwara no Tokihira, he was frightened and asked to resign. Uda, "the Cloistered Emperor," would not let Daigo accept Sugawara no Michizane's resignation.

9. Explain the circumstances of Sugawara no Michizane's exile.

A9.—Pg. 475, ¶ 3 & 4—In 901, after Michizane was denied the right to resign, Tokihira convinced the young and vulnerable Daigo that Uda and Michizane were plotting to remove him from the throne and make one of his brothers the heavenly sovereign instead. Daigo was persuaded by Tokihira to issue an imperial decree exiling Michizane from the capital city. As soon as the decree was signed Tokihira ordered Michizane and his family arrested, hauled out of the city, and sent into exile on the southern island of Kyushu.

10. How did Taira no Masakado come to call himself the "New Emperor"?

A10.—Pg. 477, ¶ 2 & 3—Masakado fought with several of his neighbors over land rights, and after he won a small local war against the landowners he directed his private army to follow him in attacking the nearest provincial governor. When he got to the royal official in charge of the province of Hitachi, the officials surrendered quickly. Masakado was so impressed with his own might that he declared himself to be the "New Emperor," capturing the surrounding royal outposts as well and starting to appoint court officials of his own to help run them.

Section III: Critical Thinking

The student may not use her text to answer this question.

Ambition is a trait that can live inside any man or woman. In the medieval world, if one had ambition to rule, he or she had to know how to work the local political system. Unfortunately for him, Taira no Masakado was not shrewd enough to recognize that the form his ambition took did not match the Japanese customs. Write a paragraph or two explaining why Taira no Masakado's hope of rising to power was doomed from the start. Make sure to include a description of how Japanese armies were raised in your answer.

Unlike power in China or Byzantium, the Japanese throne was not taken by usurpers. Yes, there were pretenders ruling the government, but in Japan they came in the form of powerful court advisors that managed puppet emperors. Jostling for power relied on manipulating the court because there was no standing army. The heavenly sovereign did not have thousands of men charged to protect his kingdom at all times. Instead, when he needed them, the heavenly sovereign drafted troops from the civilian population of free men older than twenty and younger than sixty. When they were not fighting, these men mostly remained in their own homes, carrying on with their regular lives, giving no more than about forty days a year to military service. An ambitious Japanese person could not rely on pursuing a career as a general, gaining the army's support, and using it to overthrow the ruler—the popular option in the western world.

Nonetheless, Taira no Masakado tried his hand at earning his power by might. He saw what power could do while he was at court in Heian, and when he returned to his homeland the squabbles over land rights offered him the opportunity to move up in power. He gathered a private army and won a small local war. Then he moved on to attack the governor in charge of the province of Hitachi. The governor's office did not have a standing guard, so they surrendered to Taira no Masakado quickly. These small successes gave Taira no Masakado the idea that he could rule Japan, so he named himself the "New Emperor," and started capturing more royal outposts and appointing his own officials to help run them.

The heavenly sovereign may not have had a standing army, but he did have money. Tadahira, Suzaku's Kampaku, ordered Taira no Masakado killed. He used royal money to buy up the personal armies of two great landowners, and three months after Masakado claimed his title, the armies descended upon his captured territory. Like any hired army, the men who were fighting for Masakado were not trained to fight for a living. They would go home and tend to their families when they were not actively fighting. When the sovereign's representatives attacked many men were at home; the rebellion was wiped out and Masakado was killed.

EXAMPLE ANSWER:

When Taira no Masakado went to court at Heian he was inspired and amazed by the power of the Fujiwara. Returning home, Masakado found that he could exercise his own power over local landowners that were fighting about land rights. Masakado did not understand, though, that the Fujiwara did not rule because they had a powerful army, but because they were politically shrewd. There was no standing royal army. Men were drafted from the civilian population of free men older than twenty and younger than sixty. When they were not fighting, these men mostly remained in their own homes, carrying on with their regular lives, giving no more than about forty days a year to military service. An ambitious Japanese person could not rely on pursuing a career as a general, gaining the army's support, and using it to overthrow the ruler—the popular option in the western world.

Returning home from court, intoxicated with power, Taira no Masakado gathered a private army and won a small local war. Then he moved on to attack the governor in charge of the province of Hitachi. The governor's office did not have a standing guard, so they surrendered to Taira no Masakado quickly. These small successes gave Taira no Masakado the idea that he could rule Japan, so he named himself the "New Emperor," and started capturing more royal outposts and appointing his own officials to help run them. These small wins were real, but Masakado missed the political maneuvering necessary for the real gain of power. When word of Masakado's rebellion reached Heian, Tadahira hired the private armies of two landowners to stop it. When the sovereign's representatives attacked Masakado's troops many men were at home; the rebellion was wiped out and Masakado

was killed. He might have had ambition, but relying on force to gain power meant that Masakado was doomed from the start.

Section IV: Map Exercise

1. Using a black pencil, trace the rectangular outline of the frame for Map 62.1: The Rebellion of Masakado.

2. Using a blue pencil, trace the coastline up the shore of China and around Japan. Using a black pencil, trace the region of Japan. Then, using a contrasting color, trace the outline of the region of the Kingdom of the "New Emperor." Repeat until the contours are familiar.

3. Using a new sheet of paper, trace the rectangular outline of the frame in black. Remove your tracing paper from the original. Using a regular pencil with an eraser, draw the coastline up the shore of China and around Japan, as you look at Map 62.1. Erase and redraw as necessary.

4. When you are pleased with your map, lay it over the original. Erase and redraw any lines which are more than ¼ inch off of the original.

5. Remove your map. Use your black pencil to draw over the outline of Japan. Then shade the region of the Kingdom of the "New Emperor."

6. Next study carefully the locations of Kyushu, Heian, Kanto, and Hitachi. Also study the location of Mt. Tsukuba. When you are familiar with them, close the book. Using your regular pencil, label Kyushu, Heian, Kanto, Hitachi, and Mt. Tsukuba. When you are done, lay your own map over the original. Correct any misplaced labels. If any locations are more than ¼ inch off of the original, then erase and redraw them, as you look at the map.

Chapter Sixty-Three

Basileus

The student may use his text when answering the questions in sections I and II.

Section I: Who, What, Where

Write a one or two-sentence answer explaining the significance of each item listed below.

Alexander—**Pg. 482, ¶ 3 and Pg. 483, ¶ 3—Alexander, Leo VI's brother and co-emperor, refused to give Constantine VII power when Leo VI died, and also refused to pay tribute to Simeon I of Bulgaria. Alexander did not have a chance to go to war with the Bulgarians after refusing to recognize Simeon I as basileus of the Bulgarian people because he had a stroke and died.**

Constantine VII—**Pg. 480, ¶ 6 and Pg. 485, ¶ 2—Constantine, Leo VI's son with Zoe Karbonopsina, was given the name Constantine VII Porphyrogenitus at the time of his coronation to remind all that he was supported by the court in his place as Leo VI's successor. The loyalty of the court that gave Constantine VII his legitimacy then gave credence to Romanos I's coronation, putting Constantine VII to the side as the admiral's co-emperor.**

Elena—**Pg. 484, ¶ 8—Elena, daughter of Romanos Lecapenus, was married to Constantine VII when she was nine-years-old.**

Leo Phocas—**Pg. 484, ¶ 2, 3 & 7 and Pg. 485, ¶ 3—Leo Phocas, general of the Byzantine ground forces, suffered great defeat by the Bulgarians at the Battle of Anchialus, and when Romanos Lecapenus took control of the council of regents after the defeat, Leo Phocas retreated to Chrysopolis. When Leo Phocas objected to Romanos's coronation as co-emperor, two of Romanos's men arrested and blinded him.**

Nicholas Mystikos—**Pg. 479, ¶ 3, Pg. 480, ¶ 6, Pg. 482, ¶ 3 and Pg. 485, ¶ 2—Nicholas Mystikos, patriarch of Constantinople appointed by Leo VI himself, refused to allow Leo VI a fourth marriage, and as a result was removed from his position and exiled. Nicholas Mystikos was**

recalled to duty when Leo VI's brother Alexander came into power and after Alexander's death he happily named Romanos Lecapenus Romanos I, co-emperor of Byzantium, taking power away from Constantine VII, the ruler he had always viewed as illegitimate.

Oleg of Novgorod—**Pg. 481, ¶ 4—Oleg of Novgorod, Rus nobleman and guardian of Rurik's son, took the power of the Rus for himself and moved the center of his power to Kiev. Oleg was apparently active even seventy years later, so most historians suspect "Oleg" is a title rather than the name of an actual person.**

Peter I—**Pg. 486, ¶ 2 & 3—Peter I, son of Simeon I, made a lightning-quick destructive invasion of the Byzantine territory in Macedonia and then retreated and offered to make peace. Romanos agreed, Peter I's daughter married Romanos's granddaughter, and Romanos acknowledged Peter I as basileus.**

Romanos Lecapenus—**Pg. 484, ¶ 7 to Pg. 485, ¶ 2 and Pg. 486, ¶ 3—Romanos Lecapenus, admiral of the Byzantine navy, took over the council of regents after a terrible Byzantine defeat by Simeon I, then married his daughter to Constantine VII, and finally convinced Nicholas Mystikos to name him Romanos I, co-emperor of Byzantium. After Simeon I's death and his son's quick and destructive attack on Byzantine territory in Macedonia, Romanos officially recognized Peter I as basileus, emperor of the Bulgarians.**

Simeon I—**Pg. 481, ¶ 2, Pg. 482, ¶ 4 to Pg. 483, ¶ 1 and Pg. 486, ¶ 1—Simeon I, son of the Bulgarian king Boris, advanced his forces to the walls of Constantinople in 904, resulting in a treaty that gave the Bulgarians the entire north of the Greek peninsula, making Simeon the emperor over the Slavic tribes in the lands known as the Balkans. When Alexander came to the Byzantine throne and refused to pay tribute to the Bulgarians, Simeon I demanded the Byzantine emperor recognize his power as basileus; when Alexander refused, Simeon I attacked and peace was not made until 924, when Romanos I agreed to the reinstatement of the Byzantine yearly tribute to the Bulgarians.**

Zoe Karbonopsina—**Pg. 479, ¶ 4, Pg. 480, ¶ 4 and Pg. 484, ¶ 6–8—Zoe Karbonopsina, or "Zoe the Black-Eyed," was the mistress of Leo VI, and the mother to Leo VI's successor; after Zoe gave birth to a son Leo VI married her without the permission of the patriarch. Zoe cancelled the peace treaty with Simeon I made by Nicholas Mystikos, and she was blamed for the treacherous fighting that followed between the Bulgarian and Byzantine armies; in the end she was sent to a convent by Romanos Lecapenus.**

Section II: Comprehension

Write a two or three-sentence answer to each of the following questions.

1. What did Leo VI's nickname "Leo Sophos" mean? How did he earn this nickname?

A1.—Pg. 479, ¶ 1—Leo VI's nickname "Leo Sophos" meant "Leo the Wise," or better, "Leo the Bookish." Leo loved to read and had a strong memory. He spent his evenings by writing military manuals, revising legal codes, composing hymns and poems, and preparing sermons, which he delivered on feast days and special occasions.

2. Why did the theologian Arethas of Caesarea give Leo VI another nickname—*theosophos*?

A2.—Pg. 479, ¶ 2—Arethas of Caesarea called Leo VI *theosophos*, meaning "wise in the things of God," which was code for "meddler in sacred things," because he was heavily involved in the affairs of the church. Soon after he became emperor of Constantinople, Leo VI replaced the patriarch with own brother Stephen, and when Stephen died he appointed the next two patriarchs as well.

3. Describe the Rus threat faced by Leo VI. How did he handle the threat?

A3.—Pg. 481, ¶ 5 to Pg. 482, ¶ 2—By the end of the ninth century, Rus power had spread, and neighboring Slavic tribes, including the eastern Slavic tribe of the Drevlians, were forced to pay tribute. The *Russian Primary Chronicle* lists a multitude of subjected peoples who were forced to supply troops for an attack on Constantinople—a total of two thousand ships, manned by men from twelve different nations, that could supposedly move straight from water to land because of wheels attached to their sides. Leo VI was scared of the Rus: he paid a huge tribute to them so that they would retreat from Constantinople when they attacked in 906, and in 911 he issued a second treaty that established a fragile peace between them.

4. What were Simeon I's reasons for attacking Constantinople during Alexander's rule?

A4.—Pg. 482, ¶ 3 to Pg. 483, ¶ 3—The first reason Simeon I wanted to attack Constantinople was that Alexander refused to pay him the yearly tribute his brother Leo VI had promised. Second, Alexander refused to acknowledge Simeon I as basileus, or emperor, of the Bulgarian people. Simeon I was cheated of his money and greatly insulted by Alexander, so he could justify to his people the attack on Constantinople.

5. Explain Nicholas Mystikos's awkward position as Simeon I approached the walls of Constantinople with his army.

A5.—Pg. 483, ¶ 4—Nicholas Mystikos was in an awkward position as Simeon I approached the walls of Constantinople with his army because of his relationship to Constantine VII. Nicholas Mystikos was exiled by Constantine VII's father, and if he admitted that Constantine VII was legitimate and the rightful ruler of Constantine, then he would also admit that he was wrong in denying Leo VI the right to marry Zoe Karbonopsina. How could he support an emperor the he thought was illegitimate?

6. What were the terms of the peace treaty Nicholas Mystikos made with Simeon I? Why was Nicholas Mystikos able to agree to these terms?

A6.—Pg. 483, ¶ 5 & 6—The terms of the peace treaty Nicholas Mystikos made with Simeon I were that Byzantium would pay tribute to the Bulgarians, Constantine VII would agree to take one of Simeon's daughters as his wife, and he himself, the patriarch of Constantinople, would crown Simeon as emperor of the Bulgarians. Nicholas Mystikos was able to make this treaty because he didn't believe Constantine VII had any rightful claim over the people of Constantinople, so to Nicholas Mystikos, Simeon I's parallel power was equally illegitimate.

7. What happened at the Battle of Anchialus?

A7.—Pg. 484, ¶ 3—When the Byzantine land forces met the Bulgarian army at Anchialus, the Byzantine army was slaughtered; it was the bloodiest day of fighting in centuries. Almost all of Leo Phocas's officers and tens of thousands of regular soldiers fell. The battleground was unusable for decades afterwards because of the corpses stacked on it.

8. How did Romanos Lecapenus take control of Byzantine's council of regents?

A8.—Pg. 484, ¶ 5–7—Romanos Lecapenus had sailed for Constantinople after the Battle of Anchialus, and when Leo Phocas was defeated again by Simeon I right outside of Constantinople, Romanos invited the city officials to board his flagship to discuss strategy. He then locked them in the hold, after which he marched into the city and removed Zoe and all of her supporters. He then took charge of the council of regents, promising safety and deliverance.

9. After taking control of council of regents, how did Romanos Lecapenus become co-emperor of Byzantium?

A9.—Pg. 484, ¶ 8 to Pg. 485, ¶ 2—Romanos had much popular support after taking control of the council of regents, and he took advantage of that support by sending Zoe Karbonopsina to a convent and convincing the council to name him Constantine's second-in-command. He then arranged for the marriage of his own daughter Elena to Constantine VII, making him both vice emperor and father-in-law to the emperor. Finally, he easily convinced Nicholas Mystikos, who never believed in Constantine VII's claim to the throne, to crown him Romanos I, co-emperor of Byzantium.

10. Why did Simeon I make an alliance with the Fatimid caliph al-Mahdi? How did he lose this alliance?

A10.—Pg. 485, ¶ 4–7—Simeon I needed a navy to attack Constantinople, and he didn't have one—the alliance with the Fatimid caliph al-Mahdi gave Simeon I ships. However, on their way back from North Africa the Bulgarian ambassadors that had brokered the deal were taken prisoner by Byzantine soldiers and sent back to Constantinople. Romanos then sent his own envoy to al-Mahdi, offering a tribute and guaranteed peace if the caliph would become his ally; al-Mahdi agreed and Simeon I lost his alliance.

11. For what reason did Romanos Lecapenus make an alliance with the Abbasid caliph?

A11.—Pg. 485, ¶ 6 & 7—Romanos Lecapenus wanted to make sure that neither half of the Islamic empire attacked him, so he sent a peace offering to the caliph in Baghdad as well as to the Fatimid caliph. The Abbasid caliph accepted Romanos's terms.

12. Why did Romanos agree to peace with Peter I after he attacked Byzantine territory in Macedonia? What were the terms of the peace treaty?

A12.—Pg. 486, ¶ 2 & 3—Romanos agreed to peace with Peter I because his attack on the Byzantine territory in Macedonia was quick and destructive—Romanos saw that more destruction could follow. The peace treaty arranged a marriage between Peter I's daughter and Romanos's granddaughter. More importantly, Romanos acknowledged Peter I as emperor, making the Bulgarian king equal in status to the ruler of Constantinople.

Section III: Critical Thinking

The student may not use his text to answer this question.

The power of the court was great in the medieval world. In Japan, the clan that ruled the court could always trump the heavenly sovereign, and in Constantinople, one's acceptance by the court could mean more than the voice of God's representatives on earth. Write a paragraph or two explaining the measures Leo VI took to have his son with mistress Zoe Karbonopsina accepted as his legitimate heir. In your answer make sure to explain the significance of the Purple Chamber, the name given to Leo VI's son at his birth and his coronation, and what happened to the patriarch that did not accept Leo VI's son as his successor.

Legitimacy was high currency in the medieval world. However, as the student has learned, if the circumstances of a coronation or a birth, for example, were not legitimate, the context could be shifted so a significant event could have the air of rightfulness. This is what happened with Leo VI's son. Zoe Karbonopsina was Leo VI's mistress, the woman he tried to make an heir with after three marriages. This was not a legitimate match in the eyes of the church. The patriarch of Constantinople stood by the rule that if one's spouse died, it was acceptable to marry again—but only once. Leo VI managed to get a third marriage approved by the patriarch, but a fourth seemed to be out of the question.

When Zoe Karbonopsina was pregnant with her second child by Leo VI, the emperor had her moved into the porphyry-walled palace chamber (the Purple Chamber) where empresses traditionally gave birth to royal heirs. If you were born in the Purple Room, you were admitted into court, and to be admitted into court meant a certain type of legitimacy. The court lasted through many emperors; their power as a whole was greater than any single man: as written on page 480, "the emperors of Constantinople were also hostage to the court's goodwill, and an emperor's power was only as great as the loyalty of his ministers and officers." The court's acceptance of Leo VI's son was the first step in giving the baby a legitimate place in the royal succession.

Leo VI then gave his son the royal name "Constantine," which was another way he hoped to legitimize his son with Zoe Karbonopsina. The last step to secure his baby's position was to marry the baby's mother. The patriarch Nicholas Mystikos refused to give Leo VI permission to marry Zoe Karbonopsina, so Leo VI decided he did not need the patriarch's approval and married his mistress anyway. Though the church was in an uproar over the wedding, Leo VI nonetheless introduced the mother of his baby into the palace like an emperor's wife. When Leo VI's son reached the age of six, he was crowned as co-emperor and given the name "Constantine VII Porphyrogenitus," meaning "purple-born," to remind everyone that the court had supported Constantine's right to inherit the throne.

Meanwhile, the consequences for going against the church were grave for Leo VI. Leo defied the churchmen, and as a result Nicholas Mystikos was forced to bar the emperor from entering the churches in his own city. The consequences for denying Leo VI the right to marry his wife, and then barring the emperor from worship, were also grave for the church. Leo VI, defiant, sent his soldiers to remove the patriarch and the priests who objected to Zoe Karbonopsina's coronation, and sent them all into exile. This was the price the churchmen paid for Constantine VII Porphyrogenitus's legitimacy.

EXAMPLE ANSWER:

Leo VI had no heir, so when his mistress Zoe Karbonopsina was pregnant (after previously giving birth to a girl), Leo VI took his chances and put his mistress in the Purple Chamber for the birth of their second child. The Purple Chamber was royal, the room where empresses gave birth to their kings' heirs. A child born in the Purple Chamber was accepted by the court as legitimate, and this was necessary for Leo VI because he had been married three times before trying to make an heir with Zoe Karbonopsina. He needed to work very hard to make sure if his son was a boy that he would be accepted as his legitimate heir. Luckily, Zoe Karbonopsina had a boy, and he was given the royal name Constantine. Leo VI then married Zoe Karbonopsina against the wishes of the church, welcomed her into the palace as his empress, and when their son was six-years-old Leo VI crowned him co-emperor, giving him the name "Constantine VII Porphyrogenitus," meaning "purple born." This name was given to remind the world that the power and approval of the court was behind his son's right to inherit Leo VI's throne.

Leo VI had an heir, but it came at a price. When Leo VI decided to marry Zoe Karbonopsina, the churchmen in Constantinople were outraged, and the patriarch Nicholas Mystikos was forced to bar Leo VI from entering the churches in his own city. Leo VI did not accept this punishment, nor the church's disdain for his marriage, so he sent his soldiers to remove and exile the patriarch and the priests who objected to Zoe Karbonopsina's coronation. This was the price the churchmen paid for Constantine VII Porphyrogenitus's legitimacy.

Chapter Sixty-Four

The Creation of Normandy

The student may use her text when answering the questions in sections I and II.

Section I: **Who, What, Where**

Write a one or two-sentence answer explaining the significance of each item listed below.

Charles the Simple—**Pg. 489, ¶ 4 and Pg. 490, ¶ 2—Charles the Simple, grandson of Charles the Fat, was elected ruler by the noblemen of Western Francia and he fought regularly against invading Vikings. In 911, Charles the Simple signed the Treaty of Saint-Clair-sur-Epte which created Normandy.**

Gisela—**Pg. 490, ¶ 2—Gisela, Charles the Simple's daughter, was married to the Viking warrior Rollo after he signed the Treaty of Saint-Clair-sur-Epte. Her marriage to Robert, the duke of Normandy, sealed the treaty between Western Francia and the Vikings.**

Louis the Child—**Pg. 489, ¶ 4—Louis the Child, Arnulf of Carinthia's son, succeeded his father as king of Eastern Francia. He took the throne when he was just six, and his kingdom was troubled by invading Magyars.**

Rollo—**Pg. 489, ¶ 6 to Pg. 490, ¶ 4—Rollo, a Viking chief that had spent most of his adult life fighting in Western Francia, agreed to Charles the Simple's Treaty of Saint-Clair-sur-Epte. After signing the treaty, Rollo chose the baptismal name of Robert and became the first duke of Normandy, theoretically in subjection to the king of the Franks but really ruling independently and as he pleased.**

Rudolph of Burgundy—**Pg. 489, ¶ 4—Rudolph of Burgundy, a Burgundian nobleman, led the upper part of Burgundy which remained independent after rebelling against Charles the Fat.**

Section II: Comprehension

Write a two or three-sentence answer to each of the following questions.

1. What were the terms of Louis of Provence's surrender to Berengar when he won back the Iron Crown of the Lombards in 902?

A1.—Pg. 488, ¶ 1—When Louis of Provence surrendered to Berengar in 902, he promised that he would return to his homeland. Louis promised he would be happy as being emperor of the Romans and ruling Provence as an independent king—he refused to swear allegiance to the king of the eastern Franks. He also swore he would never enter Italy again.

2. Why did the Italian nobles invite Louis back to Italy? Even though he knew Berengar would attack him, why did Louis agree?

A2.—Pg. 488, ¶ 2 & 3—The Italian nobles invited Louis back to Italy because they were sick of Berengar's meddlesome ways. The Italian nobility was used to having their independence, and unlike Berengar, Louis was a hands-off ruler. Even though he knew that Berengar would attack him, Louis agreed to return to Italy because be was guaranteed soldiers from the private armies of the Italian noblemen, and he was confident in their ability to protect him.

3. What did Louis of Provence say that got him in trouble with Adalbert and the Italian noblemen? What did Adalbert's wife think about Louis's comment?

A3.—Pg. 488, ¶ 4 & 5—Louis of Provence was taken aback by the size of the Italian private armies, and by the luxury in which Adalbert and the Italian noblemen lived. He commented to one of his generals that Adalbert lived in royal splendor, and it seemed that only the lack of a royal title kept Adalbert from being called king. Adalbert's wife took Louis's comment as a threat, and she told her husband that maybe Louis wasn't going to be as flexible of a ruler as the noblemen had hoped.

4. How did Louis of Provence become Louis the Blind?

A4.—Pg. 488, ¶ 5 to Pg. 489, ¶ 2—Hearing of the Italian noblemen's change of heart regarding Louis of Provence's leadership, Berengar offered the men a substantial bribe if they would let him into Verona late at night with his men while Louis was off guard. Berengar's men found the emperor of the Romans and brought him to Berengar, who told Louis he would spare his life but he would take his eyesight by gouging out his eyes as payment for re-entering Italy. Louis was forced to again give up the Iron Crown, as well as the title of emperor, because he could no longer function without help, but he was able to keep his rule of Provence where he would be known as "Louis the Blind."

5. Who followed Louis of Provence as the Roman emperor after he was blinded?

A5.—Pg. 489, *—After Louis of Provence was blinded, the role of emperor was not filled, and it remained vacant until 915. Berengar finally became the Roman emperor in 915, and held the title until 924.

6. What long term solution did Charles the Simple come up with in 911 for dealing with the Vikings?

A6.—Pg. 489, ¶ 5—In 911, Charles the Simple decided that instead of continuing to fight against Viking raids, he would give part of his land in Western Francia to the Viking invaders. The treaty would guarantee that in exchange for the land, the rest of his realm would be protected by the Vikings.

7. What were the terms of the Treaty of Saint-Clair-sur-Epte?

A7.—Pg. 489, ¶ 7 to Pg. 490, ¶ 2—The Treaty of Saint-Clair-sur-Epte gave the Vikings led by Rollo a homeland of their own on the western coast of Western Francia. In exchange for the land, Rollo agreed to accept Christian baptism, to be loyal to the king of the Western Franks, and to fight against any other Viking invaders who might trouble Charles the Simple's kingdom. Rollo was baptized as Robert, the first duke of Normandy, and he became the husband to Charles the Simple's daughter, Gisela.

Section III: Critical Thinking

The student may not use her text to answer this question.

Agreeing to a transfer of power on paper could mean something very different in real life. Robert of Normandy may have been a duke, but he was a Viking warrior at heart. Explain what happened when the new duke was ordered to kiss Charles the Simple's foot, and the real world meaning of Rollo's subversion.

We all know the phrase "Old habits die hard." Rollo was a Viking warrior who may have been baptized and made a duke, but that did not mean his fighting spirit was dampened. At the ceremony that gave Rollo, or Robert, his new land, he was asked by the bishop to kiss Charles the Simple's foot. To kiss the king's foot was a common gesture of respect for a subordinate ruler. Rollo refused. Pressed by the audience, he then agreed to show the traditional sign of respect, but he would not do it himself—he had one of his soldiers do it. This was already a distancing of the relationship between the king and the duke. Then, the chosen soldier took the king's foot while still standing upright, so that when he kissed the foot the king fell backwards. The crowd laughed, the king was made a fool of, and Rollo found a way around the expectation that he would bow to the king of Western Francia. Rollo's subversion at the ceremony reflected his intentions for his rule of Normandy. He was theoretically supposed to be under the rule of Charles the Simple, but Rollo would not be following orders, just as he turned the act of kissing the king's foot into a joke.

EXAMPLE ANSWER:

It should have seemed to Rollo, the Viking warrior, that he was being a given a great gift when Charles the Simple gave him a homeland and made him a duke. But following the traditions of honor meant little to Rollo. At the ceremony that gave Rollo his new land, he was asked by the bishop to kiss Charles the Simple's foot. To kiss the king's foot was a

common gesture of respect for a subordinate ruler. Rollo refused. Pressed by the audience, he then agreed to show the traditional sign of respect, but he would not do it himself—he had one of his soldiers do it. Then, the chosen soldier took the king's foot while still standing upright, so that when he kissed the foot the king fell backwards. Not only did Rollo insult the king by not kissing the foot himself, but he then made a fool of the king when his soldier caused him to fall backwards. Rollo's subversion at the ceremony reflected his intentions for his rule of Normandy. He was theoretically supposed to be under the rule of Charles the Simple, but Rollo would not be following orders. He would rule in his new homeland just as he pleased.

Section IV: Map Exercise

1. Using a black pencil, trace the rectangular outline of the frame for Map 64.1: The Creation of Normandy.

2. Using a blue pencil, trace the visible coastline on this map: the Atlantic along the continent around Britain (you need not trace Ireland at this time) and the Mediterranean visible around Italy and under Provence and Western Francia. You do not need to include islands at this time. Using a black pencil, trace the mountain peaks visible above Italy and under Western Francia. Repeat until the contours are familiar.

3. Trace the rectangular outline of the frame in black. Remove your tracing paper from the original. Using a regular pencil with an eraser as you look at Map 64.1, draw the coastline around Britain outside Eastern and Western Francia. Draw the coastline of the Mediterranean (you do not need to draw any islands at this time). Erase and redraw as necessary.

4. When you are pleased with your map, lay it over the original. Erase and redraw any lines which are more than ¼ inch off of the original.

5. Leaving your map over the original, trace the regions of the Emirate of Cordoba, Pamplona, Western Francia, Eastern Francia, Burgundy, Provence, the Kingdom of Italy, Ravenna, the Byzantine holdings in Italy, and the Papal States. Remove your map from the original. Study carefully the locations of the Emirate of Cordoba, Pamplona, Western Francia, Eastern Francia, Burgundy, Provence, the Kingdom of Italy, Ravenna, the Byzantine holdings in Italy, and the Papal States. When you are familiar with them, close the book. Using your regular pencil with an eraser, label each location inside the tracing you did of it. Check your map against the original. Correct any misplaced labels.

6. Now study the locations of Paris, Rome, Venice, and Verona. When you are familiar with them, close the book, mark the cities, and label them. When you are done, lay your map over the original. Erase and redraw any markings which are more than ¼ inch off of the original.

7. Draw the outline of Normandy. Label.

Chapter Sixty-Five

The Kingdom of Germany

The student may use his text when answering the questions in sections I and II.

Section I: Who, What, Where

Write a one or two-sentence answer explaining the significance of each item listed below.

Battle of Riade—**Pg. 494, ¶ 3 to Pg. 495, ¶ 2—The Battle of Riade was fought in 933 when Henry the Fowler brought together the armies of the German duchies to fight against the advancing Magyars. Henry the Fowler gave his men expert command, and they were able to break the Magyars: after the Battle of Riade the Magyars retreated back to the east and the German borders enjoyed a temporary peace.**

Boleslav—**Pg. 496, ¶ 1–3—Boleslav, Wenceslaus's younger brother, led the resistance against Wenceslaus, demanding he give up his alliance with Henry the Fowler and his Christianity. When Wenceslaus refused, Boleslav had his brother murdered and he declared himself prince of Bohemia which was an explicit rejection of becoming a German dukedom.**

Conrad—**Pg. 493, ¶ 4–6—Conrad, duke of Franconia, was elected king of Eastern Francia by his fellow dukes after the death of Louis the Child. Instead of ruling like a leader among equals, he insisted that the dukes of Eastern Francia obey him, which resulted in his fighting the other dukes until his death in 918.**

Drahomira—**Pg. 495, ¶ 4–6—Drahomira, Wenceslaus's mother and regent, was a believer in the ancient religions of her Slavic ancestors; she refused to be baptized and she had Wenceslaus's grandmother killed because she was raising the boy to be a Christian king. Wenceslaus refused to give up his Christianity and when he turned eighteen and took power in his own name, he had his mother exiled.**

Henry the Fowler—**Pg. 493, ¶ 6, Pg. 495, ¶ 2 and Pg. 496, ¶ 3 & 4—Henry the Fowler, duke of Saxony, was elected to be the king of Eastern Francia in 918 after Conrad's death. He led the duchies of Germany in a successful battle against the invading Magyars, he tried to**

incorporate Bohemia into Germany but failed, and when he died he broke with Frankish tradition and left his kingdom to one heir, his son Otto.

Ludmila—**Pg. 495, ¶ 4 & 5—Ludmila, the Christian grandmother of Wenceslaus, acted as one of Wenceslaus's regents when he came to the throne at fourteen. Ludmila instructed her grandson in Christianity and intended to teach him how to be a Christian king, but she was unable to do so because she was murdered by Wenceslaus's mother Drahomira because of their different religious views.**

Spytihnev—**Pg. 495, ¶ 3—Spytihnev, a Christian whose father had been baptized in Moravia by the missionary Methodius, moved his family to the west, away from the Magyar threat. With the help of Arnulf of Carinthia, he had established himself as the ruler in the new western land, the first duke of Bohemia.**

Wenceslaus—**Pg. 495, ¶ 4 to Pg. 3—Wenceslaus, grandson of Spytihnev and Christian duke of Bohemia, agreed to an alliance with Henry the Fowler to make Bohemia a part of Germany, but his brother disagreed with the alliance and had Wenceslaus killed. Because of his fierce belief in his Christian faith, Wenceslaus was taken up as a martyr for Christ.**

Section II: Comprehension

Write a two or three-sentence answer to each of the following questions.

1. Explain the difference between "duchies" and "stem duchies" and what both had to do with the long gone tribal territories of Francia.

A1.—Pg. 492, ¶ 3 & *—"Duchies" were semi-independent kingdoms that were once defined by the tribal loyalties of Germanic barbarians. "Stem duchies" were small individual realms within the larger kingdom of Eastern Francia; the name implies that each duchy's coherence came from a distant past as a single tribal unit from which its identity stemmed. In Louis the Child's time the duchies evolved as a result of his weak reign, but their origins came from the Germanic tribal territories of the past.

2. Who ruled the duchies, and who defended them?

A2.—Pg. 492, ¶ 3 to Pg. 493, ¶ 1—Each duchy was controlled by a powerful family and the head of these families, known as dukes—were both the rulers and defenders of their lands. The dukes raised their own armies, fought their own battles and ruled their own lands.

3. What happened when Louis the Child gathered an army at Augsburg to fight against the Magyars in 910?

A3.—Pg. 493, ¶ 3—Louis the Child's 910 push against the Magyars was a failure. The Magyars attacked before dawn, catching many of the soldiers still in their beds and then hours of fighting followed, with heavy casualties on both sides. Towards evening, the Magyars

pretended to retreat; when the Frankish army broke rank and chased after them, the Magyars doubled back around and attacked from behind, breaking the Frankish resistance and ending Louis the Child's fight.

4. Why did the dukes of Eastern Francia elect Conrad to be their leader after the death of Louis the Child?

A4.—Pg. 493, ¶ 4—When Louis the Child died, Charles the Simple claimed that Francia should be reunited, but the dukes of Eastern Francia, who ruled their own duchies, did not want to give up their power. Instead, they elected Conrad, a duke himself, to be their leader because they thought their individual powers would be preserved.

5. How did Henry the Fowler spend his first three years as king of Eastern Francia?

A5.—Pg. 493, 6—In his first three years as king of Eastern Francia, Henry negotiated a series of oaths between himself and the dukes of Eastern Francia. The oaths of "vassalage" laid out an almost-equal relationship; they acknowledged that both kings and dukes had responsibilities towards each other, and recognized the dukes as "senior partners" in the job of governing, with authority to administer their own laws and lands as they pleased.

7. Why did Henry the Fowler want to make Bohemia a part of Germany?

A7.—Pg. 495, ¶ 2 & 3—Henry the Fowler was able to force the Magyars to retreat after their defeat at the Battle of Riade, but he knew their absence from the German border would be temporary. In an effort to create a buffer between Germany and the Magyar advance, Henry the Fowler wanted to incorporate the dukedom of Bohemia into Germany. Bohemia was located on the eastern side of Germany, and would be a barrier between his kingdom and the Magyar invaders.

8. For what reason did some Bohemian officials disagree with Wenceslaus's decision to make an alliance with Henry the Fowler?

A8.—Pg. 495, ¶ 7 to 496, ¶ 1—Some of Bohemian officials thought Henry the Fowler was dangerous and they did not agree with the alliance Wenceslaus had forged. They saw the independence of Bohemia threatened by the Germans. Also they believed that the Christian religion, a religion that had come to Bohemia via Moravian missionaries as a tool for domination, would make Bohemia even more vulnerable to conquest by the Germans.

9. How did Wenceslaus become a famous martyr for Christ?

A9.—496, ¶ 3—Wenceslaus died because of his Christianity: when his brother demanded that Wenceslaus end his alliance with Henry the Fowler and give up his Christianity, Wenceslaus refused to do so. Wenceslaus was murdered by his brother while attending mass, and he was then hailed by the Bohemians as a martyr for Christ. Stories blossomed about Wenceslaus, turning his devotion to his faith into Christian myth.

Section III: Critical Thinking

The student may not use his text to answer this question.

In the previous chapter, we learned about the creation of Normandy. Charles the Simple could not withstand any more Viking attacks, so he turned over part of his land to the Viking warrior Rollo and hoped for the best. In this chapter, we read about the creation of Germany. Unlike Normandy, Germany was long in the making. Write a paragraph explaining how Eastern Francia organically turned into Germany. In your answer, make sure to include the significance of who Henry the Fowler chose to be his successor.

Eastern Francia formed around land that had once been populated by Germanic barbarian tribes. The land may have been conquered by the Franks, but the roots of kingdom's identity were German. As Louis the Child's grasp over his kingdom weakened, governance fell to the heads of powerful families that ruled over their duchies. The duchies had regained their semi-independence as they had once existed when they were the tribal lands. In the past, the tribes were connected by the Germanic roots, but each tribe ruled over its own territory. There was little difference with the duchies—families ruling over their own land, connected as part of a larger kingdom.

In 925, Henry the Fowler had taken part of Western Francia and added it to his kingdom, he ruled from Charlemagne's old capital Aachen, and he led the dukes of the five duchies—Franconia, Saxony, Bavaria, Swabia, and Lorraine—as equals. This was not like the rule of the Carolingian kings of Francia's past. Henry's kingdom was not a kingdom of Franks; it was a kingdom make up of duchies born of old Germanic tribal identities. His lands were German, so his kingdom became Germany. To reinforce the break from the Franks, Henry named a single heir to his throne, his son Otto. Frankish tradition was to leave a piece of one's kingdom to each of one's sons, but Henry no longer ruled as a Frank—he ruled as a German.

EXAMPLE ANSWER:

Eastern Francia formed around land that had once been populated by Germanic barbarian tribes. As Louis the Child's grasp over his kingdom weakened, governance fell to the heads of powerful families that ruled over their duchies. The duchies had regained their semi-independence as they had once existed when they were the tribal lands. In the past, the tribes were connected by their Germanic roots, but each tribe ruled over its own territory. There was little difference with the duchies—families ruling over their own land, connected as part of a larger kingdom. In 925, Henry the Fowler had taken part of Western Francia and added it to his kingdom; he ruled from Charlemagne's old capital Aachen, and he led the dukes of the five duchies—Franconia, Saxony, Bavaria, Swabia, and Lorraine—as equals. This was not like the rule of the Carolingian kings of Francia's past. Henry's kingdom was not a kingdom of Franks, it was a kingdom make up of duchies born of old Germanic tribal identities. His lands were German, so his kingdom became Germany. To reinforce the break from the Franks, Henry named a single heir to his throne, his son Otto. Frankish tradition was to leave a piece of one's kingdom to each of one's sons, but Henry no longer ruled as a Frank—he ruled as a German.

Chapter Sixty-Six

The Turn of the Wheel

The student may use her text when answering the questions in sections I and II.

Section I: Who, What, Where

Write a one or two-sentence answer explaining the significance of each item listed below.

Arinjaya—**Pg. 501, ¶ 3 & 4—Arinjaya, Gandaraditya's younger brother, heir and co-regent, ruled over Chola while his brother built temples. Arinjaya was a weak ruler and during his time in power the Pandya reclaimed some of their old land from the Chola.**

Battle of Vallala—**Pg. 499, ¶ 3 & 4—The Battle of Vallala occurred sometime around 916. The Cholas defeated the Rashtrakutas; this was the third Chola win in a row, which made king Parantaka of Chola seem unstoppable in his conquests.**

Gandaraditya—**Pg. 500, ¶ 2 and Pg. 501, ¶ 3—Gandaraditya, Parantaka's younger son and successor, was a devout follower of Shiva. Gandaraditya made the poor choice of leaving the running of his empire to his brother Arinjaya while he and his wife built new temples and repaired old ones all over Chola.**

Indra III—**Pg. 499, ¶ 2, 3 & 5—Indra III, grandson of Krishna II, faced Chola threats to his Rashtrakuta rule from the very beginning of his reign. After being defeated by the Chola at the Battle of Vallala, Indra III managed to take Pratihara for his kingdom, but he died prematurely in 929 before he could secure his conquest.**

Indra IV—**Pg. 502, ¶ 1 & 2—Indra IV was the last Rashtrakuta king. At the start of his reign he had to fight against the newly proclaimed king Tailapa II of the Western Chalukya, a struggle that continued for seven years until Indra IV decided to starve himself to death.**

Khottiga—**Pg. 501, ¶ 5—Khottiga, Krishna III's successor, faced revolt around the edges of the Rashtrakuta empire. In 972, less than five years into his rule, he was killed in battle defending the borders of his kingdom.**

Krishna III—**Pg. 499, ¶ 7 to Pg. 500, ¶ 1—Krishna III, great-nephew of Indra III, was the last great Rashtrakuta king, defeating the great Parantaka of the Chola in battle at Takkolam in 949.**

Marasimha—**Pg. 502, ¶ 1—Marasimha, Indra IV's uncle and chief ally, was so humiliated by the Western Chalukya defeat of Rashtrakuta forces that he committed the ritual suicide known as *sallekhana*.**

Parantaka—**Pg. 498, ¶ 1, Pg. 499, ¶ 4 and Pg. 500, ¶ 2—Parantaka, son of Chola king Aditya, started his reign by defeating the Pandyan resistance in the south as well as their Sri Lankan allies, and then defeating the Rashtrakuta in the north. The power of the Chola grew under Parantaka, but after his army was defeated by the Rashtrakuta under Krishna III, Parantaka grew weary and died in 950.**

Rajaditya Chola—**Pg. 499, ¶ 8 to Pg. 500, ¶ 1—Rajaditya Chola, Parantaka's son and the crown prince of the Chola, was killed in 949 in battle at the city of Takkolam. A chance arrow struck the crown prince; when he fell, his wing of the army scattered, and the Chola army was forced to retreat.**

Rajasimha II—**Pg. 498, ¶ 3 to Pg. 499, ¶ 1 & 4—Rajasimha II, king of Pandya, made an alliance with the king of Sri Lanka in an effort to defend his kingdom against the Chola king Parantaka. After Parantaka defeated Rajasimha II, the Pandyan king fled to Sri Lanka with his crown and royal regalia so that he could one day take his throne back, but Parantaka's defeat of the Rashtrakuta made Rajasimha II give up any hope of recovering his power.**

Sembiyan Mahadevi—**Pg. 501, ¶ 3—Sembiyan Mahadevi was the wife of Gandaraditya, and a devout follower of Shiva. She built new temples and repaired old ones all through Chola with her husband, stamping their names across the countryside.**

Shaivite—**Pg. 501, ¶ 2—A Shaivite was a person who was devoted to the god Shiva and his divine escort. The kings who ruled Chola after its founding were Shaivite, and the building of temples for Shiva to inhabit often acted as a symbol of the Chola king's power.**

Tailapa—**Pg. 501, ¶ 6 and Pg. 502, ¶ 2—Tailapa, a Western Chalukya war-leader, declared independence from Rashtrakuta and crowned himself Tailapa II, king of the Western Chalukya; he was the first Western Chalukya leader in two hundred years to claim sovereignty. After Indra IV starved himself to death, Tailapa II seized Rashtrakuta territory, making him the ruler of the center of India.**

Section II: Comprehension

Write a two or three-sentence answer to each of the following questions.

1. Why did Rajasimha II ask the Sri Lankan king for an alliance? What was the result of the Pandya-Sri Lankan alliance?

A1.—Pg. 498, ¶ 3—Rajasimha II needed help because he knew the Chola king was planning to attack his kingdom but because the Chola were so powerful, few kings were willing to defy Parantaka. However, Rajasimha II was able to make an alliance with the Sri Lankan king and in 909, Sri Lankan armies sailed across the water and joined with the Pandyan forces. The alliance did not help the Pandya kingdom; the Chola armies destroyed the Pandyan and Sri Lankan resistance.

2. After being defeated at the Battle of Vallala, how did the Rashtrakuta king Indra III regain some power for his kingdom? Why didn't that power last?

A2.—Pg. 499, ¶ 5 & 6—After being defeated at the Battle of Vallala, Indra III tried to regain his power by turning north against the Pratihara. He managed to fight his way all the way to the crown jewel of the Pratihara kingdom, the city of Kannauj itself, and conquer it. However, Indra III died prematurely in 929, and while his successors fought over the throne, the kingdom lost the power Indra III had just won back.

3. How did the Rashtrakuta defeat the Chola in 949 in the battle at Takkolam? What suggests that after their defeat the Chola had to pay homage to the Rashtrakuta?

A3.—Pg. 499, ¶ 8 to Pg. 500, ¶ 1—The forces between the Rashtrakuta and the Chola at Takkolam were evenly matched, so what won the battle for the Rashtrakuta was a chance arrow that hit the crown prince Rajaditya Chola. When Rajaditya was hit, the wing of the army under his command scattered, then the whole army scattered and Parantaka was forced to retreat and to hand over northern territory. Because there were no more inscriptions about the greatness of the Chola after this defeat, it seems most likely that the Chola were also forced to pay homage to Krishna III as their superior ruler.

4. In what way did the building of temples for Shiva to inhabit help substantiate Chola dominance?

A4.—Pg. 501, ¶ 2—The kings who ruled after the founding of the Chola empire were devotees of the god Shiva and his divine consort. Aditya had built temples for Shiva to inhabit all along the Kaveri River, which was a sacred watercourse. The temples were a symbol of power; while they were strong fighters, it was also a symbol of dominance for the Chola to boast of inviting the gods to come and live in their empire.

5. What happened to the Chola empire while Gandaraditya and Sembiyan Mahadevi were building temples all over the countryside?

A5.—Pg. 501, ¶ 3 & 4—While Gandaraditya and his queen were attending to the temples, Arinjaya was left to run the Chola empire. Arinjaya was not a strong ruler, and before long a relative of the Pandyan king came out of obscurity and claimed the old Pandyan lands

for himself. When Arinjaya died, the Chola empire had turned into a tiny state, with the northern territory occupied by the Rashtrakuta and the southern territory in the hands of a Pandyan pretender.

6. Define *sallekhana*. Why would Marasimha and Indra IV commit *sallekhana*?

A6.—Pg. 502, ¶ 1 & 2—*Sallekhana* was the Indian name for ritual suicide enacted via starvation. *Sallekhana* was honorable because it took courage for one to commit to it, and it offered the possibility of a permanent end to the cycle of birth and rebirth. Marasimha and Indra IV witnessed the continuous cycles of power-hungry fighting, with one empire on top and then another—*sallekhana*, by putting an end to reincarnation, meant that neither man would ever have to witness the violence of war again.

Section III: Critical Thinking

The student may not use her text to answer this question.

The reading in this chapter makes it very clear to us that there is a difference between symbols of power, and power itself. Parantaka of the Chola wanted to find the crown and royal regalia hidden in Sri Lanka by Rajasimha II of Pandya because he wanted to show the world the Chola had destroyed the Pandya. However, he didn't *need* the exiled king's belongings to be strong. Parantaka knew the symbols of Rajasimha II's power were secondary to the Chola's real power. But what happened to that power? Write a paragraph explaining how the blurring of lines between real and symbolic power—in the form of temples—was the death of the Chola after Parantaka's death.

Parantaka was a great fighter. Like the Chola kings before him, Parantaka claimed his power by right of conquest. The temples that were built in Chola were an afterthought, secondary to the power of the sword. Inscriptions tell us that Aditya, a worshipper of Shiva but also a man of war, built temples along the Kaveri River for Shiva to inhabit. These temples were built not only as a place to worship but also a symbols of power. The temples invited Shiva to come and live in the Chola empire. To house a god was a clear sign of dominance, a divine symbol of the Chola's earthly ferocity.

The temples worked as a symbol of power because the Chola were strong fighters. But when Gandaraditya came to the throne, his focus on the temples took away from the real world fighting power of the Chola, and the empire crumbled. The fixing up and building of temples made the Chola weak. While Gandaraditya worshipped, the Pandya reclaimed their land, and the Rashtrakuta grew strong in the north. Unlike Parantaka, who would have liked to have the Pandyan crown and regalia but didn't need it to prove his might, Gandaraditya relied on the symbols of power to keep his kingdom strong, and that was its ruin. Symbols did not win wars or keep an empire's borders strong. Gandaraditya's faith could not protect his kingdom, and by the end of his reign, the Chola kingdom had shrunken into a tiny state.

EXAMPLE ANSWER:

The temples that were all over the Chola empire were built as both places of worship and also as symbols of Chola power. Inscriptions tell us that Aditya, a worshipper of Shiva but also a man of war, built temples along the Kaveri River for Shiva to inhabit. The temples invited Shiva to come and live in the Chola empire. To house a god was a clear sign of dominance, a divine symbol of the Chola's earthly ferocity. When Gandaraditya came to the throne, he focused on the fixing up and building of temples without backing those temples up with conquest, and that made the Chola weak. While Gandaraditya worshipped, the Pandya reclaimed their land, and the Rashtrakuta grew strong in the north. Unlike Parantaka, who would have liked to have the Pandyan crown and regalia but didn't need it to prove his might, Gandaraditya relied on the symbols of power to keep his kingdom strong, and that was its ruin. Symbols did not win wars or keep an empire's borders strong. Gandaraditya's faith could not protect his kingdom, and by the end of his reign, the Chola kingdom had shrunken into a tiny state.

Section IV: **Map Exercise**

1. Using a black pencil, trace the rectangular outline of the frame for Map 66.1: The Height of the Chola.

2. Using a blue pencil, trace the coastline of the Arabian Sea. Include Sri Lanka. With your blue pencil, trace the Indus River, the Ganges River, the Narmada, and the Kaveri River. Use simple peaks to represent all the mountain peaks. Repeat until the contours are familiar.

3. Using a new sheet of paper, trace the rectangular outline of the frame in black. Remove your tracing paper from the original, and draw the coastline of the Arabian Sea, including Sri Lanka. Draw the Indus River, the Ganges River, the Kaveri River, and the mountains (just using simple peaks). Erase and redraw as necessary.

4. When you are pleased with your map, lay it over the original. Erase and redraw any lines which are more than ¼ inch off of the original.

5. Remove your map. Mark the Arabian Sea, the Indus River, the Ganges River, the Narmada, and the Kaveri. Study carefully the locations of Makran, Debal, Pratihara, Rashtrakuta, Western Chalukya, Chola, and Pandya. Then study the locations of the cities of Kannauj and Takkolam. Study also the locations of Mt. Kailasa and the Battle of Vallala. When you are familiar with them, close the book. On your map, mark the locations of Makran, Debal, Pratihara, Rashtrakuta, Western Chalukya, Chola, and Pandya; and the cities of Kannauj and Takkolam and also Mt. Kailasa and the Battle of Vallala. Check your map against the original, and correct any misplaced labels.

Chapter Sixty-Seven

The Capture of Baghdad

The student may use his text when answering the questions in sections I and II.

Section I: Who, What, Where

Write a one or two-sentence answer explaining the significance of each item listed below.

Abd ar-Rahman III—**Pg. 506, ¶ 3 and Pg. 507, ¶ 2—Abd ar-Rahman III, grandson and successor of the emir Abdullah of Cordoba, succeeded his grandfather as emir and used the Fatimid rebellion to declare himself to be independent, to be caliph of Cordoba.**

Ahmad—**Pg. 507, ¶ 5 & 6—Ahmad, emir of the Samanids, expanded Samanid control across the east by extending trade up the Volga river to the Khazars and the Rus and by capturing the remaining strongholds of the Saffarids. Ahmad was murdered in 914 by his servants during a rebellion in the old Saffarid province of Sistan—full of Persian speakers—because he was trying to make Arabic the official language of the Samanid court.**

Ahmad ibn Buya—**Pg. 509, ¶ 7 & 8—Ahmad ibn Buya, a Buyid general, marched into Baghdad in 945 and claimed the title "Commander of Commanders" for himself. Ahmad ibn Buya had the seated caliph deposed and blinded, and he allowed a new caliph to be elected but barred him from any participation in the government of the city.**

Alfonso III—**Pg. 506, ¶ 2—Alfonso III, king of Asturias, brought together the territories of Asturias, Leon, and Galicia into a triple-sized Christian realm known as the Kingdom of Leon. He married a Pamplona princess, creating a solid wall of Christian alliance against Cordoban power.**

Ali ibn Buya—**Pg. 508, ¶ 1 and Pg. 509, ¶ 7—Ali ibn Buya, one of Mardaviz al-Ziyar's officials, seized the city of Karaj in 932 and used it as a base to battle into the Ziyarid territory of Fars. Ali ibn Buya's brother later took the title "Commander of Commanders" in Baghdad.**

Al-Jaihani—**Pg. 507, ¶ 7—Al-Jaihani, Nasr's regent, lost Sistan to a Saffarid rebellion when the young man came to power.**

Al-Muqtadir—**Pg. 504, ¶ 5 and Pg. 508, ¶ 5—Al-Muqtadir was Abbasid caliph at the time of al-Mahdi's rule. Al-Muqtadir had remained alive as the figurehead caliph because he was content to be powerless, but in 932 he was deposed by his brother al-Qahir.**

Al-Qahir—**Pg. 508, ¶ 5—Al-Qahir, brother of al-Muqtadir, deposed his brother and ruled as caliph for two years. Al-Qahir did not act as a puppet caliph, and as s result he was deposed, blinded by his Turkish courtiers and soldiers and left to spend the last years of his life begging on the streets of Baghdad.**

Al-Qaim bi-amr Allah—**Pg. 504, ¶ 3 and Pg. 505, ¶ 2—Al-Qaim bi-amr Allah, meaning "The One Who Executes God's Command," was the title given to al-Mahdi's nineteen-year-old son when he was named co-ruler and successor of the Fatimid caliphate. As head of the Fatimid army, al-Qaim faced major defeat by the Abbasids twice and as a result he was unable to take Baghdad for his father.**

Al-Radi—**Pg. 508, ¶ 5 & 6 and Pg. 509, ¶ 3 & 6—Al-Radi, nephew of al-Qahir and son of al-Muqtadir, became the puppet-caliph after his uncle was deposed. Al-Radi was forced to make Muhammad ibn Ra'iq "Commander of Commanders," but al-Radi only lasted as caliph for two years until he was overthrown.**

Mahdia—**Pg. 504, ¶ 2—Mahdia was the capital city established by the Fatimid caliph. The city was on the North African coast.**

Mardaviz al-Ziyar—**Pg. 508, ¶ 1 & 3—Mardaviz al-Ziyar created his own emirate, the Ziyarid dynasty, by helping Samanid officials regain control of their territory near the Caspian Sea and then taking that land for himself. Mardaviz al-Ziyar gained great favor when he announced himself the restorer of the old Persian empire, a follower of Zoroastrianism, undoer of the Muslim conquest.**

Muhammad ibn Ra'iq—**Pg. 509, ¶ 2 & 5—Muhammad ibn Ra'iq, al-Radi's most powerful general, was able to get al-Radi to name him *amir ul-umara*, "Commander of Commanders"—a position that would take over the administration of the empire—by bribing the caliph with the taxes he had collected in the lands southeast of Baghdad. Ibn Ra'iq did not bring peace to Baghdad, instead struggle for control of the caliphate caused many rebellions.**

Mu'nis—**Pg. 505, ¶ 1 & 2—Mu'nis, a skilled eunuch soldier, was put at the head of the Abbasid resistance to al-Qaim's approaching army. Mu'nis defeated Fatimid forces in 915 and 920, squelching their threat to Baghdad.**

Nasr—**Pg. 507, ¶ 7—Nasr, son of Ahmad, became the Samanid emir at eight years old; his regent was al-Jaihani. The Samanid empire shrunk under Nasr when Abbasid officers in Sistan rebelled and made their own little country.**

Umar ibn-Hafsun—**Pg. 506, ¶ 1 and Pg. 507, ¶ 1—Umar ibn-Hafsun was a rebel that had been leading guerilla attacks on Cordoban forces for almost thirty years, starting during the rule of Abdullah. When ar-Rahman became emir, he launched yearly attacks against the rebel until his revolt finally disintegrated.**

Section II: Comprehension

Write a two or three-sentence answer to each of the following questions.

1. Describe the Fatimid army's march through North Africa towards Alexandria in the early 10th century.

A1.—Pg. 504, ¶ 4—In 913 al-Qaim led his army to Tripoli and forced the city to surrender after a six-month siege. Then, using Tripoli as a base, the Fatimid army marched further east along the coast into Cyrenaica, the far edge of Abbasid control. By August of the following year, Fatimid soldiers were streaming into Alexandria, in November al-Qaim arrived in the city, and with his arrival the mosques of Alexandria were ordered to honor the Shi'a rulers, not the Abbasids of Baghdad, in their prayers.

2. How did Mu'nis take down al-Mahdi and the Fatimid army?

A2.—Pg. 504, ¶ 5 to Pg. 505, ¶ 2—Al-Muqtadir's vizier and generals knew that the Fatimid armies intended to march all the way to Baghdad because al-Qaim had sent a letter to his father promising that he would spread Fatimid power all the way to the Tigris and Euphrates. Mu'nis lead the Abbasid army towards Egypt in 915 and they abruptly stopped the Fatimid expansion east. In 920, after al-Mahdi had built himself a fleet of warships and launched a second attack, the Abbasids again destroyed the Fatimid forces and depleted their new navy.

3. Who were the "counts" that were bothering the Emirate of Cordoba?

A3.—Pg. 506, ¶ 1—In the Spanish Marches, the mountainous lands between the Emirate of Cordoba and the Frankish border, independent warlords supported by the Frankish kings ruled. These warlords—who often took the title of count—threatened the emirate's lands in the northeast. The count of Barcelona was particularly troublesome.

4. Why did Ahmad want to make Arabic the official language of the Samanid court? What resistance did he face?

A4.—Pg. 507, ¶ 6—Ahmad wanted to make Arabic the official language of the Samanid court because he felt that, as a lieutenant for the caliph in Baghdad, his pieced-together Muslim kingdom should speak the language of the Muslims. The Persian speakers of the old Saffarid lands Ahmad had taken control of did not want to be part of an Arab-dominated Muslim kingdom; they wanted their own Persian lands, and language. Ahmad faced

rebellion after rebellion in the old Saffarid province of Sistan, ending only when he was murdered in his own tent by his servants.

5. How did Sistan come to be its own little country (at least until 963)?

A5.—Pg. 507, ¶ 7—After Nasr came to be the Samanid emir, with al-Jaihani ruling as his regent, Abbasid officers took advantage of this change in power to rebel and claim Sistan. They made it into their own little country, and found a Saffarid family member to install as their puppet-emir. Their arrangement lasted until 963.

6. Why did Ali ibn Buya start to call himself "shah" rather than "emir" of his newly conquered territory?

A6.—Pg. 508, ¶ 3—Mardaviz al-Ziyar played on the feelings of the people he conquered near the Caspian Sea, and announced himself restorer of their old Persian empire, and a follower of Zoroastrianism. Al-Ziyar was so successful in garnering support after his proclamation of faith to the Persian traditions that Ali ibn Buya followed his lead. Thus, he started calling himself "shah," the old Persian honorific, instead of the despised Muslim title of "emir."

7. What did al-Radi realize about the position of the caliph when he came to power?

A7.—Pg. 508, ¶ 6 to Pg. 509, ¶ 1—When al-Radi came to the position of caliph, he realized that there was no way for the caliph to continue on as head of the Abbasid state. The breaking away of the eastern territories meant that the tax base of the empire had been ruined. He could not pay his soldiers, he could barely supply his own court, and he certainly did not have the money to fight off any real challenges to his power.

8. How did Muhammad ibn Ra'iq rise up to be *amir ul-umara,* while the Abbasid caliphate came to an end in all but name?

A8.—Pg. 509, ¶ 2–4—Muhammad ibn Ra'iq had taken control of the lands southeast of Baghdad and refused to send the taxes he collected there on to the capital unless al-Radi would agree to recognize ibn Ra'iq with the title *amir ul-umara,* "Commander of Commanders." Al-Radi had no choice but to agree, so the general came into Baghdad with his handpicked band of Turkish soldiers, turned over the tax revenues and then took over the administration of the empire. This meant that the Commander of Commanders would control the remains of the empire, while the Abbasid caliph was left with little more than the title.

9. Why did ibn Ra'iq breach the Nahrawan Canal? What was the result?

A9.—Pg. 509, ¶ 5 & 6—In order to block the path of one of his challengers, ibn Ra'iq ordered the Nahrawan Canal breached. The breach temporarily blocked the advance of the threat, but it also destroyed the irrigation that kept the plains populated. The farmers who had sent their produce to Baghdad began to move away, their farms withered, and the struggle for the control of the caliphate intensified.

Section III: Critical Thinking

The student may not use his text to answer this question.

As we have been reading about the ups and downs within the Islamic empire, one thread has been consistent: the fight over who should rule has been based on sectarian politics, and not strictly on power. In this chapter we see a shift in the fight over the caliphate(s). Write a paragraph explaining why the emir of Cordoba, Abd ar-Rahman III, declared himself to be a caliph. Then explain how the caliphate became nothing more than a shell, and how it could be that the Buyid general Ahmad ibn Buya was in control of the empire.

The rise of the caliphate in Cordoba is not directly related to the rise of Ahmad ibn Buya, but the student should see the two events as connected because they both show the collapse of religious right to rule.

Abd ar-Rahman III saw al-Mahdi's declaration of the Fatimid caliphate not as a challenge to the Abbasid caliphate, but as a destruction of the sanctified role of caliph itself. He saw both existing caliphs as fictional leaders, and so instead of swearing allegiance to either one, he made himself a leader as well. On January 16, 929, ar-Rahman declared himself to be caliph of Cordoba, Commander of the Believers, Defender of the Religion of God. Unlike the Fatimid caliph, ar-Rahman was not claiming to be the one true caliph. Instead, he was declaring his complete and total independence from both the Abbasids and Fatimids. Ar-Rahman would rule on his own account, claiming his authority from his Umayyad ancestors, placing himself outside of the Fatimid-Abbasid conflict.

Abd ar-Rahman's refusal to bow to either the Abbasid or the Fatimid caliphate made real the lack of religious power behind the supposed "chosen" leader of the Muslim people. The divine thread connecting the caliph back to the Prophet had grown bare, and by the time of Ahmad ibn Buya, it had snapped. When Muhammad ibn Ra'iq demanded the title "Commander of Commanders" and the power to rule over the administration of the empire, he took away everything that made the caliph the head of state. The Abbasid caliph may have been a puppet for a long time but whoever occupied the position still pretended to rule. When the shift under Muhammad ibn Ra'iq happened, the caliph was truly disempowered, and even stopped observing the ritual responsibilities of the caliphate. The power to rule now lay in military might; this is how the Buyid general was able to take control of Baghdad. In 945, Ahmad ibn Buya marched into Baghdad and claimed the title "Commander of Commanders" for himself. The current caliph was deposed and blinded. A new caliph was elected but Ahmad ibn Buya barred him from any participation in the government of the city. The caliph was truly impotent. As stated in the final lines of the chapter: "The Buyids were in control of the empire, and Baghdad had fallen under the rule of an upstart family, one that no longer required even the meaningless approval of a powerless caliphate to claim rule."

EXAMPLE ANSWER:

Abd ar-Rahman III saw al-Mahdi's declaration of the Fatimid caliphate not as a challenge to the Abbasid caliphate, but as a destruction of the sanctified role of caliph itself. Both existing caliphs were fictional leaders, so Abd ar-Rahman decided to declare himself a caliph, too. On January 16, 929, ar-Rahman declared himself to be caliph of Cordoba, Commander of the Believers, Defender of the Religion of God. Ar-Rahman's declaration

made him independent, and put him outside of the Fatimid-Abbasid conflict. His declaration also further weakened the symbolic power of the caliphate.

The divine thread connecting the caliph back to the Prophet had grown bare, and by the time of Ahmad ibn Buya, it had snapped. When Muhammad ibn Ra'iq demanded the title "Commander of Commanders" and the power to rule over the administration of the empire, he took away everything that made the caliph the head of state. The Abbasid caliph may have been a puppet for a long time but whoever occupied the position still pretended to rule. When the shift under Muhammad ibn Ra'iq happened, the caliph was truly disempowered, and even stopped observing the ritual responsibilities of the caliphate. The power to rule now lay in military might; this is how the Buyid general was able to take control of Baghdad. In 945, Ahmad ibn Buya marched into Baghdad and claimed the title "Commander of Commanders" for himself. The current caliph was deposed and blinded. A new caliph was elected but Ahmad ibn Buya barred him from any participation in the government of the city. Because the caliph was truly impotent, and held no religious might, the Buyids were able to march into Baghdad and use force to take control of the empire.

Section IV: Map Exercise

1. Using a black pencil, trace the rectangular outline of the frame for Map 67.1: The Fatimids and Cordoba.

2. Using a blue pencil, trace the coastline around the continent from the top of the map down Germany, Western Francia, and Pamplona. You do not need to trace around Britain at this time. Trace the coastline through the Mediterranean (you do not need to trace any islands). Trace the mountain peaks. Repeat until the contours are familiar.

3. Using a new sheet of paper, trace the rectangular outline of the frame in black. Remove your tracing paper from the original. Using a regular pencil with an eraser, draw the coastline around the continent from the top of the map down Germany, Western Francia, and Pamplona. Draw the Mediterranean coastline as well, and draw the mountain peaks.

3. When you are pleased with your map, lay it over the original. Erase and redraw any lines which are more than ¼ inch off of the original.

4. Leaving your map over the original, trace the outlines of the Fatimid Caliphate, the Caliphate of Cordova, the Kingdom of Leon, Pamplona, Western Francia, Germany, Burgundy, and Provence. Study each of these locations carefully. When they are familiar, remove your map from original and close the book. Using your regular pencil, label the Fatimid Caliphate, the Caliphate of Cordova, the Kingdom of Leon, Pamplona, Western Francia, Germany, Burgundy, and Provence. Then study carefully the locations of Galicia, Leon, Asturias, the Spanish Marches, Cordoba, Barcelona, Rome, Mahdia, and Tripoli. When you are familiar with them, close the book. Using your regular pencil, mark and label each. Check your map against the original. Correct any misplaced labels.

Chapter Sixty-Eight

Three Kingdoms

The student may use her text when answering the questions in sections I and II.

Section I: Who, What, Where

Write a one or two-sentence answer explaining the significance of each item listed below.

Bei—**Pg. 514, ¶ 5 & 7—Bei, the older son of Abaoji (Taizu) and Shu-lu shih, took the land his father conquered before his death, Balhae, as his own after his brother became the emperor of Khitan. He renamed Balhae Dongdan, and ruled it as an independent kingdom until 930 when he fell out with his brother and fled to China.**

Deguang (Taizong)—**Pg. 514, ¶ 4–7—Deguang, the second son of Abaoji (Taizu) and Shu-lu shih, succeeded his father and ruled as emperor "Taizong." Taizong annexed Dongdan, added it to his old Khitan realm and created the new kingdom of the Liao.**

Gyeongae—**Pg. 512, ¶ 3—Gyeongae, king of Silla, could not hold the gates of his capital city Kyongju against Kyonhwon. After Later Baekje soldiers flooded the city, sacked and burned its buildings, killed civilians and defenders alike, and broke into the royal palace, they murdered King Gyeongae in his own banquet hall.**

Gyeongsun—**Pg. 512, ¶ 5–7—Gyeongsun, a royal cousin on Wang Kon, was made king of Silla after Wang Kon rescued the city, and was married to one of Wang Kon's daughters after his coronation. Gyeongsun was a puppet-king, and when Wang Kon needed to fold Silla into Goryeo, Gyeongsun was dethroned.**

Mu—**Pg. 513, ¶ 3—Mu was Wang Kon's oldest son and the crown prince. He was dispatched by his father to accompany Kyonhwon back into Later Baekje with ten thousand soldiers to fight his rebellious sons.**

Shu-lu shih—**Pg. 514, ¶ 4–6—Shu-lu shih, meaning "of the Shu-lu clan," was the wife of Abaoji (Taizu) and she kept her husband's newly expanded kingdom together after his death. In**

order to turn the Khitans into a true Chinese kingdom she had to be ruthless against her opposition: she would send anyone who questioned her judgment to her husband's tomb in order to ask his advice, only instead the guards who watched over the dead emperor would do away with the visitor.

Song Taizong—**Pg. 516, ¶ 3 & 4—Song Taizong, younger brother of Song Taizu, took the throne in 976 and within two years of his rule he finished his conquest of the south. In 979 Song Taizong took control of the Northern Han, spreading Song rule over the Chinese mainland.**

Taebong—**Pg. 511, ¶ 2 and *—Taebong was another name for Wang Kong's kingdom, Goryeo, the renamed Later Goguryeo.**

Taejo—**Pg. 511, *—Taejo was the title given to Wang Kon after his death. He is often referred to as "Taejo."**

Taizu—**Pg. 515, ¶ 2 & 4 and Pg. 516, ¶ 2—Taizu, a great fighter and favorite general of the Later Zhou army, was made Emperor Taizu of the Song by his army officials, and he worked to legitimize his rule by creating stories about himself that gave him a sheen of heavenly approval. Song Taizu spent his reign trying to reunify the south of China; he was able to defeat three of the six kingdoms, but he was unable to conquer the Northern Han.**

Section II: Comprehension

Write a two or three-sentence answer to each of the following questions.

1. What steps did Wang Kon take to legitimize his rule of Later Goguryeo?

A1.—Pg. 511, ¶ 2—In order to legitimize his rule of Later Goguryeo, Wang Kon worked hard to erase traces of past revolt by renaming his kingdom Goryeo. He moved the capital city to Kaesong and announced himself to be the founder of a new royal dynasty. He told his followers that by working together to look for solutions to problems in their immediate surroundings and recognizing the mutual dependence of ruler and subject, the country would be able to join together in a celebration of peace.

2. Who ruled Silla after the death of King Hyogong?

A2.—Pg. 511, ¶ 4 to Pg. 512, ¶ 1—King Hyogong of Silla died childless. There were several successors that followed Hyogong, but not one of them was able to keep the throne. Castle lords had to take matters into their own hands, making treaties with either Kyonhwon or Wang Kon, depending on who was the bigger threat at the time.

3. How was Wang Kon able to use Kyonhwon's invasion of Silla to his advantage?

A3.—Pg. 512, ¶ 4 & 5—Wang Kon used Kyonhwon's invasion of Silla to look like the kingdom's savior rather than its usurper. Wang Kon sent troops to Silla under the guise

of punishing Kyonhwon and restoring order, but when they got there what they did was drive the Later Baekje forces out, and elevate a royal cousin named Gyeongsun to the Sillan throne. Then Wang Kon married one of his daughters to Gyeongsun, garrisoned the capital city with Goryeon troops, and announced that he had rescued Silla (when he had really taken it over).

4. Why did Wang Kon depose Gyeongsun when he heard Kyonhwon's sons had turned against him?

A4.—Pg. 512, ¶ 6 & 7—Wang Kon saw an opportunity to take Later Baekje for himself when he found out that Kyonhwon's sons had turned against their father. If Wang Kon was going to take all of the peninsula for himself by taking over Later Baekje, he would first have to take Silla. He demanded the abdication of the puppet-king Gyeongsun and Wang Kon folded the remains of Silla into his own realm, making him the only other king on the peninsula.

5. How did Wang Kon get his former enemy Kyonhwon to be his ally? Why did he want Kyonhwon as an ally?

A5.—Pg. 512, ¶ 8 to Pg. 513, ¶ 1—Wang Kon was able to make Kyonhwon his ally by first helping him escape from prison, and then setting him up as a prosperous slave-master in Goryeo. Wang Kon also gave his former enemy the South palace as his official residence. He was given a position that made him superior to the other Goryeo officials, and he was given gold, silk, folding screens, bedding, forty male and female slaves each, and ten horses from the court stables. By getting him to be his ally, Wang Kon would be able to break down the power structure in Later Baekje, Goryeo's competitor on the peninsula.

6. How did Wang Kon's long game for possession of Later Baekje unfold?

A6.—Pg. 513, ¶ 2 & 3—After making Kyonhwon an ally, Wang Kon let the anger between the Later Baekje king and his sons take over. He gave Kyonhwon ten thousand troops escorted by his son Mu and his most trusted general, and the army of the rebellious sons was crushed. The three oldest brothers that led the rebellion were put to death, and while the kingdom was given back to Kyonhwon, he died of illness just days later, making Wang Kon the leader of Later Baekje and the sole king of the peninsula.

7. What did Wang Kon tell his people in a set of injunctions intended to shape the future of his newly unified country? What were the implications of what he told his people?

A7.—Pg. 513, ¶ 4—Wang Kon told his people that while the inhabitants of the peninsula had always had a deep attachment for the ways of China, their country occupied a different geographical location and the people had a different character than the Chinese. Therefore, there was no reason for them to keep copying the Chinese way. The result was that under Wang Kon the country of the Koreans took its shape as a unified nation, and it would last for the next thousand years.

8. Describe how the Khitan khan Abaoji brought Tang customs to his kingdom.

A8.—Pg. 513, ¶ 7 to Pg. 514, ¶ 1—Abaoji wanted to distance his Khitan kingdom from its nomadic past, so he borrowed from Tang custom to make his kingdom more civilized. By 918, he had given himself the Chinese royal name "Celestial Emperor Taizu," built himself a new Tang-style capital city at Shangjing, and had named his oldest son to be crown prince and heir—a departure from Khitan tradition.

9. How did Shu-lu shih reimpose the old Khitan tradition of elected succession after her husband tried to switch the kingdom over to blood succession?

A9.—Pg. 514, ¶ 4 & 5—Shu-lu shih preferred her second son Deguang to be ruler and told her court as much, but her husband had named their oldest son crown prince. Shu-lu shih assembled the tribal leaders, mounted both boys on their horses, and then told them that because she could not decide who should rule the leaders had to grasp the bridle of the son that seemed more worthy. The tribal leaders knew Shu-lu shih favored Deguang and chose the younger son; the old Khitan tradition of succession of worthiest had been reimposed.

10. Explain how Dongdan and the old Khitan realm came together to be the new kingdom of the Liao.

A10.—Pg. 514, ¶ 7—In 930, Bei fell out with his brother Taizong, so Taizong sent his own son to govern Dongdan while Bei fled to China. By 936, Taizong had annexed Dongdan and had given his empire a new name. The Khitan empire and Dongdan came together to be called the new kingdom of the Liao.

11. How was the Song dynasty formed?

A11.—Pg. 515, ¶ 2—In 960, the Later Zhou emperor died, leaving only a baby as heir and a young empress as regent. The officers of the Later Zhou army disliked the empress, who had no experience with war. Afraid that the army would lose its pre-eminent place in Northern Zhou society, they rebelled and declared their favorite general to be emperor, founder of the new dynasty: Emperor Taizu of the Song.

12. Explain what deal Song Taizu made with his army once he was firmly on the throne. Why did he let the army go?

A12.—Pg. 515, ¶ 5 & 6—Song Taizu knew that the army that made him emperor could just as easily dethrone him if they wanted to, so he made a radical move: he let them go. As soon as he was firmly on the throne, he summoned all of his officers to a banquet and made them an offer: if they would renounce their ranks, give up all military authority, and retire to the countryside, he would gift them handsome severance pay and turn over to them the best lands where they could pass their lives in pleasure and peace. Once the soldiers were living happily, he rebuilt his army from the ground up, a move which guaranteed their loyalty and stopped the cycle of revolt that had previously plagued China during the Five Dynasties and Ten Kingdoms period.

Section III: Critical Thinking

The student may not use her text to answer this question.

Perhaps you have read Aesop's fable of The Wind and the Sun. For a refresher, it goes something like this: The Wind and the Sun were arguing over who was stronger. They saw a traveller coming down the road and the Sun said, "I know how we can figure out who is stronger. Whichever of us can cause the traveller to take off his coat is the stronger of the two." The Wind agreed to the challenge. "You go first," the Sun said. So, while the Wind blew and blew the Sun waited patiently behind a cloud. With each gust of wind, the man drew his coat tighter around himself. Frustrated, the Wind gave up. The Sun then came out from behind the cloud and shone brightly. The warmth from the Sun caused the man to take off his coat, and he basked in the Sun's rays. Write a paragraph that connects Aesop's fable of The Wind and the Sun to the political tactics used by Wang Kon, Song Taizu and Song Taizong.

Aesop's fable of the Wind and the Sun shows the power of kindness over the power of force. Wang Kon, Song Taizu and Song Taizong all used kindness in certain political situations instead of force, and the outcome each time was overwhelmingly positive for their respective kingdoms.

On the Korean peninsula, Wang Kon waited for Kyonhwon to attack Silla, and then he came to Silla's theoretical rescue, kindly running out the Later Baekje invaders. Then, Wang Kon played on sympathy in order to win the alliance of Kyonhwon against his own sons. Breaking Kyonhwon out of jail, giving him a place to live in Goryeo, making him a prosperous slave-owner with a position superior to other Goryeo officials—all of these things were niceties that warmed Kyonhwon up to Wang Kon. Wang Kon even helped Kyonhwon invade his own land and fight against his rebellious sons. When Kyonhwon passed away, he was a happy man in charge of his own kingdom . . . and Wang Kon was a happy man because he was able to take that kingdom after Kyonhwon's death and add it to Goryeo without force.

In China, Song Taizu was expected to have a reign of about nine years, a ruling period typical during the Five Dynasties and Ten Kingdoms. However, Song Taizu knew that the army that had made him emperor could dethrone him just as easily. We learned on page 515 that "As soon as he was firmly on the throne, he summoned all of his officers to a banquet and made them an offer: if they would renounce their ranks, give up all military authority, and retire to the countryside, he would gift them handsome severance pay and turn over to them 'the best lands and most delightful dwelling-places,' where they could pass their lives 'in pleasure and peace.' " Then, once the former army was happy and settled, he recruited members for a new army that was built from the ground up and guaranteed him loyalty. By using kindness, Song Taizu broke the cycle of revolt.

Song Taizong followed in his father's footsteps, and showed kindness to the Northern Han once he was finally able to take their capital city of Taiyuan. A long siege followed the Song invasion into the city, and Song Taizong knew that to really win he would have to show some mercy. He offered the Northern Han ruler a golden handshake: if he would step down and hand his kingdom over, Song Taizong would reward him with safety, an estate, and a lifetime of ease. Instead of killing every last Northern Han, Song Taizong let up on the force and used a more gentle approach to take the Northern Han as his own.

EXAMPLE ANSWER:

Aesop's fable of the Wind and the Sun shows the power of kindness over the power of force. Wang Kon, Song Taizu and Song Taizong all used kindness in certain political situations instead of force, and the outcome each time was overwhelmingly positive for their respective kingdoms. On the Korean peninsula, Wang Kon did not attack Silla, but waited for Kyonhwon to attack so he could act as restorer of the peace to the kingdom. Then, he helped Kyonhwon by breaking him out of jail, giving him a place to live in Goryeo and making him a prosperous slave-owner with a position superior to other Goryeo officials. All of these things were niceties that warmed Kyonhwon up to Wang Kon. Wang Kon even helped Kyonhwon invade his own land and fight against his rebellious sons. When Kyonhwon passed away, he was a happy man in charge of his own kingdom . . . and Wang Kon was a happy man because he was able to take that kingdom after Kyonhwon's death and add it to Goryeo without too much force.

In China, Song Taizu was expected to have a reign of about nine years, a ruling period typical during the Five Dynasties and Ten Kingdoms. However, Song Taizu knew that the army that had made him emperor could dethrone him just as easily. So, he offered the men of the army handsome severance pay, the best lands he had to give, and a life of peace and pleasure if they would give up their military authority. Then, once the former army was happy and settled, he recruited members for a new army that was built from the ground up and guaranteed him loyalty. By using kindness, Song Taizu broke the cycle of revolt.

Song Taizong followed in his father's footsteps, and showed kindness to the Northern Han once he was finally able to take their capital city of Taiyuan. A long siege followed the Song invasion into the city, and Song Taizong knew that to really win he would have to show some mercy. He told the Northern Han ruler that if he would step down and hand his kingdom over, Song Taizong would reward him with safety, an estate, and a lifetime of ease. Instead of killing every last Northern Han, Song Taizong let up on the force and used a more gentle approach to take the Northern Han as his own.

Chapter Sixty-Nine

Kings of England

The student may use his text when answering the questions in sections I and II.

Section I: Who, What, Where

Write a one or two-sentence answer explaining the significance of each item listed below.

Atheling/Aetheling—**Pg. 519, ¶ 2 & *—Atheling, or aetheling, was the Anglo-Saxon word used to describe a man eligible to inherit the throne.**

Athelstan—**Pg. 518, ¶ 3 and Pg. 519, ¶ 2—Athelstan, one of Edward the Elder's eldest sons, became sole king of the Anglo-Saxons after the death of one of his brothers, with whom he was supposed to share the kingdom. After a lifetime of fighting, Athelstan brought an end to the Danelaw, forced the kings of Wales and Scotland to acknowledge his power, and became the first true king of England.**

Battle of Brunanburh—**Pg. 519, ¶ 2—The Battle of Brunanburh was fought in 936, when Athelstan attacked the alliance of Northumbrian Vikings and Scots. Athelstan crushed the resistance to his overlordship, a win so great it earned its own poem in the *Anglo-Saxon Chronicle*.**

Battle of Havsfjord—**Pg. 523, ¶ 2—The Battle of Havsfjord, fought around 900, gave Harald Tangle-Hair control of Norway. Harald Tangle-Hair defeated the armies of his most dangerous enemies, the Norse princes Thorir Long-chin and Kjotvi the Wealthy, and after this win Harald faced no more opposition.**

Constantine II—**Pg. 519, ¶ 2—Constantine II, king of the Scots, lost his son in the Battle of Brunanburh, was forced to flee, and was made to bow down to King Athelstan of England.**

Danegeld—**Pg. 526, ¶ 5 & 6 and Pg. 528, ¶ 3—Danegeld was the term used for the payment given by King Ethelred to Sweyn Forkbeard in exchange for his withdrawal from England.**

The Danegeld was paid over and over, each time with the hope of keeping the Danes away for good, but they returned again and again.

Duke Richard the Good of Normandy—**Pg. 527, ¶ 5 & 6—Duke Richard the Good of Normandy agreed to an alliance with King Ethelred of England. He would provide troops to help the English fight the Danes in exchange for his sister Emma's marriage to the English king.**

Dunstan—**Pg. 521, ¶ 2 & 3 and Pg. 522, ¶ 2—Dunstan, the English bishop at the time of Edwy All-Fair's rule, disliked the king because of reforms he made that caused suffering for England's monasteries. Later, as archbishop of Canterbury, Dunstan created a formal ceremony to recognize King Edgar's sovereignty.**

Edgar—**Pg. 521, ¶ 4 & 5 and Pg. 522, ¶ 2—Edgar, Edwy All-Fair's younger brother, became king of all England when Edwy died in 959. Edgar proved to be a strong king: he restored the monasteries of England, and by 973 he was in full control of his country with oaths of loyalty sworn by the king of the Scots and the king of the Welsh. Finally, Edgar was made the true king of England when he was crowned in a ceremony presided over by archbishop Dunstan.**

Edmund the Just—**Pg. 520, ¶ 1 & 2—Edmund, Athelstan's half-brother, inherited the English throne at seventeen and almost immediately lost the midlands of England to Olaf I, getting them back only after Olaf I died. Edmund ruled over a reunified England until 946, when he was stabbed after attacking a thief that he had previously exiled.**

Edred Weak-Foot—**Pg. 520, ¶ 3 to Pg. 521, ¶ 1—Edred Weak-Foot, Edmund's brother, took the English crown away from Edmund's five-year-old son. Edred Weak-Foot held the country together, even in the face of a revolt in Northumbria and when he died of chronic illness in 955, he passed a unified nation on to his nephew.**

Edward the Elder—**Pg. 518, ¶ 1–3—Edward the Elder, son and heir of Alfred the Great, forced the west and north to join the south under his leadership, making him the first king of all the Anglo-Saxons. Edward the Elder left his realm to his two eldest sons, following the old Germanic custom.**

Edwy All-Fair—**Pg. 521, ¶ 2–4—Edwy All-Fair, English king at fourteen and successor to Edred Weak-Foot, was a puppet of court officials and at their behest he deprived the monasteries of their tax revenues. Just two years into his rule he lost half of his kingdom to his younger brother Edgar.**

Emma—**Pg. 527, ¶ 5 & 6 and Pg. 528, ¶ 6—Emma, sister of Duke Richard the Good of Normandy, was married to King Ethelred of England in exchange for Norman troops to help the English fight off the Danes. She was crowned queen of England in 1002 and in 1013 when Sweyn Forkbeard invaded England, she was sent to Normandy with her two sons by King Ethelred.**

Eric the Red—**Pg. 524, ¶ 7 to Pg. 526, 1—Eric the Red, a Norse troublemaker, sailed from Norway to Iceland, and then from Iceland to a massive island he named Greenland. He started a small colony there that became an outpost of Scandinavian power.**

Erik Bloodaxe—**Pg. 523, ¶ 5—Erik Bloodaxe, older brother of Hakon the Good and husband to sister of the Danish king Harald Bluetooth, fought for fifteen years to take Norway's crown away from his younger brother. He died in battle against his brother in 955, but his civil war carried on via his sons, in alliance with Harald Bluetooth.**

Ethelred—**Pg. 524, ¶ 6 and Pg. 528, ¶ 6—Ethelred, son of Edgar, was crowned as king at ten years of age, and immediately faced the raiding parties of Harald Bluetooth and his son Sweyn Forkbeard. After paying the Danes over and over to withdraw from England during their various attacks, Ethelred finally lost England to Sweyn Forkbeard in 1013.**

Hakon of Hladir—**Pg. 524, ¶ 5—Hakon of Hladir, one of Harald Bluetooth's noblemen, killed the Norse king Harald Greycloak, and was given control of the upper Norse coast as a reward.**

Hakon the Good—**Pg. 523, ¶ 5 & 6—Hakon the Good, Harald's youngest son, followed Harald as leader of Norway, but he had to fight to keep his title against his brother Erik Bloodaxe and the Danish king Harald Bluetooth. Though he was as ruthless as his brother, Hakon earned the name "the Good" because of his Christian faith.**

Harald—**Pg. 522, ¶ 6 to Pg. 523, ¶ 1—Harald became ruler of the Vestfold when he was ten, and he spent the next seventy years campaigning to unite the Norse under one crown; he vowed not to cut or comb his hair until he had become the sole king of Norway, earning him the name Harald Tangle-Hair. After winning the Battle of Havsfjord, Harald Tangle-Hair became king of Norway.**

Harald Bluetooth—**Pg. 523, ¶ 5, Pg. 524, ¶ 5 & 6—Harald Bluetooth, Danish king and brother-in-law of Erik Bloodaxe, continued to fight Hakon the Good for the Norse throne after Erik Bloodaxe's death in 955. Around 976, Harald Bluetooth had Harald Greycloak murdered, he took the eastern Norse lands for himself and during the time that he was the leader of both the Norse and Danish lands he pushed his power south and west via various explorers.**

Harald Greycloak—**Pg. 524, ¶ 2 & 5—Harald Greycloak, son of Erik Bloodaxe and supported by Harald Bluetooth, seized the throne of Norway after battling Hakon the Good, and enforced Christianity in Norway by tearing down all the old places of worship in his country. Harald Greycloak was murdered around 976 by one of Harald Bluetooth's noblemen Hakon of Hladir.**

Olaf I—**Pg. 520, ¶ 1—Olaf I, king of Ireland, invaded and the took the midlands of England away from Edmund the Just.**

Olaf Tryggvason—**Pg. 527, ¶ 2 & 3—Olaf Tryggvason, a grandson of Harald Tangle-Hair, ruler of upper Norway after the death of Hakon of Hladir, leaped overboard from his own**

ship the *Long Serpent* and was never seen again after Sweyn Forkbeard's attacks on his land in 1000. For years it was rumored that Olaf would return from the depths and free Norway from its Danish overlords, but King Olaf never rose from the sea.

Sihtric—**Pg. 518, ¶ 4 to Pg. 519, ¶ 1—Sihtric, king of the Northumbrians, was married to Athelstan's sister. When Sihtric died, Athelstan invaded Northumbria in his sister's name and claimed the Danelaw for England.**

Sweyn Forkbeard—**Pg. 526, ¶ 2 & 3, Pg. 527, ¶ 1 & 2 and Pg. 528, ¶ 6 & 7—Sweyn Forkbeard, son of Harald Bluetooth, defeated his father in battle for possession of his kingdom, and then he inherited the throne of Denmark, the Danish-controlled lands in Norway and the loyalty of Hakon of Hladir, who ruled the upper Norse lands. Sweyn Forkbeard took all of Norway for himself after defeating Olaf Tryggvason in 1000 and in 1013, after invading England and making the kingdom pay him for his retreat over and over, he finally took the island for himself, making him the ruler of a North Atlantic empire that stretched across the Baltic and the North Sea.**

Section II: Comprehension

Write a two or three-sentence answer to each of the following questions.

1. What were the circumstances of Edmund the Just's death?

A1.—Pg. 520, ¶ 2—In 946, Edmund the Just was presiding over a feast in honor of St. Augustine, founder of Christianity in England, when he noticed among the guests a thief whom he had ordered exiled. The sight infuriated him. He stood up and tackled the robber, who drew out a knife and stabbed Edmund in the chest.

2. What was the supposed reason the English bishop Dunstan did not like Edwy All-Fair? What was the real reason for the bishop's gripe with the king?

A2.—Pg. 521, ¶ 2 & 3—Supposedly, Edwy All-Fair left a very important meeting on the day of his consecration to spend time with his mistress, after which Dunstan dragged him from his bedchamber to attend the meeting. In reality, Edwy was the puppet of court officials, and under their influence, he deprived the monasteries of their tax revenues, destroying the power of the abbots and monks. This decision made Dunstan dislike the young king very much.

3. How did England come to be ruled by two kings in 957?

A3.—Pg. 521, ¶ 4—Seeing an opportunity to reassert their power against the puppet king Edwy All-Fair, the Mercian and Northumbrian noblemen decided to support Edwy's younger brother Edgar for the throne and proclaimed him as his brother's rival. In 957, only two years after coming to the throne, Edwy lost a battle against his brother and his brother's

supporters at Gloucester, and the two divided the kingdom: fourteen-year-old Edgar ruled north of the Thames, and Edwy, now sixteen, ruled in the south.

4. What did Edgar accomplish in his first fourteen years of rule?

A4.—Pg. 521, ¶ 5—In his first fourteen years of rule, Edgar restored the monasteries of England, giving the abbots and monks the power to govern their own lands. This legislation at once made all of the abbots and priests in England into king's men, and gave Edgar the backing he needed to reduce the power of the court officials that previously commanded Edwy. By 973, Edgar was in full control of his country and had extracted oaths of loyalty from the king of the Scots and the king of the Welsh.

5. Describe Harald's efforts to unite Norway. To whom did he leave his newly unified country?

A5.—Pg. 523, ¶ 2–4—Harald united Norway in 900 when he defeated the armies of his most dangerous enemies, the Norse princes Thorir Long-chin and Kjotvi the Wealthy at the Battle of Havsfjord. His rule remained contested, and he fought his whole life to keep his country united, battling against western Scandinavians and Vikings while also fathering between ten and twenty sons with various wives and mistresses. When he died, no single heir was named, and the united country again fell apart into a mess of battling noblemen and princes: the noblemen vying for power over their own estates, the princes hoping to establish themselves as the next king of all Norway.

6. How did Hakon the Good earn his moniker? Why was it advantageous for Hakon the Good and Harald Bluetooth to convert to Christianity?

A6.—Pg. 523, ¶ 6 to Pg. 524, ¶ 1—Hakon the Good earned his name because of his Christian faith, learned during his time as a child at the court of Athelstan, in England. Being a Christian, even if only superficially, made it easier to deal with both the English and the merchants on the continent. The custom was that anyone who had taken the sign of the cross could mix freely with both Christians and heathens, while keeping the faith that they pleased.

7. How did Harald Greycloak force his Christian faith on the people of Norway? In addition to the forcing of the Christian faith on the Norse people, what else caused the people to dislike the king of Norway?

A7.—Pg. 524, ¶ 2 & 3—When he became king, Harald Greycloak forced the Christian faith on the people of Norway not by converting them, but by destroying all of the old temples and places of worship of the Norse people. Hard winters, poor crops and bad fishing added to the Norse people's unhappiness. Resentment grew even stronger when an unnatural cold snap caused snow in summer and grain and fish grew more scarce.

8. Who controlled Norway after the death of Harald Greycloak?

A8.—Pg. 524, ¶ 5—After Harald Greycloak was murdered around 976, the eastern Norse lands were ruled by Harald Bluetooth, and the upper Norse coast was ruled by Hakon of

Hladir. Hakon did not take the title of king, so for a time Harald Bluetooth ruled both the Danish and Norse lands with the help of his son Sweyn Forkbeard.

9. Describe the founding of Greenland.

A9.—Pg. 524, ¶ 7 to Pg. 526, ¶ 1—Eric the Red was forced to leave Norway and settle in the Icelandic colonies after a feud with another villager that ended in death. In 982 he started a brawl with one of his Icelandic neighbors and killed two of the man's sons, which forced him to leave Iceland and find a new place to live. After three years of exploring, he settled on a massive island five hundred miles to the west that was an inhospitable, bare, sandy place. However, Eric wanted to start a colony so he named it Greenland; even though it was a tough place to live, the favorable name attracted some colonists and a tiny outpost of Scandinavian power was built.

10. What were the circumstances of Harald Bluetooth's death?

A10.—Pg. 526, ¶ 2—Sweyn Forkbeard had hoped that his father would divide his realm and give part of it to him, but Harald Bluetooth had not fought for his whole life in order to yield his kingdom to his son. As his father's righthand man, Sweyn had ships of his own so he gathered them and challenged Harald Bluetooth for the throne. In a sea battle fought in 987, Harald Bluetooth turned back his son's ships, but he was badly wounded in the fighting, and died just days later.

11. What events in 991 led to Ethelred agreeing to give Sweyn Forkbeard ten thousand pounds of silver?

A11.—Pg. 526, ¶ 3–6—Sweyn Forkbeard launched relentless attacks on England, ravaging Wessex, burning the city of Exeter and pillaging Kent. The death of able-bodied Englishmen in battle and the destruction of crops plunged England into deepening famine and distress, and King Ethelred could do nothing to stop the Danes. After the East Saxon nobleman Brihtnoth was killed at Maldon in 991 while leading a massive force against the Danish enemy, Ethelred's advisors were able to get the king to agree to handing over ten thousand pounds of silver to the Danes in exchange for their retreat.

12. Though Sweyn Forkbeard had sworn at his coronation feast to take England, why did he continue to accept payment in exchange for retreat during his invasions rather than taking over the country?

A12.—Pg. 526, ¶ 6 to Pg. 527, ¶ 1 and Pg. 528, ¶ 4—Sweyn Forkbeard realized England could be far more useful as a source of income than as a conquered land. It was better to allow Ethelred to pay Sweyn Forkbeard's expenses than to try and conquer him. In 994, Sweyn returned and fought all the way to London and once again Ethelred bought him off; this cycle continued until 1013 when Sweyn Forkbeard was finally ready to claim England for his own.

13. Why did Ethelred of England make an alliance with the Normans? What were the terms of the alliance?

A13.—Pg. 527, ¶ 5 & 6—Ethelred of England made an alliance with the Normans because he needed help fighting off the Danes. In exchange for marrying Emma, sister of Duke Richard the Good of Normandy, the Normans would provide him with soldiers to help fight Sweyn Forkbeard. In 1002, Emma travelled to England for the wedding and was crowned queen of England.

14. When it became clear that the Norman reinforcements would not turn his enemies away, what was the next tactic King Ethelred used to fight the Danes?

A14.—Pg. 527, ¶ 7 to Pg. 528, ¶ 1—When it became clear that the Norman reinforcements would not turn his enemies away, King Ethelred flew into a panic and ordered a drastic step: all Danish settlers in England—man, woman and child—were to be murdered. The massacre was carried out in a single day. On November 13, 1002, the king's men spread throughout the island, slaughtering the Danes in every village; in Oxford, Danish families fled to the church of St. Frideswide and the soldiers burned it down with them inside.

15. After years of attacking, sacking and burning and then accepting payment, how did Sweyn Forkbeard finally take England?

A15.—Pg. 528, ¶ 4—In 1013, Sweyn Forkbeard arrived on the northern coast of England, his forces sweeping southward across the countryside, making the English surrender, one village at a time. Londoners fought against Forkbeard, protecting their king inside the city's walls, so he went to Bath and declared himself "King of England" and demanded that all the English recognize his title. When Sweyn Forkbeard was in Bath, Ethelred fled for the Isle of Wight leaving the Londoners with no reason to fight, so they sent tribute and hostages to Bath, acknowledging the Dane as their ruler.

Section III: Critical Thinking

The student may not use his text to answer this question.

Rituals can provide great solace for the soul, but their real world impact is often disappointing. Write a paragraph explaining how Edgar used ritual to legitimize his kingship of England, but how that ritual did little to keep him on throne, and to protect his kingdom from falling apart.

The student's paragraph should contain three main points: 1) a description of Edgar's coronation ceremony in 973; 2) making note of Edgar's death by illness just two years after his coronation; and 3) though a king now ruled England, the throne was no defense against the relentless Sweyn Forkbeard, who invaded over and over before taking England for his own in 1013.

Until Edgar, none of the kings of England had gone through a coronation ceremony. Edgar was the fourth king to rule over the entire country, but all of Alfred's descendants had reigned as warriors, wielding their power via the sword, not via ceremony. The archbishop of Canterbury, Dunstan, took Edgar's power to the next level by creating a formal ceremony that would recognize the king's sovereignty. The chronicles of Edgar's coronation even point out that the king was anointed in his thirtieth year, connecting the king's age to the age when Jesus emerged into the public eye as the Son of God. Edgar protected his kingdom in battle and secured his rule with the approval of the church through a ceremony that tied him to God. But just two years later Edgar died, killed by a swift illness. The church's consecration of his rule could not save him from disease, nor could it stop the relentless attacks of the Danes. Edgar's successor, Ethelred, spent his entire reign fighting Sweyn Forkbeard, losing his kingdom's money and men in futile battle against the warleader. Ultimately, no ritual or ceremony could stop Sweyn Forkbeard from taking England for his own North Atlantic Empire.

EXAMPLE ANSWER:

Until Edgar, none of the kings of England had gone through a coronation ceremony. Edgar was the fourth king to rule over the entire country, but all of Alfred's descendants had reigned as warriors, wielding their power via the sword, not via ceremony. In 973, the archbishop of Canterbury, Dunstan, took Edgar's power to the next level by creating a formal ceremony that would recognize the king's sovereignty. The chronicles of Edgar's coronation even point out that the king was anointed in his thirtieth year, connecting the king's age to the age when Jesus emerged into the public eye as the Son of God. Edgar protected his kingdom in battle and secured his rule with the approval of the church through a ceremony that tied him to God. But just two years later Edgar died, killed by a swift illness. The church's consecration of his rule could not save him from disease, nor could it stop the relentless attacks of the Danes. Edgar's successor, Ethelred, spent his entire reign fighting Sweyn Forkbeard, losing his kingdom's money and men in futile battle against the warleader. Ultimately, no ritual or ceremony could stop Sweyn Forkbeard from taking England for his own North Atlantic Empire in 1013, just forty years after the Edgar's coronation.

Section IV: **Map Exercise**

1. Using a black pencil, trace the rectangular outline of the frame for Map 69.1: Athelstan's England.

2. Using a black pencil, trace the coastline all around Ireland and Britain and along the visible portion of the continent. You do not need to include any islands. Repeat until the contours are familiar.

3. Using a new sheet of paper, trace the rectangular outline of the frame in black. Remove your tracing paper from the original. Using a regular pencil with an eraser as you look at Map 69.1, draw the complete coastline. Erase and redraw as necessary.

4. When you are pleased with your map, lay it over the original. Erase and redraw any lines which are more than ¼ inch off of the original.

5. Leaving your map over the original, trace the region of Britain delineated as Athelstan's England. Then remove your map from the original.

6. Study carefully the regions of Ireland, Scotland, Northumbria, Mercia, Wales, Wessex, Sussex, Essex, East Anglia, Brittany, Normandy, and Western Francia. Mark these on your map. Then study carefully the locations of Dublin, Oxford, Malmesbury, Bath, Exeter, Kent, London, and Maldon. Mark and label each on your map. Check your map against the original. Correct any misplaced labels.

7. Mark the possible location of the Battle of Brunanburh.

Chapter Seventy

The Baptism of the Rus

The student may use her text when answering the questions in sections I and II.

Section I: Who, What, Where

Write a one or two-sentence answer explaining the significance of each item listed below.

Anna—**Pg. 536, ¶ 6 and Pg. 537, ¶ 1—Anna, sister of Basil II and Constantine VIII of Byzantium, was married to Vladimir of the Rus as part of a treaty made between her brothers and the Rus king. Anna did not want to marry Vladimir, but she was convinced to do so by Basil II, who said that by marrying Vladimir, she would be doing God's work.**

Basil II—**534, ¶ 1 and Pg. 536, ¶ 6—Basil II, Romanos II's oldest son, was made co-emperor at five after his father's death, with his mother Theophano serving as his regent. After John Tzimiskes died of dysentery, Basil II became co-emperor of Consantinople with his brother Constantine VIII.**

Boris II—**Pg. 535, ¶ 4 and Pg. 536, ¶ 4—Boris II, son of Peter I of Bulgaria, was left in charge of Bulgaria after his father had a stroke following Svyatoslav's 968 invasion. Forced into an alliance with the Rus, Boris II was captured by John Tzimiskes and sent to Constantinople as a prisoner after the Byzantine army defeated the Bulgarian and Rus forces at Arcadiopolis.**

Constantine VIII—**534, ¶ 1 and Pg. 536, ¶ 6—Constantine VIII, Romanos II's youngest son, was made co-emperor at three after his father's death, with his mother Theophano serving as his regent. After John Tzimiskes died of dysentery, Constantine VIII became co-emperor of Consantinople with his brother Basil II.**

Constantine Lecapenus—**Pg. 530, ¶ 3 and Pg. 531, ¶ 2—Constantine Lecapenus, son of Romanos Lecapenus, worked with his brother Stephen to dethrone his father. Constantine and his brother were then arrested by Constantine Porphyrogenitus (who was convinced**

by his wife to do so because she saw them as a threat to her husband's power) and sent to a distant monastery.

Igor—**Pg. 532, ¶ 1 & 3—Igor, prince of Kiev, made a treaty with Constantine Porphyrogenitus that allowed Rus merchants to enter Constantinople in exchange for Rus service in the Byzantine army if the emperor needed more men. After making the treaty with Constantine Porphyrogenitus, Igor was captured by the Drevlians on the way back to Kiev and was killed.**

John Tzimiskes—**Pg. 533, ¶ 5, Pg. 535, ¶ 2 and Pg. 536, ¶ 2—John Tzimiskes, nephew of Nikephoros Phocas and his uncle's second-in-command, became Theophano's lover after his uncle's rise to emperor of Byzantium. After doing away with his uncle and becoming emperor himself, John Tzimiskes married one of Constantine Porphyrogenitus's daughters allowing him to claim, with some truth, that he was a rightful member of the imperial dynasty.**

Nikephoros Phocas—**Pg. 533, ¶ 5, Pg. 534, ¶ 3 and Pg. 535, ¶ 2 & 7—Nikephoros Phocas, a skilled officer in Romanos II's army, was proclaimed emperor of Byzantium after Romanos II's death and was crowned by the patriarch after agreeing that he would never hurt the toddler co-emperors Basil II and Constantine VIII. Nikephoros Phocas married Theophano and ruled as a Supreme Commander, compelled to expand his kingdom's borders; this made him unpopular and as a result he was murdered by his wife, nephew and a few of the royal guard.**

Olga—**Pg. 532, ¶ 4 & 5 and Pg. 533, ¶ 2—Olga, wife of Igor, took over as regent for their son Svyatoslav; her first acts as regent were to take revenge on the Drevlians for killing her husband and to divide her state into *pogosts*. Olga was baptized in 957 when she made a state visit to Constantinople; after her son took his power she spent the rest of her life trying to convert her fellow Rus.**

Pogost—**Pg. 532, ¶ 4—*Pogost* was the name for an administrative district in Rus, as divided by Olga. Each *pogost* was responsible for a set tax payment to the Rus government.**

Romanos II—**Pg. 533, ¶ 4 and Pg. 534, ¶ 1 & 2—Romanos II, grandson of Romanos Lecapenus, successor of Constantine Porphyrogenitus, was a pliable ruler more interested in luxury and unusual passions than the running of his kingdom. In 963, just four years into his reign, Romanos II died of fever, though some suspected that he was poisoned with hemlock by his wife, Theophano.**

Romanus—**Pg. 536, ¶ 4—Romanus, brother and heir to Boris II of Bulgaria, was captured by John Tzimiskes and sent to Constantinople as a prisoner after the Byzantine army defeated the Bulgarian and Rus forces at Arcadiopolis.**

Stephen Lecapenus—**Pg. 530, ¶ 3 and Pg. 531, ¶ 2—Stephen Lecapenus, son of Romanos Lecapenus, worked with his brother Constantine to dethrone his father. Stephen and his brother were then arrested by Constantine Porphyrogenitus (who was convinced by his**

wife to do so because she saw them as a threat to her husband's power) and sent to a distant monastery.

Svyatoslav—**Pg. 533, ¶ 2 and Pg. 535, ¶ 3 & 5—Svyatoslav, son of Igor and Olga, spent his first years as leader of the Rus fighting the Khazars, the Slavic tribes, and the Pechenegs, and rejecting his mother's Christianity. In 968 he was hired by Nikephoros Phocas to help him fight against Bulgaria, and after his successful campaign against the Bulgarians, Svyatoslav turned against his Byzantine employer and announced that he would march against Constantinople and capture it for himself; however, he did not capture Constantinople and was killed by his old enemy the Pechenegs on his way back from war with Byzantium at Arcadiopolis.**

Theophano—**Pg. 533, ¶ 4 & 5, Pg. 535, ¶ 2 and Pg. 536, ¶ 3—Theophano, beautiful daughter of an innkeeper and Romanos II's wife, ran the Byzantine kingdom with the help of Nikephoros Phocas while distracting her husband with licentious pleasures. After her husband's death, Theophano married Nikephoros Phocas once he was made emperor, started an affair with his nephew John Tzimiskes, helped John Tzimiskes murder Nikephoros Phocas, and was rewarded for all her slipperiness with exile on an island in the Sea of Marmara.**

Vladimir—**Pg. 536, ¶ 6 and Pg. 537, ¶ 5—Vladimir, the youngest of Svyatoslav's sons, followed his father king of the Rus in 980 and quickly negotiated a treaty with the co-emperors of Byzantium: the Rus would remain at peace with Constantinople and would supply soldiers for the Byzantine army when needed; in return, he would marry the emperor's sister Anna and convert to Christianity. After converting to Christianity, and ordering all of his people to follow him in baptism, Vladimir used the organized monotheistic religion to provide the Rus with a new and strong infrastructure that turned Russia into a state equal to the kingdoms of the west.**

Section II: Comprehension

Write a two or three-sentence answer to each of the following questions.

1. How did Constantine Porphyrogenitus come to follow Romanos Lecapenus as the emperor of Constantinople?

A1.—Pg. 530, ¶ 2 to Pg. 531, ¶ 2—Though Romanos Lecapenus had arranged coronations for his sons and grandson in order to ensure the succession of his own family, his son-in-law became the next emperor of Constantinople via the schemes plotted by his wife. Elena Lecapenus did not want to share her imperial power as wife of Constantine Porphyrogenitus with her brothers, so after they ambushed Romanos Lecapenus and put him on a boat headed for a monastery, Elena convinced her husband to have her brothers arrested. One night at a family dinner, the royal guard seized Elena's brothers as they sat down to eat and

both men, along with Romanos's grandson—who was also a co-emperor—were put on ships and sent to distant monasteries, making Constantine Porphyrogenitus the sole emperor of Constantinople.

2. Describe the Rus as the geographer Ibn Fadlan depicted them.

A2.—Pg. 531, ¶ 5—According to Ibn Fadlan, the Rus were half-wild: always armed, tattooed from neck to fingertip, living in temporary wooden shelters, copulating in public, and sacrificing to strange bloody gods. Fadlan said they were dirty creatures, sharing bath water that was dirtied further by each user because he would blow his nose and spit in the water after washing his face and hair. Fadlan described their living circumstances as transient, always travelling, buying and selling but never bothering to build and burning their dead instead of burying them in the ground.

3. What were the terms of the treaty made between Igor, prince of Kiev, and Constantine Porphyrogenitus?

A3.—Pg. 532, ¶ 1—The terms of the treaty made between Igor and Constantine Porphyrogenitus reinforced the terms of the previous treaty made in 911. Rus merchants could enter Constantinople, but they had to be unarmed and in groups of no more than fifty men; if they went back to Kiev peacefully, they would get a month of free food. In the case that Constantine Porphyrogenitus needed soldiers to keep the Bulgarians or Arabs at bay, the Rus would serve in the Byzantine army as paid mercenaries.

4. How did Olga avenge her husband Igor's death?

A4.—Pg. 532, ¶ 4—Olga avenged her husband's death when she became the regent for their son Svyatoslav. Her first act as the Rus in charge was to punish the Drevlians for killing her husband: she ordered the Drevlian city of Korosten burned to the ground and the slaughter of hundreds of Drevlians by burning and transfixing and burying them alive. She then turned the Drevlians into a *pogost*, and they became responsible for making regular tax payments to the Rus government.

5. In what way was Olga of the Kievan Rus charmed into becoming a Christian?

A5.—Pg. 532, ¶ 5—When Olga of the Kievan Rus made a state visit to Constantinople in 957, she was received as a fellow sovereign. She walked into an imperial palace strewn with roses, ivy, myrtle, and rosemary; the walls and ceilings were hung with silken drapes; a choir from the Hagia Sophia sang as she was ushered into the emperor's presence; and mechanical toy lions in the throne room roared in her honor. After being entertained and being given banquets for a week, Olga agreed to be baptized.

6. What kind of a ruler was Svyatoslav of the Rus—refined or rough? Use examples of Svyatoslav's behavior to explain your answer.

A6.—Pg. 533, ¶ 2—Svyatoslav of the Rus was an aggressive and rough ruler: unlike his mother, he acted more like a tribal chief than a king. The early years of his reign were filled

with numerous campaigns, sending messengers to other lands announcing he was going to attack them. When he was out on his expeditions, he had no prepared food or water, but rather he cut off small strips of horseflesh, game, or beef, and ate it after roasting it on the coals, and he chose to sleep not in a tent, but out in the open on a horse-blanket, with his head resting on his saddle.

7. How did the officer Nikephoros Phocas become emperor of Byzantium?

A7.—Pg. 534, ¶ 3 to Pg. 535, ¶ 1—After the death of Romanos II, Theophano sent messengers to Nikephoros Phocas that made private offers of alliance and support. Though it isn't clear what the offers promised him, Nikephoros Phocas was moved to claim the crown, so his army declared him emperor in July of 963. When he arrived in Consantinople in August of the same year, the patriarch agreed to coronate him in the Hagia Sophia in exchange for his promise that he would never harm either of his toddler co-emperors, and on August 16 he became Nikephoros II, emperor of Byzantium.

8. Describe the circumstances of Nikephoros Phocas's death.

A8.—Pg. 535, ¶ 7 to Pg. 536, ¶ 1—Nikephoros Phocas was sleeping on the floor in his bedroom in Constantinople when Theophano and John Tzimiskes broke into the room, accompanied by hand-picked members of the royal guard, leapt at him and started kicking him. Once he woke up, one of the guards struck him with a sword, but did not kill him. As Nikephoros Phocas begged for his life, John Tzimiskes pulled mercilessly on his beard while the others smashed at his jaw and knocked his teeth out until finally John Tzimiskes drove his sword through Nikephoros's brain.

9. Why was it so easy for John Tzimiskes to be crowned as emperor after the death of Nikephoros Phocas?

A9.—Pg. 536, ¶ 2—Nikephoros Phocas had grown unpopular with his people, since his expensive campaigning had forced them into higher and higher tax payments. Within seven days of Nikephoros Phocas's death, John Tzimiskes was able to convince the entire city and the patriarch to crown him as emperor in his uncle's place. The people were happy to see the warring emperor gone, to elect a new leader, and not to make a big to-do about Nikephoros Phocas's murder.

10. What happened at Arcadiopolis?

A10.—Pg. 536, ¶ 4—Boris II of Bulgaria was forced into an alliance with Svyatoslav of the Rus with the intention of taking Constantinople, and their combined armies met John Tzimiskes at Arcadiopolis. The Rus were pushed backwards while the Bulgarians retreated. John Tzimiskes followed the Bulgarians, captured Boris II and Romanus, sent them back to Constantinople as prisoners and then annexed Bulgaria.

11. Who killed Svyatoslav? What did they do to his skull?

A11.—Pg. 536, ¶ 5—On his way back to Kiev from Arcadiopolis, Svyatoslav was ambushed and assassinated by the nomadic Turkish tribe of the Pechenegs, who had been his enemies for his entire twenty-eight-year rule. The Pecheneg chief made a gold-overlaid cup out of Svyatoslav's skull and passed it around for all of his warriors to drink from.

12. What advantages for the Rus did Vladimir see in converting to Christianity?

A12.—Pg. 537, ¶ 3–5—In addition to inheriting the kingdom of God, Vladimir saw Christianity as a way to give the Rus a strong internal network of priests and scholars, giving his country stability. After ordering a mass baptism for his people, Vladimir ordered churches built, created a parish system with priests in charge of different districts throughout the country, and instituted a system of Christian education. The Christian state Vladimir developed would be able to stand as an equal to the kingdoms of the west.

Section III: Critical Thinking

The student may not use her text to answer this question.

In this chapter we saw a version of the cliché "brains over brawn" from the most surprising of exemplars, the previously barbaric Rus. Explain how Nikephoros Phocas's downfall was his "brawn." Then explain how Vladimir's successful use of "brains" turned the Rus into an upstanding state.

Nikephoros Phocas came to power because of his outstanding capabilities as a soldier. He rose to power during the reign of Romanos II. While the emperor was out cavorting, Nikephoros Phocas led the Byzantine navy in its capture of Crete, and then he led the Byzantine army in the conquest of Aleppo, retaking territory that had been lost to the Arabs for decades. After the death of Romanos II, Nikephoros Phocas was proclaimed emperor by his army. The patriarch agreed to coronate the career officer, and thus on August 16 of 963 he became Nikephoros II, emperor of Byzantium. Nikephoros Phocas saw his role as Byzantine leader not as Defender of the Faith or Chief Administrator, but as the Supreme Commander. All of his life he fought, and he would continue to do so as emperor. Nikephoros Phocas's campaigns made him unpopular with his people; war was expensive, and it was paid for by increasing taxes on the citizens of his kingdom.

In addition to fighting all the time, Nikephoros Phocas kept the old soldier's custom of sleeping on the floor. While sleeping on the ground or in a bed might not have stopped his murder, sleeping on the floor was a symbol of Nikephoros Phocas's loyalty: to the sword. Continually engaging in battle, using his "brawn" to rule, was Nikephoros Phocas's downfall. He was murdered by his wife and nephew, attacked while sleeping on the floor of his bedchamber. His death was not made a big to-do, John Tzimiskes was made emperor quickly and with the approval of the people: the big bad warrior was no longer in charge.

On the other hand, Vladimir—who one would think would be brutal and rough like the Rus before him—realized that he could turn the Rus into an equal to the kingdoms of the west by organizing, not by attacking everyone around him. After John Tzimiskes' death, Vladimir saw an opportunity to help out his realm by making a treaty with Byzantium reliant on his conversion to Christianity. But it wasn't just Vladimir that would convert, it was all of the Rus. Christianity offered a strong internal network of priests and scholars that could keep the Rus in line if they believed in the religion, so Vladimir arranged a mass baptism in the Dnieper. After the official conversion of the Rus to Christianity, Vladimir built churches, created a parish system with priests in charge of different districts throughout the country, and instituted a system of Christian education. He used his brains to create an organized government via organized religion. Vladimir's cunning use of Christianity to unify his country changed the Rus from wandering warriors to an organized and efficient state.

EXAMPLE ANSWER:

Nikephoros Phocas rose to power during the reign of Romanos II. While the emperor was out cavorting, Nikephoros Phocas led the Byzantine navy in its capture of Crete, and then he led the Byzantine army in the conquest of Aleppo, retaking territory that had been lost to the Arabs for decades. After the death of Romanos II, Nikephoros Phocas was proclaimed emperor by his army. The patriarch agreed to coronate the career officer, and thus on August 16 of 963 be became Nikephoros II, emperor of Byzantium. In his mind, Nikephoros Phocas became Supreme Commander when he was crowned. All of his life he fought, and he would continue to do so as emperor. Nikephoros Phocas' campaigns made him unpopular with his people; war was expensive, and it was paid for by increasing taxes on the citizens of his kingdom.

In addition to fighting all the time, Nikephoros Phocas kept the old soldier's custom of sleeping on the floor. Sleeping on the floor was a symbol of Nikephoros Phocas' loyalty: to the sword. Continually engaging in battle, using his "brawn" to rule, was Nikephoros Phocas' downfall. He was murdered by his wife and nephew, attacked while sleeping on the floor of his bedchamber. The people were happy the warrior was dead, and his nephew John Tzimiskes was made emperor quickly and without fuss.

On the other hand, Vladimir—who one would think would be brutal and rough like the Rus before him—realized that he could make the Rus equal to the kingdoms of the west by organizing, not by attacking everyone around him. After John Tzimiskes death, Vladimir saw an opportunity to help out his realm by making a treaty with Byzantium reliant on his conversion to Christianity. But it wasn't just Vladimir that would convert, it was all of the Rus. Vladimir arranged a mass baptism and after the official conversion of the Rus to Christianity, Vladimir built churches, created a parish system with priests in charge of different districts throughout the country, and instituted a system of Christian education. He used his brains to create an organized government via organized religion. Vladimir's cunning use of Christianity to unify his country changed the Rus from wandering warriors to an organized and efficient state.

Section IV: Map Exercise

1. Using a black pencil, trace the rectangular outline of the frame for Map 70.1: The Rus and Byzantium.

2. Using a blue pencil, trace the coastline of the Black Sea (include the Sea of Marmara), the visible portion of the Caspian Sea, and the visible portion of the Mediterranean. (Do not include any islands other than Crete, as it is labeled on the map.) Then trace the line of the Danube River, the Dnieper, and the Volga. Repeat until the contours are familiar.

3. Using a new sheet of paper, trace the rectangular outline of the frame in black. Then draw the coastline of the Black Sea (and Sea of Marmara), Caspian Sea, Mediterranean Sea, and the three rivers. Label the rivers.

4. When you are pleased with your map, lay it over the original. Erase and redraw any lines which are more than ¼ inch off of the original. Then, placing your tracing paper back over the original, trace the outlines of Byzantium, the First Bulgarian Empire, the territory seized by the Rus, and the approximate extent of Rus power.

5. Now study carefully the locations of the Slavs, the Drevlians, the Khazars, and Hamdanid territory. Label them on your map. Then study carefully the locations of Constantinople, Kherson, Kiev, Korosten, Novgorod, Baghdad, and Aleppo.

6. Finally, label the Sea of Marmara and the Battle of Arcadiopolis.

Chapter Seventy-One

The Holy Roman Emperor

The student may use his text when answering the questions in sections I and II.

Section I: Who, What, Where

Write a one or two-sentence answer explaining the significance of each item listed below.

Abbey of Cluny—**Pg. 548, ¶ 2—The Abbey of Cluny was established around 930 as a private monastery, and its founder, William the Pious of Aquitaine, had written into its charter that Cluny was to be placed directly under the supervision of the pope, meaning no secular nobleman—not even the founder or his family—had the right to interfere in its government. Cluny could offer safety to anyone who made it to the abbey's walls, no matter how unpopular the refugee was, and it was protected by threat of excommunication from being invaded, sacked, or burned.**

Gregory V—**Pg. 548, ¶ 5—Gregory V was appointed to the papacy when he was twenty-four years old by his cousin Otto III. Once he was officially recognized as the pope, Gregory V crowned Otto III as the "Holy Roman Emperor," Protector of the Church and ruler of the old Roman lands.**

Henry the Quarrelsome—**Pg. 545, ¶ 7 & 8 and Pg. 546, ¶ 7—Henry the Quarrelsome, Otto II's cousin and duke of Bavaria, was driven out of Bavaria by Otto II after he lobbied to be elected king in his cousin's place. After managing to become the guardian of Otto III, Henry the Quarrelsome agreed to give Otto III back to the care of his mother in exchange for the duchy of Bavaria, which Otto II had taken away from him.**

Hugh Capet—**Pg. 547, ¶ 2 & 3—Hugh Capet, son of the count of Paris, was made king of Western Francia after the death of Louis the Sluggard, and with his coronation came the start of a new dynasty: the Capetians.**

John XII—**Pg. 542, ¶ 3, Pg. 543, ¶ 2 & 3 and Pg. 545, ¶ 4—John XII, pope at the time of Otto I's rule, made the German and Italian king the Roman emperor in 962, but soon after he**

encouraged the Magyars to attack the emperor so that Otto I would be distracted from empire building. John XII briefly returned to Rome after fleeing from Otto I, but he was forced to flee again hearing of the emperor's anger, and he died after having a stroke in the village where he was hiding.

John XIII—**Pg. 545, ¶ 4—John XIII was appointed to the papacy by Otto I after the death of Leo VIII. John XIII agreed to crown Otto I's son and heir as Otto II, co-emperor, establishing a hereditary right to the *imperium*.**

Lél and Bulcsu—**Pg. 541, ¶ 1–3—Lél and Bulcsu were two Magyar warlords that led several attacks against the south of Germany in 955. The two warlords tried to flee Otto I after he defeated the Magyars at the Battle of Lechfeld, but they were caught, arrested and sentenced to be hanged like common felons.**

Leo VIII—**Pg. 543, ¶ 4—Leo VIII became pope in 963 after John XII was deposed by Otto I.**

Lothair IV—**Pg. 546, ¶ 7 to Pg. 547, ¶ 1—Lothair IV, king of Western Francia, was on Otto III's side during Henry the Quarrelsome's bid for the German throne. Lothair IV died in 986 and left the throne to his son Louis the Sluggard.**

Louis the Sluggard—**Pg. 547, ¶ 1 & 2—Louis the Sluggard, Lothair IV's son, succeeded his father as king of Western Francia but he was only on the throne for a year before he died, most likely because he was poisoned by his mother. Louis the Sluggard's death brought an end to the Carolingian dynasty.**

Otto I—**Pg. 542, ¶ 2 & 3 and Pg. 545, ¶ 2 & 5—Otto I led a successful attack against the Magyars at the Battle of Lechfeld, after which his subjects believed that his victory over the heathens meant that divine favor rested on him, and as a result he was made emperor of the Romans by Pope John XII in 962. Otto I made himself the holy Roman emperor by appointing Pope Leo VIII and then having Leo VIII proclaim that the emperor had the right to appoint the pope. Otto I then secured the position of the holy Roman emperor by making his son Otto II co-emperor, guaranteeing a smooth transition of the *imperium*.**

Otto II—**Pg. 545, ¶ 5 & 6 and Pg. 546, ¶ 2—Otto II, Otto I's son, heir and co-emperor, succeeded his father as king of Germany (but with no election) and emperor of the Romans (without coronation). After fighting for his right to be king of Germany, Otto II tried to do the same and muscle his way to the title of Roman emperor, but he failed and died from illness while still fighting for the title in 983.**

Otto III—**Pg. 546, ¶ 3 & 7 and Pg. 548, ¶ 5—Otto III, Otto II's son and co-emperor, lost his power when he was a baby to his relative Henry the Quarrelsome, but his power was restored after Henry the Quarrelsome returned him to his mother in exchange for the duchy of Bavaria. When he was sixteen he appointed his cousin to the papacy, after which Pope Gregory V crowned Otto III as the "Holy Roman Emperor," Protector of the Church and ruler of the old Roman lands.**

Peace and Truce of God—**Pg. 548, ¶ 2—Peace and Truce of God was a movement started in 989 by the Christian priests gathered at the Benedictine Abbey of Charroux that attempted to lay out an official policy on the difference between combatants and noncombatants in war. It took another tentative step forward in 994, when the pope announced that the Abbey of Cluny, in the eastern Frankish lands, would become a place of refuge for its followers.**

Simony—**Pg. 544, ¶ 2—Simony, named after a New Testament magician named Simon who tried to buy the divine gift of healing from the disciples of Jesus, was the practice of selling or gifting the right to appoint a priest in exchange for good will.**

Section II: Comprehension

Write a two or three-sentence answer to each of the following questions.

1. Who tamed the Magyars? What were they like after the Battle of Lechfeld?

A1.—Pg. 541, ¶ 2 to Pg. 542, ¶ 1—Otto I of Germany tamed the Magyars after his German cavalry wiped out an entire skilled class of Magyar warriors and officers at the Battle of Lechfeld. After the battle, the Magyar alliance was broken, and between 955 and the turn of the century, the Magyars settled ever more firmly into the Carpathian Basin. While the Magyars still did some mild raiding of their neighbors, Christian practices and Christian baptism began to spread into the Magyar community from the outside.

2. What oath did Otto I have to take in order to be given the title emperor of the Romans? Why was this oath so important to the pope?

A2.—Pg. 542, ¶ 4 to Pg. 543, ¶ 1—In order for Otto I to become the emperor of the Romans, he had to take an oath that stated "I will never make laws or rules in regard to the things which are under your jurisdiction, or the jurisdiction of the Romans without your consent and I will restore to you all of the lands of St. Peter that shall come into my hands." The oath also said that the lands remained in the ownership and control of the pope and that "no one of our successors shall on any pretext take from you any part of the aforesaid provinces, cities, towns, fortresses, villages, dependencies, territories, patrimonies, or taxes, or lessen your authority over them." The lands that were listed in the oath were governed by the pope and the taxes collected there went to him, so the pope needed to make sure that the new emperor did not take any of his power or money away.

3. Why did Otto I depose Pope John XII?

A3.—Pg. 543, ¶ 2-4—After Pope John XII made Otto I emperor, he worried about Otto I's growing power, so he encouraged the Magyars to attack the Germans in order to distract Otto I from empire-building. When Otto I found out about Pope John XII's maneuverings, he marched an army towards Rome in 963. In response, Pope John XII fled the city with

most of his treasury, prompting Otto I to announce John XII was no longer pope, giving Leo VIII the sacred title instead.

4. What was "lay investiture"?

A4.—Pg. 543, ¶ 7 to Pg. 544, ¶ 1—"Lay investiture" was the practice of a layman appointing a priest to work at the private church on his estate; often the priest was one of his sons, and the priesthood itself became hereditary. The churches were used by villagers and vassals nearby, but the building belonged to the landowner and he chose the priest to run the services. This was a practice common in Germany and Western Francia because for many Christian Goths and Franks, the great cities and their cathedrals were too far away to visit for regular worship.

5. Why did Otto I want to have his son named co-emperor?

A5.—Pg. 545, ¶ 5—Otto I wanted to have his son named co-emperor because that would guarantee a smooth transition of the emperorship and establish a hereditary hold on the *imperium*. Otto I wanted to establish a dynastic claim over the "Holy" Roman Empire. With the crowning of Otto II, Germany and the Holy Roman Empire would be ruled by the Ottonian or Saxon dynasty.

6. Why did Otto II face so many rebellions at the beginning of his reign?

A6.—Pg. 545 ¶ 6 & 7—Otto II became king of Germany without election and emperor of the Romans without coronation. Not all of the German nobles were happy to see their old powers of election gone, so they rebelled. Otto II faced numerous rebellions in the southern duchies of Germany, in particular, and one of the most troublesome rebels was his own cousin, duke of Bavaria, Henry the Quarrelsome.

7. How did Otto II think he was going to firm up his authority over the Romans? What actually happened?

A7.—Pg. 545, ¶ 8 to Pg. 546, ¶ 2—After successfully fighting for his right to be king of Germany and driving his cousin Henry the Quarrelsome into exile, Otto II figured he would use the same forceful tactics to assert his claim over the Romans. He planned a military campaign into Italy that would drive all remaining Byzantine control off the peninsula, putting it firmly under the Ottonian crown and Holy Roman emperor. Things didn't go as Otto II planned and after fighting a losing battle for three years he lost southern Italy and then died from an illness while still fighting.

8. What was the hiccup in the transfer of power between Otto II and Otto III?

A8.—Pg. 546, ¶ 3–7—Otto II had declared his three-year-old son Otto III to be co-emperor, but the pope declined to recognize him as Roman emperor. Henry the Quarrelsome insisted that, as the young king's nearest male relative, he should be awarded the care and control of Otto III and he was granted this request by the archbishop of Cologne. After failing to gather enough support for his bid for the throne, Henry the Quarrelsome agreed to give the

child back to his mother, and to his rightful place as king, in exchange for rule of his former lands, the duchy of Bavaria.

9. Describe the state of Western Francia when Hugh Capet became king.

A9.—Pg. 547, ¶ 3 & 4—Western Francia was a mess when Hugh Capet became king: the old Frankish kingdom had lost its eastern expanse to Germany, and the southeastern and northwestern territories of Burgundy and Normandy claimed independence. The lands that remained under the crown were engulfed by multiple currencies, a slew of languages, and a mass of independent-minded Frankish nobles. Private warfare between French dukes, private oppression of farmers by aristocrats, armed spats between men of different loyalties and languages, dishonest trade, and altered weights: all of these problems plagued Hugh Capet's Francia.

10. While the rich in Francia could hire personal armies to keep their possessions safe, what did the poor do to protect themselves?

A10.—Pg. 547, ¶ 4—The rich in Francia could hire personal armies to keep their possessions safe, but the poor could not afford such protection. Instead, they offered to serve their wealthier neighbors in exchange for security. This became the root of the later practice of feudalism: the exchange of service, on the part of the poor, for protection and provision from the rich.

11. How did the Christian priests gathered at the Benedictine abbey of Charroux in 989 hope to fix the terrible state of Western Francia?

A11.—Pg. 547, ¶ 5 to Pg. 548, ¶ 1—The Christian priests gathered at the Benedictine abbey of Charroux in 989 hoped to fix the terrible state of Western Francia by threatening to shut the gates of heaven on those who attacked the innocent. They declared that noncombatants—peasants and clergy, families and farmers—should be immune from ravages of battle. They announced that: no matter whose army he fought for, private or royal, Frankish or foreign, any soldier who robbed a church would be excommunicated; any soldier who stole livestock from the poor would be excommunicated; and anyone who attacked a priest would be excommunicated, as long as the priest wasn't carrying a sword or wearing armor.

Section III: Critical Thinking

The student may not use his text to answer this question.

The Peace of God movement was formed as a response to a world in which the possibility of salvation and the mission of the Christian church were increasingly tied to the territorial ambitions of particular kings. While the Peace of God was formed in Francia, nowhere were the fears of the group made more clear than in the exchange of power between the "Holy Roman Emperor" and the pope. The conflation of God and might was not new, but Otto I's insistence on becoming the first "holy" Roman emperor in the years just preceding the movement's start certainly intensified the relationship between the church and the state. Explain how Otto I became the Holy Roman Emperor, and what that meant for the balance of power between the church and the state. In your answer, make sure to explain the practice of lay investiture, and how that cultural practice influenced Otto I's belief that he could choose who would be the pope.

It seems that everything in Otto I's life led him to be the first holy Roman emperor. His success in battle convinced his subjects that he was protected by God, and the ordinary German practice of appointing priests made Otto feel comfortable assigning the title of "pope." Just as Otto I seemed destined for divine rule because he beat the Magyars with God on his side, he also came from the tradition of lay investiture, where choosing religious leaders was common practice. Since the king could claim to own all of the land within his kingdom, under the rules of lay investiture, he could build churches and monasteries on his own royal holdings and other parts of the country, appointing priests and abbots to run them. As king of Germany and Italy, Otto technically had the right to appoint priests in those kingdoms, but as a Papal State, Rome was not under his jurisdiction, which meant he had no right to appoint a pope.

Otto I solved the problem by having the pope he elected after John VII's deception, Leo VIII, make a proclamation that stated Otto I and all of his successors had the right to choose the successor of the pope, and of ordaining the pope, the archbishops and bishops. Otto took the power of appointing the pope away from the church; then he had his man declare that he had the power of appointment. As written on page 544, ¶ 4 "The pope, chosen by the emperor, had completed the circle of power: he had given the emperor the right to choose all future popes."

The shift in power that came with Otto I's ability to appoint the pope moved the emperor of the Romans from protector of the papacy to running the papacy. He had power over the sacred and the secular: he was not only emperor of the Romans, but the holy *emperor. In the past we read about popes and patriarchs shutting kings and emperors out of the churches. Excommunication was a tool that could be used by the Church to wield power, a balance to the king's claim that God wanted him to rule. Now, that option was off the table. If a pope wanted to excommunicate an emperor, the emperor simply had to kick him out of Rome and appoint a new pope. This is what happened to John XII. When Otto I left Rome, John XII came out of hiding after running from Otto I and declared that Otto I did not have the right to decide who was pope. He also claimed that Leo VIII's declaration of Otto I's power was bogus, and that there remained a separation of the Church and the state. But Otto I, the warrior with God on his side, returned to Rome and John XII fled for a second time. Unfortunately John XII died of a stroke, Leo VIII was reinstalled with the help of the German army, and when Leo VIII died Otto I exercised his power as the holy Roman emperor to install the next pope.*

EXAMPLE ANSWER:

It seems that everything in Otto I's life led him to be the first holy Roman emperor. His success in battle convinced his subjects that he was protected by God, and the German practice of appointing priests made Otto feel comfortable assigning the title of "pope." Otto I came from the tradition of lay investiture, where choosing religious leaders was common practice. Since the king could claim to own all of the land within his kingdom, under the rules of lay investiture, he could build churches and monasteries on his own royal holdings and other parts of the country, appointing priests and abbots to run them.

As king of Germany and Italy, Otto technically had the right to appoint priests in those kingdoms, but as a Papal State, Rome was not under his jurisdiction, which meant he had no right to appoint a pope. Otto I solved the problem by having the pope he elected, Leo VIII, make a proclamation that stated Otto I and all of his successors had the right to choose the successor of the pope, and of ordaining the pope, the archbishops and bishops.

The shift in power that came with Otto I's ability to appoint the pope moved the emperor of the Romans from protector of the papacy to running the papacy. He had power over the sacred and the secular: he was not only emperor of the Romans, but the holy emperor. In the past, excommunication was a tool that could be used by the Church to wield power, a balance to the king's claim that God wanted him to rule. Now, that option was off the table. John XII being kicked out of the papacy was a clear example of the emperor wielding his power over the Church. After John XII died, and Pope Leo VIII died, it was Otto I that chose the next pope, proving his ecclesiastical power.

Chapter Seventy-Two

The Hardship of Sacred War

The student may use her text when answering the questions in sections I and II.

Section I: Who, What, Where

Write a one or two-sentence answer explaining the significance of each item listed below.

Abu-Ishaq—**Pg. 550, ¶ 5 and Pg. 551, ¶ 1 & 2—Abu-Ishaq, son of Alp Tigin, took control of Ghazni with his brother-in-law Sebuk Tigin after Alp Tigin's death in 975. Abu-Ishaq died just after agreeing to a peace treaty with Mansur that recognized Abu-Ishaq as Ghazni's legitimate governor; his death was convenient for Sebuk Tigin, who was slated to take over when Abu-Ishaq passed.**

Alp Tigin—**Pg. 550, ¶ 3 & 4—Alp Tigin, formerly a general for the Samanid emir and chief commander of the Samanid armies, fell out of favor with the Samanids when he tried to force the election of his own son to the position of emir instead of supporting the emir's brother Mansur. Alp Tigin left the Samanid capital and conquered the city of Ghazni where he lived out his life ruling as king of a tiny empire.**

Anandapala—**Pg. 554, ¶ 4—Anandapala, son of Jayapala, followed his father in the fight against the Ghaznavids, but he could not stop Mahmud. In 1006 he lost the upper lands of the delta; in 1009, he lost the Punjab; and in 1015 he was driven completely from his lands, making him the last Shahi king.**

Jayapala—**Pg. 552, ¶ 3 to Pg. 553, ¶ 1 and Pg. 554, ¶ 2 & 3—Jayapala, Hindu king of the Shahi, fought Sebuk Tigin twice; losing both times, he was forced to pay tribute to the Ghazni king and give up the important Khyber Pass to his enemy. The continued war with the Ghaznavid empire under the leadership of Mahmud was too much for Jayapala, so after another defeat in November of 1001, Jayapala built himself a funeral pyre, entered it, and set it on fire.**

Lingam—**Pg. 556, ¶ 3—A lingam was a seamless pillar with no features that acted as a representation of the all-encompassing, transcendent essence of Shiva.**

Mahipala—**Pg. 557, ¶ 2 & 3—Mahipala, the long-lived king of the Pala, took advantage of the preoccupation in the northwest of India with invading Ghaznavids to rebuild Pala power in the northeast. Though his empire was growing strong, he could not defeat the invading Chola king Rajendra.**

Mahmud—**Pg. 553, ¶ 2, Pg. 554, ¶ 1 and 4–7—Mahmud, oldest son of Sebuk Tigin and his father's successor to the Ghaznavid throne, claimed the rest of the Samanid land north of the Oxus for the Ghaznavids after Nasr Khan took Bukhara. He spent most of his life attacking India: in 1015 he drove out the Shahi, in 1018 he moved on to Kannauj and drove the Pratihara king out of his capital, and at the height of his power in 1025 he took the Indian harbor town of Somnath where he slaughtered pilgrims, sacked the temple of Shiva, and then took the body of the statue back to Ghazni to be placed on the steps of the Muslim mosque.**

Mansur—**Pg. 550, ¶ 3 and Pg. 551, ¶ 1—Mansur, brother of the emir of the Samanids, became king of the Samanids despite Alp Tigin's attempt to put his son on the throne. Mansur made peace with Alp Tigin's successors, recognizing a legitimate governor of Ghazni in exchange for the city's loyalty to the Samanid empire.**

Nasr Khan—**Pg. 553, ¶ 3—Nasr Kahn, chief of the Turkish Karakhanids, led his men into the Samanid city of Bukhara, let them sack the city, and kept Bukhara for the Karakhanids. After the young Samanid emir withdrew to the south of the Oxus river, the Karakhanids seized the territory around Bukhara for their own.**

Rajendra—**Pg. 556, ¶ 4 & 5 and Pg. 558, ¶ 1—Rajendra, Rajaraja I's son and successor, had a long reign, was a fierce fighter and established a firm hold on the land conquered by his father. His greatest achievement was to set sail, increasing his empire's power via trade and warships and most importantly taking control of the shipping routes into southeast Asia by invading and taking tribute from Srivijaya.**

Rajadhiraja—**Pg. 558, ¶ 2—Rajadhiraja, grandson of Rajaraja I, followed Rajendra as king, making the Chola the longest ruling southern Indian kingdom and blanketing the South of India with Chola language, Chola customs and Chola power. Rajadhiraja's kingdom was wealthy enough to support poets and scholars at court, and under his patronage southern Indian literature bloomed.**

Rajaraja I—**Pg. 555, ¶ 6 to Pg. 556, ¶ 1 & 3—Rajaraja I came to power as king of the Chola in 985 and immediately began a reconquest of the south by wiping out Pandya, defeating the Eastern Chalukya and making them his vassals, and halting the spread of Western Chalukya power and sending his men into Sri Lanka. To commemorate his power over the south of India, Rajaraja I built a huge temple devoted to Shiva in Thanjavur.**

Sebuk Tigin—**Pg. 550, ¶ 5, Pg. 551, ¶ 2 & 5 and Pg. 553, ¶ 1—Sebuk Tigin, son-in-law of Alp Tigin, took control of Ghazni with Abu-Ishaq after Alp Tigin's death in 975, and then took sole control of Ghazni as the Samanid-approved governor after Abu-Ishaq's death. After**

capturing Kandahar, Sebuk Tigin pushed his expansion on, moving east into Shahi land, taking Kabul and most importantly taking the Khyber Pass for Ghazni.

Togrul—**Pg. 555, ¶ 2 & 3—Togrul, chief of the Karakhanids, broke with Turkish custom and forced respect from other Turkish chiefs through conquest. He built a realm of his own around the Oxus, claiming the Ghaznavid capital of Nishapur for his own in 1038 and crowning himself as sultan of the Turks; by 1044 Togrul's Turks controlled most of the land west of the mountains.**

Section II: Comprehension

Write a two or three-sentence answer to each of the following questions.

1. What were the terms of the peace made between Sebuk Tigin, Abu-Ishaq and Mansur?

A1.—Pg. 551, ¶ 1—Sebuk Tigin convinced Abu-Ishaq to go with him to the court of Mansur, king of the Samanids. Once there they negotiated a peace treaty where they swore loyalty to Mansur in return for recognition. Mansur agreed to make Abu-Ishaq the legitimate governor of Ghazni and to appoint Sebuk Tigin to the position should Abu-Ishaq die.

2. What was Sebuk Tigin's first act as governor of Ghazni? Why didn't the Samanids deal with Sebuk Tigin's expanding empire immediately?

A2.—Pg. 551, ¶ 2—Sebuk Tigin's first act as governor of Ghazni was to attack and capture Kandahar, making him more than just a city governor. Though Sebuk Tigin's expansion was a threat to the Samanids, they did not retaliate after he took Kandahar because northern Turkish nomads known as the Karakhanids had begun to cross the Oxus river south into Samanid land, raiding the silver mines on which the Samanids relied. The Samanid army was busy fighting for its silver and didn't have energy to spare for Sebuk Tigin.

3. Why did the Shahi kingdom's capital move from Kabul to Udabhandapura to Lahore? Though the capital had moved, why did Jayapala stay in Udabhandapura?

A3.—Pg. 551, ¶ 4—The Shahi moved their capital from Kabul to Udabhandapura after the city fell into Muslim hands in the 7th century. After launching several unsuccessful assaults against Ghazni from Udabhandapura, Sebuk Tigin attacked the western border of the Shahi and took some of Jayapala's territory away. This forced the Shahi to move their capital to the city of Lahore, but Jayapala stayed in Udabhandapura so that he could continue to fight against Sebuk Tigin's efforts to expand.

4. Though there was no clear victory for either the Ghaznavids nor the Shahis when the armies met outside of Kabul in 986, why did the Jayapala draw back first?

A4.—Pg. 552, ¶ 2—Though there was no clear victory for either the Ghaznavids nor the Shahis when the armies met outside of Kabul in 986, Jayapala was the first to draw back because of the religious fervor of Sebuk Tigin's men. Sebuk Tigin told his men they weren't

just fighting for land, but that they were fighting for Islam, protecting Islam from its universal enemies, the worshippers of images and idols. Sebuk Tigin's men would not be swayed from their duty to fight for Islam, so Jayapala told his men, who were not used to such outward religious zeal, to retreat.

5. Describe what Mahmud did when he got to the Indian harbor town of Somnath, and what happened to its famous and sacred statue of Shiva.

A5.—Pg. 554, ¶ 6 & 7—When Mahmud got to the sacred town of Somnath in 1025, he had his armies slaughter the thousands of pilgrims that were visiting, sack the temple of Shiva and topple the sacred image of the god, taking the body of the statue back to Ghazni. There, he placed it at the foot of the steps into the mosque, so that Muslim worshippers could wipe their feet on it as they entered. Putting the body of Shiva in a place where people could wipe their feet symbolized the triumph of Mahmud's god over the gods of his enemies.

6. How did Rajaraja I commemorate the triumphs that led to his domination of the south of India?

A6.—Pg. 556, ¶ 3—To commemorate the extent of his triumphs in the south of India, Rajaraja I built a huge temple in his capital city Thanjavur: a temple devoted to Shiva, with three hundred priests dedicated to the service and worship of the god and fifty musicians who were salaried to sing the sacred liturgies. A mighty lingam stood at its center and on the walls were painted scenes of Shiva as conqueror and Shiva as destroyer of cities.

7. What did Rajendra accomplish by "setting sail"?

A7.—Pg. 556, ¶ 5 and Pg. 558, ¶ 1—Rajendra sent trade ships east to the court of the Song that carried elephant tusks, frankincense, aromatic woods, and over a thousand pounds of pearls. He also sent warships across the southern strait, carrying naval forces to the island of Sri Lanka where he claimed to have captured the crown and regalia of the legitimate Pandya line. Most importantly, in 1025 Rajendra's navy invaded Srivijaya, demanded tribute from its king and took control of the shipping routes into southeast Asia.

8. Why didn't Rajendra attempt to conquer the kingdom of Pala? Why did he decide to return home?

A8.—Pg. 557, ¶ 3 & 4—Because the Chola armies were so far from home, they did not have the resources to follow up their defeat of Mahipala with an attempt at conquering the entire kingdom. Instead Rajendra pushed past it, across the Ganges delta, and forced the people along the coast to pay tribute. The Chola army decided to return home because, without resources, it would have been simple for the Pala army (or another army) to come from behind, breach the thin strip of Chola conquests along the coastline and cut them off from food and shelter.

9. How did Rajendra make up for turning away from attacking the Pala?

A9.—Pg. 557, ¶ 4 to Pg. 558, ¶ 1—Though Rajendra decided not to conquer the Pala, he made up for it by sending a naval expedition to the kingdom of Srivijaya, which dominated the

islands of Java and Sumatra. Rajendra invaded the island, demanded tribute from the Srivijayan king and took control of the shipping routes into southeast Asia.

Section III: Critical Thinking

The student may not use her text to answer this question.

At the end of the chapter we read about the southern Indian poet Tiruttakadevar. His most enduring epic told the tale of the prince Jivaka, a skilled fighter and general, who earned a kingdom and then willingly gave it up. Despite his victories, he had discovered the hollowness of all human achievement. Using examples from this chapter, write a paragraph explaining what "the hollowness of all human achievement" means in the context of conquest and empire building, even if it is in the name of religion.

The student has a lot of leeway in this "Critical Thinking" exercise. The "hollowness of all human achievement" may refer to life's fleeting nature, the uncertainty of the meaning of life, or perhaps the cost of human life in war—especially a war that is supposedly being fought in the name of one's god, but is almost always fought to win power. The student should take the time to mull the phrase over, and write a thoughtful paragraph about what the "hollowness of all human achievement" means to her.

One example from the chapter that might lend itself to explaining the phrase is the quick growth, and then reduction, of the Ghaznavids. Mahmud devastated most of northwest India. He slaughtered thousands of pilgrims at Somnath who simply wished to worship so that he could prove that his god was dominant. He broke down the sacred statue of Shiva, brought its body back to Ghazni, and encouraged Muslim worshippers to wipe their feet on the desecrated statue before going to pray in the mosque. His god, the god of the Muslims, was supposedly triumphant over the gods of the Indians.

After Mahmud's death, the Ghaznavid empire shrank. Mahmud's god was nowhere in sight when Togrul's Turks invaded the Ghaznavid capital. Mahmud's human achievement meant little after his death; while the fate of his empire was uncertain, there was no question of its human cost.

Please note—the student could answer in many different ways. As long as she provides an explanation of what she thinks the phrase "hollowness of all human achievement" means and then connects her explanation to a person or event in the chapter, she is on the right track. The example answer below is just one of many possible ways to tackle the question.

EXAMPLE ANSWER:

The phrase "hollowness of all human achievement" can mean so many things. In the context of this chapter, it seems to point to the cost of human life in the name of religion. The leaders in this chapter say they are fighting for their god or gods, but in their quest for religious dominance they kill so many people, ruin cultures, and generally act without mercy. It seems the dominance of each god or religion lasts only as long as the determined

king or warleader fighting for the cause, suggesting that humans are short-sighted rather than pious in their killing of other humans.

Mahmud of the Ghaznavids is an example of the hollowness of human achievement. Mahmud devastated most of northwest India. He slaughtered thousands of pilgrims at Somnath who simply wished to worship, so that he could prove that his god was dominant. He broke down the sacred statue of Shiva, brought its body back to Ghazni, and encouraged Muslim worshippers to wipe their feet on the desecrated body before going to pray in the mosque. His god, the god of the Muslims, was supposedly triumphant over the gods of the Indians. But after Mahmud's death, the Ghaznavid empire shrank. Mahmud's god was nowhere in sight when Togrul's Turks invaded the Ghaznavid capital. Mahmud's human achievement meant little after his death; while the fate of his empire was uncertain, there was no question of its human cost.

Section IV: Map Exercise

1. Using a black pencil, trace the rectangular outline of the frame for Map 72.2: The Spread of Chola Influence.

2. Using a blue pencil, trace the coastline of the Indian Ocean. Include only the islands which are marked as part of the extent of Chola influence. With your blue pencil, trace the line of the Sindh, the Punjab, the Oxus, and the Ganges. Trace the mountains with simple peaks. Repeat until the contours are familiar.

3. Using a new sheet of paper, trace the rectangular outline of the frame in black. Then draw the coastline of the Indian Ocean. Draw the lines of the Sindh, the Punjab, the Oxus, and the Ganges. Draw simple peaks to represent the mountains. Label the rivers. Erase and redraw as necessary.

4. When you are pleased with your map, lay it over the original. Erase and redraw any lines which are more than ¼ inch off of the original.

5. Leaving your map on the original, outline in black the areas which are part of the extent of the Chola influence.

6. Remove your map. Study carefully the locations of Kandahar, Kabul, Ujjain, Kannauj, Pala, Pandya, Thanjavur, Sri Lanka, Sumatra, Jambi, and Java. Also study the locations of the Khyber Pass and Mt. Kailasa. When you are familiar with them, close the book. Using your regular pencil, label the locations of Kandahar, Kabul, Ujjain, Kannauj, Pala, Pandya, Thanjavur, Sri Lanka, Sumatra, Jambi, Java, the Khyber Pass and Mt. Kailasa.

7. Label Togrul's Turks.

Chapter Seventy-Three

Basil the Bulgar-Slayer

The student may use his text when answering the questions in sections I and II.

Section I: Who, What, Where

Write a one or two-sentence answer explaining the significance of each item listed below.

Al-Aziz—**Pg. 563, ¶ 5—Al-Aziz, son of al-Muizz, led Fatimid armies across the Red Sea into Arabia; they took control of the holy cities Medina and Mecca and marched up into the Abbasid-held provinces of Palestine and Syria, conquering both within a year.**

Al-Hakim—**Pg. 563, ¶ 6 to Pg. 564, ¶ 1, Pg. 565, ¶ 4 and Pg. 566, ¶ 3—Al-Hakim, son of al-Aziz, was appointed caliph at eleven years old in 996, and in 1001 he finalized a treaty with Basil II, agreeing to halt the battle between the Fatimids and the Byzantines for ten years. After he destroyed the Church of the Holy Sepulchre, Golgotha, and the Jerusalem synagogue, the Muslims to the east denounced the Fatimid regime; it was a good thing they did because in 1021 al-Hakim's realm was in such a mess, and he was so deluded in his beliefs that he was divine, that he rode off into the desert alone and disappeared.**

Al-Muizz—**Pg. 563, ¶ 4—Al-Muizz, Fatimid caliph, seized control of Egypt in 969 and built a city named Cairo to be the foundation of his new territory. By 973 al-Muizz's Cairo had become the functioning capital of the Fatimid empire, but that meant he had lost control of the North African tribes in the Maghreb.**

Al-Qadir—**Pg. 565, ¶ 4—Al-Qadir, Abbasid caliph at the time of al-Hakim's destruction of Christian and Jewish places of worship, denied the legitimacy of the Fatimid caliphate in the "Baghdad Manifesto." Al-Qadir's "Baghdad Manifesto" was read out loud in mosques all throughout the Muslim world; it wrote into law the breach between the Fatimid and Abbasid caliphates.**

Bardas Phocas—**Pg. 561, ¶ 4 & 6—Bardas Phocas, nephew of Nikephoros Phocas and general for Basil IIs' army, went against the king and convinced his troops in Asia Minor to declare him**

emperor. Bardas Phocas fell dead from his saddle in his first major confrontation with Basil II at Chrysopolis in April of 989, quickly ending the resistance against the Byzantine king.

Samuel—**Pg. 560, ¶ 2, Pg. 561, ¶ 3, Pg. 563, ¶ 2 and Pg. 566, ¶ 1—Samuel, one of four brothers fighting for Bulgarian freedom, took over Bulgarian power by putting puppet king Romanus on the throne and then declaring himself king after Romanus's death. After years of battling against Basil II, Samuel's Bulgarian forces were defeated in July of 1014, and the sight of his destroyed army killed the aged Bulgarian chief.**

Skleros—**Pg. 562, ¶ 3-5—Skleros, an aging Byzantine general, surreptitiously rebelled against Basil II via guerilla tactics, like halting transport to Constantinople on the roads, seizing shipments to and from the city and waylaying royal couriers and stealing their orders. Skleros made a deal with Basil II: the general would call off his forces, give up his claim to the crown, and retire to the countryside and Basil would grant him the rank of second in the empire and give all of his supporters immunity.**

Varangian Guard—**Pg. 562, ¶ 2—Varangian Guard were the Russian bodyguards Basil II had hired from Vladimir of Kiev and then decided to keep close because he had grown suspicious of everyone. The Varangian Guard remained in the emperor's confidence and in his personal service as his most trusted companions.**

Section II: Comprehension

Write a two or three-sentence answer to each of the following questions.

1. Who were the four freedom fighters in the west of Bulgaria that challenged Byzantine rule? What did the brothers claim they wanted from Constantinople? What Basil II think they really wanted?

A1.—Pg. 560, ¶ 2 & 3—The four freedom fighters in the west of Bulgaria that challenged Byzantine rule were David, Moses, Aaron and Samuel. The brothers claimed they wanted the release of their imprisoned king Boris II. Basil II suspected that the oldest brother Samuel actually wanted to rule Bulgaria more than he wanted to have his king set free.

2. What did Basil II hope would happen after he set Boris II and his brother and heir Romanus free in 981? What actually happened?

A2.—Pg. 560, ¶ 3 to Pg. 561, ¶ 2—Basil II hoped that if the royal family actually returned to Bulgaria, Samuel would be forced to admit that he was only using them and then civil war might break out, bringing the independence movement to an end. After their release, Boris II was killed by a border guard while Romanus survived. Romanus, agreeable and not a long-term threat because he was castrated and could not produce offspring, was declared king of Bulgaria by Samuel, while Samuel himself actually kept the power in his own hands.

3. How did Basil II handle the threat posed by Bardas Phocas and his loyal Asia Minor troops?

Pg. 561, ¶ 5 & 6—Basil II asked his brother-in-law Vladimir of Kiev to supply reinforcements to battle Bardas Phocas because the Byzantine army was overextended, so Vladimir sent him six thousand Rus soldiers. In April of 989, Basil led his combined Byzantine and Russian forces into battle against Bardas Phocas at Chrysopolis. The fight was short because Bardas Phocas fell dead from his saddle as he was leading his troops towards the imperial line, after which his army quickly disintegrated and the resistance movement ended.

4. What advice did Skleros give Basil II concerning his running of Byzantium? What did Basil II do with this advice?

A4.—Pg. 562, ¶ 5 to Pg. 563, ¶ 1—Skleros told Basil II to "Cut down the governors who become overproud," and "Let no generals on campaign have too many resources. Exhaust them with unjust exactions, to keep them busied with their own affairs. . . . Be accessible to no one. Share with few your most intimate plans." Skleros's advice matched Basil II's own thoughts: to be private, withdrawn, and thoroughly in control. Basil II then ruled his empire alone from the top, introducing new measures, directing his military forces, and using his own intuition rather than law to run his civil administration.

5. What kind of a ruler was the Fatimid caliph al-Hakim? What were some of the rules he imposed on his kingdom?

A5.—Pg. 564, ¶ 3 to Pg. 565, ¶ 1—Al-Hakim was a deeply pious man who wished to establish himself as the perfect Muslim ruler: just and lawful, austere in his personal life and generous in public. Some of the rules he imposed were: the destruction of vineyards so that wine, which was forbidden to Muslims, could not be made anywhere in his realm; he decreed that women in Cairo remain in their homes, to protect their virtue; and he commanded that the marketplace in Cairo be lit and open all night, demonstrating the complete peace and safety of his realm even in the dark. His rules made sense to him, but they seemed harsh and sometimes meaningless to the public, especially to the non-Muslims who lived inside his borders.

6. Why didn't Basil II attack al-Hakim after he destroyed the Church of the Holy Sepulchre and Golgotha?

A6.—Pg. 565, ¶ 3—Basil II did not attack al-Hakim after he destroyed the Church of the Holy Sepulchre and Golgotha for two reasons. First, the treaty he made with al-Hakim bound him to peace. Second, he was getting ready to reignite the war against the Bulgarians, and he could not get diverted by invading the Fatimid realm.

7. What happened when the Byzantine army finally met the Bulgarians in battle at Kleidion in July of 1014?

A7.—Pg. 565, ¶ 5 to Pg. 566, ¶ 1—When Basil II met the Byzantine army in July of 2014, the Bulgarians were brutally defeated. Fifteen thousand Bulgarian troops were taken captive and Basil II ordered ninety-nine out of every hundred captives blinded—the hundredth

man was left with only one eye so that he could lead his comrades back to Samuel, who had remained back in the capital city of Ohrid. Samuel had a heart attack and died at the sight of his mutilated troops, and without their chief, the Bulgarian resistance to Byzantium faltered.

8. Describe al-Hakim's madness and his ultimate self-destruction.

A8.—Pg. 566, ¶ 3—The Fatimids knew Al-Hakim had gone mad when in 1016 he declared himself divine and ordered his name inserted into Friday prayers in place of Allah's. At this his Muslim subjects joined the Christians and Jews in revolt. Al-Hakim ordered vicious reprisals, but in 1021, with his realm in total chaos, he rode off into the desert alone and disappeared from view.

9. How did Basil II earn the nickname "Basil the Bulgar-Slayer"?

A9.—Pg. 566, ¶ 2 & 4—Basil II slaughtered thousands of Bulgarians after their defeat at Kleidion. In the four years that followed, Bulgarian nobles began to surrender to Basil II and by 1018, Bulgaria was again enfolded into Byzantium—this time, all the way to the Danube river. Basil II earned the nickname "Basil the Bulgar-Slayer" because of his triumphs over the Bulgarians during his life-long war against them.

Section III: Critical Thinking

The student may not use his text to answer this question.

In the last chapter you wrote about the phrase "the hollowness of all human achievement," words spoken by Jivaka, a fictional fighter and general created by the Southern Indian poet Tiruttakadevar. Now, you will continue to ruminate on Jivaka's discovery about humanity. Write a paragraph explaining how the loss of the Church of the Holy Sepulchre is a testament to "the hollowness of all human achievement." In your answer detail why the Church was destroyed, and then connect the destruction to Jivaka's sorrowful words, further explicating the your ideas from Chapter 72.

Al-Hakim's demolition of the Church of the Holy Sepulchre came at the end of a destructive spree in his territory. He was worried about the non-Muslims living within the Fatimid kingdom, and as a result destroyed their places of worship. As written on page 565, "In 1003, he ordered the church of St. Mark just south of Cairo razed, flattened the Jewish and Christian cemeteries around it, and built a mosque where the complex had stood. Throughout Egypt, Christian land was confiscated, crosses destroyed, and churches closed. And then, to discourage pilgrimage to Jerusalem, al-Hakim ordered the great Christian complex built by Constantine destroyed: the Church of the Holy Sepulchre, which protected the tomb of Jesus, commemorated as the site of the resurrection, and Golgotha, the hill of crucifixion. The enormous stones were hacked to bits with axes, and the rock itself was removed from the city." The Church of the Holy Sepulchre was built in the 4th century, standing as the greatest monument to the Christian faith; with one word al-Hakim had it leveled.

The Church of the Holy Sepulchre may have seemed like a threat to al-Hakim, but in reality it was an important monument, and mankind suffered for its loss. To make matters worse, we found out at the end of the chapter that al-Hakim was mad, declaring himself divine in 1016 and ordering his name inserted into Friday prayers in place of Allah's. Al-Hakim destroyed a monument on land that is so sacred that Israel and Palestine are still fighting over it today, all for a crazy vendetta against non-Muslims. There is perhaps no greater example of the hollowness of all human achievement. The great Church crumbled because the powerful caliph wanted to assert the might of the Muslim faith. Al-Hakim's attack on the church was devastating for history and for the possibility of religions co-existing peacefully in medieval times.

EXAMPLE ANSWER:

Al-Hakim's demolition of the Church of the Holy Sepulchre came at the end of a destructive spree in his territory. He was worried about the non-Muslims living within the Fatimid kingdom, and as a result destroyed their places of worship. He ordered the church of St. Mark just south of Cairo razed in 1013, and then he flattened the Jewish and Christian cemeteries around it. On top of those ruins he built a mosque. Following the demolition of the church of St. Mark, al-Hakim ordered Christian land confiscated, crosses destroyed, and churches closed. Finally, to stop pilgrimage to Jerusalem, al-Hakim ordered the Church of the Holy Sepulchre, which protected the tomb of Jesus, commemorated as the site of the resurrection, and Golgotha, the hill of crucifixion, destroyed. The Church of the Holy Sepulchre was built in the 4th century, standing as the greatest monument to the Christian faith; with one word al-Hakim had it leveled.

The Church of the Holy Sepulchre may have seemed like a threat to al-Hakim, but in reality it was an important monument, and mankind suffered for its loss. To make matters worse, we found out at the end of the chapter that al-Hakim was mad, declaring himself divine in 1016 and ordering his name inserted into Friday prayers in place of Allah's. The way al-Hakim used his power as caliph is perhaps the best example of the hollowness of all human achievement. The great Church crumbled because the caliph wanted to assert the might of the Muslim faith. Al-Hakim's attack on the church was devastating for history and for the possibility of religions co-existing peacefully in medieval times.

Section IV: **Map Exercise**

1. Using a black pencil, trace the rectangular outline of the frame for Map 73.1: The Fatimid Caliphate and Byzantium.

2. Using a blue pencil, trace the coastline of the Mediterranean Sea, the Red Sea, and the Black Sea. You do not need to include any islands at this time. Repeat until the contours are familiar.

3. Using a new sheet of paper, trace the rectangular outline of the frame in black. Remove your tracing paper from the original, and draw the coastline of the Mediterranean, the Red Sea, and the Black Sea.

4. When you are pleased with your map, lay it over the original. Erase and redraw any lines which are more than ¼ inch off of the original. Using a black pencil, trace the outline of the Rus and the outline of the Fatimids. Then trace the area of the Hamdanids and of the Buyids.

5. Remove your map. Study carefully the locations of North Africa, Egypt, Arabia, Palestine, Asia Minor, Thracia, and Bulgaria. Mark them on your map. Then study carefully the locations of Cairo, Mecca, Medina, Damascus, Baghdad, Antioch, Constantinople, Chrysopolis, Ohrid, and Mahdia. Mark them on your map as well. Check your map against the original, and correct any misplaced labels.

6. Mark the location of the Battle of Kleidion.

Chapter Seventy-Four

Defending the Mandate

The student may use her text when answering the questions in sections I and II.

Section I: Who, What, Where

Write a one or two-sentence answer explaining the significance of each item listed below.

Liao Shengzong—**Pg. 569, ¶ 4 and Pg. 570, ¶ 1–3—Liao Shengzong was the Liao king at the time of Song Taizong's second campaign against Liao borders. When Song Zhenzong came to power, Liao Shengzong launched a major attack on the Song, resulting in a peace treaty: the Treaty of Chanyuan.**

Song Renzong—**Pg. 572, ¶ 2–4—Song Renzong, Song Zhenzong's son and heir, made the Song people richer and richer during his reign. Song Renzong was able to use tax money for roads, buildings, schools, and books, and the technique of printing with carved wooden blocks resulted in the creation of the world's first paper money.**

Song Zhenzong—**Pg. 570, ¶ 5, Pg. 571, ¶ 3 and Pg. 572, ¶ 1—Song Zhenzong, Song Taizong's third son and successor, was forced to make a treaty in 1005 with the Liao after they attacked the northern Song border. Song Zhenzong spent the second part of his reign convincing his subjects that the Mandate of Heaven was with him, but the real reason his people supported him was because peace time brought wealth, prosperity and good health to the Song.**

Treaty of Chanyuan—**Pg. 571, ¶ 3 & 4—The Treaty of Chanyuan, signed in 1005, brought an end to the Song's first era of conquest in favor of a predictable and peaceful coexistence with its northern Liao neighbors. The terms of the agreement were as such: the Liao would give up their attempts to seize Song land; both kings would respect the border and build no more fortifications along it; the Song emperor would address the Liao ruler properly, as an emperor in his own right; and the Song would hand over two hundred thousand bolts of silk and a massive payment in silver to the Liao every single year.**

Xiao—**Pg. 569, ¶ 4 & 5—Xiao was the regent for the teenage Liao king Liao Shengzong. The empress dowager Xiao, who had a good head for war, defeated all three Song armies after their surprise attack in 986 by telling the Liao forces to retreat and then attack the Song from behind.**

Section II: Comprehension

Write a two or three-sentence answer to each of the following questions.

1. For what reasons was Song Taizong's crown in jeopardy, even though he had conquered the Northern Han?

A1.—Pg. 568, ¶ 3—Song Taizong decided to attack Liao borders after his successes against the Northern Han, but he was massively beaten just west of Beijing. Song Taizong's officers were already suspicious that the emperor murdered his brother Song Taizu for the crown, and others said Song Taizong had usurped the throne from Song Taizu's son. Song Taizong's victories against the Northern Han may have temporarily silenced his critics, but the questionable way by which he acquired the throne and his defeat by the Liao put his crown in jeopardy.

2. How could a ruler prove he had the Mandate of Heaven?

A2.—Pg. 568, ¶ 4 to Pg. 569, ¶ 1—While a ruler could be upright and live virtuously, the strongest proof that he held the Mandate of Heaven was success in battle.

3. Why did the older of Song Taizong's nephews cut his own throat?

A3.—Pg. 569, ¶ 2—Song Taizong's defeat at the Liao border tarnished the shine of the Mandate. He had listened to army gossip; he knew that his officers might lead a revolt against him at any time, and that his brother's two sons could be installed on the imperial throne in his place. When Song Taizong was safely back in Kaifeng he let the older of the young princes know he intended to kill him—instead of waiting for his uncle to strike, the young man cut his own throat.

4. How did Song Taizong manage to surprise the Liao during his second campaign against his enemy neighbor in 986?

A4.—Pg. 569, ¶ 4—In 986, three separate divisions of Song soldiers marched across the Liao border, each headed for a different pass through the mountains. Liao Shengzong and the empress dowager Xiao were taken by surprise because they had received bad intelligence. Liao Shengzong believed the Song were also going to attack by water, so he divided his army and sent half of it to the coast, allowing the Song armies to pushed quickly forward against the weakened Liao forces, taking cities in the west as they moved into Liao land.

5. How was Song Taizong able to keep his throne after his second defeat by the Liao?

A5.—Pg. 570, ¶ 1—Though the mandate did not seem to be with Song Taizong after the second Song defeat by the Liao, Song Taizong was able to keep his throne because he had killed off all of his possible rivals.

6. Describe the state of the Song kingdom when Song Zhenzong came to the throne. How did he try and deal with the mess left for him by his father?

A6.—Pg. 570, ¶ 6 to Pg. 571, ¶ 2—When Song Zhenzong took the throne, he inherited a kingdom with an enormous bureaucracy and hostile neighbors. Yearly raids from the Liao were causing increasing angst in the northern reaches of the Song empire, so Song Zhenzong's first big project to deal with the mess in the north was to build a series of canals, dikes and well-garrisoned fortresses along the Song-Liao border. The barrier would have been great, but before it was finished, Liao Shengzong launched a major attack against the Song, burst through the unfinished fortifications and swept south into Song territory.

7. What did Song Zhenzong do to prove to his people the Mandate of Heave had not deserted him?

A7.—Pg. 571, ¶ 6—In 1008, the emperor made a startling discovery: a sacred text, buried in the palace grounds, explaining that the Song dynasty reigned with heaven's favor. Then Song Zhenzong had a supernatural vision, which he described in great detail to his people: the mythical and sacred first emperor of China had appeared and explained that he, the Yellow Emperor, had been reincarnated as Zhenzong's ancestor. These two acts were supposed to prove to the Song people that not only did Zhenzong have the Mandate of Heaven, but also that his clan was descended from China's greatest ruler.

8. While Song Zhenzong worked to prove to his people that divine favor was with him, what was most likely the reason that his people continued to support his rule?

A8.—Pg. 572, ¶ 1—The Song were wealthier and more comfortable after the Treaty of Chanyuan, and as a result they were supportive of Song Zhenzong. The emperor had introduced a new kind of rice into his country: he had bought thousands of bushels of a quick-maturing, drought-resistant seed from rice-growers in the far south and imported them into the north for use by the Song farmers. The new rice grew so quickly that two crops per year could be planted and harvested, and its tolerance for dry land meant that fields farther north and higher up could now yield a crop.

9. How did peace change the book industry in Song China?

A9.—Pg. 572, ¶ 3—Without major wars to fight, tax money went not to the army but to roads, buildings, schools, and books. Books were in higher demand than ever because Song Renzong relied on the results of the civil examinations when he chose his officials, which meant that young men all over the empire were buying the standard texts from which they could study. The technique of printing books with carved wooden blocks, rather than writing them by hand, made it possible to produce multiple copies of the most popular books and to sell them for affordable prices.

10. In what way did woodblock printing prove useful in addition to the mass production of books?

A10.—Pg. 572, ¶ 4—Woodblock printing helped create the world's first paper money. Previously, Chinese merchants left their coins in special, privately run "deposit houses," received stamped receipts, and then used the receipts to buy and sell. Song Renzong encouraged trade by standardizing the receipt system: sometime early in his reign, a royal office was established in the city of Chengdu to print these receipts in set amounts, thus creating uniform paper currency.

Section III: Critical Thinking

The student may not use her text to answer this question.

Over the course of our history of the medieval world we have seen rulers make great changes in their respective kingdoms. Rarely, though, have we seen a ruler create an entirely new class of people. During the rule of Song Taizong a new class emerged in China: the class of professional bureaucrats. Write a paragraph explaining why this class came to exist and how it grew under Song Taizong.

A detailed explanation of how the class of Chinese bureaucrats developed can be found on page 570.

Song Taizong did not trust anyone of royal blood or great military power for, without the full backing of the Mandate of Heaven, they could kick him off his throne and replace him with someone else. Song Taizong instead took counsel from men who had no other kind of power but were able to pass the civil service exams. The result was a shift from the government being run by royals to the government being run by bureaucrats. The great families of China had fractured during the wars of the previous century and Song Taizong's reliance on the examination system to fill his administration further diminished the importance of noble ancestry.

The new bureaucrats were well-educated within the parameters of the civil service tests. They learned what they needed to know to pass the tests with flying colors. The goal was to master a certain amount of knowledge and parrot it back on the test to the emperor's satisfaction. The reward for passing the test was not only a position in the emperor's government, but also a personal meeting with the emperor. Song Taizong hoped to dazzle his new employees with imperial favor to foster loyalty. The process worked. In 977, five thousand men sat for the civil service exam. Over the course of fifteen years, as the bureaucracy grew, so did the people who were interested in serving their emperor. In 992, over seventeen thousand men sat for the exam. Becoming a civil servant afforded the everyman a chance to be part of a government that was once run only by those with noble blood.

EXAMPLE ANSWER:

Song Taizong did not trust anyone of royal blood or great military power for, without the full backing of the Mandate of Heaven, they could kick him off his throne and replace him with someone else. Song Taizong instead took advice from men who had no other kind of power but were able to pass the civil service exams. The result was a shift from the government being run by royals to the government being run by bureaucrats. The new

bureaucrats were well-educated within the parameters of the civil service tests. They learned what they needed to know to pass the tests with flying colors. The goal was to master a certain amount of knowledge and parrot it back on the test to the emperor's satisfaction. The reward for passing the test was not only a position in the emperor's government, but also a personal meeting with the emperor. Song Taizong hoped to dazzle his new employees with imperial favor to foster loyalty. The process worked. In 977, five thousand men sat for the civil service exam. Over the course of fifteen years, as the bureaucracy grew, so did the people who were interested in serving their emperor. In 992, over seventeen thousand men sat for the exam. Becoming a civil servant afforded the everyman a chance to be part of a government that was once run only by those with noble blood.

Chapter Seventy-Five

The New Found Land

The student may use his text when answering the questions in sections I and II.

Section I: Who, What, Where

Write a one or two-sentence answer explaining the significance of each item listed below.

Anasazi—**Pg. 577, ¶ 6—Anasazi people, who lived farther west than the Mississippian people and the Hopewell culture on the North American continent, were hunters, farmers, and turquoise-miners and their civilization reached its height just before AD 1100. They built complexes from adobe bricks of baked clay and sand: rows of linked dwellings, some with as many as seven hundred rooms, housing thousands.**

Bjarni Herjolfsson—**Pg. 574, ¶ 2—Bjarni Herjolfsson was a Norse merchant that set sail for Greenland in 985, but instead of arriving in Greenland found himself looking at an unfamiliar forested coast. Bjarni Herjolfsson did not let his crew explore the new land and instead turned around to sail back east to Greenland.**

Cahokia—**Pg. 577, ¶ 5—Cahokia was the name of a city—five square miles with perhaps thirty thousand residents—built by the Mississippian peoples around the time of Leif Ericsson's existence. The Mississippian people left behind tremendous earthen mounds, the remains of foundations and well-planned streets, tools and figurines, burial grounds and sacrificial pits.**

Dorset—**Pg. 577, ¶ 3—Dorset was the name of the seal-hunting people that lived on the northeastern American coast at the time of Thorfinn Karlsefni's settlement. The Dorset scattered into oblivion when their lands were invaded by the Thule.**

Gudrid—**Pg. 575, ¶ 6 and Pg. 576, ¶ 2—Gudrid, Leif Ericsson's sister, was married to Thorfinn Karlsefni three years after her brother Thorvald died. Gudrid went to Vinland with her husband and gave birth to her son Snorri in the new found land.**

Hopewell—**Pg. 577, ¶ 4—Hopewell is the name of a group of people that lived in what is now Ohio and Illinois, and reached their height during Leif Ericsson's day. The Hopewell builders left behind enormous tomb mounds, each a geometric set of circles and squares, and a winding mysterious earthwork, five feet tall and over a thousand feet long, in the shape of a serpent devouring an egg.**

Ipiutak—**Pg. 577, ¶ 2—Ipiutak is the name archaeologists gave to the people who settled just east of the Bering Strait five hundred years before the Greenlander settlement in North America. The Ipiutak settlement boasted more than six hundred houses and a huge cemetery, and the remains of the town are scattered with elaborate ivory carvings, knife handles, and harpoons.**

Leif Ericsson—**Pg. 574, ¶ 5 and Pg. 575, ¶ 2—Leif Ericsson, the Viking Eric the Red's son, was the first Greenlander to travel to unexplored North America in 1003 and set up camp. He returned home just before his father died in 1004 with a ship filled with virgin timber, grapes, and wine.**

Skraelings—**Pg. 577, ¶ 1 & 3—*Skraelings*, meaning the "Shriekers," was the name the Norsemen gave to the inhabitants of the new found land because they attacked the colonists while shrieking loudly. The *Skraelings* were either from the Dorset or Thule people, or possibly bands of both.**

Snorri—**Pg. 576, ¶ 2—Snorri, the son of Gudrid and Thorfinn Karlsefni, was the first European baby born in North America. He was born in Vinland during his parents' attempt at settling in the new found land.**

Tezcatlipoca—**Pg. 581, ¶ 4 & 6—Tezcatlipoca was the name of a demon in human form that refused to allow the practice of human sacrifice to stop in the city of Tula. Tezcatlipoca is the symbol of resistance from the noblemen who had been living in Tula and did not want their ways supplanted by the customs of outsiders, like the newcomer Topiltzin.**

Thorfinn Karlsefni—**Pg. 575, ¶ 6 to Pg. 577, ¶ 1—Thorfinn Karlsefni, a wealthy and experienced Norse explorer, arrived in Greenland three years after Thorvald's death and within weeks professed his love for Leif Ericsson's sister, Gudrid. Thorfinn Karlsefni took his bride to Vinland and prepared to settle for good, but was forced to return home with his family after being attacked by the *Skraelings*.**

Thorvald Ericsson—**Pg. 575, ¶ 3–5—Thorvald Ericsson traveled to Leif Ericsson's camp in North America the year after his brother's return in order to settle a permanent colony on the land that seemed uninhabited. After a year of living undisturbed, Thorvald and his men encountered inhabitants of the new found land, which they promptly attacked, causing an immediate counterattack which cost Thorvald Ericsson his life.**

Thule—**Pg. 577, ¶ 3—Thule was the name of the people that grew from the Ipiutak ruins and spread east to the coast, displacing the Dorset. Archaeologists call the people "Thule" because unlike the Ipiutak they used iron tools instead of stone.**

Topiltzin—**Pg. 581, ¶ 1, 2, 4 & 5—Topiltzin, a prince that led newcomers into the city of Tula, became king of Tula and was worshipped as the son of a god during his lifetime: his father was said to be a divine conqueror, his mother a goddess, and Topiltzin himself was given the title "Topiltzin Quetzalcoatl," high priest and earthly incarnation of the great god of wind and sky. Topiltzin left Tula voluntarily when the struggles over whether or not to sacrifice humans became too heated; some say he died when he reached the Gulf of Mexico while others say he built a raft and sailed into the light, waiting to return one day and deliver Tula from its enemies.**

Section II: Comprehension

Write a two or three-sentence answer to each of the following questions.

1. Why didn't Eric the Red accompany his son Leif Ericsson on his exploratory journey to the unknown land discovered by Bjarni Herjolfsson?

A1.—Pg. 574, ¶ 3 & 4—Eric the Red agreed, at first, to accompany his son on an expedition to the west after Bjarni Herjolfsson's discovery of an unknown land. However, on the way to the harbor where their ship lay anchored, Eric's horse stumbled and threw him, injuring his foot. Eric took this as a bad omen and went back home.

2. List Leif Ericsson's 1003 exploratory route and the names he gave to the lands he encountered.

A2.—Pg. 574, ¶ 5 to Pg. 575, ¶ 1—Leif Ericsson and his men sailed northwest until they reached the southern end of Baffin Island, and then down along the coasts of the North American islands and peninsulas. He named the lands as he passed them: inhospitable Baffin Island earned the name "Helluland," or "Stone-slab land"; forest-covered Labrador became "Markland," or "Forest land"; and Nova Scotia was named "Vinland," or "Wineland," since the explorers found grapes there and immediately put them to use.

3. Describe the weather and living conditions Leif Ericsson and his men experienced during the winter months of their first expedition to the new found land in North America.

A3.—Pg. 575, ¶ 2—Leif Ericsson and his men were expecting a cold winter, but instead they found the cold months to be not very cold at all. The men were well fed because of the abundant and large salmon found in the lake and river. The temperature never dropped below freezing, the livestock didn't need fodder during the winter, and the grass withered only slightly.

4. Why did Thorvald Ericsson and his fellow explorers think the lands near his brother's camp in North America were unclaimed? What happened that drove the men back to Greenland?

A4.—Pg. 575, ¶ 3–5—Thorvald Ericsson believed the new found land was unclaimed because for over a year he saw no signs of men or animals except for a single wood grain cover. However, during the second summer, nine men and three hide-covered boats came up to the camp and the Norsemen attacked, killing all but one of them. A counterattack followed immediately—a vast number of hide-covered boats swept down the nearest inlet, with the inhabitants raining arrows upon the Norsemen—Thorvald was struck in the armpit and died, and the Norsemen returned home after burying their leader.

5. Describe the city of Cahokia. Why do we know so little about the people who lived in Cahokia, and more generally, the people that lived in North America during the days of Leif Ericsson?

A5.—Pg. 577, ¶ 5 and Pg. 579, ¶ 1—Cahokia was a city that was about five square miles with perhaps thirty thousand residents, built by the Mississippian peoples. Cahokia was as large as the Mesoamerican city of Teotihuacan, as populous as the Zapotec city of Monte Alban and its rulers were as powerful as the Mayan sovereigns. However, without written history we know nothing of the names of their kings and queens, the nature of their gods and goddesses, the struggles of their noblemen and peasants, and the same goes for the rest of the peoples that lived in North America before and during the days of Leif Ericsson.

6. Who were the Mixtec, and what did they do with old Mayan and Zapotec land?

A6.—Pg. 580, ¶ 2—The Mixtec were hill-dwellers who had lived in scattered villages in the Oaxaca Valley and then pressed in on the land vacated by the Mayans. Unlike the Mayans, the Zapotecs had not disappeared—they no longer lived in the great city of Monte Alban but in small, prosperous, and stable settlements centered around the estates of aristocrats or wealthy farmers. The settlements were vulnerable, and the Mixtec took advantage of them, taking them over and occupying them when they could in addition to seizing fields and valleys that had once been Zapotec.

7. Describe the city of Tula. Why did the people of central Mesoamerica call the city "Tollan"?

A7.—Pg. 580, ¶ 4 and Pg. 581, ¶ 3—Tula, which sat on high ground about 150 miles from the Gulf coast, was filled with craftsmen and merchants who specialized in the trade of obsidian. Its buildings lay over five square miles, the walls of its temples were carved with jaguars and eagles, clasping human hearts in their claws and talons, and thirty-five thousand people lived within the city's walls. The people of central Mesoamerica called the city "Tollan" because it was beautiful, prosperous and secure; "Tollan" was a mythical name suggesting paradise, a place where every material need was met, where the gods had come down to teach the citizens craft and skill.

8. Why did Topiltzin have enemies in Tula? Why did he leave the city?

A8.—Pg. 581, ¶ 3 & 4—The people who lived in the city of Tula believed that human blood was a holy liquid that glued the seams of the cosmos together, and they practiced human

sacrifice in celebration. One early story tells us that Topiltzin wanted to bring peace to Tula, and so he insisted that winged creatures and reptiles—quail and butterflies, large grasshoppers and snakes—be sacrificed in the place of human captives. The story tells us that Topiltzin was opposed by Tezcatlipoca and when the struggle over whether or not to shed human blood grew more savage Topiltzin decided to leave the city for good, going into voluntary exile.

9. Why did citizens of Tula call themselves "Toltecs"?

A9.—Pg. 581, ¶ 6 to Pg. 582, ¶ 1—Citizens of Tula called themselves "Toltecs" because they believed themselves to be inhabitants of a mythical paradise where the gods came to earth: Tollan. They were inhabitants of blessed Tollan, beneficiaries of the gods. They were fortunate enough, they told themselves, to live in an earthly paradise, a physical city whose stones and walls somehow incorporated the beauty of the divine.

10. Where did the Toltecs go after the city of Tula was ruined?

A10.—Pg. 582, ¶ 2 & 3—After the city of Tula fell into ruins, the Toltecs settled in various places, some joining the populations of nearby cities, and others travelling farther south, where they mingled with the Mixtec. At least one band of Toltecs went north, broke into the largest Yucatán city of Chichen Itza, and then seized control of its throne. The conquest is depicted on reliefs and paintings throughout the city's ruins, showing houses on fire, Toltec siege towers assaulting the walls, Toltec warriors rampaging through the streets, and captives from the defeated population sacrificed to the gods.

11. Why was Chichen Itza considered a sacred city? How did the Toltecs make Chichen Itza their own?

A11.—Pg. 582, ¶ 4—Chichen Itza was home to a sacred well, an enormous sinkhole nearly two hundred feet across and over a hundred feet deep where visitors threw offerings like carvings, jewels, and keepsakes and hoped for divine guidance from the gods. Once the city was under Toltec control, human sacrifices were also thrown into the sacred well. A new temple to the god Quetzalcoatl was built near the sinkhole, and its walls were adorned with the same images of heart-devouring eagles and jaguars that had decorated the sacred surfaces of Tula, and the Toltecs built a *tzompantli*, a platform adorned with carved skulls, which held a display rack for the real skulls of sacrificial victims.

Section III: Critical Thinking

The student may not use his text to answer this question.

In general, we think abundance is a good thing. When cities are successful and they grow, we see the expansion of a culture, and even of civilization. But this was not the case for the Maya. Write a paragraph explaining how prosperity ruined the Maya.

The southern cities of the Maya collapsed because they were prosperous. The population boomed and the result was too many people to feed. Every bit of fertile land was used to grow food for the expanding population: swamps were converted to gardens, flood plains were cultivated, and forested areas were slashed and burned to create new fields. At first food production kept up with demand, but there was no extra grain left at the end of the growing season. If the weather was good, a surplus wasn't necessary. However, a drought hit in the middle of the ninth century and the Maya began to starve. We learn in the chapter that excavations in Mayan cemeteries revealed bodies suffering from malnutrition: "Adult skeletons grow shorter and shorter, signs of scurvy and anemia abound, striations in the teeth of young children testify to long periods of fasting." Mayan nobles thought they could keep their civilization strong if the aristocracy survived, so they seized rations for themselves. But there was still not enough food. All Mayans—aristocrats and commoners—were forced to leave the overcrowded cities in the hopes of finding fertile land elsewhere. One last monument was built in January of 909 in the city of Tonina, followed by silence. Any Mayan survivors moved elsewhere. Some went to the southeast and settled south of the Gulf of Honduras and others went north. Wherever they went, the great Mayan civilization was disappeared by the end of the tenth century.

EXAMPLE ANSWER:

The southern cities of the Maya collapsed because they were prosperous. The population boomed and the result was too many people to feed. Every bit of fertile land was used to grow food for the expanding population: swamps were converted to gardens, flood plains were cultivated, and forested areas were slashed and burned to create new fields. At first food production kept up with demand, but there was no extra grain left at the end of the growing season. If the weather was good, a surplus wasn't necessary. However, a drought hit in the middle of the ninth century and the Maya began to starve. Mayan nobles thought they could keep their civilization strong if the aristocracy survived, so they seized rations for themselves. But there was still not enough food. All Mayans—aristocrats and commoners—were forced to leave the overcrowded cities in the hopes of finding fertile land elsewhere. Some went to the southeast and settled south of the Gulf of Honduras and others went north. Wherever they went, the great Mayan civilization had disappeared by the end of the tenth century.

Section IV: Map Exercise

1. Using a black pencil, trace the rectangular outline of the frame for map 75.1: Settlements of the Americas.

2. Using a blue pencil, trace the coastline around the American continent. Include the large island opposite the Yucatan Peninsula and the island containing Leif's winter camp. You do not need to include all the many small islands between the main continent and Greenland, but draw the perimeter of the area, and use small circles to denote the presence of multiple smaller islands inside the area. Include the small coastline opposite the Bering Strait by the Ipiutak settlement. You do not need to trace any other islands at this time. Repeat until the contours are familiar.

3. Using a new sheet of paper, trace the rectangular outline of the frame in black. Remove your tracing paper from the original. Using a regular pencil with an eraser as you look at Map 75.1, draw the coastline around the continent, including the islands you traced, but no others. As you did when tracing, draw the perimeter of the area heavily covered in islands, and draw circles inside to denote the presence of multiple islands. Erase and redraw as necessary.

4. When you are pleased with your map, lay it over the original. Erase and redraw any lines which are more than ¼ inch off of the original.

5. Remove your map. Study carefully the locations of Greenland, Helluland, Anasazi, Markland, Dorset, Vinland, the Gulf of Mexio, the Yucatan Peninsula, and the Gulf of Honduras. Label all these locations on the map. Then study carefully the locations of Tula, Tonina, Chichen Itza, Cahokia, Leif's Winter Camp, and the Ipiutak settlement. Label them on the map. When you are done, label the movements of the Thule. Check your map against the original. Correct any misplaced labels.

6. Mark and label the Bering Straight, as well as the Valley of Mexico and the Valley of Oaxaca.

Chapter Seventy-Six

Schism

The student may use her text when answering the questions in sections I and II.

Section I: Who, What, Where

Write a one or two-sentence answer explaining the significance of each item listed below.

Benedict IX—**Pg. 590, ¶ 3–6—Benedict IX, the teenaged nephew of John XIX and his uncle's successor to the papacy, ruled in Rome as pope for a decade and a half while indulging himself in alcohol and fornication, actions that caused the people of Rome to revolt in 1045 and elect a pope of their own. Benedict IX used the power of his family to raise an army and reclaim Rome but then he sold his papacy to his godfather for a thousand pounds of silver only to try and take it back again in 1046.**

Burchard—**Pg. 588, ¶ 3—Burchard, a German priest known as the bishop of Worms, put together a twenty-volume collection of canon law asserting that anyone who resisted the power of the emperor could be excommunicated since the emperor's power came from God himself.**

Cardinal Humbert—**Pg. 593, ¶ 4—Cardinal Humbert, the senior priest of the delegation sent from Rome by Leo IX to participate in the theological arguments initiated by Michael Cerularius, was suspicious of all things eastern and anxious to take offense. After weeks of fruitless argument and growing indignation on both sides, Cardinal Humbert wrote an official excommunication of Michael Cerularius and his supporters and threw it onto the altar at the Hagia Sophia only to have Michael Cerularius burn the excommunication and, in turn, excommunicate the entire papal delegation.**

Clement II—**Pg. 591, 2—Clement II was made pope by Henry III after the German and Italian king denounced the papacies of Benedict IX, Sylvester II and John Gratian (Gregory VI). Clement II's first act as pope was to crown Henry III as Holy Roman Emperor.**

College of Cardinals—**Pg. 594, ¶ 6—The College of Cardinals, formed in 1059, was a gathering of high-ranking bishops that would come together to elect the next pope. The College of Cardinals was formed to separate the papacy from its dependency on the Holy Roman Emperor.**

Conrad II—**Pg. 589, ¶ 3 & 5—Conrad II, elected leader by his German noblemen after the death of Henry II, was the first emperor of a new dynasty called the Salians. By 1027 he was king of Germany, Italy, crowned Holy Roman Emperor and not long after he brought Burgundy and Provence into the fold. Conrad believed the church was there to do his bidding, demanding that bishops and archbishops obey without question, and if they resisted he imprisoned them or put them in exile.**

Crescentius—**Pg. 584, ¶ 4 and Pg. 585 ¶ 3 & 4—Crescentius, a Roman senator, rounded up a mob and chased Gregory V out of Rome after Otto III returned to Germany and chose a new pope with his Roman churchmen. When Otto III arrived in Rome to defend Gregory V he captured Crescentius and his allies, beheaded them, and hung them all upside down on the highest hill in Rome.**

Drogo of Hauteville—**Pg. 591, ¶ 6 and Pg. 592, ¶ 1, 4 & 5—Drogo of Hauteville, the most powerful of the Norman warriors settled in southern Italy, agreed to become Henry III's ally in return for an official title—Duke and Master of Italy, Count of the Normans of all Apulia and Calabria—making Drogo the head of an actual Norman state in the south of Italy. Drogo of Hauteville had agreed to Leo IX's oath of peace but was assassinated on his way to the church in 1051.**

Geza—**Pg. 586, ¶ 4—Geza, a Magyar prince, helped his people towards becoming the nation of Hungary by agreeing to be baptized. He may or may not have believed the creed he swore allegiance to, but his lip service to Christianity allowed Hungary to stake out its place as a Western nation, complete with a parish system and an archbishop.**

Great Schism—**Pg. 594, ¶ 2—The Great Schism was the division of the once-unified Christian church into two separate bodies, one centered in Rome and one centered in Constantinople, that would never be reunited. The year 1054 became known as the date of the Great Schism, and the two churches—already separated by theology, language, and politics—remained separated by official decree.**

Gregory V—**Pg. 584, ¶ 3 and Pg. 585, ¶ 2, 4 & 6—Gregory V was the papal name for Otto III's cousin Bruno, Otto III's hand-picked pope that was chased out of the city by Crescentius as soon as Otto III left Rome. Gregory V was able to return to Rome once Otto III killed Crescentius and mutilated Johannes Philagathos, but his time as pope was short lived because he died suddenly soon after returning to the city.**

Henry of Bavaria/Henry II—**Pg. 587, ¶ 3, Pg. 588, ¶ 2 and Pg. 589, ¶ 2—Henry of Bavaria won Otto III's empire, was elected by German nobles as King Henry II, fought for two years to be made King of Italy, and after ten years of competent rule over the two realms, was**

crowned Holy Roman Emperor by Pope Benedict VIII. In his ten years as Holy Roman Emperor, Henry II settled quarrels between monasteries, insisted that his own candidates benefit from the "free elections" of German bishops, and even tinkered with the liturgy but his reign was cut short when he died unexpectedly in 1024, ending the Saxon dynasty of emperors.

Henry the Black/Henry III—**Pg. 589, ¶ 6, Pg. 590, ¶ 2 and Pg. 591, ¶ 1—Henry the Black, son of Conrad II, crowned as co-ruler of Germany and Italy, became king Henry III of both countries at twenty-one after his father's death. Henry III expanded the Peace and Truce of God and became Holy Roman Emperor after he installed Clement II as pope in the stead of Benedict IX, Sylvester II and John Gratian (Gregory VI).**

Henry IV—**Pg. 594, ¶ 3—Henry IV, the six-year-old son of Henry III, was made king of Germany when his father died.**

Johannes Philagathos—**Pg. 585, ¶ 3 & 4—Johannes Philagathos was the pope elected by Crescentius and the Roman churchmen after they ran Gregory V out of Rome. When Otto III arrived in Rome to defend Gregory V, he spared Johannes Philagathos's life only to gouge his eyes out, cut his nose and ears off and parade him through the streets of Rome riding backwards on a donkey.**

John XIX—**Pg. 589, ¶ 4—John XIX, brother of Benedict VIII, the pope who had crowned Henry II, used his considerable personal wealth to convince the Romans that he should ascend the papal throne even though he was a layman. With Henry II's blessing, he had been run up through the ranks of the church and made pope in a single day.**

John Gratian—**Pg. 590, ¶ 5 and Pg. 591, ¶ 1—John Gratian, Benedict IX's godfather, bought the papacy from his godson for a thousand pounds of silver and was acclaimed as Pope Gregory VI. Henry III put an end John Gratian's papacy in 1046 when he marched into Rome and declared Johan Gratian and the two other claimants to the papacy, Benedict IX and Sylvester III, unfit to rule.**

Leo IX—**Pg. 592, ¶ 4, 5 and Pg. 593 ¶ 2—Leo IX, cousin of Henry III, who only took the papacy after the people of Rome gave their approval, managed to coax Drogo of Hauteville into taking an oath to halt the pillage and conquest in the south of Italy. After Drogo's assassination, Leo IX led a German army to Apulia but he was forced to surrender and give the Norman rebels led by Robert Guiscard official papal recognition of their rule over the south of Italy.**

Michael Cerularius—**Pg. 593, ¶ 4 *—Michael Cerularius, the patriarch of Constantinople, called for a series of ongoing theological arguments between the eastern and western Christian churches largely based on the question of authority—whether the pope or the patriarch ultimately had the last word on which Christian beliefs were and were not orthodox—all the while announcing that the western faith had become so corrupt that it was now heretical. After he was excommunicated by Cardinal Humbert, Michael Cerularius**

burned the paper that proclaimed the excommunication and, in turn, excommunicated the entire papal delegation.

Nicholas II—**Pg. 594, ¶ 3 & 4—Nicholas II, the bishop of Florence, was elected pope in 1059. Because there was no emperor to protect Rome and the king of Germany was a child, Nicholas II decided to make an alliance with the Normans and in 1059 negotiated the Treaty of Melfi with Robert the Fox.**

Robert Guiscard—**Pg. 592, ¶ 1 & 2 and Pg. 593, ¶ 1–3—Robert Guiscard, half-brother of Drogo of Hauteville, known as "Robert the Fox," was given a castle on the western edge of Drogo's kingdom, and Robert began to use this as a base to fight his way into the toe of the Italian boot in a vicious series of campaigns. When Leo IX led the German army into Norman land in southern Italy, Robert Guiscard fought with particular savagery, forced the pope to surrender and made Leo IX give them official papal recognition as rulers of the south; he continued his conquest in 1057, seizing the land of Humphrey, the Norman count of Apulia, after his death.**

Stephen—**Pg. 586, ¶ 5 & 7—Stephen, Geza's son, became king of Hungary after Pope Sylvester II wrote him a letter granting him the royal crown and the protection of the church. Stephen understood that the pope was recognizing him as a sovereign Christian king, and he proceeded to ignore the implication that he was subject to the emperor and the pope.**

Sylvester II—**Pg. 585, ¶ 6 & 7 and Pg. 586, ¶ 5—Sylvester II was the papal name of Otto III's old tutor Gerbert who was serving as the archbishop of Ravenna before he followed Gregory V as pope. In an effort to expand Otto III's Holy Roman Empire, Sylvester granted Stephen of Hungary his royal crown, but Stephen saw this as a recognition of his independence and legitimacy as a sovereign.**

Sylvester III—**Pg. 590, ¶ 3 & 4 and Pg. 591, ¶ 1—Sylvester III, a bishop, was elected pope in 1045 after the Romans grew fed up with Benedict IX, but he was forced to flee to a village on the edge of the Papal States—while still claiming to be pope—when Benedict IX stormed Rome with an army to reclaim the papacy. Henry III divested Sylvester III of his title, as well as Benedict IX and John Gratian, in 1046, declaring all three men unfit to rule.**

Section II: **Comprehension**

Write a two or three-sentence answer to each of the following questions.

1. How was Otto III's Rome different from Charlemagne's Rome?

A1.—Pg. 584, ¶ 2—Unlike Charlemagne's Rome, Otto III's Rome drew its identity from Christianity, not in its relation to the empire of the Caesars. Otto III's Rome was centered in Germany, not in Italy and as far as he was concerned the pope was not a religious leader but his chaplain, meekly carrying out his orders.

2. Why did Otto III think the punishments given to Crescentius and Johannes Philagathos were fair?

A2.—Pg. 585, ¶ 5—The penalties Otto III made Crescentius and Johannes Philagathos suffer seemed fair to the emperor because he was coming from the Germanic tradition. Crescentius was punished as a traitor, Philagathos was punished as a heretic. To defy the emperor's right to direct church matters was to rebel against the very essence of his rule as the Christian monarch of the west.

3. For what reasons did Gerbert take the papal name "Sylvester II"?

A3.—Pg. 585, ¶ 7 to Pg. 586, ¶ 2—The name Sylvester came from the first bishop of Rome in the days of Constantine the Great, and though he did nothing of importance during his bishopric, legends of great deeds had grown up around him. The *Acts of Saint Sylvester*, written well after his death, claimed that he had personally converted Constantine to Christianity, baptized him, and received the Donation of Constantine from the emperor's own hands. Sylvester I had shaped the emperor's faith, helped him to create the Papal States, and worked with him to make the Roman empire Christian; the implication was that Sylvester II intended to cooperate just as closely with the emperor in building a holy kingdom of their own.

4. Why was Sylvester II the one to make Stephen of Hungary king? How did Stephen of Hungary understand Sylvester II's gesture?

A4.—Pg. 586, ¶ 6 & 7—Sylvester II granted Stephen of Hungary the royal crown because it allowed the Holy Roman Empire to assert authority over the Hungarians without bloodshed. Stephen understood the gesture as an acknowledgment of his independence as a sovereign Christian king. He accepted the letter and the jeweled cross that came with it, and ignored the implication that he would be subject not just to the pope, but to the pope's patron, the emperor Otto III.

5. Why did Otto III and Sylvester II leave Rome in 1001? Why didn't Otto III return to Rome?

A5.—Pg. 586, ¶ 8 to Pg. 587, ¶ 2—The people of Rome rioted against the Frankish pope and German emperor in 1001. Otto III and Sylvester II left to go to Ravenna, where they planned to gather troops and then return to Rome to straighten out the riots. Unfortunately, while waiting for more soldiers to arrive from Germany, Otto III started to suffer from attacks of fever, "the Italian death," and he was dead by January of 1002.

6. What was on Henry II's seal when he became Holy Roman Emperor, and what did it mean? How did Henry II keep the power of his empire centered on Germany?

A6.—Pg. 587, ¶ 4 & 5—Henry II's seal proclaimed *Renovatio regni Francorum*, meaning his empire focused not on Rome but on his own German lands. Henry II used lay investiture to keep the power of his empire centered on his own German circle and he gave offices and control over churches and monasteries to men who would be loyal to him. He treated the church as a servant of the emperor and he kept churchmen in line by taking a severe stand

on clerical celibacy; priests with no children would pass their land and power not to their sons but back to the church.

7. How did Henry II make the parishes in his empire feel as if they had sovereignty?

A7.—Pg. 588, ¶ 1—Henry II was willing to give away posts, as long as the positions were going to return to his control in the future, and as long as the parishes in his domain accepted the priests he appointed without argument or question. Some churches were able to brandish charters at him that promised free elections, the right for the churches to choose their *own* bishop; Henry simply insisted that the phrase *salvo tamen regis sive imperatoris consensu* be added. While the parishes felt they had free elections, the installment of those elected always relied on imperial consent.

8. Explain how the Peace and Truce of God grew under Henry III's rule.

A8.—Pg. 590, ¶ 2—When Henry III came to rule, merchants and their goods had joined peasants, clergymen, and farmers as official noncombatants, immune from attack under the rules of the Peace and Truce of God, and certain days were now completely off limits for fighting: under threat of excommunication, no one could wage war on Fridays, Sundays, church holidays, or any of the forty days of Lent. In 1041, Henry III decreed that the Peace would be observed in Germany from Wednesday evening through Monday morning of every week of the year. In 1043, he attended a synod held in the German city of Constance and himself preached from the pulpit, imploring his people to keep a peace "unknown in previous centuries," forgiving—on the spot—all of his own enemies, including several noblemen in Swabia who had been attempting rebellion.

9. How did the Normans come to reside in Italy? How did Henry III first deal with the Normans in Italy?

A9.—Pg. 591, ¶ 5 & 6—Normans moved east to the south of Italy over the course of twenty years in an effort to avoid the chaos caused by the struggle over the title "Duke of Normandy." Norman mercenaries had settled in the south of Italy, hiring themselves out to Italian noblemen as useful private swords—while carving out little independent domains of their own. Henry III could see a welter of competing powers, ready to erupt into full-scale war, but rather than going down and attempting to conquer them all, one at a time, he made a peaceful imperial trip south, circled through the battling states, and summoned the jostling dukes, counts, and mercenaries to reaffirm their pledges to the imperial crown.

10. What were the two main issues that caused the patriarch of Constantinople to resurrect a series of ongoing theological arguments between the eastern and western Christian churches?

A10.—Pg. 593, *—The two main issues were that the western church used unleavened bread for the celebration of communion, while the east did not and that the western church spoke of the Holy Spirit as proceeding from both the Father and the Son, while the east refused to use this formulation. The eastern patriarch believed that the use of unleavened bread was too close to Jewish practice, meaning that the western church had not fully accepted the

transition from Old Testament law to New Testament grace; the eastern priests were also widely convinced that to speak of the procession of the Holy Spirit "from the Father and the Son" suggested that God the Father and Jesus Christ were separate beings in a way that violated the unity of the Trinity. However, the real quarrel between east and west was one of authority: whether pope or patriarch ultimately had the last word on which Christian beliefs were and were not orthodox.

Section III: Critical Thinking

The student may not use her text to answer this question.

In this section of *The History of the Medieval World* we are reading about crusades, or, religious wars. In this chapter, we learned about the Treaty of Melfi, which was made to separate church and state. Write a paragraph that outlines the Treaty of Melfi. Then, explain how, despite its insistence on dividing the power of religion and government, the treaty needed the two to be entwined in order for it to be successful.

The student learns about the Treaty of Melfi on page 594 of the chapter. The Treaty of Melfi was made between Pope Nicholas II and Robert the Fox in 1059. The treaty said that Nicholas II would acknowledge the Norman count as ruler of the southern Italian territories of Apulia, Calabria and Sicily, in return for Robert's willingness to accept the pope's spiritual authority. The treaty also renounced the special right of the "Roman Emperor" to protect the heirs of St. Peter. As written in paragraph 5, "In signing it, Nicholas II took away the central duty that made the office of the emperor holy. That duty had now been handed over to the Normans, who—as part of the treaty—even promised that they would fight for *the pope, and* against *any future Holy Roman Emperor, if necessary."*

The Treaty of Melfi was written so that the Holy Roman Emperor could no longer start wars in the name of the church, but the only way the treaty could be made was if Robert the Fox agreed to abide by the spiritual authority of the pope. Robert the Fox also agreed to fight in religious wars if a future Holy Roman Emperor tried to attack the pope or the Papal States. Wrapped up in the treaty is the promise of future holy war since the Normans would now act as protectors of the papacy. The condition that Robert acknowledge the spiritual authority of the Christian pope also tied church and state together, rather than tearing them apart.

EXAMPLE ANSWER:

Pope Nicholas II and Robert the Fox agreed to The Treaty of Melfi in 1059. The treaty said that Nicholas II would acknowledge Robert Guiscard as ruler of the southern Italian territories of Apulia, Calabria and Sicily, in return for Robert's willingness to accept the pope's spiritual authority. The treaty also renounced the special right of the "Roman Emperor" to protect the heirs of St. Peter. The Normans were now responsible for protecting the pope. Part of the treaty was that the Normans promised that they would fight for the pope, and against any future Holy Roman Emperor, if necessary.

The Treaty of Melfi was written so that the Holy Roman Emperor could no longer start wars in the name of the church, but the only way the treaty could be made was if Robert the Fox agreed to abide by the spiritual authority of the pope. Robert the Fox also agreed to fight in religious wars if a future Holy Roman Emperor tried to attack the pope or the Papal States. Wrapped up in the treaty is the promise of future holy war since the Normans would now act as protectors of the papacy. The condition that Robert acknowledge the spiritual authority of the Christian pope also tied church and state together, rather than tearing them apart.

Section IV: Map Exercise

1. Using a black pencil, trace the rectangular outline of the frame for Map 76.1: The Holy Roman Empire.

2. Using a blue pencil, trace the coastline of the Atlantic around Britain and down the entirety of the mainland, starting up at the top of the map with Scandinavia and running down all the way through the Mediterranean. You do not need to include all the minor islands at this time; just Sardinia, Corsica, Sicily, Crete, and Cyprus. Trace the coastline of the Black Sea. Then with your black pencil trace the mountains, using simple peaks. Repeat until the contours are familiar.

3. Trace the rectangular outline of the frame in black. Leaving your map over the original, trace with your regular pencil the regions of the Caliphate of Cordoba, the Kingdom of Leon, Pamplona, Western Francia, Burgundy, Normandy, Germany, Bavaria, the Italian Kingdom, Corsica, Norman Italy, Calabria, Hungary, Rus, and Byzantium. Trace the mountains with simple peaks.

4. Remove your map from the original. Study carefully the regions of the Caliphate of Cordoba, the Kingdom of Leon, Pamplona, Western Francia, Burgundy, Normandy, Germany, Bavaria, the Italian Kingdom, Corsica, Norman Italy, Calabria, Hungary, Rus, and Byzantium. When you are familiar with them, close the book. Using your regular pencil, label each region. Check your map against the original, and correct any misplaced labels.

5. Lay your map back over the original and trace the outline of the Holy Roman Empire with your black pencil.

6. Now remove your map from the original. Study carefully the locations of the Abbey of Cluny, Paris, Cologne, Aachen, Constance, Worms, Pavia, Augsburg, Merseburg, Novgorod, Ravenna, Florence, Spoleto, Rome, Benevento, Constantinople, and Antioch. When you are familiar with them, close the book, and label each region with your regular pencil. If necessary, study the first nine locations first and label them before you go on to study and label the last seven. When you are done, check your map against the original, and correct any misplaced locations or labels.

Chapter Seventy-Seven

Danish Domination

The student may use his text when answering the questions in sections I and II.

Section I: Who, What, Where

Write a one or two-sentence answer explaining the significance of each item listed below.

Aelfgifu—**Pg. 598, ¶ 5—Aelfgifu was Canute the Great's long-term mistress, or common law wife. She gave Canute one son the year before he married Emma and another one in the same year of their marriage.**

Alfred Atheling—**Pg. 598, ¶ 5 and Pg. 600, ¶ 6 to Pg. 601, ¶ 1—Alfred Atheling, son of Emma and Ethelred, was sent to Normandy with his brother Edmund after his father's death. After Canute's death, Edmund and his brother tried to return to their homeland but were thwarted by Godwin; Alfred was taken prisoner and blinded so ineptly that his brain was pierced, causing his painful death at age twenty-four.**

Canute the Great—**Pg. 596, ¶ 2 & 4, Pg. 598, ¶ 3 and Pg. 500, ¶ 2 to Pg. 600, ¶ 1—Canute the Great, son of Sweyn Forkbeard, claimed the crowns of Denmark and England after his father's death; he took the crown of Norway in 1028; and in 1031 he invaded Scotland and fought against Malcolm II until the Scottish armies agreed to a truce. When Canute first became the English king he was called away to Denmark, but he returned and won back half his throne from Edmund, Ethelred's successor, and when Edmund died Canute claimed the crown all for himself.**

Duncan—**Pg. 601, ¶ 5 and Pg. 602, ¶ 2—Duncan, son of Malcolm II and his successor as high king of Scotland, lost control of his subject rulers when he took the throne. When the rebel Mac Bethad mac Findlaich declined to pay taxes, Duncan marched into Mac Bethad's home of Moray to collect money from the subject king, but was killed in battle.**

Edmund—**Pg. 596, ¶ 3, Pg. 597, ¶ 2 and Pg. 598, ¶ 2 & 3—Edmund, son of Ethelred from his first marriage, given the nickname Ironside because of his strength and determination in**

war, was elected king of England by the witan in April 1016 after his father's death. Edmund was forced to make a truce with Canute and just a month after their war ended, Edmund was dead.

Edward—**Pg. 598, ¶ 5 and Pg. 600, ¶ 6 to Pg. 601, ¶ 1—A son of Ethelred, Edward was sent to Normandy with his brother Alfred after his father's death in order to keep him safe from Canute. After Canute's death, Edward and his brother tried to return to their homeland but were thwarted by Godwin; Alfred died but Edward managed to escape.**

Emma—**Pg. 596, ¶ 5, Pg. 598, ¶ 5 & 6 and Pg. 601, ¶ 3—Emma, wife of Ethelred the Unready, was forced to marry Canute after her husband's death, and after two years of marriage Emma gave birth to a son with Canute named Harthacanute. Emma left England after Canute's death and found refuge in Western Francia.**

Godwin—**Pg. 599, ¶ 1—Godwin, a native of Sussex who had supported Canute in his battle for the English throne, was given rule over the earldom of Wessex by Canute. Godwin courted and married Canute's sister, himself by blood to the foreign king.**

Harold Harefoot—**Pg. 600, ¶ 5, Pg. 601, ¶ 4 and Pg. 602, ¶ 3—Harold Harefoot, Canute's oldest son, was made "regent" by the Danish army in England after Canute's death and when Godwin's schemes against him went awry, Harold Harefoot celebrated by having himself crowned as King of England. Harold Harefoot died on his way to Scotland during a mission to get the unruly Scots back under English control.**

Harthacanute—**Pg. 598, ¶ 6, Pg. 600, ¶ 4 and Pg. 602, ¶ 3—Harthacanute, son of Emma and Canute the Great and heir to the crown of England, was sent to Denmark, where he was supposed to be watching over the double realm of Norway and Denmark for his father. Harthacanute returned to England as soon as Harold Harefoot died, and was welcomed as the new king of England and Scotland but he was very unpopular because of the severe taxes he imposed on his subjects.**

Mac Bethad mac Findlaich (Macbeth)—**Pg. 601, ¶ 6 to Pg. 602, ¶ 2—Mac Bethad mac Findlaich, king of the northern Scottish kingdom called Moray, killed the high king of Scotland Duncan in a battle over taxes in Moray in 1040. Mac Bethad claimed the high kingship of Scotland and refused to yield to the Danish king in the south.**

Magnus the Good—**Pg. 600, ¶ 4 and Pg. 602, ¶ 4—Magnus the Good, the illegitimate son of Olaf the Saint, mounted an armed challenge for the English throne after Canute's death, and was supported by much of Norway. When Harthacanute died, Magnus the Good took the throne of Denmark, which united Norway and Denmark under his rule.**

Malcolm II—**Pg. 600, ¶ 1 & 2—Malcolm II, high king of the Scots, was forced to make a truce with Canute in 1031. In his submission to Canute, Malcolm II also made Maelbeth and Iehmarc, the other Scottish kings, recognize the English king's authority.**

Olaf the Saint—**Pg. 596, ¶ 2 and Pg. 599, ¶ 2—Olaf the Saint, a Norse nobleman, reclaimed Norway after the death of Sweyn Forkbeard. In 1028, Canute forced Olaf the Saint of Norway to abdicate.**

William the Bastard—**Pg. 601, ¶ 2—William the Bastard, son of Emma's younger nephew, was acclaimed as duke of Normandy in 1035 when he was only eight years old.**

Witan—**Pg. 597, ¶ 2—Witan was the gathering of English nobility who claimed the right to choose their king.**

Section II: Comprehension

Write a two or three-sentence answer to each of the following questions.

1. What did the people of London do after Sweyn Forkbeard died? What was the result of their attack against Canute?

A1.—Pg. 596, ¶ 3—After Sweyn Forkbeard died, the people of London took courage and sent a message to Ethelred asking him to return and fight against Canute. Ethelred agreed and returned with Norman troops, and pushed Canute to retreat to Denmark around Easter in the same year he was crowned.

2. For what reason did Canute most likely return to Denmark from London?

A2.—Pg. 596, ¶ 4—Though it would be nice to think that Ethelred drove Canute out of England, Canute most likely returned to Denmark from London because his brother, who had been serving as regent in Denmark while Canute was in London, was making a play for the Danish throne. England was a prize for the Danes, but it was newly conquered and insecure, and Canute first intended to secure his homeland. Canute showed that he wasn't afraid of Ethelred by cutting the ears and noses off his English prisoners of war and dumping them on the shores right before he sailed back to his homeland.

3. Why did the witan have to elect Edmund to the throne? What were their reasons for his election?

A3.—Pg. 597, ¶ 2—The witan had to elect Edmund to the throne because Ethelred's rule had not been such a shattering success that his son could automatically claim the succession. The witan felt comfortable electing Edmund because he had outfought his father in the war against the Danes, earning himself the nickname "Ironside" due to his strength and resoluteness in war. The witan crowned him king of England and then gave him the job of driving off Canute, a necessary action in order to save their kingdom.

4. What were the terms of the truce made between Edmund and Canute that ended the war between the two kings in November 1016?

A4.—Pg. 598, ¶ 2—The terms of the truce made in November 1016 between Edmund and Canute were that the kings would divide the country: Canute would rule from Mercia to the

north, and Edmund would keep London and remain king of the south. Edmund was also forced to disinherit his own two young sons and agree to make Canute his heir.

5. What happened to Edmund Ironside's two young sons immediately after his death?

A5.—Pg. 598, ¶ 4—After Edmund Ironside's death and Canute's taking of the totality of the English crown, the new king put the two boys on a ship to Scandinavia so that they could be killed in Sweden. The king of Sweden refused to comply when he found that he was expected to put two babies to death so he sent them as far away as he could arrange—to King Stephen of Hungary, with whom he had a passing acquaintance. The journey was too much for the younger baby, who died of illness and hunger; but the toddler survived and grew up under the care of a Hungarian foster-mother.

6. Why did Emma send her sons Alfred and Edward back to Normandy after her marriage to Canute?

A6.—Pg. 598, ¶ 5—Emma sent her sons Alfred and Edward back to Normandy after her marriage to Canute because she wanted to protect her sons from the English king. Alfred was a baby and Edward was ten years old; both were healthy. She feared that her boys would be killed like other kings' sons had been, so she sent them away.

7. How was England divided under the rule of Canute the Great, and who did he choose to rule over each section of his kingdom?

A7.—Pg. 599, ¶ 1—Canute divided England into four earldoms, known as Wessex, Mercia, East Anglia, and Northumbria. He appointed Danish earls to rule over three of the realms: Thorkell the Tall over East Anglia, Siward over Northumbria, and Leofric over Mercia, which left the Anglo-Saxon Godwin to rule over Wessex.

8. Describe why Edmund and Alfred thought they could return to England, and what happened when they got there.

A8.—Pg. 600, ¶ 6 to Pg. 601, ¶ 1—After Canute's death and Magnus the Good and Harold Harefoot's fight for the English throne, Edmund and Alfred Atheling saw an opportunity to return to their homeland with the backing of a small group of unhappy Anglo-Saxons and Norman soldiers. Godwin, who had become Harold Harefoot's close friend, sent word to Edward and Alfred that he was behind their return, all the time reporting to Harold the whereabouts of the regent's younger half-brothers. The result was that when Edward and Alfred landed, their party was ambushed; though Edward escaped, his supporters and brother were captured.

9. Mac Bethad mac Findlaich was the inspiration for Shakespeare's traitorous host who killed his king in his sleep. What were the circumstances of Macbeth's real rebellion against his high king Duncan?

A9.—Pg. 601, ¶ 6 to Pg. 602, ¶ 2—Macbeth's real revolt was a perfectly routine declaration of independence, the rejection of a high king whose clan had been willing to bow to a foreign invader. Macbeth was a powerful and generous king, where Duncan was known

as a weak and ineffective ruler with nothing but his bloodline to keep him on the throne. When Duncan invaded Moray in 1040 after Macbeth refused to pay taxes to the high king, Macbeth fought, killing the high king in battle, giving Macbeth the opportunity to claim the high kingship of Scotland.

10. How did Harthacanute become immediately unpopular after he took the English throne following Harold Harefoot's death?

A10.—Pg. 602, ¶ 3—Harthacanute immediately made himself unpopular in England by starting a very severe tax on his subjects. If someone argued with the king over the tax, Harthacanute said the subject was disloyal. He made himself even more unpopular by sending his soldiers to collect the severe tax by force when the people of western Mercia were unable to pay it, and by ordering Harold Harefoot's body dug up and flung into a swamp.

Section III: Critical Thinking

The student may not use his text to answer this question.

Macbeth is one of William Shakespeare's most famous plays. As we read about in this chapter, the real story of Mac Bethad mac Findlaich was nowhere near as scandalous as the version presented by the Bard of Avon. However, real life did inspire Shakespeare's great work. In this Critical Thinking question, do a little research and find another example of a famous work of literature inspired by a real life person or event. Write a paragraph that names the work and its author, what inspired the work, and a little bit about the work itself. Do the best you can to cite the source of your information in your paragraph.

The student has a lot of freedom in this Critical Thinking question. This is an opportunity for the student to do some research and think about how to cite his sources. The student can use the internet and try some general search terms such as "great works of literature inspired by true events" or "fiction based on real people." Let the student play around and find out what works for him. When it comes time to write the paragraph, the student should—as stated above—name the work and its author, what inspired the work, a little bit about the work itself and the student should cite his source in his writing. If you are working on citation practices with the student, feel free to use a method such as MLA or Chicago style, but mentioning the source in a sentence will also suffice.

EXAMPLE ANSWER:

Arthur Miller wrote the famous play *The Crucible* in 1953. According to "Education Portal" (http://education-portal.com/academy/lesson/arthur-millers-the-crucible-summary-and-quotes.html), the play is about the hysteria over witches that took place in Salem, Massachusetts in the 1690s. However, though the play was theoretically about the historical events that took place in 17th century Massachusetts, it is said that Miller was responding to the Red Scare that took place in the 1950s in America. The Red Scare was a time when anyone in America could be accused of being a communist and put on trial, just as the accused witches were in Salem. Miller used the Salem witch trials as an allegory for the persecution of communists in America during the Cold War.

Chapter Seventy-Eight

The Norman Conquest

The student may use her text when answering the questions in sections I and II.

Section I: Who, What, Where

Write a one or two-sentence answer explaining the significance of each item listed below.

Edgar—**Pg. 607, ¶ 8 and Pg. 611, ¶ 3—Edgar, grandson of Edmund Ironside, was raised as an adoptive son by Edward the Confessor and when Harold Godwinson was killed Edgar was made king by the witan. However, Edgar did not want to suffer at the hands of William the Conqueror, so he surrendered himself and was sent to Normandy by William, where he was treated well.**

Edith—**Pg. 604, ¶ 3, Pg. 605, ¶ 2 & 3 and Pg. 606, ¶ 2—Edith, daughter of Godwin, was married to Edward in 1045, but Edith's marriage to Edward was most likely never consummated because the king was celibate. When Godwin was exiled by Edward, Edith was sent to live in a nunnery but then was brought back after Edgar was forced to reinstall Godwin as Earl of Wessex.**

Harald Hardrada—**Pg. 607, ¶ 1, Pg. 609, ¶ 2 and Pg. 610, ¶ 3—Harald Hardrada, king of Norway and successor to Magnus the Good, gave refuge to Tostig after he was forced to leave England by his brother Harold. Harald Hardrada's army, with Tostig and troops from Scotland attacked Harold near York in 1066, but the band was unsuccessful and both Harald Hardrada and Tostig were killed in battle.**

Harold Godwinson—**Pg. 604, ¶ 3, Pg. 606, ¶ 3, Pg. 607, ¶ 5 & 7, Pg. 608, ¶ 1, and Pg. 611, ¶ 2—Harold Godwinson, son of Godwin, Earl of East Anglia and Earl of Wessex (after his father's death), was made king—Harold II of England—after the death of Edward the Confessor. Harold Godwinson was unsuccessful in his fight against William the Bastard, whom he had promised the kingship of England in exchange for help after a shipwreck in Normandy, and died fighting the duke at the Battle of Hastings.**

Leofric—**Pg. 605, ¶ 3 and Pg. 606, ¶ 2—Leofric, Earl of Mercia, gave Edward the Confessor enough support to exile Godwin and all of his family, in exchange for which Edward gave Leofric's son the earldom of East Anglia. Leofric's son lost his status as earl when Edward was forced to let Godwin and his family back into England.**

Siward—**Pg. 605, ¶ 3 and Pg. 606, ¶ 4—Siward, Earl of Northumbria, gave Edward the Confessor enough support to exile Godwin and all of his family, in exchange for which Edward gave Siward treasure and a bishopric. In 1054, Siward won particular renown by killing the Scottish high king Mac Bethad in battle and forcing the Scottish once again to swear loyalty to the king of England.**

Tostig—**Pg. 606, ¶ 5 to Pg. 607, ¶ 1, Pg. 609, ¶ 2 and Pg. 610, ¶ 3—Tostig, Harold's brother and earl of Northumbria, was forced by his brother to leave England and take refuge in Norway after he began to persecute the taxpayers of Northumbria by raising the rates and then sending soldiers to collect the money. Tostig convinced Harald Hardrada of Norway to join him in battle against Harold Godwinson, a battle that killed both Tostig and his coconspirator.**

Section II: Comprehension

Write a two or three-sentence answer to each of the following questions.

1. How did Edward earn the nickname "Edward the Confessor"? In contrast, what did Edward do with his mother's goods when he was named king?

A1.—Pg. 604, ¶ 1—Edward was a withdrawn and silent man, known for piety and devotion, thus earning him the nickname "Edward the Confessor." Despite his religiosity, he was hard and unforgiving. When the witan acclaimed him as king he ordered that all of his mother's worldly goods be confiscated, all her gold, silver, gems, and precious stones, because he could not let go of the hatred that was planted in him as a young boy.

2. What did Godwin do to regain the earldom of Wessex?

A2.—Pg. 606, ¶ 1 & 2—Godwin, exiled in Western Francia, collected his supporters, sailed up the Thames before Edward could assemble a fleet to keep him out, made his case directly to the people of London and succeeded in bringing almost everybody onto his side. Though Edward could have attacked, he did not want to go against public opinion, so he made peace with Godwin. Edward restored him to the position of Earl of Wessex, and brought Godwin's family out of exile.

3. How did Harold's treatment of his brother Tostig prove the Earl of Wessex had just as much power as a king?

A3.—Pg. 606, ¶ 5 to Pg. 607, ¶ 1—When Tostig, Earl of Northumbria, began to persecute the taxpayers of Northumbria by raising the rates and sending soldiers to collect the

money, Harold took charge of disciplining him, which was normally the prerogative of the monarch. He marched against Tostig's soldiers with his own forces, defeated his brother, and forced him to leave England. Tostig fled to Norway and took refuge at the court of Harald Hardrada, and Harold proved his ability to rule as a king.

4. What happened between William the Bastard and Harold Godwinson in 1064?

A4.—Pg. 607, ¶ 5—There are nine stories about what happened between William the Bastard and Harold Godwinson in 1064, and though we can't know the truth we do know that by the time Harold left Normandy with the help of the duke, William the Bastard was determined to become the next king of England. Edward the Confessor was just past sixty and clearly uninterested in fathering an heir; William, his first cousin once removed, was his closest adult male relative. Harold's father Godwin had been a kingmaker and so Harold Godwinson could help William gain the favor of the English nobility.

5. How did Harold Godwinson become Harold II of England?

A5.—Pg. 607, ¶ 7 to Pg. 608, ¶ 1—Edward the Confessor fell ill during the Christmas festivities of 1065, and died on January 5, 1066. On the same day as Edward the Confessor's death, the witan chose Harold Godwinson to be king even though Edward the Confessor had been raising Edward Ironside's grandson Edgar as an adoptive son. At the time of Edward the Confessor's death, Edgar was only fourteen years old and essentially a foreigner after having been raised mostly in Hungary, so the witan picked the grown man who had already proved himself in battle: that is how Harold Godwinson was declared Harold II of England.

6. Why did the English read Halley's Comet as a bad omen at the start of Harold II's reign?

A6.—Pg. 608, ¶ 2—Harold Godwinson promised William the Bastard he would become king of England, but then Edward the Confessor died and Harold became king in 1066. Though winds and tides held William the Bastard off, Harold knew that the Norman duke would attack in the spring so he assembled a standing army and kept them on high alert. Halley's Comet passed over England in the last week of April and the English read it as a sign of a great threat approaching—the threat of William the Bastard and his men.

7. Describe what happened when Tostig and Harald Hardrada of Norway first landed near York in September of 1066.

A7.—Pg. 609, ¶ 2 and Pg. 610, ¶ 1—Tostig and Harald Hardrada of Norway, with the help of the Scots, landed near York after Harold II's troops broke up for the winter. A hastily assembled English army had marched out to meet them and had been slaughtered. York had agreed to a formal surrender, complete with hostages, to be carried out on September 25.

8. What stopped William the Bastard from first attacking England in September of 1066?

A8.—Pg. 609, ¶ 3—When William the Bastard tried to attack England in September of 1066 he had to sail in hostile weather. Late in the second week of September, he launched his attack fleet into the English Channel, where they were promptly battered by an enormous

storm that sank some of his ships, blew others off course, and drowned part of his invasion force.

9. What was the result of the clash between Harold II and Tostig in York?

A9.—Pg. 610, ¶ 3—Harold II barely beat Tostig and Harald Hardrada, who were both killed in the fighting. Harold II received the Norwegian surrender from Harald Hardrada's son and allowed the young man to go home. He took with him the meager remnants of the Norwegian force, just twenty-four ships out of an invasion force of more than three hundred.

10. Why was the Battle of Hastings fought?

A10.—Pg. 610, ¶ 5 to Pg. 611, ¶ 2—The Battle of Hastings was fought because William the Bastard refused to negotiate with Harold II. William insisted that Edward the Confessor had intended him to receive the crown of England, and he further accused Harold of swearing a sacred oath to hand over the crown after he saved him from the shipwreck in Normandy. A week of fruitless negotiations made it very clear that William would not leave without a fight and so on October 14 the English army—mostly foot-soldiers—met the Norman force of cavalry, infantry, and archers near the town of Hastings.

11. How did William the Bastard become William the Conqueror? How did he become William I?

A11.—Pg. 611, ¶ 2–4—William the Bastard's forces attacked Harold II's foot soldiers without mercy at the Battle of Hastings and during the fight Harold II was killed, as were his brothers. By day's end, William the Bastard had become William the Conqueror. Though the witan had crowned Edgar king, Edgar surrendered himself to William the Conqueror, making room for William to go to Westminster Abbey and be consecrated as King William I.

Section III: Critical Thinking

The student may not use her text to answer this question.

In many cultures weather can serve as an omen, a sign of good or bad fortune. Weather was particularly significant to Harold Godwinson. Write a paragraph explaining how the weather played a role in Harold's life, and his unfortunate fate.

Weather first played a role in Harold Godwinson's life when it caused him to shipwreck near Normandy. Without ship, men, or money, he was forced to appeal to William the Bastard, duke of Normandy, to provide all three so that he could get home again. In exchange for his help, Harold promised William the Bastard that he would help him become king of England.

After Edward the Confessor's death, Harold Godwinson himself became king—not William the Bastard. Harold knew William would be coming for the throne, an event magnified by the week-long flight of Halley's Comet, a spectacular natural event, over England. William decided to attack England, but bad weather, winds and tides kept the Norman duke from travelling the English channel. Harold II's troops were ready for the attack, but the delay because of the weather caused them to loosen up, and after a few months Harold II told his army to go home.

As the troops retreated, no longer waiting for William, Tostig and Harald Hardrada attacked near York, and Harold II was forced to fight a bloody battle against his brother, sacrificing many of his troops. At the same time, William the Bastard fought against the weather and managed to land in Pevensey. By the time Harold and his troops arrived to fight William, they were weak. Harold II was killed in battle, and William the Bastard had become William the Conqueror.

In summary, bad weather caused Harold Godwinson to shipwreck near Normandy and ask for help from William the Bastard. Halley's Comet acted as a warning of the great threat against England that was coming. William the Bastard's attack on England was delayed because of bad weather, causing Harold to let his guard down. Harold's weakness was taken advantage of by Tostig, which cost Harold many of his troops. The fight in York between brothers ultimately led to Harold's inability to fight against William the Bastard once he did arrive in England, and which cost Harold his life.

EXAMPLE ANSWER:

Bad weather caused Harold Godwinson to shipwreck near Normandy and ask for help from William the Bastard. William agreed to help Harold but only if Harold would help William become king of England. After Edward the Confessor's death, Harold Godwinson became king, and he knew that William would be coming. William's threat was made clear by Halley's Comet's week-long flight over England. William the Bastard's attack on England was delayed because of bad weather, causing Harold to let his guard down. Harold's weakness was taken advantage of by Tostig and Harald Hardrada, who attacked in York. Harold fought against his brother and lost many of his troops. At the same time as the fighting in York, William the Bastard showed up in Pevensey. By the time Harold and his troops arrived to fight William, they were weak. Harold was killed in battle, and William the Bastard had become William the Conqueror. The weather had never been on Harold's side, causing him to make a deal he couldn't keep and ultimately costing him his life.

Section IV: Map Exercise

1. Using a black pencil, trace the rectangular outline of the frame for Map 78.1: The Battle of Hastings.

2. Using a black pencil, trace the coastline around Ireland, Britain, Scandinavia, and down the continent. Trace the visible portion of the Mediterranean. You do not need to include any islands at this time. Repeat until the contours are familiar.

3. Using a new sheet of paper, trace the rectangular outline of the frame in black. Remove your tracing paper from the original. Using a regular pencil with an eraser as you look at the map, draw the coastline. Erase and redraw as necessary.

4. When you are pleased with your map, lay it over the original. Erase and redraw any lines which are more than ¼ inch off of the original. With your black pencil, trace the outlines of Asturias, the Caliphate of Cordoba, Pamplona, Western Francia, and Germany.

5. Remove your map. Study carefully the locations of Ireland, England, Norway, Sweden, Denmark, Germany, Western Francia, Normandy, Brittany, Asturias, Pamplona, and the Caliphate of Cordoba. When you are familiar with them, mark the locations on your map.

6. Now show the location and direction of William the Conqueror and Harold Hardrada. Show their movement with arrows on your map.

Chapter Seventy-Nine

The Kings of Spain

The student may use his text when answering the questions in sections I and II.

Section I: Who, What, Where

Write a one or two-sentence answer explaining the significance of each item listed below.

Abd al-Malik—**Pg. 614, ¶ 5—Abd al-Malik, son of al-Mansur, was forced to fight continuously to keep the borders of the caliphate out to where al-Mansur had pushed them after his father's death in 1002. Though he claimed the post of vizier and kept Hisham II out of government affairs, Abd al-Malik was too busy fighting to govern; he never got his chance because in October 1008 he died from a cough.**

Abd al-Rahman—**Pg. 614, ¶ 6 to Pg. 615, ¶ 3—Abd al-Rahman, al-Mansur's younger son, took his brother Abd al-Malik's role after his death and forced Hisham II to name him heir to the caliphate. The Umayyads revolted against Abd al-Rahman and he was killed in the fighting that followed.**

Abu-Bakr—**Pg. 620, ¶ 2—Abu-Bakr, Yahya ibn Ibrahim's brother, led the Almoravids in their conquest of most of the northwestern African coast. By 1085, under Abu-Bakr, the Almoravids built a capital city and central mosque at Marrakesh; they proclaimed their loyalty to the Abbasid caliphate in Baghdad and took for their own the existing Abbasid laws and customs.**

Al-Mu'tamid—**Pg. 618, ¶ 5—Al-Mu'tamid, ruler of Seville, was able to defeat an invasion by Granada's army because of the heroic fighting of El Cid.**

Al-Nasir—**Pg. 615, ¶ 4 & 5—Al-Nasir, a Berber solider, marched into Cordoba in 1016 at the head of his own North African forces, took Sulayman II captive, and beheaded him in public with his own hands. Al-Nasir proclaimed himself caliph and paraded around with Sulayman II's head and the heads of the Berber chiefs who went against him, but even**

though he showed all that power he couldn't stop his own assassination in the bath two years later.

Alfonso V—**Pg. 616, ¶ 2 & 5—Alfonso V, known as Alfonso the Noble, king of Leon, wanted to stop Sancho III's taking of Castile, so he offered his sister to marry Count Garcia II when he was thirteen. Alfonso V was outsmarted by Sancho III and later in 1034, when Sancho III fought against Leon as the leader of the Kingdom of Navarre, Leon was forced into exile in Galicia where he died three years later.**

Alfonso VI—**Pg. 618, ¶ 1, 3 & 4 and Pg. 622, ¶ 3—Alfonso, middle son of Ferdinand I, was driven out of Leon by his brother but then he took revenge by having Sancho II the Strong killed and returning from exile as Alfonso VI of Castile and Leon. Alfonso VI was a long-lived king; he was able to expand his Christian kingdom across most of the north of Spain, earning him the nickname "Alfonso the Brave."**

Alfonso the Battler—**Pg. 622, ¶ 3 and Pg. 622, ¶ 7 to Pg. 623, ¶ 1—Alfonso the Battler, Alfonso VI's first cousin (once removed), the king of Aragon-Navarre, began a double quest in 1104 to reconquer the Muslim south and to reverse the relationship between Leon-Castile and his own kingdom so that the larger realm paid homage to the smaller. Alfonso the Battler married Urraca, and when Alfonso VI died, Alfonso the Battler became king of Aragon and Navarre, Leon and Castile, *rex Hispania*.**

Ali ibn Yusuf—**Pg. 622, ¶ 5—Ali ibn Yusuf, son of Yusuf ibn Tashfin, inherited an Almoravid empire that had lost much of its territory to the armies of Leon-Castile during the later parts of his father's rule, when Tashfin was preoccupied with old age. In 1108 Ali ibn Yusuf was able to defeat Sancho and take Ucles.**

Ferdinand I—**Pg. 617, ¶ 3 & 4—Ferdinand, the second-born son of Sancho III and the last of the dead emperor's heirs, claimed his father's land and title for himself as Ferdinand I. Ferdinand tried to atone for the atrocities of the battles that gave him his title by giving the better part of his spoils to charity, and in 1065, when he felt himself fatally weakening, he put on a hair shirt so he could spend his last days in penance.**

Garcia II—**Pg. 616, ¶ 1–3—Garcia II, count of Castile at three, was theoretically protected by his sister's husband and his regent Sancho III. When Garcia II was arranged to marry the king of Leon's daughter at thirteen, Sancho III had the young boy killed.**

Hisham II—**Pg. 613, ¶ 2 & 4 and Pg. 615, ¶ 1–3—Hisham II, who inherited the rule of Cordoba after the death of his father in 976 when he was only ten, was controlled by his ministers and kept secluded in his old palace, proclaimed by al-Mansur his vizier to have devoted himself to good works. Hisham II's seclusion continued through the administrations of both al-Malik and al-Rahman, and he was killed because of his support of al-Mansur's sons; his naming of al-Rahman as heir to the caliphate caused a revolt by the Umayyad family, a revolt that cost Hisham II his life.**

Ibn Yasin—**Pg. 619, ¶ 4—Ibn Yasin, an imam brought to Africa by Yahya ibn Ibrahim, spent twenty years with the tribes teaching them a militant and ascetic interpretation that ordered the heterodox believers to straighten up, shun alcohol, devote their time to prayer and fasting, study the Qur'an and then to spread these practices, by force if necessary.**

Muhammad ibn Abi Amir—**Pg. 613, ¶ 2–4 and Pg. 614, ¶ 2 & 3—Muhammad ibn Abi Amir, known more widely as al-Mansur, "The Victorious," worked his way up to vizier of Hisham II in 978 after which he built a new palace and moved himself and the bureaucracy of Cordoba, except for the caliph, into it in 981. Al-Mansur proved himself to be a great strategist, having won fifty-seven battles over northern resistance and marrying the daughter of the king of Pamplona; under his rule al-Andalus prospered even with the rightful caliph under house arrest.**

Rodrigo Diaz (El Cid)—**Pg. 618, ¶ 2, Pg. 619, ¶ 1, Pg. 620, ¶ 4 and Pg. 621, ¶ 6—Rodrigo Diaz (El Cid), Sancho II the Great's military commander, inherited by Alfonso VI, became a mercenary for the Arab king of Zaragoza after being exiled by his new leader. El Cid returned to work for Alfonso VI after he signed a treaty that gave him two castles, a small territory of his own, and any land he acquired fighting the *taifa*; this is how he got Valencia, the small oasis from religious war that he created for himself where he was able to die peacefully at the age of sixty.**

Sancho—**Pg. 622, ¶ 6—Sancho, fifteen-year-old son of Alfonso VI, was sent by his father to fight the Almoravids in 1108. Though Sancho was accompanied by two experienced generals, the Almoravids were still able to defeat the Christian troops, killing young Sancho and both of his generals.**

Sancho II—**Pg. 614, ¶ 2—Sancho II, king of Pamplona, suffered a series of humiliating defeats at the hands of al-Mansur. He gave up and came to Cordoba to make peace which al-Mansur accepted, along with Sancho's daughter as his wife.**

Sancho II the Strong—**Pg. 617, ¶ 5 and Pg. 618, ¶ 3—Sancho II the Strong, oldest son of Ferdinand I, became the king of Castile after his father's death. Though Sancho II the Strong had plans to take his brothers' territory with the help of El Cid, he was outsmarted by Alfonso who, after being driven out of Leon, had his brother murdered.**

Sancho III—**Pg. 615, ¶ 7 to Pg. 616, ¶ 1, 4 & 6 and Pg. 617, ¶ 1—Sancho III, known as Sancho the Great, grandson of Sancho II, wanted to control Castile in addition to Pamplona, Navarre and Ebro, so he married the count of Castile's daughter and killed her brother. Sancho III claimed the title of emperor because he ruled over the three Christian kingdoms in the north of Spain—Leon, Castile and Navarre—as well as a few smaller Christian regions.**

Sulayman II—**Pg. 615, ¶ 3—Sulayman II became caliph after war broke out between Abd al-Rahman and the Umayyads. Sulayman II was beheaded in 1016 by the Berber soldier al-Nasir.**

Urraca—**Pg. 622, ¶ 7 and Pg. 623, ¶ 1—Urraca, Alfonso VI's widowed daughter, was married to Alfonso the Battler so that when Alfonso VI died the king of Aragon would be able to defend the realm. Urraca had a four-year-old son from her previous marriage, and this child, not Alfonso the Battler, had the right to become the next ruler of Leon and Castile so she insisted on ruling her own part of the empire without Alfonso the Battler's help.**

Yahya ibn Ibrahim—**Pg. 619, ¶ 3 & 4—Yahya ibn Ibrahim, a North African chief, went to Mecca in 1035 for the sacred pilgrimage, the *hajj* and there he discovered just how odd the western African version of Islam was. When Yahya ibn Ibrahim returned to Africa he brought with him an *imam* named ibn Yasin who spent the next twenty years with the tribes teaching them his particular brand of militaristic and ascetic version of Islam.**

Yusuf ibn Tashfin—**Pg. 620, ¶ 3, 5 & 6—Yusuf ibn Tashfin, cousin of Abu-Bakr and general of the Almoravid army, fought against Alfonso VI and on October 23, 1087 the combined armies of the *taifa* kingdoms and Almoravids defeated the soldiers of Leon and Castile in battle at Sagrajas, southwest of Toledo. The rulers of the *taifa* kingdoms made Tashfin promise he would return to Africa as soon as the Christians were defeated, but Abu-Bakr's death had left Tashfin sole ruler of Almoravid lands, a role which he used to conquer Granada, Cordoba and Seville, making southern Spain a province of the Almoravid empire.**

Section II: Comprehension

Write a two or three-sentence answer to each of the following questions.

1. How did al-Mansur manage to move himself up in the palace hierarchy of al-Andalus?

A1.—Pg. 613, ¶ 4 to Pg. 614, ¶ 1—Al-Mansur was made vizier to Hisham II in 978, after which he ordered the construction of a new palace where he moved himself and the entire bureaucracy of Cordoba into it. Al-Mansur dealt with his competitors by accusing them of heresy and disloyalty and having them put to death, and he basically had Hisham II under house arrest, having told the world Hisham II had devoted himself to good works and preferred to reside alone in the caliph's palace. After isolating the caliph and getting rid of his possible challengers, al-Mansur's name was spoken along with the caliph's in Friday prayers—proof that he had risen to the top of the palace hierarchy.

2. What made al-Mansur an excellent strategist and administrator?

A2.—Pg. 614, ¶ 2—Al-Mansur reinforced the Cordoban army with crowds of Berber soldiers, brought over from North Africa, and during his rule as vizier, the Caliphate of Cordoba triumphed in battle after battle against the Christian kingdoms to the north. Barcelona, which had been governed by independent Christian dukes for over a century, was sacked in 985 and the king of Pamplona gave himself over to al-Mansur by making peace and offering his daughter for marriage. In 999, the caliph's armies flooded over the border of the Kingdom of Leon and destroyed much of the city of Santiago de Compostela, which was

doubly embarrassing because it was not only Christian territory but also a site of pilgrimage for Christians from all over the world.

3. Why did the Umayyads revolt when al-Rahman was named heir to the caliphate by Hisham II? What happened during the revolt?

A3.—Pg. 615, ¶ 2 & 3—If al-Rahman was made caliph, the Umayyad hold on the caliphate in Cordoba would end and as a result the other members of the Umayyad family—who already resented the privileges claimed by al-Mansur and his family and disliked the high position held by so many Berbers in the army—revolted. Support was split between Hisham II and another Umayyad caliph and civil war broke out, with Abd al-Rahman and his Berbers fighting against the various Umayyad factions who wanted the caliphate back, and the Umayyads fighting against each other. In the years of struggle that followed, both Abd al-Rahman and Hisham II were killed and eventually the Umayyad claimant Sulayman II became caliph.

4. Describe the leadership of al-Andalus after the death of al-Nasir.

A4.—Pg. 615, ¶ 5—After the death of al-Nasir no caliph managed to rule in Cordoba for more than a few years and in 1031, when the last man to try to claim the title died, al-Andalus fell apart into a fragmentation of little city-states. Their kings were called *reyes de taifas*, the "party kings," each the head of his own tiny political movement. Over the next half-century, over thirty of these *taifa* kingdoms, some ruled by Arabs and others ruled by Berbers, would blanket the former territory of the caliphate.

5. Explain how Sancho III got away with murdering Garcia II and managed to unite Pamplona with Castile.

A5.—Pg. 616, ¶ 3 & 4—When Alfonso V arranged for Garcia II to be married to his sister, Sancho III pretended to be very happy and arranged to accompany Garcia II to the formal celebration of betrothal with his entire army. No sooner had they arrived in Leon than three assassins, brothers from the Castilian family of Vela, attacked the boy and stabbed him to death in front of his sister, his brother-in-law, and their entourage and then fled to Pamplona. Sancho III had hired Castillians that he could follow into Pamplona and catch in order to prove his love of Garcia II, a plan that worked because Garcia II's sister became countess of Castile, which meant that the kingdom had effectively been united with Pamplona.

6. What did El Cid do to get himself exiled by Alfonso VI?

A6.—Pg. 618, ¶ 5 to Pg. 619, ¶ 1—While working as an ambassador to the *taifa* kingdoms for Alfonso VI, El Cid protected al-Mu'tamid from attack by the army of Granada. After defeating the forces from Granada, El Cid attacked Toledo, taking seven thousand captives and wagons of treasure back to Castile and Leon with him. Alfonso VI was jealous of El Cid's reputation and popularity, and he took the attack on Toledo as an excuse to sack El Cid's home and exile the general from his kingdom.

7. Why were the *taifa* kingdoms afraid of Alfonso VI? What did they plan to do to defeat him?

A7.—Pg. 619, ¶ 2—The *taifa* kingdoms were afraid of Alfonso VI because after he captured Coria in 1079 he captured Toledo in 1085, which was the center of one of the strong *taifa* kingdoms. They feared that if Alfonso VI managed to fight his way through the *taifa* kingdoms all the way to the coast, he could divide the northern and southern *taifa* kingdoms from each other and pick them off, one at a time. The *taifa* kingdoms had to be united in order to stand a chance against Alfonso IV, so the *taifa* rulers sent an appeal for help across the Strait of Gibraltar to the North African Muslims known as the Almoravids.

8. Why did Alfonso VI want El Cid back in his kingdom? What were the conditions of El Cid's return to Alfonso VI's service?

A8—Pg. 620, ¶ 4—Alfonso VI barely survived the bloody battle between his own armies and the combined armies of the *taifa* kings and the Almoravids. The defeat frightened him so badly that he recalled El Cid from exile to fight the Almoravid threat. El Cid agreed to come home in exchange for two castles, a small territory of his own, and a written pardon from Alfonso, which stipulated that all lands and castles which El Cid might acquire by conquering *taifa* territory would belong solely to him.

9. What happened to Valencia after the death of El Cid?

A9.—Pg. 621, ¶ 6 to Pg. 622, ¶ 2—Valencia existed entirely through the strength and resolution of El Cid and as soon as he died the Almoravids marched against Valencia, invaded its territory, and besieged the city for seven months. El Cid's wife sent an appeal to Alfonso of Castile, who arrived with his army and fought his way into the city to rescue her and the body of her dead husband, but he refused to commit himself to lifting the siege. When they had all left Valencia Alfonso VI ordered the city to be burnt and abandoned but the Almoravids, who had backed away, returned and claimed the burned city.

10. In what way did the relationship between Alfonso the Battler and Urraca help the Almoravid empire keep their power?

A10.—Pg. 623, ¶ 1-3—Urraca hated Alfonso the Battler and she believed her son from her previous marriage was the rightful heir of Leon and Castile, so she insisted on ruling her own part of the empire without her new husband's help. However, Alfonso the Battler still claimed the title of king over the whole realm and during the next eight years, he fought a constant war with the Almoravid armies along the frontier, helped out by Urraca who also sent the armies of Leon-Castile against the Almoravids. Even though they both sent troops against the Almoravids, they also fought each other; the hostility between the Christian king and queen thwarted their attempts to fight the North African enemy allowing the Almoravids to keep their power a little longer.

Section III: Critical Thinking

The student may not use his text to answer this question.

The relationship between war and peace is often a confusing one. Just look at Ferdinand I, for example. War made him king of a great realm, but to find inner peace he spent his last days in the clothes of a sinner. Thinking about the relationship between war and peace, write a paragraph explaining the contradiction between how El Cid conquered Valencia and the way he used the small kingdom after he was in control.

El Cid laid siege to the city of Valencia in 1094. Once he was able to claim the city as his own, he took it according to the treaty he made with Alfonso VI. Then he conquered the area around Valencia to make himself a kingdom. The kingdom was not easily brought together. He killed the inhabitants of Valencia who opposed him, sacked villages that refused to surrender, and stole treasure from the conquered for his own personal use. But he also did not impose any religious views on the people of his new kingdom. El Cid had spent his entire life fighting for Muslim kings against other Muslims,
for Muslim kings against Christians,
for Christian kings against Muslims,
for Christian kings against their own
brothers. He was tired of war and fed
up with changing sides. Though the physical territory of Valencia was brought together through violence, and it was war that made El Cid desire a place of his own, Valencia under El Cid was a kingdom of tolerance. While he was king, El Cid made his kingdom of Valencia a place of peace that could be home to both Christians and Muslims.

EXAMPLE ANSWER:

El Cid spent most of his life fighting. He fought for Christians and for Muslims, he fought for one brother against another brother, and in the last battles of his life he fought for his own kingdom. In 1094, El Cid laid siege to Valencia and then conquered the territories around the city. He killed the inhabitants of Valencia who opposed him, sacked villages that refused to surrender, and stole treasure from the conquered for his own personal use. But all of this violence occurred so that El Cid could have a kingdom of peace. Tired of all of the fighting, El Cid allowed any Spaniard that followed his rules to live in Valencia, regardless of faith. While he was king, El Cid made his kingdom of Valencia a place of peace that could be home to both Christians and Muslims.

Chapter Eighty

The Arrival of the Turks

The student may use her text when answering the questions in sections I and II.

Section I: Who, What, Where

Write a one or two-sentence answer explaining the significance of each item listed below.

Alp Arslan—**Pg. 631, ¶ 2 and Pg. 632, ¶ 1—Alp Arslan, nephew of Togrul, inherited his uncle's power as leader of the Turks. Alp Arslan defeated Romanos Diogenes, took him prisoner, and then made the Byzantine ruler swear friendship and peace to the Turks.**

Constantine VIII—**Pg. 625, ¶ 2 & 3—Constantine VIII, brother and heir to Basil the Bulgar-Slayer, inherited the crown in 1025 when he was in his sixties. Constantine VIII spent his life hunting, horseback riding and eating, he had no governing skills and no heirs, and so in a last ditch attempt at arranging a successor, he married his daughter Zoe to Romanos Argyros.**

Constantine Doukas—**Pg. 630, ¶ 3 to Pg. 631, ¶ 1—Constantine Doukas, a bureaucrat, was crowned emperor of Byzantium after Isaac Comnenus's death. Constantine Doukas managed to stay in power for eight years, but he paid little attention to the Turkish advances in the east.**

Constantine Monomachos—**Pg. 627, ¶ 2 & 3, Pg. 628, ¶ 2 & 3 and Pg. 629, ¶ 4 & 5—Constantine Monomachos, Zoe's new lover after Michael IV stopped sleeping with her, was exiled by the emperor to the island of Lesbos and then reinstated when Zoe became co-empress; she recalled Constantine Monomachos from exile, married him, and had him crowned as emperor. Constantine Monomachos inherited a kingdom that was threatened on every side, and after making a temporary peace with the Turks, he died, suffering from a disease that slowly paralyzed him and racked him with painful muscle convulsions.**

Isaac Comnenus—**Pg. 630, ¶ 1 & 3—Isaac Comnenus, the commander of the Byzantine army, was made emperor in 1057 by the wishes of his men and became ruler after Michael Bringas**

abdicated peacefully. Though everyone celebrated the new emperor, he almost immediately made himself unpopular at court by proposing massive government reforms, and then—before he could carry most of them out—he grew ill and died.

John Orphanotrophus—**Pg. 626, ¶ 4 and Pg. 627, ¶ 1—John, brother of Michael the Paphlagonian, a powerful palace eunuch that was behind his brother's affair with Zoe, was nicknamed "Orphanotrophus" because he had charge of the official state orphanage in Constantinople. John was shrewd, meticulous and devoted to his brother's success.**

Michael V—**Pg. 627, ¶ 4–6—Michael, the twenty-five year old nephew to Michael IV and John Orphanotrophus, was adopted by Michael IV and when the emperor died he was made Michael V, emperor of Byzantium. Eager to shake off control of his powerful uncle, Michael V had John and Zoe banished, but the people loved Zoe so they hunted Michael V down after he fled Constantinople, and blinded him with a sharp iron.**

Michael VII—**Pg. 632, ¶ 2—Michael VII, eldest son of Constantine Doukas, became senior emperor in 1071. There was no chance that Michael VII could drive the Turks out of Asia Minor; the sultan of the Seljuq Turks had established a new Turkish outpost in Asia Minor and a vassal ruler, the sultan of Rum, presided over this new Turkish state, but the slaughter of Byzantine forces at Manzikert made it impossible for the Byzantines to muster a force large enough to drive the Turks out.**

Michael the Paphlagonian—**Pg. 626, ¶ 3 and Pg. 627, ¶ 4—Michael the Paphlagonian, the palace chamberlain, was married to his lover Zoe and crowned emperor Michael VI on the same day her husband Romanos III died. Michael IV's reign was shaped by his brother and his epilepsy; John Orphanotrophus ensured Michael IV had an heir so that when he died, which he did at age thirty-one, power would remain in the family.**

Michael Bringas—**Pg. 629, ¶ 5 and Pg. 630, ¶ 1—Michael Bringas, Theodora's minister, was named by the empress as her successor, and when she died he was instantly nicknamed "Michael Gerontas," or "Michael the Aged." Michael Bringas was crowned in 1056, but in 1057 the Byzantine army named Isaac Comnenus emperor; Michael Bringas abdicated peacefully and became a monk, dying two years later in his bed.**

Romanos Argyros—**Pg. 625, ¶ 3 & 4 and Pg. 626, ¶ 3—Romanos Argyros, the city governor of Constantinople and great-grandson of Emperor Romanos I was married to Constantine VIII's daughter Zoe and became Constantine VIII's successor, Romanos III. Romanos III was slowly poisoned by Zoe after his popularity plummeted and he died one morning after slipping and drowning in the bath.**

Romanos Diogenes—**Pg. 631, ¶ 1 and Pg. 632, ¶ 1—Romanos Diogenes, crowned Romanos IV in 1068, ruled as senior co-emperor of Byzantium with Constantine Doukas's sons. Though Romanos IV had some victory against the Turks, his defeat and submission to Alp Arslan caused his own people to turn against him, blind him, and to leave him in a monastery to die.**

Theodora—**Pg. 628, ¶ 1 and Pg. 629, ¶ 5—Theodora, sister of Zoe, was named co-empress after Michael V tried to have Zoe banished. Theodora was left alone on the throne, her sister and emperor having died before her, and before she died in 1056 she declared that the throne should pass to her minister Michael Bringas.**

Zoe—**Pg. 625, ¶ 3 & 4 and Pg. 628, ¶ 2—Zoe, Constantine VIII's beautiful middle daughter, was married to Romanos Argyros at forty-eight, and when her father died she became Empress Zoe, ruler of Byzantium, wife of Romanos III. Zoe remained an incredibly beautiful and powerful woman who took many lovers throughout her life, making three men emperors through marriage—Romanos III, Michael IV and Constantine Monomachos—and was named co-empress with her sister Theodora after the fall of Michael V.**

Section II: Comprehension

Write a two or three-sentence answer to each of the following questions.

1. Describe how all of Romanos III's royal dreams fell through.

A1.—Pg. 625, ¶ 5 to Pg. 626, ¶ 1—Romanos III gathered a huge army and marched against the Muslim border to the east; he raised taxes, hoping to make himself famous through enormous building projects; and he worked hard at siring an heir so that his dynasty would last forever. All of these projects backfired. The assault on the Muslim border ended with an embarrassing defeat; the new taxes made him hugely unpopular; and Zoe, who was nearly fifty, was not able to have a child no matter how many ointments or crystals were put on her body.

2. For what reasons were men castrated in Byzantium?

A2.—Pg. 626, ¶ 5—Men were castrated in Byzantium because they were made slaves or prisoners, but there were also native-born eunuchs, young boys with royal blood castrated to keep them from claiming the throne. Even more commonly, rural parents with numerous sons would castrate two or three and send them off to the capital city to make their fortunes. They couldn't all stay on the farm, and since eunuchs had no sons of their own and no ambitions to build dynasties, they had a distinct advantage at court.

3. How did Michael IV's relationship with Zoe change under the influence of John Orphanotrophus?

A3.—Pg. 627, ¶ 2—Under John's guidance, Michael began to hem Zoe in, reducing her influence at court. He confined her to her chambers and ordered that anyone visiting her had to be cleared by her honor guard. He also stopped sleeping with her, but that was most likely because his epilepsy had grown worse making him impotent.

4. How did Michael IV deal with his epileptic fits in public? What steps were taken to ensure that Michael IV had an heir?

A4.—Pg. 627, ¶ 3 & 4—Every time Michael IV went out in public he was with a band of attendants so that they could circle him if he fell into a seizure, making sure no one could see his convulsions. With is condition worsening, John Orphanotrophus suggested that Michael adopt as his son and heir their twenty-five-year-old nephew (their older sister's son), also named Michael. The adoption was completed in 1040.

5. How did Zoe and her sister Theodora come to be co-empresses of Byzantium?

A5.—Pg. 627, ¶ 5 to Pg. 628, ¶ 1—When Michael V took the throne, he ordered his uncle John Orphanotrophus and his adoptive mother Zoe banished. John Orphanotrophus was respected and Zoe was loved; a riot broke out against Michael V, with mobs in the streets armed with axes, broadswords, spears, and stones, ready to kill Michael V as soon as he showed his face. After Michael V was caught at the monastery where he was trying to hide, he was dragged away and blinded with a sharp iron and then the crowds acclaimed Zoe and her sister Theodora as co-empresses.

6. What kind of kingdom did Constantine Monomachos inherit when he became emperor of Byzantium?

A6.—Pg. 628, ¶ 3 & 4—Constantine Monomachos found himself at the head of an empire threatened on almost every side by outside powers. He was forced to deal with a rebellion by one of his generals, an attack from the Rus, a migration of Pecheneg refugees across the frozen Danube, and hostile Muslim forces to the east. Though he was able to cope with these problems, an insurmountable threat arrived in 1048 in the form of Togrul the Turk.

7. How did the Turks become strong enough to challenge Byzantium?

A7.—Pg. 628, ¶ 4—Under the leadership of Togrul of the Seljuq Turks, the Turks became a nation. Togrul led his coalition in the successful conquest of the Ghaznavid lands west of the Indus mountains, had himself crowned sultan of the Turks in 1038, and established his capital at Nishapur. Because of the nation Togrul built up, the Turks were strong enough to challenge Byzantium.

8. What happened when the Turks breached the eastern border and captured the rich border city of Erzen in 1048?

A8.—Pg. 628, ¶ 5 to Pg. 629, ¶ 1—When the Turks breached the eastern border and captured the rich border city of Erzen in 1048, Constantine Monomachos sent an army of fifty thousand to drive the invaders back. The Byzantine soldiers were badly defeated, the Seljuq Turks took thousands of prisoners including the Byzantine commanding general, and they captured the army supplies: thousands of wagons filled with food, dry goods, and money. Constantine Monomachos made a treaty with the Turks that exchanged peace and the return of the captives for land on the eastern frontier, expensive gifts for Togrul, and the promise that the Muslims would be allowed to worship freely in Constantinople.

9. How did it come to pass that Togrul was recognized in the Friday prayers?

A9.—Pg. 629, ¶ 6—In 1056 Togrul marched into Baghdad and removed it firmly from Buyid control, driving the last Buyid rulers into exile. The Abbasid caliph still lived in Baghdad and he still retained some spiritual authority, although not a shred of political power, and Togrul made a deal with him: the caliph could remain peacefully in Baghdad as long as he agreed to recognize Togrul as supreme sultan, highest authority in the Muslim world, in the Friday prayers. Once, the mention of anyone other than the caliph or his heir in the Friday prayers was treachery, but now the caliph himself would pray for the sultan.

10. How was Romanos Diogenes able to drive the Turks back across the Euphrates in 1070?

A10.—Pg. 631, ¶ 2—Romanos Diogenes recognized the danger of Turkish growth and finally organized a campaign against the eastern border. Driving forward against the Turks, he pushed into the land they had already taken and in 1070, in a series of hard-fought battles, he managed to drive them back across the Euphrates. His years of campaigning had taught him the best way to deal with the lightly armed, fast-moving Turkish cavalry: keep the army bunched together, not spread out into a line, with bowmen protecting the slow, heavily armed cavalry on all sides.

11. What happened to Romanos Diogenes's army after Alp Arslan regrouped in 1071?

A11.—Pg. 631, ¶ 4–6—When Alp Arslan advanced again into Byzantine territory in 1071, Romanos Diogenes divided his men, and then attacked and captured Manzikert. Three days after the capture, when he met what appeared to be a band of Turkish raiders, Romanos Diogenes drew up his army in a single line to drive them back, not realizing as he pursued them that they were the front edge of Alp Arslan's massive force. The Turks surrounded Romanos Diogenes's men, massacred them, and captured Romanos as a prisoner.

12. How was Romanos Diogenes treated after he was taken prisoner by Alp Arslan? How was he treated by his own people?

A12.—Pg. 632, ¶ 1—Romanos Diogenes was treated with honor by Alp Arslan, fed from the sultan's own table, and set free—after extracting from him solemn vows of friendship and peace. However, Romanos was not treated so kindly by his own people, his reputation destroyed by his captivity and oath of friendship to Alp Arslan. A handful of trusted men, including members of the Doukas family, captured Romanos Diogenes on his way home, blinded him, and left him in a monastery to die.

Section III: Critical Thinking

The student may not use her text to answer this question.

It is common sense to think that a ruler of a tribe, a nation, a kingdom, or an empire, would make decisions that would benefit his/her realm, rather than him/herself. But as we have read over and over, that is just not the case. Write a paragraph or two explaining how Constantine Monomachos and Romanos Diogenes made decisions that were in their best interest, but not the best interest for Byzantium. Then explain how those decisions led to the shrinking of Byzantium.

Both Constantine Monomachos and Romanos Diogenes had to keep their empire afloat while facing threats from the Turks. Constantine Monomachos sent an army of fifty thousand to drive Togrul back from Erzen, but he was defeated. He lost thousands of prisoners and his army supplies: thousands of wagons filled with food, dry goods and money. Instead of thinking about how to defeat the Turks, Constantine Monomachos thought about how to save his skin as emperor. As a result, he made a treaty with the Seljuq Turks. In exchange for peace and the return of the prisoners, he agreed to give up some Byzantine land on the eastern frontier. He also sent expensive gifts to Togrul and promised the he would allow Muslims to worship freely in Constantinople. Togrul accepted these terms and the fighting was over, but this wasn't the best decision for Byzantium. Though Constantine Monomachos stopped the fighting and kept his title, Byzantium shrank under his rule. Rather than building his empire up, he built himself up as emperor and sacrificed part of his territory.

Romanos Diogenes made mistakes similar to Constantine Monomachos. Romanos Diogenes was an experienced general, and he had outsmarted the Turkish army once in 1070, managing to drive them back across the Euphrates. Romanos Diogenes became too cocky as a leader and made hasty decisions that made him look powerful but ultimately led to the downfall of the Byzantine army. When Alp Arslan advanced into Byzantine territory again in 1071, Romanos Diogenes didn't know exactly where Alp Arslan and the bulk of his army had camped, and rather than holding his men together until he could get firm intelligence, he divided his army in half and sent thirty thousand men off to attack a nearby fortress. He marched with his remaining men to the city of Manzikert, right on the frontier between Byzantine and Turkish territory, and captured it. However, Alp Arslan was just beyond Manzikert, keeping tabs on the emperor's movements. Three days after the capture of Manzikert, as Romanos IV advanced cautiously into Turkish territory, he met what appeared to be a band of Turkish raiders. He drew up his army in a single line—exactly what he knew not to do when dealing with the Turkish forces—and led the Byzantine troops after the enemy, pursuing them into the late afternoon. Unfortunately the raiders were not one band but actually the front edge of Alp Arslan's massive force. As soon as the sun set, the Turks surrounded the strung-out army and massacred them in the twilight.

Romanos Diogenes made a decision that looked good for him, but not for Byzantium. If he had waited for his intelligence rather than being prideful and assuming he knew what the Turkish leader was doing, the Byzantine army might not have been slaughtered. His decision was made for himself, not for his empire. After the slaughter, Romanos Diogenes's people had him captured and blinded, then left him in a monastery to die.

EXAMPLE ANSWER:

Both Constantine Monomachos and Romanos Diogenes had to keep their empire afloat while facing threats from the Turks, but both emperors made decisions that were based on self-interest rather than on the good of Byzantium. Constantine Monomachos made a peace treaty with the Turks that required him to give up a portion of land in eastern Byzantium. He also sent expensive gifts to Togrul and promised the he would allow Muslims to worship freely in Constantinople. In an effort to keep his place as emperor, Constantine Monomachos lost some of his empire and his riches and gave up the religious standards at Byzantium's core. These were decisions made for himself, not for his realm.

Romanos Diogenes made mistakes similar to Constantine Monomachos. After a small win over the Turkish army in 1070, Romanos Diogenes made some decisions that were meant to showcase his uncanny talents as a general rather than safe decisions that would have benefitted his empire. When Alp Arslan advanced into Byzantine territory again in 1071, Romanos Diogenes didn't know exactly where Alp Arslan and the bulk of his army had camped, and rather than holding his men together until he could get firm intelligence, he divided his army in half and sent thirty thousand men off to attack a nearby fortress. This led to his army's ultimate downfall. After taking Manzikert, Romanos Diogenes was tricked into following Alp Arslan's army and soon the Byzantine forces were massacred. Romanos Diogenes made a decision that looked good for him, but not for Byzantium. If he had waited for his intelligence rather than being prideful and assuming he knew what the Turkish leader was doing, the Byzantine army might not have been slaughtered. His decision was made for himself, not for his empire. After the slaughter, Romanos Diogenes's people had him captured and blinded, and then they left him in a monastery to die.

Chapter Eighty-One

The Loss of the Song

The student may use his text when answering the questions in sections I and II.

Section I: **Who, What, Where**

Write a one or two-sentence answer explaining the significance of each item listed below.

Akuta—**Pg. 637, ¶ 2 & 5—Akuta became leader of the Wanyan clan of the Jurchen in 1115 and as leader he knew that he needed to have a ceremonial kingship in order to turn his nomads into a settled state. Akuta demanded the Liao recognize him as emperor and when they didn't, Akuta made an alliance with Song Huizong; their combined forces attacked the Liao capital in 1122 and took the emperor captive.**

Gaozong—**Pg. 638, ¶ 4—Gaozong, Qinzong's half-brother, was taken by the Song as they fled Kaifeng. He was proclaimed emperor of the Southern Song in exile at Lin'an, far to the south.**

Jin Taizong—**Pg. 637, ¶ 6—Jin Taizong, younger brother of Akuta and his successor, led the Jurchen in the attack on the Song capital of Kaifeng, the attack that brought down the Song dynasty.**

Li Deming—**Pg. 634, ¶ 2—Li Deming was the great chief of the Western Xia, nomads that Li Deming was able to organize into a state between 982 and 1032. Li Deming hoped his son would be a true monarch, educated in the ways of the Chinese aristocracy.**

Li Yuanhao—**Pg. 634, ¶ 3 to Pg. 635, ¶ 3 & 5—Li Yuanhao, son and successor of Li Deming of the Western Xia, declared by his ministers to be "Shizu, Sage of Culture and Hero of War, Originator of Literature, Rooted in Might, Giver of Law, Founder of Ritual, Humane and Filial Emperor" went to great lengths to create a civilized nation including giving himself a Chinese Buddhist education, creating a script for the Tangut language, writing to Song Renzong and asking for official recognition, and finally attacking Song Renzong in an effort to be acknowledged as leader of the Great Xia. After six years of fighting, Li Yuanhao agreed**

to a compromise with Song Renzong that gave the Western Xia an annual tribute, but not recognition of Li Yuanhao as a real emperor.

Lin Lingsu—**Pg. 637, ¶ 3 & 4—Lin Lingsu, a Taoist priest, told emperor Song Huizong that he was the incarnation of the supreme deity "Great Imperial Lord of Long Life." This convinced Huizong that he was indeed a Son of Heaven, possessor of the Divine Mandate, and led the emperor to occupy his days with painting, poetry, tea ceremonies, and Taoist rituals.**

Qinzong—**Pg. 638, ¶ 2 & 3—Qinzong, twenty-five-year-old son of Song Huizong, was forcibly made emperor after his father faked a stroke so he did not have to deal with the Jurchen attack on his kingdom. Song Qinzong was captured by the Jurchen after they took the Song capital of Kaifeng and he lived in their captivity for three decades.**

Song Huizong—**Pg. 637, ¶ 3 & 4 and Pg. 638, ¶ 2—Song Huizong, encouraged by the Taoist priest named Lin Lingsu, spent his reign building Taoist temples, endowing Taoist monasteries, and studying Taoist teachings rather than building up his military and thinking strategically. This led to Song Huizong agreeing to make an alliance with the Jurchen against the Liao, an alliance that backfired and led to the fall of the Song dynasty.**

Yun Kwan—**Pg. 636, ¶ 7 to Pg. 637, ¶ 1—Yun Kwan, Goryeon general, led a special army called "The Extraordinary Military Corps," which had a full division of cavalry, north to fight against the Wanyan that demanded the return of the Jurchen refugees that had fled into Goryeo. In 1107, the Extraordinary Military Corps pushed its way into Jurchen territory and built a series of defensive positions known as the Nine Forts in order to protect the northern territories.**

Section II: Comprehension

Write a two or three-sentence answer to each of the following questions.

1. How was Li Yuanhao able to create a past for the Western Xia?

A1.—Pg. 634, ¶ 4—Li Yuanhao made sure a script for his native Tangut language was created when he became the leader of the Western Xia. The script was a complicated system based on Chinese principles. By having history written down, Li Yuanhao created an official, written past for his people.

2. If the Song did not dominate the east, why did the Western Xia want Song Renzong's recognition?

A2.—Pg. 635, ¶ 2—Though the Song did not dominate the east, the empire's reputation was unmatched. The Song emperor had the sheen of millennia of tradition, and fledgling nations like the Liao and Western Xia wanted some of that greatness for themselves.

3. Describe the Western Xia attack on the Song between 1038 and 1042. How was Song Renzong able to avoid a war with the Liao while his armies were fighting the Western Xia?

A3.—Pg. 635, ¶ 3 & 4—When Song Renzong refused to recognize Li Yuanhao as Shizu, emperor of the Great Xia, the slighted leader's army invaded. Between 1038 and 1042, the

Western Xia overran the forts along the western frontier with Li Yuanhao advancing his men cautiously, slowly eating away at the western reaches of the Song empire. In 1042, the Liao demanded another chunk of Song territory for themselves, but rather than fighting or giving up the land, Song Renzong offered to increase the annual tribute to the Liao instead.

4. Why was the *Wujing Zongyao* written, and what information does it contain?

A4.—Pg. 635, ¶ 6 to Pg. 636, ¶ 1—The *Wujing Zongyao* was written by a band of scholars commissioned to put together a compendium on techniques of war. The *Wujing Zongyao* describes a pump-powered flame-thrower that could hurl naphtha, the same "Greek fire" used by the defenders of Constantinople, and it also explains how to make explosive black powder from coal, saltpeter, and sulfur. The *Wujing Zongyao* was the first time in history that the formula for gunpowder appears in writing.

5. How did Song Renzong use the time he bought in the truce between the Western Xia, the Liao and the Song?

A5.—Pg. 636, ¶ 2—The purchased truce gave the Song time to rebuild their military might and prepare for war. Song Renzong raised taxes to pay for the tribute as well as a newly expanded national army. He also ordered new standards put into place for new army recruits who would now have to pass an eye exam, as well as tests in running, jumping, and shooting.

6. Who was the Jurchen? What was the difference between "Civilized Jurchen" and "Raw Jurchen"?

A6.—Pg. 636, ¶ 4—The Jurchen was a tribe that came from the north at the beginning of the twelfth century that spoke a language distantly related to the Turkish tongues and lived mostly on the wooded plains north of Goryeo, in the lands later called Manchuria. The "Civilized Jurchen" were western groups that had come under rule of Liao and the "Raw Jurchen" were eastern bands that were still wild and free. The "Raw Jurchen" roamed beyond the control of both the Song and Liao emperors.

7. How did the Goryeo keep out the nomadic Jurchen to the north of their country? How did their defenses hold up against the Jurchen fleeing from the Wanyan?

A7.—Pg. 636, ¶ 6 & 7—Nomadic Jurchen horsemen attacked the northern border of Goryeo often just to rob its villages. This annoyance was dealt with in the eleventh century when the kings of Goryeo built a Long Wall that started from the mouth of the Yalu river and went over three hundred miles inland. The wall was effective against random wanderers, but it didn't keep out the flood of refugees from other Jurchen tribes that were fleeing from the Wanyan.

8. How did Akuta plan to use the Liao to turn his nomads into a settled state?

A8.—Pg. 637, ¶ 2—Akuta knew that he needed a ceremonial kingship and an established bureaucracy and history to turn his wandering nomads into a settled state. Though he wanted Song approval, he approached the Liao first, demanding that the Liao extend formal recognition that Akuta was a Great Holy and Enlightened Emperor. He wanted his clan to be

known, from now on, by the Chinese name "Great Jin"; he intended to wear royal robes and ride in a jade-encrusted carriage, and he wanted the Liao to pay an annual tribute, almost as large as the tribute the Song paid to them.

9. Why did Song Huizong agree to an alliance with Akuta? What happened when the combined armies attacked the Liao?

A9.—Pg. 637, ¶ 5—Song Huizong agreed to an alliance with the Jurchen when Akuta promised that after the joint conquest of the Liao, the Song could reclaim the southern reaches of the old Liao empire: this land had once been the Chinese "Sixteen Prefectures," and it had been in enemy hands for a century. Retaking the Prefectures would shore up the Divine Mandate with a real display of victory. In 1122, the combined armies reached the Liao capital and took the emperor captive; the remains of the Liao army and a hundred thousand refugees fled west, away from the conquerors.

10. How did Qinzong become emperor?

A10.—Pg. 638, ¶ 2—Song Huizong tried to escape from responsibility for the looming defeat at the hands of the Jurchen by faking a stroke, abdicating, and ordering the royal robes placed on his heir, his twenty-five-year-old son, Qinzong. When Qinzong refused to take the job, Huizong, who was pretending that his right side was paralyzed, wrote a message with his left hand ordering his son to take up the Mandate. Qinzong still declined, so Huizong ordered the eunuchs to forcibly carry Qinzong to Blessed Tranquility Hall and put him on the throne, where, after a struggle, the grand councilors met and congratulated him as emperor.

Section III: Critical Thinking

The student may use his text to answer this question.

A written history seems to be one key to creating a legitimate nation. Li Yuanhao made sure that a script was created for the Tangut language so the history of his people and culture could be recorded. Akuta also knew that he needed to create a history for the Jurchen people in order for them to be declared legitimate. But what good is history when a dynasty topples? Explain how the Song's intricate history and culture could not save the dynasty from being overrun by a powerful enemy, and how that history could not restore the Song once the dynasty came to an end. In your answer make sure to include some of poetry written by Zhang Xiaoxiang, found on page 639 of your text.

Imperial recognition from the Song was sought after by new nations, like the Liao, Western Xia, and Jurchen. But while other peoples wanted to be like the Song, that didn't stop outsiders from also wanting to conquer the Song. Song Huizong, encouraged by Lin Lingsu, spent his time building Taoist temples, studying Taoist teachings, painting, reading poetry and attending tea ceremonies. All of these actions enriched Song culture, but at the same the local militia and reforms made by Song Renzong during the truce between the Western Xia, Liao and Song had fallen apart. As a result, there was no one capable enough to defend the Song in battle. Customs and art could not stop the Jurchen from taking Kaifeng, raping its women and stealing its treasure, food and animals.

The Song managed to regroup and turn itself into the "Southern Song," but the northern land taken by the Jurchens was the true cradle of Chinese culture. They occupied the valley where the most honored of its divine kings had lived, the home of the great deeds that had made the ancient Chinese empire the envy of its nomadic neighbors. As we read on page 639, the poems of the Southern Song lament the loss of ancient lands, as in this example by Zhang Xiaoxiang:

I see their forts amid the forest when I gaze toward the Yellow River,
The cloud of dust darkens the sky and the frost wind is bitter,

The silence of the border region rends my heart,
The beacon fires have been extinguished,
the soldiers given rest . . .

Yet I have heard that the old who were left behind in the central plains
Constantly look toward the south
Hoping to see the decorated imperial chariots.

The ancient connection to the place where the Mandate of Heaven was descended was broken, and no amount of history or poetry could get that back for the Song.

EXAMPLE ANSWER:

History and culture could not fight battles. Though the Song was respected by all fledgling nations, its long-held traditions and admired culture could not do the same work as a well-trained army. Song Huizong, encouraged by Lin Lingsu, spent his time building Taoist temples, studying Taoist teachings, painting, reading poetry and attending tea ceremonies. All of these actions enriched Song culture, but at the same the local militia had fallen apart, meaning there was no one to defend the Song in battle. Customs and art could not stop the Jurchen from taking Kaifeng, raping its women and stealing its treasure, food and animals.

The Song managed to regroup and turn itself into the "Southern Song," but the northern land taken by the Jurchens was the true cradle of Chinese culture. They occupied the valley where the most honored of its divine kings had lived, the home of the great deeds that had made the ancient Chinese empire the envy of its nomadic neighbors. They lived in the land where the Mandate of Heaven descended, and as described in the poetry of Zhang Xiaoxiang, the Southern Song longed to return to their cultural home: "The silence of the border region rends my heart, / The beacon fires have been extinguished,/ the soldiers given rest . . ./ Yet I have heard that the old who were left behind in the central plains/ Constantly look toward the south/ Hoping to see the decorated imperial chariots." The Southern Song would never again see their imperial chariots in the valley of the Yellow River; they could only remember and write about their roots.

Chapter Eighty-Two

Repentance at Canossa

The student may use her text when answering the questions in sections I and II.

Section I: Who, What, Where

Write a one or two-sentence answer explaining the significance of each item listed below.

Anno II—**Pg. 641, ¶ 2 & 3—Anno II, the German archbishop, worked with two other powerful German counts to have King Henry IV kidnapped so that they could rule over Germany.**

Bertha of Turin—**Pg. 642, ¶ 5, Pg. 643, ¶ 2 and Pg. 645, ¶ 4—Bertha of Turin, daughter of a prominent Italian nobleman, was betrothed to Henry V at the age of five and their marriage was celebrated when Henry IV turned fifteen. Though Henry IV tried to divorce Bertha on account of the king's inability to consummate the marriage, Bertha remained married to the king, bore him two children, and accompanied him on his penitential journey to Canossa.**

Gregory VII—**Pg. 643, ¶ 3, Pg. 645, ¶ 1 & 2 and Pg. 646, ¶ 2—Gregory VII, the papal name of archdeacon Hildebrand, followed Alexander II in 1073 as pope, determined to protect the papacy from corruption and from reliance on swords and kings. Gregory VII excommunicated Henry IV after the king continued to disobey the pope's orders, but he was forced to forgive Henry IV after the king made a penitent trip to Canossa.**

Peace of Terouanne—**Pg. 642, ¶ 2 & 3—The Peace of Terouanne was made in 1063 when priests in the northern German city of Terouanne put together another set of regulations for the Peace and Truce of God. The Peace of Terouanne stated that there would be no fighting from sunset on Wednesday until sunrise on Monday and that the Peace would be observed during every day of Advent and Lent, as well as between the church feasts of Ascension and Pentecost—a schedule that made nearly three-quarters of the year off-limits for fighting.**

Philip—**Pg. 641, ¶ 1—Philip was the son and heir of the Capetian king of Western Francia. Philip, who became king at age seven when his father died in 1060, was incapable of halting the tide of private warfare that still surged back and forth across the Frankish lands.**

Section II: Comprehension

Write a two or three-sentence answer to each of the following questions.

1. Why did the German duchies gain so much power at the start of Henry IV's rule?

A1.—Pg. 641, ¶ 2—The German duchies gained so much power at the start of Henry IV's rule because, since he was only ten years old, his mother was in charge. She did not want to be queen or regent for her son, so she avoided trouble with the noblemen of Germany by granting them power. The result was that they ruled over their duchies as if they were independent kings.

2. Describe Henry IV's capture and imprisonment.

A2.—Pg. 641, ¶ 2 & 3—Right after Easter of 1062, Anno II and two powerful German counts invited the young king to come and inspect a ship that had been outfitted particularly for his use only to capture him on board and whisk him down the Rhine. Henry dove into the river in an attempt to escape, but the water was cold and swift, and he nearly drowned before one of the conspirators dragged him back out. He was then taken to the city of Cologne where he was imprisoned in Anno II's luxurious archbishop's residence.

3. How did Pope Alexander II respond to Henry IV's request to divorce his wife? Why did Henry IV accept the pope's decision?

A3.—Pg. 642, ¶ 7 to Pg. 643, ¶ 1—Pope Alexander II absolutely refused to release Henry IV from his vows. He said that a betrayal of the Christian faith via divorce by such a public figure would set a terrible example, and that person then could never be made emperor. Even though the Normans of Italy now protected the papal states, the pope did not intend to give up his right to choose the next Holy Roman Emperor, and he would certainly not choose Henry IV if the young king was divorced.

4. Why was Pope Gregory VII opposed to the idea that a layman could appoint a church official? How was this belief made papal law?

A4.—Pg. 643, ¶ 3—Pope Gregory VII opposed the idea that a layman, no matter how royal, could appoint any church official because, he argued, that was an act that would inevitably lead to corruption, to the sale of church offices, and to the domination of the emperor over St. Peter's heir. In March of 1075 he made a papal declaration that only the pope could appoint and remove bishops, call church councils, and authorize new church laws. He also wrote that because the church of Rome had never erred, and since he was the leader of the church, he also had the power to depose emperors, and that all princes should kiss his feet.

5. What was Henry IV's first rebellion against Pope Gregory VII?

A5.—Pg. 643, ¶ 4—After Pope Gregory VII made his *Dictatus papae,* Henry IV appointed new bishops to the bishoprics of Milan, Fermo, and Spoleto. This was a direct rebellion against the pope because the pope had just claimed that only he could appoint church officials.

6. What did Pope Gregory VII suggest Henry IV might do to make up for his challenge to the *Dictatus papae*?

A6.—Pg. 643, ¶ 5 to Pg. 644, ¶ 1—In late December of 1075, Pope Gregory VII wrote Henry IV a letter, offering to approve the royally chosen bishop of Milan if the king should send away from his German court five of his advisors who had been excommunicated for their involvement in selling church offices. Faithful members of the Christian church were not supposed to associate with unrepentant sinners who had been excommunicated, meaning that Henry's willingness to exile these men would be an acknowledgement that Gregory was still his spiritual father. The restrained letter was delivered by three papal envoys who added a much stronger verbal message, admonishing Henry IV to do penance for his sins and threatening that if he did not yield to the authority of the divine laws he would be excommunicated and "deprived of his entire dignity as king without hope of recovery."

7. How did Henry IV react to Pope Gregory VII's threat?

A7.—Pg. 644, ¶ 2 to Pg. 645, ¶ 1—In response to Pope Gregory VII's threat, Henry IV convened an assembly in the city of Worms in January of 1076, less than a month after Gregory VII's warning, and under Henry's direction it was agreed that two different letters should be written over the king's signature. One, sent to Rome, accused Gregory VII of seizing the papacy without due election, trampling on the rights of the bishops, and seducing an Italian noblewoman named Matilda. The second letter circulated through Germany as a bit of royal propaganda justifying Henry's defiance of the pope.

8. What happened to Henry IV's power after Gregory VII had him excommunicated from the church? What did Henry IV decide to do in order to regain his power?

A8.—Pg. 645, ¶ 3 & 4—After Gregory VII excommunicated Henry IV, which included taking away his power as king, the noblemen of Saxony rebelled against Henry IV. Henry IV was unable to overcome them because many of the German aristocrats who had supported him in the last revolt were too nervous over Gregory VII's declaration to throw their weight behind the king. The king's power was shaken, forcing him to go on a penitential journey through the Alps, with his family as his support, to beg the pope for forgiveness.

Section III: Critical Thinking

The student may not use her text to answer this question.

Is there a difference between godly power and earthly power? How can we know if power is always enacted by men of this world? While some men claim more authority than others because it is God-given, how are the rules they impose on men any different than the rules born of man's earthly desires? Write a paragraph that explains how the motivations and rules of the pope are no different than the motivations of the king or the emperor, using Popes Alexander II and Gregory VII as examples.

In this chapter we read about popes fighting for power with kings. Pope Alexander II refused to let Henry IV get a divorce. Henry IV might control his subjects, but the pope controlled the theoretical gates to heaven. Henry IV had to listen to the pope if he wanted to have a peaceful afterlife. Pope Alexander II also refused to give up his power to choose the emperor, a play in the world of earthly power. By keeping the right to name the emperor, Pope Alexander II still played a role in the political scheme and the way power was distributed to the benefit of the church.

Pope Gregory VII made similar power plays. Though Pope Gregory VII was worried about corruption and the sale of church offices, he was also worried about the distribution of power between the church and the state. His papal declaration that only the pope could appoint and remove bishops, call church councils and authorize new church laws makes some sense, but then to claim that all princes should kiss his feet shows that his papal declaration was as much about power as anything else—he was taking the power away from the emperors and kings and giving it to himself. Pope Gregory VII's declaration that Henry IV lost his rights as king after he was excommunicated was purposeful, reigniting a previous rebellion. Pope Gregory VII forced the German king to bow down to him. People may have been afraid of getting exiled, but they were more afraid of being locked out of heaven. Pope Gregory VII used his position of religious power to influence the political landscape of his time, an act not unlike one that would be made by a self-important king or emperor.

EXAMPLE ANSWER:

Pope Alexander II refused to let Henry IV get a divorce. Henry IV might control his subjects, but the pope controlled the theoretical gates to heaven. Henry IV had to listen to the pope if he wanted to have a peaceful afterlife. Pope Alexander II also refused to give up his power to chose the emperor, a play in the world of earthly power. By keeping the right to name the emperor, Pope Alexander II still played a role in the political scheme and the way power was distributed to the benefit of the church. Pope Gregory VII made similar power plays. Though Pope Gregory VII was worried about corruption and the sale of church offices, he was also worried about the distribution of power between the church and the state. His papal declaration that only the pope could appoint and remove bishops, call church councils and authorize new church laws makes some sense, but then to claim that all princes should kiss his feet shows that his papal declaration was as much about power as anything else—he was taking the power away from the emperors and kings and giving it to himself. Pope Gregory VII's declaration that Henry IV lost his rights as king after he was excommunicated was purposeful, reigniting a previous rebellion. Pope Gregory VII forced the German king to bow down to him. Pope Gregory VII used his position of religious power to influence the political landscape of his time, an act not unlike one that would be made by a self-important king or emperor.

Chapter Eighty-Three

The Call

The student may use his text when answering the questions in sections I and II.

Section I: Who, What, Where

Write a one or two-sentence answer explaining the significance of each item listed below.

Alexius Comnenus—**Pg. 648, ¶ 3 and Pg. 650, ¶ 1—Alexius Comnenus, Michael VII's general, stopped a rebellion led by John Doukas against the emperor by hiring Seljuq Turks to beef up the royal army. Alexius Comnenus became emperor of Constantinople in 1081 after marching on Nikephoros III because he had disinherited Michael VII and empress Maria's son Constantine.**

Anna—**Pg. 650, ¶ 2—Anna, daughter of Alexius Comnenus, was engaged to co-emperor Constantine after her father became emperor of Constantinople.**

Atsiz ibn Abaq—**Pg. 649, ¶ 2—Atsiz ibn Abaq, general of the Turkish armies during the rule of Malik Shah, pushed Turkish forces south all the way to Jerusalem and finally took the city for his ruler in 1077 after massacring three thousand of its inhabitants.**

Badr al-Jamali—**Pg. 649, ¶ 1—Badr al-Jamali imposed a military dictatorship that revived the Fatimid caliphate, which had lost the north of Syria to the Turks in 1070 and was badly weakened by a six-year famine and mismanagement.**

Bohemund—**Pg. 651, ¶ 6 and Pg. 652, ¶ 2—Bohemund, son of Robert Guiscard, was left in charge of the Byzantine war after his father returned to Italy to deal with the overthrow of Gregory VII. Bohemund started losing battles as soon as his father returned to Italy.**

Constantine—**Pg. 649, ¶ 6 & 7 and Pg. 650, ¶ 2—Constantine, the son of Michael VII, was promised by his father to marry the daughter of the Norman adventurer Robert Guiscard, but these plans were thwarted when Nikephoros III disinherited Constantine. After Alexius**

Comnenus became emperor, Constantine's position as co-emperor was restored, but his betrothal to Robert Guiscard's daughter was not renewed and instead Constantine was engaged to Anna, Alexius Comnenus's daughter.

John Doukas—**Pg. 648, ¶ 3—John Doukas, Michael VII's uncle, led a rebellion against his nephew the emperor in 1074.**

Malik Shah—**Pg. 648, ¶ 5, Pg. 649, ¶ 2 & 3 and Pg. 652, ¶ 3—Malik Shah, son of Alp Arslan, took over rule of the Turks in 1073, and kept the sultanate strong by taming the sultan of Rum, reinforcing the Ghaznavid border, and taking Jerusalem for the Turks in 1077. In the last years of his reign Malik Shah converted to the Shi'ite branch of Islam, the final step in making the Turks into a Muslim people.**

Maria—**Pg. 649, ¶ 4 & 7—Maria, wife of Michael VII, married Nikephoros Botaneiates after her husband abdicated and fled to a monastery. After Nikephoros III disinherited her son, Maria appealed to Alexius Comnenus to come and restore her son's rights.**

Nikephoros Botaneiates—**Pg. 649, ¶ 4 and Pg. 650, ¶ 1—Nikephoros Botaneiates, a general, was crowned emperor Nikephoros III after being declared ruler by his army, marching on Constantinople, and taking the throne from Michael VII who abdicated peacefully and entered a monastery. When Alexius Comnenus marched on Constantinople at the request of Maria, Nikephoros III abdicated, fled to a monastery, and later died there of old age.**

Rudolf of Swabia—**Pg. 650, ¶ 6 and Pg. 651, ¶ 2—Rudolf, duke of Swabia, had managed to get himself declared rival king to Henry IV by the German aristocrats in Saxony and Bavaria and the result was three years of civil war waged between 1077 and 1081. Rudolf's rebellion ended after his right hand was cut off in battle, an injury that caused Rudolf's death two days later and the end of the revolt against Henry IV soon after.**

Urban II—**Pg. 652, ¶ 5 and Pg. 654, ¶ 3 & 5—Urban II, who became pope in 1088 after Wibert was displaced because of Henry IV's loss of power in Italy, agreed to help Byzantium in its battles against the Turks while also declaring that it was time to recapture Jerusalem from the hands of the Muslims. Urban II promised that those who fought to reclaim the holy land would have immediate remission of their sins.**

Wibert of Ravenna—**Pg. 651, ¶ 1, 5 & * and Pg. 652, ¶ 5—Wibert of Ravenna, the Italian archbishop, was elected pope in May of 1080 after Henry IV's synod agreed that Gregory VII should step down. Wibert was made Pope Clement III (generally referred to as Antipope Clement III) in March of 1084 and then four years later he was removed as pope in 1088 after Henry IV's loss of power in Italy.**

Section II: Comprehension

Write a two or three-sentence answer to each of the following questions.

1. Why did Alexius Comnenus have to hire Seljuq Turks to fight for Michael VII in 1074?

A1.—Pg. 648, ¶ 2 & 3—Michael VII liked to read and write poetry; his self-absorption meant that he paid little attention to the shrinking of his empire caused by the expanding kingdoms of the west and the swelling Turkish power in the east. In 1074, Michael VII's uncle John Doukas led a rebellion against him. Michael VII's general Alexius Comnenus had to hire soldiers from the Seljuq Turks to beef up the sparse troops still loyal to the crowned emperor.

2. What did Malik Shah accomplish in the first year of his rule over the Turks? When did Malik Shah finally take Jerusalem for the Turks?

A2.—Pg. 648, ¶ 5 to Pg. 649, ¶ 3—In the first year of his rule over the Turks, Malik Shah managed to tame the sultan of Rum into temporary loyalty, reinforce the Ghaznavid border, and handle the threat from Constantinople, but that was mostly because necessity had forced Constantinople to stop its hostilities against the Turks. With the help of Atsiz ibn Abaq, Malik Shah was able to push his kingdom all the way to Jerusalem, laying siege to the city in the same year that Malik Shah took his father's place as ruler of the Turks. Fatimid resistance in Jerusalem continued until 1077, but in that year Atsiz massacred three thousand of its inhabitants—mostly Fatimid Arabs and Jews—bringing a final end to the Fatimid attempts to hold onto the city and placing it firmly under Malik Shah's command.

3. Explain the trouble caused when Nikephoros III disinherited Constantine.

A3.—Pg. 649, ¶ 6 & 7—Before his abdication, Michael VII had promised his son Constantine in marriage to the daughter of the Norman adventurer Robert Guiscard (Robert the Fox). At the same time, Michael VII had put a large army under the command of his general Alexius Comnenus to prepare for a possible Norman invasion. When Nikephoros III became emperor, he disinherited Constantine and broke the betrothal to Guiscard's daughter, which caused Guiscard to gear up for a massive invasion in revenge, while Constantine's mother Maria appealed to Alexius Comnenus to come and restore Constantine's rights.

4. Why did Alexius Comnenus have to ask Henry IV of Germany for help protecting Byzantine territory?

A4.—Pg. 650, ¶ 3 & 4—After Alexius Comnenus engaged his daughter Anna to Constantine rather than reinstating the young co-emperor's betrothal to Robert Guiscard's daughter, the Norman began a war, arriving at the Byzantine border with a monk who claimed to be the deposed Michael VII. The people of Constantinople knew the monk was an imposter but that did not stop the ferocious attacks by Robert Guiscard and the Normans of Italy. In addition, the Turks were attacking the east and the west was in bad condition; the Byzantine empire couldn't protect itself any longer, so Alexius Comnenus turned to Henry IV of Germany for help.

5. What series of events led to Henry IV's call for Pope Gregory VII to step down from his role as the Christian church's leader?

A5.—Pg. 650, ¶ 7 to Pg. 651, ¶ 1—In 1080, Pope Gregory VII decided that Rudolf of Swabia would make a better German king than Henry IV, so he had Henry IV excommunicated again and then he announced that Rudolf was the rightful king of Germany. This decision was so clearly political in nature that most of the German bishops rejected the excommunication as unlawful, as did a number of the Italian bishops. In May of 1080, Henry IV called his own synod and it was decided by the loyal bishops that Gregory VII should step down from his role as leader of the Christian church.

6. Why did Alexius Comnenus offer 360,000 gold pieces to Henry IV in support of the German king's campaign against Italy?

A6.—Pg. 651, ¶ 3 & 4—Though Henry IV had called for Gregory VII to step down, he would eventually have to go to Rome to forcefully remove the pope. Alexius Comnenus requested that Henry IV stop worrying about German civil war and go attack Italy, sweetening the offer with the massive sum of 360,000 gold pieces to support the German's campaign against Italy. The faster Henry IV got to Italy with his troops, the sooner Robert Guiscard's attention would be taken away from attacking Byzantium and turned to protecting his Italian holdings.

7. How did Henry IV finally become the Holy Roman Emperor?

A7.—Pg. 651, ¶ 4 & 5—In March of 1081 Henry IV crossed over into Italy and attacked Rome three times, failing to breach the walls but coming closer and closer to conquest each time. Robert Guiscard was over in Byzantium and did not return home to help Pope Gregory VII; in his absence, Henry IV finally broke into Rome in June of 1083. He then worked to earn the loyalty of the Roman people over the course of a year and in March of 1084 Gregory VII was deposed, Wibert was proclaimed the new pope, and a week later, on Easter Sunday, Wibert crowned Henry IV as Holy Roman Emperor.

8. In what way did Robert Guiscard live on after his death? Be sure to include some of Dante's words in your answer.

A8.—Pg. 652, ¶ 2—Robert Guiscard lived on after his death via a reputation for conquest that lasted for centuries. Two hundred years later, the poet Dante placed him in the sphere of Mars along with Charlemagne and other great commanders, and wrote of the Byzantine soldiers who "felt the thrust of painful blows
when/ they fought hard against Robert Guiscard/whose bones are still piled up/at Ceperano."

9. How did the Turks become people of the Muslim faith?

A9.—Pg. 652, ¶ 3—After Malik Shah's armies conquered Antioch they pushed steadily into Asia Minor. As the Turks spread into Muslim land, they gradually adopted Islam. In the last years of his reign Malik Shah converted to the Shi'ite branch of the faith, the final step in making the Turks into a Muslim people.

10. What happened to the Turkish alliance after the death of Malik Shah?

A10.—Pg. 652, ¶ 4—When Malik Shah died in 1092 the Turkish alliance broke into a series of independent states. Malik Shah's four sons and one brother fought over Malik Shah's domain, fracturing it into pieces. The Sultanate of Rum broke free under Malik Shah's former vassal, Kilij Arslan and Syria, Persia, Kirman (southern Persia), and Khorasan all separated from each other, each declaring itself a sovereign Turkish realm.

11. What did Pope Urban II promise would happen to any man fighting against the Muslims for power over Jerusalem?

A11.—Pg. 654, ¶ 4 & 5—Urban II promised that a man fighting for the Christian cause in Jerusalem would be transformed into a hero, no matter his station in life prior to war. He also promised that any man that died in battle against the Muslims would have immediate remission of all his sins.

Section III: Critical Thinking

The student may use his text to answer this question. The student may also look at the previous chapter's workbook answers.

When Urban II agreed to help Alexius Comnenus fight the Turks that were attacking Byzantium, he also declared that it was time to recapture Jerusalem from the Muslims. In November of 1095, Urban II announced:

"As most of you have heard the Turks and Arabs . . . have occupied more and more of the lands of those Christians, and have overcome them in seven battles. They have killed and captured many, and have destroyed the churches and devastated the empire. If you permit them to continue thus for awhile with impurity, the faithful of God will be much more widely attacked by them. On this account I, or rather the Lord, beseech you as Christ's heralds to publish this everywhere and to persuade all people of whatever rank, foot-soldiers and knights, poor and rich, to carry aid promptly to those Christians and to destroy that vile race from the lands of our friends. I say this to those who are present, it is meant also for those who are absent. Moreover, Christ commands it.

Using what you know about leadership and power, and continuing the work from the Critical Thinking question in *Chapter 82: Repentance at Canossa*, write a paragraph explaining how Pope Urban II's declaration at Clermont in 1095 had less to do with God's will than it did with his own desire for power. In your answer, make sure to use the language of Urban II's announcement to support your analysis.

In the previous chapter the student explained how the motivation to gain power was no different for a king, or an emperor, or a pope. We see a continuation of that idea in this chapter. On page 654 of the chapter, we learn that Urban II was going to "demonstrate that the authority of St. Peter's heir stretched across the world." Urban II wanted to prove he was all powerful through his position as the head of the Christian church. In the announcement made in November of 1095 at Clermont in Western Francia, Urban II used the word "I" several times, suggesting that the motivations for the attack on Jerusalem were fueled by his own desires rather than by the power of God. "I" comes before "the Lord" when Urban II asked his listeners to act as Christ's heralds: "On this account I, or rather the Lord, beseech you. . . ." He told his listeners that he was commanding them to act against the Muslims, and after that said that God demands it, too: "I say this to those who are present. . . . Moreover, Christ commands it." The placement of "I" in the announcement reinforces the will of Urban II to rule over the world. Urban II is the one who wants the Muslims out of Jerusalem and for everyone to recognize his spiritual authority.

EXAMPLE ANSWER:

In the last chapter we realized that the desire for power in a pope is really no different from the desire for power in a king or an emperor. Pope Urban II proves this once again. Like an emperor who wants more and more territory for his kingdom, Urban II wanted to show the whole world that the Christian faith dominated and that as its earthly leader he had authority over everyone. In the announcement made in November of 1095 at Clermont in Western Francia, Urban II used the word "I" several times, suggesting that the motivations for the attack on Jerusalem were fueled by his own desires rather than by the power of God. "I" comes before "the Lord" when Urban II asked his listeners to act as Christ's heralds: "On this account I, or rather the Lord, beseech you. . . ." He told his listeners that he was commanding them to act against the Muslims, and after that said that God demanded it, too: "I say this to those who are present. . . . Moreover, Christ commands it." The placement of "I" in the announcement reinforces the will of Urban II to rule over the world. Urban II is the one who wants the Muslims out of Jerusalem and for everyone to recognize his spiritual authority.

Chapter Eighty-Four

Fighting for Jerusalem

The student may use her text when answering the questions in sections I and II.

Section I: Who, What, Where

Write a one or two-sentence answer explaining the significance of each item listed below.

Adhemar—**Pg. 660, ¶ 1-3—Adhemar, a bishop that accompanied the army of Toulouse as a representative of the pope, did not believe Peter Bartholomew's story that the Holy Lance was discovered in the church of St. Peter in Antioch. Seeing, however, that Raymond of Toulouse thought the discovery was genuine, Adhemar chose to hold his tongue and go along with the tale.**

Baldwin—**Pg. 656, ¶ 2, Pg. 658, ¶ 6 and Pg. 660, ¶ 4—Baldwin, brother of Godfrey and Eustace, became a mercenary for the king of Edessa after things got bad in Antioch and then became the adopted son of the king and also his heir. Baldwin inherited Edessa and governed it as an independent Christian state.**

Edgar Atheling—**Pg. 659, ¶ 2—Edgar Atheling, heir to the English throne who had surrendered to William the Conqueror, commanded the English fleet that arrived on the Mediterranean coast with supplies to help the crusaders stationed outside of Antioch. His important role in helping the crusaders was a nice change from his history of fighting in failed wars.**

Eustace—**Pg. 656, ¶ 2—Eustace, brother of Godfrey and Baldwin, set out with his siblings as one of the first fighters in the war for Jerusalem.**

Godfrey—**Pg. 656, ¶ 1 & 2 and Pg. 662, ¶ 4 & 6—Godfrey, duke of lower Lorraine, was the first to sell his land and set out on the road to Jerusalem. Godfrey led the crusader army in triumph against the invading Fatimids outside Jerusalem and then became duke and protector of the Kingdom of Jerusalem.**

Kerbogha—**Pg. 659, ¶ 6 and Pg. 660, ¶ 3—Kerbogha, a Turkish general, led an enormous Muslim army to Antioch, arriving at the city three days after the crusaders successfully stormed its gates in June of 1098. The crusaders drove Kerbogha and his army out of Antioch after discovering the Holy Lance within the city's walls.**

Kilij Arslan—**Pg. 657, ¶ 4—Kilij Arslan, the sultan of Rum, either killed or captured the twenty-five thousand foot soldiers and five hundred knights that marched on Nicaea because they were bored waiting for the crusades to start.**

Peter the Little—**Pg. 657, ¶ 1 and Pg. 658, ¶ 5—Peter the Little, a cleric that had suffered at the hands of the Turks and who had been preaching that everyone should strive to liberate Jerusalem, was one of the first to arrive at Constantinople, leading an army that chroniclers later called the "People's Crusade." Peter the Little tried to desert the cause when things got tough at Antioch but he was hauled back by one of the captains.**

Peter Bartholomew—**Pg. 660, ¶ 1–3 and Pg. 661, ¶ 1—Peter Bartholomew, a peasant, supposedly recovered the Holy Lance from the church of St. Peter in Antioch, a feat that gave the crusaders the will to beat the Muslim army waiting outside Antioch's walls. Peter Bartholomew suffered because of his own tale, forced to walk through fire to prove his divinity and then dying twelve days later from the burns.**

Raymond of Toulouse—**Pg. 656, ¶ 2, Pg. 660, ¶ 5 and Pg. 661, ¶ 5—Raymond of Toulouse, a Frankish duke, brought ten thousand men with him to fight in the first crusade, and he carried on the mission after Antioch, leading the crusaders to Jerusalem. After the city was taken, Raymond of Toulouse refused the title of king because the slaughter of the city's inhabitants left him unsettled.**

Robert of Normandy—**Pg. 656, ¶ 2 and Pg. 660, ¶ 5—Robert of Normandy, who, as the oldest son of William the Conqueror, had inherited Normandy at his father's death in 1087, was one of the first noblemen to go off to fight in the war for Jerusalem. Robert of Normandy was paid in gold by Robert of Toulouse to continue the fight from Antioch to Jerusalem.**

Stephen of Blois—**Pg. 658, ¶ 3 & 6 and Pg. 659, ¶ 1—Stephen of Blois, a Frankish nobleman, wrote to his wife of the impenetrable nature of Antioch. After months outside the city he deserted the cause, announcing that ill health required him to leave, taking his men to more comfortable quarters on the Mediterranean coast.**

Tancred—**Pg. 660, ¶ 5—Tancred, Bohemund's nephew, was paid by Raymond of Toulouse in gold to leave his uncle and accompany him as he left Antioch and headed towards Jerusalem.**

Taticius—**Pg. 657, ¶ 6 to Pg. 658, ¶ 1 & 5—Taticius, Alexius Comnenus's most trusted general, led the Crusader army in the spring of 1097 in a victory over Nicaea and then southwards toward Jerusalem. When things got tough outside of Antioch in February of 1098, Taticius took his men from camp and headed back towards Constantinople.**

Walter the Penniless—**Pg. 656, ¶ 3—Walter the Penniless was a Frankish nobleman that was the first to arrive at Constantinople in preparation for the fight for Jerusalem. He was travelling through the old kingdom of Bulgaria in the early summer of 1096 when his small band of men, unpaid and starving, began to steal from the villages they passed and the Bulgarians retaliated by driving some of the robbers into a nearby church and setting it on fire.**

William of Normandy—**Pg. 656, ¶ 2—William of Normandy became the second Norman king of England after his father's death in 1087.**

Section II: Comprehension

Write a two or three-sentence answer to each of the following questions.

1. Why did later chroniclers call Peter the Little's army the "People's Crusade"?

A1.—Pg. 657, ¶ 2—Later chroniclers called Peter the Little's army the "People's Crusade" because it seemed to be made up of farmers and housewives. In reality, the army was made up mostly of soldiers but it lacked high-profile aristocrats, who preferred to lead their own private armies. Without big names to chronicle, historians assumed the army was made up of laymen.

2. Why did Alexius Comnenus have Peter the Little's army camp near the Byzantine frontier? Why did the armies waiting on the frontier march against Nicaea?

A2.—Pg. 657, ¶ 2 & 3—Alexius Comnenus did not want to add thousands of restless and angry men to the population of Constantinople, so he had Peter the Little's troops move on across the Bosphorus Strait and camp near the Byzantine frontier while they awaited the rest of the crusader armies. As the army waited, more men showed up—bands of soldiers without experienced, forceful leadership. Bored crusaders were motivated by their pent up aggression and headed for Nicaea looking for a fight.

3. What oath did Alexius Comnenus make each duke that arrived in Constantinople between 1096-1097 to fight in the First Crusade take?

A3.—Pg. 657, ¶ 5—When each duke arrived in Constantinople to prepare for the First Crusade, Alexius Comnenus asked him to swear an oath that any city, country or fort that had first belonged to the Roman Empire be turned back over to Byzantium after it was taken. This crusade, Alexius Comnenus reminded them, was to be fought for the benefit of Byzantium, not for personal gain.

4. How were the crusaders inside of Antioch rallied to fight the awaiting Muslim army stationed outside the city's walls?

A4.—Pg. 660, ¶ 1-3—The peasant Peter Bartholomew told Raymond of Toulouse that the Holy Lance, the spear that had pierced the side of Jesus Christ during the Crucifixion, was inside Antioch, so Bohemund took the men to the church of St. Peter, dug a pit, and though it seemed empty at first, Peter Bartholomew climbed out clutching the point of a spear. Raymond of

Toulouse embraced the discovery as genuine, word spread through the crusader army and it was believed this was evidence of God's favor. On June 28, 1098, the crusaders charged out of Antioch with the "Holy Lance" in their midst and drove the Muslim army into retreat.

5. Though Antioch was supposed to be turned over to Byzantium, who took control of the city?

A5.—Pg. 660, ¶ 4—Though Bohemund had sworn an oath to turn over cities won in the crusades to Byzantium, he never intended on keeping his promise. Bohemund claimed that because he arranged for the surrender of the city and that the city had surrendered to him, that meant the city was now his. He stayed in Antioch as its prince, ruler of a Christian kingdom in Syria.

6. What did the landscape outside of Jerusalem look like when the crusaders arrived in June of 1099?

A6.—Pg. 661, ¶ 3—When the crusaders arrived outside of Jerusalem in June of 1099, the landscape was forbidding. It was hot, water was scarce because the Turks stopped up the springs and fouled the wells near the city, and the trees, buildings, and all possible sources of timber near the city walls had been leveled so there were no materials for fire or weapons. The pack animals died because they were deprived of water and the smell from their rotting bodies polluted the air.

7. Explain how the crusaders took Jerusalem.

A7.—Pg. 662, ¶ 1 & 2—The crusaders took Jerusalem by building siege towers out of the ships that had brought their reinforcements. The northern moat of the city was filled in, the siege towers were pushed over the newly laid dirt, and the crusaders set fire to sacks of straw and cushions stuffed with cotton that caused such dense smoke to fill the city that the people defending the wall had to retreat. Once the walls were clear the attackers lowered wooden bridges to their tops, stormed across them into the city, and then slaughtered every survivor they could find.

8. What did the approaching Fatimid army have to do with the slaughter inside of Jerusalem?

A8.—Pg. 662, ¶ 3 & 4—News had reached the crusaders that a Fatimid army was on its way from Egypt to take Jerusalem, which had once been ruled by the Fatimids, so any chance of opposition had to be wiped out inside of the city. When they arrived on August 12, the city was completely under crusader control. Godfrey led the crusader army out from the city's wall and drove the Egyptian army to retreat without a second attack.

Section III: Critical Thinking

The student may use her text to answer this question.

Pope Urban II may have told the crusaders God was on their side, but that did not mean that the victories in His name would come easily. For this Critical Thinking question, you will write a detailed account of the difficulties the crusaders faced in their taking of Antioch. To answer this question successfully, go back to your text and make an outline of the events that led to the possession of Antioch for the crusaders. Then, close your textbook and write your account of the events from your notes.

This chapter focuses on the First Crusade and the process of gaining three Christian states in the Muslim east: the county of Edessa, the Principality of Antioch, and the Kingdom of Jerusalem. In the last chapter of The History of the Medieval World, *the student will read about how the ideal of the crusades was made into law. Reinforcing the lengths the crusaders would go to in order to win back their holy states will help the student to better understand how important the final transformation of religious ideal into law would be for understanding the coming history of the Renaissance world. The ordeal the crusaders went through in order to take Antioch best represents the sacrifices crusaders would make to support their cause; it shows what they would do in the name of God.*

As listed in the directions for this Critical Thinking question, the student will go back to the chapter and make an outline of the events that led to the taking of Antioch. From there, she will close her book and then use her notes to write about how the city eventually fell to the crusaders. Below you will find a digest of the events, followed by a suggested outline, and then an example answer.

The description of the fight for Antioch begins on page 658 in paragraph 3. The crusaders first laid siege to the city on October 21 of 1097. The city was well protected: Antioch was the strongest city in Syria. The walls of the city touched the Orontes river, allowing defenders inside the city a constant supply of water and an easy way to resupply the city with food and arms. Outside of the city the crusaders were tired from months of fighting and felt overwhelmed by the city's defenses. By December, the army had stripped the surrounding countryside bare of food and fuel and when a party was sent out to forage for food farther away a Turkish detachment drove them back empty-handed. Starving horses were dying off, as were the soldiers. By January only two thousand soldiers were left from the seventy thousand that had started off from Nicaea. Conditions only worsened. Rot set in: food and garments were soaked with flood waters and there was no place for anything to dry out. As a result, pestilence broke out, further ravaging the remaining men.

Things looked bleak for the men at Antioch until Edgar Atheling showed up on March 4th on the Mediterranean coast commanding a fleet of English ships. The ships had stopped at Constantinople and were commanded by Alexius Comnenus to pick up siege materials, tools and workmen. Raymond of Toulouse and Bohemund went together to bring the siege materials back to the camp. The supplies allowed the crusaders to build additional fortifications that blocked ships from refreshing Antioch's supplies from the river. Now the city began to weaken.

As the defenders inside of Antioch lost heart, Bohemund took advantage of a Turkish guard and struck a deal: if the guard let Bohemund into the city, the Norman nobleman would ensure that the guard would be made rich and given much honor. On June 2 of 1098, the gate was opened to Bohemund and he led his men into the city. They killed the guards at the large gate known as the Gate of the Bridge and opened it from the inside, allowing the rest of the crusader army into Antioch. As the crusaders stormed in they killed everyone regardless of condition, gender or age; ten thousand people were killed on that day.

The war for Antioch was not over. Three days after the taking of the city, Kerbogha showed up with an enormous Muslim army. The crusaders shut themselves inside of the city but found that conditions were even worse than in the siege camp: dead bodies lay everywhere festering in the streets, the city was empty of food, and the crusaders were reduced to eating the rotting flesh of animals dead and buried for weeks in order to survive.

As things got worse in the city Bohemund found a way to rally the crusaders. He announced that God sent a message of deliverance and assurance. Peter Bartholomew had discovered the Holy Lance, the spear that had pierced the side of Jesus Christ during the Crucifixion, at the church of St. Peter. The crusaders believed the will of God was with them and found the power to storm the Muslim troops waiting on the other side of Antioch's walls. On June 28, 1098, the crusaders drove the Muslim army into retreat and Antioch became firmly under the control of the crusaders.

OUTLINE:

—October 21, 1097: crusaders first lay siege to Antioch

—The city has strong defenses and the people inside can get food and war supplies from the Orontes river

—December of 1097: crusaders are tired, have stripped the countryside bare and come back empty-handed from a foraging mission because of a Turkish detachment

—January 1098: 2,000 of 70,000 crusaders are left

—Flood waters means everything is wet, nothing can dry out, things start to rot

—March 4 1098: Edgar Atheling shows up on the Mediterranean coast with siege materials, tools and workmen supplied by Alexius Comnenus

—Supplies for the crusaders mean additional fortifications that can block supplies into Antioch

—Bohemund makes a deal with a guard—guard will let him in in exchange for riches and honor

—June 2, 1098: gate opened to Bohemund, guards killed at the Gate of the Bridge, gate opened and the crusaders storm Antioch—10,000 killed

—Three days later Kerbogha shows up with an enormous Muslim army

—Crusaders shut themselves inside, conditions are bad: dead bodies everywhere, no food, forced to eat animals that had been buried in the ground for weeks

—Peter Bartholomew finds the Holy Lance in the church of St. Peter

—June 28, 1098: crusaders rally, attack the Muslim army and Antioch is theirs

EXAMPLE ANSWER:

On October 21, 1097 the crusaders first laid siege to Antioch. They were surprised to find the city well-defended. Also, the people inside of the city could replenish their food and war supplies because part of the city touched the Orontes river. After a few months, the crusaders stripped the countryside of food and had to go beyond their camp for supplies. That December a group of crusaders tried to travel further for supplies but a Turkish detachment drove them back to their camp empty-handed. Things were bleak; by January of 1098 only two thousand of seventy thousand crusaders were left. In addition, everything started to rot because flood waters made their camp and clothes wet and there was no place for anything to dry out. Pestilence spread. On March 4 of 1098 things started looking up when Edgar Atheling showed up on the Mediterranean coast with siege materials, tools and workmen provided by Alexius Comnenus. The supplies helped the soldiers and gave them extra fortifications to block the river and the supplies flowing into Antioch. Then, Bohemund was able to make a deal with a guard to let him into the city in exchange for riches and honor. On June 2, 1098 the gate was opened to Bohemund. The guards at the Gate of the Bridge were killed, Bohemund opened the gate and the crusaders stormed in. Ten thousand people were killed that day. But the battle wasn't over. Three days later Kerbogha showed up with an enormous Muslim army. The crusaders shut themselves inside but conditions were bad: there were dead bodies everywhere, there was no food, and they were forced to eat animals that had been buried in the ground for weeks. Then word spread via Bohemund that Peter Bartholomew found the Holy Lance in the church of St. Peter. It seemed God was back on the crusaders' side. On June 28, 1098, the crusaders rallied, attacked the Muslim army and finally took possession of the city.

Chapter Eighty-Five

Aftershocks

The student may use his text when answering the questions in sections I and II.

Section I: Who, What, Where

Write a one or two-sentence answer explaining the significance of each item listed below.

Baldwin II—**Pg. 665, ¶ 2—Baldwin II, a distant cousin of Baldwin of Edessa, took the rule of Edessa after the death of Godfrey caused his cousin to become the leader of Jerusalem. In 1118, after the death of Baldwin, the current Baldwin of Edessa became King Baldwin II of Jerusalem.**

Bernard of Clairvaux—**Pg. 666, ¶ 1—Bernard of Clairvaux, a great monastic reformer, wrote the Rule of the Knights Templar after a church council convened at Troyes in 1129 agreed to formally recognize the monastic order.**

Confraternity of Belchite—**Pg. 664, ¶ 5—Confraternity of Belchite was formed in 1122 by Alfonso the Battler to protect the area south of the Ebro river from the Almoravids. It was the first order of Christian knights to be formed and protected by law.**

Hugh of Payens—**Pg. 665, ¶ 3 & 4—Hugh of Payens, a Frankish nobleman, went to Jerusalem in 1119 looking to better his soul. He decided that protecting pilgrims who were travelling unarmed from the coast to the Jerusalem was a righteous mission so he formed a group of like-minded men, the Knights Templar, to serve as defenders of the pilgrims.**

Section II: Comprehension

Write a two or three-sentence answer to each of the following questions.

1. Why was the capture of Zaragoza considered a crusade? What were the implications of making the capture of Zaragoza an act of holy war?

A1.—Pg. 664, ¶ 1 & 2—Alfonso the Battler had been fighting for two decades against the Muslim Almoravids and he believed that recapturing Spain for Aragon-Navarre meant recapturing it for Christ. In 1118, a church council at Toulouse decreed that the capture of the Almoravid-ruled Zaragoza could be considered a crusade. One French account even says that the pope himself promised forgiveness of the sins of those willing to besiege Zaragoza and drive the Almoravid occupiers out of the city.

2. What happened to Almoravid power in Spain after the fall of Zaragoza to Christian armies in 1118?

A2.—Pg. 664, ¶ 4—After Zaragoza fell to the Christian armies in 1118, the balance of power in Spain shifted back towards the Christian kings. The Almoravid soldiers stationed there were less and less inclined to fight to the death to keep their land. Almoravid ruler Ali ibn Yusuf remained in Marrakesh and treated Spain like a distant outpost because his power there had diminished.

3. How did Alfonso the Battler turn the crusader status of his Christian armies into military orders protected by the law? What was the first order formed?

A3.—Pg. 664, ¶ 5 to Pg. 665, ¶ 1—Alfonso the Battler turned the crusader status of his Christian armies into military orders protected by the law by giving the soldiers the status of monks, full-time servants of God. The first order formed in 1122 was called the Confraternity of Belchite and its job was to protect the area south of the Ebro river. The order's charter proclaimed that imperial authority had established a Christian knighthood and a brotherly army of Christians so that they may serve God and subdue the pagans, in this case the Almoravids.

4. How did Baldwin of Edessa become Baldwin of Jerusalem, twice?

A4.—Pg. 665, ¶ 2—Baldwin of Edessa took over as king of Jerusalem after Godfrey died of typhoid. Baldwin gave the rule of Edessa over to a distant cousin, also named Baldwin. Baldwin of Jerusalem ruled for eighteen years, expanding his kingdom, and when he died in 1118 his distant cousin who governed Edessa became King Baldwin II of Jerusalem.

5. Describe the lifestyle of the group of men formed by Hugh of Payens.

A5.—Pg. 665, ¶ 3 & 4—The group of men formed by Hugh of Payens made it their life's work to protect unarmed pilgrims travelling to Jerusalem. The men lived as monks, not taking wives, not bathing and having no personal possessions whatsoever. Like monks, they took vows of poverty, chastity, and obedience but they also carried arms with which to protect the pilgrims.

6. How did the group of men formed by Hugh of Payens come to be called the Knights Templar?

A6.—Pg. 665, ¶ 4—The services performed by the group of men formed by Hugh of Payens were so greatly appreciated by travellers to Jerusalem that King Baldwin II decided to give the group a temporary dwelling place in his own palace on the north side by the Temple of the Lord. The group came to be called the Knights Templar because of their association with the accommodations provided by the king.

7. What did Bernard of Clairvaux write in the introduction to the Rule of the Knights Templar?

A7.—Pg. 666, ¶ 1—Bernard of Clairvaux wrote in the introduction to the Rule of the Knights Templar that previously secular knights should hasten to associate themselves with the Order. The knights were no longer to rob and kill, but to seek justice and to defend the poor and the churches.

8. How was the founding of military orders, like the Knights Templar, a fitting conclusion for the drama begun by Constantine at the Milvian Bridge?

A8.—Pg. 666, ¶ 2 & 3—The founding of the military orders was a fitting conclusion for the drama begun by Constantine at the Milvian Bridge because Constantine was convincing his people and himself that he was driven to battle by something higher and more important than kingly ambition. Fighting for Christianity gave Constantine freedom from guilt over his conquests and gave him the zeal that he needed to pursue war, the same zeal that fueled the First Crusade. The military orders gave the men who joined them the same purpose that Constantine felt, and a Rule to spell out exactly what they would gain in their battles for Christ.

Section III: Critical Thinking

The student may not use his text to answer this question.

You may have come to the end of your study of the Medieval World, but the history and stories of the time will follow you into the modern day. In this final chapter you read about the formation of the Knights Templar. This particular monastic order has been fodder for myths and legends that continue to show up in popular culture. For this last Critical Thinking question you will search for contemporary mentions of the Knights Templar in creative works. Find at least three different mentions of the ancient monastic order, write a sentence or two explaining each reference, and make sure to cite the sources from which the mentions were found.

In this final Critical Thinking question the student should have a little fun researching contemporary mentions of the Knights Templar. It should be relatively easy for the student to find mentions of the order. For example, an internet search for "Knights Templar in contemporary fiction" (as of January 2015) brings up a Wikipedia page titled "Knights Templar and Popular Culture." The page has an extensive list of depictions of the Knights Templar in novels, comics, films, music and games. The three examples below are just a drop in the bucket of contemporary portrayals of the Knights Templar.

Web Address for Example Answer 1
http://www.dummies.com/how-to/content/debunking-dan-brown-the-real-knights-templar.html

Web Address for Example Answer 2
http://www.washingtonpost.com/wp-dyn/content/article/2011/03/02/AR2011030206303.html

Web Address for Example Answer 3
http://www.telegraph.co.uk/news/worldnews/northamerica/usa/1452000/Ridley-Scotts-new-Crusades-film-panders-to-Osama-bin-Laden.html

EXAMPLE ANSWER:

1. Author Dan Brown puts the Knights Templar at the center of the conspiracy theory in his 2003 novel *The Da Vinci Code*. According to the website "For Dummies," the portrayal of the Knights Templar in *The Da Vinci Code* has very little to do with the real monastic order.

2. The Knights Templar show up in Deborah Harkness's 2011 book *A Discovery of Witches*. Elizabeth Hand of *The Washington Post* says the Knights Templar are the model for the religious order of which character Matthew Clairmont, a 1,500-year-old vampire, is a member.

3. The 2005 movie *Kingdom of Heaven*, directed by Ridley Scott, is a historical drama about the 12th century crusades. In the film, Charlotte Edwardes writes for *The Telegraph*, the Knights Templar are portrayed as "the baddies." The movie glorifies the Muslim cause, but the historically accurate representation, says Dr. Jonathan Philips, is that the Knights Templar were the biggest threat to the Muslims because that was their job: "their sworn vocation was to protect the Holy Land."

Student Pages

FOR

The History of the Medieval World

How To Use This Study Guide

This Study Guide for *The History of the Medieval World: From the Conversion of Constantine to the First Crusade* is designed to be used by tutors, parents, or teachers working with both individual students and groups.

For each chapter of *The History of the Medieval World,* four sets of exercises are given.

I. Who, What, Where

This section is designed to check your grasp of basic information presented in the chapter: prominent characters, important places, and foundational ideas. You should explain the significance of each person, place or idea in **one or two complete sentences**.

II. Comprehension

This section requires you to express, in your own words, the central concepts in each chapter. You may use **two to three complete sentences** to answer each question.

III. Critical Thinking

This section requires you to produce a brief written reflection on the ideas presented in the chapter.

IV. Map Work [maps found on pages 781 & following]

This section uses a traditional method to improve your geography. In his *Complete Course in Geography* (1875), the geographer William Swinton observed:

"That form is easiest remembered which the hand is taught to trace. The exercise of the mind, needed to teach the hand to trace a form, impresses that form upon the mind. As the study of maps is a study of form, the manner of studying them should be by map-drawing."

Section IV asks you to go through a carefully structured set of steps with maps (provided on perforated pages in the back of this book): tracing repeatedly, then copying while looking at the original, and finally, where appropriate, reproducing from memory. You will be asked to use a black pencil (one that does not erase easily) as well as a regular pencil with an eraser, as well as colored pencils of various kinds. Large amounts of tracing paper are needed!

Chapter One

One Empire, Under God

You may use your text when answering the questions in sections I and II.

Section I: **Who, What, Where**

Write a one or two-sentence answer explaining the significance of each item listed below.

Arius

Byzantium

Constantia

Constantine

Diocletian

Edict of Milan

Incarnation

Licinius

Maxentius

Maximinus Daia

Nicene Creed

Section II: Comprehension

Write a two or three-sentence answer to each of the following questions.

1. Why did Constantine send Maxentius's head to North Africa?

2. What made the battle between Maximinus Daia and Licinius in 313 a holy war?

3. How did Licinius guarantee Constantine's safety on the throne after defeating Maximinus Daia?

4. How do we know Constantine was not a devout Christian?

5. What excuse did Constantine use to get rid of his co-emperor Licinius?

6. What is the paradox of Christ's existence? How does Ignatius of Antioch describe this paradox?

7. Describe the difference in Christian beliefs between the Ebionites, the Docetists, the Gnostics and the Arians as described in the chapter.

8. How did Constantine come to be anti-Arian?

9. In his support of the religion, what did Constantine offer Christians who lived in the Roman empire?

10. What happened to Arius after his condemnation at the Council of Nicaea? Why might Constantia have supported Arius?

Section III: Critical Thinking

You may use your text to answer this question.

The first thing we learned in Chapter One of *The History of the Medieval World* is that when Constantine's men marched into Rome after defeating seated ruler Maxentius, they did so with the sign of Christ marked on each shield. Christianity was not only credited with helping Constantine defeat Maxentius, but also for bringing Rome together into one united empire. Write a paragraph explaining what gave Christianity the special quality that allowed Constantine to use it to keep his Roman empire together. In your answer, make sure to explain why Constantine made the Nicene Creed law.

Section IV: Map Exercise

1. Using a black pencil, trace the rectangular outline of the frame for Map 1.1: The Empires of the Romans and Persians.

2. Using a blue pencil, trace the coastline of the Mediterranean Sea. Then trace the coastline of the Black Sea. Then, using your black pencil, trace the external limits of the two empires, Roman and Persian. Trace the dotted line that separates the two empires. Repeat these until the contours are familiar.

3. Using a new sheet of paper, trace the rectangular outline of the frame in black. Remove your tracing paper from the original. Using a regular pencil with an eraser, draw the coastline of the Mediterranean Sea, the limits of the two empires, and the coastline of the Black Sea, while looking at Map 1.1. Use the distance between the map and the rectangular frame as a guide.

4. When you are pleased with your map, lay it over the original. Erase and redraw any lines which are more than ¼ inch off of the original.

5. Look back at your map and study carefully the cities of Carthage, Rome, Athens, Alexandria, Ephesus, Nicea, Byzantium, and Antioch. When you are familiar with them, close the book. Use your regular pencil to locate and label these cities on your map. Check your map against the original. If you are more than ¼ of an inch off, erase and remark the cities while looking at the original.

Chapter Two

Seeking the Mandate of Heaven

You may use your text when answering the questions in sections I and II.

Section I: Who, What, Where

Write a one or two-sentence answer explaining the significance of each item listed below.

280

Battle of the Fei River

Fu Jian

Jin Huaidi

Sima Rui/Jin Yuandi

Sima Yan/Jin Wudi

Sixteen Kingdoms

Sun En

Three Kingdoms (territory)

Three Kingdoms (story)

Tuoba Gui

Wei Yuandi

Section II: Comprehension

Write a two or three-sentence answer to each of the following questions.

1. What was Sima Yan's motivation to claim the Cao Wei crown for himself?

2. How was the Cao Wei crown passed from Wei Yuandi to Sima Yan?

3. When Jin Wudi's armies arrived outside of Dong Wu territory and found the Jianye river blocked by barriers of iron chain, how did the Jin army break through? What happened after Jin Wudi's army broke through?

4. What was the Rebellion of the Eight Princes? What caused the rebellion?

5. How did the Hanzhao take down Luoyang and begin the destruction of the Jin empire?

6. What happened to Jin Huaidi after he was taken prisoner by Liu Cong? What happened to the remaining Jin court?

7. What actions did Fu Jian take to make his barbarian kingdom more Chinese?

8. Though joining a monastic community meant renouncing the world and giving up all ownership of private property, what benefits did joining the monastery offer?

Section III: Critical Thinking

You may not use your text to answer this question.

When Jin Wudi set about trying to reunify China, he knew he needed greater justification than force to bring together his empire. As written in our chapter, "Emperors ruled by the will of Heaven, but if they grew tyrannical and corrupt, the will of Heaven would raise up another dynasty to supplant them." Years after Jin Wudi's shortly reunified China fell apart, the Jin name managed to live on. Explain why neither the Hanzhao, nor any of the other Sixteen Kingdoms, did not try to bring a final end to the Jin. Then explain how the Jin were able to justify to themselves that the Mandate of Heaven was still alive and well in the *real* China.

Section IV: Map Exercise

1. Using a black pencil, trace the rectangular outline of the frame for Map 2.1: The Three Kingdoms.

2. Using a blue pencil, trace the outline of the Yellow Sea. Using your blue pencil, trace the line of the Yellow River. Then trace the line of the Yangtze River up to the perimeter. Using your black

pencil, trace the lines delineating the Three Kingdoms, Cao Wei, Shu Han, and Dong Wu. Repeat until the contours are familiar.

3. Trace the rectangular outline of the frame in black. Remove your tracing paper from the original. Using a regular pencil with an eraser, draw the coastline of the Yellow Sea and the lines of the Three Kingdoms, while looking at Map 2.1. Use the distance between the map and the rectangular frame as a guide. Label the Yellow and Yangtze Rivers.

4. When you are pleased with your map, lay it over the original. Erase and redraw any lines which are more than ¼ inch off of the original.

5. Look back at your map and study carefully the cities of Jianye and Luoyang. When you are familiar with them, close the book. Use your regular pencil to locate and label these cities on your map. Check your map against the original. If you are more than ¼ of an inch off, erase and remark the cities while looking at the original.

Chapter Three

An Empire of the Mind

You may use your text when answering the questions in sections I and II.

Section I: Who, What, Where

Write a one or two-sentence answer explaining the significance of each item listed below.

Asoka the Great

Brahmans

Chandragupta/*maharajadhiraja*

Chandragupta II/Vikramaditya

Ghatokacha

Kalabhra

Pataliputra

Pillar Edicts

Prabhavati

Samudragupta

Satavahana

Section II: Comprehension

Write a two or three-sentence answer to each of the following questions.

1. What lands did Samudragupta conquer during his forty-five year reign?

2. Samudragupta may have called himself "conqueror of the four quarters of the earth," but he did not actually rule over all of India. How did Samudragupta justify this title?

3. Why did Samudragupta inscribe his victories on an ancient stone pillar?

4. Where did Sanskrit come from? How are the prakrits related to Sanskrit? Who used Sanskrit during Samudragupta's time, and what important works were written in Sanskrit?

5. What is the general definition of a culture's golden age, and classical period? What must a historian do in order to identify a culture's golden age or classical period?

6. Describe both the Hindu and Buddhist elements of the Guptas.

7. What do coins from the period after Samudragupta died tell us about the transfer of power that followed his rule?

8. Describe the plot of the play *Devi-Chandra-gupta*.

Section III: Critical Thinking

You may use your text to answer this question.

When Chandragupta began to grow his empire, he realized he could not actually conquer all of the far-flung Indian lands. Instead, he collected tribute from many smaller states and let the kings and tribal chiefs of these lands continue to rule per their own will. Chandragupta's son, Chandragupta II, followed in his father's footsteps and created an empire that was tied together through peace, an "empire of the mind." Using the Chinese monk Faxian's description of Indian lands, explain what life was like in Chandragupta II's empire. Then, describe how Chandragupta II's policies created an empire of the mind, and how that led to his remembrance as the wise king Vikramaditya.

Section IV: Map Exercise

1. Using a black pencil, trace the rectangular outline of the frame for Map 3.1: The Age of the Gupta.

2. Using a blue pencil, trace the coastline of the Arabian Sea and Bay of Bengal.

Use contrasting colors to designate the territories of Chandragupta, Samudragupta, Samudragupta's tributaries, and the tributaries of Chandragupta II. Use peaks to represent the mountains. Repeat until the contours are familiar.

3. Using a new sheet of paper, trace the black rectangular outline of the frame in black. Remove your tracing paper from the original. Using a regular pencil with an eraser, draw the coastline of the Arabian Sea and Bay of Bengal and the separate territories of Chandragupta, Samudragupta, Samudragupta's tributaries, and Chandragupta II, while looking at Map 3.1. Use the distance between the map and the rectangular frame as a guide. Label the Arabian Sea and Bay of Bengal.

4. When you are pleased with your map, place it over the original. Erase and redraw any lines which are more than ¼ inch off of the original.

Chapter Four

The Persian Threat

You may use your text when answering the questions in sections I and II.

Section I: Who, What, Where

Write a one or two-sentence answer explaining the significance of each item listed below.

Ammianus Marcellinus

Constans

Constantine II

Constantius

Ezana

Hurmuz

Julian

Khosrov the Short

Magnentius

Shapur II/Shapur the Great

Tiridates

Zoroastrianism

Section II: Comprehension

Write a two or three-sentence answer to each of the following questions.

1. Why didn't the Persians attack Constantine during his rise to power?

2. For what reason were the Arabs attacking Persia in the south? Why didn't Persia fight back?

3. When Shapur II was a boy, he could do nothing to help the Persians fight against the Arabs. How did he handle the problem when he attained his majority?

4. What change did Shapur II make early in his career that showed he was intelligent, shrewd and a good administrator? Hint: think of the Tigris river.

5. Why did Constantine ask Shapur II to show mercy on the Christians living in Persia? How was this act contradicted by the conversion of the African king of Axum, Ezana, to Christianity?

6. What does "Dhu al-Aktaf" mean? Why was Shapur II called "Dhu al-Aktaf"?

7. After the failed invasion of Armenia in 336, why did Shapur II crack down on Persian Christians?

8. Why was Constantine buried in a mausoleum at the Church of the Holy Apostles?

9. How did Julian become co-emperor of the Roman empire?

10. Why was Constantius's displacement of Liberius, bishop of Rome, with a pro-Arian bishop, so offensive?

11. How did the Persians re-take control of Armenia? Describe how the Persians outsmarted the Romans who invaded Armenia at the Euphrates.

12. Describe the Roman defeat at the siege of Amida.

Section III: Critical Thinking

You may not use your text to answer this question.

Before he died, Constantine was preparing a crusade against Persia. This is not to be confused with the "Crusades" of the 11th, 12th and 13th centuries. Using a dictionary, look up the definition of crusade, and explain the different between "crusade" and "Crusade." Then, explain how Constantine's planned attack on Persia was a "crusade."

Section IV: Map Exercise:

1. Using a black pencil, trace the rectangular outline of the frame for Map 4.1: The Romans and Persians.

2. Using a blue pencil, trace the coastal outline of the Mediterranean. Then trace the outline of the Black Sea, the Caspian Sea, the Red Sea, and the Persian Gulf.

3. Using your black pencil, trace the outlines of the Prefecture of Gaul, the Prefecture of Italy, and the Prefecture of the East. Using a contrasting color, trace the outline of the Persian Empire, including Axum. Use your black pencil to trace the outline of Armenia over the contrasted color you used to show the Persian Empire. Repeat until the contours are familiar.

4. Using a new sheet of paper, trace the black rectangular outline of the frame in black. Remove your tracing paper from the original. Using a regular pencil with an eraser as you look at Map 4.1, first draw the coastlines of the Mediterranean, the Black Sea, the Caspian Sea, the Persian Gulf, and the Red Sea. Then draw the outlines of the Persian Empire (again including Axum). Finally draw the outlines of the Prefecture of Gaul, the Prefecture of Italy, and the Prefecture of the East. Remember to use the distance between the map and the rectangular frame as a guide.

5. When you are pleased with your map, place it over the original. Erase and redraw any lines which are more than ¼ inch off of the original.

6. Looking at Map 4.1, study carefully the bodies of water (the Black Sea, the Caspian Sea, the Red Sea, and the Persian Gulf) and the locations of the Franks, North Africa, Italy, Rome, Asia Minor, Byzantium, Arabia, and Armenia. When you are familiar with them, close the book. Using your pencil, try to label each. Check your map against the original. If your labels are misplaced, erase and re-mark while looking at the original.

Chapter Five

The Apostate

You may use your text when answering the questions in sections I and II.

Section I: **Who, What, Where**

Write a one or two-sentence answer explaining the significance of each item listed below.

Foederati

Goths

Jovian

Libanius

Section II: **Comprehension**

Write a two or three-sentence answer to each of the following questions.

1. Why did Julian declare that no Christian could teach literature?

2. What was the effect on the Christian community of Julian's ban on Christians teaching literature?

3. How did Julian update the old Roman religion in order to compete with the unifying power of the Christian church?

4. How did Julian deal with the northern threat posed by the Germanic tribes of the Franks?

5. Who was part of Julian's 363 campaign against Persia? Were all the groups who accompanied Julian helpful? Why or why not?

6. How did Julian plan on attacking the Persian capital of Ctesiphon?

7. What did Shapur do when he saw Roman troops approaching Ctesiphon? How did Shapur get the Romans to retreat?

8. Describe the two versions of Julian's death, one Roman and one Christian, given to us in the chapter.

9. What were the terms of the treaty Jovian made with Shapur? How did the Roman public react to the treaty?

10. After making peace with the Persians, how did Jovian deal with religious tensions in Rome? Were his new policies successful?

Section III: Critical Thinking

You may use your text to answer this question.

What is an "apostate"? In this chapter, we learn that Julian earned the nickname "Julian the Apostate," for his renunciation of Christianity, and his renewed dedication to the old Roman religion. Write a paragraph that explains the meaning of "apostate," and then explain how Julian both was and was not an "apostate."

Chapter Six

Earthquake and Invasion

You may use your text when answering the questions in sections I and II.

Section I: Who, What, Where

Write a one or two-sentence answer explaining the significance of each item listed below.

July 21, 365

Alemanni

Barbarica Conspirato

Britannia

Comes Litori

Dux Britanniarum

Flavius Theodosius

Gratian

The Huns

Procopius

Quadi

Theodosius the Elder

Valens

Valentinian

Valentinian II

Section II: Comprehension

Write a two or three-sentence answer to each of the following questions.

1. What military problems did the Roman empire face at the beginning of the co-rule of Valentinian and Valens?

2. What was Valentinian's religious policy? Why did Valentinian reverse his law against sacrificing to the Roman gods?

3. What was Valens's religious policy?

4. How did the Goths and the Romans coexist before Valens declared war on the Goths?

5. Who were the tribes north of Hadrian's Wall and on the small island west of Britannia? How long had they been in Britannia, what were their names, and where did they live, respectively?

6. Describe the state of Britannia after Theodosius the Elder squashed the participants of the Barbarian Conspiracy.

7. Meaning to censure the Roman commander that killed the Quadi king, what did Valentinian actually do when he got to the spot where Romans were attacked by the Quadis?

8. Why did the Goths ask Valens for permission to settle in Roman land? Why did he grant them permission?

9. Why, even though Valens granted the Goths asylum in Roman territory, did another war between the Romans and the barbarians manage to break out?

10. What were the circumstances of Valens' death?

11. Why did the Goths withdraw from Hadrianople? From Constantinople? Though they withdrew, why were these Gothic battles so important to the fabric of Roman culture?

Section III: Critical Thinking

You may use your text to answer this question.

Since the ancient world, different cultures have had different ways of remembering the same events. Often a lost war is glossed over by the wounded nation, or a small battle is made into an epic fight by a king looking to boost his reputation. In the past few chapters, we have seen several events interpreted differently by Roman and Christian historians. One of the most important events to affect the Roman empire was an unbiased act of nature, an earthquake followed by a tsunami. However, the event was interpreted differently by the Romans and Christians. Write a paragraph giving a brief overview of the damage done by earthquake and tsunami, and then explain how the event was rationalized differently by the Romans and the Christians. Despite the different explanations from two factions, what was the common link between their explanations?

Section IV: Map Exercise

1. Using a black pencil, trace the rectangular outline of the frame for Map 6.2: The Barbarian Approach.

2. Using a blue pencil, trace the coastal outlines: the Mediterranean, the Black Sea, the Caspian Sea, the Persian Gulf, and the Red Sea. Repeat until the contours are familiar. Then, using your black pencil, trace the (bold) outline of the Roman Empire. Include the line separating east and west. Using a contrasting color, trace the outline of the Persian Empire. Repeat again until the contours are familiar.

3. Using a new sheet of paper, trace the black rectangular outline of the frame in black. Remove your tracing paper from the original. Using a regular pencil with an eraser, first draw the coastlines of the Mediterranean, the Black Sea, the Caspian Sea, the Persian Gulf, and the Red Sea. Now draw the outline of the Roman and Persian Empires, including the line separating east and west. Remember to use the distance between the map and the rectangular frame as a guide.

4. When you are pleased with your map, place it over the original. Erase and redraw any lines which are more than ¼ inch off of the original.

5. Using your regular pencil while looking at Map 6.2, label all the territories: Hispania, Gaul, Italy, Sicily, Crete, Dacia, Macedonia, Thracia, Asia, Syria, Egypt, North Africa, Armenia.

6. Now outside the perimeter of the Roman Empire, find different colors to denote the Saxons, Franks, Vandals, Bergundians, Alemanni, Quadi, Goths, and Huns. Use the color for the Huns to draw the big arrow associated with their movement.

7. Now study the cities: Rome, Milan, Corinth, Nicaea, Constantinople, Hadrianople, Thyatira, Antioch, and Alexandria. When you are familiar with them, close the book. Using your regular pencil while looking at Map 6.2, label all the cities. Check your map against the original. Erase and re-mark any misplaced labels.

Chapter Seven

Refounding the Kingdom

You may use your text when answering the questions in sections I and II.

Section I: **Who, What, Where**

Write a one or two-sentence answer explaining the significance of each item listed below.

Chimnyu

Geunchogo

Gogugwon

Goguryeo

Guanggaeto

Guanggaeto Stele

Malananda

Micheon

Naemul

Samskrita

Sosurim

Sun-do

T'aehak

Section II: Comprehension

Write a two or three-sentence answer to each of the following questions.

1. Who populated the north and south part of the Korean peninsula at the time when the Chinese dynasty of the Han was still in power?

2. What were the Chinese holdings in Korea when the Han fell?

3. What military disasters occurred while Gogugwon hid in his royal palace for thirty years?

4. Why did both the Goguryeo and the Baekje kings accept Buddhism into their kingdoms?

5. How did the king of Baekje come to pay homage to King Guanggaeto of Goguryeo?

6. How did Guanggaeto earn himself the nickname "The Great Expander"?

Section III: Critical Thinking

You may use your text to answer this question.

When King Sosurim came to Goguryeo's throne, his kingdom was a mess. The Buddhist and Confucian teachings of the monk Sun-do helped Sosurim shape the kingdom that would later become very powerful under the leadership of Sosurim's nephew, Guanggaeto. Write a paragraph explaining the Buddhist and Confucian teachings that fortified the weak Goguryeo, and how these ideas could exist together. Explain how these teachings promised future success for the kingdom while leaning on the past for support.

Chapter Eight

The Catholic Church

You may use your text when answering the questions in sections I and II.

Section I: Who, What, Where

Write a one or two-sentence answer explaining the significance of each item listed below.

Ardashir II

Emperor Theodosius I

Jerome

Section II: Comprehension

Write a two or three-sentence answer to each of the following questions.

1. What did Gratian, a devout Christian, do to show the Senate that he would not allow the Roman gods to undermine the empire's Christian faith?

2. By rejecting the Roman gods and traditions, what else was Gratian rejecting?

3. How did Theodosius deal with the destructive power of Christian division that had spread to even the lowest levels of Roman society?

4. What does "catholic" mean? What was the main tenet of the catholic Christian Church?

5. After Theodosius's law declaring that Nicene Christianity was the one true faith of the Roman empire, what legally defined heresy? According to the law, how would heretics be punished?

6. What actions did Theodosius take to enforce religious uniformity?

7. Why did Gratian hand over part of his western empire to Theodosius?

8. How did Theodosius beef up his army to fight against the Goths?

9. What were the terms of the treaty Theodosius made with the Goths in 382?

10. Why was Theodosius's 381 declaration that the bishop of Constantinople would be equal to the bishop of Rome met with an uproar? How did the bishop of Rome react to this new law?

Section III: Critical Thinking

You may not use your text to answer this question.

While Constantine realized that Christianity could be the rope that tied his empire together, he did not do away with Roman custom. Rather, he added Christianity into the mix while continuing to honor Roman traditions. Both Gratian and Emperor Theodosius I followed in Constantine's footsteps, attempting to unify their kingdoms with Christianity. Explain how these two leaders attempted to make Christianity the highest belief in the Roman empire. Then explain how Theodosius I's laws backfired, and actually caused division instead of unity within his kingdom.

Chapter Nine

Excommunicated

You may use your text when answering the questions in sections I and II.

Section I: Who, What, Where

Write a one or two-sentence answer explaining the significance of each item listed below.

Ambrose

Arbogast

Galla

Justina

Macsen Wledgi

Magnus Maximus

Quintus Aurelius Symmachus

Shapur III

Stilicho

Theodosian Decrees

Vandal

Section II: Comprehension

Write a two or three-sentence answer to each of the following questions.

1. What hint of historical truth about Magnus Maximus's reign can we find in the epic *Breuddwyd Macsen*? Why would he appear in Welsh legend?

2. Geoffrey of Monmouth's *History of the Kings of Britain* includes a story inspired by Magnus Maximus's attack on Gaul, about King Arthur sailing into Gaul, laying waste to the countryside and setting up a royal court at the old Roman fortress town Lutetia Parisiorum, on the Seine. What is the real story of Magnus Maximus's attack on Gaul?

3. When Magnus Maximus took control of Gaul, how was the whole of the Roman empire divided?

4. What were the circumstances of the alliance made between Magnus Maximus and Theodosius?

5. What were the terms of the Armenian treaty made between Shapur III and Stilicho in 384?

6. What happened when Justina sent officials to the Basilica in Milan on the Friday before Palm Sunday to change the hanging in the church?

7. What did Ambrose preach while he was staging his sit-in at the Basilica? Why was this offensive to Justina, and the Arians?

8. Even though Magnus Maximus had originally fought wars for territory in the name of the Roman god Jupiter, why did he decide to attack Valentinian II as a defender of the Nicene faith?

9. Why did Theodosius surround himself with men like Arbogast?

10. What was the theoretical imperial answer to Quintus Aurelius Symmachus's question, "Why did all Romans have to practice the same faith?"

11. Why was Theodosius excommunicated from the Christian church by Ambrose in 390?

12. After accepting several months of penance and being readmitted into the church, what did Theodosius do to assert his imperial power?

Section III: Critical Thinking

You may use your text to answer this question.

In order to use the Christian faith to unify the Roman empire, the church leaders had to be given significant power. Yet, how much was too much? If the church could make rules that trumped the law, who was really in control—the emperor, or the church? First, explain how Theodosius and Ambrose were able to work together to squelch Quintus Aurelius Symmachus and the senators of the imperial court's requests to reinstate the old Roman religion. Then explain how Theodosius's excommunication from the church showed that a bishop like Ambrose might have more power than the emperor of Rome.

Section IV: Map Exercise

1. Using a black pencil, trace the rectangular outline of the frame for Map 9.1: The Empire in Thirds.

2. Using a blue pencil, trace the outline of the Mediterranean while looking at Map 9.1. Using a black pencil, label the territories of Britannia, Hispania, Gaul, Italy, North Africa, Pannonia, Thracia, Egypt, and Syria. Then, using a contrasting color, trace the outline of the Persian Empire (including Armenia). Finally, using your black pencil, trace the territories of Magnus Maximus, Valentinian II, and Theodosius. Repeat until the contours are familiar.

3. Trace the rectangular outline of the frame in black. Remove your tracing paper from the original. Using a regular pencil with an eraser as you look at Map 9.1, draw the outline of the Mediterranean and the outlines of the territories of Magnus Maximus, Valentinian II, and Theodosius. Draw the outline of the Persian Empire as well. Erase and redraw as necessary as you look at the map.

4. When you are pleased with your map, lay it over the original. Erase and redraw any lines which are more than ¼ inch off of the original.

5. Using a blue pencil, trace the outlines of the Black Sea, the Red Sea, the Persian Gulf and the Caspian Sea.

6. Study the regions of Britannia, Hispania, Gaul, Italy, North Africa, Pannonia, Thracia, Egypt, and Syria. When you are familiar with them, close the book. Using your regular pencil, label all nine. Check your map against the original. Correct and replace any misplaced labels.

Chapter Ten

Cracked in Two

You may use your text when answering the questions in sections I and II.

Section I: Who, What, Where

Write a one or two-sentence answer explaining the significance of each item listed below.

Alaric

Arcadius

Battle of the Frigidus

Ethnogenesis

Eugenius

Honorius

Magister militum

Placida

Rufinus

Visigoth

Section II: Comprehension

Write a two or three-sentence answer to each of the following questions.

1. Why did Arbogast side with the Roman senate after Valentinian II's suicide?

2. What mystical things happened during the Battle of the Frigidus that predicted the defeat of Eugenius and Arbogast by Theodosius, Stilicho, and Alaric?

3. What might have caused the "divine wind" that blew up during the Battle of the Frigidus?

4. Why did the Christian historian Orosius call the Battle of the Frigidus a battle of "pious necessity"?

5. What were the signs that the great warrior Alaric was treated poorly by the Romans because of his barbarian blood?

6. How did the historians of the late Roman empire, in particular Jordanes and Cassiodorus, define the Goths? Before Alaric, were the Goths a real nation?

7. How did Arcadius and Rufinus handle the Visigoth threat?

8. What were the circumstances of Rufinus's death?

9. Why was Rufinius murdered, and not Arcadius?

10. Why did Eutropius have Stilicho declared an enemy to the empire?

Section III: Critical Thinking

You may not use your text to answer this question.

The trouble Theodosius faced trying to unite the Roman empire under Christianity could make it seem like bringing people together under one idea would be impossible. However, in the midst of Rome's turmoil, Alaric managed to create a new nation out of a motley group of people because of the very fact that they all did believe in the same thing. Write a paragraph explaining how Alaric was able to create a Visigoth nation. In your answer, make sure to explain how he was able to do this even though the Visigoths did not have a homeland.

Chapter Eleven

The Sack of Rome

You may use your text when answering the questions in sections I and II.

Section I: Who, What, Where

Write a one or two-sentence answer explaining the significance of each item listed below.

Aetius

Attalus

Augustine

Battle of Pollentia

Comes Africae

Constantine III

Donatists

Fravitta

Gildo

Manichaeism

Mascezel

Theodosius II

Yazdegerd I

Section II: Comprehension

Write a two or three-sentence answer to each of the following questions.

1. Briefly recap the story of Augustine's conversion from Manichee to Nicene Christian.

2. What was the dispute particular to the North African Christians that Augustine faced when he returned home from Milan?

3. What is the fundamental difference between the Donatists and the Christians of Augustine's church?

4. Why might the Donatists have insisted on the purity of their members in the time of political turmoil faced by the Roman empire?

5. What was the most immediate problem for Stilicho caused by Gildo's rebellion? How did Stilicho decide to handle the problem?

6. What were the circumstances of Mascezel's victory against Gildo?

7. What do Rufinius, Eutropius, and Gainas have in common?

8. Why did the Visigoth king Alaric invade Italy in 400?

9. Why didn't Honorius launch an attack from Ravenna on the invading Visigoths? What was the result of Honorius's inaction?

10. Explain why Arcadius bucked with tradition and did not name his son Theodosius II co-emperor when he was an infant. How did Yazdegerd I of Persia come to be the guardian of Theodosius II?

11. What were the terms of the treaty settled upon after the Battle of Pollentia?

12. What were the circumstances of Stilicho's execution?

13. After being bribed out of Rome with gold, silk, leather and pepper, why did Alaric lay siege to Rome a second time?

14. After being named Attalus's *magister militum* and given a Roman hostage to ensure good faith between the Visigoths and the Romans, what caused Alaric to attack Rome a third time?

15. How did Augustine react to Alaric's Sack of Rome?

Section III: Critical Thinking

You may use your text to answer this question.

It took Visigoth king Alaric three attacks on Rome to get his point across—not only did he deserve recognition for his leadership, but also Rome was not all it was cracked up to be. Alaric might have wanted acceptance from Roman leaders, but his Sack of Rome also showed that it was not untouchable. In the chapter we learn that Alaric's Sack of Rome was not the most devastating attack the city had seen, but it was very damaging in terms of morale. Write a paragraph explaining why Alaric's Sack of Rome was so symbolically destructive.

Section IV: Map Exercise

1. Using a black pencil, trace the outlines of the rectangular frame of Map 11.1: The Visigoth Invasion.

2. Using a blue pencil, trace the coastline of the Mediterranean and the Black Sea. (You do not need to trace the outline of the Red Sea at this time.)

3. Using a black pencil, trace the outline of the Roman Empire, east and west. Include the dividing center line between east and west. Trace the mountain peaks of the Alps, simply using small peaks. Repeat until the contours are familiar.

4. Using a new sheet of paper, trace the rectangular frame of the map in black. Remove your tracing paper from the original. Using a regular pencil with an eraser as you look at Map 11.1, draw the outline of the Mediterranean and the Black Sea. Erase and redraw as necessary.

5. When you are pleased with your map, lay it over the original. Erase and redraw any lines which are more than ¼ of an inch off the original.

6. Now carefully study the locations of Gaul, North Africa, Italy, Sicily, Illyricum, Asia, Egypt, and Syria. When you are familiar with them, close the book. Using your regular pencil with the eraser, label all eight locations. Check your map against the original. Erase and re-mark any misplaced labels.

7. Now carefully study the cities of Toulouse, Hippo Regius, Carthage, Ravenna, Milan, Jerusalem, and Bethlehem. When you are familiar with them, close the book. Using your regular pencil with the eraser, label all eight locations. Check your map against the original. Erase and re-mark any misplaced labels.

8. Now study the locations of the Franks (inside and outside the limits of the Roman Empire), the Visigoths, and the Ostrogoths. When you are familiar with them, close the book. Choose three different colors to represent the Franks, the Visigoths, and the Ostrogoths. Use these three colors to label the locations of each barbarian group. Use the color you used for the Visigoths to draw the

arrows that show their movement. Check your map against the original, and erase and re-mark any misplaced labels.

9. Study the location of the Battle of Pollentia. When you are familiar with it, close the book, and mark the location on the map. Check your final map against the original. Erase and re-mark if necessary.

Chapter Twelve

One Nature versus Two

You may use your text when answering the questions in sections I and II.

Section I: Who, What, Where

Write a one or two-sentence answer explaining the significance of each item listed below.

Avesta

Bahram

Codex Theodosianus

Council of Ephesus

Monophysitism

Nestorianism

Pulcheria

Section II: Comprehension

Write a two or three-sentence answer to each of the following questions.

1. What measures did the Persian Yazdegerd I take to keep Roman Theodosius II safe during his guardianship of the young Roman heir?

2. Why did Persians give Yazdegerd the nickname "Yazdegerd the Sinner"?

3. What spurred Yazdegerd to finally persecute Persian Christians?

4. How did Yazdegerd die? Explain the myth associated with Yazdegerd's death, and its meaning.

5. How did the fight between the Persians and the Romans that began with Theodosius II's declaration of war against Yazdegerd end?

6. What civic acts did Theodosius II undertake during the Persian-enforced peace of his early years?

7. What was the purpose of creating the university in Constantinople?

8. Why was Arianism considered the religion of the barbarians?

9. In the debate between monophysitism and Nestorianism, where did Mary fit in?

10. In what way was the decision made at the Council of Ephesus a decision about power, rather than religion?

11. Why did the bishops in the eastern empire suspect that Nestorius's two-natured beliefs were influenced by the Persians?

12. If the arguments over Christology weren't just about monophysitism versus Nestorianism, what were they really about?

Section III: **Critical Thinking**

You may use your text to answer this question.

Constantine thought belief in Christ would unite Rome. As we read more about the history of the medieval world, we see that not only would Christ *not* unite Rome, Christianity itself would be divided. Use this space to list all of the sects of Christianity we have read about up to this point, and explain the major belief of each sect. Start with the division between Arian and Nicene Christianity. You can use your text to go back and refresh your memory. Once you've made your list, explain why Constantine's idea that Rome could be united under Christianity could never last.

Chapter Thirteen

Seeking a Homeland

You may use your text when answering the questions in sections I and II.

Section I: Who, What, Where

Write a one or two-sentence answer explaining the significance of each item listed below.

Ataulf

Attila

Constantius

Wallia

Section II: Comprehension

Write a two or three-sentence answer to each of the following questions.

1. Describe the burial Alaric was given by his men. Why was this type of burial significant to Alaric's memory?

2. How did Ataulf join the Visigoth kingdom with the Roman empire without shedding any blood?

3. Why did Ataulf think Gaul would be a good place to vie for a Visigoth homeland?

4. Why did Constantine ditch his position as leader of the British in Gaul to join the church? Was this move a smart one?

5. Where did Ataulf first settle the Visigoths in Gaul, in 413?

6. How did Attalus manage to become, once again, a rival emperor to Honorius?

7. What happened when Honorius heard that Attalus and Ataulf were making a play for the Roman empire?

8. What were the circumstances of Ataulf's death?

9. Explain the terms of the deal Wallia made with Constantius and Honorius to end the war between the Visigoths and the western Roman empire.

10. What happened to Placida and Aetius when they returned to the western Roman empire?

Section III: Critical Thinking

You may use your text to answer this question.

Visions of grandeur are often paired with skewed visions of reality. Ataulf, after successfully campaigning for the Visigoths, believed he could become the emperor of Rome. Write a paragraph explaining how Ataulf's dream of being a great king of Rome ruined his chances at *actually* being a great king of the Visigoths.

Section IV: Map Exercise

1. Using a black pencil, trace the rectangular outline of the frame for Map 13.1: Visigoth Kingdom.

2. Using a blue pencil, trace the coastal outline present on the map: (the Atlantic) around Britannia and down along the shores of the Saxons and Franks and then Hispania. Continue to trace the coastline as it turns into the Mediterranean inside Hispania and North Africa and so forth. Now trace the perimeter of the Roman Empire, including the center line dividing east and west. Use a contrasting color to show the Kingdom of the Visigoths. Repeat until the contours are familiar.

3. Using a new sheet of paper, trace the rectangular frame of the map in black. Remove your tracing paper from the original. Using a regular pencil with an eraser as you look at Map 13.1, draw the complete coastal outline present on the map. Then draw the outline of the Roman Empire. Draw the outline of the Kingdom of the Visigoths and shade to delineate from the Roman Empire. Compare with the original, and erase and redraw as necessary.

4. When you are pleased with your map, lay it over the original. Erase and redraw any lines which are more than ¼ of an inch off the original.

5. Now study the locations of the barbarians: the Visigoths, the Vandals, and the Franks. Also study the locations of the cities of Toulouse, Milan, Ravenna, Rome, Hippo Regius, and Carthage. When you are familiar with them, close the book. Using your regular pencil, mark the locations of the barbarian regions, including the Kingdom of the Visigoths, and the cities. Check your map against the original. Correct any misplaced labels.

Chapter Fourteen

The Gupta Decline

You may use your text when answering the questions in sections I and II.

Section I: Who, What, Where

Write a one or two-sentence answer explaining the significance of each item listed below.

Ajanta Caves

Budhagupta

Harishena

Hephthalites

Kumaragupta

Mahayana school of Buddhism

Mekala

Narendrasena

Skandagupta

Theravada school of Buddhism

Viharas

Section II: Comprehension

Write a two or three-sentence answer to each of the following questions.

1. Describe the contradictory composure of the India that Chandragupta II left for his son Kumaragupta when he died in 415.

2. Why did the Indians call the Hephthalites *hunas* if they were not related to the Huns in the west? What two other designations were there for the Hephthalites?

3. How do Roman historians describe the Hephthalites as different from other nomadic invaders? Where did Arab geographers stand on the matter? How did the Indians see the Hephthalites?

4. What does the royal inscription about Kumaragupta, that his fame "tasted the waters of the four oceans," mean? Why is he remembered as the "lord of the earth" and the "Moon in the firmament of the Gupta dynasty"?

5. Though Kumaragupta was remembered as the "lord of the earth," what troubles did he face at the end of his reign? What do the coins from the end of Kumaragupta's reign tell us about these troubled times?

6. How do we know that religion flourished during the crumbling of the Gupta empire?

7. Why was the intersection between Harishena's victories and the cave-temples he built in Ellora a fluke?

8. Where did the monks who lived in the viharas get their food and clothing?

9. What was the relationship between Theravada Buddhism and the monastic experience?

Section III: Critical Thinking

You may not use your text to answer this question.

As we have read about the political and religious turmoil in the Roman empire, we've seen that not only did religion shape the culture of the Romans, but it also played a role in dictating who was in power. In India, we also see religion shaping culture, but it was not a player in India's politics. Write a paragraph explaining how Theravada Buddhism was a model for the way the independent entities that made up India co-existed without struggling for power and dominance.

Chapter Fifteen

Northern Ambitions

You may use your text when answering the questions in sections I and II.

Section I: Who, What, Where

Write a one or two-sentence answer explaining the significance of each item listed below.

Ciu Hao

Ge Hong

Huang

Jiapu

Jon Gongdi

Kou Qianzhi

Liu Song

Liu Yu/Song Wudi

Shao

Song Wendi

Song Xiaowu

Wei Taiwu

Section II: Comprehension

Write a two or three-sentence answer to each of the following questions.

1. In what way did the power of the aristocrats finally bring an end to the Jin?

2. Why did Liu Yu choose to make the abdication of the Jin throne legal?

3. How did Jin Gongdi die? How did Song Wudi react to the former Jin emperor's death?

4. What was the "Reign of Yuanjia"? What happened during the "Reign of Yuanjia"?

5. How was the Bei Wei kingdom under Wei Taiwu organized?

6. What type of religion did Ciu Hao practice? What is the difference between traditional Taoism and the type of Taoism Ciu Hao practiced?

7. Why did Wei Taiwu order the slaughtering of Buddhist monks in the Bei Wei empire?

8. Why did Song Wendi of the Liu Song deny Wei Taiwu's suggestion of a marriage alliance between the two empires? What did Song Wendi do after he refused the alliance?

9. How did Song Xiaowu's son react to his father's death? How does this reflect the fading of the Mandate of Heaven?

Section III: Critical Thinking

You may use your text to answer this question.

Finish the sentence: "Money can't buy you . . ." There are many ways to conclude this thought; for Wei Taiwu, money couldn't buy him an authentic Chinese identity, or empire. Wei Taiwu did his best to infuse the Bei Wei with Chinese tradition—hiring a Chinese advisor, bringing Chinese administration to Bei Wei and ruling his empire with Chinese law. Write a paragraph explaining how Wei Taiwu's institution of a state religion, and the obtaining of the charm book, could also be understood as an effort to duplicate Chinese culture; in this case, the Mandate of Heaven.

Chapter Sixteen

The Huns

You may use your text when answering the questions in sections I and II.

Section I: Who, What, Where

Write a one or two-sentence answer explaining the significance of each item listed below.

Bleda

Burgundians

Dioscorus

Eugenius

Geiseric

Gundahar

Leo I

Nibelungenlied (Song of the Nibelungs)

Orestes

Suevi

Valentinian III

Section II: Comprehension

Write a two or three-sentence answer to each of the following questions.

1. What was the state of the western Roman empire at the time of Honorius's death?

2. How did Aetius force his way into the role of Valentinian III's *magister militum*?

3. Before 434, why hadn't the Huns launched a sustained attack on the Romans?

4. Why was Leo I upset with the bishop of Thessalonica? What was Leo I's reasoning as to why the bishop of Thessalonica could not act the way that he did?

5. Why did Dioscorus, bishop of Alexandria, call together a hasty church council in Ephesus to affirm his version of monophysitism as orthodox? Why did Dioscorus excommunicate Leo I at the church council?

6. Why was the council held in Ephesus by Dioscorus called the "Robber Council," or the Latrocinium?

7. What was Honoria's motivation for sending a marriage proposal to Attila the Hun?

8. After Theodosius II's death, who did Pulcheria choose as a husband to help her rule the eastern empire? What were the terms of their marriage?

9. How did Pulcheria and Marcian manage to avoid an attack by the Huns after refusing to pay Attila the bribes Theodosius II had been shelling out to keep Constantinople safe?

Section III: Critical Thinking

You may use your text to answer this question.

Until the rule of Rua, the Huns had not been able to sustain a prolonged attack on Rome because they were not a single unified force. Rua was able to extend his power to Hun tribes unrelated to his own, increasing the strength of the Huns and creating something like a nation. When Attila took over, he continued to grow the power, size and strength of the Huns. Write a paragraph describing Attila's headquarters, and then explain how the village he built as his temporary capital exemplified the rising force of the Huns.

Section IV: Map Exercise

1. Using a black pencil, trace the rectangular outline of the frame for Map 16.1: The Approach of the Huns.

2. Using a blue pencil, trace the coastlines of the Atlantic, the Mediterranean, the Black Sea, the Sea of Azov, the Caspian Sea, the Persian Gulf, and the Red Sea. Include the coastline of Britannia. Using your blue pencil, trace the path of the Danube along the perimeter of the Roman Empire. Using a black pencil, trace the perimeter of the Roman Empire, including the line dividing east and west. Then trace the outline of the Persian Empire. Repeat until the contours are familiar.

3. Using a new sheet of paper, trace the rectangular frame of the map in black. Remove your tracing paper from the original. Using a regular pencil with an eraser as you look at Map 16.1, draw the complete coastal outline present on the map: the Atlantic around Britannica, and above the region of the Saxons down through the Mediterranean. Include the Black Sea, the Sea of Azov, the Caspian Sea, the Persian Gulf, and the Red Sea. Then draw the outline of the Roman Empire and the outline of the Persian Empire. Draw the outline of the Kingdom of the Visigoths and shade to delineate it from the Roman Empire. Using your blue pencil, draw the line of the Danube along the perimeter of the Roman Empire. Refer to the map as necessary as you draw. Compare with the original, and erase and redraw as necessary.

4. When you are pleased with your map, lay it over the original. Erase and redraw any lines which are more than ¼ of an inch off the original.

5. Study carefully the regions of Iberia, Gaul, Illyricum, and North Africa. When you are familiar with them, close the book. Using your regular pencil, mark all four on the map. Check your map with the original, and make any necessary corrections.

6. Study carefully the regions of the Huns, the Goths, the Vandals, the Visigoths, the Burgundians, the Alemanni, the Franks, and the Saxons, as well as the Suevi. Take especial note of the Kingdom of the Visigoths and the Kingdom of the Vandals. Note the movement in the map from the Huns to the left of the map down through Iberia, including the movement of the Vandals to their kingdom in North Africa. When you are familiar with these, close the book. Using your regular pencil, label each area with its barbarian inhabitants, and indicate the barbarian movement with arrows as is done on the original map. Check your map against the original. Correct any misplaced labels. When your map is complete, shade the Kingdoms of the Visigoths and the Vandals.

Chapter Seventeen

Attila

You may use your text when answering the questions in sections I and II.

Section I: **Who, What, Where**

Write a one or two-sentence answer explaining the significance of each item listed below.

Ildico

Merovech

Salians

Theodoric I

Thorismund

Section II: **Comprehension**

Write a two or three-sentence answer to each of the following questions.

1. After Attila took Metz for the Huns, how far did his territory reach? Who did Aetius get to help him defend Rome's capitals against Attila?

2. Why did the Salian chiefs grow their hair long?

3. What war strategy did Aetius use when he met Attila in June of 451 in battle at Châlons-sur-Marne?

4. Describe the losses suffered on the Roman side during and after the battle at Châlons-sur-Marne.

5. Describe Attila's attack on Italy after the Huns' defeat at Châlons-sur-Marne. What stopped Attila's ravaging of Italy?

6. What were some of the otherworldly explanations that the Romans came up with to explain Attila's agreement to a peace after meeting with Leo the Great?

7. What were the plausible reasons for Attila's agreement to a peace with Rome?

8. How did Attila the Hun die?

9. What happened to the Huns after Attila's death?

Section III: Critical Thinking

You may use your text to answer this question.

Leo the Great, the bishop of Rome and the first pope of the Catholic church, may seem like an unlikely candidate to make peace between the Roman Empire and Attila the Hun. But, he did just that. Write a paragraph explaining why Leo the Great was able, as a spiritual leader, to take such an active political role at the time of Attila's aggression.

Chapter Eighteen

Orthodoxy

You may use your text when answering the questions in sections I and II.

Section I: Who, What, Where

Write a one or two-sentence answer explaining the significance of each item listed below.

Battle of Vartanantz

Vartan

Yazdegerd II

Section II: Comprehension

Write a two or three-sentence answer to each of the following questions.

1. Describe the state of Christianity in the Roman empire when Marcian called a church council at Chalcedon in 451. For what religious reason did Marcian call the council?

2. What were Marcian's beliefs about Christ's two natures? Why did this complicate Marcian's dealings with the various bishops of the Roman empire?

3. For what political reason did Marcian call the 451 church council at Chalcedon? Why did Marcian want the council held at Chalcedon?

4. What did Leo expect to happen after his statement on Christ's two natures was read at the Council of Chalcedon? What actually happened?

5. How was the Syrian Orthodox Church formed?

6. For how long did Yazdegerd II's welcome of Christians from Rome after the Council of Chalcedon last?

7. Why did Yazdegerd II declare Zoroastrianism as the single faith of the Persian empire? How did the Armenians react to his decree?

8. After putting down rebellious Christians in Armenia at the Battle of Vartanantz, what further measures did Yazdegerd II take to prevent challenges to the orthodoxy of Zoroastrianism?

Section III: Critical Thinking

You may not use your text to answer this question.

This chapter is titled, "Orthodoxy." To be orthodox means to adhere to what is commonly accepted, what is customary or traditional. Yet, in our chapter, we did not read about people of the medieval world adhering to custom; we read about powerful figures establishing laws that were meant to create orthodoxy, and their subjects rebelling against these decrees. Write a paragraph explaining how the imposition of orthodoxy in the Roman empire actually created division instead of unity. In your answer, explain why the growing power of the clergy prompted Marcian to fight for the increased power of the bishop of Constantinople, and how that added to the divisions within the Roman empire.

Section IV: Map Exercise

1. Using a black pencil, trace the rectangular outline of the frame for Map 18:1.

2. Using a blue pencil, trace the coastline of the Mediterranean, the Black Sea, and the small corner of the Red Sea visible towards the bottom of the map. Still using your blue pencil, trace the outline of the Nile river. Then trace the outline of the Tigris and Euphrates. Repeat until the contours are familiar.

3. Using your black pencil, trace the dotted outline of the Eastern Roman Empire. Then, using a contrasting color, trace the outline of the Persian Empire. Use your black pencil to trace the outline of Armenia inside the Persian Empire. Repeat until the contours are familiar.

4. Using a new sheet of paper, trace the rectangular frame of the map in black. Remove your tracing paper from the original. Using your regular pencil with an eraser, trace the coastal outlines and the outlines of the Roman and Persian empire.

5. When you are pleased with your map, lay it over the original. Erase and redraw any lines that are more than ¼ inch off of the original.

6. Label the Eastern Roman Empire and the Persian Empire and then the regions of Thracia, Egypt, and Armenia.

7. Study carefully the locations of Rome, Constantinople, Chalcedon, Alexandria, and Ctesiphon. Study also the location of the Battle of Vartanantz. When you are familiar with their locations, close the book. Using your regular pencil, mark each location on your map. Check your map against the original and correct any locations that were mislabeled.

Chapter Nineteen

The High Kings

You may use your text when answering the questions in sections I and II.

Section I: Who, What, Where

Write a one or two-sentence answer explaining the significance of each item listed below.

455

Connachta

Cunedda

Hengest and Horsa

Nennius

Niall of the Nine Hostages

Patricius

Venii/Feni

Vortigern

Section II: Comprehension

Write a two or three-sentence answer to each of the following questions.

1. Though Ireland was never occupied by Roman soldiers, how was the island still touched by the Roman empire?

2. What did Niall have to accomplish in Ireland before launching raids on Gaul and Britain? How did he build enough support to start his campaigns?

3. Saint Patrick is credited by Christian historians with driving the snakes out of Ireland, but the reality is that there were no snakes in Ireland. Explain what the Christian historians really meant when they said Saint Patrick rid Ireland of snakes.

4. How was Ireland divided up by Niall's sons after Patricius's death, around 493? Though he is long dead and his kingdom was divided, in what way is Niall still with us in the modern world?

5. What other Irish clans existed alongside the Ui Neill dynasty? How did one of these tribes end up in the area we now know as Wales?

6. What happened to rule in Britain after the departure of Constantine III in 410? What enemies did Vortigern first face when he was elected warleader by the minor kings and tribal chiefs of Britain?

7. Having received no reply from the Roman *magister militum* Aetius in his request for help against the Picts, what strategy did Vortigern devise in an effort to squelch his northern opponents?

8. How did Vortigern's plan to allow Saxons and Angles to settle in the south of Britain in exchange for help fighting the Picts and the Irish backfire?

9. Describe the prolonged invasion of Britain by the Saxons, Angles and Jutes.

10. In what way does Nennius's *History of the Britons* suggest that Vortigern and his court were driven to drastic and ancient strategies to defend their country? Describe what sacrifice was to be made, and what course of action took place instead of the sacrifice.

Section III: **Critical Thinking**

You may use your text to answer this question.

As we know from our histories of both the Ancient and Medieval worlds, history and myth are often combined into powerful folklore that cannot be dismissed as mere fiction. Irish history is no different. Though we cannot be sure of the exact accomplishments of Niall of the Nine Hostages, we can surmise through a reading of "The Adventures of the Sons of Eochaid Mugmedon" that his rise to power was a bloody one. Write a paragraph that paraphrases "The Adventures of the Sons of Eochaid Mugmedon" and then write a paragraph that explains how the story showcases Niall's ambition to rule.

Section IV: Map Exercise

1. Using a black pencil, trace the rectangular outline of the frame for Map 19.1: Ireland and Britain.

2. Using a black pencil, trace the coastline in its entirety: around the continent, into the Baltic Sea, and around Britain and Ireland. You do not need to trace all the islands outside Scotland. With your blue pencil, trace the line of the Rhine on the continent and the line of the Thames in Britain. Repeat until the contours are familiar.

3. Trace the rectangular outline of the frame in black. Remove your tracing paper from the original. Using a regular pencil with an eraser, draw the coastline along the continent and around Britain. Remember to use the distance from the frame of the map as a guide.

4. When you are pleased with your map, lay it over the original. Erase and redraw any lines which are more than ¼ inch off of the original.

5. Study carefully the big regions of Ireland, Britain, and Gaul. Also study the regions of the Picts, Saxons, Angles, and Jutes. Be sure to study the locations of the Saxons, Angles, and Jutes in Britain as well as on the continent. When you are familiar with them, close the book. Mark the locations of Ireland, Britain, and Gaul on your map. Then mark the locations of the Saxons, Angles, and Jutes both on the continent and in Britain. Check your map with the original, and correct any misplaced labels.

6. Then study carefully the locations of the Eoghanach, the Connachta, the Ulaidh, the Midhe, and the Laighn. Also study the locations of Hadrian's Wall, Gwynedd, Essex, Kent, and Londinium. When you are familiar with them, close the book. Mark each location with your regular pencil. Check your map against the original, and erase and re-draw any misplaced labels.

7. Finally study and label the Irish Sea, the English Channel, the North Sea, and the Baltic Sea.

Chapter Twenty

The End of the Roman Myth

You may use your text when answering the questions in sections I and II.

Section I: Who, What, Where

Write a one or two-sentence answer explaining the significance of each item listed below.

April 22, 455

Alypia

Anthemius

Avitus

Eudocia

Julius Nepos

Libius Severus

Majorian

Marcian

Odovacer

Orestes

Petronius Maximus

Ricimer

Riotimus

Romulus

Section II: Comprehension

Write a two or three-sentence answer to each of the following questions.

1. Why, in 454, did Aetius arrange for the engagement of his son to Valentinian III's daughter?

2. What happened to Valentinian III's empire during the thirty years of his reign?

3. What were the circumstances of Aetius's death?

4. Why didn't Geiseric and his Vandal invaders try to hold Rome?

5. How did Avitus lose the support of both the Visigoth army that backed his takeover of the western throne, and the support of the Roman people?

6. What trouble with the Visigoths inspired Ricimer to appoint a new emperor, after eighteen months of ruling without the myth of royalty?

7. What happened in the battle between the Britons and the Visigoths?

8. What were the circumstances of Anthemius's death?

Section III: Critical Thinking

You may not use your text to answer this question.

It finally happened . . . we have been waiting for this moment in our reading: the disintegration of the myth of the western Roman empire. As we read in the last paragraph of this chapter, the death warrant for the western empire was signed by Constantine over a century before Odovacer's declaration that he was the "King of Italy." The decline of the western empire has been dragging out over our chapters, and now we see how the myth of Roman greatness failed. Write a paragraph explaining how Ricimer's eighteen-month emperor-less rule was a sign of western Rome's imminent end. Make sure to explain why Ricimer did eventually decide to appoint Anthemius emperor after eighteen months of being without a figurehead. Then, write a paragraph explaining why Odovacer decided to call himself "King of Italy" rather than *imperator.*

Chapter Twenty-One

The Ostrogoths

You may use your text when answering the questions in sections I and II.

Section I: Who, What, Where

Write a one or two-sentence answer explaining the significance of each item listed below.

Alans

Ariadne

Aspar

Athalaric

Basiliscus

Benedict of Nursia

Isaurians

Leo the Thracian

Leo II

Theoderic the Ostrogoth (Theoderic the Great)

Zeno

Section II: Comprehension

Write a two or three-sentence answer to each of the following questions.

1. When and how did the Theodosian dynasty in eastern Rome end?

2. Why did Leo the Thracian ally himself with the Isaurians?

3. Why did Odovacer, king of Italy, ask Zeno the Isaurian to be his overlord and emperor?

4. What was Odovacer's new title after he became part of Zeno's empire? What happened after Odovacer received this new title?

5. What are the differences between Theoderic the Ostrogoth and Theoderic the Squinter?

6. How did Zeno try to pacify Theoderic and the Ostrogoths as they advanced towards Constantinople in the years between 478 and 488?

7. How did Theoderic the Ostrogoth come to attack Italy? Who went along with Theoderic in his pursuit of the peninsula?

8. What were the circumstances of Odovacer's death?

9. Why did the monks at a monastery near Subiaco ask Benedict to come and live with them, and then try to poison him?

10. What were the circumstances of the founding of Monte Cassino?

11. What were the rules, or "the Rule of St. Benedict," by which the monks in Monte Cassino lived?

12. If a monk broke one of Benedict's rules, what was the punishment? How did Benedict know that the rules were being broken?

Section III: Critical Thinking

You may use your text to answer this question.

As the Roman empire crumbled, the myth of Roman superiority hung on tight. While the idea of Roman sophistication still lingered, there was no doubt that real power lay in the hands of cunning strategists and successful warriors. Write a paragraph explaining how Theoderic's actions after becoming king of Italy weakened the idea of Roman greatness. Then, explain how the argument over the education of his son, Athalaric, became symbolic of the struggle between real and imagined power.

Section IV: Map Exercise:

1. Using a black pencil, trace the rectangular outline of the frame for Map 21.1: Odovacer's Kingdom.

2. Using a blue pencil, trace the outline of the Mediterranean. At this time, you do not need to include the various islands except for Sicily. Be sure to include the coastline all the way up to the Black Sea. Trace the outline of the Black Sea as well. Repeat until the contours are familiar.

3. Using a black pencil, trace the dotted outline of the Eastern Roman Empire. Then trace the outline of Odovacer's kingdom. Trace the shading lines denoting the kingdom of the Vandals. Repeat until the contours are familiar.

4. Using a new sheet of paper, trace the rectangular frame of the map with a black pencil. Remove your tracing paper from the original. Using a regular pencil with an eraser as you look at the map, draw the coastlines of the Mediterranean and Black Sea. Then draw the outline of the Eastern Roman Empire and the outline of Odovacer's kingdom. Shade the Kingdom of the Vandals.

5. When you are pleased with your map, lay it over the original. Erase and redraw any lines which are more than ¼ inch off of the original.

5. Remove your map. Label Sicily, Dacia, and Asia Minor (if necessary, study first and then label). Then study carefully the regions of the Apennines, Moesia, and the Isaurians. When you are familiar with them, close the book. Mark the location of each. Check your map with the original, and correct any misplaced labels.

6. Now study carefully the cities of Carthage, Cassino, Rome, Nursia, Ravenna, Verona, and Constantinople. When you are familiar with them, close the book. Using your regular pencil, label all eight on your map. Compare with the original, and erase and re-mark your labels as necessary.

Chapter Twenty-Two

Byzantium

You may use your text when answering the questions in sections I and II.

Section I: Who, What, Where

Write a one or two-sentence answer explaining the significance of each item listed below.

Anastasius

Balash

Mazdak

Na'man of al-Hirah

Nevarsek Treaty

Justin

Justinian

Kavadh

Peroz

Zamasb

Section II: Comprehension

Write a two or three-sentence answer to each of the following questions.

1. Describe the difficulties Persia faced during Peroz's twenty-seven year reign.

2. Explain how Peroz was tricked by the Hephthalites in battle in both 471 *and* in 484.

3. How did Persia become a subject of the Hephthalites?

4. How did Kavadh's contemporaries react to his reforms based on Mazdak's ideas? What do their reactions suggest Kavadh was actually trying to achieve in his reforms?

5. In what way did Kavadh's reforms help his rule? Why did the Persian nobles resent Kavadh's reforms, and what did they do with their anger about the reforms?

6. Who helped Kavadh escape from the "Fortress of Oblivion"?

7. What were the conditions of Kavadh's return to the Persian throne after being locked away in the "Fortress of Oblivion"?

8. Why did the war between the Romans and the Persians end? What were the terms of the treaty made between the two empires?

9. Describe who fans rooted for in medieval Roman chariot-racing.

10. Explain how chariot-racing turned Constantinople into a city so dangerous its citizens raced home at sunset so they would be off the street before dark.

Section III: Critical Thinking

You may use your text to answer this question.

Tracking the developments of known civilizations during the medieval world can sometimes be mind-boggling: empires split up, nations absorbed one another, some barbarians found homelands and others were kicked out of what they thought was their own soil. In this chapter, we learned about the further disintegration of what was known as the Roman empire, and the formation of Byzantium. Write a paragraph or two, starting with the Slavs, that explains how barbarian invasions eventually led to the creation of Anastasius's Long Wall, and finally Byzantium. In your answer, make sure to explain the difference between the Slavs and Germanic peoples, why Anastasius uprooted the Isaurians, and how the Bulgars played into the formation of Byzantium.

Section IV: Map Exercise:

1. Using a black pencil, trace the rectangular outline of the frame for Map 22.1: Persia and the Hephthalites.

2. Using a blue pencil, trace the coastlines of the Mediterranean (the white portion inside the Byzantine Empire), the Red Sea, the Persian Gulf, the Caspian Sea, and the Black Sea. With the blue

pencil, trace the line of the Nile, the Danube (what is visible), the Tigris, the Euphrates, and the Oxus. Repeat until the contours are familiar.

3. Using a black pencil, trace the outlines of the Persian Empire and the Byzantine empire. Use a contrasting color to show Armenia. Show the Carpathian mountains and the Caucasus mountains with simple peaks. Repeat until the contours are familiar.

4. Trace the rectangular outline of the frame in black. Remove your tracing paper from the original. Using a regular pencil with an eraser as you look at the map, draw the outlines of the Mediterranean, the Red Sea, the Persian Gulf, the Caspian Sea, and the Black Sea. Draw the lines of the Nile, the Danube, the Tigris, the Euphrates, and the Oxus. Draw the outlines of the Persian Empire, Armenia, and the Byzantine Empire. Show the Carpathian mountains and the Caucasus mountains with peaks as you did before.

5. When you are pleased with your map, lay it over the original. Erase and redraw any lines which are more than ¼ inch off of the original.

6. Remove your map. Study the regions of the Byzantine Empire, Arabia, the Persian Empire, Armenia, Khorasan, Bactria, and the Hephthalites. When you are familiar with them, close the book. Label them all, and then check your labels with the original. Erase and redraw any misplaced labels.

7. Then study carefully the locations of Constantinople, Amida, Edessa, Harran, Ctesiphon, the Fortress of Oblivion, and the Caspian Gates. When you are familiar with them, close the book, label each, and check your labels against the original. Erase and redraw any misplaced labels.

Chapter Twenty-Three

Aspirations

You may use your text when answering the questions in sections I and II.

Section I: Who, What, Where

Write a one or two-sentence answer explaining the significance of each item listed below.

Ado

Chijung

Feng

Jangsu

King Pophung

Wei Xiaowen

Wei Xuanwu

Section II: Comprehension

Write a two or three-sentence answer to each of the following questions.

1. Why did the Tuoba clan decree that the mother of the crown prince be executed? How did Feng manage to escape this fate?

2. How did Wei Xiaowen and Feng transform the Bei Wei court into an essentially Chinese court?

3. Why is Taoism so important to ancient Chinese medicine?

4. In what way was Confucianism important for the formation of the Bei Wei government?

5. Explain the legendary Buddhist origins of Kung Fu.

6. What did Wei Xiaowen tell his clan leaders when he suggested they move the Bei Wei capital from Pingcheng to Luoyang? Why did Wei Xiaowen want to move the capital?

7. Describe the Bei Wei capital city of Luoyang at its peak.

8. Where was the Goguryeon capital when Guanggaeto ruled? Why did Jangsu move the capital to Pyongyang?

9. Why were Baekje and Silla alarmed by the move of the Goguryeon capital to Pyongyang? What happened to Baekje after the move?

10. What actions did Chijung take when he came to Silla's throne in 500 that turned Silla into a thriving nation?

11. How did Buddhism come to Silla?

Section III: **Critical Thinking**

You may use your text to answer this question.

Taoism and Confucianism were both important to the transformation of the Bei Wei into a seemingly traditional Chinese culture. Buddhism, however, turned out to be key in moving the Bei Wei towards a more Chinese way of life. Buddhism also helped the young nation of Silla form its identity and become more Chinese. Write a paragraph that explains how Mahayana Buddhism shaped the Bei Wei during Wei Xiaowen's rule. Make sure to describe the structure of Mahayana Buddhism, and how the bodhisattvas provided a model of rule for Wei Xiaowen. Then, explain how King Pophung of Silla also used Buddhism to reinforce the strength of his small nation.

Section IV: **Map Exercise**

1. Using a black pencil, trace the rectangular outline of the frame for Map 23.1: The East in the Era of King Jangsu.

2. Using a blue pencil, trace the outline of the East China Sea. You do not need to include islands at this time. Then trace the lines of the Yangtze and Yellow rivers. Using a black pencil, trace the outlines of the Bei Wei and the Liu Song. Repeat until the contours are familiar.

3. Using a new sheet of paper, trace the rectangular outline of the frame in black. Remove your tracing paper from the original. Using a regular pencil with an eraser as you look at Map 23.1, draw the coastline of the East China Sea, up through the Yellow Sea and into the bay above. Lightly draw the perimeters of the regions of the Bei Wei and the Liu Song.

4. When you are pleased with your map, lay it over the original. Erase and redraw any lines which are more than ¼ inch off of the original. When you are done, lightly shade the areas of the Bei Wei and the Liu Song inside their respective perimeters.

5. Remove your map. Study carefully the locations of Goguryeo, Silla, Baekje, and the Gaya Confederacy. When you are familiar with them, close the book. Label each on your map. Then check your map with the original, and erase and correct any misplaced labels.

6. Next study closely the locations of Chang'an, Pingcheng, Luoyang, Ungjin, Pyongyang, and Guknaesong. Also study closely the location of Mount Song Shan. When they are familiar for you, close the book, and label each one. Then compare with the original. Erase and remark any misplaced labels.

Chapter Twenty-Four

Resentment

You may use your text when answering the questions in sections I and II.

Section I: Who, What, Where

Write a one or two-sentence answer explaining the significance of each item listed below.

Erzhu Rong

Erzhu Zhao

"Inattentive Empress"

Liang Wudi

Qi Gaodi

Qi Hedi

Qi Mingdi

Qi Wudi

Wei Xiaoming

Wei Xiaozhuang

Wei Xuanwu

Section II: Comprehension

Write a two or three-sentence answer to each of the following questions.

1. List the emperors of the ill-fated Liu Song dynasty that ruled after Song Xiaowu. In your answer, include how long each emperor ruled and if possible, why his reign ended.

2. Why did Xiao Yan act as prime minister, and support the rule of Qi Hedi's sixteen-year-old brother in his claim to the throne, after the Idiot King's death?

3. What bureaucratic and military accomplishments did Liang Wudi make during his reign as emperor of the Southern Liang dynasty?

4. How did Buddhism shape Liang Wudi's China?

5. Why was being a virtuous ruler so important to Liang Wudi?

6. How did Liang Wudi's Buddhism conflict with his rule of the Southern Liang dynasty? What won out in the end, the temple or the throne?

7. What is the *juntian*, or "equal-field" system? What was the purpose of the "equal-field" system?

8. How did the "equal-field" system redistribute private armies?

9. What was the Bei Wei strategy for dealing with nomads that attacked the kingdom's northern borders?

10. Why was assignment to the northern frontier, once an honor, seen as a punishment during Wei Xuanwu's rule?

11. Why did a proposal that did not pass—that soldiers would no longer be eligible to hold government offices—cause fighting between the Bei Wei and its own border guard?

12. What were the circumstances of the Heyin Massacre?

13. What was the cause of the Bei Wei civil war? What was the result of the civil war?

Section III: Critical Thinking

You may not use your text to answer this question.

The Bei Wei were in between two worlds: the nomadic and barbarian world of their past, and the aristocratic and refined Chinese world of their future. The transition between these two worlds was not smooth, as evidenced by the civil war that eventually split the Bei Wei in two. Explain how the conflict between the Bei Wei's past and present manifested itself in the land disputes of the Bei Wei tribal leaders. Write a paragraph that explains the plight of the "local aristocrats," how their desires conflicted with the desire of the emperor, and how their desire to be Chinese ultimately led to the sacrifice of their local power.

Chapter Twenty-Five

Elected Kings

You may use your text when answering the questions in sections I and II.

Section I: Who, What, Where

Write a one or two-sentence answer explaining the significance of each item listed below.

Aelle

Amalaric

Ambrosius Aurelianus

Childebert

Childeric

Chlodomer

Chlothar

Clotild

Clovis

Theuderic

Theudis

Section II: Comprehension

Write a two or three-sentence answer to each of the following questions.

1. Though he claimed to be "King of the Franks," who did Childeric truly rule over? Why didn't he rule over all of the Franks, and who did he have to fight with during his rule?

2. Describe Gregory's account of Clovis's conversion to Christianity.

3. What did Christianity offer to the Franks and that Roman-ness could not?

4. How did the Franks take the Arian Visigoths of Hispania? When the Visigothic court scattered from Toulouse, who did they take with them?

5. How did the Italian Ostrogoths get into the fight between the Franks and the Arian Visigoths of Hispania? What was the end result of their battle?

6. How did Clovis become "Augustus, Consul of the West"? Even though this title was not meant for Clovis why did the eastern Roman emperor allow Clovis to continue to call himself as such?

7. What did Clovis do after he became "Augustus," victorious Christian and Roman king?

8. Even though Vortigern had managed to kill one of the invading Saxon generals in 455, why was he remembered so bitterly? What kinds of tales were spread about Vortigern?

9. What are some of the stories that have circulated about the Battle of Mount Badon? Despite the contradictory accounts, what is the one constant among the different tales?

10. When King Clovis, Augustus, Consul of the West, died in 511, why did he leave his kingdom to his four sons?

Section III: Critical Thinking

You may use your text to answer this question.

The American poet Gertrude Stein once wrote, "A rose is a rose is a rose;" there is no variation, a rose is what it is: a rose. For the 5th century British, a king was a king was a king. Explain the difference between ideas of British kingship as described in the chapter and the ideas behind kingship in Rome. Then, explain how Geoffrey of Monmouth challenged the British idea that a king was a king was a king.

Section IV: Map Exercise

1. Using a black pencil, trace the rectangular outline of the frame for Map 25.1: Clovis and His Neighbors.

2. Using a blue pencil, trace the coastline all the way down the coast to Hispania, into the Mediterranean, and up around Britain. You do not need to include islands at this time. Repeat until the contours are familiar.

3. Choose four contrasting colors. Use each to trace the territories of the Ostrogoths, the Franks, the Vandals, and the Visigoths. Use horizontal lines as the map-maker did to indicate the area conquered by Clovis. Repeat until the contours are familiar.

4. Trace the rectangular outline of the frame in black. Remove your tracing paper from the original. Using a regular pencil with an eraser, draw the coastal outline around Britain and down the continent and around the Mediterranean as you look at Map 25.1. As before, you need not draw islands at this time. Erase and redraw as necessary.

5. When you are satisfied with your map, lay it over the original. Erase and redraw any lines which are more than ¼ inch off of the original.

6. Remove your map. Mark (study first if necessary) the areas of England, Gaul, and Hispania on your map. Then study carefully the locations of the Saxons, Angles (on the continent and in Britain), Jutes, Thuringii, Burgundians, and Alemanni. When you are familiar with them, close the book, mark them on your map, and then check and make any needed corrections.

7. Now study the locations of Mount Baden, Camlann, Sussex, Cambrai, Soissons, Reims, Paris, Orleans, Tours, Toulouse, Rome, and Carthage. When you are familiar with them, close the book. Using your regular pencil, mark the location of each on your map. Then check your map against the original. If the city or the labels are more than ¼ inch off, erase and remark while looking at the original.

Chapter Twenty-Six

Invasion and Eruption

You may use your text when answering the questions in sections I and II.

Section I: Who, What, Where

Write a one or two-sentence answer explaining the significance of each item listed below.

Aryabhata

Bhanugupta

King Candrawarman

Mihirakula

Narasimha

Toramana

Suryawarman

Section II: Comprehension

Write a two or three-sentence answer to each of the following questions.

1. What happened to Chandragupta II's empire in the time since his passing to the reign of Narasimha?

2. How does *The Questions of King Milinda* describe Toramana's capital city of Sakala?

3. Despite Toramana's taste for the finer things in life, as evidenced by the upkeep of Sakala, what aspects of his empire still had nomadic qualities?

4. Why did Mihirakula want to get rid of Buddhism in India?

5. What is the difference between Manichaean, Chalcedonian and Nestorian Christianity?

6. How did Hinduism prosper under Mihirakula's rule?

7. What land did the Guptas rule over during the reign of Mihirakula? Why was Mihirakula threated by a group with such a small domain?

8. Though Mihirakula was not targeting Hinduism in his religious battles, why were the Hindu Indians in his empire angered by Mihirakula's "high-handed" ways? How did his prosecution of Buddhism ultimately drive Mihirakula to control a diminished kingdom?

9. What happened to power in northern India after Mihirakula was banished to the north of the Punjab?

10. Where were Sumatra and Java located in relation to the southeastern Indian coast? What cities were found on these islands, and where was Krakatoa located in relation to the two islands?

11. What piece of information from *The Book of Ancient Kings* suggests that Sumatra and Java may have been a single island at one time?

Section III: **Critical Thinking**

You may use your text to answer this question.

While men with appetites for land, gold and power were very dangerous in the medieval world, sometimes there was nothing more treacherous than Mother Nature. Describe the explosion of Krakatoa and the fallout that came after the volcano's eruption. In your answer, make sure to explain how the aftermath of Krakatoa's eruption affected a much wider landscape than just Sumatra and Java.

Section IV: **Map Exercise**

1. Using a black pencil, trace the rectangular outline of the frame for Map 26.1: India and Its Southeast Trading Partners.

2. Using a black pencil, trace the coastal outline in its entirety. You do not need to include all the islands at this time, but do include Sumatra and Java. Use your black pencil to outline the visible perimeter of the Persian Empire. Also use your black pencil to draw simple peaks to represent the mountains. Repeat until the contours are familiar.

3. Using a new sheet of paper as you look at the map, trace the rectangular outline of the frame in black. Remove your tracing paper from the original. Using a regular pencil with an eraser, draw

the coastline of the mainland and the islands Sumatra and Java. Draw the perimeter of the Persian Empire and the mountain peaks.

4. When you are pleased with your map, lay it over the original. Erase and redraw any lines which are more than ¼ inch off of the original.

5. Remove your map. Study carefully the locations of the Hephthalites and the Guptas. Also study the locations of Sakala, Eran, Kantoli, and Tarumanagara. Study carefully also the location of Krakatoa. When you are familiar with them, close the book. Using your regular pencil with the eraser, mark the location of each on your map. Then check your map against the original. If the city or the labels are more than ¼ inch off, erase and remark while looking at the original.

Chapter Twenty-Seven

The Americas

You may use your text when answering the questions in sections I and II.

Section I: Who, What, Where

Write a one or two-sentence answer explaining the significance of each item listed below.

The Maya

Monte Alban

Sacred Round

Teotihuacan

tonalli

The Zapotec

Section II: Comprehension

Write a two or three-sentence answer to each of the following questions.

1. What is an "El Niño" event? What are some of the consequences of an "El Niño" event?

2. Why don't we know anything about the Americas before 600 AD?

3. How was the writing in the Americas different from the writing across the ocean in the great urban civilizations of Rome and Egypt?

4. How long did it take for the cycle of the Sacred Round to match up to the Earth's rounding of the sun? How did the Maya and the Zapotec view all the days in between the matching up of the two calendars?

5. How did the Maya and the Zapotec view the passage of time?

6. How did Teotihuacan grow to be such a big city?

7. Describe how the construction of Teotihuacan was a matrix in which sacred time met earthly existence; how its observation of sacred time was built directly into its streets and walls.

8. Explain how Quetzalcoatl restored life to humanity after all men and women had been destroyed in a battle between rival gods.

9. What the did the cycle of droughts and storms that began in the 530s mean to the Teotihuacans? Why was the cycle so devastating for the city?

10. What was the cause for the massive riot that broke out in Teotihuacan around 600? What damage was caused by the riot?

11. Why were the people of Teotihuacan ready to revolt against their rulers, in addition to fear and rage over deaths caused by the bad weather cycle?

12. What happened to the population of Monte Alban between 550 and 650?

13. Who was Sky Witness, and Lord Water? Why is Cancuen important, and what is the significance of Chichen Itza? Why do all of these things mean little when considering 6th century Mayan history?

Section III: Critical Thinking

You may not use your text to answer this question.

The Sacred Round of the Maya and the Zapotec and the cycles of their calendar placed each day in the context of the past: a king in central America always ruled in the footprints of the king who had come before him in the previous cycle. As we read on page 190, ¶ 2, "each of the milestones of his rule—birth, marriage, coronation, conquest, death—occupied a particular slot on [the] elaborate calendar." Most importantly, each day according to the Sacred Round was a site of both past and present events. Write a paragraph explaining how the past and present affected the way the Maya and the Zapotec worshipped. In your answer, explain why the corners of the Pyramid of the Feathered Serpent were filled with sacrificial victims, and why a new king would cut himself on top of a pyramid at the beginning of his rule.

Chapter Twenty-Eight

Great and Holy Majesty

You may use your text when answering the questions in sections I and II.

Section I: Who, What, Where

Write a one or two-sentence answer explaining the significance of each item listed below.

April 1, 527

Caleb

Code of 529

Dhu Nuwas

Ghassanids

Himyar

Lakhmids

Macedonia

Mecca

Mundir

Najran

Theodora

Section II: Comprehension

Write a two or three-sentence answer to each of the following questions.

1. Why were the people of Himyar, Axum and the Bedouins alike? Why were they different?

2. What threats did Dhu Nuwas see facing his kingdom? What action did Dhu Nuwas take in an effort to get ahead of these threats?

3. How did Dhu Nuwas think Judaism would help him to get ahead of Persia and Byzantium?

4. Who did Dhu Nuwas target as enemies of his state after his conversion to Judaism?

5. What was the source of hostility between the Persians and the people of Byzantium that came about when Justin became emperor?

6. When the Lakhmids were negotiating with the Byzantine ambassador, a letter arrived describing the massacre in Himyar: what did it say? What did King Dhu Nuwas want from King Mundir?

7. What happened to the Himyarite kingdom after Dhu Nuwas's massacre of the Christians of Najran?

8. Explain the rumor that still lives on, started by the letter that Dhu Nuwas sent to King Mundir.

9. Why did Kavadh lose his Arab mercenaries after the fall of Himyar?

10. How did Theodora end up working as an actress, and then end up in the company of an informant for Justinian's secret police?

11. Why was Alexandria a welcome haven for those who found themselves out of step with the Chalcedonian Christianity of Constantinople and Rome? Why was it so important to the Christians in Alexandria that Jesus and God be seen as one person?

12. What obstacles did Theodora and Justinian have to overcome before they could be married?

13. What caused the shutdown of the academy at Athens? Where did the faculty go?

Section III: Critical Thinking

You may not use your text to answer this question.

Justinian's marriage to a former prostitute was not the only wild thing we read about concerning Constantinople's past in this chapter. Knowing Roman history and the inability of emperors to use the force of Christ to keep their empires together, it is just as wild that Justinian was able to make his word valid as secular *and* sacred law. Write a paragraph that explains how Justinian was able to make himself the arbiter of laws both secular and sacred.

Section IV: Map Exercise

1. Using a black pencil, trace the rectangular outline of the frame for Map 28.1: Arab Tribes and Kingdoms.

2. Using a blue pencil, trace the coastal outlines of the Mediterranean Sea, the Black Sea, the Red Sea, the Caspian Sea, and the Arabian Sea, including the Persian Gulf. You do not need to include islands at this time. With your blue pencil, trace the line of the Nile down from Alexandria parallel to the Red Sea. Use your blue pencil also to trace the line of the Oxus River. Use small peaks to represent the mountains. Repeat until the contours are familiar.

3. Using a new sheet of paper, trace the rectangular outline of the frame in black. Remove your tracing paper from the original. Using a regular pencil with an eraser as you look at the map, draw the coastlines of the Mediterranean, the Black Sea, the Red Sea, the Caspian Sea, and the Arabian Sea, including the Persian Gulf. Remember to use the distance from the rectangular frame as a guide. Draw the line of the Nile and the line of the Oxus. Draw the mountains with small peaks. Erase and redraw as necessary. When you are done, label each body of water.

4. When you are pleased with your map, lay it over the original. Erase and redraw any lines which are more than ¼ inch off of the original.

5. Remove your map. Study carefully the locations of Byzantium, Arabia, Axum, Himyar, Syria, the Ghassanids, the Lakhmids, the Persian Empire, Khorasan, Bactria, and Kashmir. When you are familiar with them, close the book. Using your regular pencil, label Byzantium, Arabia, Axum, Himyar, Syria, the Ghassanids, the Lakhmids, the Persian Empire, Khorasan, Bactria, and Kashmir. Check your map against the original. Correct any misplaced labels.

6. Now study closely the locations of Athens, Constantinople, Alexandria, Halikarnassos, Chalcedon, Edessa, Antioch, Amida, Mecca, Najran, Balkh, and Eran. When you are familiar with them, close the book. Using your regular pencil, label each location. Check your map against the original, and correct any misplaced labels.

Chapter Twenty-Nine

Pestilence

You may use your text when answering the questions in sections I and II.

Section I: Who, What, Where

Write a one or two-sentence answer explaining the significance of each item listed below.

al-Mada'in

Anthemius of Tralles

Belisarius

Gelimer

Hagia Sophia

Hypatius

Khosru

Theodahad

Totila

Witigis

Section II: Comprehension

Write a two or three-sentence answer to each of the following questions.

1. What deal was made between the Persian and Byzantine emperors in 532? What was it called, and how long did it last?

2. Why was it risky for Justinian to rely on the loyalty of the Blues in regards to the taxes he imposed for great building projects in Constantinople and reclamation of land lost in the west?

3. How did the Blues and Greens come to riot together against the government of Constantinople in 532?

4. Describe the rioting by the factionists in Constantinople in 532.

5. Why didn't Justinian flee Constantinople during the rebellion, even though he wanted to?

6. How did Justinian and Belisarius put down the rebellion of 532, also known as the "Nika" revolt?

7. What were the circumstances of Justinian's reclamation of Carthage?

8. Describe how Belisarius was able to reclaim Italy, even if only for a moment, for Justinian?

9. What provisions did Justinian take to ensure that Italy would be reabsorbed into the Byzantine empire, rather than, say, being taken by Belisarius or by other wandering peoples?

10. What happened to control of Italy once Belisarius departed for Constantinople?

11. Why did Khosru march into Syria and sack the ancient city of Antioch in June of 540? How did Justinian put Khosru off from doing further damage?

12. Before the bubonic plague hit the Byzantine empire, what actions did Khosru take that anticipated the end of the Eternal Peace and the beginning of war between Persia and Byzantium?

13. How did Khosru plan to take Edessa in 544? How did the people of Edessa defeat Khosru and his men?

14. How was peace reached between Edessa and Khosru's Persian army, and then between Khosru and Justinian?

15. What is the legend of the Mandylion?

16. How did the Mandylion supposedly save Edessa from defeat by Khosru?

Section III: Critical Thinking

You may use your text to answer this question.

As we read in Chapter Twenty-Six, the effects of Krakatoa's eruption in 535 spread far and wide, both around the medieval world and forward through time. How is Krakatoa related to the pestilence that spread across Constantinople in 542? Write a paragraph explaining their connection; then, describe the plague, its cause and its eventual end.

Section IV: Map Exercise

1. Using a black pencil, trace the rectangular outline of the frame for Map 29.1: Constantinople.

2. Using a blue pencil, trace the coastline of the Mediterranean (include the large islands of Sardinia, Corsica, Sicily, Crete, and Cyprus, but not the smaller islands), the Red Sea, the Black Sea, and the Caspian Sea. You do not need to trace the western coastline of the Atlantic at this time. With your blue pencil, trace the line of the Nile, the Tigris and Euphrates, and also the Danube, the Rhine, the Loire, and the Seine to the west. Show the Carpathian mountains with simple peaks. Repeat until the contours are familiar.

3. Now using your black pencil, trace the outline of the empire of Justinian. Trace the outline of the Persian Empire and the regions of the Franks as well. Use lines as the mapmaker did for the area of the Visigoths. Repeat until the contours are familiar.

4. Trace the rectangular outline of the frame in black. Remove your tracing paper from the original. Using a regular pencil with an eraser as you look at Map 29.2, draw the coastline of the Mediterranean (including only the islands which you traced), the Red Sea, the Black Sea, and the Caspian Sea. Draw the lines of the Nile, the Tigris and Euphrates, the Danube, the Rhine, the Loire, and the Seine. Draw simple peaks to represent the Carpathian mountains. Then draw the outline of the empire of Justinian, the outline of the Persian Empire, the region of the Franks, and the region of the Visigoths (use lines as you did while tracing). Erase and redraw as necessary as you look at the map.

5. When you are pleased with your map, lay it over the original. Erase and redraw any lines which are more than ¼ inch off of the original.

6. Remove your map from the original. Mark the regions of North Africa, Sicily, Egypt, Syria, and Asia Minor (study the map first if necessary). Mark the rivers and bodies of water. Then study carefully the locations of the Burgundians, the Alemanni, the Lombards, and the Ghassanids. When you are familiar with them, close the book, mark them on your map, and then check and correct any misplaced labels.

7. Next study carefully the locations of the following cities: Tours, Paris, Arles, Carthage, Naples, Rome, Ravenna, Constantinople, Edessa, Antioch, Caesarea, Petra, al-Rumiyyah, Nisbis, Ctesiphon, and Derbent. When you are familiar with them, close the book. Using your regular pencil, mark the locations on your map. **(If these are too many to learn at one time, first learn the cities up through Ravenna and then learn the remaining, starting with Constantinople.)** When you are pleased with your map, check it against the original. Erase and replace any misplaced cities or labels.

Chapter Thirty

The Heavenly Sovereign

You may use your text when answering the questions in sections I and II.

Section I: Who, What, Where

Write a one or two-sentence answer explaining the significance of each item listed below.

Bambetsu

Chinhung

Ezo

Jomon

Jushichijo no Kempo

Kimmei

Konwon

Ojin

Seong

Shinto

Shotoku Taishi

Sogo no Iname

Soga no Umako

Suiko

Sushun

Tenno

Uji

Wa

Wideok

Yamato

Yayoi

Section II: Comprehension

Write a two or three-sentence answer to each of the following questions.

1. Why were the Silla, Baekje and Goguryeo always at war?

2. For what reason, around 540, did King Seong of Baekje move his capital from Ungjin to Sabi?

3. Why was Goguryeo a bitter enemy of the northern Chinese kingdoms? Why wasn't King Seong of Baekje afraid of making an alliance with the northern Chinese?

4. Why did Seong of Baekje ally himself with Chinhung of Silla? How did the alliance backfire?

5. What were the two historical parts of the Yamato dynasty? Why were the parts named in this way?

6. What happened when the gifts—a statue of the Buddha made of gold and copper and books of Buddhist scriptures—sent by Seong arrived in Japan in 552? Why were some of the Japanese clans against keeping the gifts, while some were for it? What decision was made in the end?

7. What was the result of King Seong's attack against the Kwansan Fortress, the keystone to the defense of the Silla frontier?

8. Describe the difference between the localized religious practice of the Shinto and the universal religious practice of Buddhism.

9. How did Kimmei ensure that his legacy would keep the Soga clan close to the throne?

10. When Shotoku Taishi was in his thirties, he hit his ruling "stride." What actions did Shotoku take to increase Yamato power?

Section III: Critical Thinking

You may not use your text to answer this question.

When a statue of the Buddha made of gold and copper and a book of Buddhist scriptures arrived in Japan in 552, the Yamato ruler had to decide whether or not to accept the Baekje's gifts. However, the decision was not the heavenly sovereign's to make: he had to ask the clan leaders what they thought. This check on the leader's power was meant to be ameliorated with the institution of the Jushichijo no Kempo in 602. Write a paragraph explaining the meaning of the Jushichijo no Kempo, and how even though it seemed to give the leader of the Yamato dynasty carte blanche, it also very much limited the sovereign's power.

Section IV: Map Exercise

1. Using a black pencil, trace the rectangular outline of the frame for Map 30.1: The Far East in the Sixth Century.

2. Using a blue pencil, trace the coastline. You do not need to include all islands at this time; just include all the land down to Kyushu. Be sure to include the Inland Sea. Using your blue pencil, trace the line of the Yellow River and the Han River (in Silla). Repeat until the contours are familiar.

3. Using a black pencil, trace the line of the Great Wall. Then trace the outlines of Silla, Goguryeo, and Baekje. Repeat until the contours are familiar.

4. Using a new sheet of paper, trace the rectangular outline of the frame in black. Remove your tracing paper from the original. Using a regular pencil with an eraser as you look at Map 30.1, draw the coastline of China all the way around the Yellow Sea, up past Goguryeo, and down and around Kyushu and the Yamato Plain. Erase and redraw as necessary as you look at the map.

5. After completing the coastline, draw the Great Wall and Han and the Yellow Rivers, looking at the map and correcting as you go. Then draw the outlines of Goguryeo, Silla, and Baekje.

6. When you are satisfied with your map, lay it over the original. Erase and redraw any lines which are more than ¼ inch off of the original.

7. Remove your map from the original. Label the Great Wall, the Yellow River, the Yellow Sea, and the Goguryeo, Silla, and Baekje regions.

8. Now study carefully the areas of the Eastern Wei, the Southern Lang, Hokkaido, the Yamato Plain, and Kyushu. When you are familiar with them, close the book. Using your regular pencil, label each area on your map. Then study carefully the cities of Luoyang, Pyongyang, and Unjin, as well as Kwanson Fortress. When you feel confident with them, close the book and label each city. Check your map against the original, and correct any misplaced labels. Then lay your map over the original and erase and redraw any cities which are more than ¼ inch off of the original.

Chapter Thirty-One

Reunification

You may use your text when answering the questions in sections I and II.

Section I: Who, What, Where

Write a one or two-sentence answer explaining the significance of each item listed below.

Eulji Mundeok

Gao Huan

Gao Ying

Gaozu (Tang Gaozu)

Hou Jing

Jian (Liang Jian Wendi)

Li Delin

Liang Yuandi

Sui Yangdi

Yang Jian (Sui Wendi)

Zhou Jing

Zhou Wu

Zhou Xuan

Section II: Comprehension

Write a two or three-sentence answer to each of the following questions.

1. How did the Northern Qi dynasty come into existence?

2. According to Yang Xuanzhi, who recounted a sixth-century dispute between a drunken Southerner and the palace master of the north, why should the Southern "Chinese" have stopped thinking of the Northerners as "barbarians"?

3. What were the circumstances of Liang Wudi's death?

4. When did the Southern Chen dynasty come into existence?

5. How did the Northern Zhou dynasty come into existence? How did China move from having three ruling dynasties to two during this same period?

6. Who was Yan Zhitui and what can we learn about the prejudices of the Southern Chinese against the Northern Chinese from the rules he wrote down for his sons?

7. What actions proved that Zhou Xuan was more interested in his own immediate power than reuniting all of China?

8. How did Yang Jian become regent for Zhou Jing?

9. What did the document say that was signed by Zhou Jing in September of 580? Why was this document important to Yang Jian's establishment of his own rule?

10. What steps did Yang Jian take in order to make his role as emperor legitimate, and to eliminate any challenges to his power?

11. How was China reunited under the leadership of Sui Wendi?

12. Why did Sui Wendi deprive everyone (except for the army) in newly reunited China of weapons? Why did he rebuild the Great Wall, and build canals between the Yellow and the Yangtze rivers?

13. What did Sui Wendi do to the governments of North and South China upon reunification? What was his "New Code," and why was it created?

14. Why did Sui Wendi start a war with the Korean kingdom of Goguryeo after reuniting China?

15. Describe the canals between the Yangtze and Yellow rivers. How were they built, and where did the money come for their construction?

16. How did Sui Yangdi handle the problems he inherited with his Chinese crown?

17. What was the state of China when Tang Gaozu began his rule, and his new dynasty?

Section III: Critical Thinking

You may not use your text to answer this question.

In the previous chapter we learned that there *isn't* much to learn about the history of ancient Japan because there are so few written records from that time. No matter how mighty their rulers may have been, we don't know about those leaders because we can't read about them. Stories influence what we know about the past and how we think of the future—Yang Jian certainly understood that. Write a paragraph or two explaining how Yang Jian took advantage of the power of words to become emperor and reunite China.

Section IV: Map Exercise

1. Using a black pencil, trace the rectangular outline of the frame for Map 31.1: The Grand Canal.

2. Using a blue pencil, trace the coastline from Goguryeo down to the bottom of the frame. Using a black pencil, trace the outline of the shaded portion of the map. Repeat until the contours are familiar.

3. Using a new sheet of paper, trace the rectangular outline of the frame in black. Remove your tracing paper from the original. Using a regular pencil with an eraser as you look at Map 31.1, draw the coastline and then the shaded portion of the map. Erase and redraw as necessary.

4. When you are pleased with your map, lay it over the original. Erase and redraw any lines which are more than ¼ inch off of the original. Label Sui.

5. Remove your map from the original. Looking back at Map 31.1, study carefully the locations of Chang'an, Luoyang, and Nanjing. When you are familiar with them, close the book.

6. Looking back at Map 31.1, draw the lines of the Yellow River, the Yangtze River, and the approximate course of the Grand Canal. Label each. Draw the outline of the border of Goguryeo and label as well. Erase and redraw to be as correct as possible.

Chapter Thirty-Two

The South Indian Kings

You may use your text when answering the questions in sections I and II.

Section I: Who, What, Where

Write a one or two-sentence answer explaining the significance of each item listed below.

Chalukya

Harsha Carita

Harsha Vardhana

Kannauj

Kirtivarman

Mahendravarman

Mangalesa

Pallava

Pulakesi

Pulakesi II

Rajyasri

Section II: Comprehension

Write a two or three-sentence answer to each of the following questions.

1. What did conquering land on the western coast of India do for Chalukya? What else did Pulakesi do to prove his worth as king of Chalukya?

2. What made Mahendravarman, or "Vichitrachitta," the man with new-fangled ideas, stand out among the south Indian kings?

3. Why do we know so little about Mahendravarman's accomplishments?

4. Why did Mangalesa believe he deserved to be king of the Chalukya?

5. What did Pulakesi II do once he came to the Chalukya throne?

6. How did Harsha Vardhana come to claim the country of his sister's king for himself?

7. What was Pulakesi II's strategy to bolster his army when facing Harsha Vardhana's hundred thousand horsemen, hundred thousand foot soldiers and sixty thousand elephants?

8. While drunken courage may have helped Pulakesi II's army, what really helped the king defend Chalukya territory? After their battle, what became Harsha Vardhana's southern border?

9. How did Pulakesi II add Vengi to his territory?

Section III: Critical Thinking

You may use your text to answer this question.

The ancient Hindu ritual of the horse-sacrifice was intended to bring health and strength to the people by channeling it through the king. Write a paragraph explaining what the ritual entailed, and then explain how the horse-sacrifice gave Pulakesi II the power to defeat his various enemies and to grow a strong Chalukya kingdom.

Chapter Thirty-Three

Two Emperors

You may use your text when answering the questions in sections I and II.

Section I: Who, What, Where

Write a one or two-sentence answer explaining the significance of each item listed below.

Alboin

Athanagild

Bumin Khan

Ergenekon

Gokturk Khaghanate

Justin II

Leovigild

Mukhan

Narses

Quraysh

Sophia

T'u-chueh

Tiberius

Section II: Comprehension

Write a two or three-sentence answer to each of the following questions.

1. Where might the Lombards have come from? What evidence is there that they might have come from this place?

2. Who helped Narses attack Rome in 551? What happened at Rome, and then at Ravenna, with Narses leading the Byzantine army?

3. What was an exarch, and what was his job when it came to Italy?

4. What price did Justinian pay for regaining the heart of the Roman empire?

5. How did Justinian recapture southern Hispania by 554?

6. How did Belisarius end up in jail, rather than in retirement, in the years before he died? What was the state of Justinian and Belisarius's relationship when both men died in 565?

7. What threatened Byzantine domination in Italy after Justin II's accession to the throne?

8. Why did the Lombards want to expand into Italy?

9. What was left of Byzantium's hold in Italy after the Lombards moved in en masse in 568?

10. What is the difference between Sasanian Persia and the ancient Persian empire?

11. How did Khosru reorganize the vast expanse of land that he controlled after many successful campaigns?

12. Why did Axum want to attack Mecca?

13. While God may have stopped Abraha of Axum from invading Mecca once, what stopped a repeat attack against the city?

14. Describe the good Khosru did for Persia before his death in 579, during his forty-eight-year reign.

Section III: Critical Thinking

You may not use your text to answer this question.

We have all heard the phrase "God works in mysterious ways." According to the Qur'an, it was God that stopped Abraha of Axum from conquering Mecca by blighting his forces with the plague. The presence of God also affected how things were run in Mecca. Write a paragraph describing how the government in Mecca was structured. In your answer, explain why, in a religious center such as Mecca, all of the tribes were bound together even if there was no common law and no central authority.

Section IV: Map Exercise

1. Using a black pencil, trace the rectangular outline of the frame for Map 33.2: The Gokturk Khaghanate.

2. Using a blue pencil, trace all the coastline visible on the map (the areas shaded with horizontal lines). Include Lake Baikal. Using your black pencil, trace the perimeters of the Northern Zhou, the Southern Chen, and the Northern Qi. Then trace the outline of the shaded area showing the approximate extent of the Gokturk Khaghanate. Trace the Himalaya mountains and the Altay mountains with simple peaks. Repeat these tracings until the contours are familiar.

3. Take a new sheet of paper. Using a black pencil, trace the rectangular frame of the map in black. Remove your tracing paper from the original. Using a regular pencil with an eraser as you look at the map, draw the visible coastline, including Lake Baikal. Then draw the perimeters of the Northern Zhou, the Southern Chen, and the Northern Qi. Draw the outlines of the approximate extent of the Gokturk Khaganate. Finally draw the mountain peaks of the Himalaya and the Altay mountains.

4. When you are pleased with your map, place it over the original. Erase and redraw any lines which are more than ¼ inch off of the original.

5. Remove your map from the original. Study the locations of the Gokturk Khaganate and also Northern Zhou, the Southern Chen, and the Northern Qi. Also study carefully the locations of the Great Wall, the possible location of Ergenekon, and the area of the T'u-hueh. When you are familiar with them, close the book. Using your regular pencil, draw and label the Great Wall and label the locations of the Gokturk Khaganate and also Northern Zhou, the Southern Chen, and the Northern Qi. Also mark and label the possible location of Ergenekon and the area of the T'u-hueh. Check your map against the original. If your labels are misplaced, erase and remark while looking at the original.

Chapter Thirty-Four

The Mayors of the Palaces

You may use your text when answering the questions in sections I and II.

Section I: Who, What, Where

Write a one or two-sentence answer explaining the significance of each item listed below.

Aquitaine

Brunhilda

Charibert

Childebert II

Childebert the Adopted

Chilperic

Chlothar II

Clovis II

Dagobert

Dagobert II

Edict of Paris

Erchinoald

Fredegund

Galswintha

Grimoald

Guntram

Pippin the Elder

Rado

Sigebert

Sigebert III

Song of the Nibelungs

Theudebert II

Theuderic II

Warnachar

Section II: Comprehension

Write a two or three-sentence answer to each of the following questions.

1. How long did Chlothar I's rule of the unified Franks last? Why did the Frankish nation split again after Chlothar I's death?

2. Why did Sigebert marry the Visigothic princess Brunhilda?

3. What deal did Chilperic of Neustria make with King Athanagild in order to gain the hand of Galswintha? What happened once Galswintha arrived in Neustria?

4. What were the circumstances of Sigebert's death in 575?

5. How did Childebert II become the heir of Burgundy?

6. Why did Fredegund need three bishops and three hundred of the more important leaders in Neustria to assure the public that Fredegund's baby was fathered by Chilperic?

7. How did the Frankish nation come to be ruled by two women that hated each other?

8. Why did Fredegund and Chlothar II decide to seize Paris? What stopped the consummation of full-fledged war between Fredegund and Brunhilda?

9. Why did Theuderic II plan to marry the Visigothic princess Ermenberga? How did the arrangement fall apart?

10. Describe the events that led to Theudebert II's murder in prison at the request of Brunhilda.

11. What does the term "mayor of the palace" mean?

12. How did the Franks come to be united under Chlothar II?

13. Explain these terms, found on page 252: *Francia, Austrasia, Neustria.* How did these terms come to be?

14. Why did Dagobert make his three-year-old son, Sigebert III, king of Austrasia?

15. What does it mean to be "tonsured"?

Section III: **Critical Thinking**

You may not use your text to answer this question.

The chronicle of the rise of the Merovingian *rois faineants*, or "do-nothing kings," is a complicated one. Yet, the premise behind why these "do-nothing kings" came about is simple: the mayors of the palaces wanted more power. Explain how putting a single king on the throne of the united Franks actually made it very easy for the majors of the palaces to decentralize royal rule and claim more power for themselves. In your answer, first write a paragraph describing how Chlothar II became king of all the Franks. Then explain the Edict of Paris, the 617 declaration that followed, and finally how these two laws rendered the Frankish king essentially powerless.

Section IV: **Map Exercise**

1. Using a black pencil, trace the rectangular outline of the frame for Map 34.1: Territories of the Franks.

2. Using a blue pencil, trace the coastline around Britannia and up the coastline of the continent. You do not need to include any islands at this time. Then trace the lines of the Loire, the Seine, the Rhine, the Rhone, and the Danube. Trace the mountains with simple peaks. Using your black pencil, trace the perimeter of the approximate extent of Frankish rule. Repeat until the contours are familiar.

3. Trace the rectangular outline of the frame in black. Remove your tracing paper from the original. Using a regular pencil with an eraser as you look at the map, draw the coastline and then the approximate extent of Frankish rule. Draw the mountain peaks as well. Erase and redraw as necessary.

4. When you are pleased with your map, lay it over the original. Erase and redraw any lines which are more than ¼ inch off of the original.

5. Remove your map from the original, and label the different rivers.

6. Now study carefully the locations of Aquitaine, Neustria, Burgundy, and Austrasia. When you are familiar with them, close the book, and mark them on your map. Check your map against the original, and correct if necessary.

7. Now study carefully the locations of the cities of Tours, Orleans, Paris, Soissons, Reims, Metz, Cologne, and Mainz. When you are familiar with them, close the book. Using your regular pencil, mark each city on your map and label it. When you are done, lay your map over the original. Correct any misplaced labels, and erase and redraw any cities which are more than ¼ inch off of the original.

Chapter Thirty-Five

Gregory the Great

You may use your text when answering the questions in sections I and II.

Section I: Who, What, Where

Write a one or two-sentence answer explaining the significance of each item listed below.

Agilulf

Augustine

Authari

Bertha

Ethelbert

Gregory the Great

Rosemund

Section II: Comprehension

Write a two or three-sentence answer to each of the following questions.

1. What were the circumstances of the Lombard king Alboin's death? How did Alboin's death lead to Rosemund's death?

2. What happened to the Lombard kingship after Alboin's death? How were "duchies" and the "Rule of the Dukes" related to the disintegration of the Lombard kingship?

3. How did the areas of Lombard territory in the south of Italy come to be known as Duchy of Spoleto and Duchy of Benevento?

4. Describe the state of Rome at the time of Pope Pelagius II's death.

5. How did the monk Gregory become the pope after Pelagius II, even though he did not want to be pope?

6. Why did everyone in Rome—the people, priests and officials—turn to Gregory for guidance after he was made pope?

7. Explain the Lombard threat that faced Rome in 593. How did Gregory handle the threat?

8. Why wouldn't the exarch at Ravenna agree to a truce with Agilulf? How was peace negotiated between the Byzantines and Lombards when Callinicus came into power?

9. What happened to Christianity in Britain after the collapse of the Roman empire?

10. What was the cultural makeup of Britain at the end of the sixth century, when Gregory took it upon himself to bring the island back into the kingdom of God?

11. How did Augustine end up with the title "bishop of the Angles at Canterbury"? How did he end up living in Britain?

12. Why did Augustine express concern about living with his monks in Britain? How did Gregory convince Augustine to stay and live with his converts?

Section III: Critical Thinking

You may not use your text to answer this question.

Gregory the Great did not ask to become pope, but it happened anyway. As pope, he was tasked with not only the religious protection of Rome, but also with the safety of its people. Protecting Rome against the Lombards was a victory, but Gregory longed to get back to the work of God. Explain how, through his guidance of Augustine, Gregory the Great was able to fulfill his spiritual responsibilities by spreading Christianity in Britain. In your answer, make it clear how Ethelbert had a hand in making sure the Saxons under his rule also found salvation in Christ.

Section IV: Map Exercise

1. Using a black pencil, trace the rectangular outline of the frame for Map 35.2: Saxon Kingdoms.

2. Using a black pencil, trace the coastline all around Britannia and what is visible of Ireland. You do not need to include any islands at this time. Then, with your black pencil, trace the outline of the British (the shaded area). Repeat until the contours are familiar.

3. Trace the rectangular outline of the frame in black. Remove your tracing paper from the original. Using a regular pencil with an eraser as you look at the map, draw the coastline. Erase and redraw as necessary.

4. When you are pleased with your map, lay it over the original. Erase and redraw any lines which are more than ¼ inch off of the original.

5. Label the Irish Sea, the North Sea, and the English Channel. Draw and label Hadrian's Wall. Draw and label the Thames River.

6. Remove your map from the original. Looking back at Map 35.2, study the areas of the British, the Angles, the West Saxons, and the East Saxons. Also study the locations of Sussex, Kent, Canterbury, London, and Thanet Island. When you are familiar with them, close the book. Using your regular pencil, label the areas of the British, the Angles, the West Saxons, and the East Saxons and the locations of Sussex, Kent, Canterbury, London, and Thanet Island. Check your map against the original and correct any misplaced labels or cities.

Chapter Thirty-Six

The Persian Crusade

You may use your text when answering the questions in sections I and II.

Section I: Who, What, Where

Write a one or two-sentence answer explaining the significance of each item listed below.

Bahram Chobin

Bonus

Heraclius

Hurmuz

Kavadh II

Khosru II

Kubrat

Narses

Phocas

Samo

Sergius

Sisebut

Theodosius

Section II: Comprehension

Write a two or three-sentence answer to each of the following questions.

1. Why did Hurmuz send Bahram Chobin a dress?

2. Why did Khosru II flee into Byzantine territory after he was threatened by Bahram Chobin? What were the results of Khosru II's negotiations with Maurice?

3. Why did Maurice decide to head back to Constantinople, rather than face the Slavs invading the Danube with his soldiers? What did Maurice give his soldiers in his place?

4. What happened in 599 that made Maurice very unpopular with his troops? What made him even more unpopular in 602?

5. Why did Maurice arm the Blues and the Greens when he heard that Phocas had been declared general of the Byzantine army? What was the result of arming the gangs?

6. Explain the circumstances of Maurice's death, and his son Theodosius's death.

7. Describe the killing spree Phocas embarked upon at the start of war with Persia in 605, and his political ban on the Greens.

8. How did Heraclius come to be elected emperor of Byzantium?

9. Describe the state of Byzantium when Heraclius was crowned emperor. In your answer, make sure to include the state of Byzantine relations with Persia and the Visigoths at the start of Heraclius's rule.

10. What happened when Heraclius asked Khosru II to bring an end to the war in exchange for a tribute? What did Khosru and his Persian army do next to solidify his empire's warring stance?

11. Why did Heraclius think his empire was doomed, and what did he do with all of Constantinople's treasures? What happened to these treasures?

12. What made Heraclius recommit to war with Khosru II? How was the war funded?

13. What was Heraclius able to buy with the church's money?

14. Why did Heraclius sail to Asia Minor, to the Cilician Gates, instead of meeting the Persians straight on at Chalcedon?

15. Describe the progress of the war between Heraclius and Khosru II after the Byzantine army successfully defeated the Persians in their first meeting outside of Armenia. What drastic move did Khosru II make in 626 in order to bring the war to an end?

16. Describe Khosru II's attack on Constantinople in July of 626.

17. What tactical mistake did the Persian general in charge of the attack on Constantinople make during the siege on the city? How did this mistake cost the Persians victory?

18. Who were the Khazars, and why were they important to Heraclius?

19. What were the terms of the peace made between Kavadh II and Heraclius in 628? When was the True Cross returned to Jerusalem?

Section III: Critical Thinking

You may not use your text to answer this question.

Khosru II had mighty ambitions for Persia, and for his own power. Khosru II's early victories against Edessa, Caesarea and Jerusalem suggested the gods were on his side. He was even able to take two precious Christian relics—the Mandylion and a fragment of the True Cross—into Persian possession. But claiming divine intervention as the reason for his success was a misstep on Khosru II's part. Explain why turning the Persian war against the Byzantine empire into a crusade was a mistake, and how religious fervor was actually exactly what Persia's opponent—Byzantium—needed in order to defeat Khosru II.

Chapter Thirty-Seven

The Prophet

You may use your text when answering the questions in sections I and II.

Section I: Who, What, Where

Write a one or two-sentence answer explaining the significance of each item listed below.

Abu Bakr

Abu Talib

Ali

Ansar

The Hijra

Khadija

Muhammad

Muslim

Sacrilegious War

Umma

Zaid

Section II: Comprehension

Write a two or three-sentence answer to each of the following questions.

1. What is a *wadi*? Why was the dam at the Wadi Dhana so important to the people of Marib?

2. Why was the third breach of the dam at the Wadi Dhana in 590 so significant to the history of medieval southern Arabia?

3. How was Medina affected by the third dam breach at the Wadi Dhana? Why was Medina already an important city on the Arabian peninsula?

4. Explain the social divisions of clans (*banu*) and tribes in Arabian culture, using the clans and tribes of Mecca as your example.

5. What four sacred months of the year were the Arabic tribes supposed to observe? Were these months of observation fixed?

6. How did Muhammad come to work in the caravan business?

7. Why did the wall around Ka'aba have to be rebuilt? Why did Muhammad take part in the rebuilding?

8. What was Muhammad doing when he was given a vision of the angel Gabriel in 610?

9. What did Gabriel say to Muhammad during his vision? What words did Muhammad read in his vision?

10. Describe the basic tenets of the religion that was given to Muhammad in his vision of 610. What is *al-mar'ruf* and how did this relate to Muhammad's new religion?

11. Explain the core of the message Muhammad received from Allah in 613. Who followed Muhammad when he started to proclaim his message in public? Who resented Muhammad's faith?

12. What happened to the followers of Muhammad in Mecca? Where did they go when conditions in Mecca worsened?

13. What revelation was Muhammad given while surviving in the wretched conditions in Mecca, during which time his wife and uncle died?

14. When was Muhammad given permission by God to leave Mecca?

15. When did Muslim identity truly take shape? What was the Muslim identity based on?

Section III: Critical Thinking

You may use your text to answer this question.

In this chapter we read about several visions received by Muhammad that were directly related to the conditions of living in Mecca. For example, when he was being persecuted by the Quraysh clan leaders, he was given the vision that those who were wronged and driven from their home could fight back. When Muhammad found out his assassination was being planned, he had a revelation that God gave him permission to migrate. Write a paragraph explaining how the system of Arabic clans in Mecca was related to Muhammad's first revelation. Then explain how Muhammad's first vision influenced his own leadership in Medina.

Section IV: Map Exercise

1. Using a black pencil, trace the rectangular outline of the frame for Map 37.1: Muhammad's Arabia.

2. Using a blue pencil, trace the coastline along Arabia and the outline of the Black Sea, the Caspian Sea, the Red Sea, and the visible portion of the Mediterranean. Then select four contrasting colors. Use these respectively to trace the Persian Empire, the Byzantine Empire, Himyar, and Axum. Repeat until the contours are familiar.

3. Using a new sheet of paper, trace the rectangular outline of the frame in black. Using your regular pencil with an eraser as you look at Map 37.1, draw the coastline along Arabia. Then draw the outlines of the Black Sea, the Caspian Sea, the Red Sea, and the visible portion of the Mediterranean. Then trace the outlines of the Persian Empire, the Byzantine Empire, Himyar, and Axum. Erase and redraw as necessary while looking at the map.

4. When you are pleased with your map, lay it over the original. Erase and redraw any lines which are more than ¼ inch off of the original. When your map is correct, shade each area as the map maker does. Shade Axum and cross with diagonal lines. Shade Himyar very lightly. Shade the Byzantine Empire less lightly and the Persian Empire most heavily of all. If you have trouble making your shading tones distinct, you can substitute horizontal or hatched lines to distinguish each area.

5. Remove your map from the original. Study closely the locations of Jerusalem, Damascus, Medina, Mecca, Marib, Ctesiphon, Wadi Dhana, and Marib Dam. When you are familiar with them, close your book. Mark each on your map, and label it. Then check your map against the original. If your locations or labels are misplaced, erase and remark while looking at the map.

Chapter Thirty-Eight

Tang Dominance

You may use your text when answering the questions in sections I and II.

Section I: Who, What, Where

Write a one or two-sentence answer explaining the significance of each item listed below.

Battle of Baekgang

Battle of Hwang San Beol

Buyeo Pung

Gaozong (Tang Gaozong)

Gar Tongtsen

Hsieh-li

Kotoku

Li Shimin (Tang Taizong)

Mangson Mangtsen

Munmu

Muyeol the Great

Naka no Oe

Nakatomi no Kamatari

Namri Songtsen

Saimei

Soga no Emishi

Soga no Iruka

Songtsen Gampo

Su Dingfang

Uija

Wen-ch'eng

Wu Zetian

Section II: **Comprehension**

Write a two or three-sentence answer to each of the following questions.

1. In what ways did Tang Gaozu relate to his neighbors in the Eastern Khaghanate?

2. How did Li Shimin stop a full Eastern Khaghanate invasion of Tang territory?

3. Describe Li Shimin's rise to the Tang throne as Tang Taizong.

4. After his coronation, how did Tang Taizong once again stop the invading Eastern Turks?

5. How did Tang Taizong become "Heavenly Khan of the Eastern Turks"? How did Tang Taizong make himself popular with his new subjects?

6. Where did the Tibetan tribes come from? Where did the Tibetan tribes reside during Tang Taizong's rule?

7. How did Songtsen Gampo use both war and alliance to bring coherence to the Tibetan tribes?

8. How did northern Chinese culture and Indian culture infiltrate Songtsen Gampo's Tibetan empire?

9. Where did Baekje rebels go for help after Muyeol the Great of Silla proclaimed himself king of Silla and Baekje?

10. Why did the Japanese Soga clan want to keep Saimei on the throne?

11. Despite King Munmu's bringing Silla into dominance on the Korean peninsula, why was Silla still not fully sovereign after entering the Unified Silla period?

12. How did King Munmu manage to regain some Tang-controlled land for Silla? What happened to Tang's Protectorate General in Silla?

Section III: Critical Thinking

You may not use your text to answer this question.

Japan's powerful Soga clan was the only thing that stood between Naka no Oe and the throne. When Naka no Oe managed to get rid of Soga power, the result was not what he expected. Explain the "Isshi Incident," and how, by taking command and doing what had to be done, Naka no Oe actually lost his right to take the title of Heavenly Sovereign.

Section IV: Map Exercise

1. Using a black pencil, trace the rectangular outline of the frame for Map 38.1: The East in the Seventh Century.

2. Using a blue pencil, trace the coastline. You do not need to include any islands at this time other than Japan; be sure to include the entirety of Japan. Then with your blue pencil trace the outline of the Caspian Sea. Trace the line of the Yellow River and the Yangtze River. Trace the mountain peaks of the Himalaya mountains and the Altay mountains. Repeat until the contours are familiar.

3. Now with your black pencil trace the areas of Western Khaganate, of Eastern Khaganate, of Tang, and of the Persian Empire. Lightly trace the perimeter of the shaded area of Tibet. Trace the areas of Goguryeo, Baekje, and Silla. Repeat until the contours are familiar.

4. Trace the outline of the course of the Grand Canal until familiar. Trace the outline of the Great Wall repeatedly until it is familiar.

5. Using a new sheet of paper, trace the rectangular frame of the map in black. Using a regular pencil with an eraser as you look at the map, draw the coastline up and around through Japan. Draw the Caspian Sea, the Yellow River, the Yangtze River, the Great Wall, the Grand Canal, and the Himalaya and Altay mountains. Then draw the areas of the Western Khaganate, the Eastern Khaganate, Tang, and the Persian Empire. Lightly draw Tibet. Then draw the areas of Goguryeo, Baekje, and Silla.

6. Finally, check your map against the original. Erase and redraw as necessary as you look at the map.

Chapter Thirty-Nine

The Tribe of Faith

You may use your text when answering the questions in sections I and II.

Section I: Who, What, Where

Write a one or two-sentence answer explaining the significance of each item listed below.

Abu Sufian

Aishah

Ali ibn Abu Talib

Battle of the Trench

Constans II

Constantine III

Heraklonas

Khalid

Khalifat ar-rasul Allah

Martina

Muhajirun

Ridda

Rothari

S'ad

Umar

Yazdegerd III

Section II: Comprehension

Write a two or three-sentence answer to each of the following questions.

1. What did Muhammad expect from non-Muslims in the city of Medina?

2. What is the content of the revelation Muhammad received that appears as Surah 2 in the Qu'ran? How did this revelation relate to Muhammad's frustration with those outside the *umma*?

3. How did the *umma* become the most powerful "tribe" in Medina? What was one disingenuous reason some Arabs were converting to the Muslim faith?

4. What message was Muhammad sending to Mecca by raiding the caravans that passed between Mecca and destinations to the north?

5. Why was Muhammad upset by the death of a Quraysh merchant during a raid on a passing caravan?

6. What was the revelation that Muhammad received after the death of the Quraysh tradesman during the sacred month? What was the implied meaning of that revelation?

7. How did Muhammad manage to win the fight against the Meccans at the Wells of Badr on March 17, 624?

8. Why were the Jews driven out of Medina? What happened to them?

9. How was Muhammad able to justify his large attack on Medina? What kind of troops did he assemble for the fight by 630?

10. What happened when Muhammad arrived at the walls of Mecca with his massive army?

11. When did Mecca become the core of Islam? How was Muhammad's influence spreading?

12. Where does the division between Sunni Muslims and Shi'ite Muslims stem from?

13. How did Abu Bakr deal with the resistance to his leadership? How did this lead to a united Arabian peninsula?

14. Why did Abu Bakr start wars with Persia and Byzantium in 633?

15. What made Abu Bakr take troops away from the Persian front and send them to the Byzantine front? What was the result of this military move?

16. What title was Umar given when he took Abu Bakr's role as leader of the Arabs? Why was his title changed, what was it changed to, and why was this change significant?

17. Despite gathering an army of 150,000, what happened to Heraclius and his Byzantine holdings in the battle with the Arabic forces at the Yarmuk river in Syria? What was Heraclius's one victory?

18. What was the symbolic purpose of slitting Heraklonas's nose? What did the mutilation of Heraklonas suggest about the emperor's role in Byzantium?

Section III: **Critical Thinking**

You may not use your text to answer this question.

When Muhammad became a religious leader, he preached inclusivity and rights for all. But by the time Muhammad became the political leader of Medina, one had to be part of the *umma* in order to be protected by Muhammad. Write a paragraph explaining what happened to the Jews that were living in Medina. Then, explain how their treatment contradicted Muhammad's basic message of equality as espoused in his farewell sermon.

Section IV: **Map Exercise**

1. Using a black pencil, trace the rectangular outline of the frame for Map 39.1: The Conquests of Muhammad and Abu Bakr.

2. Using a blue pencil, trace the visible portion of the Mediterranean, the Black Sea, the Caspian Sea, the Red Sea, and the coastline around Arabia. Also trace the lines of the Tigris and Euphrates. Select four contrasting colors. Use each respectively to trace the Persian Empire, the Byzantine Empire, Muhammad's conquests, and Abu Bakr's conquests.

Repeat until the contours are familiar.

3. Using a new sheet of paper, trace the rectangular outline of the frame in black. Remove your tracing paper from the original. Using a regular pencil with an eraser, draw the visible portion of the Mediterranean, the Black Sea, the Caspian Sea, the Red Sea, and the coastline around Arabia. Also draw the lines of the Tigris and Euphrates. Then draw the Persian Empire, the Byzantine Empire, Muhammad's conquests, and Abu Bakr's conquests. Erase and redraw as necessary.

4. When you are pleased with your map, lay it over the original. Erase and redraw any lines which are more than ¼ inch off of the original. When your map is correct, shade the areas of the Persian Empire, the Byzantine Empire, Muhammad's conquests, and Abu Bakr's conquests as the mapmaker has done: darker for the Persian Empire, lighter for the Byzantine Empire, and contrasting lines for Muhammad and Abu Bakr's conquests.

5. Remove your map. Label the Black Sea and the Caspian Sea. Study carefully the locations of Egypt, Palestine, Syria, Yemen, and Oman. When you are familiar with them, close the book, and label each. Check your map against the original, and correct any misplaced labels.

6. Then study closely the locations of Alexandria, Damascus, Yarmuk, Jerusalem, Medina, Mecca, and Ctesiphon. When you are familiar with them, close the book. Mark each location on your map, and label it. Then lay your map over the original. Correct any misplaced labels, and erase and redraw any cities which are more than ¼ inch off of the original.

Chapter Forty

Intersection

You may use your text when answering the questions in sections I and II.

Section I: **Who, What, Where**

Write a one or two-sentence answer explaining the significance of each item listed below.

al-Hakam

Kannauj

Makran

Manavamma

Pandya

Paramesvaravarman I

Rasil

Sangam

Shahi

Sindh

Vikramaditya

Vinayaditya

Section II: Comprehension

Write a two or three-sentence answer to each of the following questions.

1. How were the kingdoms of Makran, Sindh and Shahi related?

2. Why didn't the Shahi assist the Makran and Sindh when the Arabs attacked? What was the result of the attack?

3. What stopped Umar from expanding the edge of his kingdom from the Makran further into India?

4. In what way did the kingdoms of the Shahi and the Sindh protect Harsha's northern Indian kingdom from Arab invasion?

5. What was Harsha's relationship like with the Chinese, and why were the Chinese (via Xuan Zang) impressed with his ruling style?

6. What happened to Harsha's Northern Indian kingdom after his death in 647?

7. Despite taking the throne in 655, what losses did Vikramaditya suffer at the start of his reign? How did these losses divide the Chalukya kingdom?

8. How did the Pandya get involved in the fight between the Western Chalukya and Pallava?

Section III: Critical Thinking

You may not use your text to answer this question.

Political and religious practices were rarely separated in the medieval world. Similarly, the personal beliefs of rulers usually influenced the beliefs and rituals of their realms. This was no different in Harsha's northern Indian kingdom. Write a paragraph explaining how Harsha's personal history with his sister affected the kingdom's Hindu religious beliefs. Make sure to explain the meaning of shakti, and to recap the play written by Harsha, *Nagananda*. Then write a few sentences explaining how Harsha's Buddhist beliefs affected the laws of his kingdom.

Chapter Forty-One

The Troubles of Empire

You may use your text when answering the questions in sections I and II.

Section I: Who, What, Where

Write a one or two-sentence answer explaining the significance of each item listed below.

Abn 'Amir

Battle of the Camel

Berbers

Fitna

Fostat

Hasan

Kharijis

Muawiyah

Saqiba

Uthman

Section II: Comprehension

Write a two or three-sentence answer to each of the following questions.

1. What were the circumstance of Umar's death, and the naming of his successor?

2. Why did the council of six Muslims choose to name Uthman the next caliph rather than Muhammad's son-in-law Ali ibn Abu Talib?

3. What was Uthman's vision for the organization of the entire Arabic conquered realm? How did he enact this vision?

4. In what way did occupying Alexandria benefit the Arabic empire, other than increasing its size? What was the first conquest of Muawiyah's navy?

5. Describe what happened to Yazdegerd III's court in Khorasan, and the Persian king's murder on the banks of the Murghab river. What did this mean for the Persian empire?

6. What relation did the signet ring of the Prophet have to do with the difficulties in Uthman's rule? In your answer, make sure to describe the signet ring and its significance.

7. What territorial problems did Uthman face in the second part of his reign?

8. Why did Uthman create a definitive version of Muhammad's teachings?

9. How was the stage for revolt against Uthman set in the city of Kufa?

10. Describe the circumstances of Uthman's death.

11. What happened to Uthman's body after he died?

12. Why did Aishah oppose Ali as the next caliph? Why was her argument flawed?

13. What was Aishah's real purpose in trying to keep Ali out of the seat of Arab power?

14. Why did Ali move the seat of his caliphate from Medina to Kufa? Who did not support Ali?

15. What happened when Muawiyah and Ali met for battle on the upper Euphrates in July of 657? What was the result of their truce?

16. In what way did Uthman's murder haunt Ali's time as ruler? How did Ali die?

Section III: **Critical Thinking**

You may not use your text to answer this question.

Like all the charismatic and engaging rulers we've read about before him, Muhammad was able to keep his rapidly expanding empire together largely because of his personality. The caliphs that followed Muhammad barely held the empire together, and by the time Ali ibn Abu Talib was caliph, a piece of the empire had essentially split itself off from the whole. Write a paragraph that explains all the ways the different caliphs tried to keep the Arabic empire together. Then explain why it was so difficult to create cohesion. Make sure to include how issues of both nationality and religion upset Arab unity.

Chapter Forty-Two

Law and Language

You may use your text when answering the questions in sections I and II.

Section I: Who, What, Where

Write a one or two-sentence answer explaining the significance of each item listed below.

Abd al-Malik ibn Marwan

Alcek

Aripert

Asparukh

Bayan

Constantine IV

Dome of the Rock

Grimoald of Benevento

Justinian II

Kotrag

Kouber

Kubrat

Leontios

Musa bin Nusair

Section II: Comprehension

Write a two or three-sentence answer to each of the following questions.

1. How did the Arab invasions affect the Lombards of Italy?

2. What did Rothari hope to do by creating a set of laws for the Lombards in 643? What was his code called? What are some examples of the laws Rothari came up with?

3. According to the Edict of Rothari, how were outsiders supposed to act once they entered the Lombard kingdom? Why was this law important for the realization of Lombard Italy as a nation?

4. Describe the medley of religions that existed within the Lombard kingdom, and how the Lombard religious mix moved towards Catholicism.

5. Why did Constans II move his headquarters to Tarentum in 661?

6. Who was in charge of Benevento at the time of Constans II's approach? What happened to Constans II's planned attack of Benevento once Grimoald was summoned?

7. How long did Constans II stay in Rome? What did he do while he was in Rome? Where did he go next and what did he do from there?

8. What happened to the Shahi kingdom as the Arabs moved east into India in 670?

9. How was Constantine IV able to defend Constantinople against the Arab attacks that started in 674? In your answer, make sure to explain "Greek fire," and how it caused Arab troops to withdraw from the city.

10. What did Kubrat tell his sons on his deathbed, according to Nicephorus in the *Chronographikon syntomon*? How did his prophecy come true?

11. How did Constantine IV come to make a peace treaty with Asparukh? What were the terms of the treaty, and what was the outcome of the treaty for the Bulgarians?

12. How did Abd al-Malik ibn Marwan spend the first years of his caliphate? How did the circumstances of Abd al-Malik ibn Marwan's first years of rule lead to peace with the Byzantines?

13. Describe the organization of Byzantium as it existed when Justinian II came to power. In your answer, make sure to explain how the military was organized as well.

14. Why were Abd al-Malik ibn Marwan and Justinian II so eager to go to war? What was the cause of their war, and how did Justinian II plan on defending Byzantine land?

15. Why did the Bulgarian mercenaries abandon Byzantine troops at the Battle of Sebastopolis in 694? What was the result of the battle?

16. How did the tribal structure of the Berbers help hasten the Islamic conquest of North Africa?

17. What did Abd al-Malik ibn Marwan do during his rule to create a more coherent Arab nation?

Section III: **Critical Thinking**

You may not use your text to answer this question.

The idea of Rome's greatness has done more harm to its various leaders than actually bringing them any kind of glory or triumph. Constans II was seduced by the image of Rome in his mind, and it was his ultimate undoing. Write a paragraph explaining why Constans II left Constantinople, what he hoped to find in Rome, and what he actually found there. How was Constans II's end perfectly suited to the kind of ruler he turned out to be?

Section IV: **Map Exercise**

1. Using a black pencil, trace the rectangular outline of the frame for Map 42.1: Byzantium, the Arabs, and the Bulgars.

2. Using a blue pencil, trace the coastline of the Atlantic around the continent and then the Mediterranean. You do not need to include Britain or islands other than Sardinia, Corsica, Sicily, Crete, and Cyprus at this time. Also with your blue pencil, trace the outline of the Black Sea, the Azov Sea, and the Caspian Sea. Trace the lines of the Danube, the Dniester, the Donets, the Don, and the Volga. Then trace the lines of the Tigris and Euphrates. Repeat until the contours are familiar.

3. Select three contrasting colors (or seven if you have them). Use these respectively to trace the areas of the Visigoths, the Franks, Lombardy, Byzantium, the Khazars, the First Bulgarian Empire, and the Arab Empire. Either use seven contrasting colors to distinguish the regions, or use three contrasting colors for the different shaded areas and then draw different lines across the areas as the mapmaker did for the remaining four regions. Be sure to include the islands of Sardinia, Corsica, Sicily, Crete, and Cyprus, showing which territory each belongs in. Repeat until the contours are familiar.

4. Using a new sheet of paper, trace the rectangular outline of the frame in black. Remove your paper from the original. Using a regular pencil with an eraser as you look at Map 42.1, draw the entire coastline, again including only the islands of Sardinia, Corsica, Sicily, Crete, and Cyprus. Then draw the Black Sea, the Azov Sea, and the Caspian Sea. Draw the Danube, the Dniester, the Donets, the Don, and the Volga. Draw also the Tigris and Euphrates. Now draw the outlines of the territories of the Visigoths, Lombardy, Byzantium, Khazars, the First Bulgarian Empire, and the Arab Empire. Erase and redraw as necessary while looking at the map.

5. When you are pleased with your map, lay it over the original. Erase and redraw any lines which are more than ¼ inch off of the original.

6. Finally draw the arrows showing the Bulgar movements.

Chapter Forty-Three

Creating the Past

You may use your text when answering the questions in sections I and II.

Section I: Who, What, Where

Write a one or two-sentence answer explaining the significance of each item listed below.

Fujiwara

Gemmei

Gensho

Jimmu

Mommu

Shomu

Tenji

Section II: Comprehension

Write a two or three-sentence answer to each of the following questions.

1. How did Tenji's (then Naka no Oe) attempt to help the Baekje against the Tang-Silla alliance end up reinforcing Japan's isolationist policy?

2. Why did then crown prince Naka no Oe and Nakatomi No Kamatari create the Great Reform, or "Taika reforms"?

3. What did the first Reform Edict declare, and how did this reform change the law associated with titles and land ownership?

4. From where did the idea of the Great Reform come? What model was it based on?

5. What is a "polestar monarchy"? How did Tenji try and influence the culture of Japan in his role as "polestar monarch"?

6. Why did Tenji attempt to set down a written legal code for all of Japan?

7. How was the rule of Japan laid out in the Taiho ritsu-ryo different from the reality of how Japan was governed?

8. Why was Gemmei's capital city special? What new name was the city given, and what changes were made to enhance the city?

9. How did the capital at Nara help to extend the heavenly sovereign's power from the divine to the real world?

10. What was the Yoro Code?

Section III: Critical Thinking

You may not use your text to answer this question.

External conquest was *de rigueur* in the medieval world. In this chapter, however, we see the infiltration of Chinese ideas into isolated Japan, and rather than breaking Japan apart, this infiltration actually strengthened the multiple-island nation. Write a paragraph explaining the historical myth that was produced to give a foundation to Japanese kingship. In the second part of your answer, explain how the myth justified internal conflict for the sake of a united Japan.

Section IV: Map Exercise

1. Using a black pencil, trace the rectangular outline of the frame for Map 43.1: The Nara Period.

2. Using a blue pencil, trace the coastal outline up the coast of China and around the coast of Japan. You need not include any islands other than Japan at this time, but do include the Inland Sea. Using your blue pencil, trace the line of the Yellow River. Then, using a black pencil, trace the line of the Great Wall. Repeat until the contours are familiar.

3. Using a new sheet of paper, trace the rectangular outline of the frame for Map 43.1 in black. Remove your tracing paper from the original. Using a regular pencil with an eraser, draw the coastal outline around China and Japan, including the Inland Sea. Draw the line of the Yellow River and the Great Wall.

4. When you are pleased with your map, lay it over the original. Erase and redraw any lines which are more than ¼ inch off of the original.

5. Now study carefully the locations of the Yellow Sea, Hokkaido, Nara, the Yamato Plain, Kyushu, and the Inland Sea. When they are familiar to you, close the book. Label each location, and then check your map against the original. Erase and remark any misplaced locations.

Chapter Forty-Four

The Days of the Empress

You may use your text when answering the questions in sections I and II.

Section I: Who, What, Where

Write a one or two-sentence answer explaining the significance of each item listed below.

Empress Wei

Khitan

Khri-'bring

Li Chongzhao

Mo-ch'o

Ruizong

Tang Xuanzong

Tridu Songtsen

Xue Huaiyi

Zhongzong

Zhou

Section II: Comprehension

Write a two or three-sentence answer to each of the following questions.

1. In addition to naming his heir apparent, and heir apparent grandson, what else did Tang Gaozong order before his death? How did Wu Zetian take advantage of this decree?

2. How did the decree, the "Act of Grace," affect the royal court in Tang China? What did the decree symbolize?

3. Why was it relatively easy for Wu Zetian to make so many changes within Tang China?

4. How did Wu Zetian solve the problem of resentment felt by aristocrats of the court over a former concubine rising to the power of empress and leader?

5. In addition to making common people officials, what else did Wu Zetian do to ensure support of her rule?

6. How did Wu Zetian come to accept the title "Emperor, Son of Heaven"?

7. How did Mo-ch'o most likely orchestrate and use the triple uprising in the north against Wu Zetian to his advantage?

8. How did Zhongzong become heir apparent to the Chinese throne, after once being emperor, and then how did he become emperor once again?

9. What happened to the Zhou dynasty after Wu Zetian's passing?

10. What caused Ruizong to give up his role as Tang emperor?

11. How did Tang Xuanzong fix the mess made by the emperors before him?

Section III: Critical Thinking

You may not use your text to answer this question.

In this chapter we read about two brilliant emperors, though only one was given that nickname. Tang Xuanzong may have brought the Tang dynasty to greatness, but Wu Zetian, once a concubine, managed to convince the empire that she could be a masculine emperor even though she was a woman. Explain how Wu Zetian was able to manipulate the system and turn herself into an emperor. Why were the Chinese people able to accept her in this role?

Chapter Forty-Five

Paths in Europe

You may use your text when answering the questions in sections I and II.

Section I: Who, What, Where

Write a one or two-sentence answer explaining the significance of each item listed below.

Al-Andalus

Al-Ghafiqi

Al-Samh

Alpaida

Busir Glavan

Charles Martel

Egica

Leo III

Odo

Pelayo

Pippin the Fat

Plectrude

Ruderic

Suleiman

Tariq bin Ziyad

Tervel

Theodosius III

Theuderic III

Tiberios III

Umar II

Walid I

Wittiza

Section II: Comprehension

Write a two or three-sentence answer to each of the following questions.

1. What was Justinian the Noseless's first plan to get back the Byzantine throne? How was that plan derailed?

2. How did Justinian manage to get back onto the throne at Constantinople? What were the consequences of his siege?

3. What special appendage did Justinian the Noseless wear during his second reign? What was his main objective during his second reign, and how did it end?

4. Why did Musa ibn Nusair and Tariq bin Ziyad want to take Tangiers for the Islamic holdings in North Africa?

5. What rules were made about Visigoth kingship at the Fifth and Eighth Councils of Toledo? What do the Toledo decrees tells us about where the Visigoths hoped to find stability?

6. What caused civil war amongst the Visigoths during Ruderic's rule?

7. What might have made it easier for Tariq bin Ziyad to fight against the Visigoths led by Ruderic? What was the result of the Battle of Guadalete on July 19, 711?

8. How did the Battle of Guadalete bring an end to the Visigothic kingdom in Spain?

9. How did Leo III drive back the first round of Arab ships that tried to attack the entrance into the Golden Horn?

10. What happened when Umar II took up the siege against Constantinople started by his cousin Suleiman?

11. Why did Pippin the Fat start calling himself *dux et princeps Francorum*, "Duke and Prince of the Franks"? What did the label mean?

12. How does Fredegar's account of what happened at the battle between the Arabs and the Franks at Poitiers differ from what really happened?

13. How did Charles Martel earn the nickname "The Hammer"? Why was this a misnomer?

Section III: Critical Thinking

You may not use your text to answer this question.

Great and loyal leaders are not always remembered as such, especially if historical accounts decide to leave their bravery out of the chronicles. Fredegar did a good job of glorifying Charles Martel, "The Hammer," in his history of the Franks, but he did not give Odo the attention he was due. Now is the chance for Odo to get the recognition Fredegar denied him. Write a paragraph that praises Odo and all that he did for the survival of Aquitaine and the Frankish nation.

Section IV: Map Exercise

1. Using a black pencil, trace the rectangular outline of the frame for Map 45.1: The Arab Advance.

2. Using a blue pencil, trace the coastline from the Atlantic on the west into the Mediterranean. You do not need to trace the coastline of Britain at this time. Trace the coastline of Sardinia, Corsica, Sicily, Crete, and Cyprus, but you do not need to trace any other islands. Trace the coastline of the Black Sea, the Caspian Sea, and the Azov Sea. Trace the lines of the Danube, the Donets, the Don, and the Volga. Then trace the lines of the Tigris and Euphrates. Repeat until the contours are familiar.

3. Select six contrasting colors (or use lines and shading to distinguish the regions) to trace the Franks, Lombardy, Byzantium, Khazars, the First Bulgarian Empire, and the Arab Empire. Trace the different regions with a corresponding color for each, or use lines and shading like the mapmaker to distinguish the regions. Repeat until the contours are familiar.

4. Using a new sheet of paper, trace the rectangular outline of the frame in black. Remove your tracing paper from the original. Using a regular pencil with an eraser as you look at the map, draw the coastline around the continent and through the Mediterranean. (Again, do not draw the coastline of Britain, but do draw that of Sardinia, Corsica, Sicily, Crete, and Cyprus. Do not draw any other islands.) Draw the coastline of the Black Sea, the Caspian Sea, and the Azov Sea. Draw the lines of the Danube, the Donets, the Don, the Volga, the Tigris, and the Euphrates. Erase and redraw as necessary. Then lay your map over the original and correct any lines which are more than ¼ inch off of the original.

5. Next, using a regular pencil as you look at the map, draw the perimeters of the territories of the Visigoths, Franks, Lombardy, Byzantium, Khazars, First Bulgarian Empire, and the Arab Empire. Erase and redraw as necessary.

6. When you are pleased with your map, lay it over the original. Erase and redraw any lines which are more than ¼ inch off of the original.

7. Next, create a coding system similar as the mapmaker did on the original map to show which color (or shading or lines, depending on what you used) corresponds to which region. Provide labels to identify each color (or shading/lines).

8. Next, as you look at your map, label the regions of Ifriqiya, Libya, Egypt, Syria, Armenia, Asia Minor, Thracia, Macedonia, Greece, Pannonia, Austrasia, Neustria, Aquitaine, Asturias, and Al-Andalus. Then label the locations of Tangiers, Toledo, Bourdeaux, Poitiers, Tours, Cologne, Ravenna, Rome, Benevento, Naples, Syracuse, Carthage, Tarentum, Constantinople, Jerusalem, Damascus, Kufa, Medina, and Mecca. (Because there are so many locations on this map, you will be studying the battle locations instead of the city locations. You are marking city locations here for reference.)

9. Study carefully the locations of the Battle of Guadalete, the Battle of Toulouse, the Battle of the River Garonne, and the Battle of Tours. When you are familiar with them, close the book. Using your regular pencil, label the location of each battle. Check your map against the original, and correct any misplaced labels.

10. Mark the location of the Dardanelles and the Sea of Marmara.

Chapter Forty-Six

The Kailasa of the South

You may use your text when answering the questions in sections I and II.

Section I: **Who, What, Where**

Write a one or two-sentence answer explaining the significance of each item listed below.

Al-Hajjaj

Brahmanabad

Dahir

Dantidurga

Dhruva

Howdah

Kailasa (Krishnesvara)

Kirtivarman II

Krishna I

Muhammad bin Qasim

Nagabhata

Vikramaditya II

Section II: Comprehension

Write a two or three-sentence answer to each of the following questions.

1. How did al-Hajjaj and his son Muhammad bin Qasim trick Dahir into a fight? Why did they need a reason to attack Debal?

2. Describe the Arabs' attack on Debal. What were the results of the attack?

3. How did bin Qasim move the battle at Debal so that it followed Dahir over the Indus? What was the result of the battle?

4. Though conquest of the Sindh was once abandoned because the land seemed barren, how did its eventual conquest benefit the Arabs?

5. How was it that Dantidurga had Chalukya blood in his veins?

6. What three groups had a stake in protecting the northern city of Kannauj?

Section III: Critical Thinking

You may not use your text to answer this question.

Power and conquest often mean more when they are backed by the gods. The creation of the Rashtrakuta kingdom was incomplete when Dantidurga died, not only because he wasn't able to fill out the borders he'd carved, but also because he did not declare a spiritual center for his kingdom. Write a paragraph explaining how Krishna I fortified the Rashtrakuta kingdom through both conquest and spiritual grounding.

Chapter Forty-Seven

Purifications

You may use your text when answering the questions in sections I and II.

Section I: Who, What, Where

Write a one or two-sentence answer explaining the significance of each item listed below.

Eutychius

Constantine V

Germanos

Hodegetria

Liutprand

Mo-chi-lien

Pope Gregory II

Pope Gregory III

Yazid II

Section II: Comprehension

Write a two or three-sentence answer to each of the following questions.

1. What was the "head tax" Muhammad instituted during his reign? How did later officials take advantage of the "head tax"?

2. Why did Umar II do away with the "head tax"? What was the result of its repeal?

3. What was the reason for the non-Arab tribes in Khorasan to rebel against Yazid II? Who did they go to for help in their rebellion?

4. Why did the Jews leave Byzantium around the time of the fight between Khorasan and the Arab empire?

5. What is the meaning of the Greek word eikon? What was the purpose of an icon, for example, a painting of the Virgin Mary?

6. Why was Leo III opposed to icon worship? After the eruption of the volcano on Thera in 726, how were Leo III's fears about his people's overreliance on icons justified?

7. What resulted from Leo III's taking down of the icon of Christ that hung over the Bronze Gate?

8. Explain the difference between iconoclasts and iconodules. How did iconodules twist Leo III's ban of icons into a political battle?

9. What was Pope Gregory II's reaction to Leo III's ban on the use of icons?

10. How did the Byzantine cities in Italy react to Leo III's declaration that banned the use of icons?

11. What was the Sutri Donation, and why was it so important to the papacy?

12. How did Leo III react to Pope Gregory III's 731 excommunication of all icon-destroyers?

Section III: Critical Thinking

You may use your text to answer this question.

The debate over the worship of icons in Christianity has its roots in the separation of Christianity from the old Roman religion. The debate is also an echo of Nestorianism versus monophysitism. Explain why the worship of icons was frowned upon at first, at the beginning of Christianity, and then explain how the use of icons reflected different views about the true nature of Christ. You may go back to *Chapter 12: One Nature versus Two* for help.

Section IV: Map Exercise

1. Using a black pencil, trace the rectangular outline of the frame for Map 47. 2: The First Papal State.

2. Using a black pencil, trace the coastline around Italy, Sicily, Sardinia, and Corsica. Repeat until the contours are familiar.

3. Select three contrasting colors. Use each respectively to trace the regions of the Lombard Kingdom, Byzantium, and the first papal state. Repeat until the contours are familiar.

4. Using a new sheet of paper, trace the rectangular frame of the map in black. Remove your tracing paper from the original. Using a regular pencil with an eraser as you look at the map, draw Italy, Sicily, Sardinia, and Corsica. Then draw the regions of the Lombard Kingdom, Byzantium, and the First Papal State. Erase and redraw as necessary.

5. When you are pleased with your map, lay it over the original. Erase and redraw any lines which are more than ¼ inch off of the original.

6. Study carefully the locations of Milan, Venice, Ravenna, Sutri, Rome, and Naples. Then study the locations of the Duchy of Spoleto and the Duchy of Benevento. When you are familiar with them, close the book. Using your regular pencil, label each city and the Duchy of Spoleto and of Benevento. When you are done, lay your map over the original. Erase and redraw any cities that are more than ¼ inch off of the original. Correct any misplaced labels.

Chapter Forty-Eight

The Abbasids

You may use your text when answering the questions in sections I and II.

Section I: Who, What, Where

Write a one or two-sentence answer explaining the significance of each item listed below.

Abd ar-Rahman

Abu al-Abbas

Al-Mansur

Gao Xianzhi

Hashimites

Hisham

Khan Bihar

Marwan II

Qadi

Shi'at Ali

Tzitzak

Yusuf al-Fihri

Section II: Comprehension

Write a two or three-sentence answer to each of the following questions.

1. What caused aggression between the Khazars and the Arabs? When Hisham came to power, what were the two empires fighting over?

2. According to the account of one of the Jewish kings of the Khazars, how did Khan Bihar come to the conclusion that he should convert his empire to Judaism? In what way was this a very smart political decision?

3. List the caliphs that followed Hisham, the length of their leadership, and the circumstances of their death or their loss of the caliphate.

4. How did Constantine V's defeat of the Arab navy in a 747 sea battle near Syria affect Marwan II's rule? What was the cause of the main opposition to Marwan II's leadership?

5. What happened when Marwan II's hundred thousand men met Abu al-Abbas's troops just east of the Tigris in early 750?

6. Why did Abd ar-Rahman flee from Damascus? Describe his escape with his brother and Greek servant.

7. How did al-Abbas deal with the Umayyads that remained in his realm?

8. Why was Gao Xianzhi's army able to get as close to the Islamic empire as Sogdiana? What happened at the Battle of Talas in 751?

9. Why did al-Mansur move the capital of the Arab empire to Baghdad?

10. What did Abd ar-Rahman call himself when he became ruler of al-Andalus? Why was his rule of al-Andalus so significant?

11. How did al-Mansur begin his caliphate? For what reason did people believe he had a magic mirror that told him who was loyal and who was planning revolt?

Section III: Critical Thinking

You may not use your text to answer this question.

Before Muhammad was given a vision of the angel Gabriel, he was already disconcerted by the growing divide between the rich and poor in Mecca. Once he received his vision, Muhammad preached purity, piety and morality. In the decades after his rule, the caliphate moved further and further away from Muhammad's original teachings. Write a paragraph explaining how the break from the Umayyad caliphate was meant to be a return to Muhammad's original role as spiritual ruler, but ended up being even further from Muhammad's teachings by the time of al-Mansur's rule.

Section IV: Map Exercise

1. Using a black pencil, trace the rectangular outline of the frame for Map 48.1: The Battle of Talas.

2. Using a blue pencil, trace the coastline along Persia. Using a black pencil, trace the mountain peaks. Using your blue pencil, trace the line of the Oxus and Indus rivers. Using a black pencil, trace the outline of the Abbasid Caliphate. Using a contrasting color, trace the area which is the approximate extent of the eastern Khaghanate. Repeat until the contours are familiar.

3. Using a new sheet of paper, trace the rectangular outline of the frame in black. Remove your tracing paper from the original. Using a regular pencil with an eraser, draw all the visible coastline. Draw the mountain peaks and the three rivers. Then draw the perimeters for the Abbasid Caliphate and the approximate extent of the eastern Khaghanate. Erase and redraw as necessary.

4. When you are pleased with your map, lay it over the original. Erase and redraw any lines which are more than ¼ inch off of the original.

5. Looking at your map, label the Khyber Pass. Label all three rivers.

6. Study carefully the regions of Persia, Khorasan, Pratihara, Rashtrakuta, Pala, Tibet, and Tang. When you are familiar with them, close the book and mark each on your map. Check your map against the original, and make any needed corrections.

7. Now study carefully the locations of the cities of Debal and Kannauj. When you are familiar with them, close the book. Mark each on your map. Then lay your map over the original. Erase and redraw any locations which are more than ¼ inch off of the original.

Chapter Forty-Nine

Charlemagne

You may use your text when answering the questions in sections I and II.

Section I: Who, What, Where

Write a one or two-sentence answer explaining the significance of each item listed below.

Aistulf

Carloman (of Charles Martel)

Carloman (of Pippin the Younger)

Charles/Charlemagne

Childeric III

Desiderius

Donation of Constantine

Hildegard

Irminsul

Iron Crown of the Lombards

Pippin the Younger

Pope Stephen II

Pope Zachary

Song of Roland

Sulayman al-Arabi

Section II: Comprehension

Write a two or three-sentence answer to each of the following questions.

1. Why didn't Charles Martel appoint a new king of the Franks after Theuderic IV's death in 737?

2. What was the cause of tension between Pope Gregory III and Liutprand in 738? Who did Pope Gregory III go to for help and what did he promise in exchange for aid?

3. Why did Charles Martel refuse to help Pope Gregory III in his battle against Liutprand?

4. What was the significance of Pope Gregory III's appeal to Charles Martel for help in the fight against Liutprand?

5. Why did Pippin the Younger need Pope Zachary's permission to take the Frankish throne?

6. How did Pippin the Younger become the *de facto* ruler of Italy?

7. Why did Desiderius want to destroy Charles? Despite the threat from the Lombard king, how was Charles's marriage to Hildegard advantageous for the Frankish king?

8. What made Charles head for Saxon territory in 772? Why did Charles want to make sure his men destroyed the Irminsul?

9. Describe Charles's conquest of the Lombards. What was his "crowning" achievement?

10. What was supposed to happen when Charlemagne arrived at the city of Zaragoza in al-Andalus, and what really happened? After leaving Zaragoza, why did Charlemagne sack Pamplona?

11. Why was Charlemagne's sacking of Pamplona a miscalculation? How did the Vascones get their revenge on the Frankish king?

12. Why was the Vascones' ambush on Charlemagne's men so devastating to the Frankish king? In what way did time and distance theoretically heal Charlemagne's wounds?

Section III: Critical Thinking

You may not use your text to answer this question.

We know from our readings that kings and emperors will invoke the power of the heavens to justify their rule on earth. In this chapter, we read about two popes that took advantage of earthly power to ensure their place as religious leaders. Explain how the power of the pope and the power of the Frankish king merged, and how this merge benefitted both parties.

Section IV: Map Exercise

1. Using a black pencil, trace the rectangular outline of the frame for Map 49.1: Charlemagne's Kingdom.

2. Using a blue pencil, trace the coastline of the Atlantic and the Mediterranean. Include the coastline of Britain and the islands of Sardinia, Corsica, and Sicily, but do not include any other islands. Trace the Alps and the Pyrenees mountains with simple peaks with a black pencil. With your blue pencil, draw the lines of the Loire, Seine, Rhone, Rhine, Elbe, and Danube. Repeat until the contours are familiar.

3. Using a new sheet of paper, trace the rectangular outline of the frame in black. Remove your tracing paper from the original. Using a regular pencil, draw the coastline as you traced it while you look at Map 49.1. Show the Alps and the Pyrenees mountains with simple peaks, and draw the lines of the rivers Loire, Seine, Rhone, Rhine, Elbe, and Danube. Erase and redraw as necessary.

4. When you are pleased with your map, lay it over the original. Erase and redraw any lines which are more than ¼ inch off of the original.

5. Remove your map. Study carefully the areas of Asturias, the Emirate of Cordoba, Aquitaine, Neustria, and Austrasia. When you are familiar with them, close the book and label them on your map. Check your map against the original, and correct any misplaced labels.

6. Then study carefully the locations of Cordoba, Zaragoza, Pamplona, and Soissons. Also study the locations of Milan, Venice, Pavia, Ravenna, Rome, and Naples. Study the locations of the Duchy of Spoleto and the Duchy of Benevento. When you are familiar with them, close the book. Using your regular pencil, mark the cities of Cordoba, Zaragoza, Pamplona, Soissons, Milan, Venice, Pavia, Ravenna, Rome, and Naples. Then mark the Duchy of Spoleto and the Duchy of Benevento. Check your map against the original. Correct any misplaced labels.

7. Mark the locations of the Pass of Roncesvalles and the Breton Marches.

Chapter Fifty

The An Lushan Rebellion

You may use your text when answering the questions in sections I and II.

Section I: Who, What, Where

Write a one or two-sentence answer explaining the significance of each item listed below.

An Lushan

Geluofeng

Gyeongdeok

Li Bai

Li Linfu

Mun

Piluoge

Tang Daizong

Tang Suzong

Wang Wei

Wu Daozi

Yang Guifei

Yang Guozhong

Zhang Jiuling

Section II: Comprehension

Write a two or three-sentence answer to each of the following questions.

1. Describe the greatness of the Tang empire as it thrived under the leadership of Tang Xuanzong.

2. What was the cost of China's expanding empire, according to the poet Li Bai? How was this cost affected by Tang Xuanzong's preoccupation with Yang Guifei?

3. How did the Nanzhao kingdom come to be? How did Tang Xuanzong view Piluoge's strengthening domain?

4. In what way did the Tang conflict with Nanzhao allow An Lushan to declare his challenge to the emperor's power?

5. Describe the beginning of An Lushan's advances against The Brilliant Emperor. How did Gao Xianzhi suffer as a result of An Lushan's uprising?

6. What was Yang Guozhong's plan to fight An Lushan? What was the result of his plan?

7. How did the An Lushan rebellion end?

8. Who were the Uighur people, and where did they come from? What was the relationship between the Uighur and Tang China like before the An Lushan rebellion?

9. How did the Balhae form? Why was the Balhae a threat to Unified Silla?

Section III: Critical Thinking

You may not use your text to answer this question.

Often when we think of singular events reshaping the ancient or medieval world, we think of great natural disasters that forced peoples to rethink their way of life. The An Lushan rebellion was a singular event that altered life for many peoples in the same way that the Great Flood, or the explosion of Mount Vesuvius, altered the lives and customs of people in the past. Write a paragraph or two explaining how the one An Lushan rebellion ended up reshaping an entire system of political relations. In your answer, make sure to explain the concrete effects of the rebellion on the relationship between Tang China and its surrounding peoples.

Section IV: Map Exercise

1. Using a black pencil, trace the rectangular outline of the frame for Map 50.1: New Kingdoms and the Tang.

2. Using a blue pencil, trace the coastline as far as it is visible. You do not need to include any islands at this time. Trace the line of the Yangtze River and the Yellow River. Mark Lake Erhai and Lake Kokonor. Using your black pencil, trace the Himalaya mountains with simple peaks. Repeat until the contours are familiar. Then trace the regions of the Tang, the land lost by the Tang, Tibet, and Balhae. Repeat until the contours are familiar.

3. Trace the rectangular outline of the frame in black. Remove your tracing paper from the original. Using a regular pencil with an eraser as you look at Map 50.1, draw the coastline, the Yangtze River, the Yellow River, and the mountains. Draw the perimeters of the regions of the Tang, the land lost by the Tang, Tibet, and Balhae. Mark and label Lake Erhai and Lake Kokonor. Erase and redraw as necessary.

4. When you are pleased with your map, lay it over the original. Erase and redraw any lines which are more than ¼ inch off of the original.

5. Remove your map. Study carefully the regions of Uighur, Fanyang, Khitan, and Unified Silla. Also study the locations of Nanzhao and Weicheng. When you are familiar with them, close the book, and mark the locations on your map. Check your map with the original, and make any necessary corrections.

6. Now study the locations of Ordu-Baliq, Fanyang, Chang'an, Luoyang, and Beijing. Also study the locations of the Battle of Talas and the Battle of Xiaguan. When you are familiar with them, close the book. Mark the locations on your map. Check your map with the original, and correct any misplaced locations or labels.

7. Mark the locations of Lake Erhai and Lake Kokonor as you look at the map. Then draw and mark the Silk Road and the Great Wall.

Chapter Fifty-One

Imperator et Augustus

You may use your text when answering the questions in sections I and II.

Section I: Who, What, Where

Write a one or two-sentence answer explaining the significance of each item listed below.

Alcuin

Alfonso II

Al-Mahdi

Charles the Younger

Constantine VI

Irene

Kardam

Leo IV

Louis the Pious

Nikephorus

Nikephoros I

Pippin

Rotrude

Widukind

Section II: Comprehension

Write a two or three-sentence answer to each of the following questions.

1. Why was Constantine V planning to go to war against the First Bulgarian Empire in 775? What stopped him from attacking?

2. Why did Irene ask Charlemagne to betroth one of his daughters to the eleven-year-old Byzantine king Constantine VI?

3. Describe the reach of Charlemagne and his family's power when he received the request from Irene to marry one of his daughters to the young Constantine VI.

4. Why would an alliance between the Carolingians and the Byzantine emperors be a real challenge to the power of the Arabs?

5. Why did Irene break the engagement between Constantine VI and Rotrude?

6. How did Charlemagne come to be called "King David" by his royal circle of scholars and clerics? How did King David spark the "Carolingian renaissance"?

7. Why did Charlemagne attack the Saxons in 782? What rules did the Saxons have to abide by after Widukind's capture?

8. How were the religious rules imposed upon the Saxons part of Charlemagne's forceful evangelism? In what way did Alcuin suggest Charlemagne be a little less forceful?

9. What actions did Irene of Byzantium take to prove she held the highest God-sanctioned position of authority in the known world?

10. How did Constantine VI react when he found out there was a plot to take him off of the throne?

11. What happened when Kardam threatened to invade Thracia unless Constantine VI paid him tribute? How did Kardam eventually get his tribute?

12. Why did Charlemagne consider the throne of Constantinople to be empty? How did Charlemagne respond to the Second Council of Nicaea?

13. What did the title *imperator et augustus* mean to Charlemagne? How was the crowning of Charlemagne viewed in Constantinople?

14. What were the terms of the agreement made between Nikephoros I and Charlemagne called the *Pax Nicephori*? Why wouldn't Nikephoros I acknowledge Charlemagne as "Emperor" when he signed the treaty?

Section III: Critical Thinking

You may not use your text to answer this question.

In 799, Pope Leo III was attacked by a band of his enemies, who tried to cut out his eyes and tongue. Pope Leo III managed to escape his attackers, and he went immediately to Charlemagne, asking the Frankish king to help him drive out his enemies from Rome. Write a paragraph explaining why Charlemagne had to think hard about his decision to send soldiers to Rome. Then write a paragraph explaining what Charlemagne decided to do, and the unexpected reward he received for helping Pope Leo III.

Chapter Fifty-Two

The New Sennacherib

You may use your text when answering the questions in sections I and II.

Section I: Who, What, Where

Write a one or two-sentence answer explaining the significance of each item listed below.

Abu'l-Abbas

Harun al-Rashid

Michael Rangabe

King Offa

Krum

Leo V

Omurtag

Staurakios

Section II: Comprehension

Write a two or three-sentence answer to each of the following questions.

1. Why did Harun al-Rashid pursue a friendly relationship with Charlemagne?

2. Why did Harun al-Rashid move his court from Baghdad to Ar Raqqah?

3. How was it that Arab merchants were able to trade with Scandinavian merchants? What did the Scandinavian merchants have to offer, and what did they want from Arab merchants?

4. Describe how peace with Charlemagne allowed the Arabs unhindered access to trade routes via water. In what way did peace and healthy trade with the Arabs benefit Charlemagne?

5. How did Harun al-Rashid keep his Abbasid empire safe during his reign?

6. What important declaration did al-Rashid make in 807 regarding Christian holy sites in Jerusalem? What is the significance of al-Rashid directing this declaration towards Charlemagne, and not the pope?

7. Why did Nikephoros I declare war on the Bulgars? What happened when Nikephoros I finally got his troops on the road?

8. What happened to Nikephoros I and his army in his second siege against Krum?

9. Why wouldn't Michael Rangabe make a truce with Krum?

10. What were the terms of the treaty between Michael Rangabe and Charlemagne?

11. What happened to Michael Rangabe and his family after his failed 813 campaign against the Bulgarians?

12. How did Krum react after Leo V failed to kill him under the flag of truce?

Section III: Critical Thinking

You may use your text to answer this question.

The Abbasid caliph Harun al-Rashid did not expand the borders of his kingdom through conquest. Yet the reach of his empire penetrated several borders, and even transcended time. Explain how healthy trade routes allowed Harun al-Rashid's empire to grown in space and in time. In your answer, make sure to include the stories of the "OFFA REX" coin and the *Arabian Nights.*

Section IV: Map Exercise

1. Using a black pencil, trace the rectangular outline of the frame for Map 52.1: Expansion of the First Bulgarian Empire.

2. Using a blue pencil, trace the coastline from the Baltic Sea down the Atlantic around Britain and into the Mediterranean. Include as usual the islands of Sardinia, Corsica, Sicily, Crete, and Cyprus, but you do not need to include any other islands at this time. Then draw the coastline of the Black Sea, the Azov Sea, the Caspian Sea, the Red Sea, and what is visible of the Persian Gulf on the far right of the map. Repeat until the contours are familiar.

3. Now try to find six contrasting colors to delineate the Empire of Charlemagne, the Papal States, Byzantium, Khazars, the First Bulgarian Empire, and the Abbasid Empire. Trace each with its respective color until the contours are familiar.

4. Using a new sheet of paper, trace the rectangular outline of the frame in black. Remove your tracing paper from the original. Using a regular pencil with an eraser as you look at Map 52.1, draw the coastline from the Baltic Sea around Britain and down the continent through the Mediterranean, including the five major islands. Draw the Black Sea, the Azov Sea, the Caspian Sea, the Red Sea, and the Persian Gulf. Then draw the six different territories of the Empire of Charlemagne, the Papal States, Byzantium, Khazars, the First Bulgarian Empire, and the Abbasid Empire. Erase and redraw as necessary.

5. When you are pleased with your map, lay it over the original. Erase and redraw any lines which are more than ¼ inch off of the original.

6. Looking at your map, label the regions of Ifriqiya, Libya, Egypt, Syria, Armenia, Asia Minor, Khazars, Thracia, Macedonia, Pannonia, Scandinavian traders, Saxons, Austrasia, Burgundy, Neustria, Aquitaine, Asturias, Al-Andalus, and Mercia.

7. Study carefully the locations of Pliska and Serdica. When you are familiar with them, close the book. Using your regular pencil, label both cities. Check your map against the original, and correct if necessary.

8. Finally trace the lines of the Dniester and Danube rivers. Label each.

Chapter Fifty-Three

Castle Lords and Regents

You may use your text when answering the questions in sections I and II.

Section I: Who, What, Where

Write a one or two-sentence answer explaining the significance of each item listed below.

Aejang

Akira Keiko

Chang Pogo

Fujiwara no Mototsune

Fujiwara no Yoshifusa

Heian Period

Heizei

Heondeok

Heungdeok

Kammu

Junna

Kim Ujing

Montoku

Munseong

Ninmyo

Saga

Seiwa

Seol Chong

Soseong

Takaiko

Wonseong

Yozei

Section II: Comprehension

Write a two or three-sentence answer to each of the following questions.

1. In eighth century Sillan culture, what did "bone rank" mean? What were the various ranks within bone rank, and what rank was currently in power?

2. Why was one able to move up in status in Chinese society, but not in eighth century Sillan society?

3. What did candidates have to do in order to pass King Wonseong's new examinations? What did King Wonseong want the candidates to prove during these examinations?

4. When did Silla's Late Period start? What was the defining characteristic of the Late Period? Use the beginning of King Heondeok's reign as an example.

5. In the Late Period turmoil in Silla, how was it that Munseong was able to hold onto the throne for almost two decades?

6. Describe the state of Silla after the death of Chang Pogo. What were "castle lords," who was managing the Buddhist monasteries, and what did farmers and tradesmen do for protection?

7. Why was the Fujiwara clan such a threat to Kammu?

8. Describe Kammu's move to Nagaoka. Was the move successful in distancing the Heavenly Sovereign from the Fujiwara?

9. Why did Kammu move the capital a second time? Where was the new capital city, and what was it renamed?

10. How did the two moves of the capital and the corrupt tax practices of the Fujiwara affect the peasants who lived along the Kamo river?

Section III: Critical Thinking

You may not use your text to answer this question.

In this chapter we learned that by the middle of the 9th century, United Silla was not united at all. Power had moved away from the king to nobles that ruled over small enclaves, creating their own mini-kingdoms, and the Buddhist monasteries took government accounting into their own hands, collecting land and revenues taxes for themselves. The shift away from a concentrated center of power in United Silla was mirrored in Japan. Explain the dimming light of the polestar, and connect it to the shifts in power in United Silla.

Section IV: Map Exercise

1. Using a black pencil, trace the rectangular outline of the frame for Map 53.1: Unified Silla and Japan.

2. Using a blue pencil, trace the coastal outline around the Yellow Sea and up and around Japan. You do not need to include any islands at this time other than the main islands of Japan, but do include the Inland Sea. Then trace the line of the Yellow River. Repeat until the contours are familiar.

3. Using four contrasting colors, trace the perimeters of the regions of Unified Silla, Japan, Balhae, and Tang. Repeat until the contours are familiar.

4. Using a new sheet of paper, trace the rectangular outline of the frame in black. Remove your tracing paper from the original. Using a regular pencil with an eraser, draw the coastline, including the Inland Sea, and the Yellow River. Then draw the outlines of the four regions. Erase and redraw as necessary.

5. When you are pleased with your map, lay it over the original. Erase and redraw any lines which are more than ¼ inch off of the original.

6. Remove your map. Study carefully the locations of Ch'ungju, Kyongju, Wando, Hokkaido, and Kyushu. When you are familiar with them, close the book. Using your regular pencil, label each location. Check your map against the original. Correct any misplaced labels.

7. Draw the line of the Great Wall. Draw the arrows showing the Khitan.

Chapter Fifty-Four

The Triumph of the Outsiders

You may use your text when answering the questions in sections I and II.

Section I: Who, What, Where

Write a one or two-sentence answer explaining the significance of each item listed below.

Abaoji

Ch'oe Chi'won

Fanzhen

Gyeongmun

Heonggang

Huang Chao

Hyogong

Jinseong

Kungye

Kyonhwon

Later Three Kingdoms

Li Keyong

Muzong

Shatuo

Tang Aidi

Tang Jingzong

Tang Wenzong

Tang Xianzong

Tang Xizong

Tang Zhaozong

Wang Kon

Yanggil

Zhu Wen

Section II: Comprehension

Write a two or three-sentence answer to each of the following questions.

1. Despite a healthy salt trade and an effective system of tax collection, why was Tang rule still shaky after the An Lushan rebellion?

2. Who really ran China during the reign of Tang Wenzong? What stroke of luck kept China prosperous?

3. Why was Huang Chao so upset after he took the civil service examination in 874? How did he make up for his failure?

4. What happened when Tang troops were dispatched from Chang'an to put down Huang Chao and his gang?

5. How were Tang Xizong, Li Keyong and Zhu Wen able to defeat Huang Chao and his rebel army?

6. Using the words of poet Wei Zhuang, describe the state of Chang'an after the fighting between Huang Chao and Tang Xizong.

7. Explain how both Li Keyong and Zhu Wen gained more power in the years after putting down Huang Chao's rebellion through the time of Tang Zhaozong's death.

8. What period did the abdication of the last Tang emperor mark in Chinese history? Why was the period given this name?

9. Why did King Gyeongmun's two queens want to murder Kungye and his mother? Were they successful?

10. What kinds of things did Heonggang do during his reign to make it seem like all was well in Silla? What was the reality of the state of Silla outside of the capital city?

11. How was Queen Jinseong described in contemporary accounts of her rule? Why was she described in this way?

12. In what way did Queen Jinseong's crackdown on taxpayers to fund her government backfire?

13. What happened to Kungye after he formed Later Goguryeo?

Section III: Critical Thinking

You may use your text to answer this question.

This chapter is full of usurpation and murder, a reflection of the chaotic leadership in 9th century China and Korea. The Confucian scholar-poet Ch'oe Chi'won was so distraught by the turmoil that he decided to trade in doomed palace life for the monastery. Using what you learned about Ch'oe Chi'won's life, and some of the words from the verse below, explain why Ch'oe Chi'won decided to leave politics to practice a life of peace.

> The frenzied rush through the rocks roars at the peaks,
> and drowns out the human voices close by.
>
> Because I always fear disputes between right and wrong
> I have arranged the waters to cage in these mountains.

Chapter Fifty-Five

The Third Dynasty

You may use your text when answering the questions in sections I and II.

Section I: Who, What, Where

Write a one or two-sentence answer explaining the significance of each item listed below.

Al-Amin

Al-Mamun

Al-Mutasim

Tahir

Talhah

Section II: Comprehension

Write a two or three-sentence answer to each of the following questions.

1. How did Harun al-Rashid die? What did he leave behind?

2. Why was al-Rashid torn between who to appoint as heir? How did he solve the problem?

3. Why did al-Amin want al-Mamun to come to Baghdad? What did al-Mamun do instead?

4. What were the circumstances that led to war between al-Amin and al-Mamun?

5. Describe what happened to Baghdad and its surrounding cities while it was under siege during the Abbasid civil war.

6. How did Tahir claim his own independence? Why was this independence so short lived?

7. How did the Tahirids come to be?

Section III: Critical Thinking

You may use your text to answer this question.

The Muslim empire, created by Muhammad with unity in mind, was by the beginning of the 9th century fractured in three. Squabbles over rightful heirs were at the root of both divisions. Explain how fighting over the right to rule caused the first break in the Muslim empire, and then explain how warring over the right to rule was also the cause of the second split.

Section IV: Map Exercise

1. Using a black pencil, trace the rectangular outline of the frame for Map 55.1: The Tahirids.

2. Using a blue pencil, trace the visible coastline: the Mediterranean Sea (you do not need to trace any islands), the Black Sea, the Caspian Sea, the Red Sea, and the Persian Gulf. Then trace the line of the Nile, the Tigris and Euphrates, and the Oxus rivers. Show the Caucasus mountains with simple peaks. Repeat until the contours are familiar.

3. Select three contrasting colors. Use them to trace respectively the perimeters of Byzantium, the Abbasid Empire, and the Tahirids. Repeat until the contours are familiar.

4. Using a new sheet of paper, trace the rectangular outline of the frame in black. Remove your tracing paper from the original. Using a regular pencil with an eraser, draw the coastline of the Mediterranean, the Black Sea, the Caspian Sea, the Red Sea, and the Persian Gulf. Draw the Nile, Tigris and Euphrates, and the Oxus. Draw the Caucasus mountains. Then draw the perimeters of Byzantium, the Abbasid Empire, and the Tahirids. Erase and redraw as necessary.

5. When you are pleased with your map, lay it over the original. Erase and redraw any lines which are more than ¼ inch off of the original.

6. Remove your map. Study carefully the locations of Alexandria, Fostat, Antioch, Constantinople, Chalcedon, Antioch, Edessa, Amida, Baghdad, Kufa, Basra, Medina, Mecca, Hamadan, Tus, and Balkh. When you are familiar with them, close the book. Using your regular pencil, label each location. Then check your map against the original. Erase and remark any misplaced labels.

7. Label the areas of Fars, Mirman, and Khorasan.

Chapter Fifty-Six

The Vikings

You may use your text when answering the questions in sections I and II.

Section I: Who, What, Where

Write a one or two-sentence answer explaining the significance of each item listed below.

Abd ar-Rahman II

Charles

Garcia I

Inigo I

Lothair

Louis

Michael III

Ordono I

Pippin

Pippin II

Ragnar Lodbrok

Rhos/Rus

Rurik

Section II: Comprehension

Write a two or three-sentence answer to each of the following questions.

1. Describe the reach of Charlemagne's imperial power and kingdom by 813.

2. What were the terms of Charlemagne's 806 will?

3. Why was Charlemagne's 806 will thrown out?

4. With what long title did Charlemagne refer to himself? How did Louis the Pious change this title, and what did the change signify?

5. How did Louis the Pious treat his sons once they were all crowned as kings of their various domains? How did the sons react to his treatment?

6. Why was Lothair upset when Louis the Pious made Charles the king of Alemannia? How was Lothair able to convince his brothers to go to war against their father?

7. What happened during the third year of the civil war between Louis the Pious and his sons?

8. Why were Louis the Pious's sons forced to make a treaty in the middle of their very bloody civil war? What was the name of the treaty, and what were its terms?

9. What was the Medieval Warm Period, also known as the Medieval Climactic Anomaly? How did the Medieval Warm Period contribute to Viking exploration?

10. Who did the Vikings attack between 844 and 860?

11. What did Charles the Landless start to built in 860 to fortify his land against the Viking invaders? Did his plan work?

12. Who made up the people that spoke Finno-Ugrian? What did they call the later Scandinavian travellers who came through their villages?

13. How did Michael III's regents explain the retreat of the Vikings after their vicious attack on the area outside of the walls of Constantinople? What was most likely the real reason for the Vikings's retreat?

Section III: Critical Thinking

You may not use your text to answer this question.

The Rus were an adaptable people. They made their way down from Scandinavia, adopted their name from the Finno-Ugrians, with whom they intermarried, and formed a new state centered around Gorodishche with its own khagan. The khagan was easy going, exercising loose and informal control over the mix of Scandinavian newcomers and Finno-Ugrian natives who lived around him. Write a paragraph explaining how the Rus khagan avoided Viking attack around 860. Then write a paragraph explaining how the flexibility of the Rus saved them from being destroyed by the Vikings in 862.

Chapter Fifty-Seven

Long-Lived Kings

You may use your text when answering the questions in sections I and II.

Section I: **Who, What, Where**

Write a one or two-sentence answer explaining the significance of each item listed below.

Aditya

Amoghavarsha

Chola

Devapala

Dhruva

Karka

Krishna II

Mihirbhoj

Nagabhata II

Section II: **Comprehension**

Write a two or three-sentence answer to each of the following questions.

1. What is another name for the Pratihara? Where did this name come from?

2. Why was Kannauj a special city? What happened each time Kannauj was taken over by a different Indian king?

3. What previous successes occurred in Nagabhata II's reign that made him believe he could take Kannauj away from Devapala?

4. How do we know that Nagabhata II had taken some of Amoghavarsha's territory when he took control of Kannauj? Why wasn't Amoghavarsha able to protect Rashtrakuta from Pratihara attacks in the beginning of his reign?

5. How did Mihirbhoj get the Pala back for taking away land from the Pratihara kingdom early in his reign?

6. How did the Srivijayan empire come to be? What was the relationship between the Srivijayan empire and the Chola?

Section III: **Critical Thinking**

You may not use your text to answer this question.

At some point in your secondary education it has most likely been pointed out to you that, while you are wonderful and unique, in many ways you are very much like everyone else completing *their* secondary education (and we may be referring in particular here to looming college applications . . .). How can you distinguish yourself? What makes you *more* wonderful and unique than someone else in your same shoes? This is an ancient question, and one that was particularly important for the long-lived kings of 9th century India. Explain why the Indian kingdoms were all very much alike, and how it was possible for those kingdoms to set themselves apart from the others. In your answer, use at least two specific examples of how individual kings were able to set their kingdoms apart from the others on the Indian subcontinent.

Section IV: **Map Exercise**

1. Trace the rectangular outline of the frame for Map 57.1: The Rise of the Chola in black.

2. Using a blue pencil, trace the coastal outline of the Indian Ocean. You need only include islands which are part of the Rashtrakuta territory, as well as Sri Lanka. Trace the Sindh and the Punjab. Using a black pencil, trace the mountain peaks. Repeat until the contours are familiar.

3. Now trace the outlines of the Rashtrakuta territory, the Srivijaya Empire, and the Pratihara territory. Repeat until the contours are familiar.

4. Using a new sheet of paper, trace the rectangular outline of the frame in black. Remove your tracing paper from the original. Using a regular pencil with an eraser, draw the coastline, rivers, and mountains as you look at Map 57.1. Then draw the outlines of the Rashtrakuta territory, the Srivijaya Empire, and the Pratihara territory. Erase and redraw as necessary.

5. Remove your map. Study closely the areas of Makran, Central Asia, the Tibetan Plateau, the Himalaya mountains, Sri Lanka, Sumatra, and Java. Then study closely the locations of Ujjain, Kannauj, Ellora, Thanjavur, and Jambi. When you are familiar with them, close the book. Using your regular pencil, mark the location of each place on your map. Check your map against the original. Correct any misplaced labels while looking at the original.

7. Mark the location of Krakatoa. Mark the direction of Chola expansion and trade routes with arrows as the mapmaker did.

Chapter Fifty-Eight

Foreign and Domestic Relations

You may use your text when answering the questions in sections I and II.

Section I: Who, What, Where

Write a one or two-sentence answer explaining the significance of each item listed below.

Basil

Boris

Cyril

Cyrillic

Eudokia Dekapolitissa

Eudokia Ingerina

Glagolitic

Leo

Methodius

Mojmir

Rastislav

Svatopluk

Section II: Comprehension

Write a two or three-sentence answer to each of the following questions.

1. Describe the state of Constantinople in 856, when Michael III assumed power.

2. Why did Louis the German ensure that Rastislav was placed on the Moravian throne following his uncle Mojmir's death?

3. For what political reason did Rastislav ask Michael III of Byzantium for help with his country's religious practice?

4. What major obstacle did Cyril and Methodius face when they arrived as missionaries in Moravia?

5. Why did Michael III decide to invade Bulgaria?

6. Explain Boris/Michael I of Bulgaria's wavering faith after his conversion and baptism in Constantinople.

7. Why would twenty-seven year old Michael III adopt fifty-six year old Basil as his son?

8. What was the low point in the conflict between Byzantium and the Abbasid empire during Basil's reign? What was Basil's greatest project as emperor?

9. How did Basil die?

10. To where did Leo move Michael III's final resting place? Why was this move significant?

Section III: Critical Thinking

You may not use your text to answer this question.

Going to earthly battle in the name of a heavenly power was commonplace in the Medieval world. In 862, Michael III had an opportunity to strengthen his kingdom in the name of God, but without the conflict. Write a paragraph explaining how Michael III's mission in Moravia had more to do with power than with God. Then explain how religious freedom ended up being bestowed on Bulgaria, rather than greater political power on Byzantium.

Section IV: Map Exercise

1. Using a black pencil, trace the rectangular outline of the frame for Map 58.1: Moravia.

2. Using a blue pencil, trace the coastline of the Mediterranean. Include Sardinia, Corsica, and Sicily, but no other islands at this time. Include the coastline of Britain and the coastline up and around the North Sea. Then trace the outline of the Black Sea.

3. Using a new sheet of paper, trace the rectangular outline of the frame in black. Remove your tracing paper from the original. Using a regular pencil with an eraser, draw the coastlines of the Mediterranean, Atlantic, North Sea, and Black Sea as you look at Map 58.1. Erase and redraw as necessary.

4. When you are pleased with your map, lay it over the original. Erase and redraw any lines which are more than ¼ inch off of the original.

5. Remove your map. Study carefully the regions of Mercia, Western Francia, the Kingdom of Italy, Eastern Francia, Moravia, the Rus, the Slavs, the Khazars, the First Bulgarian Empire, Byzantium, the Papal States, Sicily, and the Abbasid Empire. When you are familiar with them, close the book. Using your regular pencil, label each region. Check your map against the original, and correct any misplaced labels.

6. Next, study closely the locations of Rome, Spoleto, Benevento, Syracuse, Thessalonica, and Constantinople. When you are familiar with them, close the book, mark each location on your map, and label. When you are done, lay your map over the original. Erase and redraw any locations which are more than ¼ inch off of the original.

7. Draw and label the Loire and the Rhine.

Chapter Fifty-Nine

The Second Caliphate

You may use your text when answering the questions in sections I and II.

Section I: **Who, What, Where**

Write a one or two-sentence answer explaining the significance of each item listed below.

Al-Muntasir

Al-Mutamid

Al-Mutasim

Al-Mutawakkil

Al-Mutazz

Imams

Ismail

Ja'far al-Sadiq

The Maghreb

The *mihna*

Mu'tazilism

Muhammad

Nasr

Ubaydallah al-Mahdi

Ya'qub-i Laith Saffari

Section II: Comprehension

Write a two or three-sentence answer to each of the following questions.

1. What were the five foundational principles of Mu'tazilism?

2. What were the duties of a Mu'tazilite leader?

3. What was the difference between the authority of a Sunni caliph and a Shi'a imam?

4. Why did al-Mutasim decide to go to war against his own people?

5. From where did al-Mutasim find the men for his army?

6. What was al-Mutasim's reason for moving his capital to Samarra? Why did he isolate his Turks from the rest of the population, and what was the result?

7. How was the caliph that followed al-Muntasir chosen? What happened to this caliph, and how did the political center of the caliphate move back to Baghdad?

8. What was the significance of al-Mutazz's brutal murder by the Turks?

9. Why did Ya'qub-i Laith Saffari want to storm Baghdad? Why did he want the caliph's approval?

10. Describe the succession of caliphs that followed al-Mutamid. Who had power during this succession of caliphs?

11. What did all Shi'a Muslims agree upon as far as where the designated line of *imams* began? At what point did the Shi'a Muslims disagree?

12. What did Ubaydallah al-Mahdi's role as the Fatimid caliph mean for the Islamic empire?

Section III: Critical Thinking

You may not use your text to answer this question.

On June 29, 2014, the militant group known as the "Islamic State of Iraq and Syria" (ISIS) proclaimed Abu Bakr al-Baghdadi to be its caliph. The caliph took a new name, Amir al-Mu'minin Caliph Ibrahim, and the group renamed itself the "Islamic State." The group's aim is to establish a ruling caliphate where the Sunni majority resides in both Iraq and Syria. The names of the ISIS caliph, and the fighting over Muslim majority/minority beliefs must seem familiar to you: the fighting that goes on in the Middle East over the Muslim faith started so long ago, with the arguments over who was Muhammad's true successor. Though we have been reading about this fight over the course of several chapters of our history, understanding it is perplexing. Do your best to write a paragraph—without looking at the text—that explains the differences within the Muslim factions up to this point in our medieval history. First, write a shorthand answer for each listed question. If you need to reference the text after you've taken a stab at answering the questions, then you may do so. Once you have a brief answer for each question, write your paragraph.

- What were the main beliefs of the Sunnis? What clan ruled the Sunni starting in 750?
- What were the main beliefs of the Shi'a? What leader did they follow?
- Who were the Ismailis and what were their main beliefs? Who was their leader?

Chapter Sixty

The Great Army of the Vikings

You may use your text when answering the questions in sections I and II.

Section I: Who, What, Where

Write a one or two-sentence answer explaining the significance of each item listed below.

Alfred

Cinaed mac Ailpin

Edward

Ethelred

Guthrum

Halfdan

Ivar

Odda

Odin

Oswiu

The Scoti

Treaty of Wedmore

Ubbe

Section II: Comprehension

Write a two or three-sentence answer to each of the following questions.

1. Name the seven English kingdoms that existed in ninth century Britain. Who ruled in the north? Who ruled on the southwestern coasts?

2. What physical separation existed between Mercia and Wales, and how did it come about?

3. How did the southeast of England come to be united under the king of Wessex?

4. Explain the significance of Ivar's Raven Banner.

5. Describe the religious fabric of England in the ninth century.

6. What happened when the Vikings first landed in East Anglia in 865? What happened at the end of 867 between the Vikings and the king of East Anglia?

7. How did the Vikings come to control the north and part of the east of England? How did Mercia and Wessex manage to circumvent Viking control through 867?

8. Describe the battles between the Vikings and the English during the year of 871.

9. How did Alfred react to the seemingly inevitable takeover of England by the Vikings? Why did he react this way?

10. What happened after the Viking defeat at Edington in 878?

11. What was the more plausible reason for the Viking concession to sign a treaty other than their defeat at Edington?

12. Though the Treaty of Wedmore divided England between the Anglo-Saxons and the Vikings, how was it an unprecedented win for Alfred?

Section III: Critical Thinking

You may not use your text to answer this question.

Myths and legends that are passed down through time often tell us as much, or more, about history than the actual history books themselves. In this chapter you read about two interesting tales that have survived the test of time. Write a short recap of the story of *Beowulf* and then explain how the story reflected ninth-century religious anxiety. Then, write a short recap of the story about Alfred, the housewife, and the burnt cakes, and explain how the story shows how Alfred was viewed by contemporaries despite constant defeat by the Vikings.

Section IV: Map Exercise

1. Using a black pencil, trace the rectangular outline of the frame for Map 60.1: The Treaty of Wedmore.

2. Using a black pencil, trace the coastline around Ireland, Britain, and the continent. You do not need to trace any minor islands at this time. Using your blue pencil, trace the lines of the Loire and the Seine in Western Francia. Repeat until the contours are familiar.

3. Place a new sheet of paper over the map, and trace the rectangular outline of the frame in black. Remove your tracing paper from the original. Using a regular pencil with an eraser, draw the coast all around Ireland, Britain, and the continent. Draw the lines of the Loire and the Seine on the continent. Erase and redraw as necessary.

4. Study the regions of Ireland, the Picts, Northumbria, Mercia, Wales, Wessex, Sussex, Kent, Essex, East Anglia, Britanny, Western Francia, and the Kingdom of Italy. When you are familiar with them, close the book. Using your regular pencil, label Ireland, the Picts, Northumbria, Mercia, Wales, Wessex, Sussex, Kent, Essex, East Anglia, Britanny, Western Francia, and the Kingdom of Italy. Now study the locations of Scone, York, Nottingham, Edington, Basing, Ashdown, Reading, London, Rouen, and Paris. When you are familiar with them, close the book. Then, on your own map, label Scone, York, Nottingham, Edington, Basing, Ashdown, Reading, London, Rouen, and Paris. When you are done, lay your map over the original. Correct any misplaced labels. Erase and redraw any locations that are more than ¼ inch off of the original.

5. Mark the locations of Offa's Dike, the Battle of Cynuit, and the Monastery of Whitby.

Chapter Sixty-One

Struggle for the Iron Crown

You may use your text when answering the questions in sections I and II.

Section I: Who, What, Where

Write a one or two-sentence answer explaining the significance of each item listed below.

Adalbert

Arnulf of Carinthia

Arpad

Berengar of Friuli

Carloman

Charles the Fat

Formosus

Gisela

Guy of Spoleto

Lambert

Louis of Provence

Louis the Stammerer

Louis the Younger (Louis III)

Louis II the Younger

Stephen V

Section II: Comprehension

Write a two or three-sentence answer to each of the following questions.

1. How did Charles the Landless become emperor of the Romans?

2. Why was Louis the German so upset when Charles the Landless was named emperor? Did he get his revenge on Charles the Landless?

3. How were the Frankish kingdoms divided after Louis the Stammerer's death?

4. Why did the pope crown Charles the Fat emperor of the Romans in 881? What came of the pope's plan?

5. Describe the major threat to Charles the Fat's reign that began just a year after he became king of his enormous empire in 885. How did he deal with the threat?

6. How did Charles the Fat manage to lift the Viking siege on Paris? How did this strategy affect his rule?

7. For what reason did Pope Formosus want Arnulf of Carinthia to be named the Roman Emperor?

8. According to Liudprand of Cremona, what were the circumstances of Lambert's death?

9. What did Arnulf of Carinthia have to do with the Magyar attacks on Italy?

10. How did Berengar of Friuli lose his title as "King of Italy"?

Section III: Critical Thinking

You may not use your text to answer this question.

There is a fine line between justice and revenge. Lambert could not punish Pope Formosus for naming Arnulf of Carinthia king of Italy and emperor of the Romans while he was alive, so he found a way to do it after his death. Explain how Lambert enacted justice (or revenge) on Pope Formosus during the "Trial of the Cadaver." In your answer, define "synod." You may use a dictionary to look up its definition.

Chapter Sixty-Two

Kampaku

You may use your text when answering the questions in sections I and II.

Section I: Who, What, Where

Write a one or two-sentence answer explaining the significance of each item listed below.

Ariwara no Narihira

Daigo

Fujiwara no Tadahira

Hiromi

Koko

Suzaku

Sugawara no Michizane

Taira no Masakado

Tokihira

Uda

Section II: Comprehension

Write a two or three-sentence answer to each of the following questions.

1. What power was held by the *Kampaku*? Why was this position invented?

2. Describe Yozei's psychopathic tendencies. How was Mototsune able to get Yozei off the throne?

3. What happened to Yozei after he was dethroned?

4. Why did Mototsune resign from his position as Kampaku after Koko's death? Why did he expect to get his position back?

5. What position did Uda offer to Mototsune in his new administration? How did Mototsune react to the offer of this new role?

6. Describe the circumstances of Mototsune's reinstatement as Kampaku. What did Mototsune's reinstatement prove about the distribution of power in Japan?

7. What major reforms did Uda make before abdicating his throne?

8. Why did Sugawara no Michizane want to resign from his position in Daigo's court? How was his plea answered?

9. Explain the circumstances of Sugawara no Michizane's exile.

10. How did Taira no Masakado come to call himself the "New Emperor"?

Section III: Critical Thinking

You may not use your text to answer this question.

Ambition is a trait that can live inside any man or woman. In the medieval world, if one had ambition to rule, he or she had to know how to work the local political system. Unfortunately for him, Taira no Masakado was not shrewd enough to recognize that the form his ambition took did not match the Japanese customs. Write a paragraph or two explaining why Taira no Masakado's hope of rising to power was doomed from the start. Make sure to include a description of how Japanese armies were raised in your answer.

Section IV: Map Exercise

1. Using a black pencil, trace the rectangular outline of the frame for Map 62.1: The Rebellion of Masakado.

2. Using a blue pencil, trace the coastline up the shore of China and around Japan. Using a black pencil, trace the region of Japan. Then, using a contrasting color, trace the outline of the region of the Kingdom of the "New Emperor." Repeat until the contours are familiar.

3. Using a new sheet of paper, trace the rectangular outline of the frame in black. Remove your tracing paper from the original. Using a regular pencil with an eraser, draw the coastline up the shore of China and around Japan, as you look at Map 62.1. Erase and redraw as necessary.

4. When you are pleased with your map, lay it over the original. Erase and redraw any lines which are more than ¼ inch off of the original.

5. Remove your map. Use your black pencil to draw over the outline of Japan. Then shade the region of the Kingdom of the "New Emperor."

6. Next study carefully the locations of Kyushu, Heian, Kanto, and Hitachi. Also study the location of Mt. Tsukuba. When you are familiar with them, close the book. Using your regular pencil, label Kyushu, Heian, Kanto, Hitachi, and Mt. Tsukuba. When you are done, lay your own map over the original. Correct any misplaced labels. If any locations are more than ¼ inch off of the original, then erase and redraw them, as you look at the map.

Chapter Sixty-Three

Basileus

You may use your text when answering the questions in sections I and II.

Section I: Who, What, Where

Write a one or two-sentence answer explaining the significance of each item listed below.

Alexander

Constantine VII

Elena

Leo Phocas

Nicholas Mystikos

Oleg of Novgorod

Peter I

Romanos Lecapenus

Simeon I

Zoe Karbonopsina

Section II: Comprehension

Write a two or three-sentence answer to each of the following questions.

1. What did Leo VI's nickname "Leo Sophos" mean? How did he earn this nickname?

2. Why did the theologian Arethas of Caesarea give Leo VI another nickname—*theosophos*?

3. Describe the Rus threat faced by Leo VI. How did he handle the threat?

4. What were Simeon I's reasons for attacking Constantinople during Alexander's rule?

5. Explain Nicholas Mystikos's awkward position as Simeon I approached the walls of Constantinople with his army.

6. What were the terms of the peace treaty Nicholas Mystikos made with Simeon I? Why was Nicholas Mystikos able to agree to these terms?

7. What happened at the Battle of Anchialus?

8. How did Romanos Lecapenus take control of Byzantine's council of regents?

9. After taking control of the council of regents, how did Romanos Lecapenus become co-emperor of Byzantium?

10. Why did Simeon I make an alliance with the Fatimid caliph al-Mahdi? How did he lose this alliance?

11. For what reason did Romanos Lecapenus make an alliance with the Abbasid caliph?

12. Why did Romanos agree to peace with Peter I after he attacked Byzantine territory in Macedonia? What were the terms of the peace treaty?

Section III: Critical Thinking

You may not use your text to answer this question.

The power of the court was great in the medieval world. In Japan, the clan that ruled the court could always trump the heavenly sovereign, and in Constantinople, one's acceptance by the court could mean more than the voice of God's representatives on earth. Write a paragraph or two explaining the measures Leo VI took to have his son with mistress Zoe Karbonopsina accepted as his legitimate heir. In your answer make sure to explain the significance of the Purple Chamber, the name given to Leo VI's son at his birth and his coronation, and what happened to the patriarch that did not accept Leo VI's son as his successor.

Chapter Sixty-Four

The Creation of Normandy

You may use your text when answering the questions in sections I and II.

Section I: **Who, What, Where**

Write a one or two-sentence answer explaining the significance of each item listed below.

Charles the Simple

Gisela

Louis the Child

Rollo

Rudolph of Burgundy

Section II: **Comprehension**

Write a two or three-sentence answer to each of the following questions.

1. What were the terms of Louis of Provence's surrender to Berengar when he won back the Iron Crown of the Lombards in 902?

2. Why did the Italian nobles invite Louis back to Italy? Even though he knew Berengar would attack him, why did Louis agree?

3. What did Louis of Provence say that got him in trouble with Adalbert and the Italian noblemen? What did Adalbert's wife think about Louis's comment?

4. How did Louis of Provence become Louis the Blind?

5. Who followed Louis of Provence as the Roman emperor after he was blinded?

6. What long term solution did Charles the Simple come up with in 911 for dealing with the Vikings?

7. What were the terms of the Treaty of Saint-Clair-sur-Epte?

Section III: Critical Thinking

You may not use your text to answer this question.

Agreeing to a transfer of power on paper could mean something very different in real life. Robert of Normandy may have been a duke, but he was a Viking warrior at heart. Explain what happened when the new duke was ordered to kiss Charles the Simple's foot, and the real world meaning of Rollo's subversion.

Section IV: Map Exercise

1. Using a black pencil, trace the rectangular outline of the frame for Map 64.1: The Creation of Normandy.

2. Using a blue pencil, trace the visible coastline on this map: the Atlantic along the continent around Britain (you need not trace Ireland at this time) and the Mediterranean visible around Italy and under Provence and Western Francia. You do not need to include islands at this time. Using a black pencil, trace the mountain peaks visible above Italy and under Western Francia. Repeat until the contours are familiar.

3. Trace the rectangular outline of the frame in black. Remove your tracing paper from the original. Using a regular pencil with an eraser as you look at Map 64.1, draw the coastline around Britain outside Eastern and Western Francia. Draw the coastline of the Mediterranean (you do not need to draw any islands at this time). Erase and redraw as necessary.

4. When you are pleased with your map, lay it over the original. Erase and redraw any lines which are more than ¼ inch off of the original.

5. Leaving your map over the original, trace the regions of the Emirate of Cordoba, Pamplona, Western Francia, Eastern Francia, Burgundy, Provence, the Kingdom of Italy, Ravenna, the Byzantine holdings in Italy, and the Papal States. Remove your map from the original. Study carefully the locations of the Emirate of Cordoba, Pamplona, Western Francia, Eastern Francia, Burgundy, Provence, the Kingdom of Italy, Ravenna, the Byzantine holdings in Italy, and the Papal States. When you are familiar with them, close the book. Using your regular pencil with an eraser, label each location inside the tracing you did of it. Check your map against the original. Correct any misplaced labels.

6. Now study the locations of Paris, Rome, Venice, and Verona. When you are familiar with them, close the book, mark the cities, and label them. When you are done, lay your map over the original. Erase and redraw any markings which are more than ¼ inch off of the original.

7. Draw the outline of Normandy. Label.

Chapter Sixty-Five

The Kingdom of Germany

You may use your text when answering the questions in sections I and II.

Section I: Who, What, Where

Write a one or two-sentence answer explaining the significance of each item listed below.

Battle of Riade

Boleslav

Conrad

Drahomira

Henry the Fowler

Ludmila

Spytihnev

Wenceslaus

Section II: Comprehension

Write a two or three-sentence answer to each of the following questions.

1. Explain the difference between "duchies" and "stem duchies" and what both had to do with the long gone tribal territories of Francia.

2. Who ruled the duchies, and who defended them?

3. What happened when Louis the Child gathered an army at Augsburg to fight against the Magyars in 910?

4. Why did the dukes of Eastern Francia elect Conrad to be their leader after the death of Louis the Child?

5. How did Henry the Fowler spend his first three years as king of Eastern Francia?

7. Why did Henry the Fowler want to make Bohemia a part of Germany?

8. For what reason did some Bohemian officials disagree with Wenceslaus's decision to make an alliance with Henry the Fowler?

9. How did Wenceslaus become a famous martyr for Christ?

Section III: Critical Thinking

You may not use your text to answer this question.

In the previous chapter, we learned about the creation of Normandy. Charles the Simple could not withstand any more Viking attacks, so he turned over part of his land to the Viking warrior Rollo and hoped for the best. In this chapter, we read about the creation of Germany. Unlike Normandy, Germany was long in the making. Write a paragraph explaining how Eastern Francia organically turned into Germany. In your answer, make sure to include the significance of who Henry the Fowler chose to be his successor.

Chapter Sixty-Six

The Turn of the Wheel

You may use your text when answering the questions in sections I and II.

Section I: Who, What, Where

Write a one or two-sentence answer explaining the significance of each item listed below.

Arinjaya

Battle of Vallala

Gandaraditya

Indra III

Indra IV

Khottiga

Krishna III

Marasimha

Parantaka

Rajaditya Chola

Rajasimha II

Sembiyan Mahadevi

Shaivite

Tailapa

Section II: Comprehension

Write a two or three-sentence answer to each of the following questions.

1. Why did Rajasimha II ask the Sri Lankan king for an alliance? What was the result of the Pandya-Sri Lankan alliance?

2. After being defeated at the Battle of Vallala, how did the Rashtrakuta king Indra III regain some power for his kingdom? Why didn't that power last?

3. How did the Rashtrakuta defeat the Chola in 949 in the battle at Takkolam? What suggests that after their defeat the Chola had to pay homage to the Rashtrakuta?

4. In what way did the building of temples for Shiva to inhabit help substantiate Chola dominance?

5. What happened to the Chola empire while Gandaraditya and Sembiyan Mahadevi were building temples all over the countryside?

6. Define *sallekhana*. Why would Marasimha and Indra IV commit *sallekhana*?

Section III: Critical Thinking

You may not use your text to answer this question.

The reading in this chapter makes it very clear to us that there is a difference between symbols of power, and power itself. Parantaka of the Chola wanted to find the crown and royal regalia hidden in Sri Lanka by Rajasimha II of Pandya because he wanted to show the world the Chola had destroyed the Pandya. However, he didn't *need* the exiled king's belongings to be strong. Parantaka knew the symbols of Rajasimha II's power were secondary to the Chola's real power. But what happened to that power? Write a paragraph explaining how the blurring of lines between real and symbolic power—in the form of temples—was the death of the Chola after Parantaka's death.

Section IV: Map Exercise

1. Using a black pencil, trace the rectangular outline of the frame for Map 66.1: The Height of the Chola.

2. Using a blue pencil, trace the coastline of the Arabian Sea. Include Sri Lanka. With your blue pencil, trace the Indus River, the Ganges River, the Narmada, and the Kaveri River. Use simple peaks to represent all the mountain peaks. Repeat until the contours are familiar.

3. Using a new sheet of paper, trace the rectangular outline of the frame in black. Remove your tracing paper from the original, and draw the coastline of the Arabian Sea, including Sri Lanka.

Draw the Indus River, the Ganges River, the Kaveri River, and the mountains (just using simple peaks). Erase and redraw as necessary.

4. When you are pleased with your map, lay it over the original. Erase and redraw any lines which are more than ¼ inch off of the original.

5. Remove your map. Mark the Arabian Sea, the Indus River, the Ganges River, the Narmada, and the Kaveri. Study carefully the locations of Makran, Debal, Pratihara, Rashtrakuta, Western Chalukya, Chola, and Pandya. Then study the locations of the cities of Kannauj and Takkolam. Study also the locations of Mt. Kailasa and the Battle of Vallala. When you are familiar with them, close the book. On your map, mark the locations of Makran, Debal, Pratihara, Rashtrakuta, Western Chalukya, Chola, and Pandya; and the cities of Kannauj and Takkolam and also Mt. Kailasa and the Battle of Vallala. Check your map against the original, and correct any misplaced labels.

Chapter Sixty-Seven

The Capture of Baghdad

You may use your text when answering the questions in sections I and II.

Section I: Who, What, Where

Write a one or two-sentence answer explaining the significance of each item listed below.

Abd ar-Rahman III

Ahmad

Ahmad ibn Buya

Alfonso III

Ali ibn Buya

Al-Jaihani

Al-Muqtadir

Al-Qahir

Al-Qaim bi-amr Allah

Al-Radi

Mahdia

Mardaviz al-Ziyar

Muhammad ibn Ra'iq

Mu'nis

Nasr

Umar ibn-Hafsun

Section II: Comprehension

Write a two or three-sentence answer to each of the following questions.

1. Describe the Fatimid army's march through North Africa towards Alexandria in the early 10th century.

2. How did Mu'nis take down al-Mahdi and the Fatimid army?

3. Who were the "counts" that were bothering the Emirate of Cordoba?

4. Why did Ahmad want to make Arabic the official language of the Samanid court? What resistance did he face?

5. How did Sistan come to be its own little country (at least until 963)?

6. Why did Ali ibn Buya start to call himself "shah" rather than "emir" of his newly conquered territory?

7. What did al-Radi realize about the position of the caliph when he came to power?

8. How did Muhammad ibn Ra'iq rise up to be *amir ul-umara,* while the Abbasid caliphate came to an end in all but name?

9. Why did ibn Ra'iq breach the Nahrawan Canal? What was the result?

Section III: Critical Thinking

You may not use your text to answer this question.

As we have been reading about the ups and downs within the Islamic empire, one thread has been consistent: the fight over who should rule has been based on sectarian politics, and not strictly on power. In this chapter we see a shift in the fight over the caliphate(s). Write a paragraph explaining why the emir of Cordoba, Abd ar-Rahman III, declared himself to be a caliph. Then explain how the caliphate became nothing more than a shell, and how it could be that the Buyid general Ahmad ibn Buya was in control of the empire.

Section IV: Map Exercise

1. Using a black pencil, trace the rectangular outline of the frame for Map 67.1: The Fatimids and Cordoba.

2. Using a blue pencil, trace the coastline around the continent from the top of the map down Germany, Western Francia, and Pamplona. You do not need to trace around Britain at this time.

Trace the coastline through the Mediterranean (you do not need to trace any islands). Trace the mountain peaks. Repeat until the contours are familiar.

3. Using a new sheet of paper, trace the rectangular outline of the frame in black. Remove your tracing paper from the original. Using a regular pencil with an eraser, draw the coastline around the continent from the top of the map down Germany, Western Francia, and Pamplona. Draw the Mediterranean coastline as well, and draw the mountain peaks.

3. When you are pleased with your map, lay it over the original. Erase and redraw any lines which are more than ¼ inch off of the original.

4. Leaving your map over the original, trace the outlines of the Fatimid Caliphate, the Caliphate of Cordova, the Kingdom of Leon, Pamplona, Western Francia, Germany, Burgundy, and Provence. Study each of these locations carefully. When they are familiar, remove your map from original and close the book. Using your regular pencil, label the Fatimid Caliphate, the Caliphate of Cordova, the Kingdom of Leon, Pamplona, Western Francia, Germany, Burgundy, and Provence. Then study carefully the locations of Galicia, Leon, Asturias, the Spanish Marches, Cordoba, Barcelona, Rome, Mahdia, and Tripoli. When you are familiar with them, close the book. Using your regular pencil, mark and label each. Check your map against the original. Correct any misplaced labels.

Chapter Sixty-Eight

Three Kingdoms

You may use your text when answering the questions in sections I and II.

Section I: Who, What, Where

Write a one or two-sentence answer explaining the significance of each item listed below.

Bei

Deguang (Taizong)

Gyeongae

Gyeongsun

Mu

Shu-lu shih

Song Taizong

Taebong

Taejo

Taizu

Section II: Comprehension

Write a two or three-sentence answer to each of the following questions.

1. What steps did Wang Kon take to legitimize his rule of Later Goguryeo?

2. Who ruled Silla after the death of King Hyogong?

3. How was Wang Kon able to use Kyonhwon's invasion of Silla to his advantage?

4. Why did Wang Kon depose Gyeongsun when he heard Kyonhwon's sons had turned against him?

5. How did Wang Kon get his former enemy Kyonhwon to be his ally? Why did he want Kyonhwon as an ally?

6. How did Wang Kon's long game for possession of Later Baekje unfold?

7. What did Wang Kon tell his people in a set of injunctions intended to shape the future of his newly unified country? What were the implications of what he told his people?

8. Describe how the Khitan khan Abaoji brought Tang customs to his kingdom.

9. How did Shu-lu shih reimpose the old Khitan tradition of elected succession after her husband tried to switch the kingdom over to blood succession?

10. Explain how Dongdan and the old Khitan realm came together to be the new kingdom of the Liao.

11. How was the Song dynasty formed?

12. Explain what deal Song Taizu made with his army once he was firmly on the throne. Why did he let the army go?

Section III: Critical Thinking

You may not use your text to answer this question.

Perhaps you have read Aesop's fable of The Wind and the Sun. For a refresher, it goes something like this: The Wind and the Sun were arguing over who was stronger. They saw a traveller coming down the road and the Sun said, "I know how we can figure out who is stronger. Whichever of us can cause the traveller to take off his coat is the stronger of the two." The Wind agreed to the challenge. "You go first," the Sun said. So, while the Wind blew and blew the Sun waited patiently behind a cloud. With each gust of wind, the man drew his coat tighter around himself. Frustrated, the Wind gave up. The Sun then came out from behind the cloud and shone brightly. The warmth from the Sun caused the man to take off his coat, and he basked in the Sun's rays. Write a paragraph that connects Aesop's fable of The Wind and the Sun to the political tactics used by Wang Kon, Song Taizu and Song Taizong.

Map Exercise

1. Using a black pencil, trace the rectangular outline of the frame for Map 69.1: Athelstan's England.

2. Using a black pencil, trace the coastline all around Ireland and Britain and along the visible portion of the continent. You do not need to include any islands. Repeat until the contours are familiar.

3. Using a new sheet of paper, trace the rectangular outline of the frame in black. Remove your tracing paper from the original. Using a regular pencil with an eraser as you look at Map 69.1, draw the complete coastline. Erase and redraw as necessary.

4. When you are pleased with your map, lay it over the original. Erase and redraw any lines which are more than ¼ inch off of the original.

5. Leaving your map over the original, trace the region of Britain delineated as Athelstan's England. Then remove your map from the original.

6. Study carefully the regions of Ireland, Scotland, Northumbria, Mercia, Wales, Wessex, Sussex, Essex, East Anglia, Brittany, Normandy, and Western Francia. Mark these on your map. Then study carefully the locations of Dublin, Oxford, Malmesbury, Bath, Exeter, Kent, London, and Maldon. Mark and label each on your map. Check your map against the original. Correct any misplaced labels.

7. Mark the possible location of the Battle of Brunanburh.

Chapter Sixty-Nine

Kings of England

You may use your text when answering the questions in sections I and II.

Section I: Who, What, Where

Write a one or two-sentence answer explaining the significance of each item listed below.

Atheling/Aetheling

Athelstan

Battle of Brunanburh

Battle of Havsfjord

Constantine II

Danegeld

Duke Richard the Good of Normandy

Dunstan

Edgar

Edmund the Just

Edred Weak-Foot

Edward the Elder

Edwy All-Fair

Emma

Eric the Red

Erik Bloodaxe

Ethelred

Hakon of Hladir

Hakon the Good

Harald

Harald Bluetooth

Harald Greycloak

Olaf I

Olaf Tryggvason

Sihtric

Sweyn Forkbeard

Section II: Comprehension

Write a two or three-sentence answer to each of the following questions.

1. What were the circumstances of Edmund the Just's death?

2. What was the supposed reason the English bishop Dunstan did not like Edwy All-Fair? What was the real reason for the bishop's gripe with the king?

3. How did England come to be ruled by two kings in 957?

4. What did Edgar accomplish in his first fourteen years of rule?

5. Describe Harald's efforts to unite Norway. To whom did he leave his newly unified country?

6. How did Hakon the Good earn his moniker? Why was it advantageous for Hakon the Good and Harald Bluetooth to convert to Christianity?

7. How did Harald Greycloak force his Christian faith on the people of Norway? In addition to the forcing of the Christian faith on the Norse people, what else caused the people to dislike the king of Norway?

8. Who controlled Norway after the death of Harald Greycloak?

9. Describe the founding of Greenland.

10. What were the circumstances of Harald Bluetooth's death?

11. What events in 991 led to Ethelred agreeing to give Sweyn Forkbeard ten thousand pounds of silver?

12. Though Sweyn Forkbeard had sworn at his coronation feast to take England, why did he continue to accept payment in exchange for retreat during his invasions rather than taking over the country?

13. Why did Ethelred of England make an alliance with the Normans? What were the terms of the alliance?

14. When it became clear that the Norman reinforcements would not turn his enemies away, what was the next tactic King Ethelred used to fight the Danes?

15. After years of attacking, sacking and burning and then accepting payment, how did Sweyn Forkbeard finally take England?

Section III: Critical Thinking

You may not use your text to answer this question.

Rituals can provide great solace for the soul, but their real world impact is often disappointing. Write a paragraph explaining how Edgar used ritual to legitimize his kingship of England, but how that ritual did little to keep him on throne, and to protect his kingdom from falling apart.

Chapter Seventy

The Baptism of the Rus

You may use your text when answering the questions in sections I and II.

Section I: Who, What, Where

Write a one or two-sentence answer explaining the significance of each item listed below.

Anna

Basil II

Boris II

Constantine VIII

Constantine Lecapenus

Igor

John Tzimiskes

Nikephoros Phocas

Olga

Pogost

Romanos II

Romanus

Stephen Lecapenus

Svyatoslav

Theophano

Vladimir

Section II: Comprehension

Write a two or three-sentence answer to each of the following questions.

1. How did Constantine Porphyrogenitus come to follow Romanos Lecapenus as the emperor of Constantinople?

2. Describe the Rus as the geographer Ibn Fadlan depicted them.

3. What were the terms of the treaty made between Igor, prince of Kiev, and Constantine Porphyrogenitus?

4. How did Olga avenge her husband Igor's death?

5. In what way was Olga of the Kievan Rus charmed into becoming a Christian?

6. What kind of a ruler was Svyatoslav of the Rus—refined or rough? Use examples of Svyatoslav's behavior to explain your answer.

7. How did the officer Nikephoros Phocas become emperor of Byzantium?

8. Describe the circumstances of Nikephoros Phocas's death.

9. Why was it so easy for John Tzimiskes to be crowned as emperor after the death of Nikephoros Phocas?

10. What happened at Arcadiopolis?

11. Who killed Svyatoslav? What did they do to his skull?

12. What advantages for the Rus did Vladimir see in converting to Christianity?

Section III: Critical Thinking

You may not use your text to answer this question.

In this chapter we saw a version of the cliché "brains over brawn" from the most surprising of exemplars, the previously barbaric Rus. Explain how Nikephoros Phocas's downfall was his "brawn." Then explain how Vladimir's successful use of "brains" turned the Rus into an upstanding state.

Section IV: Map Exercise

1. Using a black pencil, trace the rectangular outline of the frame for Map 70.1: The Rus and Byzantium.

2. Using a blue pencil, trace the coastline of the Black Sea (include the Sea of Marmara), the visible portion of the Caspian Sea, and the visible portion of the Mediterranean. (Do not include any islands other than Crete, as it is labeled on the map.) Then trace the line of the Danube River, the Dnieper, and the Volga. Repeat until the contours are familiar.

3. Using a new sheet of paper, trace the rectangular outline of the frame in black. Then draw the coastline of the Black Sea (and Sea of Marmara), Caspian Sea, Mediterranean Sea, and the three rivers. Label the rivers.

4. When you are pleased with your map, lay it over the original. Erase and redraw any lines which are more than ¼ inch off of the original. Then, placing your tracing paper back over the original, trace the outlines of Byzantium, the First Bulgarian Empire, the territory seized by the Rus, and the approximate extent of Rus power.

5. Now study carefully the locations of the Slavs, the Drevlians, the Khazars, and Hamdanid territory. Label them on your map. Then study carefully the locations of Constantinople, Kherson, Kiev, Korosten, Novgorod, Baghdad, and Aleppo.

6. Finally, label the Sea of Marmara and the Battle of Arcadiopolis.

Chapter Seventy-One

The Holy Roman Emperor

You may use your text when answering the questions in sections I and II.

Section I: Who, What, Where

Write a one or two-sentence answer explaining the significance of each item listed below.

Abbey of Cluny

Gregory V

Henry the Quarrelsome

Hugh Capet

John XII

John XIII

Lél and Bulcsu

Leo VIII

Lothair IV

Louis the Sluggard

Otto I

Otto II

Otto III

Peace and Truce of God

Simony

Section II: Comprehension

Write a two or three-sentence answer to each of the following questions.

1. Who tamed the Magyars? What were they like after the Battle of Lechfeld?

2. What oath did Otto I have to take in order to be given the title emperor of the Romans? Why was this oath so important to the pope?

3. Why did Otto I depose Pope John XII?

4. What was "lay investiture"?

5. Why did Otto I want to have his son named co-emperor?

6. Why did Otto II face so many rebellions at the beginning of his reign?

7. How did Otto II think he was going to firm up his authority over the Romans? What actually happened?

8. What was the hiccup in the transfer of power between Otto II and Otto III?

9. Describe the state of Western Francia when Hugh Capet became king.

10. While the rich in Francia could hire personal armies to keep their possessions safe, what did the poor do to protect themselves?

11. How did the Christian priests gathered at the Benedictine abbey of Charroux in 989 hope to fix the terrible state of Western Francia?

Section III: Critical Thinking

You may not use your text to answer this question.

The Peace of God movement was formed as a response to a world in which the possibility of salvation and the mission of the Christian church were increasingly tied to the territorial ambitions of particular kings. While the Peace of God was formed in Francia, nowhere were the fears of the group made more clear than in the exchange of power between the "Holy Roman Emperor" and the pope. The conflation of god and might was not new, but Otto I's insistence on becoming the first "holy" Roman emperor in the years just preceding the movement's start certainly intensified the relationship between the church and the state. Explain how Otto I became the Holy Roman Emperor, and what that meant for the balance of power between the church and the state. In your answer, make sure to explain the practice of lay investiture, and how that cultural practice influenced Otto I's belief that he could choose who would be the pope.

Chapter Seventy-Two

The Hardship of Sacred War

You may use your text when answering the questions in sections I and II.

Section I: Who, What, Where

Write a one or two-sentence answer explaining the significance of each item listed below.

Abu-Ishaq

Alp Tigin

Anandapala

Jayapala

Lingam

Mahipala

Mahmud

Mansur

Nasr Khan

Rajendra

Rajadhiraja

Rajaraja I

Sebuk Tigin

Togrul

Section II: Comprehension

Write a two or three-sentence answer to each of the following questions.

1. What were the terms of the peace made between Sebuk Tigin, Abu-Ishaq and Mansur?

2. What was Sebuk Tigin's first act as governor of Ghazni? Why didn't the Samanids deal with Sebuk Tigin's expanding empire immediately?

3. Why did the Shahi kingdom's capital move from Kabul to Udabhandapura to Lahore? Though the capital had moved, why did Jayapala stay in Udabhandapura?

4. Though there was no clear victory for either the Ghaznavids nor the Shahis when the armies met outside of Kabul in 986, why did the Jayapala draw back first?

5. Describe what Mahmud did when he got to the Indian harbor town of Somnath, and what happened to its famous and sacred statue of Shiva.

6. How did Rajaraja I commemorate the triumphs that led to his domination of the south of India?

7. What did Rajendra accomplish by "setting sail"?

8. Why didn't Rajendra attempt to conquer the kingdom of Pala? Why did he decide to return home?

9. How did Rajendra make up for turning away from attacking the Pala?

Section III: Critical Thinking

You may not use your text to answer this question.

At the end of the chapter we read about the southern Indian poet Tiruttakadevar. His most enduring epic told the tale of the prince Jivaka, a skilled fighter and general, who earned a kingdom and then willingly gave it up. Despite his victories, he had discovered the hollowness of all human achievement. Using examples from this chapter, write a paragraph explaining what "the hollowness of all human achievement" means in the context of conquest and empire building, even if it is in the name of religion.

Section IV: Map Exercise

1. Using a black pencil, trace the rectangular outline of the frame for Map 72.2: The Spread of Chola Influence.

2. Using a blue pencil, trace the coastline of the Indian Ocean. Include only the islands which are marked as part of the extent of Chola influence. With your blue pencil, trace the line of the Sindh, the Punjab, the Oxus, and the Ganges. Trace the mountains with simple peaks. Repeat until the contours are familiar.

3. Using a new sheet of paper, trace the rectangular outline of the frame in black. Then draw the coastline of the Indian Ocean. Draw the lines of the Sindh, the Punjab, the Oxus, and the Ganges. Draw simple peaks to represent the mountains. Label the rivers. Erase and redraw as necessary.

4. When you are pleased with your map, lay it over the original. Erase and redraw any lines which are more than ¼ inch off of the original.

5. Leaving your map on the original, outline in black the areas which are part of the extent of the Chola influence.

6. Remove your map. Study carefully the locations of Kandahar, Kabul, Ujjain, Kannauj, Pala, Pandya, Thanjavur, Sri Lanka, Sumatra, Jambi, and Java. Also study the locations of the Khyber Pass and Mt. Kailasa. When you are familiar with them, close the book. Using your regular pencil, label the locations of Kandahar, Kabul, Ujjain, Kannauj, Pala, Pandya, Thanjavur, Sri Lanka, Sumatra, Jambi, Java, the Khyber Pass and Mt. Kailasa.

7. Label Togrul's Turks.

Chapter Seventy-Three

Basil the Bulgar-Slayer

You may use your text when answering the questions in sections I and II.

Section I: Who, What, Where

Write a one or two-sentence answer explaining the significance of each item listed below.

Al-Aziz

Al-Hakim

Al-Muizz

Al-Qadir

Bardas Phocas

Samuel

Skleros

Varangian Guard

Section II: Comprehension

Write a two or three-sentence answer to each of the following questions.

1. Who were the four freedom fighters in the west of Bulgaria that challenged Byzantine rule? What did the brothers claim they wanted from Constantinople? What Basil II think they really wanted?

2. What did Basil II hope would happen after he set Boris II and his brother and heir Romanus free in 981? What actually happened?

3. How did Basil II handle the threat posed by Bardas Phocas and his loyal Asia Minor troops?

4. What advice did Skleros give Basil II concerning his running of Byzantium? What did Basil II do with this advice?

5. What kind of a ruler was the Fatimid caliph al-Hakim? What were some of the rules he imposed on his kingdom?

6. Why didn't Basil II attack al-Hakim after he destroyed the Church of the Holy Sepulchre and Golgotha?

7. What happened when the Byzantine army finally met the Bulgarians in battle at Kleidion in July of 1014?

8. Describe al-Hakim's madness and his ultimate self-destruction.

9. How did Basil II earn the nickname "Basil the Bulgar-Slayer"?

Section III: Critical Thinking

You may not use your text to answer this question.

In the last chapter you wrote about the phrase "the hollowness of all human achievement," words spoken by Jivaka, a fictional fighter and general created by the Southern Indian poet Tiruttakadevar. Now, you will continue to ruminate on Jivaka's discovery about humanity. Write a paragraph explaining how the loss of the Church of the Holy Sepulchre is a testament to "the hollowness of all human achievement." In your answer detail why the Church was destroyed, and then connect the destruction to Jivaka's sorrowful words, further explicating the your ideas from Chapter 72.

Section IV: Map Exercise

1. Using a black pencil, trace the rectangular outline of the frame for Map 73.1: The Fatimid Caliphate and Byzantium.

2. Using a blue pencil, trace the coastline of the Mediterranean Sea, the Red Sea, and the Black Sea. You do not need to include any islands at this time. Repeat until the contours are familiar.

3. Using a new sheet of paper, trace the rectangular outline of the frame in black. Remove your tracing paper from the original, and draw the coastline of the Mediterranean, the Red Sea, and the Black Sea.

4. When you are pleased with your map, lay it over the original. Erase and redraw any lines which are more than ¼ inch off of the original. Using a black pencil, trace the outline of the Rus and the outline of the Fatimids. Then trace the area of the Hamdanids and of the Buyids.

5. Remove your map. Study carefully the locations of North Africa, Egypt, Arabia, Palestine, Asia Minor, Thracia, and Bulgaria. Mark them on your map. Then study carefully the locations of Cairo, Mecca, Medina, Damascus, Baghdad, Antioch, Constantinople, Chrysopolis, Ohrid, and Mahdia. Mark them on your map as well. Check your map against the original, and correct any misplaced labels.

6. Mark the location of the Battle of Kleidion.

Chapter Seventy-Four

Defending the Mandate

You may use your text when answering the questions in sections I and II.

Section I: Who, What, Where

Write a one or two-sentence answer explaining the significance of each item listed below.

Liao Shengzong

Song Renzong

Song Zhenzong

Treaty of Chanyuan

Xiao

Section II: Comprehension

Write a two or three-sentence answer to each of the following questions.

1. For what reasons was Song Taizong's crown in jeopardy, even though he had conquered the Northern Han?

2. How could a ruler prove he had the Mandate of Heaven?

3. Why did the older of Song Taizong's nephews cut his own throat?

4. How did Song Taizong manage to surprise the Liao during his second campaign against his enemy neighbor in 986?

5. How was Song Taizong able to keep his throne after his second defeat by the Liao?

6. Describe the state of the Song kingdom when Song Zhenzong came to the throne. How did he try and deal with the mess left for him by his father?

7. What did Song Zhenzong do to prove to his people the Mandate of Heaven had not deserted him?

8. While Song Zhenzong worked to prove to his people that divine favor was with him, what was most likely the reason that his people continued to support his rule?

9. How did peace change the book industry in Song China?

10. In what way did woodblock printing prove useful in addition to the mass production of books?

Section III: Critical Thinking

You may not use your text to answer this question.

Over the course of our history of the medieval world we have seen rulers make great changes in their respective kingdoms. Rarely, though, have we seen a ruler create an entirely new class of people. During the rule of Song Taizong a new class emerged in China: the class of professional bureaucrats. Write a paragraph explaining why this class came to exist and how it grew under Song Taizong.

Chapter Seventy-Five

The New Found Land

You may use your text when answering the questions in sections I and II.

Section I: Who, What, Where

Write a one or two-sentence answer explaining the significance of each item listed below.

Anasazi

Bjarni Herjolfsson

Dorset

Gudrid

Hopewell

Ipiutak

Leif Ericsson

Skraelings

Snorri

Tezcatlipoca

Thorfinn Karlsefni

Thorvald Ericsson

Thule

Topiltzin

Section II: Comprehension

Write a two or three-sentence answer to each of the following questions.

1. Why didn't Eric the Red accompany his son Leif Ericsson on his exploratory journey to the unknown land discovered by Bjarni Herjolfsson?

2. List Leif Ericsson's 1003 exploratory route and the names he gave to the lands he encountered.

3. Describe the weather and living conditions Leif Ericsson and his men experienced during the winter months of their first expedition to the new found land in North America.

4. Why did Thorvald Ericsson and his fellow explorers think the lands near his brother's camp in North America were unclaimed? What happened that drove the men back to Greenland?

5. Describe the city of Cahokia. Why do we know so little about the people who lived in Cahokia, and more generally, the people that lived in North America during the days of Leif Ericsson?

6. Who were the Mixtec, and what did they do with old Mayan and Zapotec land?

7. Describe the city of Tula. Why did the people of central Mesoamerica call the city "Tollan"?

8. Why did Topiltzin have enemies in Tula? Why did he leave the city?

9. Why did citizens of Tula call themselves "Toltecs"?

10. Where did the Toltecs go after the city of Tula was ruined?

11. Why was Chichen Itza considered a sacred city? How did the Toltecs make Chichen Itza their own?

Section III: Critical Thinking

You may not use your text to answer this question.

In general, we think abundance is a good thing. When cities are successful and they grow, we see the expansion of a culture, and even of civilization. But this was not the case for the Maya. Write a paragraph explaining how prosperity ruined the Maya.

Section IV: Map Exercise

1. Using a black pencil, trace the rectangular outline of the frame for map 75.1: Settlements of the Americas.

2. Using a blue pencil, trace the coastline around the American continent. Include the large island opposite the Yucatan Peninsula and the island containing Leif's winter camp. You do not need to include all the many small islands between the main continent and Greenland, but draw the perimeter of the area, and use small circles to denote the presence of multiple smaller islands inside the area. Include the small coastline opposite the Bering Strait by the Ipiutak settlement. You do not need to trace any other islands at this time. Repeat until the contours are familiar.

3. Using a new sheet of paper, trace the rectangular outline of the frame in black. Remove your tracing paper from the original. Using a regular pencil with an eraser as you look at Map 75.1, draw the coastline around the continent, including the islands you traced, but no others. As you did when tracing, draw the perimeter of the area heavily covered in islands, and draw circles inside to denote the presence of multiple islands. Erase and redraw as necessary.

4. When you are pleased with your map, lay it over the original. Erase and redraw any lines which are more than ¼ inch off of the original.

5. Remove your map. Study carefully the locations of Greenland, Helluland, Anasazi, Markland, Dorset, Vinland, the Gulf of Mexico, the Yucatan Peninsula, and the Gulf of Honduras. Label all these locations on the map. Then study carefully the locations of Tula, Tonina, Chichen Itza, Cahokia, Leif's Winter Camp, and the Ipiutak settlement. Label them on the map. When you are done, label the movements of the Thule. Check your map against the original. Correct any misplaced labels.

6. Mark and label the Bering Strait, as well as the Valley of Mexico and the Valley of Oaxaca.

Chapter Seventy-Six

Schism

You may use your text when answering the questions in sections I and II.

Section I: **Who, What, Where**

Write a one or two-sentence answer explaining the significance of each item listed below.

Benedict IX

Burchard

Cardinal Humbert

Clement II

College of Cardinals

Conrad II

Crescentius

Drogo of Hauteville

Geza

Great Schism

Gregory V

Henry of Bavaria/Henry II

Henry the Black/Henry III

Henry IV

Johannes Philagathos

John XIX

John Gratian

Leo IX

Michael Cerularius

Nicholas II

Robert Guiscard

Stephen

Sylvester II

Sylvester III

Section II: Comprehension

Write a two or three-sentence answer to each of the following questions.

1. How was Otto III's Rome different from Charlemagne's Rome?

2. Why did Otto III think the punishments given to Crescentius and Johannes Philagathos were fair?

3. For what reasons did Gerbert take the papal name "Sylvester II"?

4. Why was Sylvester II the one to make Stephen of Hungary king? How did Stephen of Hungary understand Sylvester II's gesture?

5. Why did Otto III and Sylvester II leave Rome in 1001? Why didn't Otto III return to Rome?

6. What was on Henry II's seal when he became Holy Roman Emperor, and what did it mean? How did Henry II keep the power of his empire centered on Germany?

7. How did Henry II make the parishes in his empire feel as if they had sovereignty?

8. Explain how the Peace and Truce of God grew under Henry III's rule.

9. How did the Normans come to reside in Italy? How did Henry III first deal with the Normans in Italy?

10. What were the two main issues that caused the patriarch of Constantinople to resurrect a series of ongoing theological arguments between the eastern and western Christian churches?

Section III: Critical Thinking

You may not use your text to answer this question.

In this section of *The History of the Medieval World* we are reading about crusades, or, religious wars. In this chapter, we learned about the Treaty of Melfi, which was made to separate church and state. Write a paragraph that outlines the Treaty of Melfi. Then, explain how, despite its insistence on dividing the power of religion and government, the treaty needed the two to be entwined in order for it to be successful.

Section IV: Map Exercise

1. Using a black pencil, trace the rectangular outline of the frame for Map 76.1: The Holy Roman Empire.

2. Using a blue pencil, trace the coastline of the Atlantic around Britain and down the entirety of the mainland, starting up at the top of the map with Scandinavia and running down all the way through the Mediterranean. You do not need to include all the minor islands at this time; just Sardinia, Corsica, Sicily, Crete, and Cyprus. Trace the coastline of the Black Sea. Then with your black pencil trace the mountains, using simple peaks. Repeat until the contours are familiar.

3. Trace the rectangular outline of the frame in black. Leaving your map over the original, trace with your regular pencil the regions of the Caliphate of Cordoba, the Kingdom of Leon, Pamplona, Western Francia, Burgundy, Normandy, Germany, Bavaria, the Italian Kingdom, Corsica, Norman Italy, Calabria, Hungary, Rus, and Byzantium. Trace the mountains with simple peaks.

4. Remove your map from the original. Study carefully the regions of the Caliphate of Cordoba, the Kingdom of Leon, Pamplona, Western Francia, Burgundy, Normandy, Germany, Bavaria, the Italian Kingdom, Corsica, Norman Italy, Calabria, Hungary, Rus, and Byzantium. When you are familiar with them, close the book. Using your regular pencil, label each region. Check your map against the original, and correct any misplaced labels.

5. Lay your map back over the original and trace the outline of the Holy Roman Empire with your black pencil.

6. Now remove your map from the original. Study carefully the locations of the Abbey of Cluny, Paris, Cologne, Aachen, Constance, Worms, Pavia, Augsburg, Merseburg, Novgorod, Ravenna, Florence, Spoleto, Rome, Benevento, Constantinople, and Antioch. When you are familiar with them, close the book, and label each region with your regular pencil. If necessary, study the first nine locations first and label them before you go on to study and label the last seven. When you are done, check your map against the original, and correct any misplaced locations or labels.

Chapter Seventy-Seven

Danish Domination

You may use your text when answering the questions in sections I and II.

Section I: Who, What, Where

Write a one or two-sentence answer explaining the significance of each item listed below.

Aelfgifu

Alfred Atheling

Canute the Great

Duncan

Edmund

Edward

Emma

Godwin

Harold Harefoot

Harthacanute

Mac Bethad mac Findlaich (Macbeth)

Magnus the Good

Malcolm II

Olaf the Saint

William the Bastard

Witan

Section II: Comprehension

Write a two or three-sentence answer to each of the following questions.

1. What did the people of London do after Sweyn Forkbeard died? What was the result of their attack against Canute?

2. For what reason did Canute most likely return to Denmark from London?

3. Why did the witan have to elect Edmund to the throne? What were their reasons for his election?

4. What were the terms of the truce made between Edmund and Canute that ended the war between the two kings in November 1016?

5. What happened to Edmund Ironside's two young sons immediately after his death?

6. Why did Emma send her sons Alfred and Edward back to Normandy after her marriage to Canute?

7. How was England divided under the rule of Canute the Great, and who did he choose to rule over each section of his kingdom?

8. Describe why Edmund and Alfred thought they could return to England, and what happened when they got there.

9. Mac Bethad mac Findlaich was the inspiration for Shakespeare's traitorous host who killed his king in his sleep. What were the circumstances of Macbeth's real rebellion against his high king Duncan?

10. How did Harthacanute become immediately unpopular after he took the English throne following Harold Harefoot's death?

Section III: Critical Thinking

You may not use your text to answer this question.

Macbeth is one of William Shakespeare's most famous plays. As we read about in this chapter, the real story of Mac Bethad mac Findlaich was nowhere near as scandalous as the version presented by the Bard of Avon. However, real life did inspire Shakespeare's great work. In this Critical Thinking question, do a little research and find another example of a famous work of literature inspired by a real life person or event. Write a paragraph that names the work and its author, what inspired the work, and a little bit about the work itself. Do the best you can to cite the source of your information in your paragraph.

Chapter Seventy-Eight

The Norman Conquest

You may use your text when answering the questions in sections I and II.

Section I: Who, What, Where

Write a one or two-sentence answer explaining the significance of each item listed below.

Edgar

Edith

Harald Hardrada

Harold Godwinson

Leofric

Siward

Tostig

Section II: Comprehension

Write a two or three-sentence answer to each of the following questions.

1. How did Edward earn the nickname "Edward the Confessor"? In contrast, what did Edward do with his mother's goods when he was named king?

2. What did Godwin do to regain the earldom of Wessex?

3. How did Harold's treatment of his brother Tostig prove the Earl of Wessex had just as much power as a king?

4. What happened between William the Bastard and Harold Godwinson in 1064?

5. How did Harold Godwinson become Harold II of England?

6. Why did the English read Halley's Comet as a bad omen at the start of Harold II's reign?

7. Describe what happened when Tostig and Harald Hardrada of Norway first landed near York in September of 1066.

8. What stopped William the Bastard from first attacking England in September of 1066?

9. What was the result of the clash between Harold II and Tostig in York?

10. Why was the Battle of Hastings fought?

11. How did William the Bastard become William the Conqueror? How did he become William I?

Section III: Critical Thinking

You may not use your text to answer this question.

In many cultures weather can serve as an omen, a sign of good or bad fortune. Weather was particularly significant to Harold Godwinson. Write a paragraph explaining how the weather played a role in Harold's life, and his unfortunate fate.

Section IV: Map Exercise

1. Using a black pencil, trace the rectangular outline of the frame for Map 78.1: The Battle of Hastings.

2. Using a black pencil, trace the coastline around Ireland, Britain, Scandinavia, and down the continent. Trace the visible portion of the Mediterranean. You do not need to include any islands at this time. Repeat until the contours are familiar.

3. Using a new sheet of paper, trace the rectangular outline of the frame in black. Remove your tracing paper from the original. Using a regular pencil with an eraser as you look at the map, draw the coastline. Erase and redraw as necessary.

4. When you are pleased with your map, lay it over the original. Erase and redraw any lines which are more than ¼ inch off of the original. With your black pencil, trace the outlines of Asturias, the Caliphate of Cordoba, Pamplona, Western Francia, and Germany.

5. Remove your map. Study carefully the locations of Ireland, England, Norway, Sweden, Denmark, Germany, Western Francia, Normandy, Brittany, Asturias, Pamplona, and the Caliphate of Cordoba. When you are familiar with them, mark the locations on your map.

6. Now show the location and direction of William the Conqueror and Harold Hardrada. Show their movement with arrows on your map.

Chapter Seventy-Nine

The Kings of Spain

You may use your text when answering the questions in sections I and II.

Section I: Who, What, Where

Write a one or two-sentence answer explaining the significance of each item listed below.

Abd al-Malik

Abd al-Rahman

Abu-Bakr

Al-Mu'tamid

Al-Nasir

Alfonso V

Alfonso VI

Alfonso the Battler

Ali ibn Yusuf

Ferdinand I

Garcia II

Hisham II

Ibn Yasin

Muhammad ibn Abi Amir

Rodrigo Diaz (El Cid)

Sancho

Sancho II

Sancho II the Strong

Sancho III

Sulayman II

Urraca

Yahya ibn Ibrahim

Yusuf ibn Tashfin

Section II: Comprehension

Write a two or three-sentence answer to each of the following questions.

1. How did al-Mansur manage to move himself up in the palace hierarchy of al-Andalus?

2. What made al-Mansur an excellent strategist and administrator?

3. Why did the Umayyads revolt when al-Rahman was named heir to the caliphate by Hisham II? What happened during the revolt?

4. Describe the leadership of al-Andalus after the death of al-Nasir.

5. Explain how Sancho III got away with murdering Garcia II and managed to unite Pamplona with Castile.

6. What did El Cid do to get himself exiled by Alfonso VI?

7. Why were the *taifa* kingdoms afraid of Alfonso VI? What did they plan to do to defeat him?

8. Why did Alfonso VI want El Cid back in his kingdom? What were the conditions of El Cid's return to Alfonso VI's service?

9. What happened to Valencia after the death of El Cid?

10. In what way did the relationship between Alfonso the Battler and Urraca help the Almoravid empire keep their power?

Section III: Critical Thinking

You may not use your text to answer this question.

The relationship between war and peace is often a confusing one. Just look at Ferdinand I, for example. War made him king of a great realm, but to find inner peace he spent his last days in the clothes of a sinner. Thinking about the relationship between war and peace, write a paragraph explaining the contradiction between how El Cid conquered Valencia and the way he used the small kingdom after he was in control.

Chapter Eighty

The Arrival of the Turks

You may use your text when answering the questions in sections I and II.

Section I: Who, What, Where

Write a one or two-sentence answer explaining the significance of each item listed below.

Alp Arslan

Constantine VIII

Constantine Doukas

Constantine Monomachos

Isaac Comnenus

John Orphanotrophus

Michael V

Michael VII

Michael the Paphlagonian

Michael Bringas

Romanos Argyros

Romanos Diogenes

Theodora

Zoe

Section II: Comprehension

Write a two or three-sentence answer to each of the following questions.

1. Describe how all of Romanos III's royal dreams fell through.

2. For what reasons were men castrated in Byzantium?

3. How did Michael IV's relationship with Zoe change under the influence of John Orphanotrophus?

4. How did Michael IV deal with his epileptic fits in public? What steps were taken to ensure that Michael IV had an heir?

5. How did Zoe and her sister Theodora come to be co-empresses of Byzantium?

6. What kind of kingdom did Constantine Monomachos inherit when he became emperor of Byzantium?

7. How did the Turks become strong enough to challenge Byzantium?

8. What happened when the Turks breached the eastern border and captured the rich border city of Erzen in 1048?

9. How did it come to pass that Togrul was recognized in the Friday prayers?

10. How was Romanos Diogenes able to drive the Turks back across the Euphrates in 1070?

11. What happened to Romanos Diogenes's army after Alp Arslan regrouped in 1071?

12. How was Romanos Diogenes treated after he was taken prisoner by Alp Arslan? How was he treated by his own people?

Section III: Critical Thinking

You may not use your text to answer this question.

It is common sense to think that a ruler of a tribe, a nation, a kingdom, or an empire, would make decisions that would benefit his/her realm, rather than him/herself. But as we have read over and over, that is just not the case. Write a paragraph or two explaining how Constantine Monomachos and Romanos Diogenes made decisions that were in their best interest, but not the best interest for Byzantium. Then explain how those decisions led to the shrinking of Byzantium.

Chapter Eighty-One

The Loss of the Song

You may use your text when answering the questions in sections I and II.

Section I: Who, What, Where

Write a one or two-sentence answer explaining the significance of each item listed below.

Akuta

Gaozong

Jin Taizong

Li Deming

Li Yuanhao

Lin Lingsu

Qinzong

Song Huizong

Yun Kwan

Section II: Comprehension

Write a two or three-sentence answer to each of the following questions.

1. How was Li Yuanhao able to create a past for the Western Xia?

2. If the Song did not dominate the east, why did the Western Xia want Song Renzong's recognition?

3. Describe the Western Xia attack on the Song between 1038 and 1042. How was Song Renzong able to avoid a war with the Liao while his armies were fighting the Western Xia?

4. Why was the *Wujing Zongyao* written, and what information does it contain?

5. How did Song Renzong use the time he bought in the truce between the Western Xia, the Liao and the Song?

6. Who were the Jurchen? What was the difference between "Civilized Jurchen" and "Raw Jurchen"?

7. How did the Goryeo keep out the nomadic Jurchen to the north of their country? How did their defenses hold up against the Jurchen fleeing from the Wanyan?

8. How did Akuta plan to use the Liao to turn his nomads into a settled state?

9. Why did Song Huizong agree to an alliance with Akuta? What happened when the combined armies attacked the Liao?

10. How did Qinzong become emperor?

Section III: **Critical Thinking**

You may use your text to answer this question.

A written history seems to be one key to creating a legitimate nation. Li Yuanhao made sure that a script was created for the Tangut language so the history of his people and culture could be recorded. Akuta also knew that he needed to create a history for the Jurchen people in order for them to be declared legitimate. But what good is history when a dynasty topples? Explain how the Song's intricate history and culture could not save the dynasty from being overrun by a powerful enemy, and how that history could not restore the Song once the dynasty came to an end. In your answer make sure to include some of poetry written by Zhang Xiaoxiang, found on page 639 of your text.

Chapter Eighty-Two

Repentance at Canossa

You may use your text when answering the questions in sections I and II.

Section I: Who, What, Where

Write a one or two-sentence answer explaining the significance of each item listed below.

Anno II

Bertha of Turin

Gregory VII

Peace of Terouanne

Philip

Section II: Comprehension

Write a two or three-sentence answer to each of the following questions.

1. Why did the German duchies gain so much power at the start of Henry IV's rule?

2. Describe Henry IV's capture and imprisonment.

3. How did Pope Alexander II respond to Henry IV's request to divorce his wife? Why did Henry IV accept the pope's decision?

4. Why was Pope Gregory VII opposed to the idea that a layman could appoint a church official? How was this belief made papal law?

5. What was Henry IV's first rebellion against Pope Gregory VII?

6. What did Pope Gregory VII suggest Henry IV might do to make up for his challenge to the Dictatus papae?

7. How did Henry IV react to Pope Gregory VII's threat?

8. What happened to Henry IV's power after Gregory VII had him excommunicated from the church? What did Henry IV decide to do in order to regain his power?

Section III: Critical Thinking

You may not use your text to answer this question.

Is there a difference between godly power and earthly power? How can we know, if power is always enacted by men of this world? While some men claim more authority than others because it is God-given, how are the rules they impose on men any different than the rules born of man's earthly desires? Write a paragraph that explains how the motivations and rules of the pope are no different than the motivations of the king or the emperor, using Popes Alexander II and Gregory VII as examples.

Chapter Eighty-Three

The Call

You may use your text when answering the questions in sections I and II.

Section I: Who, What, Where

Write a one or two-sentence answer explaining the significance of each item listed below.

Alexius Comnenus

Anna

Atsiz ibn Abaq

Badr al-Jamali

Bohemund

Constantine

John Doukas

Malik Shah

Maria

Nikephoros Botaneiates

Rudolf of Swabia

Urban II

Wibert of Ravenna

Section II: Comprehension

Write a two or three-sentence answer to each of the following questions.

1. Why did Alexius Comnenus have to hire Seljuq Turks to fight for Michael VII in 1074?

2. What did Malik Shah accomplish in the first year of his rule over the Turks? When did Malik Shah finally take Jerusalem for the Turks?

3. Explain the trouble caused when Nikephoros III disinherited Constantine.

4. Why did Alexius Comnenus have to ask Henry IV of Germany for help protecting Byzantine territory?

5. What series of events led to Henry IV's call for Pope Gregory VII to step down from his role as the Christian church's leader?

6. Why did Alexius Comnenus offer 360,000 gold pieces to Henry IV in support of the German king's campaign against Italy?

7. How did Henry IV finally become the Holy Roman Emperor?

8. In what way did Robert Guiscard live on after his death? Be sure to include some of Dante's words in your answer.

9. How did the Turks become people of the Muslim faith?

10. What happened to the Turkish alliance after the death of Malik Shah?

11. What did Pope Urban II promise would happen to any man fighting against the Muslims for power over Jerusalem?

Section III: Critical Thinking

You may use your text to answer this question. The student may also look at the previous chapter's workbook answers.

When Urban II agreed to help Alexius Comnenus fight the Turks that were attacking Byzantium, he also declared that it was time to recapture Jerusalem from the Muslims. In November of 1095, Urban II announced:

"As most of you have heard the Turks and Arabs . . . have occupied more and more of the lands of those Christians, and have overcome them in seven battles. They have killed and captured many, and have destroyed the churches and devastated the empire. If you permit them to continue thus for awhile with impurity, the faithful of God will be much more widely attacked by them. On this account I, or rather the Lord, beseech you as Christ's heralds to publish this everywhere and to persuade all people of whatever rank, foot-soldiers and knights, poor and rich, to carry aid promptly to those Christians and to destroy that vile race from the lands of our friends. I say this to those who are present, it is meant also for those who are absent. Moreover, Christ commands it."

Using what you know about leadership and power, and continuing the work from the Critical Thinking question in *Chapter 82: Repentance at Canossa*, write a paragraph explaining how Pope Urban II's declaration at Clermont in 1095 had less to do with God's will than it did with his own desire for power. In your answer, make sure to use the language of Urban II's announcement to support your analysis.

Chapter Eighty-Four

Fighting for Jerusalem

You may use your text when answering the questions in sections I and II.

Section I: Who, What, Where

Write a one or two-sentence answer explaining the significance of each item listed below.

Adhemar

Baldwin

Edgar Atheling

Eustace

Godfrey

Kerbogha

Kilij Arslan

Peter the Little

Peter Bartholomew

Raymond of Toulouse

Robert of Normandy

Stephen of Blois

Tancred

Taticius

Walter the Penniless

William of Normandy

Section II: Comprehension

Write a two or three-sentence answer to each of the following questions.

1. Why did later chroniclers call Peter the Little's army the "People's Crusade"?

2. Why did Alexius Comnenus have Peter the Little's army camp near the Byzantine frontier? Why did the armies waiting on the frontier march against Nicaea?

3. What oath did Alexius Comnenus make each duke that arrived in Constantinople between 1096–1097 to fight in the First Crusade take?

4. How were the crusaders inside of Antioch rallied to fight the awaiting Muslim army stationed outside the city's walls?

5. Though Antioch was supposed to be turned over to Byzantium, who took control of the city?

6. What did the landscape outside of Jerusalem look like when the crusaders arrived in June of 1099?

7. Explain how the crusaders took Jerusalem.

8. What did the approaching Fatimid army have to do with the slaughter inside of Jerusalem?

Section III: Critical Thinking

You may use your text to answer this question.

Pope Urban II may have told the crusaders God was on their side, but that did not mean that the victories in His name would come easily. For this Critical Thinking question, you will write a detailed account of the difficulties the crusaders faced in their taking of Antioch. To answer this question successfully, go back to your text and make an outline of the events that led to the possession of Antioch for the crusaders. Then, close your textbook and write your account of the events from your notes.

Chapter Eighty-Five

Aftershocks

You may use your text when answering the questions in sections I and II.

Section I: **Who, What, Where**

Write a one or two-sentence answer explaining the significance of each item listed below.

Baldwin II

Bernard of Clairvaux

Confraternity of Belchite

Hugh of Payens

Section II: **Comprehension**

Write a two or three-sentence answer to each of the following questions.

1. Why was the capture of Zaragoza considered a crusade? What were the implications of making the capture of Zaragoza an act of holy war?

2. What happened to Almoravid power in Spain after the fall of Zaragoza to Christian armies in 1118?

3. How did Alfonso the Battler turn the crusader status of his Christian armies into military orders protected by the law? What was the first order formed?

4. How did Baldwin of Edessa become Baldwin of Jerusalem, twice?

5. Describe the lifestyle of the group of men formed by Hugh of Payens.

6. How did the group of men formed by Hugh of Payens come to be called the Knights Templar?

7. What did Bernard of Clairvaux write in the introduction to the Rule of the Knights Templar?

8. How was the founding of military orders, like the Knights Templar, a fitting conclusion for the drama begun by Constantine at the Milvian Bridge?

Section III: Critical Thinking

You may not use your text to answer this question.

You may have come to the end of your study of the Medieval World, but the history and stories of the time will follow you into the modern day. In this final chapter you read about the formation of the Knights Templar. This particular monastic order has been fodder for myths and legends that continue to show up in popular culture. For this last Critical Thinking question you will search for contemporary mentions of the Knights Templar in creative works. Find at least three different mentions of the ancient monastic order, write a sentence or two explaining each reference, and make sure to cite the sources from which the mentions were found.

Maps to Accompany The Study and Teaching Guide for the History of the Medieval World

All Maps Designed by Susan Wise Bauer and Sarah Park

Address permission requests to Peace Hill Press, 18021 the Glebe Lane, Charles City, VA 23030

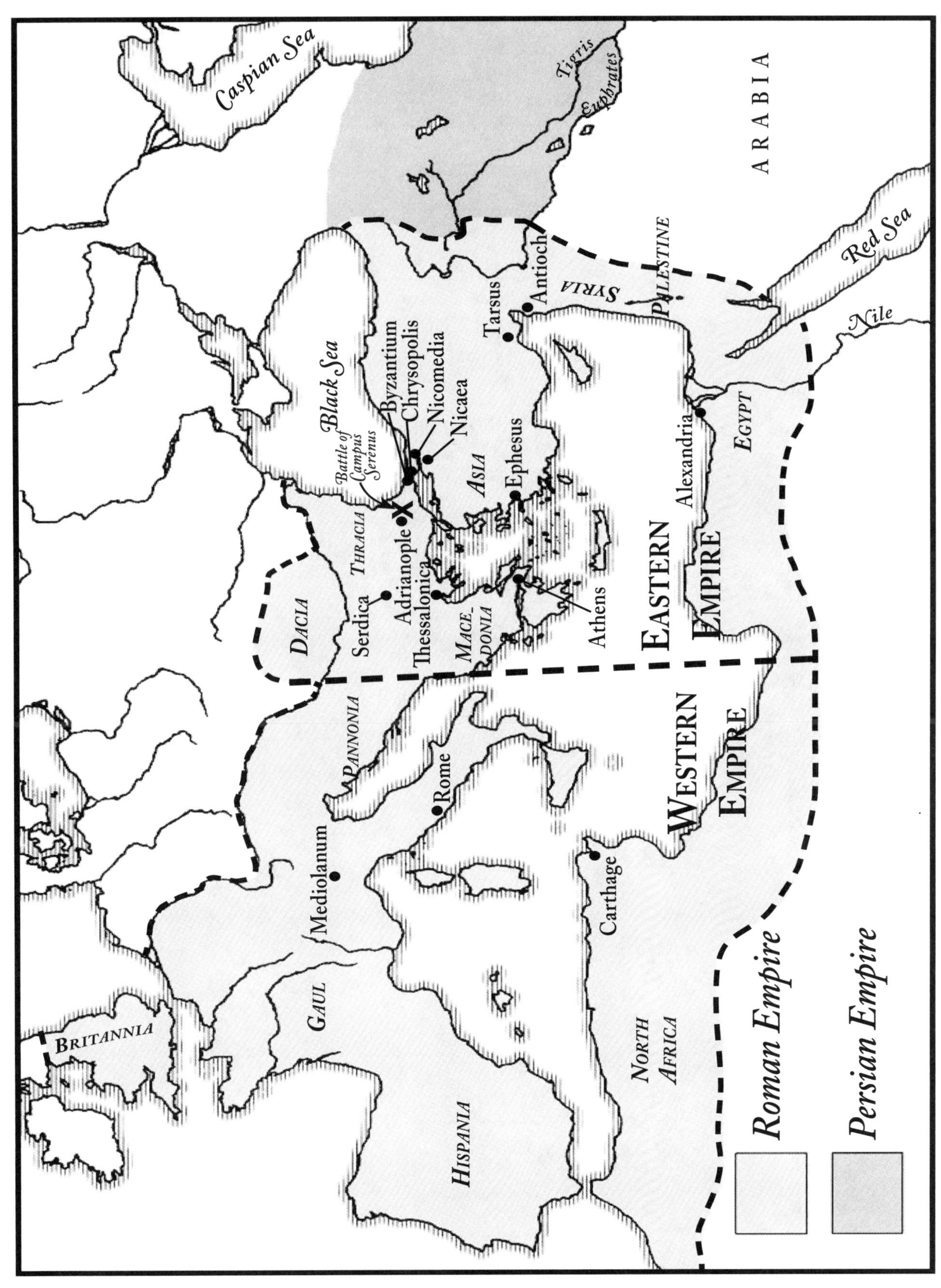

Map 1.1: The Empires of the Romans and Persians

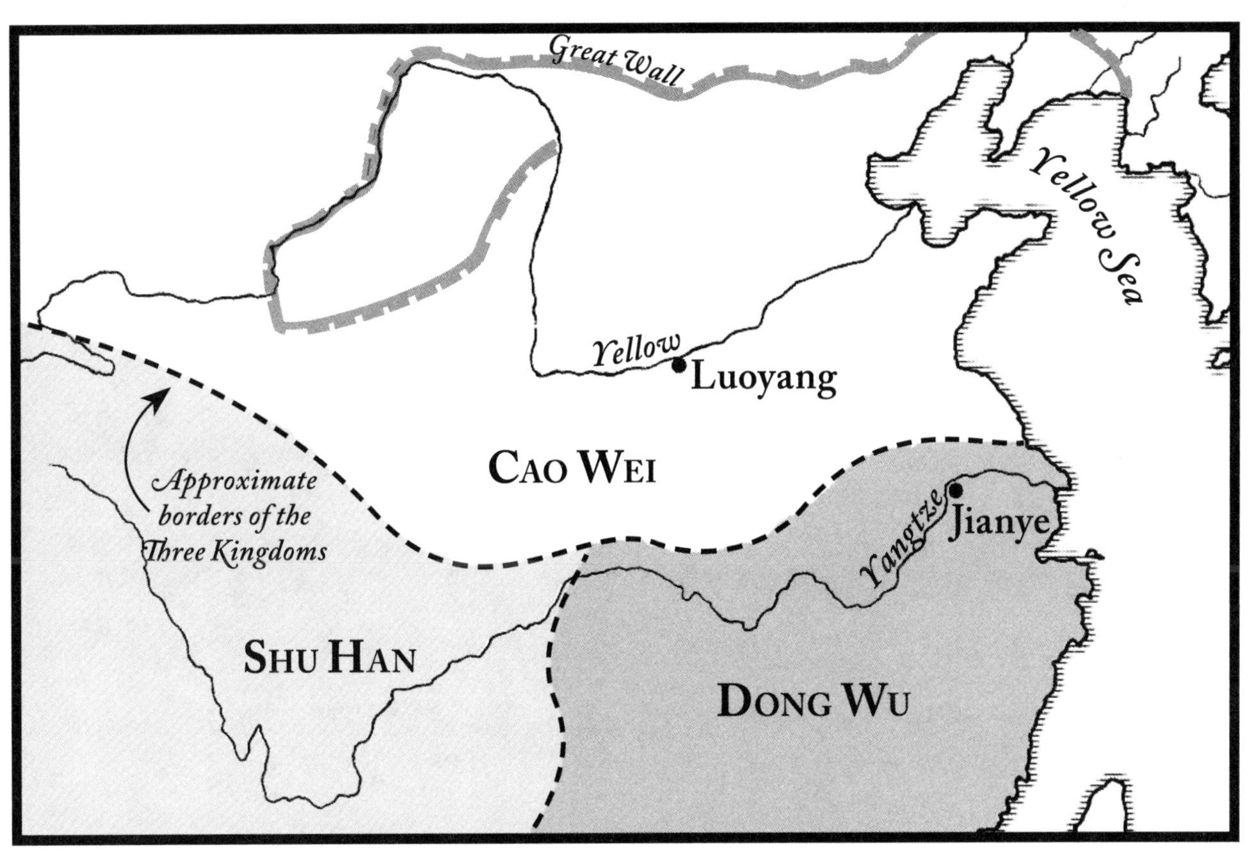

Map 2.1: The Three Kingdoms

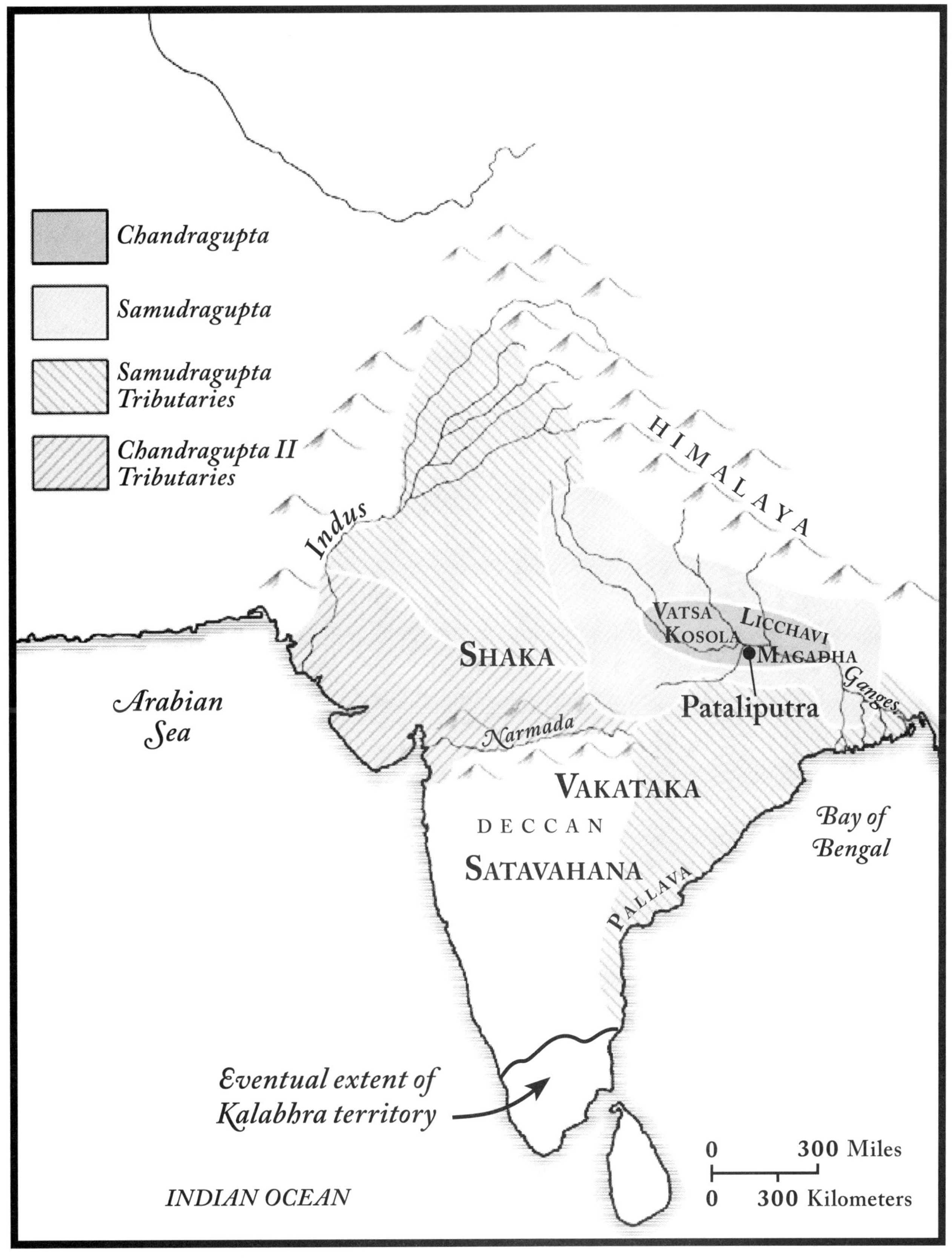

Map 3.1: The Age of the Gupta

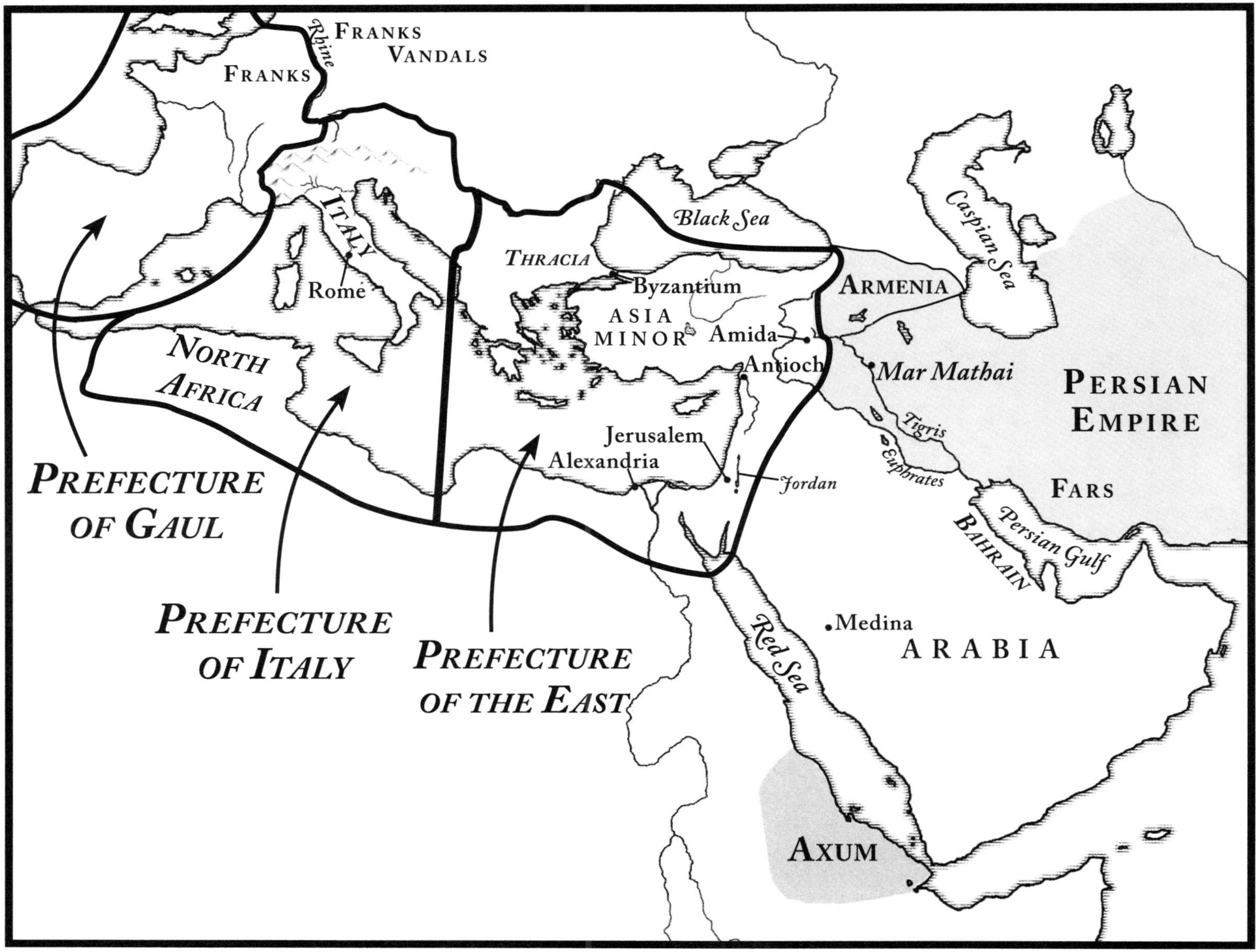

Map 4.1: The Romans and Persians

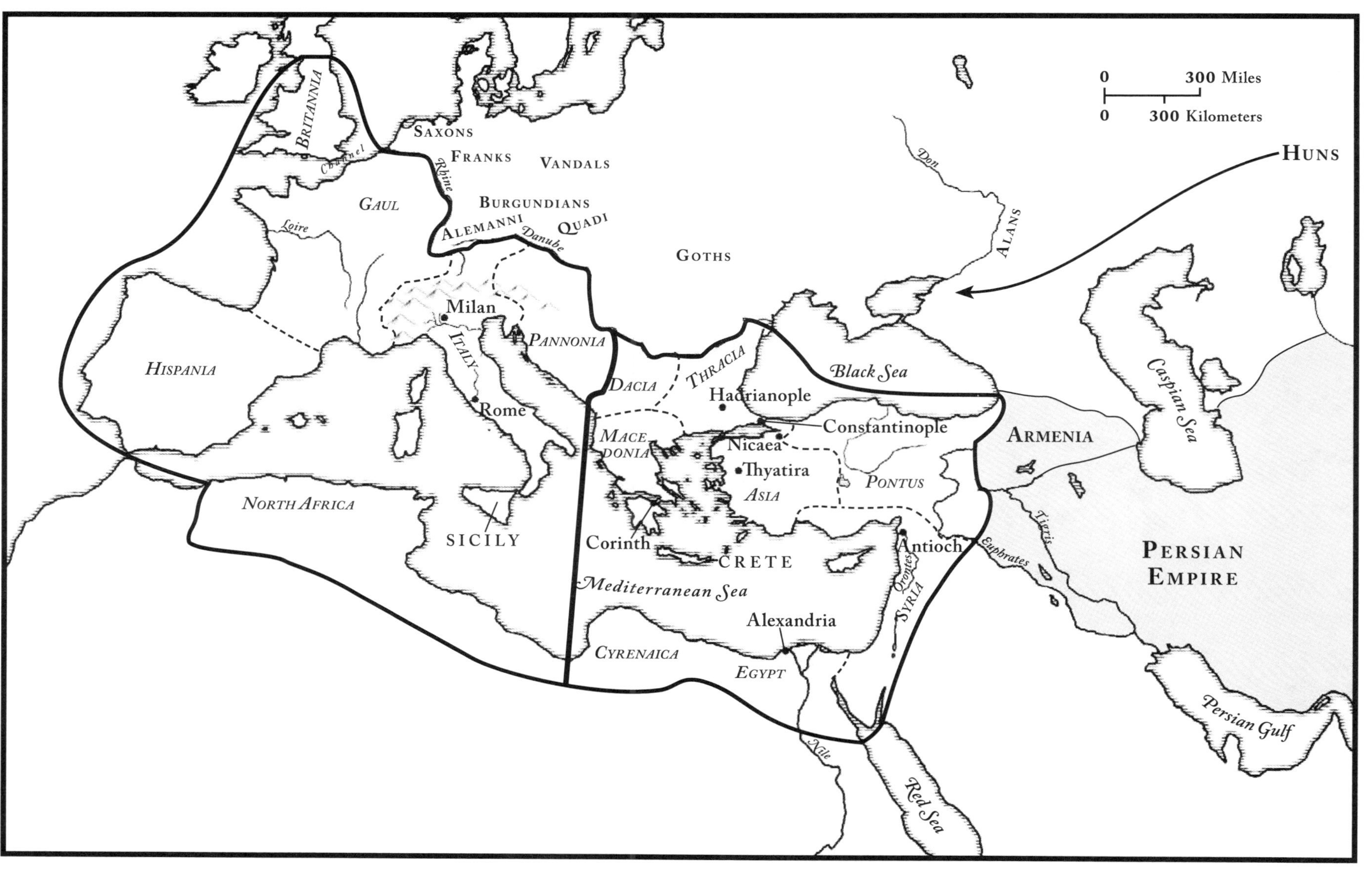

Map 6.2: The Barbarian Approch

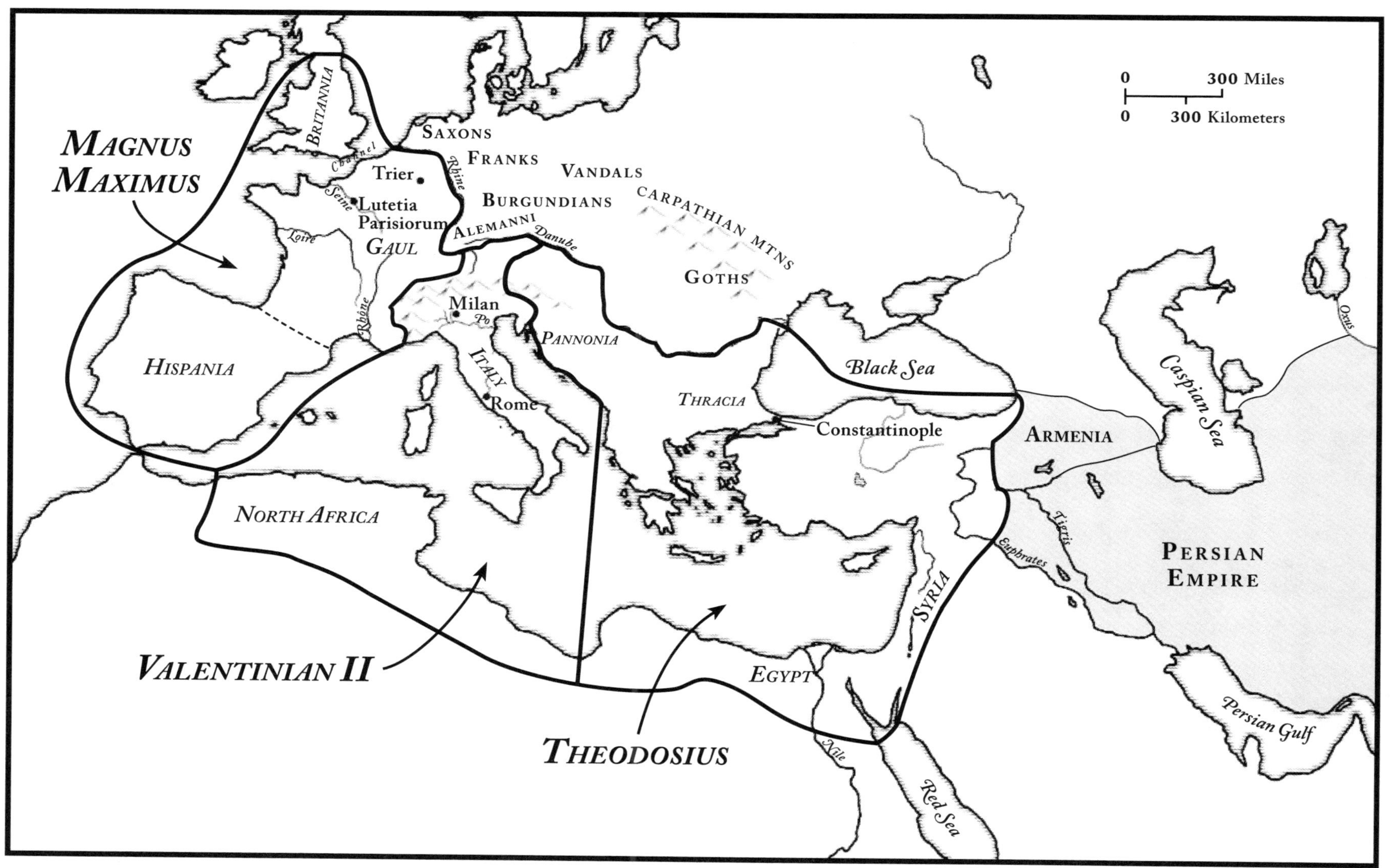

Map 9.1: The Empire in Thirds

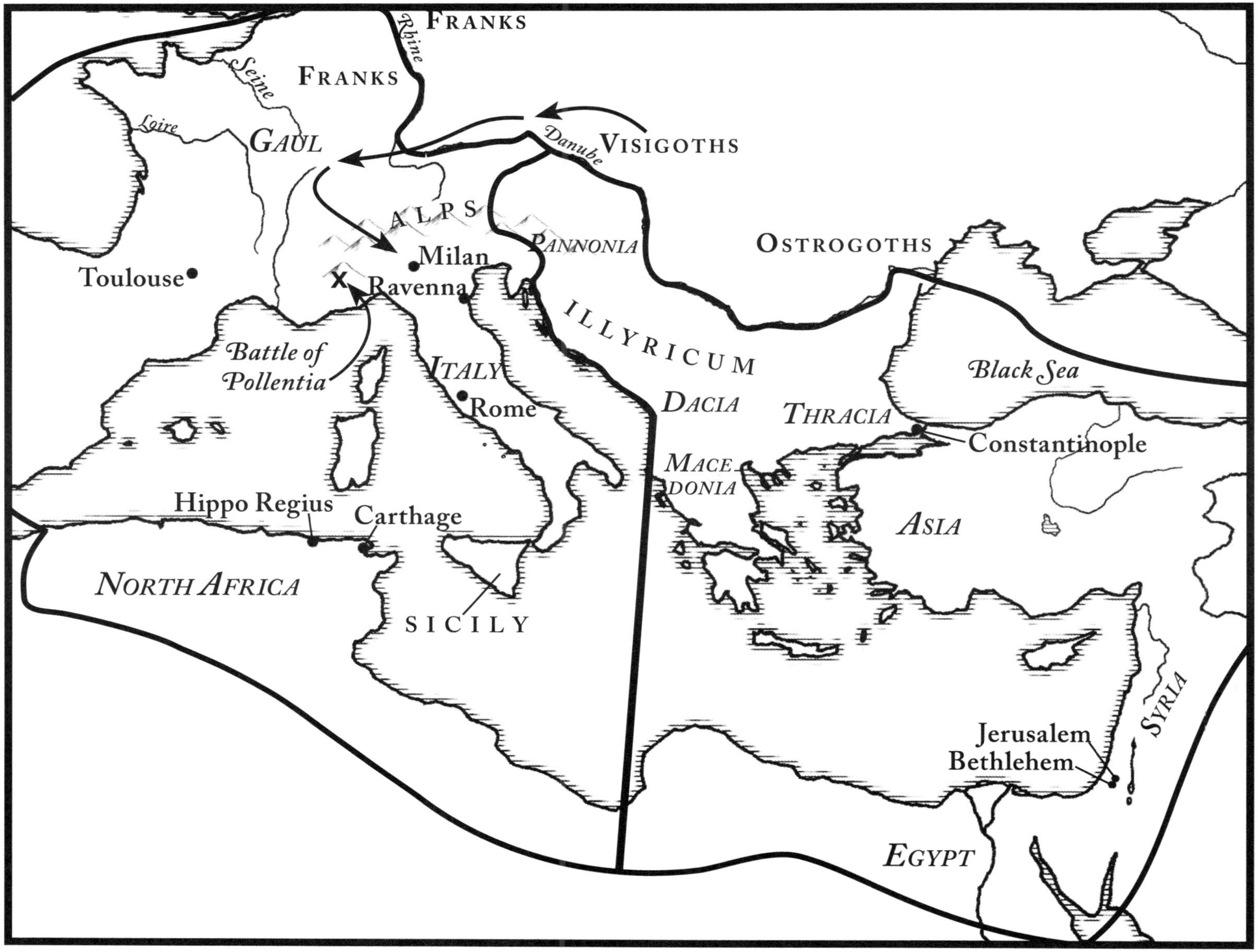

Map 11.1: The Visigoth Invasion

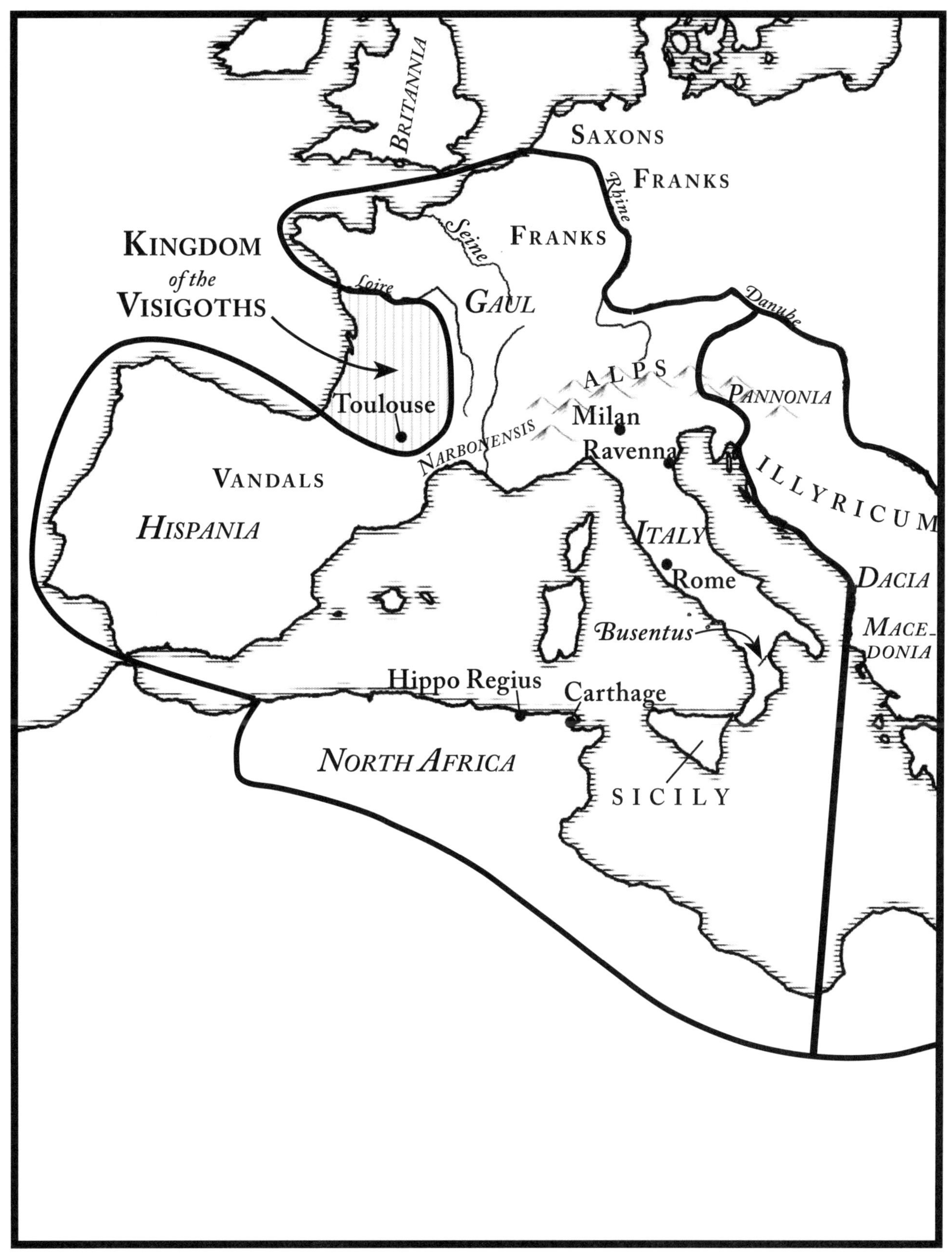

Map 13.1: Visigoth Kingdom

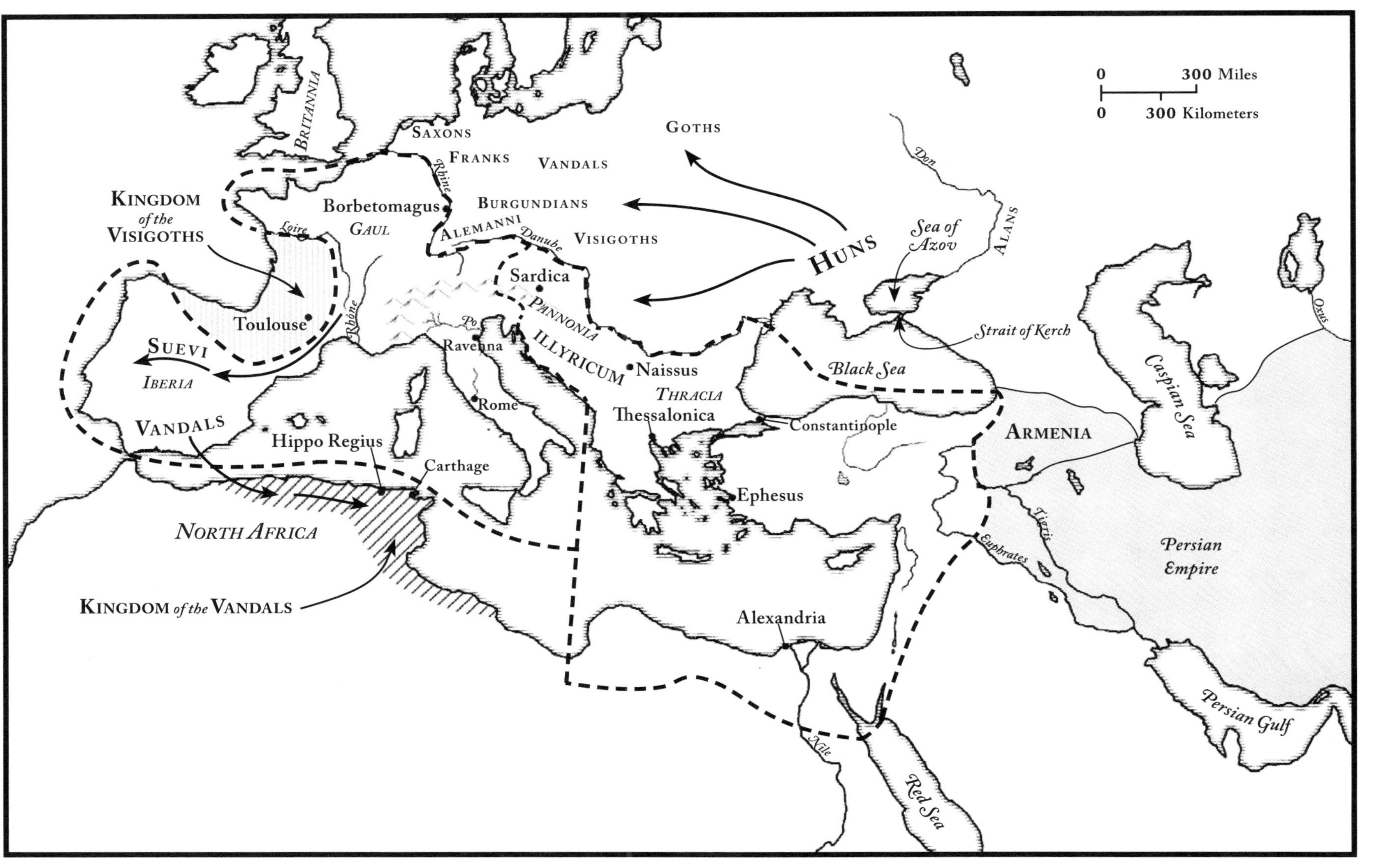

Map 16.1: The Approach of the Huns

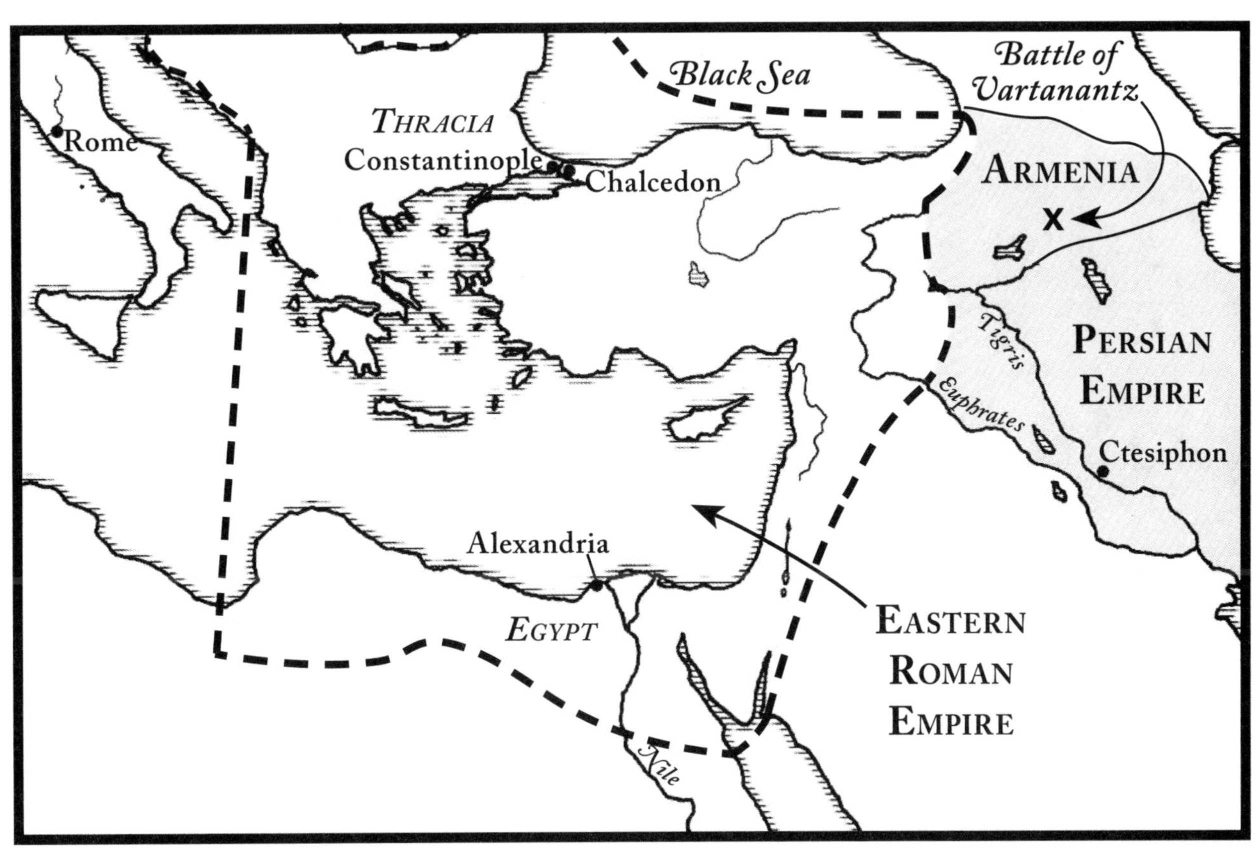

Map 18.1: The Battle of Vartanantz

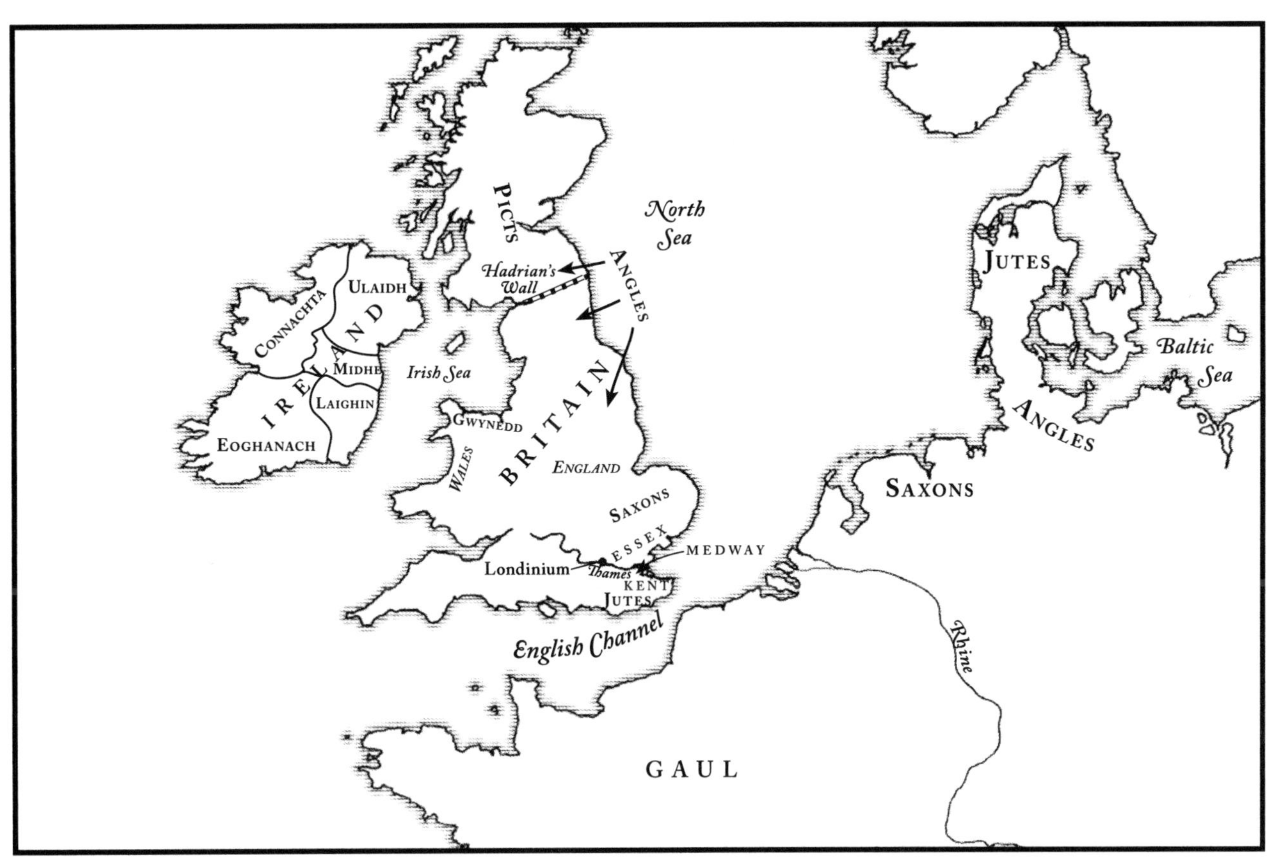

Map 19.1: Ireland and Britain

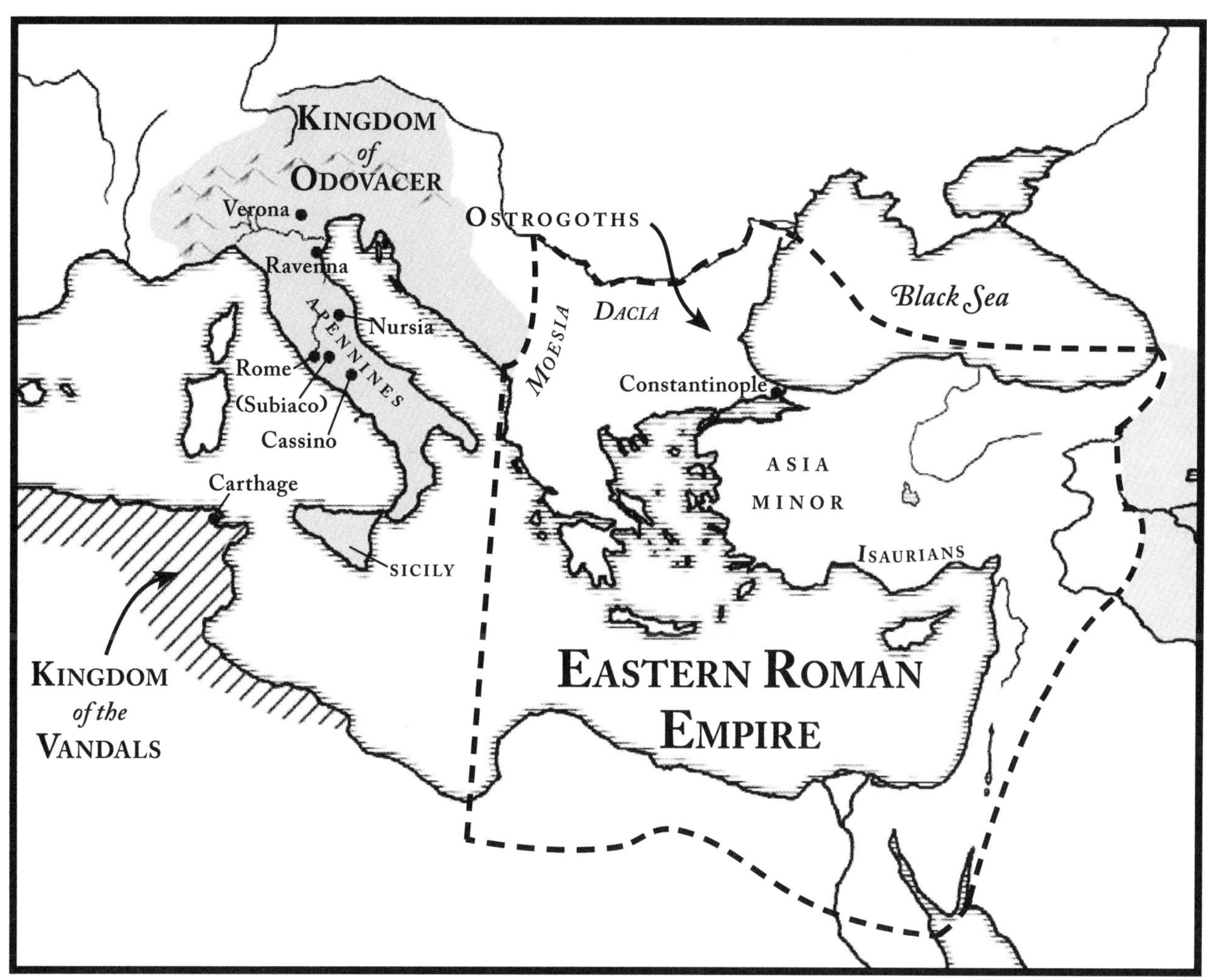

Map 21.1: Odovacer's Kingdom

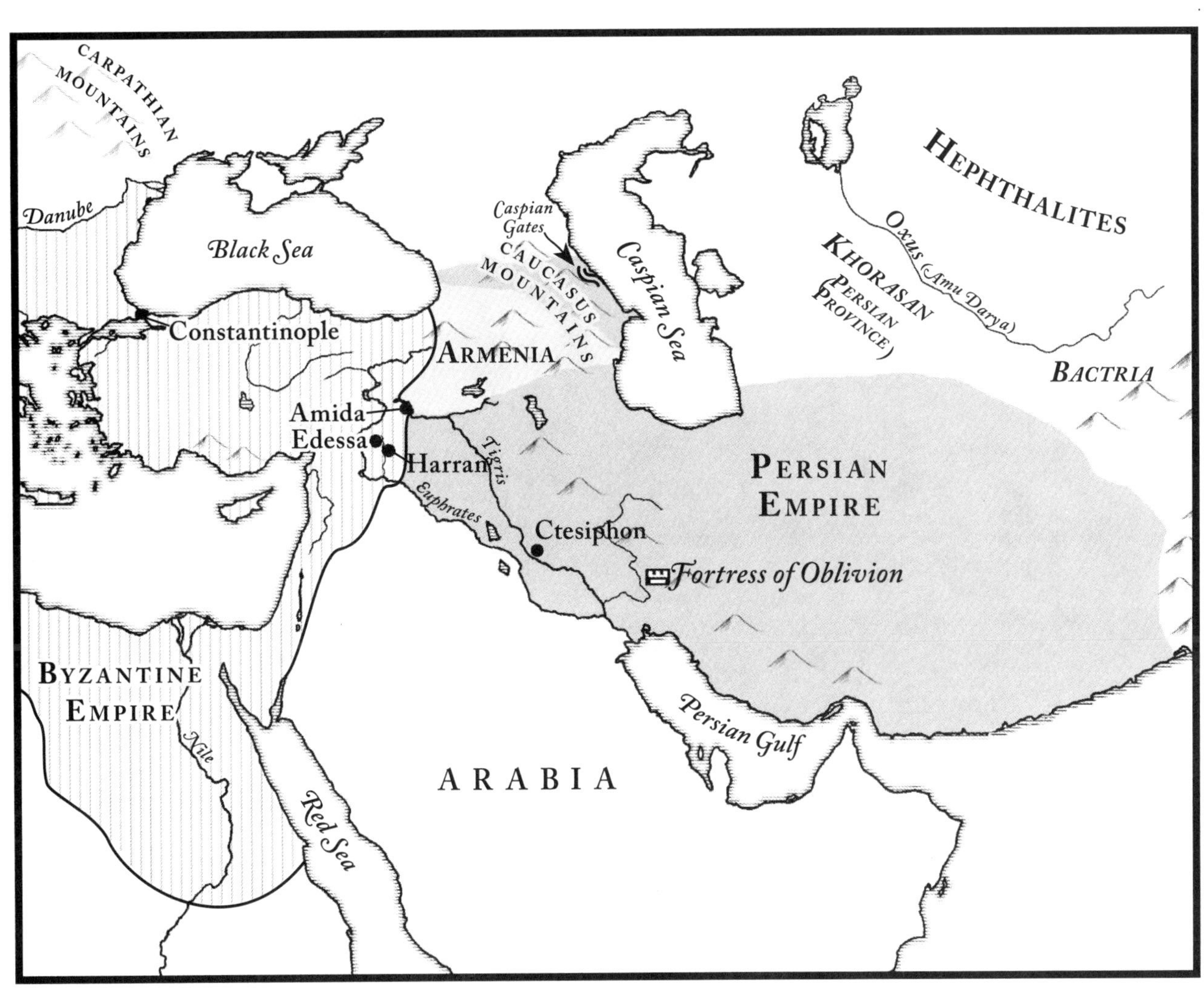

Map 22.1: Persia and the Hephthalites

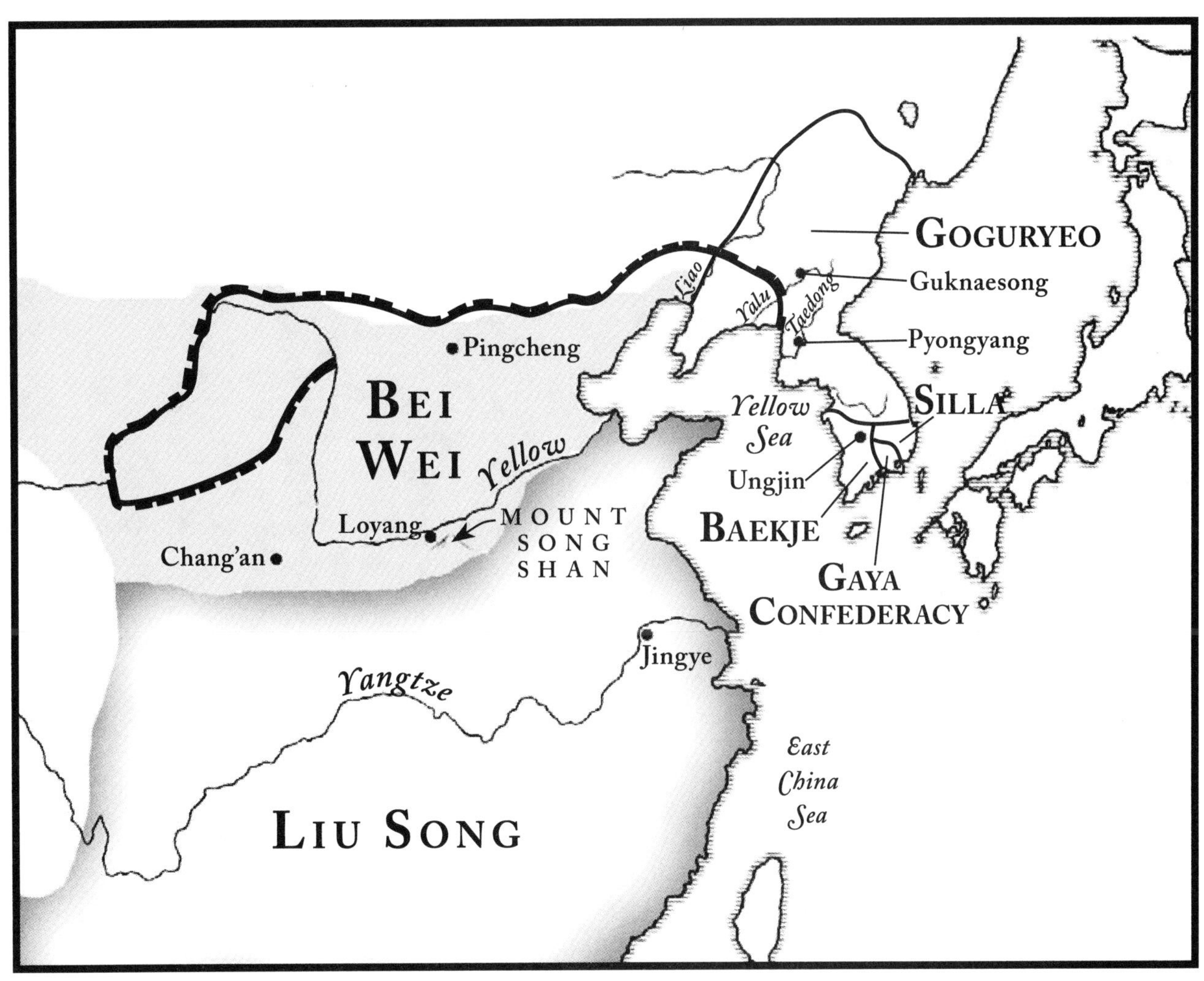

Map 23.1: The East in the Era of King Jangsu

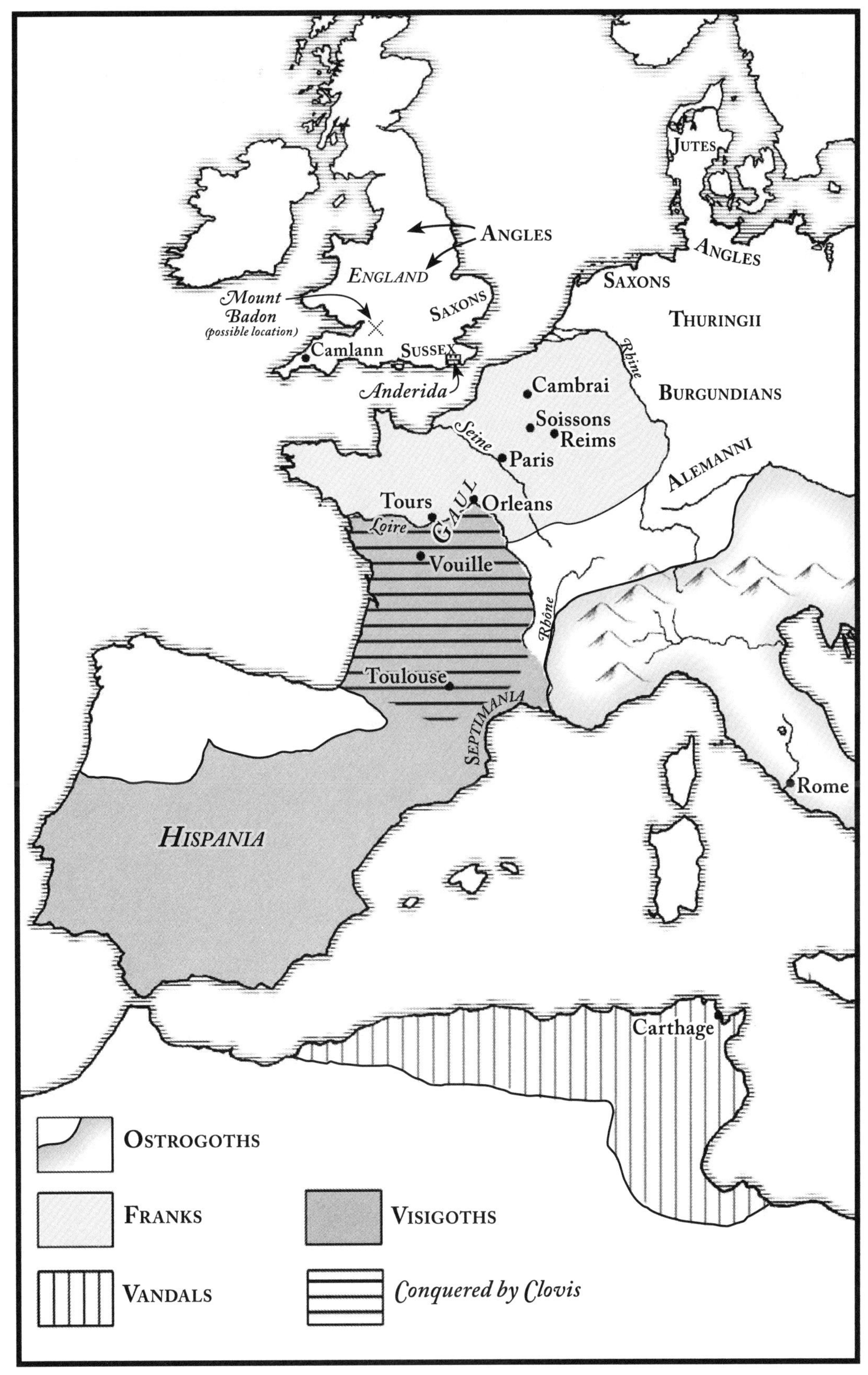

Map 25.1: Clovis and His Neighbors

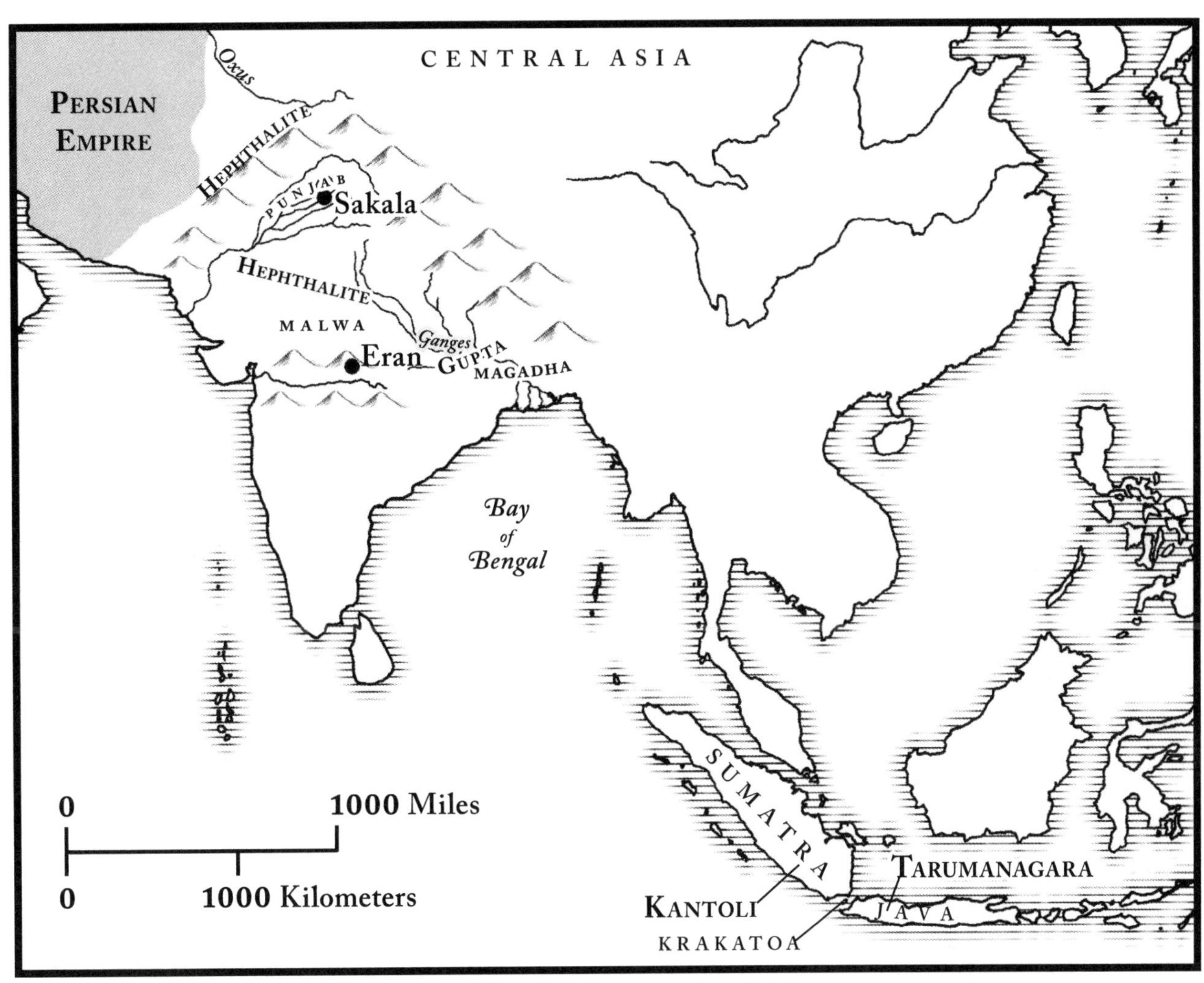

Map 26.1: Xia and Shang

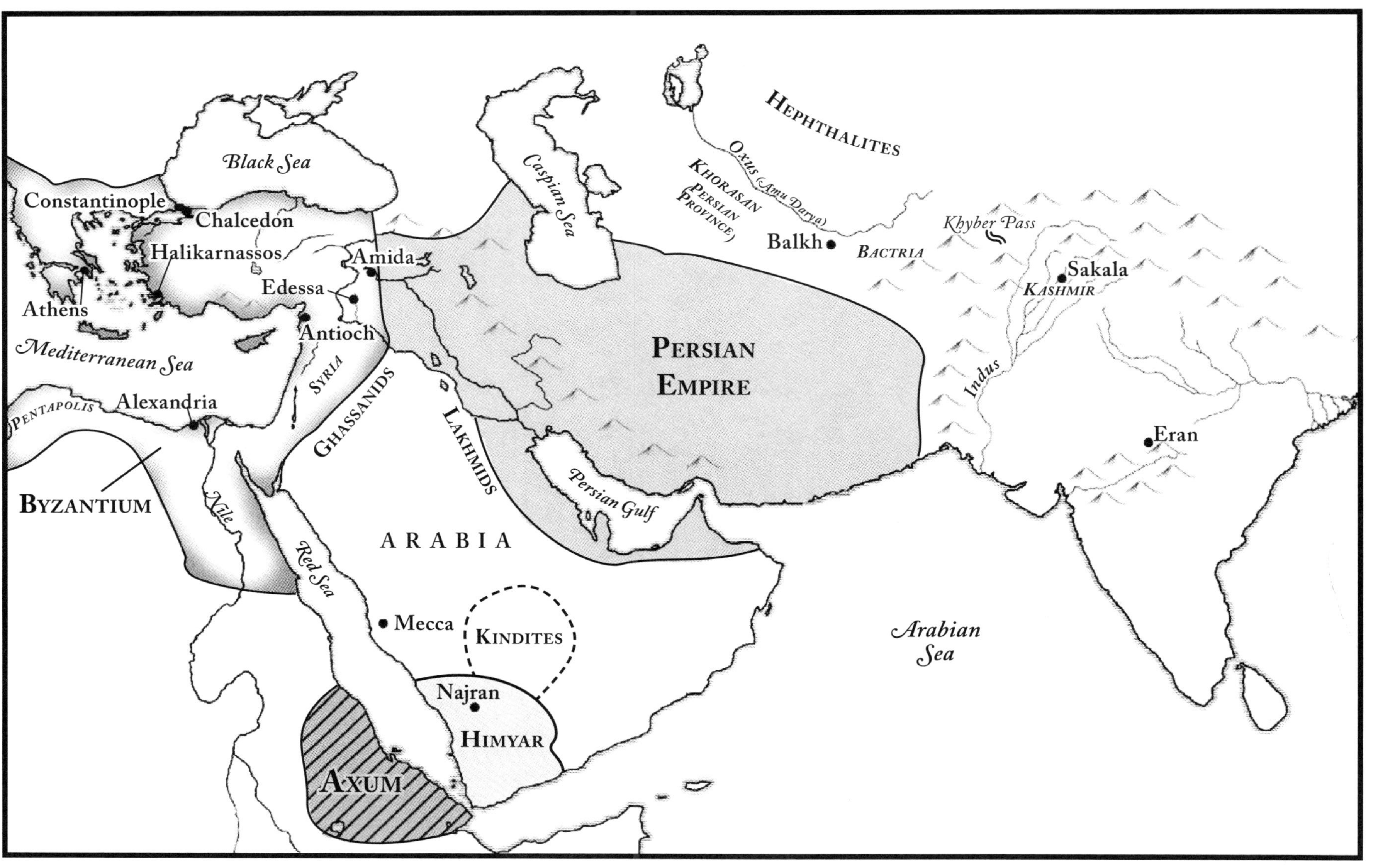

Map 28.1: Arab Tribes and Kingdoms

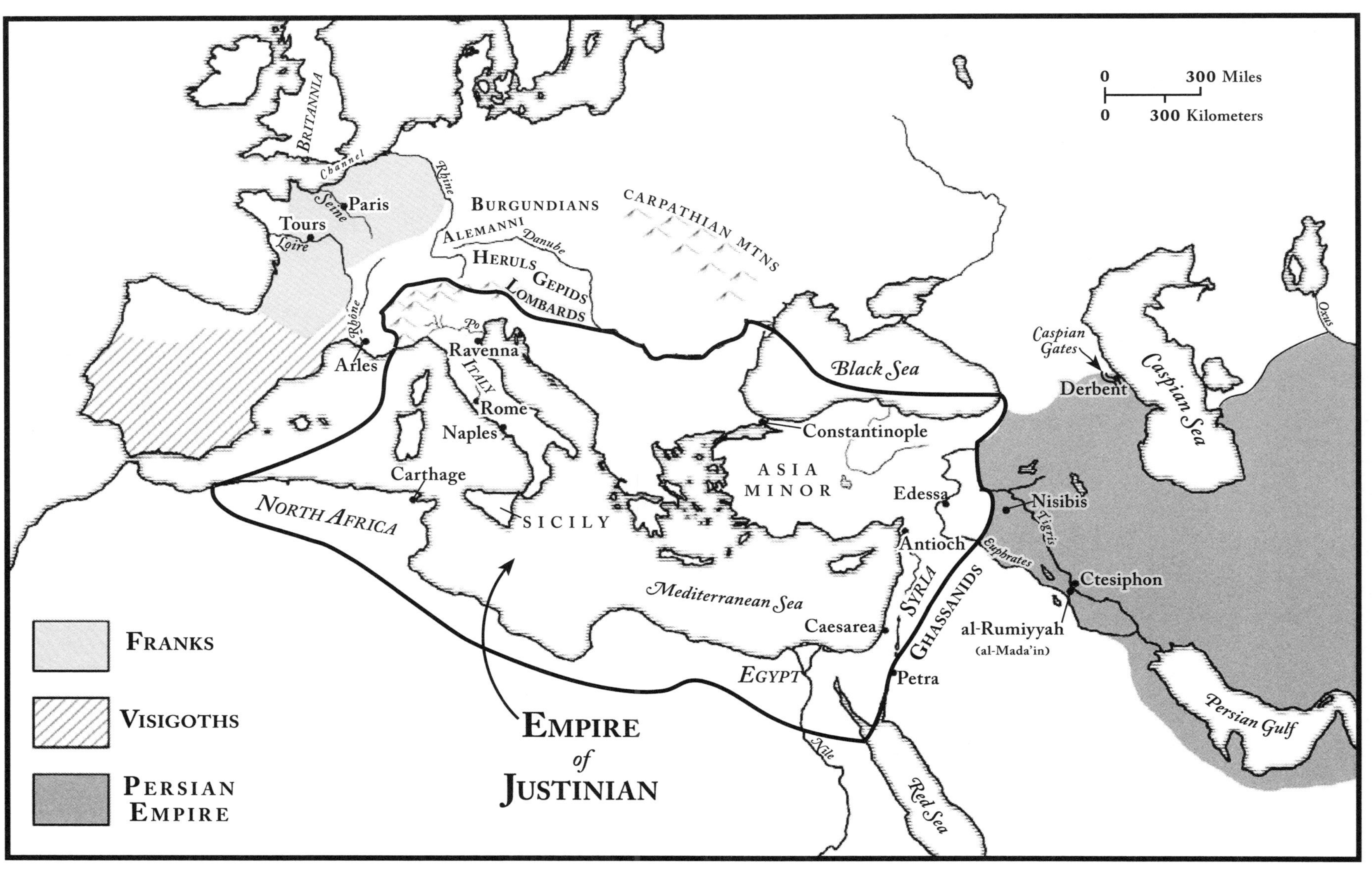

Map 29.2: The Reconquest of Roman Land

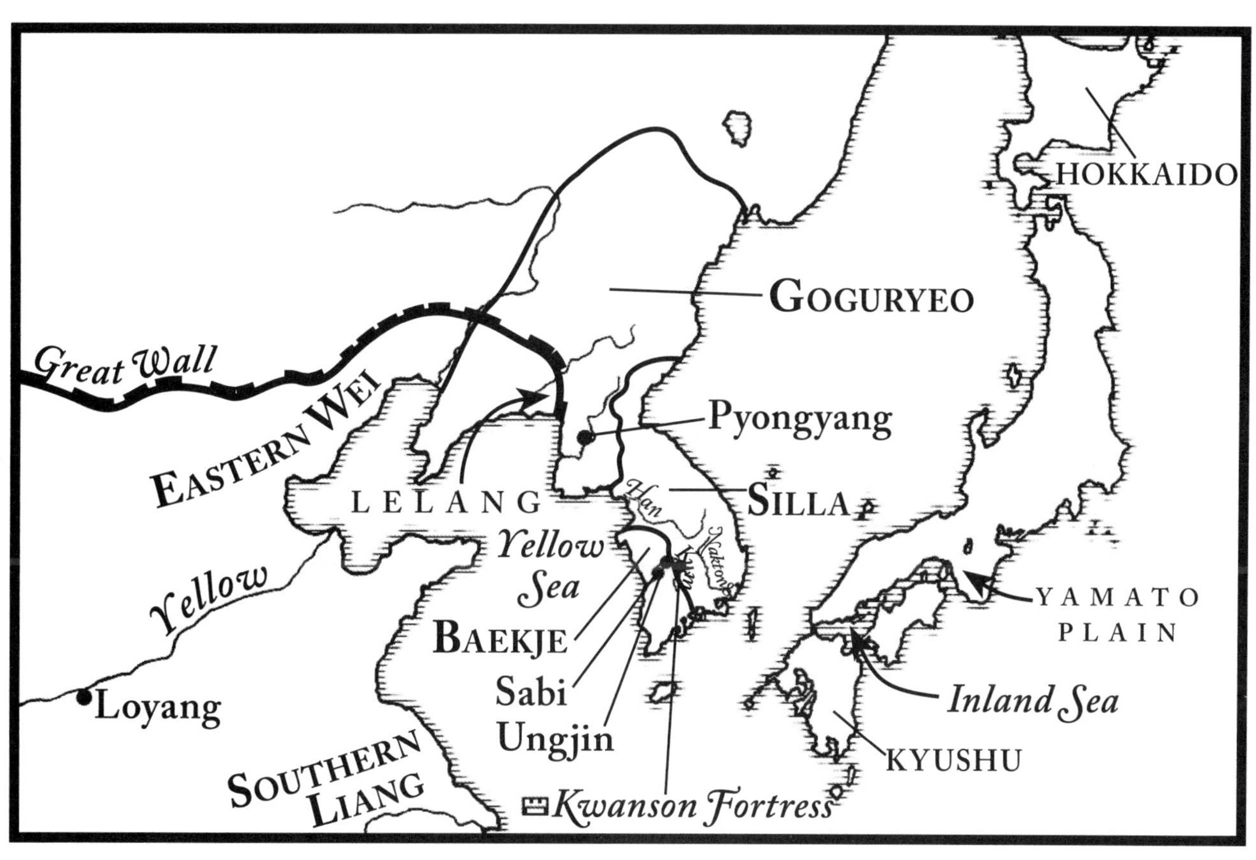

Map 30.1: The Far East in the Sixth Century

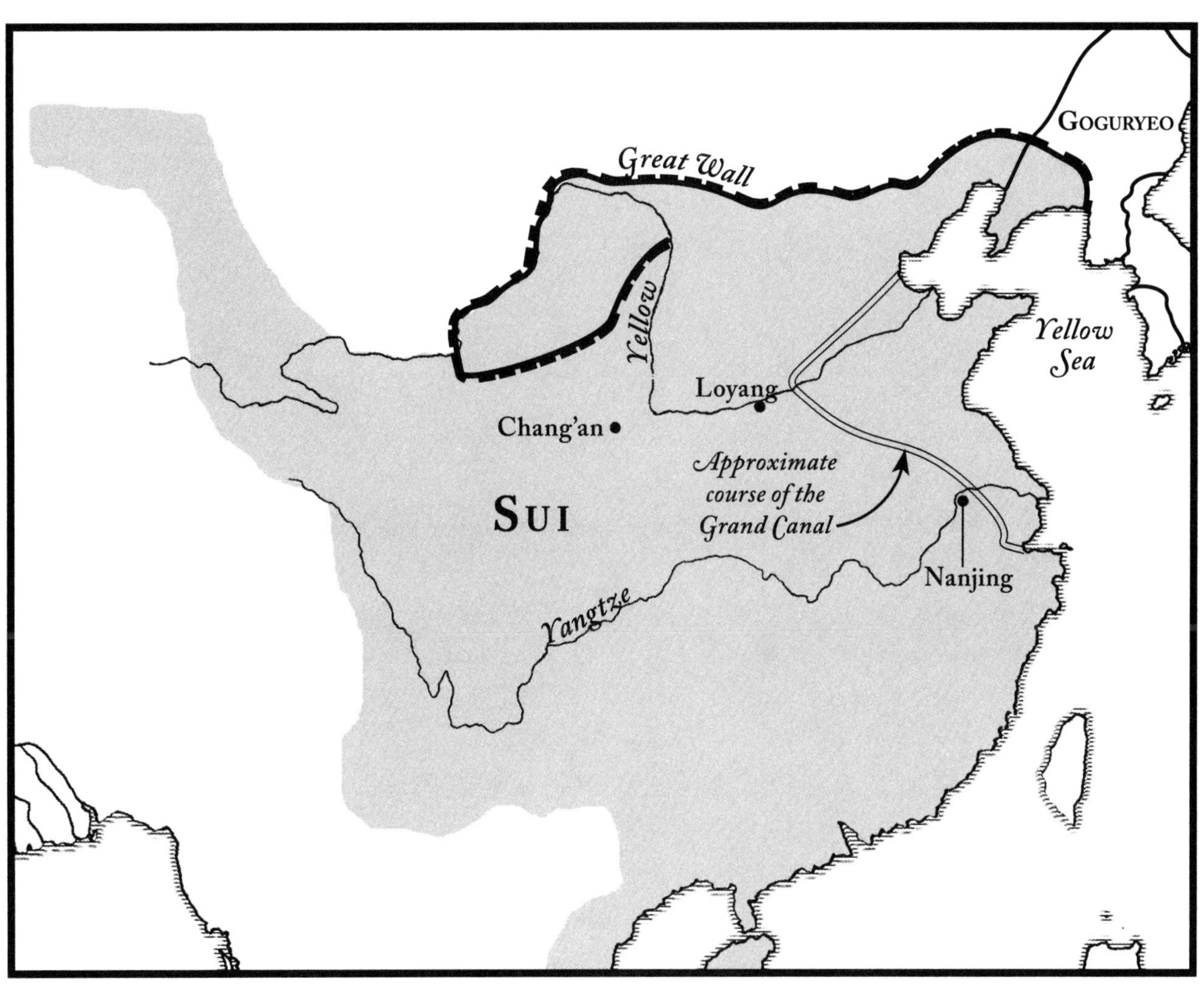

Map 31.1: The Grand Canal

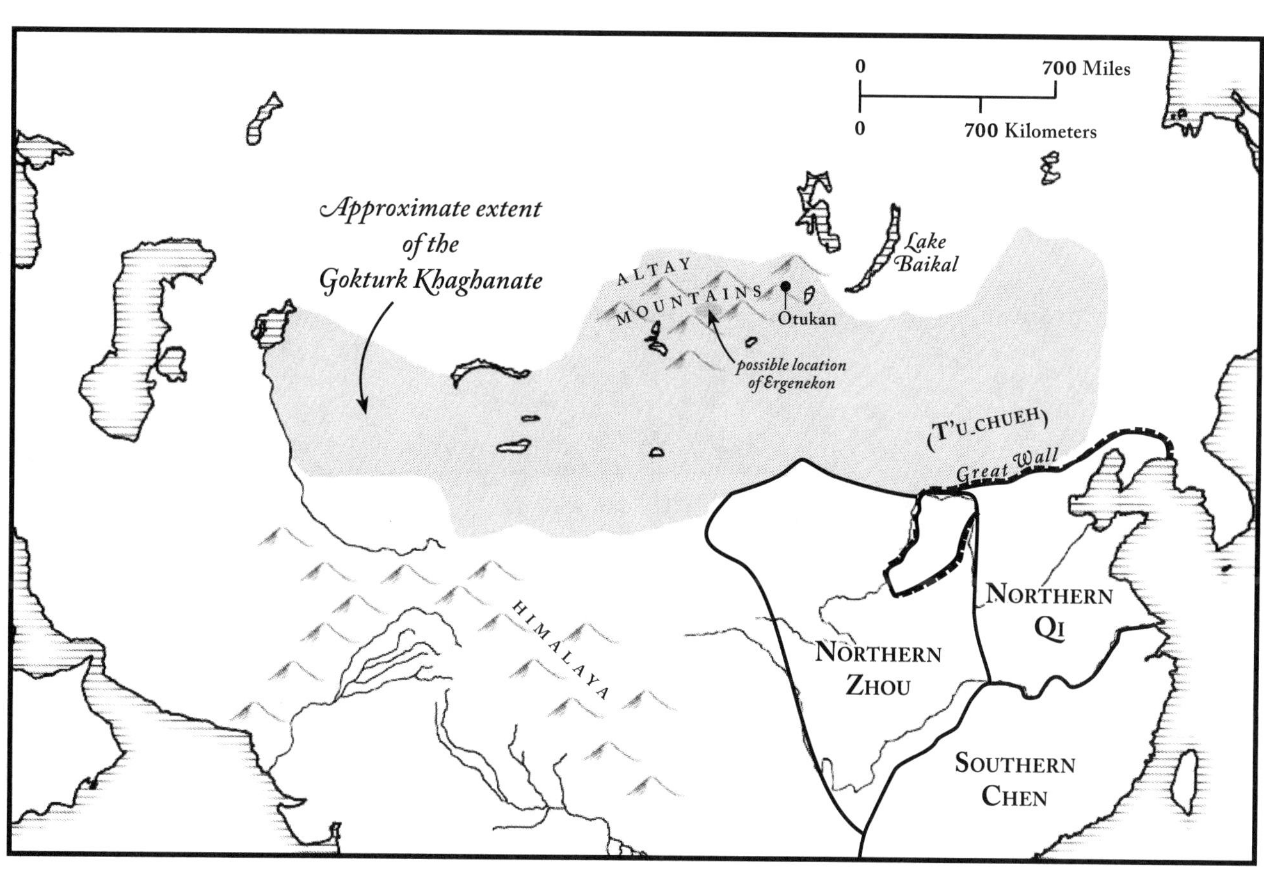

Map 33.2: The Gokturk Khaghanate

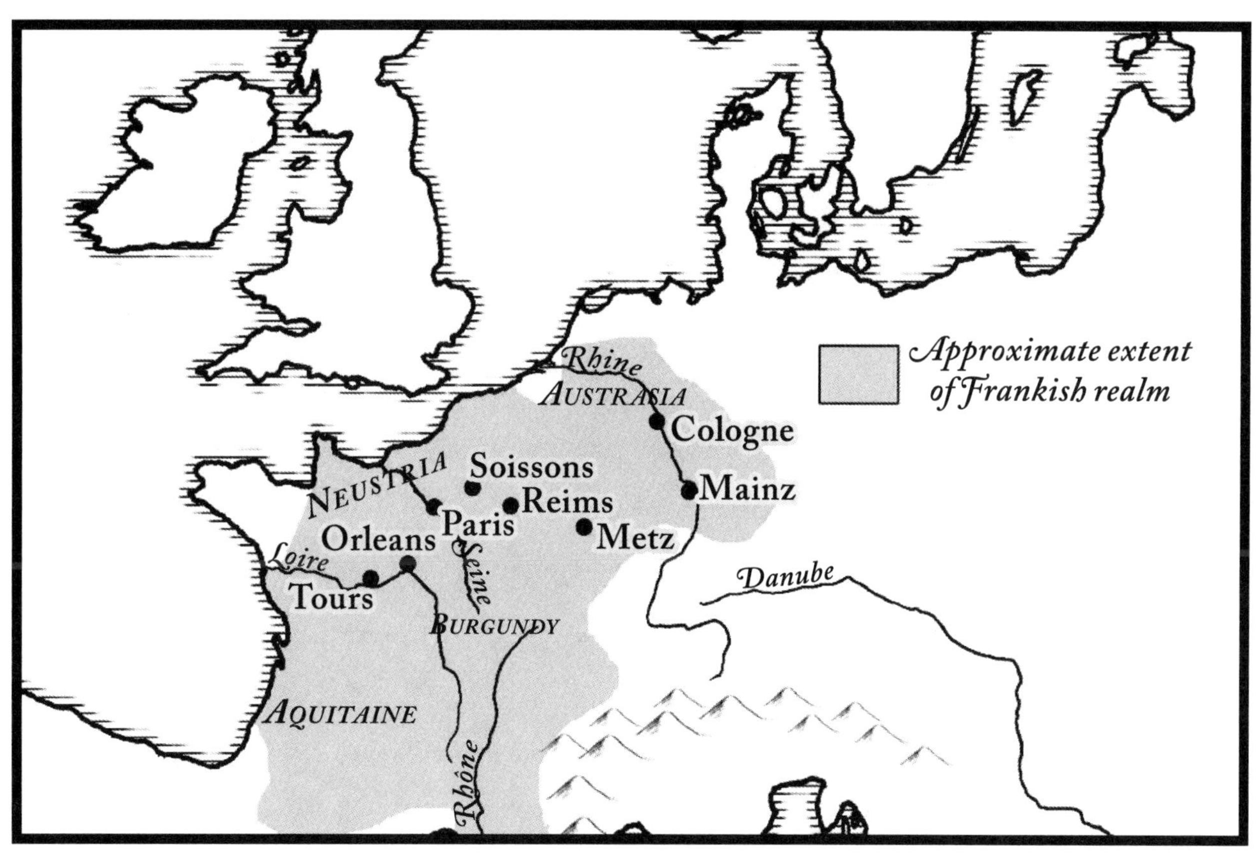

Map 34.1: Territories of the Franks

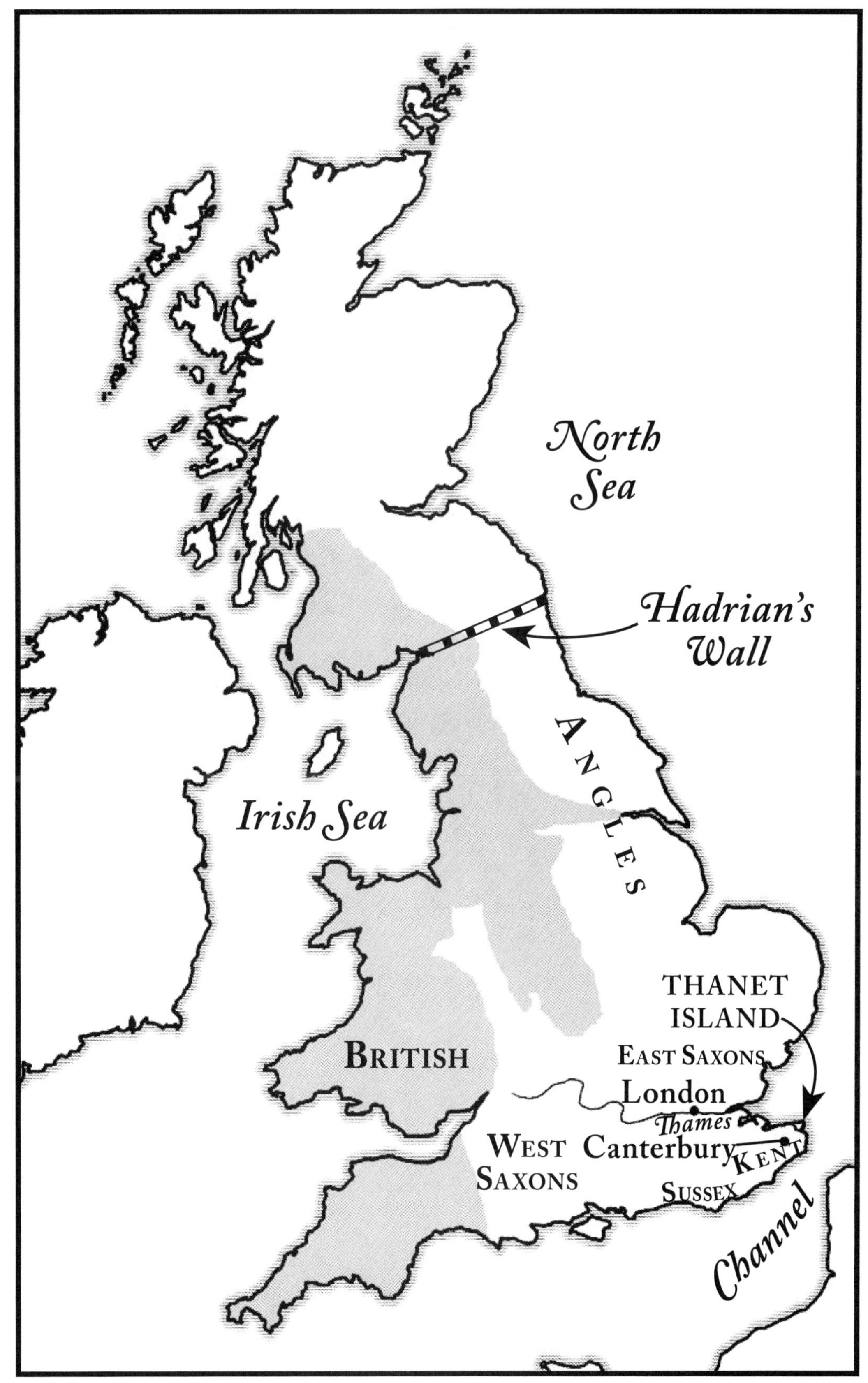

Map 35.2: Saxon Kingdoms

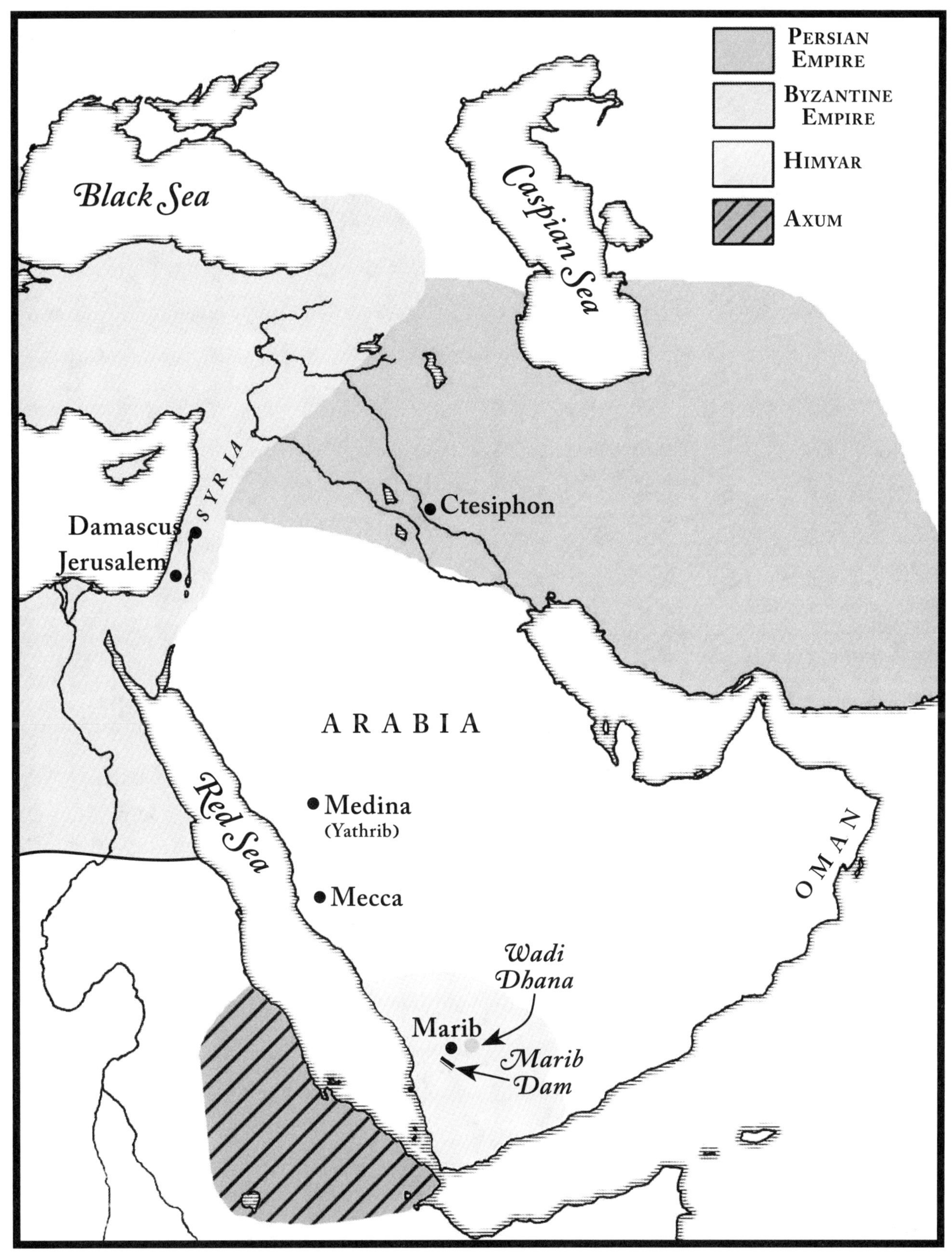

Map 37.1: Muhammad's Arabia

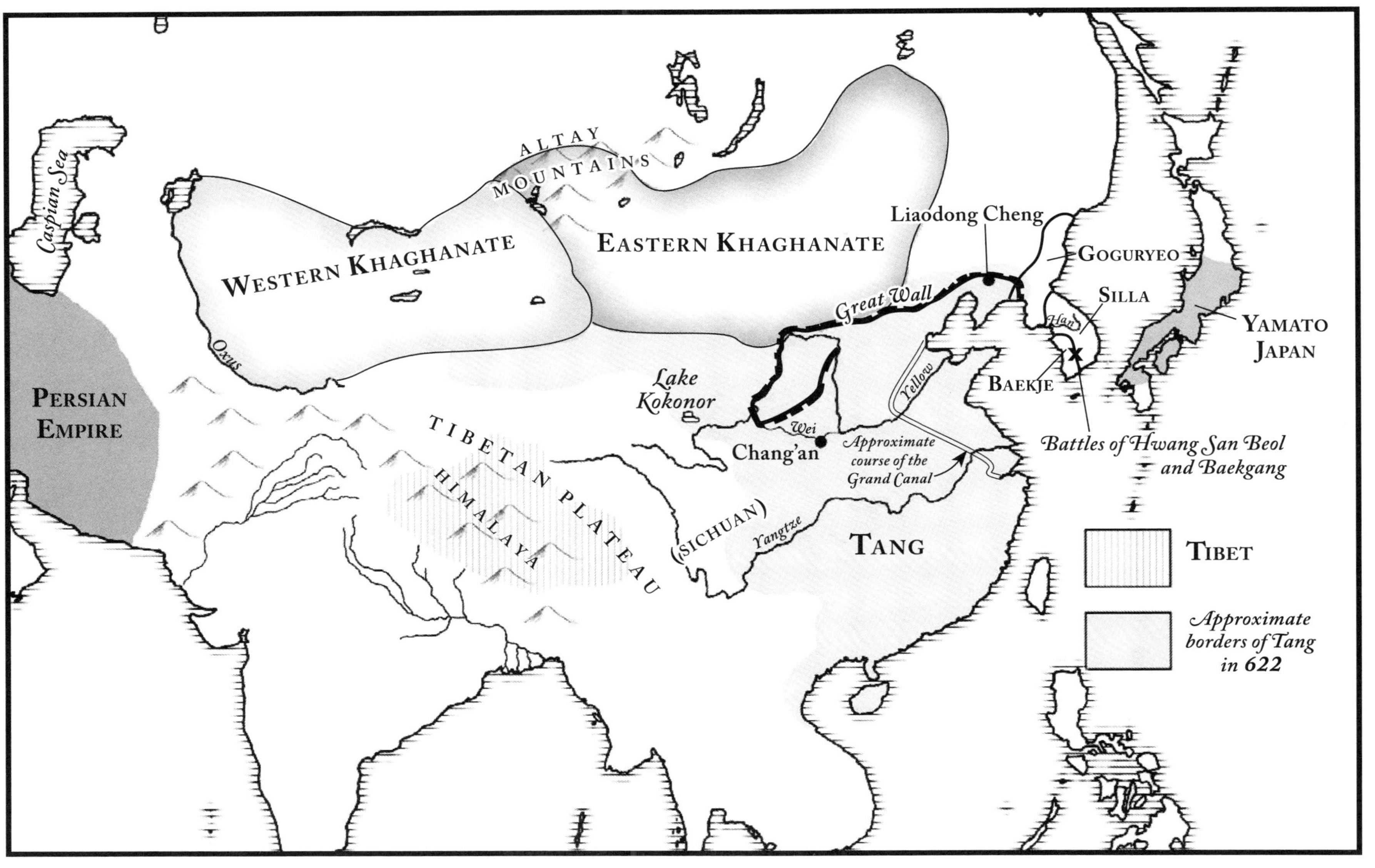

Map 38.1: The East in the Seventh Century

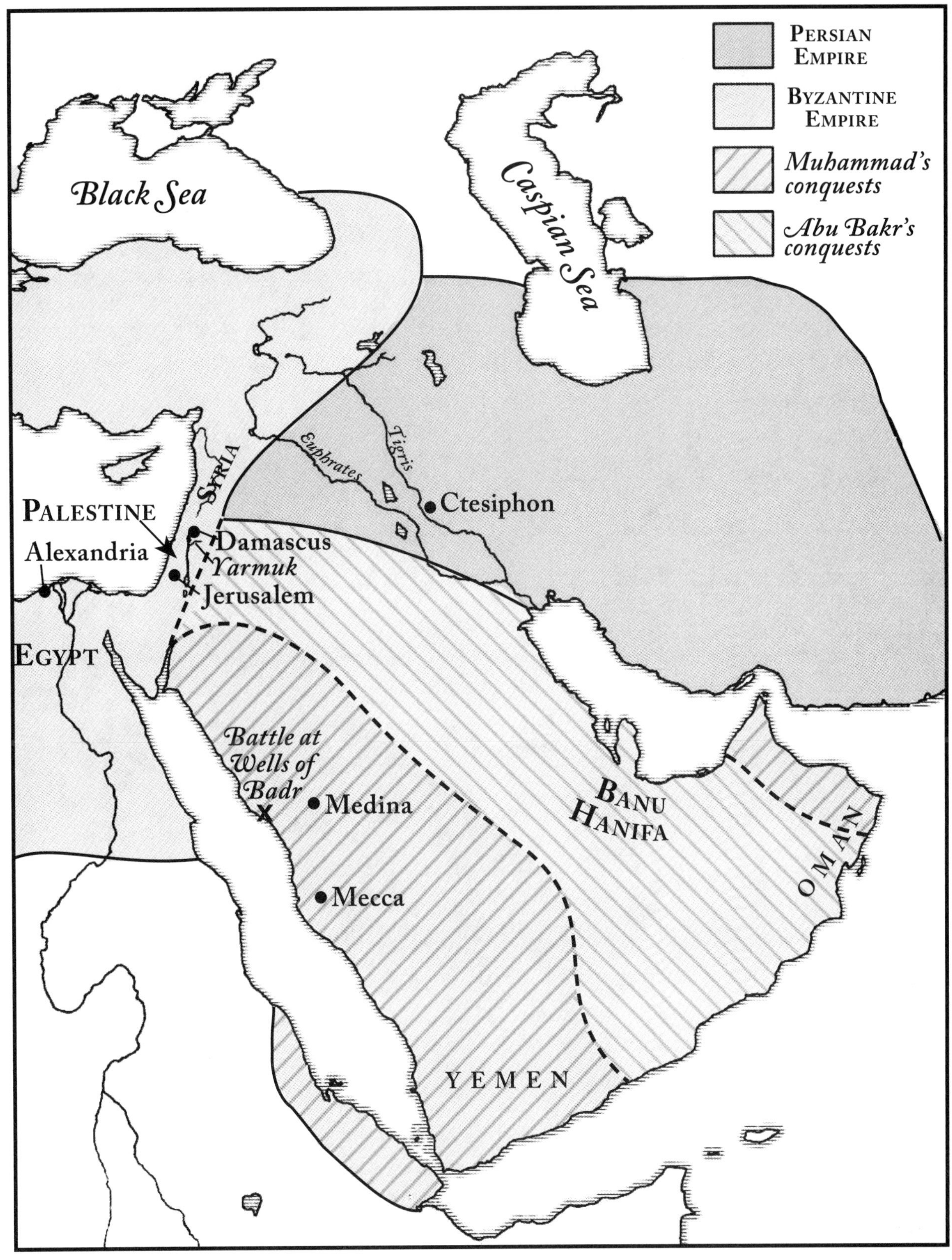

Map 39.1: The Conquests of Muhammad and Abu Bakr

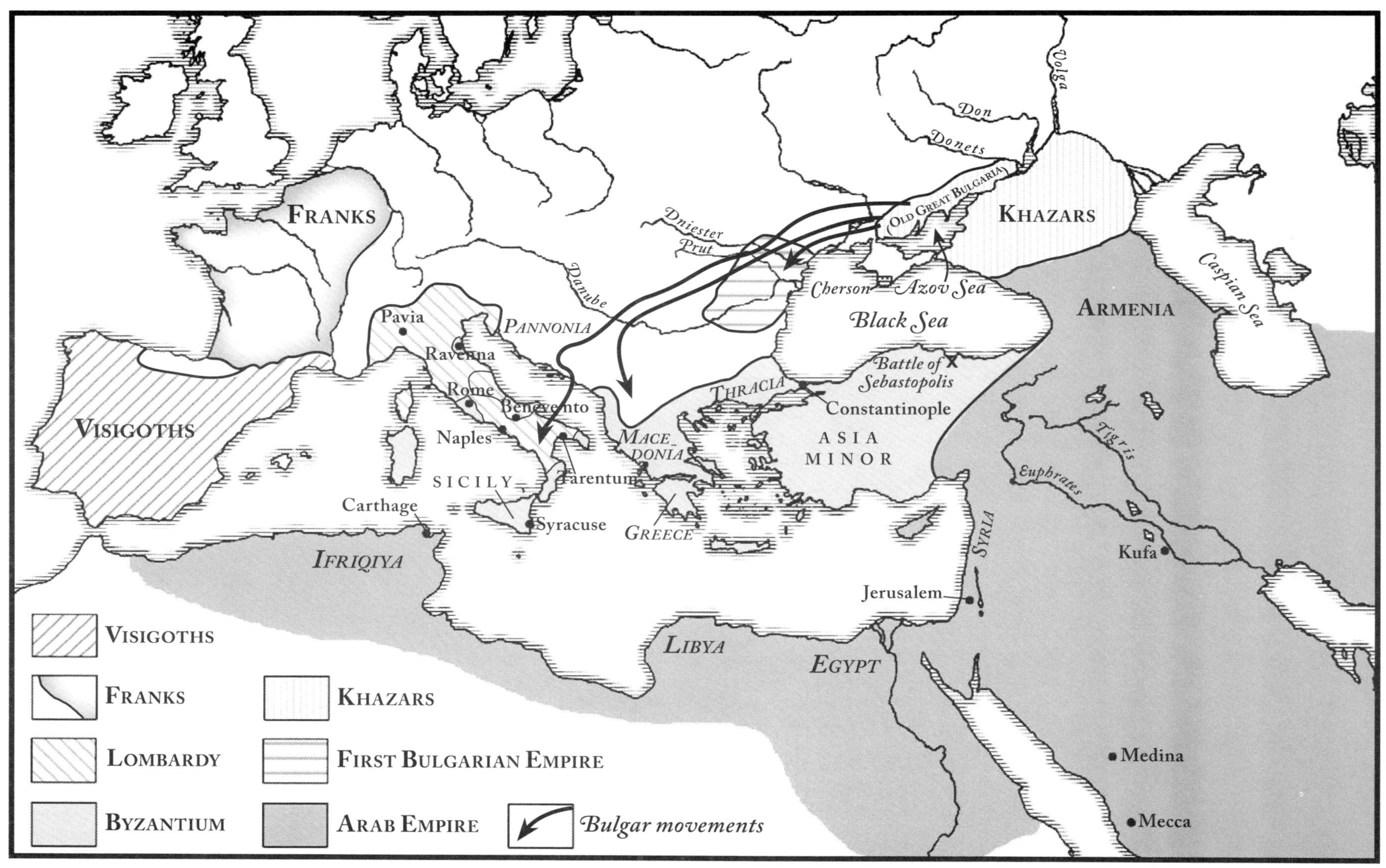

Map 42.1: Byzantium, the Arabs, and the Bulgars

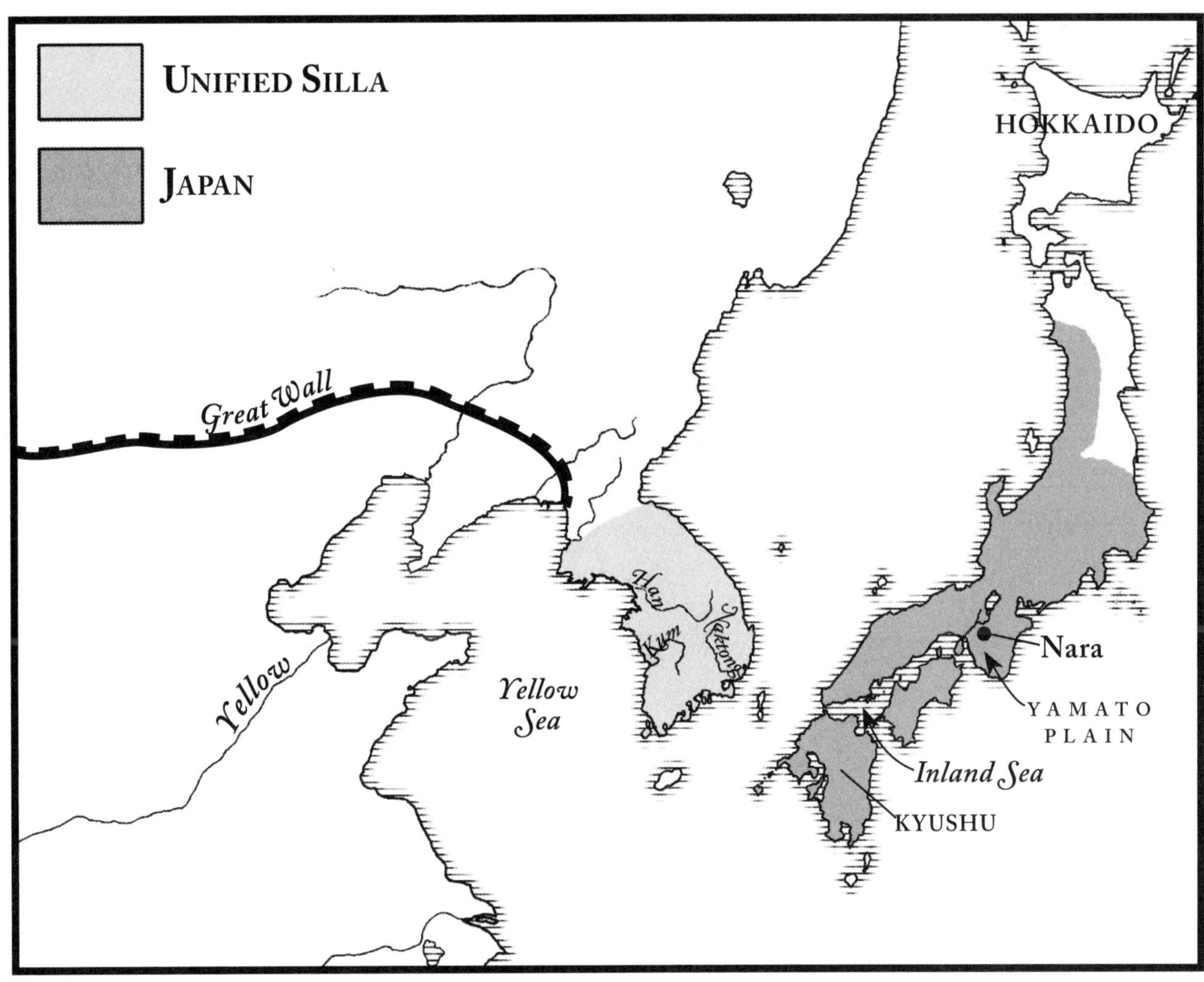

Map 43.1: The Nara Period

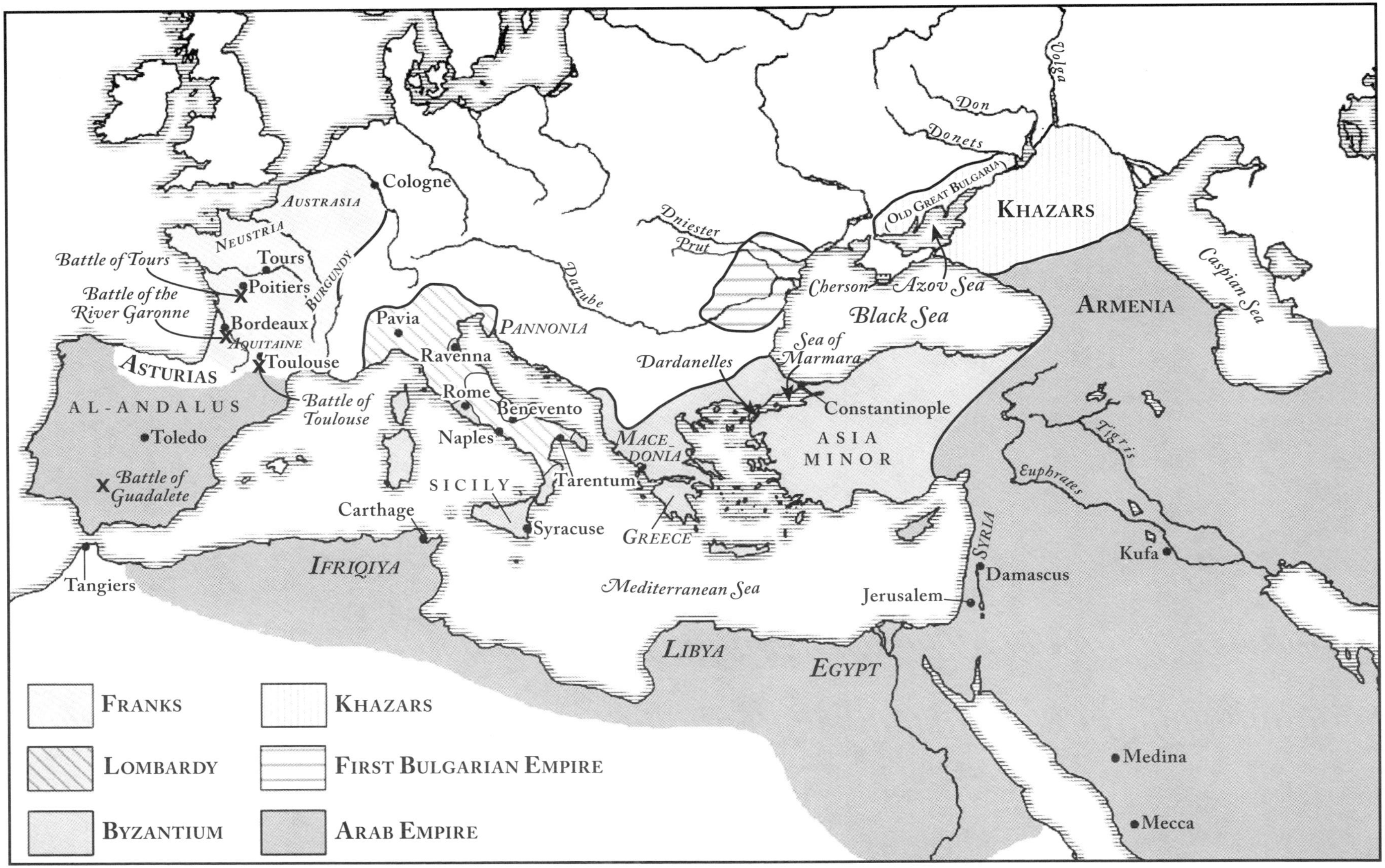

- Franks
- Lombardy
- Byzantium
- Khazars
- First Bulgarian Empire
- Arab Empire

Map 45.1: The Arab Advance

Map 47.2: The First Papal State

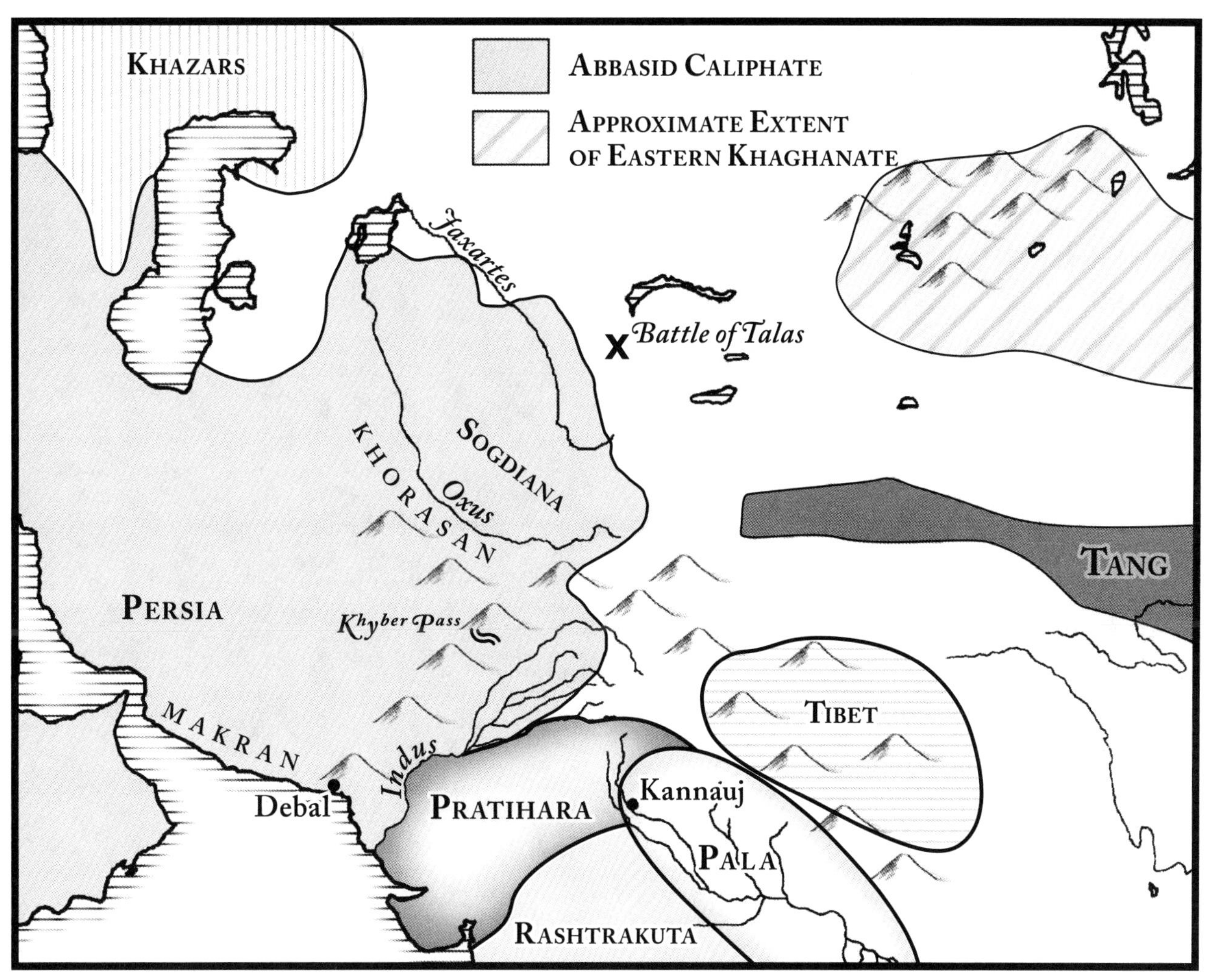

Map 48.1: The Battle of Talas

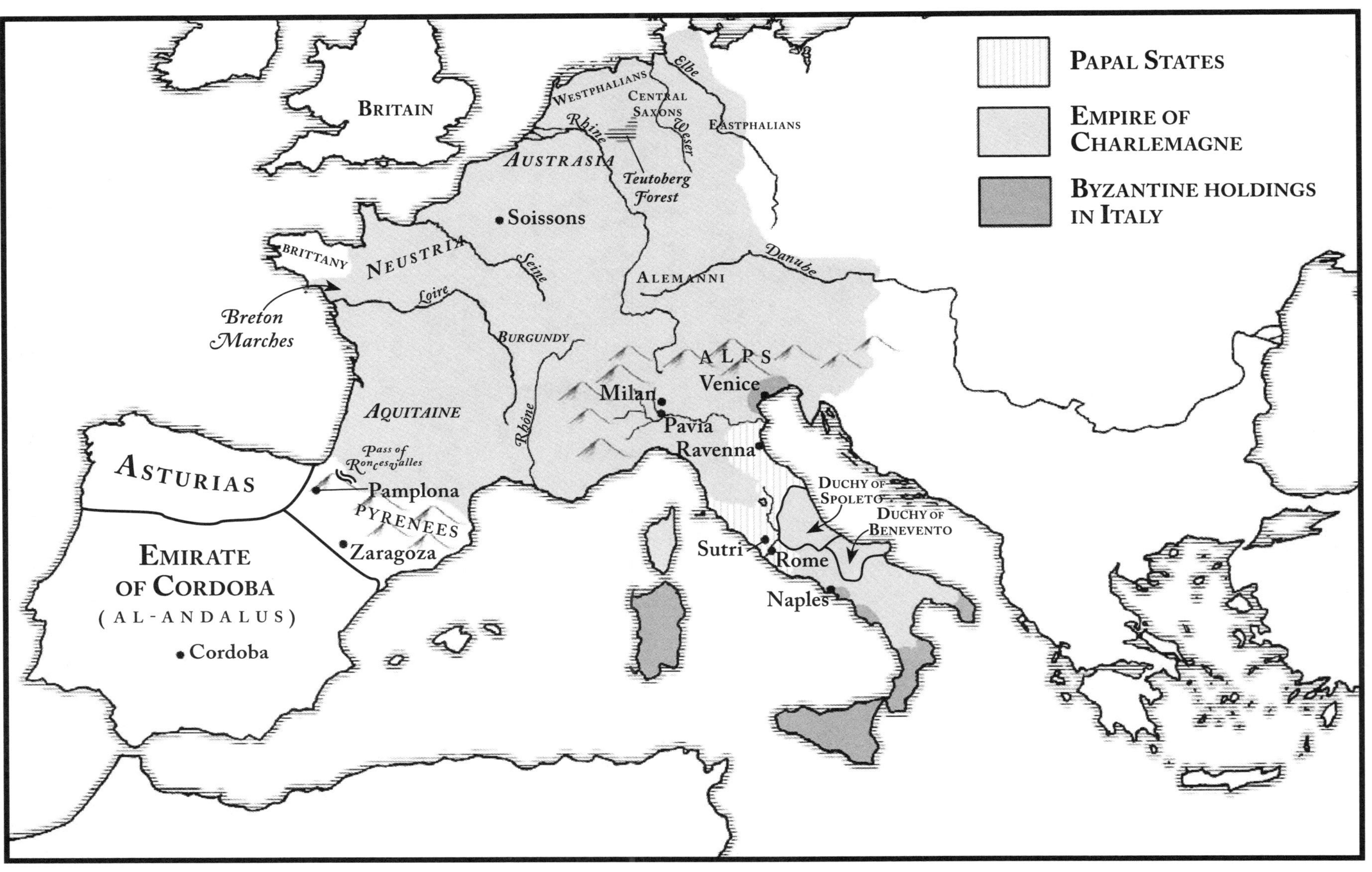

Map 49.1: Charlemagne's Kingdom

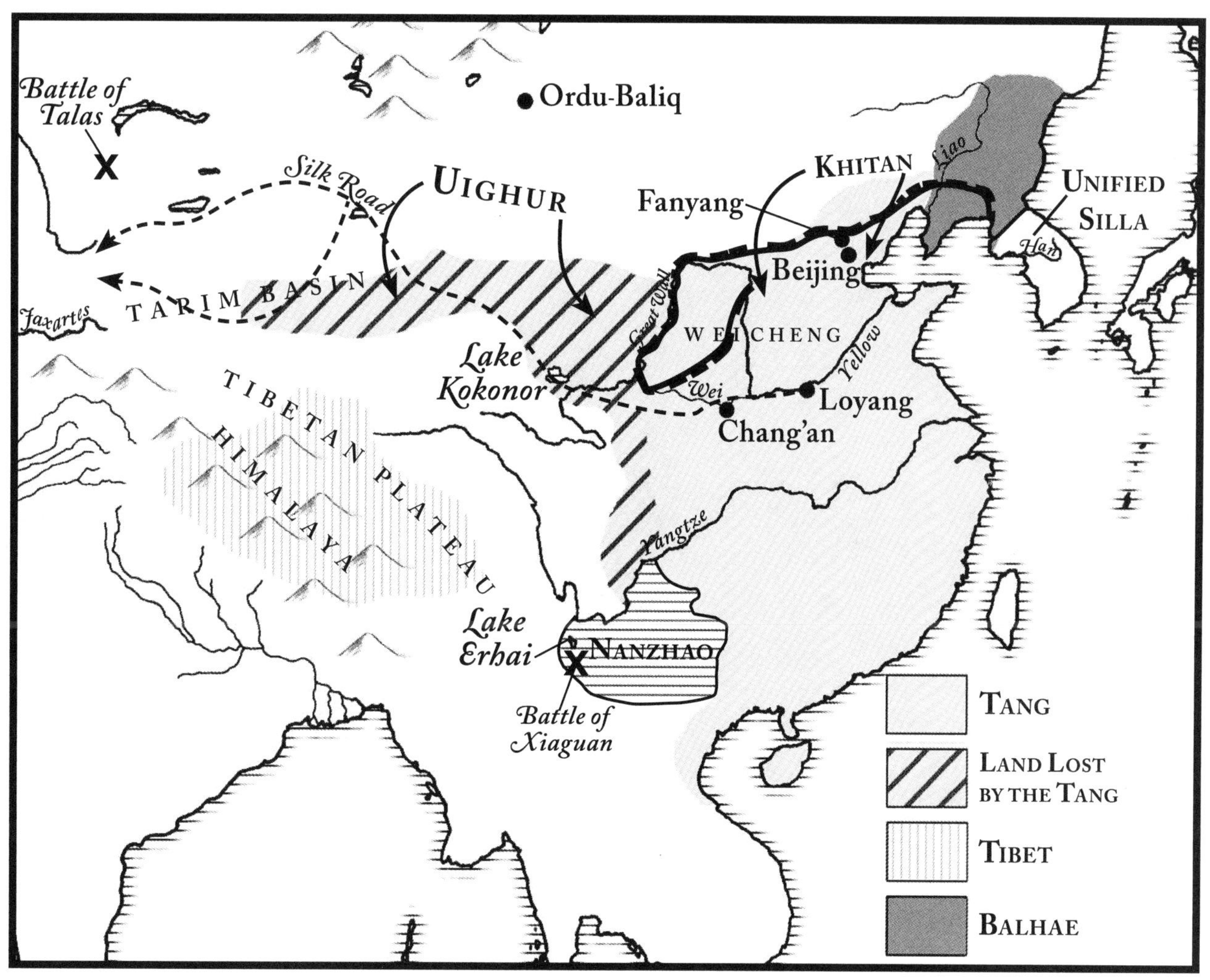

Map 50.1: New Kingdoms and the Tang

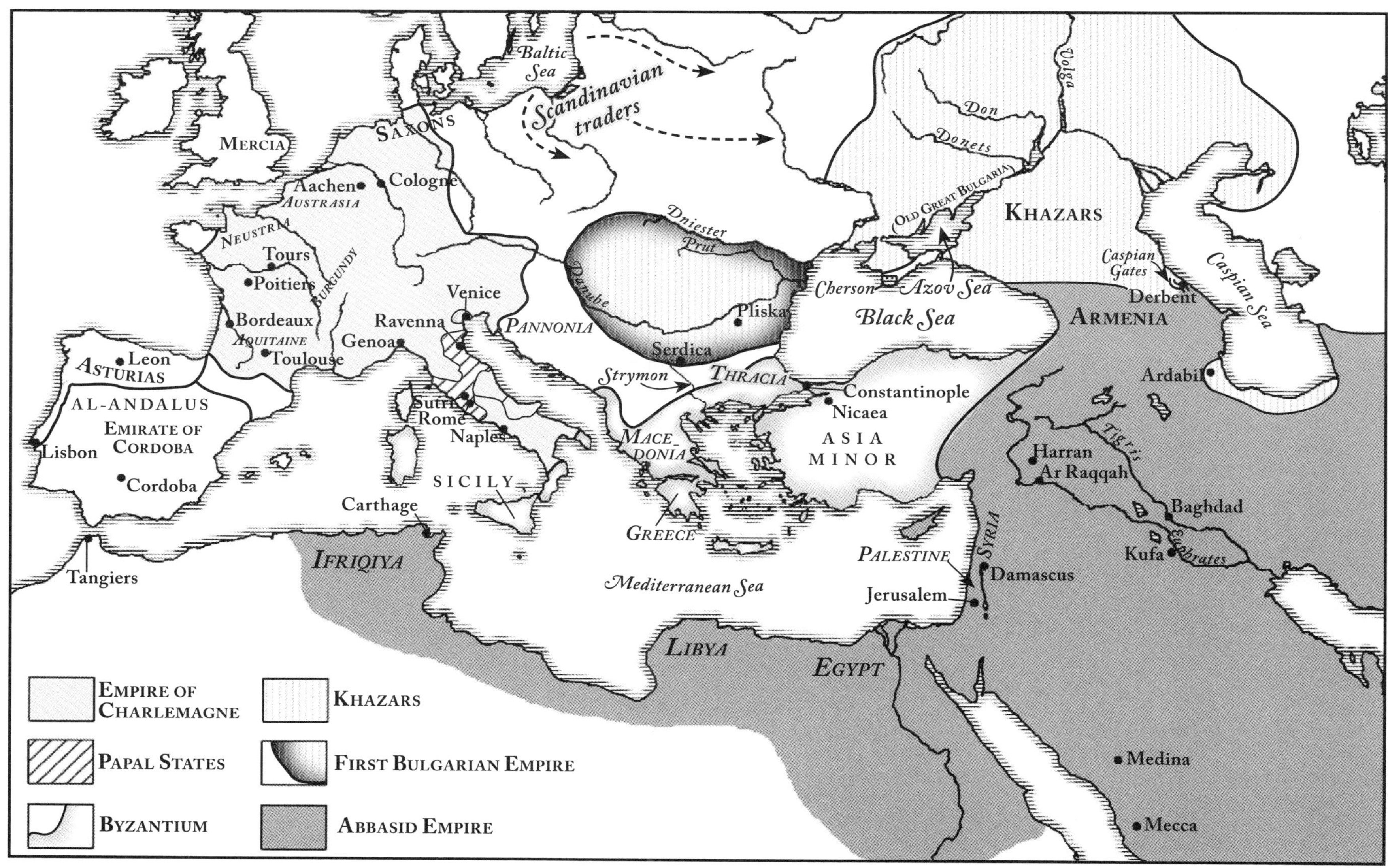

Map 52.1: Expansion of the First Bulgarian Empire

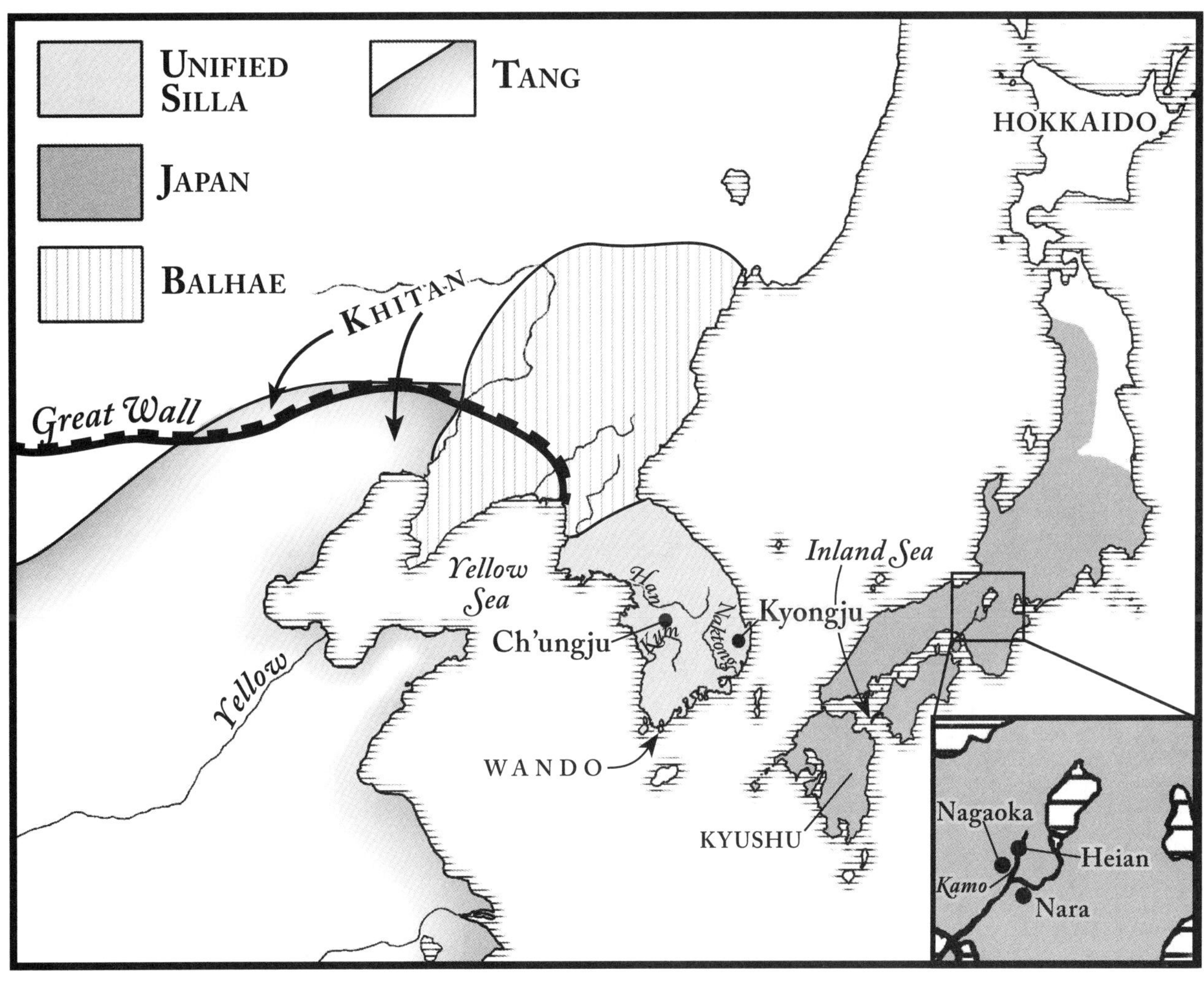

Map 53.1: Unified Silla and Japan

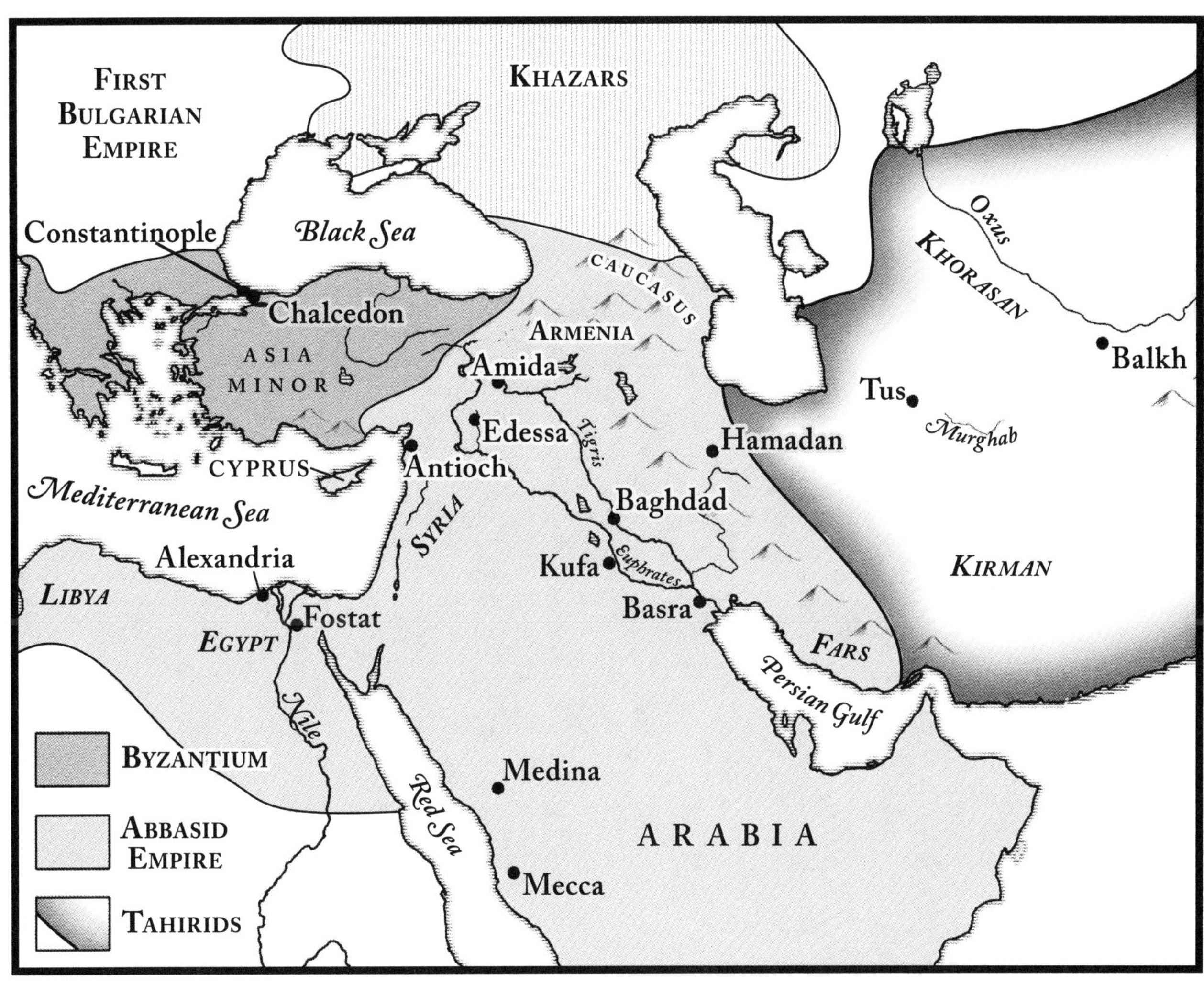

Map 55.1: The Tahirids

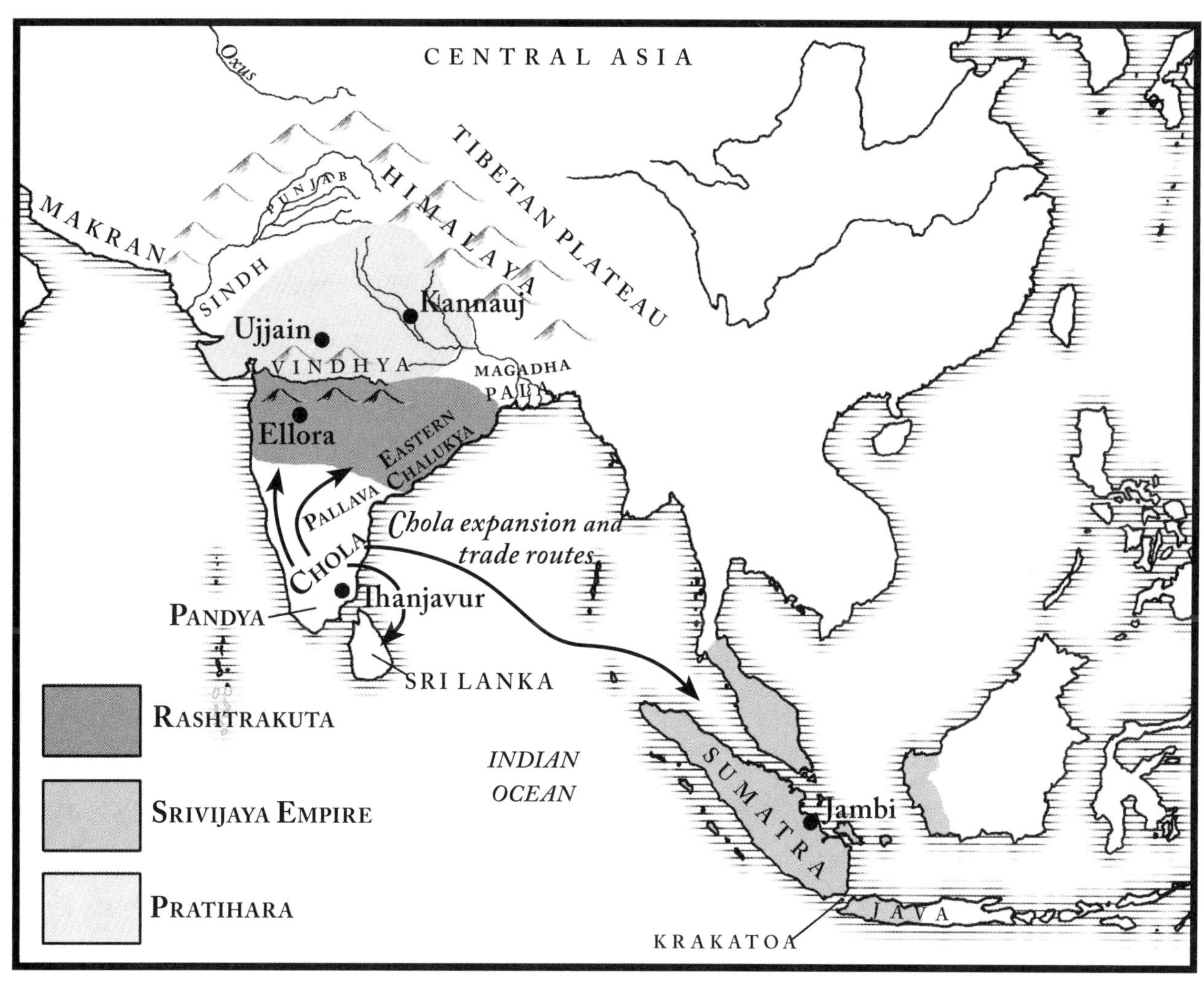

Map 57.1: The Rise of the Chola

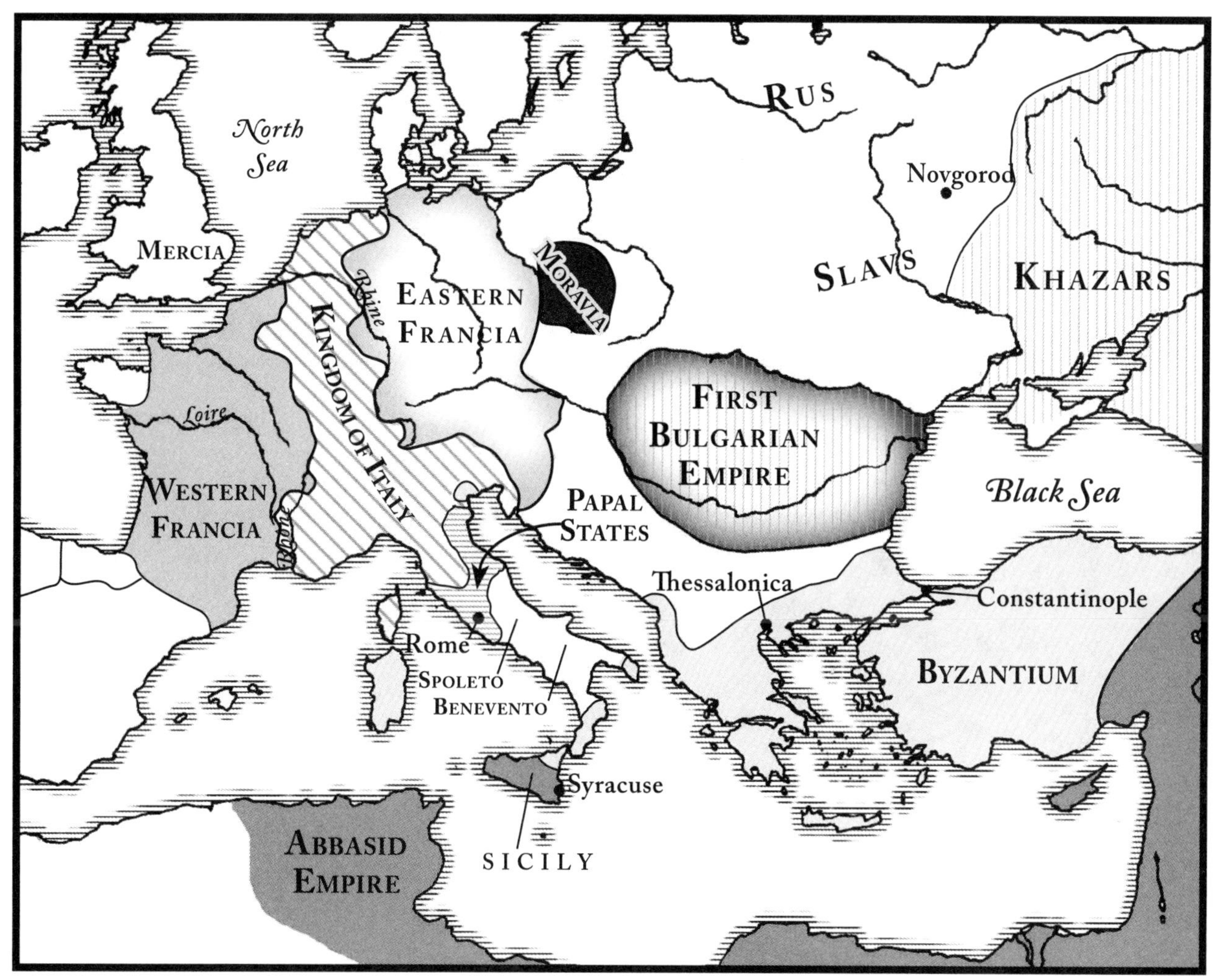

Map 58.1: Moravia

Map 60.1: The Treaty of Wedmore

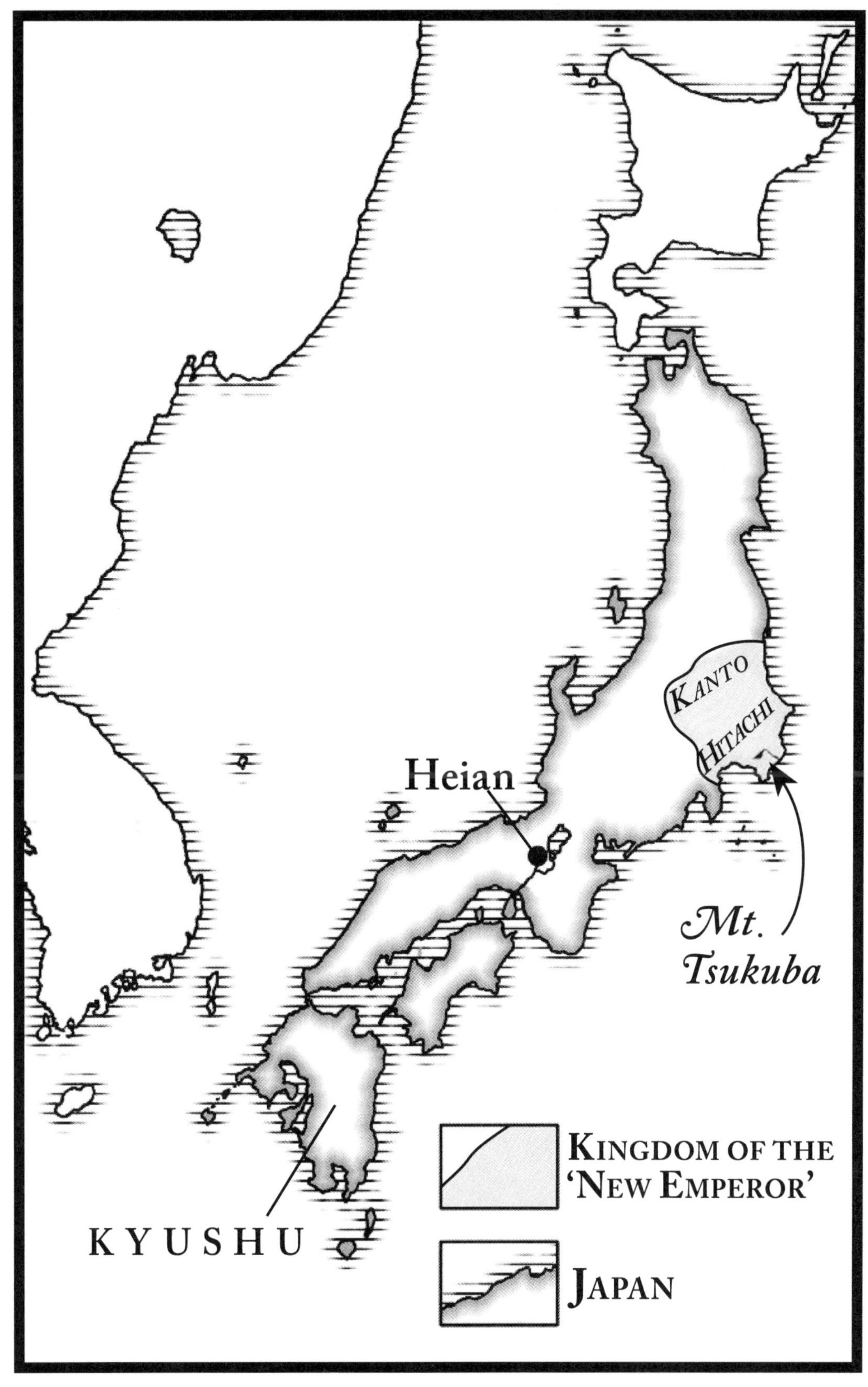

Map 62.1: The Rebellion of Masakado

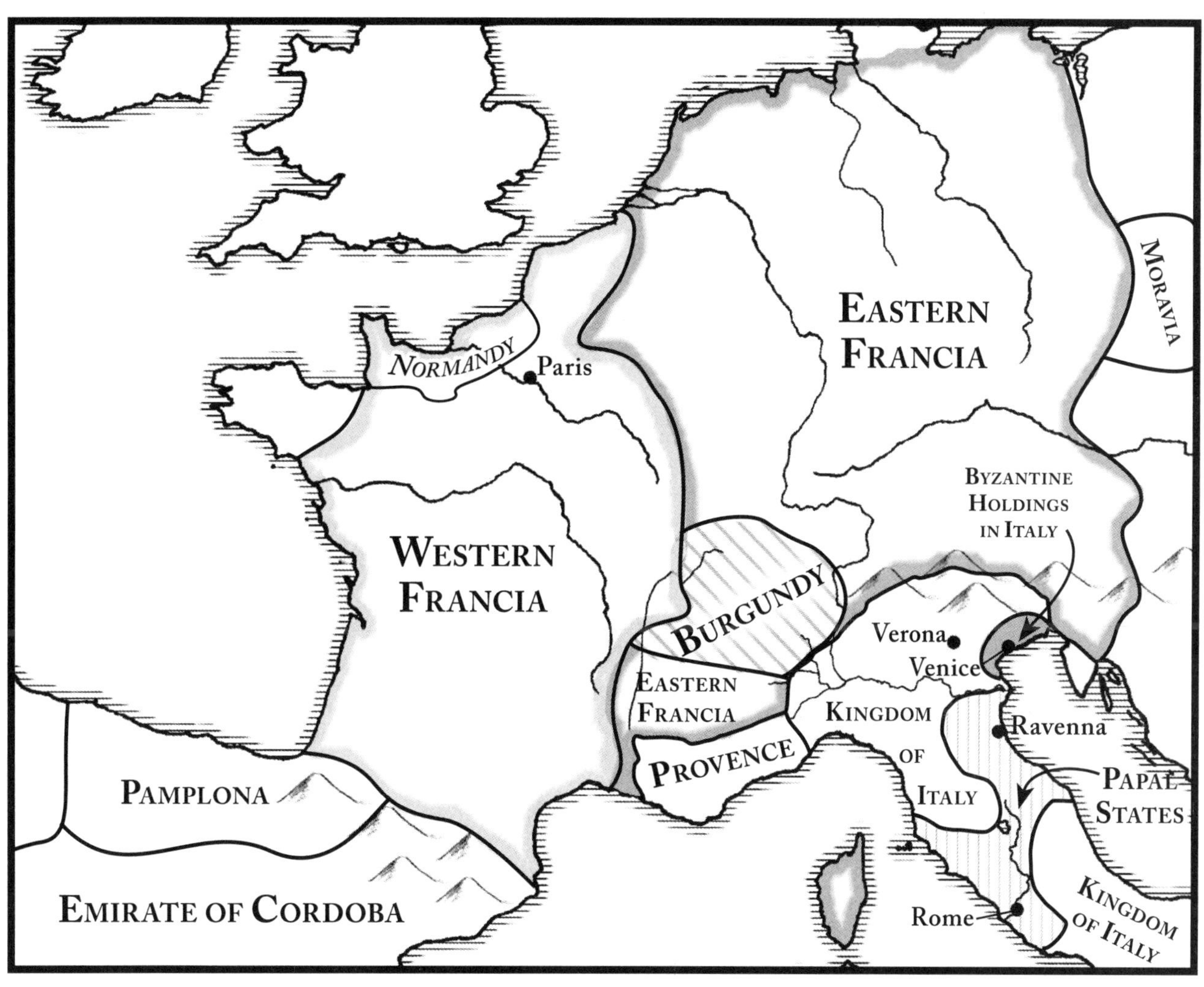

Map 64.1: The Creation of Normandy

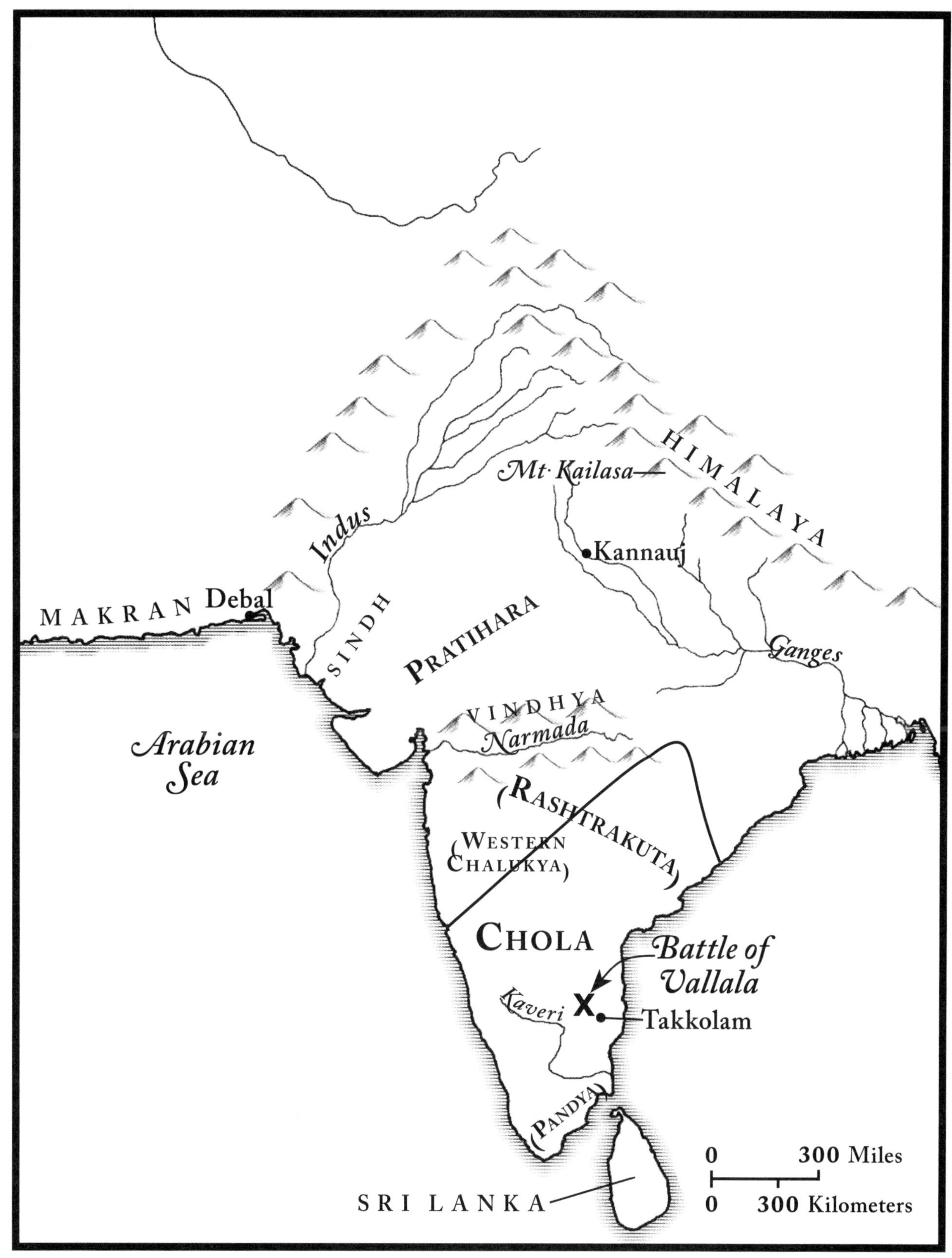

Map 66.1: The Height of the Chola

Map 67.1: The Fatimids and Cordoba

Map 69.1: Athelstan's England

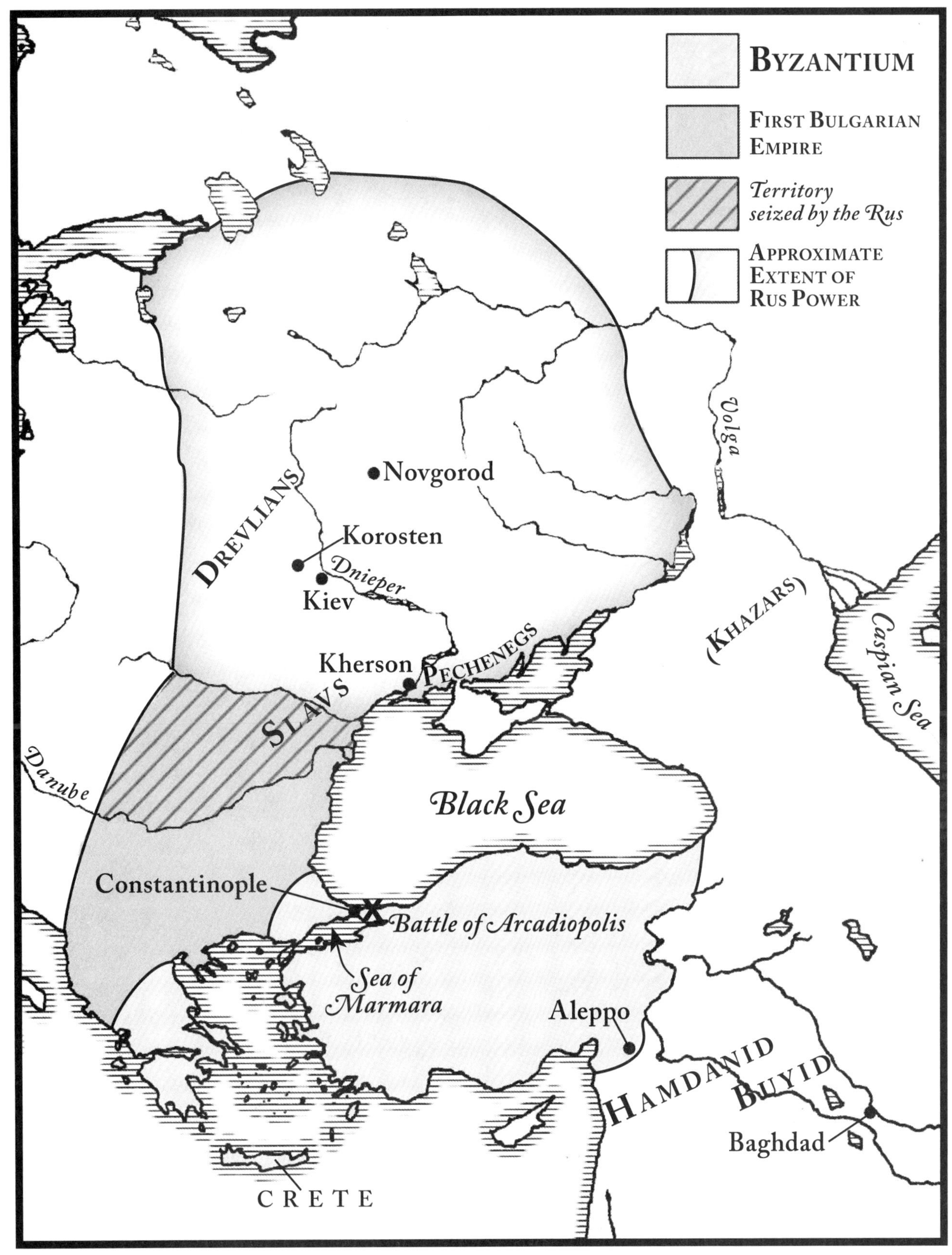

Map 70.1: The Rus and Byzantium

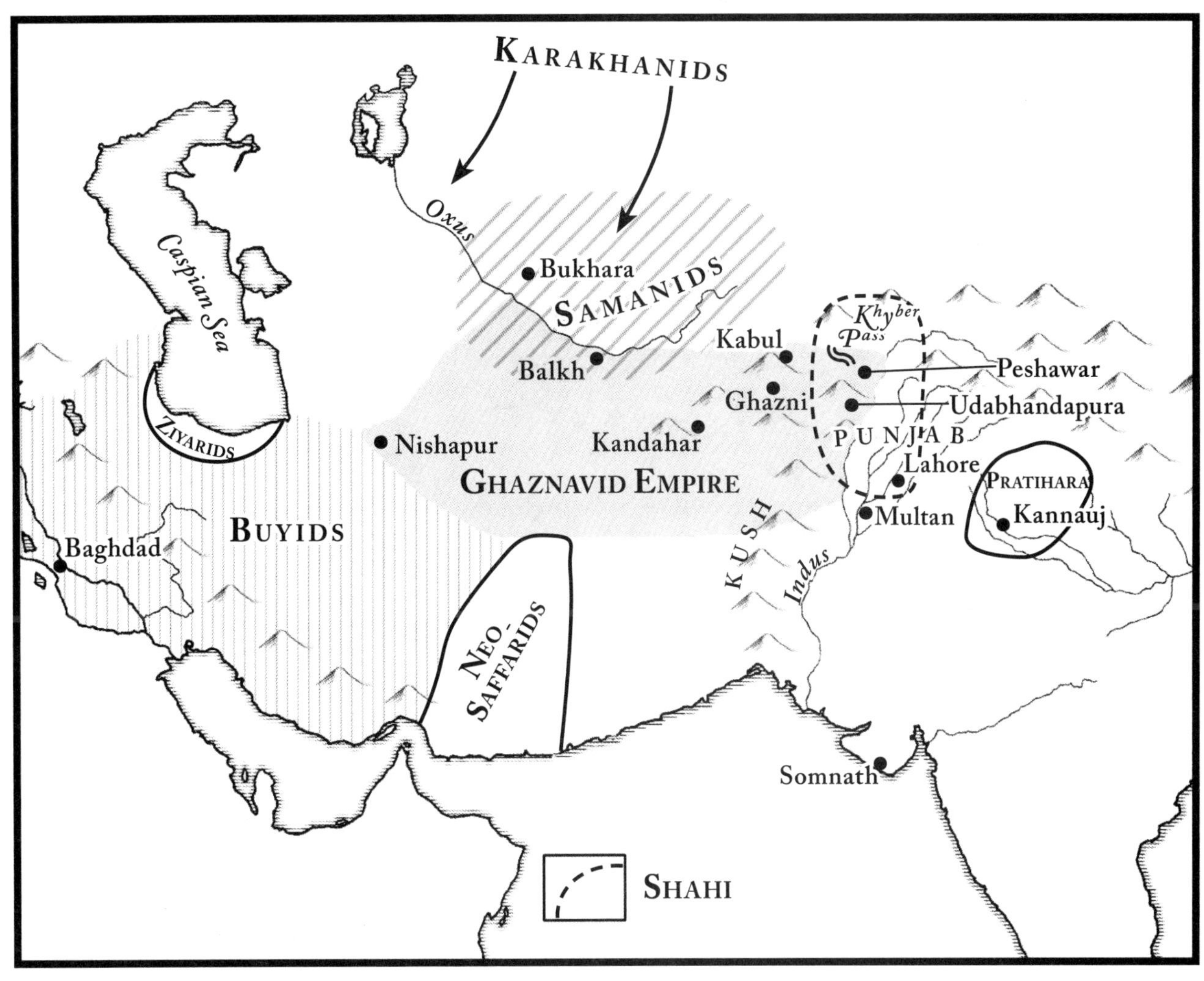

Map 72.1: Expansion of the Ghaznavids

Map 73.1: The Fatimid Caliphate and Byzantium

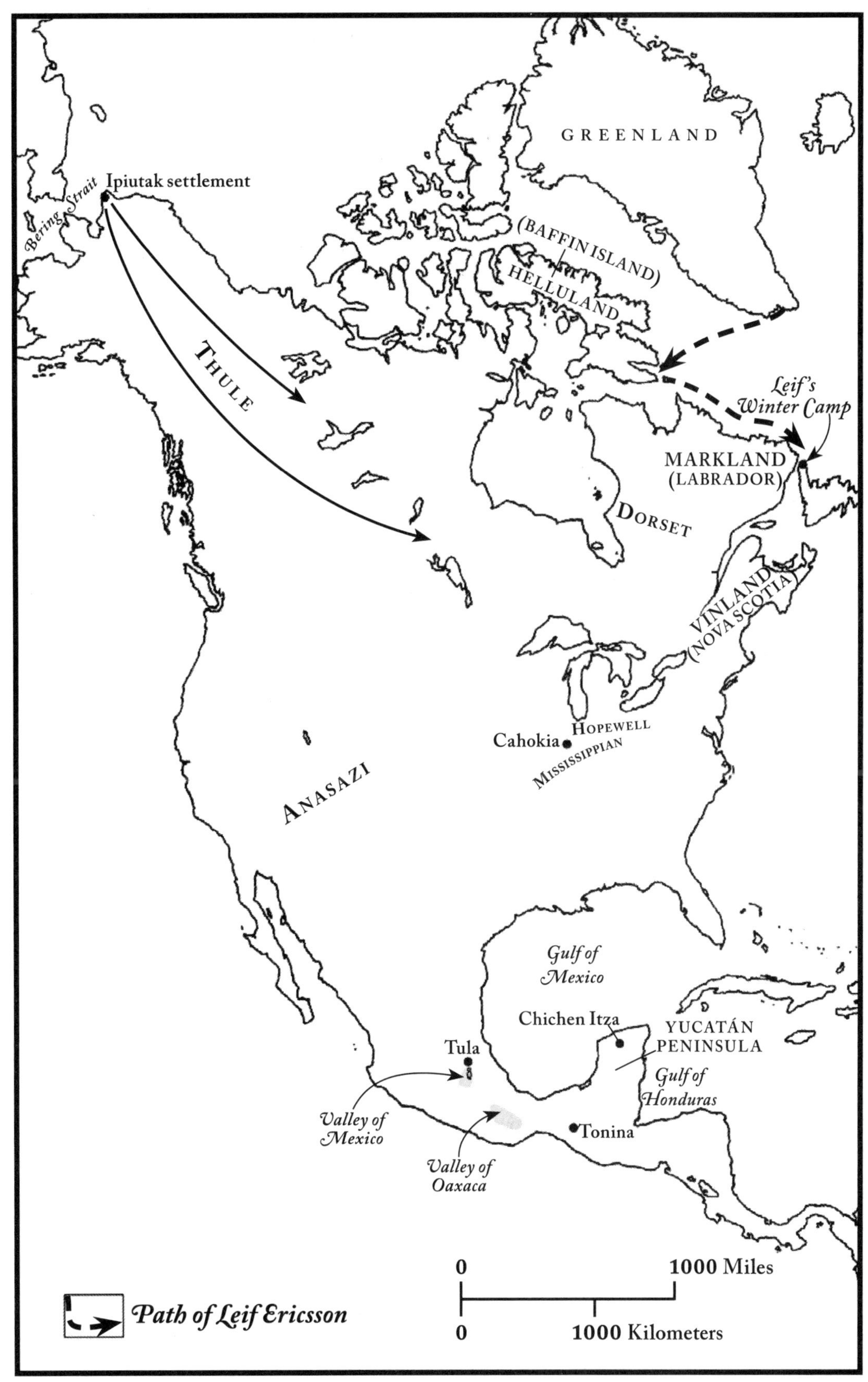

Map 75.1: Settlements of the Americas

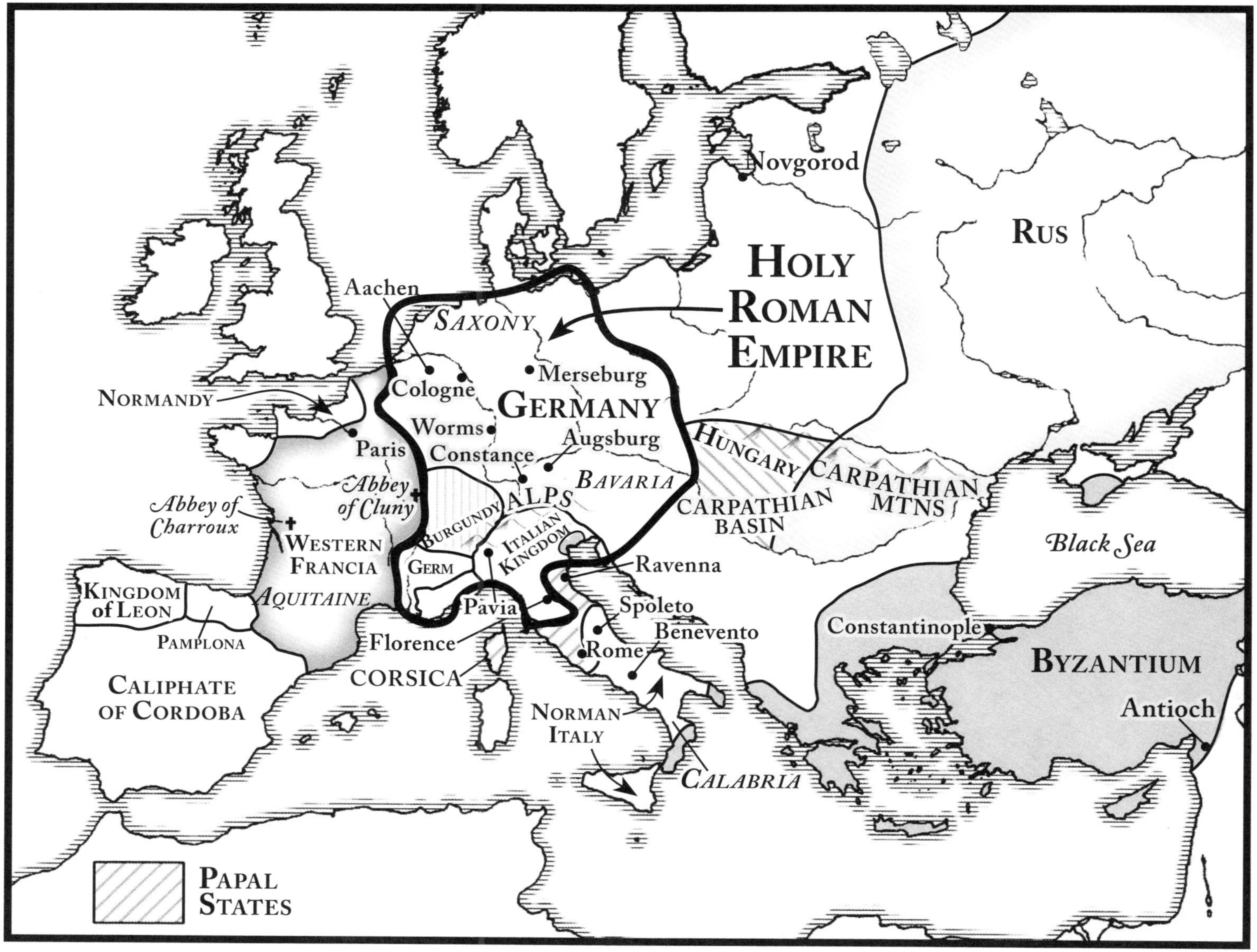

Map 76.1: The Holy Roman Empire

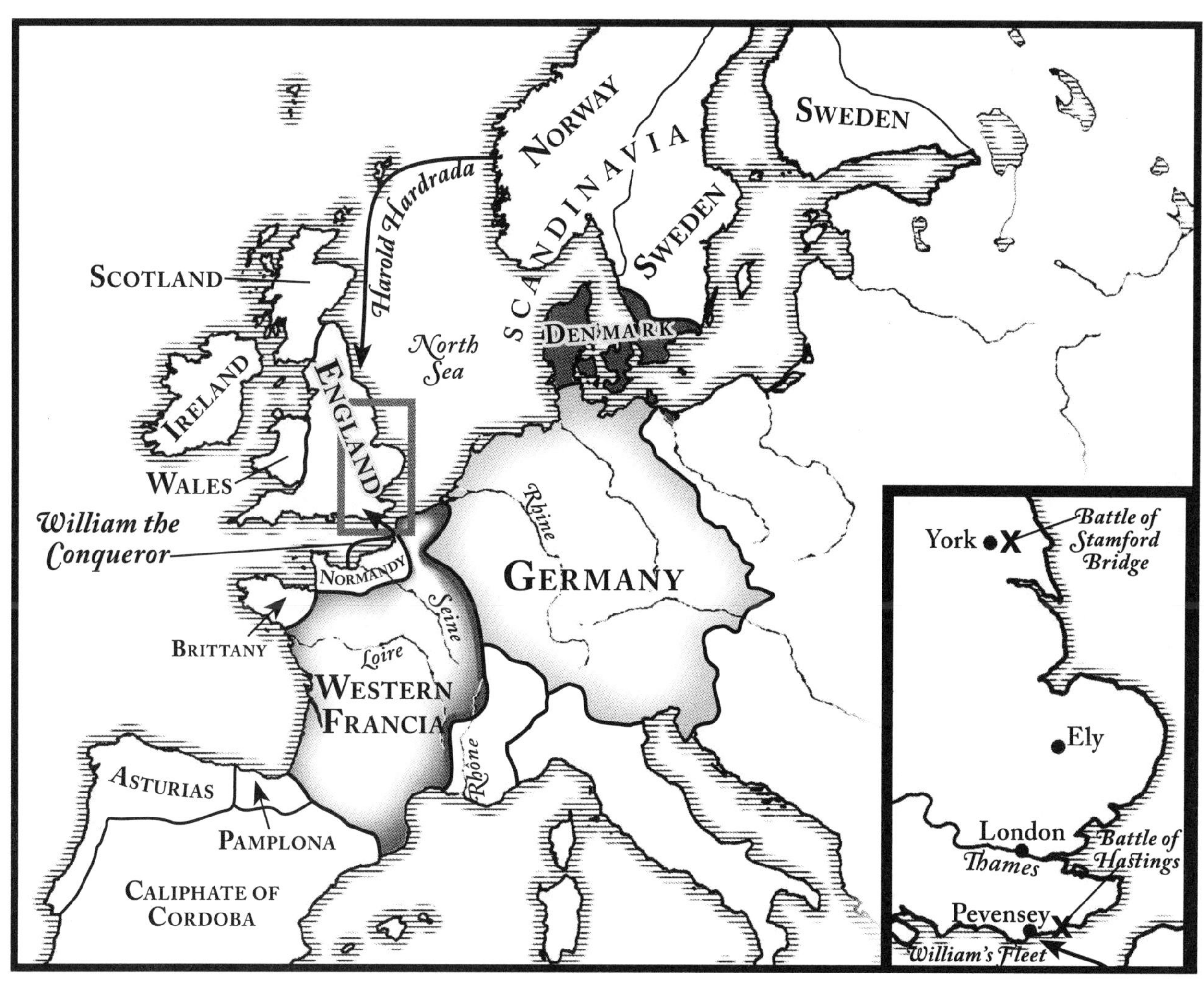

Map 78.1: The Battle of Hastings

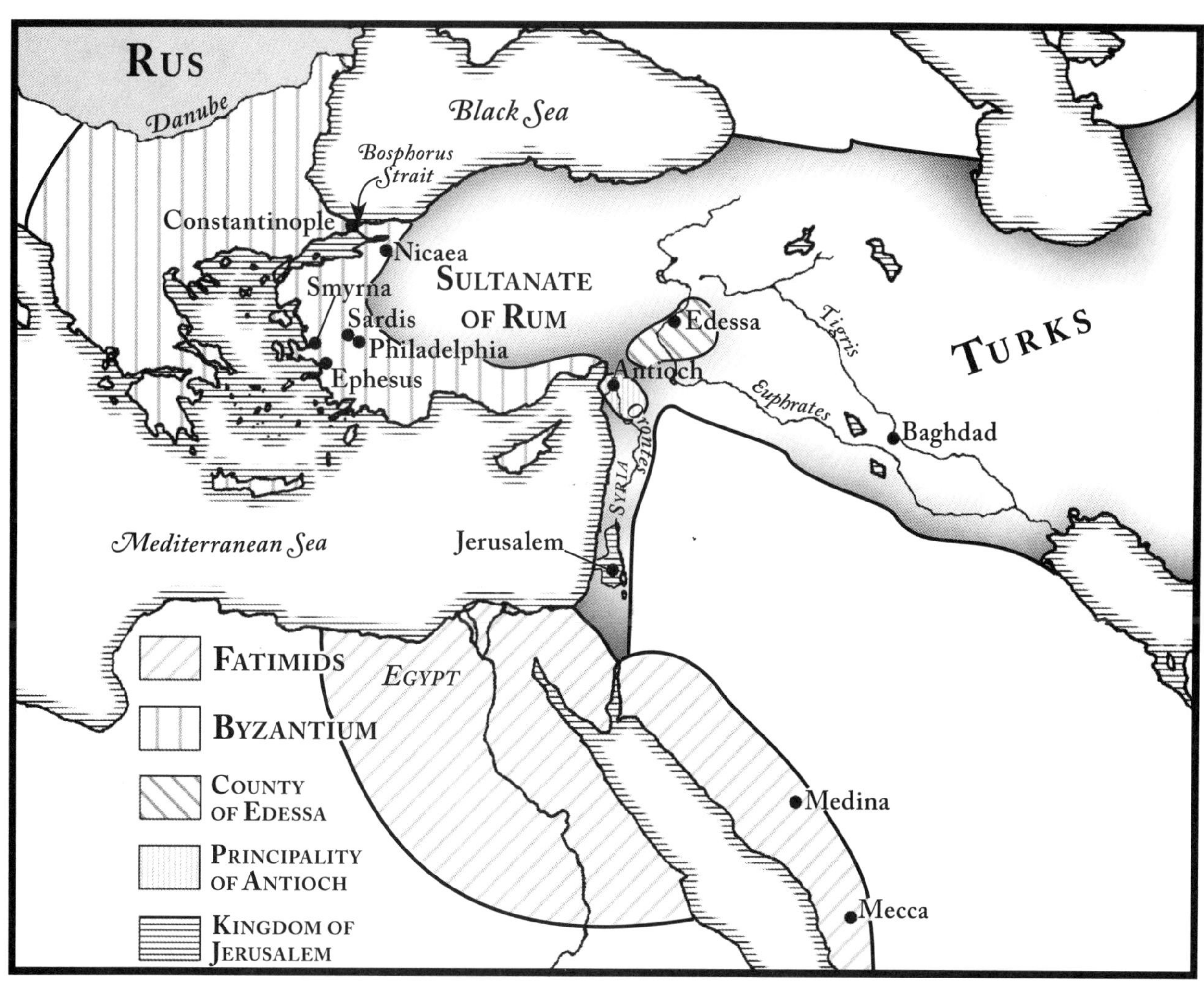

Map 84.1: The Crusader States